# WORLD TRAVEL ADVENTURES

**True Encounters From Over 100 Countries By An Ordinary Guy With Extraordinary Experiences**

**Steve Freeman**

authorHOUSE®

*AuthorHouse™*
*1663 Liberty Drive*
*Bloomington, IN 47403*
*www.authorhouse.com*
*Phone: 1-800-839-8640*



*Published by AuthorHouse 10/2/2012*

*ISBN: 978-1-4772-3729-8 (sc)*
*ISBN: 978-1-4772-3728-1 (dj)*
*ISBN: 978-1-4772-3727-4 (e)*

*Library of Congress Control Number: 2012912346*

# Table of Contents

# Introduction

## Who Am I And Why Am I Writing This Book?

Hello, my name is Steve, and I will be your tour guide throughout this book. My travel resume includes visiting 112 countries, all 7 continents, and each of the 50 states at least 4 times, including all 50 state capitals. It sure has been an amazing experience around the world and learning so much about other people, places, and things! I kept detailed journals about these trips during and immediately after my travels, primarily so I could preserve these memories which added so much happiness to my life. It is from these that I write this memoir.

I had no plans to write a book or any articles to do with these experiences. I was content with just telling family and friends what happened, and keeping my journals private. Then a funny thing happened. When others heard about my experiences, person after person was fascinated, whether they were 20, 90, or any number in-between. They found what I had done and the way I presented it to be extremely interesting, from casual traveler to world traveler, and from college student to Chief Executive Officer. Several people assumed I had already written a book, and others figured I was planning to write one. When the answer was no to both, many people insisted I write one as in: "How can you not do this?" My answer was simple: I'm not a professional writer, photographer, or traveler; I don't have the time; and, being a private person, I don't have the desire. Later, as my travels grew, some people were very persuasive in getting me to reconsider, and I got to at least thinking about it. They related to my travels, aspired to them, or both.

One day, just for kicks, I mentioned the book idea to four local bookstores (including a large one), and each buyer enthusiastically stated he or she would purchase it. A couple of store managers said that I had lived their dream and were eager to read the book. Finally, I contacted the publisher of this book. Strong interest was expressed because no-one else had written such a book and they were allowing me to tell my story my way, which was essential to me. A few situational factors came together that provided me with the opportunity, and I also started thinking philosophically about what my legacy here on Earth would be. So, to make a long story short, I decided to move ahead with the project and, ironically, see where this book would lead me.

*From Ordinary To Extraordinary*

You might find the chronology interesting, from college to present day. In the beginning I was not eager to travel, and even after the first couple of trips overseas I was not very interested in continuing. I initially traveled with a friend who cajoled me into going to Europe with him, to English-speaking countries, staying in safe areas. Later I traveled with family, a girlfriend, and solo – mostly the latter since almost always few or no others had the time and money to travel, or a matching schedule. I've taken "comfort" vacations such as to the Caribbean and on world cruises, and extreme ones such as to Antarctica by small ship with fewer than 100 passengers. Through this book you will travel to over 100 countries with me, see what I saw, learn what I learned, and mingle with the locals. By air, by land, by sea, and by mule.

These were extraordinary travels, yet I am just an ordinary guy, so if I can do it you can, too. There is nothing special about me that allowed me to travel the world: I am average height, average weight, and speak only two languages: English and "Brooklynese" (if you can read this book with a Brooklyn accent, all the better ☺). So don't think you're not "prepared" or "equipped" to travel. You are, and you should; just pick a level that's comfortable for you. I remained single which helped financially, but I learned many money-saving tips and others that I will pass along to you. I am telling you all this so that you realize the perspective I am writing from throughout this book. My lifestyle and experiences may not be the same as yours, but you will be able to take away valuable information from my travels no matter your background. So come along for the ride, sit back, relax, and prepare for your reading adventure.

*What This Can Mean To You*

Some people consider travel a hobby or interest. So did I. But after doing so much traveling it has become a pillar, a foundation like education, career, family, and friends. It changed my perspective and attitude. It geometrically increased my knowledge and happiness. I'm not a mathematician, either, but I figure that I'm at least twice as happy as I would have been during my entire life due exclusively to traveling. Travel can be life-changing in the best of ways, but like anything in life you have to pay the price. You need a few essentials to do it well, the level of which depends on you: free time, discretionary income, health, desire, and stamina for starters. I wanted to travel while younger rather than older, if I could, because I knew of the commitment it would take per the above, and I put myself in a position to do it. I was often told by retirees not to wait until I'm retired if possible; they'd say "do it while you're young" (to which I'll add the Nike slogan "Just do it™!" versus not doing it at all). Use this book as a portal for what's out there. If you decide to disembark and test the waters, I wish you a fantastic experience that is bound to be enriching and might change your life!

*Can't Start A Fire Without A Spark – How I Became Interested In Travel*

I am often asked how I became interested in travel. I gave it a lot of thought because no-one in my family does much of it. Nor do my friends or others I know. This was a seemingly simple question but had a complex answer, because there was no encouragement to do it, no reward for doing it, and early on I had better things to do – like look for girls and a job, not necessarily in that order. Being a deep thinker at times, I dived into this one because I like to figure out why I do what I do. So, to figure this out, I had to start at the beginning. What I discovered was very revealing, especially how it built in chronological order. Maybe some of this will relate to and resonate with you, too, or with others you know. To pique your interest, two major factors were a jigsaw puzzle and an old man I didn't even know.

*And The Answer Is...*

When I was a very young kid, my parents bought me a jigsaw puzzle of the United States. Each piece represented a state and was in a color representing that state (e.g., blue for Minnesota, which has so many lakes). Printed on each state's piece was only one word, the name of the state capital. Thinking back, I believe this laid a subconscious groundwork for my desire to visit each state – and its capital. In fact, when I subsequently arrived at the state border and capital decades later, I instantly recalled that puzzle piece. So can early childhood learning be a factor in later decisions? Absolutely!

My dad was a travel agent at the American Automobile Association (AAA®), from his high school graduation until retirement 47 years later. You would think travel would be a main source of discussion in our home, but this was never the case. Dad, a family man, kept work and family separate. So that wasn't a factor. But in looking back on it a major source was that from senior year of high school through my first year of graduate school I worked at the AAA travel agency during summers while paying my way through school. That's where I met others who came in for travel-related purposes (trip routings, cruise reservations, passport photos, travelers checks, etc.) - and where I may have caught the travel bug. Young and old alike, men and women, people of many nationalities – they all seemed happy about traveling, anticipating it, and talking about it with enthusiasm and cheerfulness. Some would even send me a post card and tell me how much they were enjoying their travels. I started thinking about travel but wasn't there yet, literally or figuratively.

It was around this time that I joined a college fraternity for camaraderie, when going to a strange new place (college) outside of my beloved Brooklyn neighborhood. Travel did not factor into my decision to join the fraternity. But, as it turned out, the fraternity traveled to other chapters, and this had a major effect on me as you will read. That it corresponded with adulthood also played into my enjoyment of this new-found freedom.

A few years later, early into my career in marketing, dad and I took a cruise together from New York to Bermuda. He had taken this cruise with mom a few times, and mom didn't want to go again. So with his travel agent's discount in tow, he asked me to go and I happily accepted. This wasn't my first big trip, but it was my first cruise. The significant thing about this cruise was that dad and I sat with an older couple, John, age 80, and Mary, age mid-60s, at a table for 4 during the dinners. I thought I'd be bored by the old-folks' talk (about the wars, etc.) – but John was a fascinating guy because he had been to 80 countries. I wasn't really interested at first, but his stories began to greatly interest and impress me. Mary, an attractive, intelligent woman, was totally enthralled by his travels, and although she seemed to just be his companion I thought, "Well, if he can get a very nice-looking lady like that to accompany him, maybe there's something to this." John, the world traveler, seemed very contented. Mary seemed happy to be with John. Dad, a travel agent, seemed happy with his job and when he was traveling. These and other factors will be discussed more fully in the pages to follow.

*About This Book*

I had no plans to write this book, but was prodded into it by just about everyone hearing my stories. I'm talking about from college students who aspire to travel, to people in their 90s who have been all over the world but not had the experiences I've had. That's because I was literally "out there," mixing with the locals, trying activities not found in the tour book, finding new experiences via the locals that even the tour guides didn't know about, and slowly but surely absorbing other cultures into my being to weave the mosaic that I am today. I never considered myself an expert at travel, but I will say that even travelers who have been to 80 or 90 countries ask my advice. Therefore, after lots of cajoling to write a book about it, here it is.

I'm going to break a few rules with this book. I was told to make this book relevant to the audience. Heck, I don't know who's going to read this book or anything about you. You could be any age, male or female, from the U.S. or China. Therefore, I am simply going to write this book from my actual experiences, telling it as I have to so many others who found it fascinating, and you can extract or extrapolate from it what you will as fits your situation and desires. I am a single guy from New York City. Chances are you are not. And even if you are, we are probably very different. However, I believe there's a lot you will learn, aspire to do, and be inspired to do based on my experiences. I will generally keep the numbers below 10 spelled out, except 8; this was such an important and lucky number for me that I want it to stand out, as it deserves to. The book is like a locomotive, in that it starts off slowly, and then picks up steam as we travel around the world together – exploring, learning, and expanding – until maximum speed is reached. Also, I will begin selected sentences with "And" or "But," which I was taught not to do in school. But that was years ago. And that's the way I speak (and write).

Because I've been so many places, I am going to focus this book on my international travels only, taking you vicariously through my journeys chronologically with the hope of motivating and inspiring you to go travel at the level in which you and/or others who may accompany you are comfortable. I've met senior citizens who want to go via all comfort and college students who want to rough it – and vice versa. There is no one "right way" to do it. But there is often a choice whether to do it. And to that I say go – find your passion, find yourself, and find your bliss. Life is short, and I hear a lot of people often say, "I wish I had done this sooner" or worse, from those who haven't even tried traveling, "I regret not taking a cruise or traveling in general." Don't let that person be you. If you have any desire to go, then try it. But I warn you: it is addictive and can be very contagious via the enthusiasm with which it is conveyed to others! I traveled solo almost all the time except where noted. Part of this was preference after a while, but do not confuse alone with lonely because that I surely was not.

Just so you know what's in store, here are a few words about what to expect and not expect from this book:

***This Book Is Not Meant To Be:***

An encyclopedic reference – climate, politics, geography, history, etc. Selected information in these areas may be included as related to the specific adventure

A ratings guide – hotels, restaurants, etc. which is better left to the professionals

A great literary effort I'm hoping will win a prize or critical acclaim - I write the way I speak, and that is conversational in plain English, with some funny stuff

A how-to – there is no right way or wrong way – it's up to you. What worked or didn't work for me may or may not for you. But you can learn from what I did and how I did it

A kiss-and-tell book – as somewhat of a gentleman, I'll take the juicy kiss and leave out the juicy details (but use your imagination); you will probably be able to know what happened with whom when reading about it

An endorsement of anyone or anything I've encountered – my opinion may not be the same as your opinion, and it's a good thing I didn't listen to others' opinions before or during my travels or I would have missed some great experiences (in fact, had I listened to some people I would not have traveled at all due to the "dangers," "terrorists," and other great tragedies that didn't happen)

***This Book Is Meant To Be:***

One man's opinion – a normal, everyday guy who was smitten by travel, became a road warrior of sorts, and wants to relate his experiences to others. Emphasis will be on the way travel shaped my thoughts, opinions, and actions - as they may yours after reading this

Informative from the personal experience standpoint – my experiences will probably not be the same ones you encounter given the myriad of variables unique to each trip, but it is hoped you will glean from them key points you may use in your travel decisions – money-saving tips included, and not necessarily the usual ones

A glimpse into the country – given the vastness of my travels, I write about activities, experiences, and insights of selected places visited to provide a sense of what it's like, overall impressions, and how it affected me or others I encountered

Entertaining, amusing, and educational – based on what I learned/ discovered and am sharing with you; also, astonishing and hair-raising where appropriate, based on real-life situations encountered by an ordinary person who, for better or worse, often didn't know what he was getting himself into

Inspirational – the #1 comment I hear after sharing my stories and showing my photos is without question, "I want to go!" If this book has that effect on you, then I consider it a success irrespective of sales, critical judgment or any other measure. If I can help you improve your life by leading the way, then your happiness is sure to follow and I'm happy for you

I am writing this book to have as a memory of my travels, legacy within my family, and for others who may want to follow in my footsteps. I have changed the names in most cases but the information is factual. For statistical information, note that Wikipedia® was my main source cited as well as others listed in the reference section.

So, here's what happened when I traveled around the world.

# Chapter 1

## From Here To Fraternity

To understand why and how I did what I did, you, the reader, need to understand a bit about me. As I think back to my childhood, I realize that there were several aspects that helped mold me into the traveler I would later become. Aside from the puzzle of the United States I had as a kid, there were other factors that would become imbued into my travel persona. In retrospect, everything in this chapter played a part.

I grew up in a middle-class neighborhood on East 88$^{th}$ Street in the Canarsie section of Brooklyn, New York. While there were tree-lined streets and it was generally safe, it was also between where Mike Tyson grew up in Brownsville and where John Gotti grew up in Howard Beach, Queens. Canarsie itself had its share of "tough guys," albeit on a much lesser scale, and you had to be careful. Fortunately, I was a good athlete, strong for my size, and was aligned with strong friends – all important in that time and place. I could handle myself in tough situations, and this extra layer of toughness would come in handy later on when I needed to be tough and even fearless in my travels.

Many people have asked me if I grew up in a wealthy family. Far from it. Dad and mom worked full-time as travel agent and office manager (up from administrative assistant), respectively. My younger brother and I shared a small bedroom with one black-and-white TV. All of us shared one telephone (with a cord – how prehistoric!). My brother, friends, and I bought baseball cards from Topps, Bazooka bubble gum, and lots of candy. Grandparents, aunts, uncles, and cousins all lived in close proximity. We were close with each other as family, too, being very tight-knit; if we were any more tightly-knit we'd be a sweater. We lived in a two-family house and had the same landlord for 34 years. They were very nice people and like a second family to us, including their loveable basset hound, Zoi (what a howl!). My younger brother and I attended public school all the way through high school, after which I was the first in my immediate family to attend college. I graduated from a city university (all we could afford) and I then went to a state university for graduate school (all I could afford).

There were 8 guys in total who made up my circle of friends, and we spent a lot of time just doing what street kids do, playing ball, roaming around, looking for stuff to do, trying new activities, seeing who was strongest, toughest, fastest, so that the hierarchy could be established. We especially played the popular neighborhood games stoopball, punchball, and stickball which I thought every kid played but later learned most didn't know what these games were. Being athletic was very important for the guys, especially in Brooklyn. "Doofuses" got picked on; you didn't want to be one of them. If you were a relatively smaller kid like me, you were still respected if you were a good athlete for your size. I was a good athlete, including doing 40 push-ups in a row every morning, starting at age 15. One friend was able to do 100 in a row back then. He was very protective of us younger kids; I was second-youngest in the group. I still do 40 push-ups to this day, every day. Being strong counted then, and I never forgot that. It later also counted if you were good with the ladies. I wasn't in the beginning, but learned to be better. In retrospect, both of these then-important factors would become possible explanations for why I did some of what I did later on when traveling.

Many of us were in organized Little League baseball. I played for four years as third-baseman, outfielder, and pitcher, because I had a strong arm. I either batted leadoff because I was a fast runner, or fifth because I had power. Later, I played on adult softball teams in these same positions. Being a smart kid was OK, but it wasn't important, and would even work against you if you were nerdy/non-athletic. I excelled in school, but my circle of friends did not talk about academics. My friends and I also collected things back then: sports cards, stickers, coins, and my favorite, Wacky Packages® cards and stickers, which spoofed consumer products. Ironically, I would end up working for the company that manufactured these! During the summer, I often went to camp. Most years it was local, where I could still be with my friends and family, but a couple of years I went to sleepaway camp upstate. I did not enjoy sleepaway camp because I disliked being away from home. In retrospect, this was a deterrent to my interest in traveling later on. So was delivering circulars for a nominal wage as a teen, because I got lost a lot and once even had to call my dad to pick me up. Overall, however, I had a wonderful childhood, and would not trade it for anything in the world. It built character – and many would say that I later became one as well (a Brooklyn wise-guy).

The roots of my travel interest may have started in elementary school, where I had a friend named Barry. Unlike all the other kids, Barry and I would go out of the school yard during lunch break and explore the neighborhood. This was Barry's idea, and I just went along for the walk. We had no idea where we were going but just roamed around seeing what's out there – the stores, houses, stray cats, and anything else. There was no purpose, and we were not looking for anything in particular. But we both got bored easily, were somewhat adventurous, and this was a good way to talk without distraction. If it were not for Barry, I would have been in the school yard with the others. Exploring seemed better, however. I was a standout in elementary school because I was captain of the vaunted punchball team, and my team won the school championship. I hit two home runs, and for the first time had girls interested in me. I also won the school spelling bee, and placed 4th in the district finals out of 18 school champions. Athletics, attention from girls, and exploring outside of my comfort zone during lunch breaks, a nice trifecta! But that was as good as it got for a while.

I was lost in junior high and high school, and don't remember much from that period except rooting for the New York Yankees, bowling, and trying to figure out what I wanted to be. I skipped 8th grade which meant I was good with school work but, in retrospect, this wrecked my social life for a while. The girls were thus older and taller than me. I dated a bit, but not as much as I would have liked. I kept away from the bad stuff: drugs, alcohol, gambling and was basically a "good" kid. I had my moments though, and went through the teenage angst years trying to find myself. It wasn't until college that I did.

In high school I was given your standard aptitude test. I only remember one thing from the results: there was a bar on the graph that was at least twice as high as any other, and under it read the word "Adventure." I thought nothing of it at the time and my guidance counselor didn't make any recommendations based on this. I didn't consider myself particularly adventurous, no-one in my family was, and I even asked the counselor if she was sure that was my chart. It was. I learned later on: <u>listen to your test results</u>! I made the school bowling team and did well there with a 162 average, which I maintained or bettered in several leagues during that time. At this point I liked trying new experiences and excelling at them. I didn't need to be great at any one, but being good in several different ones was a challenge and its own reward.

Baruch College was in Manhattan, surrounded by corporate buildings and small businesses, hustle and bustle, and had no campus except for the concrete jungle. I lived at home and rode the "L" train, also known as the Canarsie Line, back and forth to the college five days a week. I had to walk 15 minutes to a bus stop, take the bus another 15 minutes to the train station, and then take the train for an hour to reach the college. This process was reversed at the end of each day, so there were three hours of travel involved in going to college and back. In my freshman year, I was the new kid on the block with most students being older than me. I wasn't sure what to major in, but received good grades in my writing classes and settled on Journalism. Later I would switch to Business, encouraged by a friend's dad who gave me a motivating speech about not ending up selling jack-in-the-boxes near Penn Station. All of my neighborhood friends went to a different college or did not go to college. I was the first in my immediate family to go to college and there was no-one to guide me. I sought an anchor of some sort, maybe the same "strong-friends" type of protection I had back in Canarsie somehow, but who and what?

Then I saw a sign to join a fraternity, Sigma Alpha Mu. The fraternity was founded by 8 guys in 1909 and the governing body to this day is called "The Octagon." So there was another "8" that attracted me, and turned out to be a good thing. I met with the guys and we liked each other. Most were juniors or seniors, while I was a freshman; I saw this as a learning opportunity about not only the fraternity but about the college and life in general (I had no older siblings). So I became a "brother" and had the guidance, friendship, and security I was seeking. There could be some wild times in New York City back in the day, and "Animal House" was all the rage when I was most involved in the fraternity. Which leads me to another important component to this brotherhood: "Sammy" was a national fraternity, and the brothers often traveled to different chapters (our chapter had no house). Sometimes it was for a regional conclave or national convention, but mostly it was a road trip that was like a rite of passage to being an adult. Yes, there was partying, girls, loud music, and everything else you'd expect.

This traveling didn't matter to me when I joined, but it would soon make a huge impact. You see, I went on my first such road trip only two months after starting college. The timing was Halloween weekend and we went by train to Philadelphia (University of Pennsylvania Chapter). There I got my first taste of what both fraternity and travel were all about. Unlike at Baruch, which was a commuter school with no campus, Penn had a real university campus – and a frat house! In which they had parties...with alcohol... and girls...and....music...and fun! Blue Oyster Cult's "The Reaper" was blasting out of the fraternity house when we arrived – and always will remind me of that very moment when you could say I moved across that imaginary line into adulthood. Travel was part of that fun, excitement, and "maturity." This helped give me my identity, separating me from what my family and friends did. I would later travel extensively – but not expensively – with the fraternity. After graduation, I'd stay in various Sammy houses across the U.S. for free (the membership is lifetime). More good experiences and fun! And one of the best investments I ever made.

My first trip out of the U.S. was with the fraternity to its national convention in Toronto, Canada. I had a wonderful time there as one of two representatives of my chapter, "Alpha." I met other Sammies from around the country and we shared stories about our colleges and chapters. I thought this was great, and later learned that a cousin by marriage was also a Sammy. The next year I also had a great time at the national convention, in Chicago, as the lone "Alpha Chapter" representative. I ended up making two friends there from other chapters I would keep in contact with for more than 10 years (one from California and one from Michigan, who later moved to California).

Another important development in retrospect was that being from and living in New York City – a very multi-cultural place - I dated many gals who were not, or whose parents were not, from the U.S. These gals were Italian, Irish, Latino, Chinese, Jewish, Indian, and Polish among others. My mom liked to say I was "dating the United Nations." I have to say that all these gals were pleasant, pretty... and interesting. This may have been a seed that blossomed later on because I did think of these gals when visiting their respective home countries years later, and often did recall some of the information they had told me about them. Few of my friends back then dated a foreign-born gal, so this was unusual within my peer group. My Indian girlfriend lasted one year, while the relationship with the Polish gal lasted four years, on-and-off, beyond college. I never did see them again after we each moved on. But, unknown to me at the time, just interacting and being comfortable with them played a part in my development as the traveler I would become. At this same time an aunt who did some traveling would bring me back foreign coins for a collection I started keeping. This wasn't a big deal to me (I threw them in a shoebox) but was another exposure to international things that perhaps became a travel trigger later on.

I worked at several jobs while attending college. Dad, who worked for the AAA as a travel agent, helped me obtain jobs within his company which would last seven summers (full-time) and a couple of winters (part-time) at various AAA locations in New York City. This put me around travel a lot, and undoubtedly had a major influence on my later decision to travel. These jobs included, in chronological order:

accounts payable clerk at the West 62nd Street office in Manhattan; emergency road service clerk taking calls from stranded motorists and passing them along to a dispatcher in the Statler Hilton Hotel near Penn Station; mail room clerk refilling trip-ticket racks for the travel counselors and lifting heavy boxes (65-70 hours/week), also at the Statler; and finally, receptionist in the Brooklyn office (where dad worked) for four summers selling new memberships, renewing memberships, taking passport photos, and providing members with tour books and maps as requested. This was a shirt-and-tie job that made me feel as if I was a somebody. During the down times, I would read the tour books and study the maps. To this day I can remember the specific internal number associated with each tour book and the states it included.

Although most of this work was menial, the important takeaway for me was the cheerfulness AAA members had when coming into the office and planning their trips. There were lots of smiles, happiness, and enthusiasm. They were jovial in general. Some even had their favorite travel agent and only wanted to see that person. Others would tell me how great their last trip was, and how they're returning for another one. I even saw some of my college classmates come in to plan a road trip. Still other members sent me post cards with interesting photos on the obverse, and pleasantries on the reverse about their trip.

I became inspired to travel, and in retrospect this helped me study harder to fulfill that dream. I ended up graduating college with honors and winning an Advertising scholarship of $5,000 awarded to only two students in the country - without which I could not afford to attend graduate school – and being the only student to speak at my college graduation ceremony based on successful combination of academics, work experience, and student leadership. I had been an officer in five student organizations, including eventual President (called "Prior") of the local fraternity chapter, and also in the Advertising Society, in which I would meet my eventual best friend and future travel buddy, Mike. I wrote for three school newspapers, a local Manhattan newspaper as college intern (Heights-Inwood News), and even had an article published in an international magazine called Advertising World at which I was an unpaid college intern for a year.

I liked writing and thought I'd become a journalist, having won two college awards for it. But, as mentioned, a friend's dad convinced me to major in Business and that was good advice. I ended up with a BBA in Marketing, with a specialization in Advertising, and a second major in Journalism.

Baruch College offered me a $5,000 research assistantship to return to graduate school there, big money in those days. The assistantship was renewable for a second year, so that was $10,000! Combined with my Advertising scholarship, this would have easily paid for my entire graduate school education. Almost everyone I asked said I should return to Baruch, especially since I had done so well there. Baruch also had a fine business school reputation, and of course my family and friends were right there in New York City.

That was the problem. By that time I had a hunger for being somewhere different. Perhaps it was due to the AAA experience, or fraternity visits to other chapters. Or to my good friend and eventual fraternity brother, Harvey, who was interested in campus life. He went to Baruch with me but did not end up going for his master's degree (CPA instead), thus never going to a college with a campus as he dreamed. Harvey reveled in the University of Pennsylvania trip we took as freshmen and later University of Maryland trip as well, which both had an excellent campus and provided that college "feel" that we never had. His enthusiasm for big-name colleges, including their sports teams/stadiums, and collegiate campus life in general got me enthusiastic about this, too. Despite having the Baruch assistantship in hand, I applied to several out-of-state colleges to get this life experience, and ended up going to Michigan State University for my MBA degree. Because I had little money - and in fact took out loans taking 10 years to pay off - I ended up living in the Sigma Alpha Mu Fraternity house off campus there with 18 "brothers." I was the "old" guy at 22; all the other guys were undergraduates, and almost all were from Michigan. That in itself was quite an experience!

My formal education was excellent; Michigan State had a top-10 marketing program at the time, and I completed the program in near-record time of 1-1/2 years, graduating with honors, taking maximum credit loads every term except the last when I didn't need to. But the real experience I remember was that of being on my own, living in a new place, meeting new people, and literally having Joy (the name of my girlfriend) there from all this. There were parties with the sorority girls, beer parties, every type of party, and the Michigan State Spartans sports teams/stadiums just as Harvey had described, with 80,000 fans cheering like crazy. To this day I still play the MSU "Fight Song" during football season and watch the Spartans on TV. The fraternity guys all had nicknames. Mine was "Alpha" because I was from the founding chapter, Alpha, at Baruch College (then called City College when founded in 1909). The skinny guy with the big 'fro was called "Q-Tip." There was the big lumberjack-looking guy from Western Michigan ("Yukon John"), sloppy guy ("Slimey") and "No witz in bed," a play on words based on one of the brother's names. We called each other only by these names in the fraternity house, but were more formal when visitors came over, especially a brother's parents, in which case it was the equivalent of an Eddie Haskell-like, "Hello Mrs. Cleaver, you look lovely this evening." After that, all bets were off, and it was "Animal House," or beyond, at times (did anyone say, "food fight!").

In sum, I went to Michigan State for the life experience, to see how I'd like being on my own and handle it. Looking back on it, this too was raw material for my desire to travel away from home later on. It gave me confidence to do so. I learned that the real value can come from what we experience informally as much as learn in a classroom. The former is just as, if not more, important. All these years later I remember the thrill of the collegiate experience more than what I learned in the classroom. Both served me well, and it was a good life decision to go there. Ironically, as mentioned 10 years earlier, my parents had sent me to sleepaway camp for two summers. I did not like it there because I was uncomfortable on my own. Had I shunned going away to Michigan State because of this I would have missed out on a valuable education and life experience. People change. So if there's something in your background that causes you to shun travel, give it another try. If you're in that situation, getting over that hump is the first step you ought to make on the road to travel bliss.

# Chapter 2

## Runnin' Down A Dream: Early Travels

After college and graduate school, I still had almost no interest in travel. I focused on my career and started working for a New York City advertising agency on Nabisco snack cracker products, including Wheat Thins® and Triscuit®. The job was interesting; the company was jointly owned by Nabisco and Don Ohlmeyer, a high-profile producer and originator of Monday Night Football. There was some glitz to this job; I had a small office in the ritzy Avon building that overlooked Central Park. I also got to attend the first two MTV Music Video Awards at Radio City Music Hall, and brought a beautiful girl to each (one was a model). Life was good. But what made this job even better was the free travel. As a Junior Account Executive I would go out to the client in New Jersey a lot, but also on some limited trips elsewhere by car to research the snack crackers category.

I did not own a car in New York City during my entire life there (many people do not given the extensive mass transit system), so renting one for business or pleasure was a treat. It was the freedom I didn't have as a teenager, so in looking back there might have been a latent teenage thrill. Perhaps if I'd had a car when younger the thrill would have been long out of my system by then; instead, my desire to travel increased with each successive car rental at a time when I was starting to make some decent money. At night, I would take out the AAA maps and look to see where I could drive to. To this day, if someone asks me to name a weakness, I say "maps," because when I see one it's inevitable that I'd be going somewhere soon.

As my business career progressed, so did the money I made and the travels I could now afford. There was a nice balance of business and pleasure travel as a result. I worked at another (larger) ad agency on Good Humor® Ice Cream, after which I made the switch to marketing and worked at Pfizer. After that I found my niche at Topps where I was the marketing manager for the confectionery business, notably Ring Pop® and Push Pop® lollipops, as well as assisting my boss on Bazooka Bubble Gum®. Also lots of licensed new products tied to movies like Batman®, Teenage Mutant Ninja Turtles®, New Kids On The Block® and The Flintstones®. I loved that job because I was a big kid at heart, and even invented an interactive product that became patented (Roller Pop® candy with fruit-flavored powder). By virtue of conceptualizing this product that sold in the millions I was rewarded by the company with a trip to China to work with the manufacturing people. I stayed in the expensive and exquisite Peninsula Hotel on Kowloon Island in Hong Kong, and enjoyed both the business and personal portions of this trip. I would later return to China on pleasure, and enjoy it even more.

At Topps I did the most traveling, the vast majority being domestic, which included regional and national sales meetings; working with individual sales reps across the country to help sell the products into the retail stores; and the annual national candy convention in Chicago, which I would end up attending for nearly 15 years. There was even an international candy convention in Cologne, Germany I attended at which you could sample some of the world's finest chocolates! I then worked for other confectionery companies in Colorado Springs and Northern California at even higher levels. But Topps was my favorite, and included a very fun corporate culture. I would later take Bazooka Joe in my pocket all over the world with me, and see the product sold in many faraway places.

Back in the U.S., I began my leisure travel during vacation time, usually only two weeks a year (I would later envy Europeans who often received six weeks of vacation a year). However, I got a taste of Europe without leaving the U.S., when an out-of-state friend from grad school contacted me and said his friend Paul was relocating to

New York. Paul was a fun, innovative guy who worked near me in Manhattan, a good-looking Black guy who did part-time modeling. We had lunch a few times and soon became friends. Paul used his innovative ways in dating. He loved blondes, and as such went to the Church of Sweden to post placards about his upcoming party Friday nights in his Manhattan apartment. The sign said he needed beautiful women to be there based on the surplus of guys who would be attending. He often received many acceptances - and then had a dilemma. He had no party planned until he had a lot of women who accepted. Then he would call his guy friends at the last minute and tell them to bring their male friends as needed. The incentive: he was going to have dozens of beautiful Swedish women there! I was a regular attendee and brought friends to what I affectionately called the "ya-ya room."

We would be buzzed-in to Paul's upscale apartment building, knock on the door, and there it was before us: dozens of gorgeous Swedish women in their 20s, mostly au-pairs (nannies to wealthy families), mingling and saying "Ya, ya" while sipping their alcoholic beverage. They were svelte, easy to talk to, fun, friendly, and enjoyed my sense of humor - plus many had a good one of their own. Several were among the most beautiful women I had ever seen – and I preferred brunettes! Often, they went to the small bathroom/single toilet together which I thought was strange, but they were from a different culture which I would soon find very intriguing. One beauty named Katarina was particularly alluring and had the brightest blue eyes I had seen to that point, like that of a Siberian Husky, yet brighter. It was a wild time there each and every time, and when Paul approached me that first time no words were exchanged: he just laughed, harder and harder, as if to say, "Just look at this – pretty amazing, huh?" I just laughed along with him and admired what he had done. I later nicknamed my new friend "Saint Paul" which was ironic because there were many Swedes living in Minnesota. Many of the gorgeous blondes looked like they could be twins (baseball team) or descended from Vikings (football team). None looked like Timberwolves (basketball team), and that was a good thing.

I found this whole Euro-Manhattan experience wonderfully bizarre. I had not thought about vacationing in Europe, but then my friend Mike from Baruch asked if I'd be interested in going to England and Holland with him. I wasn't sure, but my interest was piqued since I liked domestic travel. Plus, Mike and I were similar in personality, both from Brooklyn, and liked new experiences. But we were also different. He was very interested in culture; I was not. He was interested in travel overseas; I was not. But he was very persuasive and got me to consider it. I liked the idea of going with someone I knew, with whom I could split expenses, and where English was the, or one of the, main language(s). And I was often up for a challenge, and an adventure. So we planned our vacation for nine days to England and Holland.

We went during the off-peak season in November when the prices were lower. I was still paying back my student loans and we were not yet too established in our careers. We first arrived in Amsterdam. In general we had good weather during this vacation – and I must emphasize that throughout nearly all my travels I had superb weather, making the experience that much more enjoyable and a "meant to be."

We settled into our hotel and shared a room, which we did throughout the trip and most of our travels together. The room was small, much smaller than the typical hotel room in the U.S. Although we had taken an overnight flight for 10 hours and there was a 6-hour time difference forward, the experience of being in Europe (Mike's first time, too) was so energizing we didn't even nap much before venturing out soon after arrival.  One thing I noticed right away about Amsterdam was all the bicycles – thousands of them, it seemed. There were lots of canals, museums, and antique shops. We moseyed around and just took it all in. I enjoyed taking photos even back then and took many, even of basic things, because it was all so new and exciting! In retrospect, this was the genesis of the acronym for the life I was starting to lead, especially when it came to travel, which was **FINE** – "**F**un, **I**nteresting, **N**ew and **E**xciting!"

There were a few must-sees in Amsterdam that we explored: Anne Frank house, Van Gogh Museum (which locally is pronounced Van Goff), Rikjsmuseum, Vondelpark, the Red Light district, and sightseeing historical buildings. In the U.S. we get excited if a building is 100 years old; in Europe, 1,000 years old is no big deal, and I would later see buildings that were 2,000 years old in other parts of Europe!

There were lots of coffee shops and cafés. Marijuana was legalized in Amsterdam and people there were smoking it (neither of us did that). The attitude was very liberal in general. I was thrilled just to be there, in a place so far away and different. I came to see that there were differences – choices – and appreciate them. The important thing to me was that people seemed relaxed, comfortable, and happy in general. Smiles. Cheerfulness. Friendliness. No rushing around frantically. European accents, food, art... I felt like I was somewhere different...invigorating all my senses. This was all quite a contrast to the fast-paced, high-pressured New York City lifestyle I was then living. Not necessarily better or worse, just different, and something to think about as being a big-picture person.

Mike and I were getting along well (you never known with friends and travel), and we generally stayed together the entire time in Amsterdam. However, in England we would spend most of our time together, but then separate for a while due to our different interests. We arrived in London, where we would spend the majority of our nine-day vacation. Mike was right – London is a lot like New York City, and, as with Amsterdam, English being a predominate language was a big help. The city was multicultural with loads of historical buildings, fashion, comedy clubs, pubs, and double-decker buses. It was a good thing I was taught to look both ways before crossing, because there the traffic comes from the "opposite" direction than it does in America, so if you only look left it could be an issue. And the cars there can whip around quickly so you need to be on your toes.

Mike and I did not take any organized tours but instead found our way around on foot, by taxi, and via public transportation – as we were comfortable doing in New York City. We went to Buckingham Palace on a clammy, rainy day where there was an Armistice Day celebration. Although I was the main photographer, I give Mike full credit for a photo he took of the motorcade that captured Queen Elizabeth in the back seat of a car. Most press photographers there didn't think she was in that one as they chased other cars that whisked by earlier in the procession. Thanks, Mike, for catching this!

We admired Westminster Abbey, the Crown Jewels, Hyde Park, walked around Kensington where our hotel was located, rode the train (called the "tube" there), and of course the double-decker bus. Pretty amazing. At the train station there were signs posted reading "Mind the gap." At first I wasn't sure what that meant but then realized it's the gap between the platform and train, so be careful when stepping onto the train so as not to get caught in, or fall into, the gap. I later wondered if the famous ad slogan for Gap stores, "Fall into the Gap™," was sparked by this.

Mike wanted to see a lot of the art and history the country had to offer, and I accompanied him to several museums and galleries. The British Museum and Tate Museum were foremost among these, and were impressive. However, Mike was really into art and I got bored of it after a while. So we split up one day and I took a train out to Stratford-Upon-Avon where I went to Shakespeare's birthplace and Anne Hathaway's cottage, enjoying views of the charming countryside en route. I enjoyed both tourist sites, but especially the empowerment of taking a long train ride by myself in a foreign country. Yes, it was England where English was spoken, and yes, I was comfortable being on trains, but the two combined in a foreign country were a first for me, enlivening my senses. I met some interesting people during this excursion who briefed me on the country and its culture. This, too, would become an important preference that would last until this day: Instead of reading books and taking trip advice from other Americans, I preferred to just land at my destination, find some locals, and ask them what's best to do given my personal preferences. I never had any trouble getting good answers, and realized that being from New York City there's often the tourist's version and the local's version. The local's version is often best. Thus I was led to the Jack the Ripper walking tour and museum, which was educational. Later I went to Madame Tussaud's Wax Museum, at which I have a photo straightening out Humphrey Bogart's bowtie.

Mike and I met up at night, had dinner, and exchanged the day's events. I believe it's a good idea not to spend all your time with one person or group of people on your vacation because no-one has the same exact tastes as you, and therefore you should maximize your own experience. But I understand that many, if not most, people are uncomfortable breaking away to be on their own in a foreign country. What I did with this long train ride was just a baby step – but that first step is the most important. In fact, I would split with Mike one other time and go to Oxford University by train while he went to more museums and galleries. Again, we both had a nice day, and I have to thank Harvey once again for piquing my interest in universities. Interestingly, Mike would marry an artist – and I would continue on to teach at a university in both Colorado (part-time) and California (full-time). At Oxford I bought a blue sweatshirt with the Oxford name and emblem on it. This was high-quality, and expensive at $20 U.S. at the time, but so durable that it lasted for nearly 15 years and became an enduring reminder.

Mike and I took a tour together outside of London to Bath, Salisbury, and Stonehenge which was excellent. Bath was beautiful, and was my first sight of incredible architecture like I hadn't seen before, with a huge crescent of buildings that was awesome! The highlight of course was the Roman Baths from back in the day. These were huge – the size of a large swimming pool! – and was a fine example of both engineering and preservation. There was steam coming off of the baths, and it was amazing to think that this is where Romans were 2000 years ago. I was awed – I had never seen anything like this.

Salisbury didn't seem like much at first. My initial impression was "old churches" although impressive architecturally. Churches and architecture weren't my thing – but I'd soon learn in my vast subsequent travels that you're going to see a lot of them on tours, so be prepared. As we exited the bus, however, I saw that this was a lovely town, with potted plants hanging out the windows, cobblestone streets, and lots of shops. The place was delightful, and we walked around for a couple of hours. I generally do not do sit-down meals on tours with limited roaming times, preferring to walk around, meet the locals, and take photos instead. Somehow I felt that this was England, unlike London, just as in the U.S. there was New York City and the rest of the U.S. was different. There was a fairy-tale charm to this place, and with lots of history, too. OK, better than I thought.

But the best was yet to come. A 20-minute drive away was the world-famous Stonehenge, and it was magnificent! When I first saw the large circular stones I thought, "What the heck is this?" To this day, people aren't sure and there are many theories. Religious site? Burial site? Scientific observatory? Temple? Magic powers? Method of communication with beings from outer space? To me, it seemed like the Earth had some eruption and these giant stones just landed this way, improbable as that may be. Sort of like if you tried tossing a coin to get it to land on its side, it may take thousands of attempts but perhaps it would happen (or maybe I watch too much "Twilight Zone" in which there was an episode based on this). The age is also a question mark, somewhere between 2000 and 3000 B.C., or twice as old as the Roman baths! I'd never seen anything this old, and they did make the Roman baths look modern by comparison. Mike and I walked around the monuments and took photos. There were no fences or protective barriers back then, which I found to be very unusual for a world-famous landmark such as this. (When I returned nearly 20 years later there was a fence around it, and workers there apportioned the massive crowds so it didn't get too crowded at any one time.)

As in Amsterdam, Mike and I were out almost all the time except to sleep. In London, we saw the plays "Starlight Express" and "Cats" on successive nights (both excellent). We also went to a pub or two or three, although we're not really drinkers. We had the fish 'n chips (good but not great, and overpriced) and some beer which was very good. It was there that I realized that we have several U.S. states that are derivatives from England: New York, New Jersey, and New Hampshire named after the same British cities that are, I suppose by default, the "old" or original versions, namely York, Jersey, and Hampshire. I would later mention this to many Americans and fellow travelers not from the U.S. who would ponder this with nodding agreement. Ironically, I would briefly live in New Mexico which many Americans I met years later did not realize was a U.S. state (some even asked me, "What's the country code, so I can call you there?").

Regarding another ponderable while in England, I was asked if the United States is like 50 countries in 1. Interesting that people in Europe might think of us that way, since Europe is sort of like our United States but with many different cultures, languages, currencies, etc. – and how ironic that these days Europe is trying to emulate the U.S. with its one euro currency. I replied that it's not like 50 countries, but you could make a case for there being at least 8 distinct sections including New York, California, and Texas as their own "country," so to speak. These might also include New England, the Deep South, Midwest, Northwest, and Southwest. At any rate, it was an interesting question that got me thinking how diverse we are as a country. Starting around this time I would travel around the U.S. extensively as well, and get a first-hand experience of these different "countries within a country," as I called them. But that's for another discussion, and perhaps another book down the road.

I have to give Mike kudos regarding the last night of my stay with him, when we went to the very hot Hippodrome nightclub downtown that featured a fantastic laser show. The doorman was snobby and was letting in only the elite. We had almost no chance. Mike can be bold when needed and besieged the doorman by telling him that this was my last night in London after a week there, and how we would love to get into the club and compare it to New York City nightclubs that we had gone to. Somehow he convinced the guy and we were let in. Interesting crowd, to say the least (lots of Boy George wannabes), great music, and light show. This club rivaled those that were popular in New York City back then, including The Palladium, Area, and 1018 (corner of 10$^{th}$ Avenue and West 18$^{th}$ Street in Manhattan).

My first Euro vacation ended, and was revealing as to "what's out there." Mike worked it out with his employer to stay on an extra week, during which time he went to Liverpool to learn more about his beloved Beatles. He later said this lived up to his expectations. While in retrospect I do not consider this one of my favorite vacations (because I had so many others henceforth that were fantastic), I do consider it a success and the first step in what would become a wonderful international travel odyssey. I was refreshed, relaxed, energized, full of new knowledge, desiring to learn more, and Mike and I had gotten along well. I was "running down a dream" but hadn't yet realized how long this dream would last. As it would end up, I would do a lot of domestic traveling while working my way up the corporate ladder, and not return to Europe until 8 years later, again with Mike. But I was starting to groove to travel at this early stage in my 20s, and compared it to trying a food you haven't eaten before, not knowing what it is, but liking it and wanting to try it again. Food for thought early in my travel career.

# Chapter 3

## Mexico And "Club Med Vacation – The Antidote To Civilization"

The next year I took a late vacation, in November. Potential travel partners were unable to accompany me due to their individual situations, so I would be going solo and seeking a warm-weather destination. My decision was to visit Cancun, Mexico given the popular beach, and the relative inexpensiveness due to the great exchange rate of pesos for U.S. dollars. I stayed at the Suites Brisas hotel for a week and had a marvelous time. There I went parasailing and snorkeling at a famous dive site called Xel-ha. The weather was terrific, I saw amazingly colorful fish, and I got both the worst sunburn ever followed by the best tan ever during this trip. The sunburn occurred when I first arrived and the sun was nearly setting. I sat on the beach for only 10 minutes with no lotion figuring it's November and very late in the day, so what's the worst that can happen? I sure found out in a hurry, ouch! Fortunately, this didn't peel but turned tan. I ended up with such a good reddish-brown color that, upon return, my fair-skinned supervisor at the ad agency, Sharon, said, "You should find a way to bottle that tan and sell it." Lesson learned, however, about going into the sun without proper protection; it could've turned ugly, literally.

I took a tour of the area including the Indian ruins in Tulum. Other tourists I'd met encouraged me to go to the more popular site, Chichen Itza, which was further away and more crowded. I wasn't too interested in Indian ruins at the time and went to Tulum precisely because it was closer and less crowded. I would see many more Indian ruins in years to come, more than I could have imagined back then, and with a lot more interest as well.

A funny little thing happened there when I was on the Xel-Ha snorkeling excursion. On the boat taking us there, I met a nice guy named Gerhardt who was the German ambassador to a Central American country. He spoke little English but enough to get by. He had a beautiful blonde daughter circa age 18, whom he encouraged me to take to a disco that had a laser show, much like at Hippodrome. We went around together and had a good time. It seemed that Gerhardt wanted to speak to me a lot, at length, but we did not have much in common. I was not into history, politics, culture, or other topics he brought up. Then he hit upon one commonality: sports, in particular American baseball. He knew a lot about only one team, the Atlanta Braves, who were a last-place team back then, and not much about other teams including my favorite, the popular New York Yankees. As it turned out he only had access to TBS, Ted Turner's cable TV station in Atlanta that showed the Braves games because Ted Turner owned the team. So it was unusual to hear a German guy have so much in-depth knowledge about a last-place team and not much at all about any other.

Now, looking back on it, I figured out why Gerhardt may have wanted to speak with me so much, and why he wanted me to spend time with his daughter. He may have wanted his daughter to also be exposed in front of me – to English, that is. As I would learn later on, there are many foreigners - especially professionals - who want to learn English. The best way is to speak to someone who is fluent. I would later realize the possibility that many others engaged me in conversation as well for this purpose, from all around the world. Then again, if I wanted to learn another language I'd be looking to do the same thing after perhaps taking a course in the basics.

The best was yet to come, although I didn't see it coming. In fact, it saw me. I was walking along the beach on my next to last day, and a couple of gals in bikinis said hi to me. We started talking. They said they were part of Club Med and I responded, "Oh, so you're nurses?" They giggled and explained that Club Med is a France-based company with the full name Club Méditerranée and resorts all around the world in exotic locations. They were there on vacation from Boston, and said that many who came there were from my hometown of New York City! After chatting with them a while, I spoke with the representative at the Club and agreed to pay $35 to spend half a day there as a trial. This included lunch, dinner, and the theater show at night, among other activities.

I went water-skiing there that afternoon and learned another important lesson: not to go water-skiing because, as I was later informed by my physician, from the way I'm built I'm likely to do a split which is exactly what happened several times. But everyone was very encouraging and nice, letting me jump ahead in the line to try again despite repeatedly falling on my face. I also liked that the average age of vacationers was in the 20s, this was a "singles" club (most were not), many girls were gorgeous and from all around the world, and I felt extremely comfortable there. Once again, lots of fun, smiles, and happiness which is all I really wanted out of life. Plus, there was chocolate bread – both white and dark chocolate varieties – which was, and is to this day, the best-tasting bread I've ever had! Just as the pretty gals on the beach inadvertently acted as a lure for me to check out Club Med, I would use the chocolate bread as a lure to get Mike to go with me to Club Med a couple of years later since he and I were both choco-holics. I had a wonderful time in Cancun, but the real find was Club Med – to which I would go 15 more times as of this writing, 13 of which were to Turks & Caicos Islands starting the next Spring.

So just a few months later I again went solo on a vacation, to this recommended Club Med village – on a trip that would change my life. Why Turks & Caicos? I heard that not only was there a charter flight directly from New York City to the village on the island of Providenciales, but the ratio of gals to guys there was 5:1. I had left my job at the ad agency soon before this trip and landed a job at Pfizer, Inc. at the world headquarters in Manhattan, representing a career change to corporate marketing. I took a week off during this transition and wanted to go to a fun, happy place to get recharged. Club Med was just the ticket. Wow! Gorgeous beach, loads of pretty women, excellent food, great weather, and tons of activities. The water was the most beautiful color I had ever seen, and looked like it could almost glow as it faded from blue to green, hence the name "Turkoise" for this particular village. Back then the theme was "Club Med vacation - the antidote to civilization," and the Club did not have clocks or televisions or even locks in the rooms. You were to lose all perspective of time and get out there to do things – activities, meet people, eat/drink/be merry! The staff did a wonderful job of facilitating this.

I was surprised to learn that Club Med had so many upscale people who vacationed there – especially doctors, lawyers, nurses, teachers, pilots, and others from high-stress professions. Word had gotten around that this was the place to go to totally unwind, relax, act silly, and forget about life for a while. And get drunk or laid, if that was what you were after, or just plain act stupid without having to worry about your family/friends/colleagues finding out – these were the days before camera-phones, the Internet and YouTube®.

The French who ran the Club village pronounced it "Turkwaz" instead of "Turkoise," giving it that little extra international flair. At night there were the traditional dances to the songs "Hands Up" by Ottawan and "Crazy Signs" among many others. The music played during my stay in general was so good that I had the DJ make me a recording of it. I play it to this day when I need a lift. While envisioning Club Med is not as good as being there, this helps it remain the gift that keeps on giving in my mind's eye. The song "La Isla Bonita" by Madonna, popular at that time, still whisks me away mentally to this village whenever I hear it.

Without going into detail, I met a nice gal there my age who was a psychologist from New York City I'll call Debbie. "Sex on the Beach" wasn't just a name of a drink there (along with "Screaming Orgasm") but a lifestyle at the Club. I not only bonded with Debbie but made a new friend with my roommate (agreed to this option to reduce expenses), a physician my age from Long Island I'll call Dr. Dave. Dave didn't want to tell any gals he was a doctor to avoid them liking him merely for his income potential. Everyone we encountered there could not believe we had just met at the Club; we got along so well that we were perceived as lifelong friends. Soon Dave and I combined to meet several gals, and we ended up becoming a group of 8 people (6 gals, 2 guys) who hung out together, dined, danced, swam, and had lots of fun. To this day, that vacation was as close to Nirvana as I have ever experienced. That vacation was also the best experience I had the entire year (stock market crash, among other things). And so I held a special affection for Club Med and Turks & Caicos that would last to this day. By the way, I did see Debbie when back in New York, and arranged a double-date between me and her, and my brother-her sister, both about the same age. It went OK, but didn't have the magic of Club Med once we had returned to reality. Perhaps if we had gone to the beach at night...

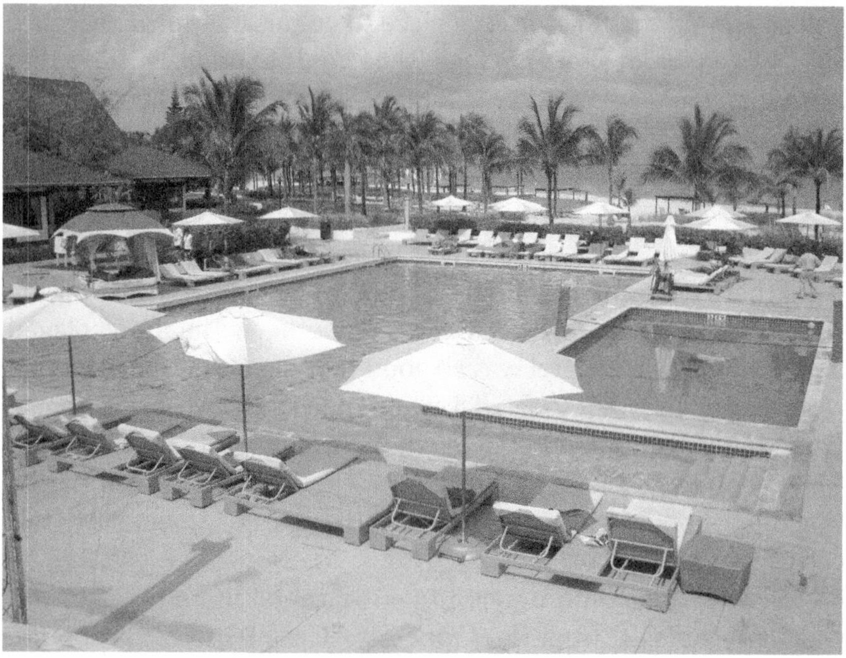

Club Med - Turkoise, in the Turks & Caicos Islands, Caribbean. They sell few post cards there because just about any landscape photo you take could be one at this picture-perfect tropical resort.

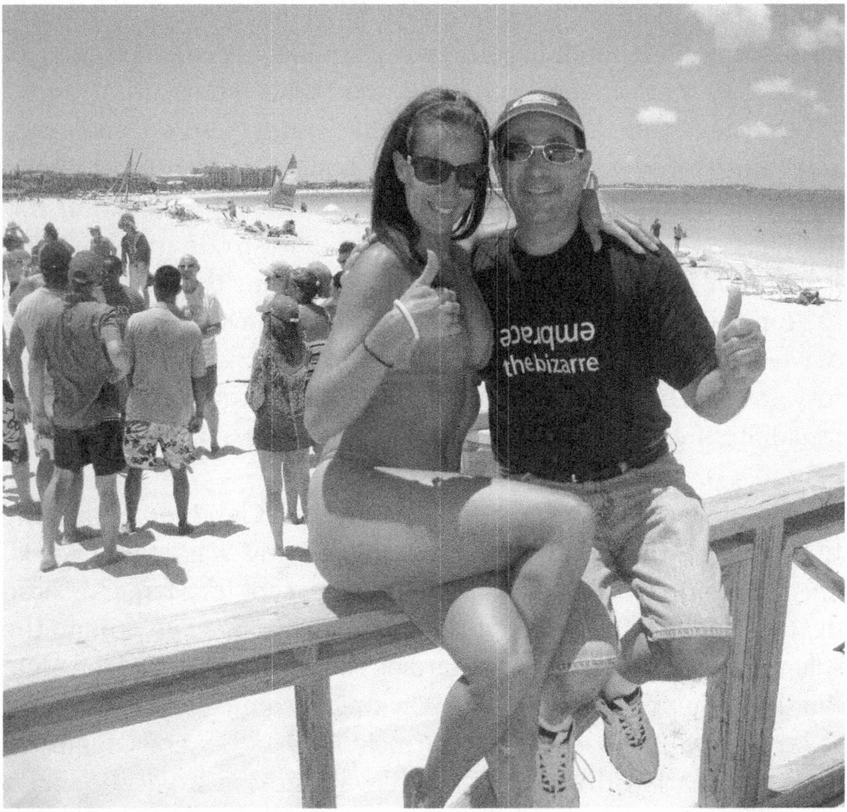

Now I know why they call it Paradise - sun, sand, and sexy. Award-winning beach, great food, and fun staff. No wonder I have been to Club Med - Turkoise over a dozen times.

Naturally, when I returned to New York I raved about this trip. Mike wanted to go, and we went the next year – but to the Club in St. Lucia which had more activities that appealed to him. I said OK and figured it would be good to try another Club Med village to see if it was the same experience. While this was an excellent trip as well, it didn't measure up to Turks & Caicos for me. At St. Lucia, what stands out today was doing the trapeze. I completed the acrobatics – but had such a funny look on my face while doing them that the Club photographer took a picture of me and put an 8x10 in a showcase the next day for all to see. I don't think I could make that same face again – surprise, concern, am I really doing this? ouch, my stomach! – but it was worth it. I may have had a similar look on my face during water-skiing in Cancun a couple of years earlier had a photographer captured my expression before doing a face-plant in the ocean. Mike and I met a couple of trauma nurses from Pittsburgh (ironic given my initial misunderstanding of what "Club Med" meant) and had a good time with them.

One night there were lots of piggyback rides going on, and a cute small but sturdy gal beckoned me to hop on by bending forward and slapping her lower back. I wasn't sure what to make of this (perhaps a silly bet?) and so hopped on. She strode me around in front of the limbo contest finals on stage, causing the French emcee to stop the festivities and say, "What do we have here, a horsie?" at which time the gal's knees buckled and we almost went tumbling forward. The gal and I just laughed with no-one getting hurt. Camp for adults, if you will, where you can just let yourself go, literally and figuratively.

About a year later, Mike and I returned to Club Med – this time to Huatulco, Mexico which had just opened (this was its first week). This trip was fairly dull in the first few days except for a large Mexican fiesta including hundreds of us guests (giant conga line around the village) and some festivities regarding the new opening of the Club. But then it happened. It was the "Olympics" contest and I was about to be an unwitting participant. The male "G.O." ("General Organizer" staff member) with French accent was seeking a vacationer to compete in the hula-hoop contest against Vanessa, a G.O. from the U.K. who was hula-hooping effortlessly on stage in a daunting way. This was the evening's main event after dinner and so there were hundreds of people standing there. Nobody raised his or her hand to hoop against her, and it took a while before anyone would be selected. That person was me!

Mike recalled that I mentioned I'm still a good hula-hooper, and won a contest at Club Getaway (mini-version of Club Med but no relation) in Connecticut a few months earlier. He grabbed my arm and raised it, laughing as the G.O. ran over and shouted in his French accent, "It's a guy!" At first I resisted, but was literally dragged toward the stage as the crowd was hooting. Upon questioning when on stage I said where I'm from, and got a big roar from about 300 other New Yorkers at the Club. I could see Mike with a goofy grin on his face – sort of like the character in "Animal House" who says, "This is gonna be great!" before Belushi and the boys go bonkers on the campus. I was handed a hula-hoop (no practice) and The DJ played the Chubby Checker song "The Twist." Vanessa and I started hula-hooping and the crowd went nuts as we both ramped up to full-swing. I wondered if this was because of Vanessa having all the right parts shaking (pretty blonde); seeing a guy who can hoop well (a rarity); or because they were drunk (probably some combination of these). Then I thought, "Hey, with all these pretty girls seeing how I can move my pelvis, maybe this isn't such a bad thing after all!" So, I just got into the flow and watched the crowd watching us. Several girls did stare at me and I just smiled back. I just let go of any inhibitions knowing the song was ending very soon, and it would be over.

But...so did the G.O. running the event, and since Vanessa and I were both going strong he said to the D.J. "Play the song again!" to which the crowd went wild. So we continued...til the end of the song again, at which point the G.O. shouted enthusiastically in his French accent, "One-More-Time!!!" The crowd was now in a frenzy, with "The Twist" being played a third time. Halfway through the song, the G.O. announced that this is a new Club Med record. The song ended after the third time around, and everyone went nuts as Vanessa and I were still hooping. Soon afterwards, Vanessa hugged me, the G.O. shook my hand vigorously before raising the hands of Vanessa and I simultaneously, and the Club photographer took photos including both of us in the same hoop that was posted up the next day. And so began and ended my 15 minutes of fame. This one event helped make an otherwise lackluster vacation into one with an outstanding memory. Interestingly, I would take up hula-hooping again many years later when my physician said that while I'm in very good shape I have a slight middle-aged spread and by some chance am I good at hula-hooping? I said yes, got one custom-made (a "man-hoop" in guy colors), and hooped a lot. It worked! So, Club Med not only can take the weight off your shoulders (i.e., relieve your stress), but off your midsection, too!

Inspired by Club Med vacations my philosophy of life was changing from corporate MBA ("greed is good") to just wanting to have fun and enjoy life. It was therefore especially important to have a job that I enjoyed, maybe in a fun industry...like candy! That's when

I found Topps, makers of the baseball and football cards I collected as a kid, and especially the "Wacky Packages" cards and stickers that I believe to this day contributed to my decisions to major in and work in advertising. During the job interview, my soon-to-be boss, Alan, and I clicked. He was smart and had done volunteer work, same as I was doing at the time. We made puns and jokes during the interview. I could easily see working with and for him. And to this day, many years later, we remain friends. I would later describe this job as "the most fun you could have without being arrested," and worked there nearly a decade – my longest in any company before restlessly moving on (mainly with other confectionery companies around the U.S.).

I soon returned to Club Med – Turkoise solo, and had another fantastic time. This time I met Janelle, a cute blonde lawyer from Washington, D.C. but originally from New York City. We had fun in the sun and would see each other a few times back in the U.S. when she visited me in New York and I visited her in D.C. In a funny coincidence, her dad was a major distributor of Topps products! Janelle was pretty well distributed, too, and sweet as well. All my subsequent vacations to Club Med were to the Turkoise village – I had such great times there!

I returned there again two years later, this time with Mike, and we had another good time. We met girls, danced, partied, played sports, and spent time at the beach and pool. I met a girl there from Vancouver named Sandy, a pretty brunette. Lightning would strike twice; a few years later one of the Topps sales guys would meet her in a Detroit bar, mention that he works for Topps, and she asked him if he knows me – which he did! Small world. There must be some cosmic connection between Topps and Club Med. I never did recapture the lightning in a bottle of my first vacation there – but several came close and were delightful as well. That year I won a "Name That Tune" contest at the Club. Oldies music was a passion of mine, and I named many songs within the first few notes, winning the contest easily. Mike later said he heard me calling out the titles very quickly from where he was sunbathing on the beach. I didn't win anything significant, but music is still a strong interest to this day – as evidenced by the many song connections in this book you will encounter.

The next year wasn't one of my better vacations there but had some moments typical of the hijinks that went on at the Club. I went solo again and was paired with a good-looking roommate named Karl who was 10 years younger than me. This was good news/bad news for me: he attracted a lot of beautiful women when we walked around together, but almost all were attracted to him. During the second night of the trip when I returned very late to the room, I was very quiet so as not to awaken Karl and fell asleep in my bed. I knew he was already sleeping because I could see his silhouette by the window. A short while later I heard a female's voice coming from Karl's bed – this gal was obscured from my view when I had glanced over but she sure was there – and they started having sex (presumably again). I think they were both drunk. I ignored it for a while but did need to get some – sleep that is, since I had an early sailing lesson the next morning. So I casually said, "Oh hi Karl, aren't you going to introduce me to your friend?" They both jumped up. Karl said, "Oh shoot, I forgot I had a roommate" and the gal said, "Now you tell me!" grabbed her clothes and ran out. Karl and I both apologized to each other but we agreed that it's best to get separate rooms since he wanted his freedom to have girls stay in the room overnight. And so it was, starting the next day.

As fate would have it, the next morning I was sitting at breakfast alone getting ready for the early sailing lesson when the G.O.'s do what they normally do and seat random people at your large, circular table so that you're not dining by yourself. There were two cute gals, followed by a couple of more gals and then two guys, all of whom I didn't know. After some light chit-chat (I was tired and barely spoke) one of the gals livened things up when saying, "You'll never guess what happened to me last night. I met this really cute guy, we got drunk, and we ended up going back to his room. We had sex, fell asleep, and then his roommate walks in. He didn't tell me he had a roommate! And the roommate didn't know that his roommate had a girl in the bed with him!" Everyone started laughing and was very interested in what happened next. I thought about saying something like, "Let me guess: the roommate says, "Hi Karl, aren't you going to introduce me to your friend?" but of course I didn't do that. In fact, I didn't say another word because she then might recognize my voice and get embarrassed. I just rolled with it. I didn't see this gal again, but I did see Karl. We were cordial to each other, chatted, and upon parting I wished him a "bon jovi," not knowing what that meant but it sounded good at this French Club. This was ironic, because another French connection was about to come my way.

My new roommate moved in that night, a new arrival and well-to-do French guy named Francois who dressed in the latest fashions. He was also a nice-looking guy, closer to my age, and we got along well. At least in the beginning. As it turned out, Francois was married and living with his wife in New York, not far from where I was then living at the time. His wife didn't know he was at Club Med, and he went chasing after just about every gal there – especially the Asian ones, whom he adored in general. Unlike Karl, however, Francois was clown-like and turned off most of them.

Once I was talking to a couple of pretty gals outside the dining hall who seemed very interested in me. Francois saw me talking to them and shouted from across the way in his French accent, "That is my room-mate"– his pitch rising with each syllable. "How are you doing with the ladies, room-mate?" he asked gleefully in front of them. Well that about ruined everything, especially because Francois tried picking them up already and they practically ran away. "<u>That's</u> your roommate?" one said disdainfully. "Oh no, he's coming over" the other said. The two gals just walked away briskly. Francois arrived and I didn't have the heart to tell him why they had left. So, we went to dinner and sat at a table of 8, as usual. I could see the two gals I'd just spoken to at a distance – they too headed for the dinner hall.

Francois and I got our food at the buffet and were seated. The place was crowded. Francois then got up, started banging his fork on the table to get everyone's attention, and said, "Ladies and gentlemen, I am sorry to disturb your dinner – but I am homeless and need money. If you would be so kind, please place your money in the hat I am passing around in any currency you may have with you. Thank you." Fortunately he passed the hat to the person nearest him on the opposite side of where I was seated. This was all a crock and

I don't think he got a dime (or franc or drachma or kroner). There seemed to be a high need for being the center of attention, but if that was the worst thing about him I could live with that. He did not have sex with any women that I'm aware of, and certainly not in the room we shared. I didn't mind if he put the emphasis on "mate" in the word "room-mate," because it was better than my previous roommate putting his mate in our room!

But that wasn't all. On the last day of the trip I said goodbye to Francois and wished him well, then darted out. I was in the van with a few others from the Club heading to the airport. OK, done with him I thought, and now it's back home to New York City and the fun factory that was my job at Topps. Just then I heard someone frantically calling, "Wait! Wait I am coming" at which time a passenger told the driver to stop. I knew from the voice who it was, and when he got into the van after storing his luggage in the back, guess who he sat next to without first looking. That's right, moi. "Hi Francois" I said. "That is my room-mate!" he happily proclaimed to the rest of the passengers (I was waiting for the "pass the hat" con to pay the fare, but he didn't pull this stunt). Francois then sat next to me on the four-hour flight to JFK Airport in New York. We had a good conversation, and he sort of charmed me like he did most others. When we arrived in New York, Francois followed me past Customs and asked if we could share a cab. I said OK, and his stop was first. When we arrived there, however, he became frightened and said, "I cannot go inside my home right now; would you mind if we went to your stop and I will buy you lunch?" I said no, thanks but he wouldn't take no for an answer, telling me he would be in big trouble if he went inside just then. He was serious for the first time. Finally, I said OK and we had lunch at a restaurant at which the hostess watched our luggage.

Francois noticed there was a fine men's shop across the street and insisted we go in there together. He practically dragged me in there. He pointed out which fashions were good and why, teaching me a few things. He then saw a pricey shirt he thought would be great on me...and without even asking just bought it for me. He insisted on doing this based on my kindness (and tolerance, I would add). I thanked him and treated him to dessert at a nearby café.

Francois made a few phone calls and, apparently when the coast was clear, said he could leave now to go home. We parted and ended on good terms, although neither of us initiated staying in contact with the other (can you hear the "Odd Couple" theme song playing)?

As a final thought on this trip, Francois was right – the shirt looked very good on me, became one of my favorites, and helped me socially based on the compliments it engendered from several women. I still have the shirt and it still fits. Thanks, Francois – "that is my room-mate!"

Perhaps this experience scared me off because I did not return to Club Med for another five years, still my longest gap between Club Med vacations to present day. I decided to give it another try, and it was like an old friend welcoming me back; I had a fantastic time! I remember one gal telling me on the beach there, "This is paradise, why go anywhere else?" At that time to me she was right. That beach, that food, those gorgeous sunsets and great-looking people, who could argue with perfection?

I had another excellent time at Club Med – this time with my own room having recalled the last roommate experience. The crowd during that particular vacation was very lively. The late-night parties were awesome, including midnight swims in the pool. Everyone it seemed was having a great time, and I realized that I should do this more often. Soon afterwards, that's what I did, but the next time with a girlfriend. Club Med was still the antidote to civilization, and I was loving my freedom. Soon, however, I would enjoy it in a new way.

Due to job commitments, I did not take much vacation the next couple of years, but when I had the next one coming I knew just where I was going. I met a nice Irish girl from Buffalo, New York named Doreen who was as sweet as could be and 11 years younger than me. We became involved in an exclusive relationship (more about that later). I convinced Doreen to join me on a Club Med vacation. All it took was a few photos from previous trips there (sans the girls I met) and she was in. We went to Turkoise and had a truly wonderful time. Seeing Doreen all jazzed up about the Club reinvigorated my passion for it, too. As a couple, we attracted other couples to hang out with. A few singles, too. So once again, as during the first time there, I found myself in a group of 8 dining and doing activities together. There were all the usual suspects on this trip: beautiful beach, sunny days, blue skies, happy faces, and great food. Doreen fell in love – with Club Med (OK, make that her second love). This had a whole different vibe to it for me but I was comfortable either way, as a single or as a couple.

Doreen and I returned the next year as well. This time my friend Mark from Topps joined us with his friend. Mark had an excellent time on this trip and later told me he would think of this beautiful place to ease an excruciating pain. Proof again that the Club Med experience can extend far beyond its physical borders. Mark would also return and become a fan of the Club. In fact, Club Med – Turkoise never disappointed anyone I know who went there. Doreen later told me she took out the photos from Club Med to look at them during dreary winter weather when feeling blue. She'd then smile and have happy memories. Club Med will do that to you when thinking about it. The only blue you'll feel is the sapphire from the ocean and the azure from the sky.

Over the years Club Med has changed with the times. Televisions in every room, clocks, Internet access, and more. I can understand it, I suppose, but still feel that the other way was best, when you lose all sense of time and self. Others I spoke to who predated all the updates agreed. I feel privileged to have experienced that because it may never return in today's frenzied, techno-reliant, and 24/7 world. The chocolate bread and fun songs/dances still remain – although I may now be doing them with the offspring of those I danced with in the beginning. But I'm not alone in my revisits to the Club – the average age has moved up from mid-20s to mid-40s. There are many I meet who have been to Club Med (all villages combined) 30 – 50 times to my meager 15. Many have repeatedly returned to Turkoise. Seems I'm not the only one who appreciates a good thing when I experience it. And Turkoise is one of the few remaining Club Med villages in the world that is geared for singles. That in itself may keep me returning to this "Isla Bonita" as warranted by my situation. To me, despite all the changes, Club Med is still the "antidote to civilization" and may even prevent a lot of what ails you in the first place. Club Med would come to my rescue again, but more about that later.

Soon after my first Club Med in Turks & Caicos, Mike and I went on another brief vacation with a French theme, this time for a long weekend to Montreal, Quebec. Neither of us spoke French but this did not seem to matter; most people there spoke English, and as long as you made an attempt to speak French they helped you out. We walked around the old section of downtown, noting the historical buildings and little shops. We sampled various restaurants and enjoyed the French cuisine. This was a pleasant city with charming and quaint little sections, a delightful place albeit a bit cold in November (I was underdressed, not realizing how cold it gets with the wind). We walked around McGill University since I liked campuses, and found this also to be historic yet charming. My fraternity had recently installed a chapter up there so at least I was familiar with the name. I didn't find any of the "brothers" on campus while there since they didn't have a house yet.

At night, Mike and I checked out a few nightclubs, and that's where something unfamiliar to me popped up. A local gal I met there named Emma and I got into a good conversation about Canada and travel in general. She was impressed that I, as an American, had traveled around a bit including to other parts of Canada and Europe. She said to me that many Americans ask her if Canada has a King or a Queen. She seemed upset about this and claimed that Americans were ignorant about Canada. At the time I wondered about that myself – not whether Americans were ignorant about Canada, but whether they had a King or a Queen. She said, "Of course you know that we have a Prime Minister, you seem like a smart guy." "Oh sure," I said, "a Prime Minister." "Mulroney's been in office for a while now, and we like him," she said. "Oh yeah, Mulroney," I retorted, having no clue about this but sounding like I did. I was tempted to ask if they had American bacon there since we have Canadian bacon in the U.S. but didn't go there with that question. I realized that despite having traveled I really didn't know that much about other cultures; I was mainly there for the sightseeing. Did I care to learn about them? Not really, at that time. But by osmosis, I would learn whether I wanted to or not. Later on, I'd want to.

# Chapter 4

## Back To The Future In Europe

As mentioned, after my first Europe trip with Mike there were several Club Med vacations and the cruise to Bermuda with dad afterwards. I had been inspired by cruisemate John, age 80, to become worldlier like he was. I aspired to become "that guy" who had been to over 80 countries, was impressive to others, and had a nice-looking younger lady on his arm (perhaps why I went for Doreen who was 11 years younger than me). So I was ready to return to Europe, and so was Mike 8 years after we first went. We got a good deal with the airlines in November to go to Italy and Switzerland. This was more of Mike's idea for the culture, but I was starting to get really into travel.

We started in Rome and saw all the usual sights on our own: the Coliseum, Trevi Fountain, the Vatican, Forum, Pantheon, and a lot more. There was history all over. Being from Brooklyn, which has a lot of Italians, we were comfortable with both the big-city beat of Rome, and the people. The Italian food was excellent, albeit served in smaller portions than in the U.S., and we found some terrific restaurants at very reasonable prices. I still prefer New York City pizza to that in Italy based on the doughier crust and more flavorful sauce, but Mike likes thin-crust pizza so to each his own. We had terrific gelato afterwards that was very flavorful and came in a multitude of varieties. The women didn't disappoint either: very beautiful, and among my top-10 even after traveling to over 100 countries! Our hotel room that we shared was small, with garish clashing colors, but we weren't there to spend time in it so no matter.

Instead of taking organized tours, Mike and I were comfortable getting around on our own. We knew to be careful and walk with purpose, looking like we knew where we were going even if we didn't. In Rome, telling people I was from "Brooklyn" was a plus; several people told me they had relatives there and were warmer to me as a result. I found most people there very helpful and many spoke English fairly well (we did not speak Italian). However, I found in almost all international countries to which I traveled, that you are much better off if you speak a little of the language or at least try. Importantly, at least know the local words for "please," "thank you," and "toilet."

At Vatican City, Mike and I climbed an enormous amount of steps and overlooked the city – or should I say, country. That's because Vatican City is technically a country – with its own post office, banking system, and even army made up of Swiss guards! Most people I met didn't know that, and this factoid would come into play in a later trip discussion. The views were excellent from this vantage point. You have to be in at least good shape to climb to the top, but the views are well worth it on a clear day.

Mike and I took the museum tour before I split off and did my own thing. I had a better appreciation for art at this point and marveled at that in the Sistine Chapel, among many others. I went around the city with my camera photographing everything interesting – architecture, statues, people, foods, and more. I found all this exhilarating and didn't mind the cold weather at all (similar weather pattern to New York City). I was impressed by many well-dressed Italians who looked as if they popped out of a fashion magazine. "Dress makes the man," I was told. And it made the women, too. I also liked the large tinted sunglasses, adding to the Mediterranean atmosphere.

I was well-aware of pickpockets there and took the same precautions that had served me so well during riding the New York City subways without incident for 20 years: wallet in front pocket, never show money, and tuck away any jewelry. If you have any luggage, keep it in front of you at all times, and do not accept anything (e.g., packages) from anyone you don't know. These rules applied everywhere, not just in Italy. I was also not pickpocketed anywhere else overseas by observing these precautions (not that they're any guarantee). As I would soon learn, anything can happen anywhere at any time, including crazy drivers, vehicles jumping the curb, and even calamities occurring when everything seemed to be "normal."

Such was the case when I had a bizarre incident happen on the way back to the hotel in Rome. I was on a city bus in heavy traffic, when a male passenger said something to the bus driver that really set him off. The two started arguing and it escalated from there, almost coming to blows. The driver got so upset that he left the bus – and never returned! Myself and most others stayed on the bus for a while thinking he would. Horns were honking from behind us, and the other passengers were talking amongst themselves in Italian. Utto, this wasn't good! I asked if anyone spoke English, but no-one responded; panic was setting in. Finally, everyone got off the bus and the driver was nowhere to be found. I had no idea where I was, but fortunately had taken a card from the front desk of the hotel upon arriving which had the name, address and phone number on it. I hailed a taxi which brought me there for about $20. I learned to always take the hotel's card or other documentation with me including the name, address, and phone number – and would do this for every hotel, motel, hostel, and other dwelling I would stay in subsequently. This was a lifesaver that day because I wasn't even sure of the hotel we were staying in (this was before cell phones so I couldn't even call Mike), and due to the time difference our travel agency was closed. I was glad to be back safe and sound; the situation could have just as easily gone in a different direction even with a bus that didn't move in any.

Our next stop via Eurail train was Florence, or Firenze as they call it there. This was important to know because the station at which we needed to disembark had a sign reading "Firenze," not Florence. I kept this in mind afterwards throughout my world travels because a few cities are not named what we call them in the U.S., as will be identified later. The Eurail train ride was a special treat. Comfortable seats, excellent scenery, food car, upscale-looking people, and a smooth ride all on schedule. Mike and I would ride this later as well, and I would subsequently ride it through other parts of Europe (or Europa, as it is called there).

I loved Firenze, which to this day is one of my favorite cities. It had a different vibe than "Roma," not nearly as frenetic or crowded. There was art and fashion all over the place. Mopeds, too, and these motorists drove like crazy New York City taxi drivers except down narrow cobblestone streets, so beware! But there were quieter streets after you crossed the Ponte Vecchio Bridge, a very old one that harkens back to Firenze's medieval days. A few times I witnessed "That's amore!" with young couples making out by the Ponte Vecchio (one couple even posed for my photo). Lots of black leather, too. Again, similar to Brooklyn, but with a historic, artistic flair and ambiance. I was even working at Topps at the time with a guy from Brooklyn whose last name was Vecchio, so I was comfortable with everything there.

Afterwards, Mike and I went to the world famous Uffizi gallery to look at paintings and sculptures. The art was beautiful, but I had seen enough and wanted to sightsee on my own. I thoroughly enjoyed this sojourn, and took some magnificent photos of the Duomo, a beautiful, large domed basilica built starting in the 13$^{th}$ century. There was also a picturesque bell tower, Boboli Gardens and Pitti Palace. Lots of fine shopping, too, including the all-important leather Italy is known for. Beautiful stuff, really. I feel the same about shopping as I do about the art galleries. Some is fine, more could be good depending, but after a while that's it, "no mas." I'm there to be out and about, especially outdoors and mingling with the locals. This mingling skill would later become invaluable in subsequent travels; I learned a lot from the locals who knew the scoop about their city as no other person or printed matter could convey. I still have some of these people as online friends today. Ironically, I would meet some on-bus, on-train, and on-plane, too. Mike got around on his own as well, and saw the highlights that interested him.

Then we were off to Switzerland by Eurail – which was my favorite part of the trip. Switzerland was the real prize, and the part I pushed for when Mike and I had planned the vacation. Taking the Eurail through the snow-capped alps was simply amazing, and a photographer's paradise! Mike and I took a series of trains up

Europe's tallest peak in Switzerland called Jungfrau (pronounced Young-frow) which offered incredible views, weather permitting. We started our ascent up at Kleine Scheidegg and ended up about 10,000 feet high to the summit via cog railway when the ride was done. I clearly remember people on the train talking about the weather, and whether or not we would be able to see anything. Then, a couple of Italian guys who were at the front of the train and got the initial view ran back into our car excitedly screaming to their friends, "Spettacolare! Spettacolare!" Even those of us who didn't speak Italian understood that and were very excited!

Mike and I exited the railway and yes, it was "spectacular!" To this day, that clear mountain view is one of my favorites. These days you can go online and see for yourself, but back then there was no such thing. And I can tell you that even photos do not do it justice. You see giant snow-capped mountains, especially the Eiger; a huge, long ice riverbed; and the observatory from which on a clear day like that you could see four countries (Austria, France, Italy, and Germany). Wow! Even my enthusiasm was lifted to a new peak! Mike and I just took it all in. I shot about 75 photos in an hour wanting to capture the majesty of this breathtaking sight, the most beautiful I had ever seen to that point. I would later live in Colorado Springs, Colorado, at the foot of Pike's Peak (tallest peak in the U.S.) and take in the views from there. No comparison; Jungfrau was way better. I would recommend this to anyone looking to see one of the world's most "spectacular" views, for its beauty was breathtaking in any language.

Mike and I spent the night in Interlaken, which is the conduit city from which you get to Jungfrau. The name translates to "between the lakes" since the city is surrounded by Lake Brienz and Lake Thun. There are spectacular mountains nearby. I learned that there was an ancient festival there called the Alpine Shepherds' Festival, which would not have been of interest to me back then. But today I have a quirky interest in unusual museums and festivals, so this would have been of utmost interest. Perhaps if I return I'll check it out.

Our next stop via Eurail was Zurich. I remember seeing cathedrals with pointy steeples along Lake Zurich, the city having a real European charm to it, and everything looking incredibly clean.

Several merchants meticulously cleaned the glass windows of their stores prior to opening and during the day. To this day, those were the cleanest windows I've ever seen, and the owners took a lot of pride in it. There was an old town Mike and I went to where we browsed in bookstores and art galleries. I recall the absolutely beautiful watches, like I'd never seen before, some looking like they were out of NASA with all sorts of dials. They were expensive, as was everything in Switzerland. Zurich, more than any place else I'd been 'til then, made me feel like I was in what my image was of Europe before I ever set foot in it. There were even lots of blonde gals looking like Heidi, just like you see on TV or on a packet of Swiss Miss® chocolate!

And this caused me to make a faux pas. As Mike and I were getting ready to board the train in Zurich we saw two cute blonde-haired girls our age with their hair in braids, looking Heidi-like. I saw this as an opportunity for us to meet them and learn more about the culture from the locals, so I approached. I wasn't sure if they spoke any English so I slowly said, "Hi, my name is Steve and this is my friend Mike. We are Americans, from New York. Do you speak any English?" The two girls just looked at each other and smiled. One then said to me in a familiar accent, "Yeah, we're from New Jersey." Mike just burst out laughing. I was so embarrassed to the point of just slinking away. The girls did let me take a photo of them as the train was pulling into the station. As I told Mike after the photos were processed, "They're Swiss girls, OK, if anyone asks. Their names are Heidi." "Both of them?" Mike asked. "Yeah" (because I couldn't think of another Swiss female name). "They're sisters, too." Mike just laughed, and would good-naturedly razz me about it later.

As we walked around, Mike and I split up to do our own thing, in my case, sightsee and take photos. Mike found and went into the Lindt chocolate factory, and I never saw him look so happy as when he was coming out with two full bags and a big smile. We both appreciated a great piece of chocolate and went on our own sampling spree in Zurich; it was fantastic! (Nestle is based in Switzerland.) White chocolate was in vogue at the time and there were many samples of these, with and without nuts. Mike told me the chocolate factory also had a museum that showed old chocolate-making equipment and promotional materials. Since he was the only one there during the visit, Mike was allowed into the company employee store, where he spent almost all his money he had at the time on the discounted chocolate. That seemed to make his day, and we called it a day soon after that, walking around the city at night and having a good, fine-dining meal. As an aside, the tipping in Europe is different than in the U.S., and is not standardized across each country. Many restaurants build the tip into the menu price; for others, 5%-10% is sufficient for good service. You might want to check into the rules before you go, which also may include tipping for lavatory attendants, hotel porters, and others that may be different than in the U.S.

Finally, we went to Lucerne, which was a charming and incredibly expensive city. Lucerne featured more gorgeous mountains, lakes, and shops. On the Eurail ride through the magnificent Alps we had a nearby seatmate from England named Malcolm, whom Mike and I goofed on. He was so straight-laced and we acted so goofy, but it was fun. Malcolm did us a big favor by taking a photo of Mike and I waving as we stuck our heads out two adjoining windows of the train car as it was pulling out of the station. This is a classic photo I still enjoy viewing. There was more Alpine splendor in Lucerne, and especially beautiful watches – the best I've ever seen. This was a sparkling, clean city, run very efficiently, including the Eurail which was always right on time throughout our trip. One last cup of hot cocoa for me and then a good night's sleep was a sweet ending to my second very good trip to Europe. It would be three years before I returned to the continent again on leisure, during which time I explored a lot more of the U.S., soon visiting every state with a trip to Hawaii the following year.

I returned to New York while Mike stayed on a few extra days once again, and went to Geneva, among other places. He later came back with an excellent photo of the stone Geneva Lion. As it turned out, this was the last vacation Mike and I would take together: conflicting vacation schedules, job priorities, dating relationships, and Mike's eventual marriage a few years later (I was best man at the wedding), followed by my subsequent long-term relationship with Doreen. Interestingly, I would not only go it alone on most subsequent vacations, but prefer it since I was getting the hang of overseas travel and liked the flexibility of being on my own. There were also a few business trips I would take overseas, so these European vacations were a good training ground for those as well.

Soon after this trip ended, Mike landed an advertising copywriter job in Toronto, Canada. He invited me up and I flew into Toronto to stay over a couple of nights. This, too, was a beautiful, clean city that reminded both of us of New York. Lots to do, and Mike had a nice apartment at The Esplanade. In a strange way, Toronto seemed like a cross-section between Switzerland and New York City since it, too, was surrounded by a lake and had a bustling city life. Toronto had several fine restaurants that we sampled. Mike guided me around, and I liked what I saw of this city. We even checked out a Yankees-Blue Jays baseball game at the Sky Dome downtown. As it turned out, this visit to Mike portended what was to come for me. I visited again a year later, this time flying into Buffalo, New York and renting a car to drive up to Toronto (90 minutes). Only a few years later I would relocate to Buffalo for a job – and drive into Toronto quite often, although by that time Mike had returned to New York City and got married.

The following year was an interesting one for travel, including my first overseas business trip to the International Candy Expo in Cologne, Germany on the Rhine River. I was working at Topps, and by then had done well in the candy business by branding Ring Pop and Push Pop lollipops primarily through TV advertising. Part of my mission there was to look for competitive knockoffs which might be illegal, in addition to new product ideas or even manufacturing sources overseas since Ring Pop was becoming maxed-out in the company's U.S. capacity to produce it. At this show, candy manufacturers had samples at their respective booths, and thus I was again able to sample some exquisite chocolates. There were Swiss, German, Belgian, Italian and many other fine chocolates. It's amazing that I didn't gain 10 pounds during that short trip; walking the immense show helped take off this weight gain.

That was my first trip to Germany but wouldn't be my last. Since I was on business, I just got to visit Cologne during very limited free time, at the end of January and only for a few days. I remember this timing because the Super Bowl was on – starting around midnight with the time difference – and I watched it in my hotel room broadcast in German despite having to wake up only a few hours after the game was over to go back to the candy show. After walking the candy show, I walked around the city. There were cathedrals and bridges, and a historical feel to the surroundings. I really felt I should return there someday to see it as a tourist – and later would do just that to better judge the city. So if you go somewhere on a business trip you should probably return as a tourist if you can to see what you've been missing. That goes for places that may seemingly have little to offer, for as I learned, everywhere has something of value – you just have to find it.

Later that year I ended up inventing a new candy product called Roller Pop candy. I was inspired by this idea by literally watching a painter roll his paint roller along a wall outside my office at Topps. I recognized the paint roller shape as that of a Push Pop lollipop turned on its side, and figured maybe the Push Pop could be affixed to a plastic paint roller handle and come with a plastic paint tray into which some fruit-flavored powder with color rub-off effect could be poured. Finally, in keeping with the "paint" theme, the pop would be rolled into the candy powder and the two combined would turn the kid's tongue colors as he or she "paint-rolled" the pop on the tongue. The product idea was patented by Topps with me listed as inventor, advertised on TV in selected markets, and sold fairly well as a candy novelty. I mention this here for two reasons: first, as a reward for doing this, Topps sent me to Asia to oversee its production along with Push Pop manufacturing (Shanghai, China and Bangkok, Thailand). Second, because five years later another candy company, in Colorado, would hire me I believe partly as a result of inventing Roller Pop. This product was similar to a product the company was looking to bring to market, called Lollipop Paint Shop. This invention thus changed my life, especially via the new job opportunity, but moreover there also was a job-altering/life-altering situation as described next.

My boss who hired me at Topps, Alan, was leaving for another position as Vice President of a toy company, and I would be getting a new boss named Charlie who was highly experienced in marketing. Alan's departure led to a senior management change in the confectionery group. Charlie and I remained in this new scenario, but left Topps for better positions in separate companies over a year later, continuing our successful business careers afterwards and to this day. Coincidentally, Alan would return in a new role, and remain at Topps for the next 15 years and counting. Had Alan not left in the first place, I probably would have remained at Topps, and everything you read in this book henceforth starting 15 years ago would not have happened. So, I have to thank Alan for leaving Topps and then returning, resulting in a string of excellent jobs for me (including at the Colorado candy company), incredible travels I was soon to encounter, and for enabling me to make a new friend in Charlie as well. I am also friends with Alan to this day, and he remains one of the finest people I have ever known.

I was traveling extensively around the U.S. during this time, mainly on business, but would stay over on weekends to check out these destinations on my own by renting a car. It didn't matter if it was in Louisville or Louisiana, I was just interested in exploring, meeting the locals, learning about the area, and getting a feel for what life was like there. I'd been doing this for about the previous 10 years, and ended up reaching a milestone when vacationing in Hawaii, my 50th state visited, for a week via flight to Honolulu and side trip to Maui. This was appropriate because I loved the old "Hawaii Five-O" TV series, the show's star was named Steve, and I was born the same year that Hawaii became a state. I had a great time there – and would visit Hawaii three more times as of the writing of this book.

Not only would I visit every state by the end of that year, but I ended up as of this writing being in every state a minimum of 4 times, including visiting all 50 state capitals - quite a difficult feat since many are not in the places you'd expect and are out of the way. This was not to set any records but because I was really into seeing the country, admiring its beauty, and seeing the treasures. That jigsaw puzzle of the U.S. also probably had something to do with this. I also had a penchant for going to unusual museums and small venues popular with the locals. I ended up at several offbeat places, but these were learning opportunities as well, including museums devoted to roller skating, toys, swimming, and even UFOs among many others. Maybe I was truly a "ramblin' man, trying to make a living and doing the best I can" as the Allman Brothers sang. And speaking of "when it's time for leavin'..."

I was off to China on business the following year. Initially I was to go to Taiwan to meet a colleague at a factory there, but had my first travel snafu. My passport was going to expire in three months, but the business trip was going to be over within a week. No problem, right? Wrong. As it turned out, I could not enter Taiwan unless my passport was good for another six months. The corporate travel agent didn't realize this and so no warning was given for me to get a new passport. Thus, on the flight to Taiwan I was forced to get off at the stopover city, Hong Kong, at which I needed a new passport to remain in China as well. I called my colleague who was already in Taiwan and he told me to stay in Hong Kong while he takes care of the business in Taiwan for a couple of days, then we'll meet in Shanghai as planned. It was a bit unnerving getting off the plane alone in China, not speaking the main language, or even knowing where I was going. I had to learn on-the-fly and did this after some difficulty. The situation was daunting at first, and I remember thinking that maybe I shouldn't be traveling overseas alone if things could get this complicated. But I worked my way through it, and it turned out to be a very good trip, both professionally and personally.

Topps was gracious enough to put me up in the Peninsula Hotel on Kowloon Island in Hong Kong at $400/night – to this day the ritziest hotel at which I ever stayed! You could do anything in the room by remote control including open and close the curtains. I was surprised it didn't pee for you, too. I played with it as if it were a toy thinking it could spark another new-product idea, but it didn't. The hotel was in a great location for sightseeing, which is what I did for two days after completing my take-along work. The island was beautiful, and I took a tour that allowed me to see the highlights, especially the tram up to Victoria Peak that overlooked the harbor (beautiful, clear weather once again). This was almost the warm-weather equivalent of the view from Jungfrau, but with water instead of the ice river, and sun-drenched mountains instead of snow-capped peaks. Really spectacular and a must-do if you go there. There was also a beach area called Repulse Bay that was picturesque as well.

Because Hong Kong was still British then, I had no problems finding people who spoke English and were able to help me locate whatever I needed. I learned how to say a couple of words in Chinese just in case. I was startled a few times when hearing Chinese people talk to me with a British accent; I guess hearing a British person with a Chinese accent would be even stranger. I was certainly learning that things are not always the way you think they're going to be. Some overall impressions there included lots of people on cell phones, which were fairly uncommon then; lots of smokers; and lots of people in general. At 5'8" I was much taller than many people there, the first time this had happened. There were also lots of dragons – statues, paintings, and other art. I was literally the "accidental tourist" in Hong Kong, but this turned out well. In addition to enjoying Italian food, I love Chinese food, too. I found the Chinese food better there than that in New York City – more flavorful, but could be a bit salty, too.

I obtained my new passport in Hong Kong (black & white photo) and met my business associate in Shanghai. The business part of our trip went well. We stayed in a nice hotel there, and from our hotel's restaurant window during breakfast high above the waterway watched well-dressed people disembark from a boat to go to work. This was sort of like the Staten Island ferry taking people into Manhattan but a lot more picturesque. What wasn't like New York City was the dining experience I had with Chinese executives there. We went to a fancy seafood restaurant, and while the seafood in particular was delicious, I was not enamored with some of the other delicacies. The way it worked was there was a big spinner plate put in the middle of the table with various foods in the compartments, like a Lazy Susan. One included eel, one included turtle (with its head on and staring straight at you), and more. I sensed that my business hosts would be offended if I didn't eat each one, so I did (yes, eeeew!). They didn't taste horrible; I pretended it was calamari because in this case I needed it to be mind over matter. I survived – but never had either one again.

One of the Chinese businessmen seated next to me was a marketing person who worked in Shanghai for the candy manufacturer. This company produced candy for Topps, but was not an official part of the company. He asked me a lot of questions about marketing in the U.S. I gave him the basics that any introductory American marketing textbook would have provided. He took copious notes. Ironically, almost exactly 10 years later I would be teaching these same concepts to college students in a new career, and watching them take copious notes as I lectured. So at this restaurant I'd be having an entrée in more ways than one.

Finally, my colleague and I went to Bangkok, Thailand. This was scenically my favorite part of the trip. We stayed in the Royal Orchid Hotel, another top-notch place. The landscaping and floral arrangements were gorgeous. I had my first taste of Thai food there and man was it spicy! I think I drank a pitcher of water with it. As with the other parts of this business trip, the Bangkok part went well, too, and I learned a lot in the process. I saw some unusual machines such as one I call the taffy stretcher, and saw hundreds of people in one room wrapping Push Pops faster than a machine could do it! I was a bit tired from this trip, enjoyed it but wished I had more time for sightseeing all the cities I visited. Little did I realize that I would return to these countries later as a tourist and be very impressed by what they had to offer. People often ask me how many of my overseas travels were for business. The answer is very few; after this business trip, there would only be one more overseas, and that would be over a decade later. The rest were all my own doing – for better or for worse.

I caught that lightning in a bottle again the following year, and it couldn't have come at a better time. I was looking for a great adventure to counter-balance an increasing work load and add some sizzle to my life. In fact, unknown to me at the time, this vacation I planned would become a major turning point in my business career, travel career, and life in general. In retrospect, this trip launched me as the traveler I would become afterwards. The first two vacations to Europe with Mike were very good, but I had not been back to Europe on vacation in a few years. No friends or others were available to travel with me at this time, so I decided to just wing it alone and see what would happen. I wasn't a highly experienced traveler at this point but was spreading my wings, so to speak. But where to go and what to do? Those were the questions.

Since I was traveling solo this time I was seeking a travel company that was turnkey, where I could just fly to a destination and be escorted around. I went to my local travel agency, was given some brochures, and decided to take a budget-oriented motor coach tour to see what that was all about. I ended up selecting Cosmos Tours going to Sweden, Denmark and Norway for nine days. I took the roommate option to reduce the cost but had other reasons as well: the "luxury" tour operators did not offer a roommate option; and I was told by the tour operator prior to my leaving that if the roommate situation does not work out and there is another room available, I could switch to a single and pay the differential. Also, if I couldn't be paired with a suitable roommate, I'd get a single room but only be charged for the less-expensive share option. That sounded good to me. Note that cost was very important to me because while I was making good money at the time I was contemplating leaving my job even without another one secured; and my philosophy was to apply my trip savings to more travels in the future. I would continue with this economic philosophy throughout my travel career, learning many cost-savings measures which I will share with you later in this book.

As it would turn out, a wonderful experience was waiting, as great as the initial Club Med vacation, which was still the undisputed champion to that point.

I arrived in Copenhagen and took a taxi to the designated hotel the night before the tour began, arriving near dinner time. The tour leader had left a notice for all passengers on this tour that was given to us upon check-in. It told of a group dinner in the hotel, after which the details of the vacation would be discussed in a meeting room near the dining room. I immediately went to my hotel room. My roommate was already there, napping after for his long flight. His name was Jerok (pronounced Jer-roke) from South Korea. I'd had a hit-and-miss experience with roommates at Club Med, and knew that they could be built-in friends or pains in the butt. I'd soon find out about my compatibility with Jerok. At the dinner the tour leader, Lisa, a well-dressed woman in her early 50s, provided the itinerary by day, hotel list, and planned activities. I was surprised there were no formal introductions; I was interested in who my 40 tourmates were, where they were from, why they were taking this tour, and more – especially since I had never been on one of these. As with being in the fraternity/starting college, I was hoping that someone could show this rookie the ropes. The vast majority of those on my tour were people in their 60s and older, retirees I suppose. I could tell by the accents that there were several different countries represented. A major positive that developed from the cross-section was that the few "younger" people – in their 20s and 30s, all single – immediately banded together. Interesting that this happened by age and not by country of origin, e.g., but as a marketer familiar with demographics perhaps I shouldn't have been surprised.

The one-hour introductory meeting ended at about 8:30 p.m. Lisa asked if there's anything anyone would like to add before we meet for breakfast the next morning at 7:00 a.m. I hesitated in doing this, but stood up and requested that anyone who wanted to stay on after this meeting, and get to know each other better, come to the seating area in the lobby. I didn't expect anyone to show up; many were tired having arrived that day, and probably wanted to get settled in their rooms if not done already. I was surprised when nearly 20 people showed up! There was a good cross-section of male and female, older and younger, married and single, and from several different countries. They all looked at me, so I guess I was Master of Ceremonies. I winged it and just asked everyone to be seated and we'll introduce ourselves. I started, stating my name, where I'm from, and why I'm taking this trip. I also mentioned that I'd been to Europe three times before and now wanted to explore these Scandinavian countries. Each person spoke for about two minutes. Main reasons for taking this tour included: desire to see a different part of Europe; an organized tour taking care of all the details; "right time, right price"; liking Cosmos as a tour operator based on previous trips; and wanting to see/meet/photograph beautiful Swedish women (OK, that one was me, but the other single guys agreed).

It was a beautiful thing to watch this unfold because even those who lingered in the back, appearing bewildered, nervous, or even shy about their English, opened up. There were some fascinating details revealed, including from one regal-appearing, somewhat shy Indian gal who was descended from royalty and explained the genealogy. I was very encouraging, made a few good jokes, lightened the mood, and generated lots of laughs and smiles. Others did the same. You would never have known that we all just met! We stayed there chatting away for three hours. I especially enjoyed hearing about the others' home countries and travels, including to exotic places in Europe, Asia, and even Africa. This made for interesting and lively discussions. In retrospect, this not only helped out Lisa the tour guide (and the bus operator Franz) in creating a good mood, but also greatly assisted the passengers to feel comfortable with each other. By the end of the trip Lisa sincerely praised our group for being among her best ever, which included people being on time and following instructions, in addition to the cordiality and enthusiastic discussions amongst us. We all had a very good time.

Jerok, my South Korean roommate, was particularly impressed by what I had done. He was sort of shy and had trouble meeting people. He also shared that the reason he selected the roommate option was to potentially have a friend right away on the tour, sort of my thinking as mentioned (assuming the fit was right). Now he was very happy I was his roommate because I also exposed him to many others with whom he may not have spoken. As it turned out, Jerok also was looking for someone who could take photos of him; he had a fancy camera but was traveling alone, making it difficult at times to be in the photos because he didn't have a tripod. I felt the same way, so we agreed to do this for each other, which made him (and me) very happy. We got along extremely well, and we were both happy about that (Jerok never had a roommate).

Ironically, just as at the Club Med – Turkoise village during my first visit there, on this trip 8 of us hung out together, split evenly between guys and gals – all the youngest people on this tour, with me being the eldest of the group. It's hard to describe how truly marvelous our time together was, because unlike at that Club Med village where the 8 of us were all Americans and basically from the New York metro area, here we represented six different countries, three different continents (most were from Asia), spanned two decades in age, and grew together as a tour group (within a group) for nine days. Nine days does not sound like a lot, but it sure can be. It goes much faster, however, when you're having fun. The 8 of us shared information about our cultures, jokes, experiences we had traveling, sightseeing/photo opportunities the others may have missed, and more. We were cordial to the other tour members, but went on most excursions as our own mini-group. I ended up being the unwitting ringleader throughout the trip; I found it interesting that a few people in the group initially said to me when decisions needed to be made (e.g., where we should go), "You're from America, so naturally you're the leader." Oh, really? Funny how my country's world leadership position translated to my being the group leader. That was my first experience of "you are what your country represents" (my words) with many more to follow. I also learned that this tour was representative of many other international ones I would later take: on average, only 10% were Americans! The most-represented countries on my tours would be (as a percent of the passengers): United Kingdom, Canada, and Australia. There were several Asians, especially Japanese, too, depending on tour location.

My favorite person in the group was not Jerok, although I greatly enjoyed his company, but a very cute Japanese college student named Akiko, who liked to be called Akko. She wore a backpack everywhere and was just like a ray of sunshine, always smiling and amenable to just about anything you asked. Akko and I made a deal, that we would take a photo together at every beautiful sight during the tour. I didn't really think this would happen, but it was funny how it did. A lot of times Akko would call out to me to come over for the "photo op" (expression I taught her) but she was so soft-spoken that sometimes she had one of the other tourmates come over and get me for it. I was a little less demure about it. When I saw a beautiful sight, say a gorgeous mountain range, I would yell, "Akko, photo op!" and she would drop her backpack, come speeding toward me with her head down, stand next to me for the photo (always on my right so the photo is in size-order when processed), then when the photographer (usually Jerok) was finished, Akko would reverse the process and speed back with her backpack on, to where she was before. This was so cute and funny. What a sweet girl, so full of life! Just a pleasure to be with. And always smiling.

In Copenhagen, our first city, the highlight was the amusement park Tivoli Gardens. Based on its world-famous reputation, I expected it to be huge like Disneyland® or Great Adventure®. It was surprisingly small with not nearly as many rides as I'd thought. Although charming with its decorations (especially bulbous lights), overall it was somewhat disappointing. We also passed by some palaces but I wasn't impressed with these, either. Maybe it was just me. No-one from the group raved about anything in Denmark either, so perhaps not. The main attraction for me was the Mermaid Statue by the water, which was cool. As they say, "When in Rome..." so I did have the "Danish" (pastries) there and the beer (Carlsberg). Both were very good. Hans Christian Andersen was from Denmark but I did not see too many sights with a fairy tale quality. A couple of locals I asked about Denmark's history complained that Denmark used to be a superpower but now is much smaller based on losing a lot of wars and territories. This seemed to still bother them. We didn't spend much time in Denmark, but the better news was that Sweden and Norway were much better.

Next we rolled into Stockholm, Sweden – and this was everything I hoped it would be, sort of like a giant Minneapolis with large lakes and gorgeous blondes – or was it gorgeous lakes and large blondes? OK, both! It was here I developed my favorite camera stunt that I continue to use to this day: I would ask a gal I wanted to meet to take my photo, since I'm a tourist all by myself. Almost all the time the gal would agree, and most of the time she would ask me where I'm from afterwards. If she didn't, I'd tell her, and would ask if she's a local. If so, I'd ask her to recommend places at which to eat, things to do, etc. This worked well on several levels: it got a conversation going; it let me know quickly if she was friendly or unfriendly toward Americans; it provided some very good recommendations; and it often ended in a good photo op with the gal, that often times included her friends as well. Best of all, it led to some awesome times that will be described later.

On the topic of photographs during this trip, a funny event happened that captures the friendliness of the people there and just the funny little things that happened to make this trip so wonderful. The 8 of us were walking around during some free time and happened onto a combination zoo and open-air museum - showing how Swedes used to live - called Skansen (I like that name – makes you feel like you're away in Scandinavia). The place was akin to Colonial Williamsburg in the U.S. We wanted a group photo in front of this big semi-circular sign with the Skansen name in yellow letters, but there was no-one coming by to take it (none of us had a tripod). Finally, a guy came by who looked like someone out of a Mentos® commercial, mid-30s, blond hair with big white-toothed smile, and dressed nicely. Akko and another Japanese gal in the group, Misaki, whom I emboldened during this trip, asked him if he wouldn't mind taking our group photo. He was at first taken aback and looked over to the rest of us. I just smiled and shrugged as the ladies charmed him (I don't think anyone could turn down Akko). He then happily obliged. Then Rashmi (Indian royalty gal) asked if he could do the same with her camera. Same response. Then Jerok. Then me. And so on. He ended up taking 8 photos, all with a different camera. Instead of getting agitated this guy was amused, even charmed, and went to extra lengths to get the right angle for the best photo, ultimately getting on one knee despite wearing nice trousers. He was so nice about it, all with a big smile, too. We each shook his hand and said "thank you" in our native language, which I suggested. It just made everyone feel good. Interesting how happiness transcends culture, age, religion, and so on. This wasn't just a vacation, but an education as well, and just plain fun.

The Swedish people were very friendly in general, but many were sort of shy at first. You had to work at it a bit. What I liked most was that many (mostly the younger people) were free-spirited and lively, unlike others I'd met in Europe who were more subdued in general. I liked the liberal attitudes, flamboyance, beautiful smiles, and general happiness. As I stated before, I just want to be happy. This sounds so simple but look how elusive it is in the world! Stockholm in particular was awesome, a beautiful city in general and not all that big. Some people called it the Venice of the North. I really liked the area down by the harbor which is right near a metropolitan part of the city. Great views, boat cruises, and just pleasant strolls in general. I met so many nice people there who were so congenial and welcoming. I noticed, however, how tall the people were! I'd say the average guy was about 6 feet tall and the average gal 5'8", or so it seemed. In fact, later in the trip I was walking down the street alone and three women were coming toward me from the distance. They were arranged in size order from left to right as I viewed them. I played a mind game in guessing that they were, 5'1", 5'5" and 5'8," respectively. As they passed me I'd realized I was way off; they were approximately 5'8, 6'1" and 6'5" respectively (all were in heels)! Pretty, too. Some people there had the blondest hair I had ever seen, some had the bluest eyes, some had the smoothest skin (by appearance), and some had all three. I'm surprised I didn't get whiplash from all the head-turning! Unlike Tivoli Gardens, Swedish women lived up to the hype and exceeded it.

I reveled in being in a place so different; unlike in New York City, e.g., if you had dark hair in Sweden you were in the minority (the same if you were under 5'10" it seemed). It's one thing to be away, say in London which is similar to the U.S. in language, or in Rome, whose people look similar to those in Brooklyn, but this was the most "away" I'd felt except for the trip to Asia which was corporate-controlled. This feeling of being on my own and away to a much different sort of place would become pivotal in future travel decisions. I felt free, empowered, happy, and charmed.

One thing I didn't like about Sweden and Scandinavia in general was all the smokers. It seemed that everyone did it and there were butts everywhere (the type you find on the cigarette, that is). I would often grin and bear it, but also went out of my way to avoid it where possible. This was hard to do because you could smoke almost anywhere there, unrestricted, including in restaurants. Thankfully, there was no smoking allowed on the tour bus (I asked before signing up).

At this point all the stress from my job in New York was gone. I was totally focused on the wonderful time I was having, and feeling great! Money couldn't buy this feeling, I was in another zone! Strangely, I remembered that when I got the "aha!" idea for Roller Pop I was also in this zone (was having a really good day). To this day I believe that if I can get back into that elevated zone on a "natural high" amazing things can happen. In retrospect, that "Skansen" day or the day I thought of Roller Pop would have been good days to play the lottery!

Our group's happiness, silliness, and giddiness seemed to rub off on the rest of the passengers, and Lisa and Franz. I wouldn't say that I learned that happiness is contagious, but that I forgot it is. We continued to just enjoy the moment, this twinkle of bliss that was so elusive, and as my supervisor at the ad agency had told me a decade earlier, I wished I could have bottled it. I was reinvigorated-squared.

Our next stop was Gothenburg, called Goteborg there, second largest city in Sweden. This city was nice but nothing like Stockholm. There was a relatively new opera house and some good shopping along a major boulevard. Some museums, modern buildings mixed with the old, but nothing memorable for me. It was there that I noticed my first "funny" word: "infart" which means "drive" or "approach," usually leading into a parking lot, e.g. There would be many more" farts" to follow. So, the trip included lightning in a bottle and some rolling thunder, you might say.

Speaking of rolling along, next stop: Norway. One thing I immediately noticed: they also love their ice hockey there! As I'd learned to do I exchanged U.S. dollars to have at least a small amount of local currency with me for incidentals. Our tour leader told us we would get a better exchange rate at the hotel, or even better at the bank if we had time. I usually did the exchanges at these places but if there were no opportunities I'd pay the extra at the airport or other convenient border location. Note that most banks back in the U.S. do not take back the coins, so it's a good idea to have only bills to exchange back into U.S. currency. However, I purposely kept some coins for the foreign coin collection I was building started when, as mentioned, my aunt would bring these back for me from her travels when I was a kid (I plan to pass these along to the next generations).

We went to Oslo and Bergen, plus a few smaller places including the Telemark area, with its winding roads and scenic mountains. Some highlights for me included visiting the ski lift from the 1932 Olympics in Oslo, and some interesting sculptures, including of three giant men with hammers in their hands, which reminded me of boss Charlie's famous expression during crunch time at the office, "It's hammer time!" But the best of this was in a sculpture park called Froggenparken (Frogner Park) which featured some of the best statues I'd ever seen. These included a man carrying a woman on his back, and a man picking up a baby. A couple of them even looked pornographic, which others noted, too. There were a lot of statues with naked people merged together. You could tell that some of these statues were, um, erected in a big way. The exhibit was bold and interesting, liberal and naughty, not something you saw a lot of out in the open. I've been to several sculpture parks afterwards, and this one remains the best. I spent about an hour just admiring these statues and taking photos (yes, including with Akko). There were also gnome statues throughout Norway, which added a little accent to the trip. Bergen was a nice little college town on the water with its own charm. I wasn't much for architecture back then, but I liked what they had there, especially as set against the green mountains and lake. More photo ops. I wrote in my journal that there was a "subdued vibrancy" to this city, if that made sense, based on the energy of the college students, yet relative conservatism compared with Sweden.

The trip ended and I have to say that I had the most wonderful time – literally – as in full of wonders! The scenery, weather, tourmates, tour leadership, photo ops, beautiful women, and more! It just all came together and would have a halo effect for many years to come. Anything to do with Sweden, college towns, even sculpture parks were of strong interest to me. I coincidentally would end up living near my second favorite sculpture park, called Griffis, outside of Buffalo, New York in New Springville. If you're anywhere near the area I would highly recommend seeing it.

This vacation was also a pivotal point for a couple of other reasons, and would slingshot me in an entirely different direction. First and foremost I decided I wanted to leave my job, which was no longer fun. Simple as that. Soon afterwards I did that. This vacation also taught me that I could have a great time traveling alone to another continent, on a tour, by myself, and even be a galvanizer of others from disparate backgrounds. Thus, I would take many more of these motor coach trips, particularly with Cosmos but others as well – and find not only great value, but great learning and happiness as well.

# Chapter 5

## Shoveling Off To Buffalo...

Early the next year I ended up in Buffalo, New York, 425 miles west of New York City – the first of what would end up being two job relocations there. It sounds odd that I would even relocate there from New York City, one of the premiere cities in the world, but there were several reasons why the opportunity and timing were right: a persistent recruiter highly recommended a frozen foods company there looking for someone with my skill set; I was warned about being pigeon-holed as just a "candy guy" since I had been at Topps, marketing confectionery products, for 8 years; my immediate family had recently moved out of Brooklyn to Southern Florida so I'd be without them in New York City anyway; the cost of living was very low; I had negotiated being paid my New York City salary; I had ended a dating relationship; Buffalo was within an easy drive to Toronto, Canada, a premiere city I liked a lot; and I wanted to try living out of New York City. Was I the consummate New Yorker, or could I now live and adapt elsewhere? That was a big question for me.

I visited Buffalo for the job interview, and was very surprised that it was much nicer than I'd thought; there is a lot to do there if you know where to look (the city is not good at promoting itself). This is where I would meet Doreen, my longtime girlfriend, but not for another year. I accepted the job and was relocated out by a company that made inexpensive frozen dinners, and also had a canned chicken line that a colleague of mine managed. The job was "OK" but dull compared to the fast-paced and innovative candy business. The marketing budget wasn't there, either, so I became bored with the job (but not Buffalo) and left in a couple of years.

But the fun was just beginning. I bought my first car in Buffalo, after having been a lifelong train commuter in New York City where most people don't own cars. I still have my 15-year-old Toyota Camry and maintain it well as the original owner. As of today I've put 170,000 miles on it and have driven it in 38 states (despite never driving it cross-country). I spent my first year driving around and exploring Buffalo and vicinity. The freedom was wonderful. There was a lot to do including museums/galleries, beach area (yes, there are several nice beach areas there), sporting events, parks, harbor front, bowling, bars/restaurants (some of the finest), and even sunset viewing areas from which I saw some of the most spectacular sunsets I've ever seen to this day from Erie Basin Marina. There was outstanding architecture, too, including several Frank Lloyd Wright homes. I also drove to all four major sports' Halls of Fame from Buffalo: Baseball (Cooperstown, New York); Football (Canton, Ohio); Basketball (Springfield, Massachusetts); and Hockey (Toronto, Canada). There's even an International Boxing Hall of Fame Museum I drove to three hours away that is not advertised, but was wonderful. And by the way, the weather was not bad at all! I had two "El Niño" winters while up there, among the warmest on record in Buffalo and the entire northeast! As mentioned, I've had fantastic success with weather, and this helped make my two-year stay in Buffalo that much better. This winter, as I'm writing, typing, and editing this book, is the warmest ever for Buffalo, and featured a record-breaking 82-degree day in mid-March, which was still technically in winter!

I was also extremely active in the community teaching as a volunteer in local high schools, taking pledges for the local PBS station, and involved with the Kids Escaping Drugs program. I made some good friends, joined a bowling league, and was enjoying life. I had several visitors who all were impressed with Buffalo, including Mike and his then-new wife (who went to college in Buffalo). Another visitor was a former girlfriend I'd met in New York City the previous year who was originally from Hungary. She noted how Buffalo's architecture reminded her of Budapest. I just shrugged, not knowing.

A few years later I would see that she was right. Soon afterwards, I met Doreen. Interestingly, although she grew up in the Buffalo area, she hadn't ventured out to explore much and I ended up showing her around many cool sites I found in the city. From there a romance blossomed on the shores of Lake Erie despite our differences in age, religion, small-town (her) versus large city (me) orientation, and education levels. Opposites attracted, and we hit it off. I would soon take Doreen well beyond her comfort zone which added a whole new dimension to the relationship.

I spent a lot of time up in Toronto, Mike's old stomping grounds, where I had visited him. I felt comfortable in Toronto for a number of reasons: Mike provided some new places to go based on his contacts still there; Hothouse was one of my favorite restaurants anywhere and, ironically, was near a building that looked a lot like the Flatiron Building in New York City near where Mike and I went to college; and, strange as this may sound, Toronto had a large international population, and I met many people there from other countries, particularly in Europe and Asia. I'd soon leave Buffalo, but before going I'd become thoroughly familiar with Toronto as well, including the downtown area, Chinatown, beach area, parks, university, and Casa Loma, an impressive medieval castle of a wealthy industrialist that overlooks Toronto. So, whoever thinks "there's nothing to do in Buffalo" (common complaint among the locals) isn't looking hard enough, or at all.

# Chapter 6

## From New York To New Zealand

I was now soon to be 40 and became contemplative about life. I had a feeling the best was yet to come. Or, more appropriately, I decided to make it happen. For many people turning 40 is depressing. I remember my grandmother, a very wise woman, telling me when I was in college that the 40s should be the best time of your life (her son and daughter were in their 40s then). I paid no attention to it then since it seemed so far away, but would now see what she meant. I considered myself "old enough to know what's right but young enough not to choose it" as the Rush song goes. I felt good and had orchestrated my freedom from a job I didn't enjoy. As such, I decided to reinvent myself. Good thing, too, because that year turned out to be outstanding. I visited my family in Florida – by which time my brother and his wife had one-year-old twin daughters, and were living there as well. As it turned out, the Super Bowl was being played in Miami a few days later, the Atlanta Falcons vs. the Denver Broncos. I had no intention of even trying to go. Then my friend Mark from Topps happened to mention that a high-level guy from the company, who liked me a lot, named Ty Franklin was down in Florida and going to the game. Ty once said to me, upon hearing that I was leaving Topps, that if I needed anything to let him know – and his administrative assistant, who overheard this, told me immediately afterwards that if he said this he really meant it.

So...I decided to call his office and find out where he was in the slim hopes of maybe being able to get a ticket. I was given his Florida hotel's phone number and called. I figured, "What the heck?" Ty was happy to hear from me, said he just got a request from another person he knows for a ticket, is having lunch with the #2 guy at the NFL that day, and asked me for a callback phone number which I provided. The next day, the day before the Super Bowl, he called to say, "When do you want to pick up your ticket?" I was speechless – he did it! I went over there, just 20 minutes away, in a flash and couldn't thank him enough. I wondered if he wasn't my guardian angel. I had a wonderful time at the game and sat next to a beautiful woman who he had obtained the other ticket for (excellent seats as well). The Denver Broncos won the game 33-19 and, as it turned out, that would be future Hall of Fame quarterback John Elway's last game; he would announce his retirement shortly.

I turned 40 soon afterwards, and had various parties thrown by family and friends marking the milestone. I welcomed the opportunity to make the most of life in my prime; to start off my 40s with a special occasion; and was inspired by the George Bernard Shaw quote, "Life is not about finding yourself. Life is about creating yourself." I wanted to explore the world and visit new places as best I could, to create a **f**un, **i**nteresting, **n**ew and **e**xciting life. So, after doing some research, I decided on heading to Australia and New Zealand, where it was warm that time of year, and go on tour again with Cosmos.

The flight from New York City to Sydney lasted 24 hours, with a brief stopover in Los Angeles. As with the trip to China, it was difficult being confined for such a long time, especially for an active person like me. But I managed through it with the help of three things: sleeping for nine hours; watching a couple of in-flight movies; and a long conversation with the gal in the seat next to me, an American attending Wollongong University, Rebecca, who was also looking for a way to pass the time. We chatted for seven hours, basically telling each other our life's stories. I would later do the same with many other seatmates I would encounter. She told me a bit about the history of Australia, too, including that it was a penal colony where British ships went to leave excess convicts that were too numerous for the British prisons. It was founded in 1788, soon after the U.S. got its independence from the British, so it sounded like the British had their hands full back then.

Further, I was becoming what I'll call a "travel athlete" – being able to endure long flights including curling up properly to sleep in the coach-class seat, and pacing myself (literally – up and down the aisles to get the circulation going) with a balance of reading, chatting, and watching movies. This travel skill was important, because if I couldn't endure long flights this would have curtailed my travels; but because I could endure them, even as I got older, this opened up the world to me as far as getting there. But I'm 5'8," and this was in the days before some airlines started putting less space between seats. It would get tougher in coach class based on this seat spacing, but I managed. How anyone six-feet or taller manages in these coach-class seats still mystifies me – but people do it (these days it's not just the feet of the person behind you on your chair, but the knees in some cases). Note that I always traveled in coach class (even for business trips) through present day, and reminder that the money saved in so doing was applied to more travels.

Landing in Australia was weird because I actually went forward in time by about 16 hours, plus the 24-hour travel, so if I left on a Tuesday night I arrived Thursday afternoon there (circa noon). I took a taxi to my hotel, had lunch on my own, and walked around the city. I had no jet lag, and never did get this affliction. I also was able to stay awake all day, and go to bed at my usual hour local Australia time, despite being very tired. I found that if I went to bed upon arrival in the new country this would mess-up my ability to acclimate to the new time zone. Fortunately, I acclimated well throughout my travels, including adjusting to the meal-time differences as well (again done according to the new local time zones, although I'd usually first eat something light).

The first thing I noticed in Australia was the funny accent of the people – most guys sounded like "Crocodile Dundee" but often more nasal, and most gals sounded like Olivia Newton-John to me. It was interesting that, because I was beneath the Equator, the water in the toilet bowl swirled from right to left, and that the weather got <u>warmer</u> as you headed <u>north</u>. This was exciting to me; just as there was an exhilaration about just being in Europe during my first trip, I needed something more potent now to create that same exhilaration, and this was it. The city looked beautiful, and the temperature was in the 80s – in February! I took an organized tour on my own before meeting up with my tourmates at night, circling Sydney by boat, much as I had taken the Circle Line around Manhattan. This was well worth it – the day was clear and we had great views of the Sydney Opera House, an architectural wonder with its shell-like roofs that looked like a ship in full sail mode when you viewed it from the side. It seemed like most things worth visiting there were easy to get to, near the harbor, including the Opera House. Sydney reminded me of a combination of New York City and Southern California; that is, lots of hustle and bustle among the business people, and yet an appreciation for down time and the beach. The buildings also looked like a hybrid of some from each place. Seemed like my kind of city, and perhaps a subconscious seed that was planted for a later move to California a few years hence.

The Harbor Bridge was also highly visible and accessible. This is a steel bridge that connects the city to areas north and can be climbed to the top of its arch. I did not do this based on time considerations, but it sounded wonderful. What a photo op that must be on a clear day! I've also heard that the bridge can shoot off fireworks as well. What a bridge!

Then there was the Sydney Tower, which looked very similar to the ones I saw in Shanghai, China and Toronto, Canada. I went up and took in a great view. My camera got a good workout once again. Soon afterwards, it was time to meet my tourmates and get briefed. This time there would be no repeat of the wonder-trip I'd taken with the younger people; this trip included mostly much older people, and so I often took off on my own when I could after the basic included tour (no disrespect, they were lovely people but I was looking for more action). There was only one younger person near my age, a male farmer from a very small Midwestern U.S. town, but we were total opposites, including my speaking fast and him speaking slowly. It was somewhat interesting learning about grains, commodities, pork bellies, price fluctuations, and other farm issues during the long motor coach rides...but not really. This tourmate, Gary, probably wasn't interested in my New York City stories, but was pleasant about listening to them. We were cordial to each other throughout the trip and talked mostly about the tour sites each day. This reminded me of my college days when there was an instructor from the Midwest who taught a business class. Smart guy, but he didn't resonate with the New York City students. The average grade on one of his exams was maybe 50 and he was gone in a year (thankfully, there was a steep curve). This difference of people, places, and things within the U.S. would be a topic I'd later discuss with numerous locals from foreign countries, who thought that people in the U.S. were mostly the same.

We were given lots of time on our own to roam around Sydney (not so much in the other cities on the tour), and I really liked that instead of the "if-it's-Tuesday-this-must-be-Belgium" approach that many tours have. On my own I went to the Taranga Zoo, on an island, by ferry from Sydney, and saw some unusual species I hadn't ever seen such as pandas, koalas, and kangaroos. I would later see a kangaroo roaming around an unsecured area of the zoo and was warned not to go near it, that one of its kicks could kill you. The kangaroo seemed so docile and fun-looking I really wanted to pet it, but heeded the advice.

My favorite part of Sydney was Bondi (pronounced Bond-eye) Beach – which I went to on my birthday. Not only was it beautiful and surrounded by mountains like in Southern California, but I was laying on my back getting a suntan in the middle of February – how grand was that while still living in Buffalo, New York? The weather was again magnificent throughout the entire trip – greatly enhancing it – and I met a lot of cute gals on the beach and hung out with them. The people there in general were as curious about the United States as we can be about Australia. I answered their questions as best I could. I love the U.S. so I presented it in a very positive light. People in general – if they don't dislike America – aspire to at least visit the U.S., if not live here. So not only was I becoming a travel athlete, but an unofficial U.S. ambassador as well. This would intensify as I traveled more – and I realized that every American becomes an ambassador (even unwitting) when he or she travels. In many cases, you are the only contact the locals may ever have with an American, and their impression of you becomes their impression of the United States. No pressure here, LOL (Lots Of Laughs).

I was educated a lot by the locals about Australia, but that stuff didn't interest me back then and I forgot most of it. There was mention of something about the Maori tribe who are the natives, and how they vie for political power in Australia, or something like that. Subsequently, however, I'd yearn to learn more about most things international. Note that the biggest criticism I've heard about the American people is that we're ignorant about what goes on in the rest in the world; in addition to meeting Americans (like me back then) who often didn't know basic things about the local country, there's plenty of American TV they watch as fodder for this as well, programs that demonstrate our ignorance by asking Americans basic questions even about their own country which they don't know the answers to. So, in the absence of meeting an educated American who knows about world politics, geography, history, etc., many international people I met, rightly or wrongly, think we're dummies and only care about ourselves. Keep this in mind relative to some subsequent travel stories I will mention in this book.

Next it was off to Melbourne, a city that most reminded me of New York City based on its downtown commerce and fashion areas. Lots of guys in suits and ties rushing around, looking harried. Yet there was a certain business-like sophistication about them I recognized having grown up in New York City, and this made me feel comfortable. I heard there was a good zoo there but I already was to the one in Sydney and probably wouldn't have had time to go to that one with the schedule of the tour. Instead of taking an optional tour around the city, I opted to just walk around the drop-off point downtown (as did several others), and mingle with the locals. The people there were crazy about their Australian Rules Football; they talked a lot about the Melbourne Cup (horse racing); and politics (none of these interested me). There was also a big international community there. I just liked hearing the accents, answering questions about the U.S., learning more about their culture in general (musical tastes for example – current artist Kylie Minogue is from there), and just sampling the city.

Being from New York City, I knew that there is the tourist's New York and the local's New York – and the two can be very different. In fact, when people often comment to me how expensive it is to live in New York City, I inform them of very worthwhile experiences they can do for little or no cost that most often are not mentioned in the tour books, such as a rowboat ride around Central Park, window-shopping, discount theater tickets, and great restaurants that aren't advertised much and are very reasonably priced (Mike and I often explored these). I also recommended Greenwich Village, Circle Line Tour, the great museums, trips to the other boroughs, and the convenient, inexpensive subway system with selected stations near selected sites (tourist, and local-known – the latter being the best). Many wrote down what I suggested.

Our last stop in Australia was Cairns (pronounced "Can"), where I snorkeled the Great Barrier Reef – the largest coral reef in the world. I was among the few from my tour group who did this, although I really wasn't in the mood to do it. It was another of those "when in Rome" moments. The tour leader advised us to put lots of suntan lotion on our backs due to the water reflecting the sun, there being a thin ozone layer there, and that we would be floating face down a lot looking at the reef and marine life. Sounded good to me – except that I was in an isolated section of the boat with a group of only 8 (there's that number again) cute Japanese gals in their 20s near me who were preoccupied putting lotion on each other. When they were done, I asked if they spoke English (would have been funny if they said, "Yeah, we're from New Jersey!"). They didn't, and here's where I would become good at charades – which I would later need for being in many other international places.

I showed them my suntan lotion and indicated I would like one of them to put some on my back. The girls all looked at each other and the one I was directing the request to motioned for me to turn around. I did – and soon I felt 8 pairs of hands rubbing this all over my back! These gals were giggling, and one took a photo with her camera. Just then several of my tourmates came over to see what the commotion was all about (a lot of people were looking; I guess word got around). One guy in his 50s, Roger, laughed his head off and said someone should get a photo of this. I asked him to grab my camera and take one. He did. It's still a treasured photo. Others on my tour also took a photo. The gals even posed and smiled, hands still on me. I also went snorkeling with these gals, holding hands with them so we wouldn't float too far away from the boat (as once happened to me). This was fun, too – no complaints.

The reef and fish were awesome – fantastic colors and so clear! I thought I'd get a sunburn on my back but didn't, fortunately. A couple of others on the excursion weren't so fortunate, especially the fair-skinned people. It's very important to be careful out in the sun and not over-do it. I still have some remnants of the Cancun burn. But anyway, I'd had a great time! I rarely snorkeled but when I did what fun times – Xel-Ha and meeting the German ambassador and his lovely daughter; a fun time snorkeling in Turks & Caicos; and now the 8 Japanese gals in Cairns, Australia! I was into my happy zone again, defined as a "10" or in words, euphoric. It didn't take a lot to make me happy; the "**FINE**" acronym I mentioned was just fine with me. Unfortunately, just as I had to emerge from the sensational snorkeling, I would emerge from this happy zone, too – but it was great just being there.

My story about having the Japanese gals rubbing suntan lotion on my back made the rounds with the rest of my tourmates – and during the rest of the trip I was often kiddingly (and maybe enviously) teased about my "geisha girls." I took it in stride, and with a big smile, I assure you. Good things came in eights and would continue to do so. Even the word "geisha" contained five letters from the word "eights," and that was "**FINE**" with me.

Next we flew to New Zealand, which I enjoyed even more than Australia. It was just beautiful with its lush, rolling hills. One immediate impression was all those sheep, at a 10:1 ratio to humans! They were everywhere. Interestingly, there is a large supermarket chain in Australia and New Zealand called Woolworth's that has no ties to the similarly named store in the U.S. that is now out of business here. But the name certainly fit the environment. We visited both the North and South islands of New Zealand (remember that the North island is warmer since we were below the Equator). On the North island, we visited Auckland and Rotorua.

Auckland was yet another place with a sky tower from which you observe spectacular views, and on yet another clear day it didn't disappoint! There was also the Auckland Harbor Bridge, which looked like a longer version of the Harbor Bridge in Sydney (a little rivalry, perhaps?). The people there, called Kiwis, seemed more relaxed than Australians, more like Californians. I heard there were excellent beaches in New Zealand as well, but I didn't have time to go to any based on our schedule and other activities I wanted to do. The locals were interested in what I was doing there; I told them I'm on tour with many others primarily from Europe. The locals seemed intrigued and welcoming. They joked with me about the sheep before I could even bring it up. I would only make one of my usual "baaad" puns about it, talking about having "shear" delight in being there. They may have heard this all before but laughed anyway.

Along this line, I remember thinking, "Now I've been from Oakland to Auckland," then "and from Dover, Delaware to Dover, England," then "and from old York in England to New York in the U.S." before my brain told itself to knock it off. However, the song "Wooly Bully" by Sam Sham and the Pharaohs kept going through my head based on all the sheep there. In retrospect, I was in the early stages of Musicales Ridiculitis – the immediate association of rock 'n roll lyrics befitting the new location or situation I was in.

Next we went on a long motor coach ride to Waitomo Glow Worm Cave, in which we then took a boat through the cave and received a history via tour guide. It was cool inside so a light jacket was recommended. The black cave featured one million wide-spread, green-colored glow worms that made it look like you were viewing the constellations. This phenomenon illuminated the limestone formations, giving an eerie, drippy feeling to it all. But it was quite a spectacle. We walked around and admired the stalactite and stalagmite structures. Stalactites form on the roof and hang down, usually in cone shapes, while stalgmites form on the floor and extend upwards. The Brooklyn wise-guy came out of me and I asked about "vegemites" in the cave (vegemite is an Australian spread, like a salty cream cheese). Several of my tourmates chuckled, and the guide stuffily said, "There are no vegemites here that I'm aware of." Well, we were "down under" – literally, in the cave.

We then rolled into Rotorua (pronounced Roto-rua). This geothermal marvel is still on fire from when the Earth was formed, and there were lots of geysers and bubbling mud pools to prove it. It smelled awful, like rotten eggs, and the smell got to me at one point causing me to gag and walk away from the group for a bit. Phew, el stinko! My associative mind immediately connected this to Yellowstone National Park, where I observed geysers and mud pools there. I had to tame my mind again when it connected Rotorua with Roto-Rooter and started playing the company's jingle from my childhood. This connection of songs, jingles, and what have you to locations I was in would continue unabated with successive travels, and get fairly creative in some cases. Very weird. I wouldn't even want to think of these songs but they would automatically pop into my head; many will be listed later at the appropriate time in this book. Fortunately or unfortunately, I am a music aficionado so there was a large mental catalog to choose from. I took it as a good thing; I was not only connecting the dots in the world but with appropriate melodies, too, ultimately forming a memorable mosaic that would keep me connected to my wonderful travels long after the trips had ended.

The South island was my favorite of the two, and was the larger one as well. We visited Christchurch and Queenstown. I don't remember too much about Christchurch except it was known for its gardens, hence the nickname "the garden city." It seemed lovely with great shopping and picturesque streets. But what I recall most was being taken to a few historical areas, notably churches, which didn't particularly interest me. A lot of people on my tours were interested in this, but I often would get "churched-out" because it seemed every city's tour guide wanted to show you the churches. While lovely, you can overdose on them if they're not your thing. I usually take that cue to go off on my own and meet the locals for the hour or two. The tour guides were not crazy about me leaving to do something else, and if I sensed there was any issue with this escape I would just take the scheduled tour. Most of the time, however, I would veer off on my own, stay close by, and be "back on the bus" at the designated time. Often times my chats with the locals were one of the best parts of the trip. In this case I even learned what lupins (a local flower) were – beyond the only other time I'd heard of them via Monty Python's Flying Circus TV show. In fact, I liked them a lot based on their color and unusual style. I was building an appreciation for nature's beauty, and would see much more of it as we progressed in our sojourn. I'd later become very interested in nature's beauty, which hadn't so much interested me previously. Ironically, being exposed to so much beauty was one of the beautiful things about travel in general – the world has an abundance, but not all in the same place. Speaking of which...

Queenstown (not to be confused with Queensland, Australia which is pretty in its own rite) is still one of my favorite places in the world today, even after visiting 100+ countries. I was amazed at its beauty – beaches surrounded by mountains – and all the activities there were to do in such a relatively small area. The view from above was spectacular via the tram. As for activities, it's almost easier to list what's not there. Some activities this tiny area was known for were bungee jumping, jet skiing, white water rafting, aerial trips, boating, hiking and biking, and more. There was ample shopping, too, and it was a pleasure to stroll around on this picture-perfect day with the temperature of 18 degrees Celsius or about 70 degrees Fahrenheit. Let me repeat – in February – and I was living in Buffalo, New York at the time. What a difference! It was amazing just to be there, and all my senses were heightened by the newness of everything. The more amazing, the better! Traveling in general became an adrenaline rush for me. And this was sure it – with the fantastic views from atop and afar. Queenstown was a wow! And I look forward to going back there some day, perhaps on a special anniversary of this initial visit.

Finally, there was an optional tour to Milford Sound, which was supposedly gorgeous. Well, I wouldn't know because it rained the few hours that we drove around (there went my streak of great weather on trips). I later learned that this is not only one of the wettest spots in New Zealand, but in the world! It can rain 10 inches in a 24-hour period. It wasn't pouring when we were there but it was enough of a rain to obscure any beautiful views. From what I could see there were a few steep waterfalls, and of course beautiful mountains. It looked sort of like Alaska's mountains on a clammy, rainy day. If I do return to New Zealand I might take this tour again – and check the weather forecast ahead of time. Weather can make a huge difference in your trip – especially if you like taking photos.

The trip ended and was well worth it. And I don't say that sheepishly! If you get the chance to go down under I highly recommend it. Every Olivia Newton-John song now reminds me of this trip, and that too is a good thing. The more audio-visual sync (marketing term connecting visual and audio cues), be it from a radio or my own mind, to hit the pleasure button, the better. Travel provides the raw material for this, so if you want to have a big, healthy, put-a-smile-on-your-face life, then travel when you can and lock-in those beautiful memories!

# Chapter 7

## Blue Skies And A Whole New Vista

Returning home to New York I flew backwards in time and arrived nearly two days earlier. I was thinking if I'd just got the winning lottery numbers in New Zealand before leaving maybe I would be a millionaire and could continue traveling forever! Alas, things don't work that way.

My friends and others back in Buffalo commented on the nice tan I had – what they didn't know was that I had one even better on my back (from snorkeling). I didn't rub it in, and just said I'd "been away" to those I didn't tell where I had gone. I met many travelers who wanted to make others envious, even with just suntans, but I was not one of them. There were consequences to doing such things, as will later be discussed.

A flow-through effect of this trip was also an interesting revelation to me in hindsight, and yet another benefit of traveling. I was on a natural high and began my job search immediately. I believe that the euphoria I had from this Australia-New Zealand trip was a factor in getting my next job, because I was "in the zone," my happy zone. I was confident and enthusiastic when talking, and the boss who later hired me noticed that I had a good attitude. Not only that, but soon afterwards I had a good altitude as well – a mile high – for this company was in Colorado Springs, Colorado. When I later heard the address was 888 Garden of the Gods Road, that clinched the deal for me – those "8's" once again! I would start there in April and the temperature was 75 degrees compared to 25 degrees in Buffalo. I was going to ask Doreen to go with me, but she beat me to it by asking me. Due to a developing situation with her job she would not join me until later – on her 30th birthday in November. We would live in New Mexico briefly before the company relocated to its new Colorado digs. New Mexico was fine; I had a friend there, liked the state a lot, and it was nice and warm! We then lived together, a new experience for both of us, for the next four years.

Doreen and I got along very well during our time together. We built our relationship and those with others. We made new friends, explored new places, and each had a good job. We traveled to 12 other states (including Florida and California) plus Canada (Vancouver), Mexico (Puerto Vallarta), and the Caribbean (two Club Med vacations to Turks & Caicos – Turkoise). Doreen enjoyed these vacations a lot, and I thought she would be the gal I'd marry. But I gave it a bit longer and found that once around with the travels was enough for her, and that at heart she was a stay-at-home type while I still had a lot of get-up-and-go, literally. I came to a crossroads in seeing that Doreen and I were opposites; as much as she and I wanted it to work out between us, we were just very different people and we split. I was heart-broken for a while but eventually "just picked myself us and got back in the race" as the song "That's Life" goes. I had not traveled overseas since we lived together and thought about doing that again. This turned out to be one of the best decisions I ever made. Having a committed relationship and traveling the world the way I ended up doing would have been mutually exclusive for me: you can't have your "Caicos" and eat it, too.

My job wasn't the same, either; after five years at both this company and in Colorado (which were fine for that amount of time) I was ready for a change. Something had to give. I decided to leave my job and just wing it, literally, flying to my destinations and my destiny. I had done well, made excellent money, and even accumulated a bunch of frequent flyer travel miles that would help fund future trips. No girl, no job, but no dependents, no responsibilities, and a clear blue sky. What to do?

I had been in this situation before and knew the answer: travel! This was soon after 9/11, and I was later asked if 9/11 was a factor in my decision to travel the world at a relatively young age. The answer was and is yes, but I would have done it anyway. I grew up in New York City and, although I lived in Colorado at the time the event happened, I was deeply affected by it being an American and especially a New Yorker. I did not know anyone who was killed in the tragedy, but knew people who did. But up through the ashes of this devastation can rise a new sense of self and purpose given this perspective, and so this heightened my desire to travel the world – see it before maybe we can't, enjoy it while it's still here, understand it if at all possible, remember it, and have it become a part of me. And I wanted to become a part of it, spreading the good things I had to offer. I was even inspired by the fortune inside a fortune cookie that read, "A part of us remains wherever we have been." It was time to start planting the seeds.

I started off slowly, going a lot to Canada over the next year. I had been to Ontario (Toronto) and Quebec (Montreal) with Mike, and also to British Columbia with ex-girlfriend Joy from grad school whose brother taught near Vancouver. I also went to Canada with Doreen many years later with a female friend of ours in Colorado named Lexi who liked hanging out with us. Her parents had a summer home in Montana and she invited us up to go on vacation with her from there. The three of us departed for a week-long wonderful vacation to Glacier National Park in Montana, then Banff and Lake Louise in Alberta, Western Canada. So having already been to all 50 states, I thought about going to all 10 Canadian provinces, making that my mission. I accomplished this with very nice trips to Eastern Canada (Newfoundland, New Brunswick, Nova Scotia, and Prince Edward Islands), followed by Western Canada (Alberta again, Manitoba and Saskatchewan) driving on my own through all of them.

Canada is very scenic and photogenic. I liked the three largest cities best: Toronto, Montreal, and Vancouver. Toronto reminded me of a cleaner, smaller, less wild & crazy New York City; Montreal was historical and French with excellent cuisine; and the Vancouver area featured one of my all-time favorite places, the Butchart Gardens in Victoria, with its incredible floral arrangements and illuminations at night (I was not big on botanical gardens until I went there). I also was fascinated with Newfoundland and its Viking heritage; this would lay the groundwork for later trips which would be among my favorites. I also greatly enjoyed Banff and Lake Louise in Alberta, which had "radiator-green"-colored rivers. However, the U.S. had many similar places, so I was not in awe of anything in Canada but enjoyed the peacefulness and historic charm there combined with its scenic landscapes.

The people in Canada were generally very nice, proper, and helpful. However, I ran across a few who did not like Americans because they said we ask ignorant questions about their country (similar to what was mentioned to me in Montreal about Americans thinking Canada has a King or a Queen). Really? First in Australia and now in Canada. Were we perceived that badly regarding this? I'd later find out in other countries: generally, yes. I must admit that I was surprised to learn that Canada did not become a country until 1867. I also found some of the people baffled as to why I wanted to visit all 10 provinces (to this day, I have never met anyone else who has done that, including Canadians – which surprised me). I would tell them, "To learn about your beautiful country," which generally satisfied them, and may have given pause to those thinking poorly of Americans in general based on our lack of knowledge about their country. I never did make it up to the Northwest Territories, however. I have a soft spot for Native Americans, and came away with the same for the Indian tribes in Canada as well. I could write a lot about Canada, but since brevity is a byproduct of vigor and there are so many other countries to write about, suffice it to say I liked it up there.

Once again, I had great weather for my trips, which totally enhanced the magnificent beauty that was already there and made for great photos. In fact, often times when I picked up my photos at the local photo lab one of the technicians would come out and tell me how good my photos look, and that the technicians often quibble over who gets to process my orders. "I'd rather be looking at a beautiful beach, beautiful girl, and beautiful sunset than more photos that have cut-off arms, legs, and even heads that we get here every day," one technician named Dan told me. He then asked what I do for a living. I said, "Nothing – right now I'm not working, but I will be soon." And sure enough I would be when ready. Next time he saw me he rushed up to the counter and said, "You must be working, I haven't seen you in a while." I'd say, "Yeah, time to refuel, but I keep dreaming about my next vacation." "Me, too," he said, "But thanks for taking me on yours" after handing him my rolls of film. "Where are we going this time?" he asked playfully. "I'll let that be a surprise," I replied with a wry smile. He would soon vicariously travel with me yet again.

A new year had arrived and I could easily get another job since I was an accomplished marketer, but decided after considerable thought...not just yet. There were several reasons why. As mentioned, you need free time, discretionary income, health, desire, and stamina to travel the world the way I wanted to. I now had all of these, plus there were other factors. I was now a healthy 45 years old and heard about a lot of people waiting to retire and then travel, but never making it (serious illness, even death before or soon after retirement). Such was the case with a close neighbor I knew back in Brooklyn. Also it was post 9/11 and I realized the world was forever changed. I wanted to see as much of it as soon as possible. Things weren't going well environmentally or politically, and I thought that my choices could be limited in the near future. Further, I had nearly 400,000 frequent flyer airline miles which would be expiring in the near future (worth about $100,000 if you were to buy them online). Plus, I was financially OK for a while if I remained single and lived modestly well as I had. I would later be very diligent about obtaining more frequent flyer miles, realizing their tremendous value if you had the means to use them.

In retrospect, that year marked the beginning of what I would call my "big bang" of travel, began a whole new wonderful chapter of my life (when some people go into mid-life crisis), and propelled me to yet an even higher plateau. People often ask me, "How do you do it, continue to have so many good things happen to you?" It's based on knowing who you are and what you truly want out of life. I was still single with no responsibilities, and decided to go for it, to leverage my freedom, excellent health, and other assets. It just felt right to me. And so began a new era of travel. I had one final decision to make...

Where to next?

The answer was a place that would later be ranked as one of my favorite countries to visit, which would shock most people: Iceland! Yes, Iceland! A few veteran travelers had mentioned this country to me as a premiere place to travel, and I thought nothing of it since I had already been to Sweden, Denmark, and Norway. But what I learned was that Iceland is nothing like those countries; in fact, the guy who discovered it purposely gave it this daunting name to keep others away from this beautiful place. So I was already intrigued. What's Iceland really like?

Since I was going to Iceland, I thought why not go to Finland, too, and thus get to all the Scandinavian and Nordic countries having already been to Sweden, Denmark and Norway? I called several major airlines but by this time in early Spring there were no reasonably priced flights to Iceland, nor could I use my frequent flyer miles since few airline carriers went there. It didn't look good for going there then. So I called Iceland Air on a whim, and the reservationist couldn't be nicer. This was another trip that was meant to be because the airline had been all booked up for a couple of months since Iceland has only a small window of decent weather. As I was chatting with the phone attendant a flight opened up out of Boston to Reykjavik, Iceland's capital and the northernmost one in the world. The reservationist excitedly said this never happens, and I believed it. She also was able to get me to Finland, then back to the States in the one-week time frame I was seeking – and also made a recommendation of where to stay in Iceland inexpensively in the middle of the city: the Salvation Army Guest House. This turned out to be an excellent choice for two reasons: Iceland was very expensive and this "inexpensive" room was only $75/night compared with minimum $200 anywhere else decent; and, because it was centrally located, I did not need a car, saving even more.

So, in May, it was off to Boston and then to Iceland, as a solo act by choice. I was surprised how short the flight was: under five hours, closer than California! On the plane I talked to a few people familiar with the country. I was told that part of Iceland is technically in North America, since this is where the Euro-Asian and North American tectonic plates meet. I thought that was interesting, which in itself was a revelation because in the past I wouldn't have cared.

They told me stories about how Iceland and Greenland got their names, discovered by the explorer Leif Ericsson and his father Eric the Red. I was told they named them as such because these explorers wanted the best place, Iceland, for themselves and pointed others to Greenland, which was mostly ice, thus naming it. So Greenland is ice and Iceland is green! There was some disagreement about this story, but no matter, I got the gist of it that Iceland was purposely misnamed. The passengers I spoke with did, however, agree on one thing: I must go to the Blue Lagoon – a huge, natural, outdoor geothermal spa surrounded by volcanoes and lava rocks, located near the airport. You go into the lagoon, and there's a healing effect based on the natural water. This sounded interesting and I wanted to check it out; fortunately, I almost always pack a bathing suit because you never know when you'll need one. We arrived at Keflavik Airport in Reykjavik, and I joined several passengers in a taxi heading directly to the Blue Lagoon, 15 minutes away.

Well, this place was quite a sight, one I'll never forget. It was cold outside, maybe 50 degrees in May, but there were people swimming in a huge, light-blue colored basin of seawater with views of mountains and geysers in the background. It was too cold for me to go in, but I decided to do it when others in there told me that the water is "very warm and good for your body, mind and soul." They had a white milky substance on their face, like cold cream, which they said is abundant from the rocks in the lagoon and "facilitates this unity." OK, whatever. This was another "when in Rome" moment along with a Kodak® one, so on went the bathing suit and out came the camera. I went in and thoroughly enjoyed it! The people in there – men, women, and children – all seemed very happy. Again, lots of smiles and laughter. I was surprised that most people spoke English fairly well. I "got into it" in more ways than one, swimming around, mingling with the people, laughing and joking around. What spectacular views, too! All this before I even got to my hotel! I did something I was later told I shouldn't have done, but fortunately there was no damage: I brought my camera into the Blue Lagoon. The seawater is very bad for it. But I protected it as best I could regardless, because I didn't want it to get wet.

Soon I was feeling magnificent – the people, the views, the friendliness – even without the white stuff on my face. A great start to what would be an outstanding vacation. It's amazing how a good vacation can take your mind off of things if you just relax and let it happen. And when it happens, you get relaxed. A nice full-circle, including a Blue Lagoon cap I would buy there and wear proudly to this day.

So, this is the Blue Lagoon in Iceland! Contrary to the country name, this huge geothermal spa has a water temperature of approximately 100 degrees. And what a view, amidst billowing steam, volcanoes, and lava rocks, as you sip a drink or swim around to meet others visiting from all over the world.

The Salvation Army Guest House was in a great location – easy walks to restaurants, shopping, and selected attractions. In the lobby there were games and other recreations – which was a mecca to meet other travelers who hung out there, mostly 20-somethings from all over the world who were interesting people. There I met a male college student who asked me if I wanted to play a game of Skak with him. "Skak?" I asked. He then held up the box it came in; it was chess based on the photo. I hadn't played in years and passed it up, but we had a lively, brief conversation. It turns out that Icelanders have their own language, Icelandic, and that many words, unlike Skak, are incredibly long! One such name that later came to international prominence was Eyjafjallajökull, an erupting volcano which not only disrupted travel over Western Europe, but also wreaked havoc with its mispronunciations by American newscasters. Street names I saw there had at least as many letters. I took several photos of these long-worded signs because they were so different – and again, made me feel like I was in a faraway place. My hotel room was tiny, and you had to share a hallway bathroom dorm style, but so what? I had the same situation living in the fraternity house at Michigan State with no problem. Besides, I wasn't there to stay in the room.

As in Sweden, the gals there were gorgeous. Unlike in Sweden, however, when I wasn't as courageous, I asked several Icelandic women if I can photograph them because they are so beautiful. All said OK, and I have a montage of these in my photo album. They were very friendly, too! One sexy blonde gal worked as a server in a pizza restaurant named Hot or Not? She had this name on the back of her shirt. When she asked me if I like my pizza hot or not, I looked up at her and said, "Definitely hot!" We smiled. She probably heard that a lot. I was also smiling thinking of the Rolling Stones song "I'm so hot for her but she's so cold" - especially if she brought me a cold pizza instead of a hot one (I was surprised there was such a choice). The young people there seemed very liberal and bohemian, and loved talking about music and drinking. There was a surprisingly terrific nightlife in Iceland that didn't start until around midnight on the weekends. I saw many smartly dressed guys and gals, and even couldn't resist taking a photo of a great-looking couple (with their permission) in black leather jackets getting ready to do the town. I can't recall anyone there denying my request to take his or her photo, and they seemed happy to oblige. I would say "takk" meaning thank you in their language, which was appreciated with a friendly smile – even if they spoke English. It was important to learn how to say key words and phrases in the local language of other countries I visited. While not mandatory, it helps; note that in many countries the younger people tend to speak English (taught in schools) while older people not so much, depending where you are. For this reason

I often approached younger people to ask directions, request them to take my photo, etc.

Topographically, Iceland was the most diverse place I had ever seen. I was fascinated by all the different features in this one relatively small country: glaciers, mountains, volcanoes, lava rocks, geysers, beaches, waterfalls and more. I remember thinking this is like Alaska and Hawaii combined. As a person who likes photography, this was fascinating. I traveled around Reykjavik, including part of the 800+-mile Ring Road that circles the country. I saw and felt the spongy tundra (similar to the North Pole in Alaska), lots of lava rocks, and learned about its volcanic history. A local gal I asked to take my photo told me about a local guy who is a volcano-chaser; he had a small theater in his home in which, for a nominal fee, he shows home-made movies he and his dad videotaped of volcanic eruptions. I went there and was stunned by the magnificence of this footage; it was as if you were right there with him! From that day on I had a keen interest in volcanoes, and the next year would take a helicopter over one in Hilo, Hawaii which was also a "wow!"

Since the landscape was a major attraction in Iceland, I wanted to not only see it by land but by air. There was an air tour that cost $200 for 45 minutes – but there was no guarantee that you would get a good view of Iceland. I asked how the weather had been the past week or so regarding visibility. I was told not so good – lots of rain. It was mostly cloudy but I was told that doesn't mean much regarding how it will be above the clouds for viewing Iceland. I was very hesitant about doing this for the money but was told that if you do get a good view this is a memory of a lifetime. My instincts took over and I decided to chance it given my track record of having great weather on vacations – and it turned out to be truly fantastic!

There were not a lot of passengers, meaning I would be able to get a window seat for taking photos – essential to my decision to take the tour. The pilot was a middle-aged nice guy who spoke English well, and looked like a cross between Captain Stubing of "The Love Boat" and the President of Topps when I was there (tall, bald, bright blue eyes). This made me feel comfortable somehow. We chatted and joked a bit right before take-off. He reiterated that we won't know how good the view will be until we get above the clouds.

I sat in a row that was empty on both sides, at the left-side window seat, so I could toggle back and forth from the left side to the right side of the plane as needed; I did not know which attractions I'd see from either side of the plane – assuming I could see any at all based on visibility.

The plane rose above the clouds and the pilot excitedly said "Clear!" preceded by an Icelandic expression that I assume meant the same thing. I looked out the window, saw this incredible view, and the first thing I thought of was the Italian guy who shouted "Spettacolare! Spettacolare!" upon the first view of Jungfrau in Switzerland. I immediately got out my camera and could not stop taking photos. Every view seemed like a post card. Mountains, glaciers, lush green rolling hills, volcanoes, the Blue Lagoon and more. I was so excited – as was everyone else, especially the pilot! Despite many of us passengers being from different parts of the world and speaking different languages, there was a communal sense of "wow!" that transcended everything. At this moment we were all in awe. The pilot continued the fly-around and I will never forget how he turned back to glance at me and emphatically point to the other side of my row with his eyes all wide. I scrambled to the seat by the right window. There was a magnificent view of Gullfoss waterfalls in a canyon surrounded by green hills – reminding me a lot of a mini Niagara Falls, which I had lived near in Buffalo, New York and visited many times. I took a lot of photos of this as well. Immediately afterwards there was another sight that reminded me of the U.S. – geysers that looked like the ones I had seen in Yellowstone National Park. I soon learned that our word "geyser" comes from the Icelandic word "geysir" after a 14$^{th}$ century eruption there. The rest of the scenery was just breathtaking, and I again was in my happy zone – that place in my mind that represents the summit of self-actualization, a mental orgasm if you will (these can be addictive!).

Upon landing, I totally wanted to see these attractions close-up, and arranged to do so. The geysers were incredible. These weren't as stinky as in Rotorua (rotten egg smell from hydrogen sulfide gas). If you haven't seen a geyser in action, I recommend it, assuming you have the stomach for the smell. Next up was Gullfoss – and it was every bit as good as it looked from the air. Yep, like a mini

Niagara Falls. It's incredible to think that Iceland has so many natural wonders in one place! How come I didn't know this sooner? Little or no promotion by its tourist bureau? Many people not having been there so little word of mouth? No matter; I felt like I was really onto something here. Plus, the weather was holding up nicely – although I did experience all four seasons in one day (30 degrees to 75 degrees)! I really felt like I was in an otherworldly place, something akin to another planet. It would be less than a year before I would *really* feel like I was on another planet, but more about that later.

An interesting attraction while there was the Perlan, a glistening, round-shaped building nicknamed the Pearl, which overlooks the city and has a revolving restaurant. The building also houses the Saga Museum, featuring replicas of Iceland's historical figures, notably Vikings. This got me interested in Vikings in general – but not enough to convert me from being a Bears football fan, LOL.

The city tour around Reykjavik was worth taking to get a sense of the area. I found some unusual architecture as well such as the Hallgrimskirkja church. To this day I haven't seen much quite like its rocket-ship-shaped exterior. There was an excellent view of the city and harbor from atop it. I wasn't wild about the food. There were some unusual combinations such as pizza with sardines and, for whatever reason, black licorice was all the rage – including enrobed in chocolate. As a veteran of the candy business I knew that black licorice wasn't a big seller in the U.S., but if anyone here manufacturing it was looking for a new market, Iceland was it. I saw a display of Jelly Belly® jelly beans there. I thought nothing of it at the time but this would come into play later in the year.

Finally, on my way back to the airport, I left extra time to go into the Blue Lagoon once again. I didn't need to stick a toe into the water, literally or figuratively, and just went right in there to absorb the healthful water and admire the view, albeit on a cloudy day with a few sprinkles. More nice people, happy faces, photos, and fun! Back to my happy zone. I would have liked to stay and see the Northern lights, and also go to Greenland but tours up to there weren't running just yet. That gave me the incentive to return – but not for a long time. There was too much of the rest of the world to see, and I was now interested in getting to as many countries as possible. But I would never forget Iceland, a magnificent tapestry of amazing sights!

If interested, I hope that you get there someday, but caution you not to be overly optimistic. Everything was just right for me, and my likes may not be the same as yours. However, that said, after becoming a veteran traveler and extolling Iceland to others, some were surprised but many were not. There were a lot of world travelers I met who also loved Iceland both before and after I went there. Not many I met had been there, but those who had raved about it, as I did. Don't judge Iceland by its name, or you too would have been punked by Eric the Red and son. Ironically, I have a close friend named Harvey with the same situation – old-fashioned name, mellow-looking guy, but an extremely interesting person whose hobbies include salsa dancing, martial arts, rap music, and Calcio (Italian soccer), with a high level of knowledge and/or proficiency in each.

So, Iceland – who knew?

Next stop was a flight to Finland, which I figured to be like Iceland. Ironically, this country was the polar opposite of Iceland – relatively dull with many drab people, more Soviet Russian than Scandinavian. Even the weather was drab, cloudy and cool (high 40s). Then I learned something interesting: Denmark, Sweden and Norway are technically the Scandinavian countries; Iceland and Finland are not. But all five are part of the Nordic region. So Scandinavian and Nordic are not interchangeable. Yet Iceland and Finland are so different as to not even be put into the same classification, at least culturally. Upon arrival in Helsinki, I noticed right away that even people's body language was different, more rigid and systematic, for example, than in Iceland. It was difficult making conversation, too. People just wanted me to cut to the chase, so if I needed directions they would provide it but if I asked if they are from this country I might get a "yes" and that's all. My ever-associative mind flashed back to a date I'd had with a Finnish gal in New York City, an au pair (nanny) who was beautiful with bright blue eyes and reddish-brown hair. When I complimented her on her beauty she said a line to me that is among the most stunning I have ever been told to this day: "I do not need compliments, I know who I am." Few times was I rendered speechless; that was one of them (Harvey still reminds me of it to this day). In retrospect, I don't think she meant to be condescending, but was just very direct in expressing her feelings. When I finally responded, "Well, you know who you are but I'd like to get to know you," it was met with an icy stare. That was a date from Hel-sinki.

I kept thinking that I would meet others who were more gregarious, but this rarely happened. The only time it did was with a pretty blonde named Anneli I met on the steps of the capital building, who was friendly and indirectly led me to another country I'd visit. She told me about the history of Finland and how much they love saunas. She was familiar with the Blue Lagoon in Iceland, but had never been there. Anneli told me how cold it gets in Finland, and that people there drink a lot of coffee. Later on I did notice this. I haven't been back there in a while, but if Starbucks® isn't there yet it should be. When I asked what there was to do that's fun and different, the best answer was to sit there and watch the people, or go watch the kayakers, or take a boat ride to nearby Estonia. "Estonia?" I said. What could there be in Estonia, which sounded primitive to me just by the name. But as soon as I thought that I remembered about Iceland and learned not to judge a country by its name. I thanked Anneli and then departed. I took a city tour of Helsinki but nothing stood out except a mermaid fountain. There were many churches, cathedrals, and other statues at the Market Square. I returned to the capital building a couple of other times and sat on the large steps, but nothing doing. So, it was off to Estonia which, I have to admit back then, I didn't realize was a country (I'd later have the same non-recollection about Macedonia).

I took a ferry from Helsinki to the capital of Estonia, Tallinn, and planned to spend a full day there. I didn't stay over because my hotel in Helsinki was fully prepaid, I didn't know if I'd even like Estonia (or how safe it was, e.g.), and I didn't like the idea of taking luggage on a ferry/walking around the city with it. It was a two-hour ride and I sat next to a lady about my age traveling with her niece who was age 12. They were very pleasant and responsive to my questions, and very interested in the U.S.; we got into a nice chat, and per my inquiry the lady told me they were from Estonia. She told me a lot about the city of Tallinn and it sounded interesting.

Sure was, and a pleasant surprise. There was a historic Old Town near the ferry dock at which you're greeted by a man and woman in medieval garb who hand out brochures about Tallinn (800 year-old history, attractions, etc.). Lots of restaurants, shops and more right there, semi-ruined by a giant McDonald's® staring you in the face (it's just not the place for it, in my opinion). There's a fairy-tale charm to this area, with lots of brick roads and pathways, castles, and a fortress with very impressive wall. Yet...nearby New Town was an upscale, modern part with outdoor cafés rivaling the upper West side of Manhattan. The food was excellent, too. Trams, buses, trolleys, well-dressed people, and lots of foreign-sounding conversation (Estonia and Finland have their own language). Great! And then my mind had at it - just as I was getting into the sightseeing and observing the happy people around me, it started playing the Bob Dylan lyrics, "Well I would not feel so alone, everybody must get Es-stoned." I could not get this song out of my head for the remainder of the trip. I walked around a lot, took many photos, spoke to several people, and saved one of the costumed workers from getting soaked during a freak brief rainstorm by sharing my umbrella, which she appreciated. I walked around the ferry dock a while just soaking it all in, then took the ferry back to Helsinki. So go figure, Tallinn was the highlight of my visit to Helsinki!

Overall, I had a wonderful time, especially in Iceland and to a lesser extent, Tallinn. Oh what the Hel-sinki, that had some nice parts, too. And so "Finnished" my Nordic (but not Scandinavian) adventure.

I'd had an excellent trip and thirsted for more. This was an important turning point because I now realized there was so much to see and do in the world, so much beauty, so many interesting people, places, and things of which I was completely unaware, and I had the resources to see and do even more. I now had an insatiable desire to explore and live my life to the maximum. While others were having a mid-life crisis I was in the midst of what would be a terrific 10-year explosion to the upside, the best time of my life, in my 40s, true to grandma's words over 20 years ago. I began seeking out tours that cut across Europe, and had the idea of traveling "buffet style" – meaning I'd get a sampler of a lot of places and later return to the ones I liked to explore in-depth, resources permitting. I returned to Cosmos which had a tour for 8 European countries. There was my magic number again, and I booked it. Hello world, I'm coming to visit you again!

The tour focused on the capitals of various countries, encompassing England, France, Belgium, Germany, Austria, Hungary, Slovakia and Czech Republic - quite a whirlwind in 16 days. Two weeks was about the maximum I could take on any motor coach tour, based on all the confining to the coach, but I was up to the challenge mainly because I was so goal-oriented. Not only did this get me to a lot of countries in one tour, but I was interested in U.S. state capitals and had been to almost all of them by this time. Once again Cosmos came through with an excellent tour providing great value. The group of 45 or so met at a London hotel. Many had arrived a day or two early to spend more time in the city while I arrived the night before and spent the next day touring London on my own before meeting the group for dinner. This was my first time back there in 19 years; it seemed familiar. I went to the usual tourist places, not wanting to risk anything extreme before joining the (prepaid) tour. So I went on my own to Buckingham Palace, Big Ben, Tower Bridge (which is also known as London Bridge), Harrods world-famous luxury retail store, a couple of parks and also the delightful aquarium. Once again, lots of photos and nice weather this early summer's day. That night, we had our dinner and orientation – with formal introductions this time, and received our marching orders for the next morning's journey. I had booked a hotel room share and wondered who I'd get. To my surprise, because there wasn't a suitable roommate on this tour to be had for me, I was given a single room for the discounted price of a share. Nice!

I was surprised at how few Americans there were, only 5 of 45, so the "10% Americans" percentage was holding and would continue to do so throughout almost all of my subsequent tours. The vast majority of my tourmates were from Canada, Australia, and other primarily English-speaking countries, with a few also from Japan. Most were older, 50s, 60s, 70s, with some married, most traveling with someone else, and the rest singles. Each crowd differs, and whenever you get a large group such as this – be it in a classroom, work office, social gathering or other, you get a variety of personalities, attitudes, and in this case cultures. It's important to oblige the tour leader and the rules set forth. In general, there were no major issues on this tour.

One such rule, which was a good thing, was to rotate seats throughout the trip so that every person had a window seat at some point. This was important to me for shooting photos out the window. Sometimes my seatmate would switch with me if he/she was not a sightseer or photographer. In fact, I happened onto a good thing when noticing that our motor coach had a large back window. Often times the back seats running across the bus were empty, and when I didn't have a window seat I would sit back there and take photos out of that window. This was not the first time I had done such a thing; I went to Alaska with a girlfriend, and while everyone was jockeying for position at the front of the ship to photograph the glaciers, I went to the back of the ship, which I had all to myself and shot some magnificent photos! Here, too, I did the same, but others soon noticed; sometimes it was a race to the back row. We were all cordial to each other, taking turns as needed.

We did a little sightseeing in England, where I had some time on my own. In a strange situation, I was walking around a historic old English pub taking photos both inside and out as a tourist. An older gentleman was intrigued by me, and invited me over to have a beer with him. He was well-dressed and seemed OK so I figured, sure, why not? I soon got the answer to that question. After some chit-chat in which he asked me where I'm from and what brought me to England, he began questioning me about my "motive" for taking so many photos, and my "plans" for what I was going to do with them. I politely responded that I'm just a tourist and plan to put the photos in a nice album when I get home. As it turned out, this guy formerly worked for Scotland Yard and, this being not too long after 9/11 and other terrorist attacks, he was suspicious of me. I assured him that "I'm on tour" and abruptly left. In retrospect, he did me a favor because this was a "snapshot" of future occurrences in which I would be wrongfully suspected of being something other than a tourist, and was moderately mindful of this possibility throughout my future travels.

We then headed to France. It was a bit misleading to put France on the itinerary since what we basically did was take a ferry from Dover, England to Calais, France. We did not tour Calais but instead motored right into Belgium without stopping. So does this count as having been in France? I brought this up on our motor coach ride to Belgium, and this created quite a stir! I was shocked at the discussion that ensued. Many people said no, it doesn't count because all we did was wait for a ferry. Others said it does count because we were "standing on the land in France." This led to a larger discussion of what constitutes having been "in" a country, for country-counting purposes (I was surprised by how many people kept count). It seemed everyone had an opinion. We settled on "counting it" being determined by doing at least a meaningful activity there that provides some sense of the culture. To some this meant dining out, others going to a museum, and others mingling with the locals. I'll let you determine what "meaningful" means, if you even agree with that (I do). I did not realize this was such a hot button – and would find it to be a lightning rod on subsequent tours, when I would bring up similar issues to both pass the time and learn as well.

Also to pass the time, the tour leader would hand out reading materials of interest about the places we were headed that day. There were also funny handouts, such as poor translations from a foreign language to English, including the sign in a Japanese hotel that read, "Please feel free to take advantage of our chambermaid." Back in Buffalo there's a famous one that reads: "Wally's Cleaners: Please drop your pants here for faster service."

Our tour was such a whirlwind that, literally, "if it's Tuesday this must be Belgium." That was our next stop, in Brussels (on a Tuesday). There was a large parliamentary square called The Grand Palace with beautiful architecture, among the best I've ever seen. There were restaurants and shops all around, and vending carts from which I bought waffles (another "when in Rome" moment) which were delicious! I never did like waffles because we usually had only the frozen kind at home, and I thought that's what all waffles tasted like. Now that I had great waffles, I'd have them every so often during subsequent travels in the U.S. – most often when my motel was located right near a Waffle House®. The Brussels stock exchange was nearby and looked a lot like the New York stock exchange from the exterior. This plaza looked "grand' in design, and gave you a feeling of history and luxury. It made a statement, and you felt special just being there. A good start to what would be a "go with the flow" part of the tour.

There were also impressive statues all over, but one that stood out – literally – and is famous in Brussels, is that of "Piss Boy," known there as Manneken Pis. I thought this was made-up like a fairy tale, but the locals said it's true. The story goes that in the 14th century Brussels was under attack from foreigners who planned to put explosives around the city to blow it up. A little boy named Julian peed on the burning fuse and saved the city. Another story has it that he peed on a witch's doorstep and she was so angry that she turned him into a statue. There are many statues of this peeing little boy around Brussels, including several fountains with the water pouring from you know where. I immediately liked Brussels based on this; the place had a sense of humor and history. "Piss Boy," now that was a real pisser! And yes, I did think about the Men At Work song with the line, "Buying bread from a man from Brussels/He was six feet four and full of muscles" - which I also thought about in Australia since that's where the band is from. I had to have Belgian chocolates, too, and they did not disappoint! I enjoyed the people of Belgium; they seemed lively and fun. Good food, scenery, and photo ops, too. Works for me.

Every two hours or so there was a rest stop, and with all the liquids I had in Belgium I was turning into a "piss boy," too, so these stops were much needed and appreciated. Next we rolled into Germany. We would see the country in two stages, part now and part later after crisscrossing other countries in-between, but I will include all my memories and impressions of Germany on this trip in this one section. Heading toward Frankfurt we came upon an ancient city called Trier, which was founded in roughly 2000 B.C. There is a Roman gate (one of four originally) there that is now a World Heritage site for its historic significance called Porta Nigra. It looks far older than any building I'd ever seen. We heard the history, took photos, and moved on quickly. I soon learned what a huge country Germany is; we spent a lot of time there. It had many interesting and beautiful cities and sights. We traveled along the Rhine River and ended up in Frankfurt, where we overnighted.

The next day we rolled through Bavaria, starting in Nuremberg, known mostly for its trials of Nazi criminals after World War II. That was all I knew about it before visiting so I figured it to be a mundane place - but it wasn't. Instead, it was a beautifully developed city featuring stunning architecture. The city had wide cobblestone streets, huge immaculate buildings, extreme cleanliness, and a market plaza area. It was there that I had my first frankfurter in Germany – and it was to this day the best-ever ("when in Frankfurt…"). In fact, on every subsequent trip I made to Germany I would be sure to get one. Not only were they very flavorful, but I connected with the way they were cooked from my elementary school days in Brooklyn. Back then I went to a nearby restaurant called Dard's (later called Hutter's) that made their hot dogs by cutting them in half, grilling them face-down, and serving them face-down on a hamburger bun. They were delicious, and after the restaurant closed I could never find a hot dog that tasted nearly as good. Until now. I had two for lunch, and would continue to have these as long as we were in Germany.

Dresden was another German city visited with a historic past, but a renewal as well. The city was bombed in 1945 during World War II and still showed some of the effects. However, it was rebuilt well and had many fine features including distinctive architecture and boats sailing along the river. There was an expansive open area which I liked, great for two things I enjoyed: freely roaming around and taking photos. I was surprised that there were a lot of Turkish people. I learned that Turks were sent to Germany after World War II to help rebuild the city. Many stayed, and had offspring there, I suppose. There were a lot of German students in general (I met several smart ones), and many who were Turkish and of other non-German backgrounds. I was impressed with how many languages some can speak; most spoke at least two and up to five or so. But that's the way Europe is configured. Imagine if you went to the next state over and had to speak another language, and use another currency (pre-euro). And maybe needed a passport or visa to enter. The concept seemed weird to me, being from the U.S. Why couldn't they all band together like we did? And have one King or a Queen? Yes, I was that simplistic back then.

We rolled on through Bavaria, where I was further in-spired (pun intended) by the pointy-spired cathedrals, castles, and other magnificent buildings throughout the region. Very picturesque and it seemed like a fairy tale. A good segue into Hamlin, Germany, a gorgeous and picturesque historic city that has a statue of the Pied Piper who supposedly hails from there. The statue isn't very large but he's playing his flute and is well-crafted. There were a few "Pied Piper"-named places nearby including a restaurant, city museum, and his supposed house, plus performers in character. More great architecture and a river surrounded by mountains. If you're near this area, check it out. Easy to overlook, but also easy to over-look for a great view.

Another small city I'd later pass through was Dortmund. I wondered why that name sounded so familiar. I then saw a sign that read, "Dortmund, sister city to Buffalo, New York." Then I remembered seeing a similar sign for Dortmund in Buffalo. Was there any connection? I'd later learn that a Dortmund native was an exchange teacher in Buffalo in the early 1970s and noticed the similarity between Buffalo and Dortmund in size, and also that both cities produced steel. The idea of a "sister city" was brought up to the German counsel, and eventually to the mayor of Buffalo who adopted it. An "Erie" coincidence to be in Dortmund and see this; later I would see lots of "sister city" signs throughout my travels. Which makes me wonder: can a city have more than one "sister city?" And what about a "brotherly" city (like Philadelphia, "city of brotherly love"?). What would constitute a brother-sister combination? And where are the parents in all this? I wondered if I should initiate this discussion on the motor coach as well...or send the idea into the producers of "Seinfeld." Interestingly, there is a town south of Buffalo called Hamburg, and a large Oktoberfest celebration in Buffalo as well. Years later I would attend this and have a great time. Perhaps someday I'll attend one in Germany – that must be awesome! I wonder if they serve "Rhine"-gold beer there (for those of you old enough to remember the brand).

Berlin was interesting. There was lots of history there yet it's a fairly modern city with impressive art throughout. I found the food to be pretty good as well (especially the hot dogs!). Throughout Germany, I found the people there surprisingly reserved, not what I expected (probably because of its violent history). They were also generally helpful and polite, educated and funny, and in some cases even orderly and deferential, with English widely spoken. I enjoyed it there and learned a lot. There was a line demarcating East from West Berlin, and I got a photo with one foot on each side. Graffiti covered remnants of the wall, and there were many tourists doing what I did – taking lots of photos. Another lesson learned came when I realized that I should notice what others were photographing – sometimes there were excellent nearby photo ops that I didn't see. When I noticed the other photographers pointing their cameras in that direction, I too would notice what they did. I "shudder" to think how many good photo ops I might have missed to that point.

We also visited the Reichstag and Brandenburg gate, and heard about the evolution of those as well. Slowly but surely I was becoming more interested in the history of the world. It was fascinating to see these things, and learn. I had heard of these before but paid no attention since, quite frankly, they were from a long time ago and didn't affect me. However, seeing them in reality and hearing the stories brought it all to life. Interestingly, despite being 45 years old then, I was being mentally molded by what I was seeing and being a part of. You're never too old to learn, or just like some ancient mountains I had seen, be molded by forces beyond your control. The experiences of travel are among them, and in retro-, present- and future-spect I'm extremely happy that I morphed into the person I am today by virtue of having experienced what I have through travel. I went from having no interest in it to thirsting for more, and as a byproduct also infused myself with a twist of historical awareness as well. It was interesting to note how things changed with me 180 degrees: I received a 'C' in World History (in which I had no interest) during college, and now I loved traveling the world. People change, so don't be daunted by past failures or lack of interest. Giving it the "old college try" later on can make a world of difference.

Back on the motor coach there was a bit of a latent buzz about Piss Boy after so many tourmates drank so much German beer. Then we rolled into Austria, with its own rich history as well. There was something quirky/funny about Austria in general, in keeping with the scatological theme – a whole lot of "fahrt"ing going on. This especially included signs reading "gute fahrt" which literally translated means "drive safely" but is more commonly used to mean "bon voyage" or "have a nice trip." At the group lunch one of my tourmates commented on seeing German road signs reading "ausfahrt" which means exit (would that also mean there's a "gas" station there?). We would see some of these same signs in Austria as well. There's a silent "h" in the Austrian "fahrts" but none in the "farts" I noticed in Sweden. Anything "silent" when it comes to "fahrting" could spell trouble. And if they'd had a Jack the "Ripper" Museum there, I surely would have fled! But enough of that...

I collect post cards, which I later use in photo albums, and was startled by one I saw. It read: "There are no kangaroos here." I guess many vacationers confuse Austria with Australia. I couldn't pass up buying this one. I wondered if there was one in Australia that read: "There are no famous waltzes from here." Somehow I don't think this is the case. A local shopkeeper told me that the post card was created based on Americans in particular asking about the kangaroos. I was tempted to ask about the Austrian Outback, but didn't want to exacerbate the situation.

Vienna was beautiful, just like its music and waltzes. I had a first-hand experience seeing these when I attended a performance by the Vienna Symphony Orchestra. This was an optional tour that cost additional money, but was another "when in Rome" experience I couldn't pass up. Prior to this, my main classical music interest was the one album I had by Vivaldi which was given to me as a gift from a girlfriend who was into classical music and wanted me to appreciate it, too (I rarely listened to it). I didn't like classical music all that much but since this orchestra is world-famous I wanted to see if this was really a "wow!" It totally was, and afterwards I began listening to classical music a lot more to get that audio-visual sync and reconnect mentally with this particular event. Everything went right at this symphony. There was no assigned seating, and since

I arrived very early I got a seat in the first row. The performance was absolutely magnificent with the best acoustics I'd ever heard! One of the musicians looked identical to me, and we looked at each other a lot. I really wondered if we were related, but we never got to speak. I'm not sure if he's from Austria, but part of my ancestry is from there so maybe we're from the same tribe way back when. A lady sitting next to me noticed that we looked alike and asked me if we're related. I replied, "I don't know, maybe." I really wanted to get a photo with him but didn't see him after the show ended (I would later learn the art of waiting around after performances and getting great photos with the actors, dancers, etc.). I would later run across similar-looking people to me (and my dad) in Romania – where my dad's father was from before coming to the U.S. in the 1920s. I found this very interesting – there, but for the grace of a grandparent's bravery, and maybe explorer spirit, go I.

There were many beautiful songs by Mozart and Tchaikovsky, but the finale, Blue Danube Waltz by Johann Strauss who was born in Vienna, just blew me away. People were waltzing after the performance; they couldn't control themselves. It was so harmonious and magnificent I couldn't imagine music getting any better than that. I would go to a few more symphonies after that but nothing came close to what I'd just witnessed. There was well-deserved thunderous applause after the concert, and I certainly was among those giving a standing ovation – sharing glances with my look-alike as well. Yes, that was a "wow!!!"

With some free time we had in Vienna, called Wien there (another Firenze moment), I took the metro train downtown to walk around and mingle with the locals. Of course, by then I knew to take the hotel's card with me and also write down the train directions to and from the hotel. I exited (or "fahrted"?) the train at Schwedenplatz station, and noted the irony of the "Sweden – Austria" connection again. I was soon to encounter a Vienna-U.S. connection as well. A young lady of about 15 was hanging out with her friend and overheard me asking someone if there are a lot of Swedes living in Vienna. The older woman I asked said that she's not aware of this, and looked at me sort of funny. Just then the teenage girl said, "Excuse me, are you from the U.S.?" I said yes and she told me that she is, too, "from Virginia but I've lived all over." Jill desperately wanted to talk to me because she was an army kid - I'd say "brat" but she was very sweet - and missed the U.S. She seemed lonely, yet outgoing, maybe because she had to be meeting new people all the time after all those moves. Jill explained that Vienna is a nice city, but she's bored with it.

She recommended I see the palaces there, one of which was extremely impressive called Schonbrunn, which I soon did with the tour group (enormous and with immaculate gardens). I asked about the Sweden connection. She wasn't aware of any but said there's a lot of Eastern Europeans there coming for work. Jill kept bringing the conversation back to the U.S. She wanted to know what's going on there. I gave her a briefing of what I thought would interest a 15-year-old, and answered her other questions as best I could. She later said she enjoyed talking to me just to hear an American accent. We parted and thanked each other. In one respect I thought "poor kid," but in another I thought how she has an exciting life compared to many others. I wondered if she joined the military later on.

I wandered around the city which was safe and clean. Basset hounds are my favorite – my landlord in Brooklyn had an adorable one for 12 years. I came across a variation of one that was much thinner than the ones I'd seen in the U.S. and England, yet still with those long, floppy ears. I'd thought all basset hounds more or less looked alike, but guess not. I continued to learn about things that I thought I knew a lot about, which made traveling all the more interesting. Wandering further, I tried the sausages in Vienna, although I don't usually eat this food. These were very good. Same with the wiener schnitzel. I tried the hot dogs, too, hoping maybe they would be as good as in Germany. They were good, but not quite as good as from Germany. The Frankfurt frankfurter was still "top dog."

There were more musical merriments to come when the tour group went to Salzburg, Austria. There we took a tour of the Mozart House, called Mozarts Geburtshaus, in a large yellow building with impressive large and meticulously clean windows. Several on my tour (including me) had our photo taken from street level as we stuck our head out the window. Inside was relatively barren, a re-creation from back in the day I suppose, and there was a museum on one of the floors - lots of paintings of the young prodigy, old musical composition sheets, a violin, piano, and other memorabilia. The marketer in me thought that there should be some of his music played in the birth house and/or museum for that audio-visual sync, which would have enhanced the experience. Even still, it was good to see this house and museum.

There literally was "The Sound of Music" when our tour group visited the hill on which some famous scenes from the movie were shot. There was a dedication sign at the entrance to the von Trapp mansion, and more sites up on a hill overlooking the city. I wasn't a big fan of the movie but this helped make me one; I was only six when the movie was released and a dear aunt brought me to see it. I'd see it on TV occasionally, watch it for a little bit, then change the channel. But as with classical music, this experience brought it to life, and my associative mind began playing some of the songs I'd long forgotten as we toured the filming locations for the movie. I continued learning how <u>experiencing</u> travel brings things in your life to life – past, present, and probably future as well. A friend once introduced me at a first dinner party by saying, "Everybody, this is our friend Steve – some people think about it, some people talk about it, Steve does it" - which I took as a supreme compliment. In the same way regarding travel, I was realizing that some people read about it, some people view it (e.g., online or TV), and some people do it – which is best of all.

Being there live and in-person created an additional connectivity that was unattainable by any other means; when I watched "The Sound of Music" on TV about a year later I felt a new sense of involvement with it, especially during the scenes where I had visited those very sites. I knew from my marketing experience that television is an excellent medium to use in reaching an audience because it combines sight, sound, and motion. Traveling to and experiencing these places also added <u>emotion</u> to the mix. I learned that travel was an enhancement to my life in general; the more touch points I had, the more vivid and robust life would be. And the more I did at a relatively young age, the longer these magnificent memories would last!

At night, in honor of being mesmerized by the Blue Danube Waltz, I took an optional cruise on the Blue Danube River and saw the illuminated buildings along the way – once I learned that the weather was expected to be good. This tour was excellent, and the music from the symphony orchestra went through my mind (no recording with headset needed). Just a wonderful ending to an unexpected charming time in Austria – even if there were no kangaroos!

Next we went to Central Europe, my first time there and a whole different vibe. Our first stop was Budapest, in which we took a local city tour. I was very impressed with the castles there, one of which looked like it was right out of Disneyland. Another, called Fisherman's castle, was all white with a pointy top looking like a party hat. There were also impressive statues, churches, and palaces, among the most impressive I'd seen to date. Lots of graffiti, too, some fairly artistic. I quickly learned that Hungary had a battle-scarred history with Romans, Mongols, Ottomans, Turks, Austrians, Russians and others over several centuries. There was an uprising against the Communists in 1956 and there are signs with this year at various points in the city as a remembrance, along with many monuments and statues. The city is built along the Danube – and if it was supposed to be blue, it sure wasn't; polluted green was more like it. I was surprised to learn that Buda and Pest (pronounced Pesht) are actually two separate and distinct cities: Buda is hilly on the west side of the Danube while Pest is flat and on the right side. There is a landmark suspension bridge there separating the two called the Chain Bridge, which physically reminded me of the Verrazano Bridge in New York City that connects Brooklyn to Staten Island. You can walk across the Chain Bridge on which there are merchants selling various items off to the side (try that on the Verrazano and you'd be crushed like an ant). It takes about 30 minutes to walk across the bridge from Buda to Pest or vice-versa. From the bridge you get a great view of the magnificent parliament building, its big red dome in the center reminding me of Il Duomo in Florence, Italy. I still think of this prevalent structure when I think of Budapest.

At the entrance to the bridge on either side were two stone lions, and there was a history with these as well as related by the tour guide. The sculptor was very proud of his work and invited other sculptors from around the world to see it. It was noticed that the lions had no tongues, and the sculptor was so humiliated that his creation was mocked that he jumped off the bridge into the Danube and killed himself. There is some dispute about the veracity of this story; it is said that the lions do indeed have tongues that can be seen from above. I couldn't see them, but I only viewed the lions from ground level. In any event, the lions are exquisitely crafted – the best I've ever seen to this day. Since that time I made a habit of checking out and photographing lion sculptures, many from around the world (I may make a photo album out of all these eventually). I did not notice if they all had tongues or even tails.

The people in Budapest were less affluent than their Western European counterparts. They appeared very liberal and liked to drink and laugh a lot. I went to a nightclub on my own and there was sake flowing everywhere, poured from this long tube by the waiters into anxiously-awaiting patrons' glasses. The crowd was so much fun; after several musical acts people happily danced the night away – including to the Blue Danube waltz. One older lady taught me how to waltz, and I wasn't bad (was taking swing dancing lessons at the time). There was lots of whirling and twirling, with many smiles and merriment that transcended every language. English wasn't as well-spoken there, but enough people did speak it so as not to be a problem for me. I saw a few people from my tour group there, said hi, and met a few local girls from the club on my own. They were pretty, pleasant, and interested in the U.S. We chatted and danced a little. The females there talked like Zsa Zsa Gabor, who by then was well into her 80s. However, Zsa Zsa might as well have been Queen of Hungary because of the affection and reverence with which people spoke about her.

As in Vienna just a few days ago, I took the local train downtown from our hotel to explore Budapest on my own. I'd heard that this metro system was the second oldest in the world after that in England, which I had also been on, and with my New York City subway experience I felt comfortable riding the system. I was good at reading subway maps and quickly figured out how to get to where I wanted to go. I bought my ticket from a booth attendant and not from the machine because the signage was all in Hungarian. As it turned out, the booth attendant didn't speak English - and this ended up costing me, literally.

I took the transit system, and needed to switch trains to get to my ultimate destination. But when I exited the second train there were two local police officers, a male and female, running behind me and blowing their whistles. I thought there was something that happened ahead of me, and looked to see what it was. But the police caught up with me and started questioning me in Hungarian - and not politely. I just looked stunned and said, "English." The female cop spoke English well and wanted to see my train ticket. I showed it to her and said, "I paid for this." She examined it and said, "Yes, but it is not stamped for this connecting ride," and explained that the train switch I made is considered another separate ride requiring a separate fare. I showed her my passport as requested (always carry this or at least a copy with you!) and even my hotel card while telling her I'm on tour with a group. We discussed the situation and she seemingly let me off the hook with only a $10 fine, payable to her in local currency cash, right then and there. On my return trip, I made sure I found someone who spoke English to assist me with buying the ticket back to the station near my hotel. This time I used the machine, and had the ticket stamped properly.

In-between the train rides, I had a very good time strolling around Budapest. There was terrific architecture, and I really liked the thermal pools (somewhat reminiscent of Iceland) outside of various ornate buildings around town. A "cool pool" is what I called it. I would have liked to go swimming in them, but there wasn't time. This really helped give Budapest its character. As did some ornate Gypsy homes that I went to see with the tour group the next day; these were really magnificent, and made for some great photos. I did note a slight resemblance to Buffalo, New York, as my Hungarian ex-girlfriend noted when visiting me there, but Budapest was much more scenically symmetrical.

A word of caution here: occasionally, when going to a particular city, the tour leader warns you about safety issues based on research or reports. We were warned about pickpockets in Central Europe, and to wear our money belts under our clothes. I have never worn a money belt and here's why: in speaking to other veteran travelers they told me that pickpockets and other thieves can tell if you're wearing a money belt – thus making you more of a target. I carry my wallet in my front hip pocket only (never the back) – and rarely carry the wallet at all since, as with a money belt, it could be noticeable. The couple of times I did get pickpocketed, which were in New York City, were when I wore slacks or shorts that were loose-fitting and a wallet could easily be removed without you feeling it. So, on these trips, I almost always wore jeans or tight-fitting shorts and never had a problem with pickpockets. I also always kept my luggage in front of me and never unattended – not only could it be taken if left alone, but in airports, for instance, it could be picked up by Security given its suspicious nature.

At night, I took the optional dinner cruise and another ride along the Danube. This time it rained, so I didn't get many photos of the illuminated buildings. But the food was good, and it was fun nonetheless. I got a good night's sleep and prepared for going to the Czech Republic and Slovakia, which was next-up. Importantly, I was having such a good time on this trip that I didn't even think about anything else – just enjoying, which was exactly what I wanted and needed. A byproduct of traveling is that so much new stimuli are bombarding you that it's often hard to worry about anything back home.

Our last stops on the tour before looping back to London were in the former country of Czechoslovakia, now the Czech Republic and Slovakia. We went to the capitals of each, first Prague, then Bratislava. Once again we were reminded about pickpockets and protecting our valuables. Fortunately, no-one on the tour ran into any such situations.

Prague is to this day one of the most beautiful cities I have visited, breathtaking in its architecture, a mix of ancient, Gothic, modern, and futuristic including "twisted" buildings! There was an incredible symmetry to the city between the buildings, bridges, parks, fountains, and just overall style. These were ineffably clean and well-preserved. Later in my travel career, when a group of us veteran travelers would chat, Prague would inevitably come up as one of the most beautiful cities to which we had been. There were three bridges that you could walk across; as in Budapest, there are excellent views and merchants along each. It was a pleasure just walking around the city – the glass windows of the storefronts were super-clean and glistening, like in Switzerland, and there were ornate, beautifully-manicured gardens. The people there took a lot of pride in their city and it showed. I considered it a privilege to be walking around it, and wouldn't even think of littering there. In fact, if I saw any litter (which I rarely did), I immediately picked it up and tossed it.

We took a city tour during which, as usual, I took lots of photos, including the Old Town Jewish ghetto section. There was definitely a sense of history there, yet you also sensed a move toward modernization, a turnover or maybe it's a congealing. Then I went off on my own to see what I could find. I came across something interesting in a not-so-obvious street location: 12 artistically painted, wooden cows arranged in a circle. They were brightly colored and had everything from maps to graffiti to ornate decorations on them. It was quite a sight and photo op. When I'd first lived in Buffalo, New York the city had lots of buffalo (the animal) statues around in plaster, bronze, stone, and other materials. I had taken pictures of as many as possible and planned to put them in an album someday. Now I could combine those with the cows, and no sooner did I think of that then the song "Grazing in the Grass" by Hugh Masekela came to mind. If it were Sunday I might have been "Groovin' on a Sunday afternoon" to the Rascals as well because I was once again getting into my happy zone, simply admiring this faraway place I hadn't known anything about. As usual, I sought out younger people to speak with since they spoke English and liked learning more English by speaking to an American. I also spoke with older people I asked to take photos of me, because I only wanted to give my camera to people I thought I could outrun in case they took off with it! I'm only half-kidding; you have to think ahead.

The people there were friendly and seemed to love their beer, especially Pilsner which I had and was good. I conversed with more locals and was provided with graphic details about the country's fight for independence against the Soviets. This made me realize how fortunate we Americans were and are to have been on the winning side so many times. I really didn't appreciate the freedoms we have until hearing these stories, and later I would hear about even worse atrocities from locals in other countries.

Back on the coach we exchanged details of our day's events, and I told of the artistic cows. My tourmates seemed very interested, but because I didn't have a digital camera I couldn't show them any photos. Many had gone to see more churches and shopping (and said the souvenir stores weren't that good) but said they would have liked to roam around freely like I had. Some asked the tour leader if she had known of the artistic cows. She said no, but it wasn't her fault; some things are not in the tour books, and you just have to discover them for yourself. I never did find out why the cows were there or who did them, but they were awesome! My pun on the tour bus got some laughs and some groans, about there being three types of Czechs: wheat, rice and corn (like the cereal, Chex®). One guy also wisecracked about bounced, canceled, and returned. Another guy called his wife his Czech-mate. While an older woman, not paying attention to our discussion, coincidentally happened to mention then to her seatmate that she's going to her doctor for a "check-up" when she returns home. She got the biggest laugh, and laughed herself when we told her why. Some of it was silly, but you can get that way after hours of riding on the motor coach. We all got along well on the tour, and by this time knew many or most of each other's names. I didn't do my "intro" routine as in Sweden, but camaraderie evolved eventually and naturally on this tour. During the long ride I kept notes about the trip to later write into my journal back home. It's good I did this because I would not have remembered a lot of what happened. It wasn't just the "itinerary items" that were essential to the trip; there were the little things as well that added so much enhancement, such as the people I met, the funny experiences, and the conversations with tourmates as well that really made it sparkle.

Finally, we went to the capital of Slovakia, Bratislava (which I had never heard of until this trip). This too had an old town, as did many cities we visited, with a local tour guide who gave us the historical perspective. There were cafés, restaurants, shops, bars, and nightclubs along the Danube (man, that's a long river). There was an impressive castle nearby, atop which you can get an excellent panoramic view of the city (it was said that on a clear day you could see Hungary and Austria), a Presidential palace fit for a king, and another suspension bridge, which was prevalent in the cities we visited. We were escorted inside several museums including a Jewish Museum of Culture. There were several Gothic buildings and modern buildings, too. The outdoor cafés again reminded me of the upper west side of Manhattan – and Tallinn, Estonia.

This was another case of old meets new, and a seeming yearning to bust out of old tradition, yet respect it if that makes sense. This city had a lot of youthfulness and energy you could feel. I walked around and attempted to mentally impress images in my mind, as if photographing them by staring and storing - lots of cobblestone streets as in Prague and other old European cities. Of course, I took the photos as well. There were several unusual bronze statues; I was into collecting photographs of anything unusual or different. I recall that there was one of the most interesting statues I'd ever seen, to this day, of a sewer worker protruding up from the ground with the manhole cover behind him. You could easily trip over this if you weren't observant.

We completed seeing all the countries on our tour, and headed back to London with various stops and overnights along the way. Fortunately, once again we had very good weather. Overall, this was a very interesting, educational, and intriguing trip with a wide exposure to new places, people, and things. And addicting – I wanted more. Not only was my world expanding, but my mind was, too. I was finding travel to be a defining period of my life, my next 'big thing.' And I was ready for the transition – ready, willing, and able based on the resources I had available, including having total freedom. I found it all exciting and thrilling!

# Chapter 8

## "California Here I Come"... But There I Go, Again

As mentioned (or in this case, recorded), music played a role in my trips, with various songs coming to mind along my travels that corresponded with both my emotions and geographical locations. So, too, this would happen with my next job opportunity. I wanted to try living in California at some point in my life. Soon after my return I began hearing a lot California-related songs on the radio, especially "California Dreamin'" (Mamas and Papas), "Lights" (Journey – re: San Francisco), and "Ventura Highway" (America). I can't remember a time when I heard so many California-themed songs in such a short span. There seemed to be a cosmic message here, and there was – one that would again change my trajectory. I had applied to a few California-based companies for an executive marketing job, and ended up at a premiere one in the confectionery industry in Northern California, Jelly Belly. This was ironic because, as mentioned, I had seen a Jelly Belly display in Iceland, which I mentioned during the job interview. I figured it was a good sign that I was now at a company related to Iceland, the "halo effect" if you will. The job wouldn't be available for a few weeks, and I had to relocate. That gave me time for one last vacation before starting, and I couldn't think of a better place than Club Med - Turks & Caicos Islands once again to rest and relax before I began my new life in California. I might as well get a good tan, I thought, and look the part upon arrival. It was the

10-year anniversary of Mr. "that is my room-mate..." Frenchman, and strange things were known to happen to me around anniversaries. Fortunately, he wasn't there. The crowd seemed rather reserved, and getting older (like me). Also, the ratio of gals to guys was now about even so I didn't have the odds stacked in my favor as before. No matter; I had a wonderful time anyway. I didn't realize how much I missed the chocolate bread, and had a loaf prepared for me to take home. Delicious! Surprisingly, due to my exercise routines, I did not gain much weight.

Two events stand out to me about that trip. As I was taking sunset photos, a young married couple from the U.S. approached me, told me their wedding photographer didn't show up, and asked, "Would you mind taking a few photos of us at sunset that you could mail to us?" (I still did not have a digital camera.) I said, "Sure" and did so. They appreciated it at the time. I never did hear back from them, however, so I hope they received the photos.

Also, there was a theater production being put on by the "G.M.'s" (Club members), and one of the "G.O.'s" (employees) asked me if I'd like to play Julius Caesar in the play "Ben Hur." I politely declined, having never acted. She said all I'd have to do is dress in Roman garb and start the chariot race by saying "Let the race begin." It sounded easy enough, and I'm always up for a new experience. Plus, this gal was very cute, persistent and persuasive, so why not? I did this, and all went well. Gee, that was easy, and now I had the regal-looking "Cleopatra" standing beside me who was another Club Med member and looking pretty good. We stayed in costume and did some "roamin'" around the village. I'd never actually dressed up for Mardi Gras or even Halloween to any great degree, so this was cool. We just had to beware of Brutus who was looking for his Cleopatra, but were able to evade him.

So with another Club Med vacation done, I was rested, relaxed, and ready to go to the Golden State near the Golden Gate. The job at Jelly Belly lasted a while and was a good steppingstone, but I wanted more out of life, having had such wonderful travel experiences. Somehow, one week's vacation after one year of work didn't thrill me (in Europe, some countries provide five or six weeks' vacation per year – now that's a work-life balance schedule that appealed to me!).

After an amicable departure from the company, I then took time off to explore California and overseas travel yet again. In retrospect, this decision to leave the corporate world turned out to be a great move, giving me the freedom I needed for not only more wonderful travels, but a beneficial, meaningful career change I would soon be making as I became more philosophical about life. I'd seen a sign in a pub that read, "It's five o'clock somewhere in the world," legitimizing the bar patron's reason to drink at any time of day or night. I wasn't a drinker, but applied this logic to my next trip: there's a great vacation for me somewhere in the world. Florida was always an option, where my family was, but I had been there and done that a lot (and would do that plenty more). Club Med? I was just there and didn't want to return so soon. Europe? Too cold at that time of year. Somewhere in the Southern hemisphere, hmmm...

I talked to various travel agents. One mentioned South America, and in particular, Argentina, and further in particular, Buenos Aires, which literally translates to "fair winds" in Spanish. The temperature in winter is similar to that of Miami. This sounded fine to me. I checked into which tour operators go there and ended up talking with Gap Adventures in Toronto. I liked Toronto from my previous experiences in the city, and Gap Adventures had been conducting this tour for a while. The company generally had budget tours, mainly for younger people in their 20s and 30s, and several of their tours required you to be in good physical shape. I was intrigued. To make a long story short, Gap had a tour that went to Argentina and... Antarctica! Now that got my icebergs flowing! Here I was collecting countries, and now I had an opportunity to get to two new continents! Also, unlike cruise ships which would circle the peninsula but not let passengers off the boat, Gap's expedition had several landings on the continent, weather permitting. The more I looked into this, the more excited I became. The price was right, too. I was offered a roommate option to keep the price down and, despite what happened at Club Med on a couple of occasions, I decided to take it. You have to sign away all liability – any harm, including falling into crevasses in the ice (which can kill you), is all your responsibility. Lots of other calamities could happen, too, as I would soon learn.

I bought cold-weather gear and hot-weather clothing, too. The range in temperature itself of well over 125 degrees between the high in Argentina and the low in Antarctica was going to be an endurance test. I found myself looking forward to this trip more and more each day. Unlike previous vacations, this time I asked a lot of questions about Antarctica in particular, but also about Argentina before departing. I knew nothing about either one. The Gap travel agents were excellent advisors about the trip. Few others knew much about Antarctica – which made going there even more appealing. There was a pre-trip "rush" to doing something this extraordinary, something like when I did a skydive in Colorado, which back then went from confident-panic-elation all in 20 minutes. There was a lot of potential danger with Antarctica, and I remembered an old poster for the movie "Alien" that had the slogan, "In space no-one can hear you scream." So could it be with this trip because a rescue in Antarctica, if needed, was a very involved and maybe impossible process depending on the situation. One thing I'd learned about myself is that once I decide to do something, I do it. I gave myself more credit for trying and failing than not trying at all. I was strongly anticipating this expedition, and by all accounts, it exceeded even the highest of expectations.

# Chapter 9

## Amazing Adventure To Argentina and Antarctica!

Although I had been traveling for about 20 years, I never experienced anything like Antarctica! One of my top resolutions for the year was to "Find the wow!" I sure did, and then some, thanks to this trip!

"Wow! I'm beyond superlatives" is how one person on my expedition to Antarctica put it. Not only did he find his "wow!" too, but everyone on this trip did as well. I'll detail this fantastic trip so you, too, can perhaps find a "wow!" if even vicariously. I'll begin at the beginning. One of my life's goals was to visit all seven continents. Before this trip I had been to four, and this expedition provided the opportunity to add two more, at which point all I'd be missing is Africa. The "summer" in Antarctica ends mid-March and I was just in time to take advantage. I found a tour operator, Gap Adventures, which charged a lot less than the luxury tour operators if you're willing to rough it. Sign me up on both counts; what's a trip to Antarctica without the rough part? The itinerary for me was to fly from San Francisco to Dallas (no plane change) to Buenos Aires, Argentina; after two days there I would take a four-hour charter flight to Ushuaia ("Oo-shweye-ah"), Argentina, the world's' southernmost city, then go aboard the Explorer ship to Antarctica for 10 days before returning to Ushuaia and then Buenos Aires for more sightseeing. From there I'd return to San Francisco, and still have a two-hour ride back home. Most meals were included as were all 14 nights' lodging.

Later on, when I asked people what they thought a trip like this cost, many answered in the $20,000+ range. The trip cost me a lot less, assisted by use of free airline frequent flyer miles I had accumulated, and a great travel deal I obtained.

Before leaving on such a major trip I was given a preparation course by my travel agent, which I'll pass along to you based on my experience. Included was some general information as well. I made sure I was fully vaccinated as needed, and received my "yellow card" from my health care provider to show upon request. Some of the vaccinations I ended up receiving in general were for Hepatitis-A, Hepatitis-B, Tetanus, Typhoid and Yellow Fever. There is no vaccination for malaria but I took pills with me as needed for later trips. Check with the Center for Disease Control to find out which vaccinations you may need before traveling overseas, and know when these vaccinations expire (many are good for at least five years). It was miraculous that in all my travels I did not get ill, but I met many who did. I credit getting appropriate vaccinations and taking other medications when needed for part of this health success. In my case, I needed all the health I could get as I often traveled to remote places, alone, and not knowing anyone there. Further, make sure to bring your passport, and in some rare cases, make sure you have two facing pages that are blank, required by some countries. Check the specifics before you leave, and ask lots of questions. Not having the right documentation is another way to ruin your trip. Passport pages can be added, so check where in your area this can be done. I had mine expanded at the local post office. As mentioned, ensure that your passport remains valid for the required length of time, which may extend months beyond your return date.

Being an inquisitive guy, I wondered what the difference was between a passport and a visa, and why you may need both. I learned that a passport identifies you and your citizenship, while a visa may or may not be required by certain countries for entry. If needed, however, this is temporary permission by that country's government allowing you to visit. There is a stamp or sticker placed in or on the passport. Also ensure that you have the proper visas; you won't be let into certain countries without these, and especially make sure that you have multiple-entry visas instead of single-entry visas as needed. I met a few people who had the wrong visa, were denied re-entry to the country, and had to pay a lot out-of-pocket to get to where they needed to go. Reconfirm everything – airline and hotel reservations in particular. Last-minute changes are frequent, so don't be left holding the bag – as in your bags of luggage, at the airport or elsewhere, because you don't have the reservation you thought. So, with all that out of the way, and everything reconfirmed, I was off to the coldest, driest, most remote place on Earth – but before that was Buenos Aires, a place that was quite the opposite.

My flight from San Francisco to Buenos Aires via Dallas lasted 10-1/2 hours. I sat next to a guy my age from Lake Tahoe named Marcus. We chatted for a while; he told me about life in California, and I told him about life in New York City. He liked skiing, I liked bowling, and there were additional vast differences. He was taking a break from his self-employed stressful job and I told him I left mine to continue my travels until I find a job better suited for me. He thought this was very admirable and cool. We didn't really talk a whole lot. He was going "all around Argentina, and other places" and I said, "me, too" without giving detail (we both really wanted to nap, and he also wanted to read his book). Marcus and I said so long to each other after a pleasant and lengthy conversation, after the plane landed in Argentina. We did not exchange contact information. It was nice meeting him, though. Interesting guy, a very outdoors type.

As stated, I speak only two languages: English and Brooklynese. But I knew a little Spanish from high school and retained a lot of it. This would come in handy. I made my way to the luggage area, but my luggage never arrived! Naturally, I freaked out! The airline rep, who also spoke English, said she would check into it and let me know. I said I'd be in Buenos Aires for only the next two days before leaving for Ushuaia and then Antarctica, so I really needed my luggage quickly. Not an auspicious start. Fortunately, I had insurance and was able to buy several items until my luggage showed up – two days later in Ushuaia, only one hour before the ship was leaving for Antarctica!!! As it turned out, there was a married couple on my tour whose luggage also was lost and did not make the ship to Antarctica. We all felt sorry for them and helped if we could (they were from

Wales in the United Kingdom, and remained surprisingly calm under the circumstances).

In Buenos Aires we had a free day to explore the city. The first thing I did was find an Internet café so I could email my brother to let him and my parents know I was OK (my parents did not have Internet or know how to use it). Internet cafés were plentiful there, and cheap, too. There were roughly 45 of us on this tour in Buenos Aires; more tourmates would meet us in Ushuaia for the eventual trip to Antarctica. Buenos Aires is nicknamed "The Paris of South America" based on its wide streets, architecture, and outdoor Parisian-style cafés. The city reminded me a little bit of those I'd been to in Mexico with lots of plazas, statues, parks, little shops, major retail stores – like any major city. Most people spoke English, and the exchange rate was very favorable for U.S. currency – three Argentine pesos (dollars) for every U.S. dollar. It was hot there in more ways than one – weather and women. At the end of February it was 85 – 90 degrees. It was strange going from winter – even if it was in Northern California – to summer. I was tired, but after the brief city tour I walked around on my own by choice for four hours. The time change was California time plus five hours. I didn't get much sleep at all except briefly on the plane, but just being in this new environment energized me. I returned to my hotel near dinner time. There I met my roommate, Sebastian, from Holland. He was close to my age with a brownish-gray moustache and ponytail. If he had said, "There is my room-mate!" I would have probably flown back to San Francisco. But Francois's antics were mild compared with another "issue" Sebastian and I would have to work out: he did not like Americans, to put it mildly. More about that later. Because Sebastian had paid for a higher cabin class than I did aboard ship, he and I would only be roommates on land in Argentina; on the Explorer ship I would be roomed with another guy, this one much younger than me. As it turned out, thankfully, both guys were very good roommates despite our cultural differences.

The next day I met the rest of the people in my tour group as more arrived; we would meet the balance in Ushuaia, who had gone there instead of Buenos Aires to spend additional time. As it turned out, some of these people were much older than I'd thought, 40s and up, although there were certainly many younger ones in their 20s and 30s. I spoke with many of these people; all were nice and interesting, including one of the few Americans who was a prison guard. Most others were from the U.K. and Australia. The "10% Americans" tour number would hold up there, too, including when we met up with the balance of the tour members in Ushuaia. It amazed me how few Americans traveled internationally relative to others; then again, we do have so much in our own country and even I, a world traveler, had been to every state at least twice by this time. But there would be no place comparable to Buenos Aires, Ushuaia, or especially Antarctica.

The following day we were briefed on what to expect from the trip – itinerary, rules & regulations, introductions, cautions, and more. I roamed around the city on my own once again. There were some similarities to New York City in that there were lots of buses and a train system (I didn't take them); crowds (three million people lived there); and especially that there were many different neighborhoods as you walk the city – my favorites were Recoleta and La Boca. The former had an "old meets new" feel to it with great sculptures along the way, while the latter featured very colorful buildings and people dancing tango in the street. Lots of action, fun and, liveliness, which I like. I learned that Buenos Aires has a very European feel to it; most people from Buenos Aires are of European descent, mainly Spanish and Italian, and 40% of Argentina's population is in this one city. And what we in the U.S. call soccer they call fútbol – and it's huge there! Many people walked around with jerseys of their local team. And if you're wearing an opposing team's jersey or even colors, look out! Before going to a soccer/fútbol-crazy city, you might want to learn which colors are best to wear to fit into the sports culture, and which colors not to wear so as not to offend these people (seriously).

I felt very comfortable there, again mingling with the locals and admiring the stunningly beautiful women (you can't help but notice). I again used my camera caper to meet many of them, as I did in Sweden, asking the ladies to take my photo and then engaging in conversation. Back with the tour group, we were told that the people there are generally perceived as arrogant, vain, and self-centered – and there is even supposedly a famous portrayal of an Argentine person in the form of a cat looking into a mirror and seeing the reflection as a lion. I did not encounter this at all, or didn't notice it if it was there. Also, I judge people based on my observations and personal interactions, not on what others say. My instincts were usually correct, maybe fueled by so many experiences I'd already had, so I let my interactions be my guide on this and all other travels.

There was some talk about safety there and taking precautions. Being from a big city, I felt safe walking around Buenos Aires and sampled various foods along the way including empanadas, ice cream (helado), and alfajores, which are two round hard cookie biscuits filled with dulce de leche (caramel jam). These were all pretty good. What wasn't so good was the ravioli I had for lunch, although I didn't expect it to be much. For $3 U.S. I had a big portion that tided me over to dinner. Note that although I tend to overeat/ snack on vacations, I keep in shape by <u>walking around a lot</u> and thus rarely gain significant weight on these trips. Often times I even lose weight depending on how much walking I do. I was brought up in a "walking city" (New York) so this was very natural to me. I returned to the hotel, from which we left for a group dinner at an outstanding steak house (Argentina is the steak capital of the world). We were advised to order the "Bife de Lomo" steak (filet) which was among the finest in the world. I did, and it was so incredibly good; to this day, it is the best steak I've ever had, and I've been to many of the finest steak houses in the U.S. Several people in our group, including myself, said the same thing and took photos of the steak! And it only cost the equivalent of $10 U.S. with all the fixins! I enjoyed Buenos Aires, and would end up going back there twice after this trip. It's still one of my favorite places.

After a good night's rest, I met the tour group early the next morning. Sebastian and I began hanging out together because we had both arrived alone and were roommates. He seemed more of a loner type, but once you got to know him you could tell he was very intelligent and worldly; as it turned out, he was a major world traveler.

We boarded our plane with the others on tour and flew four hours south to Ushuaia – where it was <u>colder</u> since we were far beneath the Equator. One guy on my tour said as we exited the plane, "Bundle up, we're heading south" which sounded weird, albeit true. The temperature was nearly 40 degrees cooler there than in Buenos Aires, but still pleasant at roughly 55 degrees during the day and 40 degrees at night (similar to San Francisco at that time of year). We met with the rest of the tour group, another 30 or so people who had bypassed the Buenos Aires portion of the tour and instead spent these two days in Ushuaia. In general they were much younger than in the group I was with in Buenos Aires, with many in their 20s. There was a tall guy I saw in the distance who looked familiar, and as we drew closer to each other we just stared and gaped – it was Marcus, my seatmate on the plane out of San Francisco! He was on my tour and would be on my ship going to Antarctica! This never came up in our discussion on the plane; we had just talked about traveling around Argentina and vicinity. We just laughed at the coincidence. He introduced me to a few people on our tour who he met in Ushuaia, and I did the same with people who were with me in Buenos Aires, notably Sebastian, who was standing next to me. Marcus had arranged to meet a female friend from England on this tour to whom he introduced me (she was nice); I had thought he was traveling alone like me. So I really didn't hang out with him during the trip, but he would factor into an incident involving Sebastian pretty soon afterwards.

Meanwhile, after we went to the hotel, the group met to go to Tierra del Fuego National Park as part of our tour package, about an hour's drive. There were over 70 of us now, so we all had to stick together. Sebastian and I stayed close to each other; however, as usual, I veered off from the group to take photos and was mildly criticized for wandering away at times. Sebastian was an excellent photographer and we photographed each other against selected landscapes. The park reminded me of Yellowstone National Park – forest, mountains, lakes, and more. I learned that this place was discovered by Magellan who named it this (translation is "ring of fire") because the indigenous people set a lot of fires. I thought if we could just get to the other side of this park I could get into yet another country to help reach my life's goal of 50 (50 countries, 50 states). But it was also at the base of the Andes Mountains which separated Argentina from Chile, so there went that idea; we weren't about to scale any mountains. Fortunately, the weather was good and relatively clear. My tourmates immediately noticed I take a lot of photos, and teased me about this. They would see me take a lot more, and why wouldn't you on a trip like this? Shame on you if you didn't! I would end up taking nearly 1,000 photos on this two-week trip, which by my standards today is low. The cost to process all of these was only about 5% of the overall trip cost, a significant amount of money, but it can't compare to the value of capturing priceless memories.

The park was excellent, and we returned to Ushuaia where I walked around by myself by choice. I bought several post cards and again took a lot of photos – especially of the sign reading that this is the southernmost city in the world. The city itself was very small and quaint; it reminded me of towns I'd been to in Alaska with great mountain views. There were lots of mansions, lots of geese, and lots of souvenir shops. There were also lots of penguins in a nearby colony that I decided not to see on optional tour since there would be plenty in Antarctica. We were in Ushuaia the next day as well, and I continued walking around and exploring. Several of the tour members had formed their own little posse and roamed around together; they wanted me to join them. Interestingly, I would be the $8^{th}$ member (the good-luck number which seemed to beckon me). I joined them for some of the walk-around, but many wanted to shop versus sightsee; one gal smoked (I avoid it); and I really wanted to maximize my photo ops, especially from the higher elevations overlooking the city which took time to do. I climbed up several hills on my own to get the overview, which looked marvelous. I joined the group for lunch, at which they attempted to guess my age – as a group, they decided on "35" – 11 years younger than my true age. I never did tell them my age, which boggled their mind – but this intrigue regarding my age would later be a "bonus question" for my future students that would boggle their minds as well (not one of them guessed right – almost all guessed roughly 10 years younger).

At night, we all gathered one last time before we set sail the next morning, and had a nice dinner. There was a lot of anticipation about this trip; to my knowledge, none of us had been to Antarctica before. I was not nervous in the least, and was very excited and motivated. If I thought Iceland was a big deal, I was in for an even more magnificent vacation to follow...

The next morning we boarded the red Explorer ship and were on our way! This was a relatively small ship needing to go through the narrow waterways we would be encountering. There was no TV, radio, or Internet. Good thing I'd brought a book to read. Lots of us stood on deck and just admired the scenery, which seemed to get better and better. We were welcomed by the captain and the crew, and given a lecture about Antarctica in general – history, terrain, preparing to walk on the continent, safety precautions, and other aspects. Wow, we were about to enter a prehistoric land that's 4.5 million square miles of 98% ice and 2% rock. The ice sheet is 1-1/2miles thick. Also, 70% of the Earth's fresh water supply is in the ice there. Amazing. I soon learned there were various experts aboard the ship who would later provide lectures about the continent's history, wildlife, botany, geology, and more. In fact, there was a member of the tour who was a scientist from Italy who had special permission from the government to take home a soil sample; she later gave a lecture about the terrain. Surprisingly, there are no polar bears in Antarctica, they are only in the Northern Hemisphere; and there are no penguins at the North Pole, they are only found in the Southern Hemisphere. I wanted to see the two together, but that wasn't going to happen.

A couple of friends of mine including Mike had asked me to bring them home a rock from Antarctica, but I learned that nothing could be taken from the continent. I also learned there was a movement to keep Antarctica as pristine as possible, and, as such, reduce the number of ships and therefore passengers who can visit. As it stands now there are only 3,500 people living on Antarctica – almost exclusively scientists and military. Tour boats have been going there for 20 years bringing an average of 15,000 visitors per year. It was said that only about 10% of these visitors were American and that only 75% of these visitors actually set foot on Antarctica. For kicks I did the math and realized that I'd be 1 of only 22,500 Americans to ever set foot on the continent to that point. One last number: there were 99 of us on the ship, including staff and crew. Small ship, small number of people, potentially rough seas. This was going to be an experience in many ways.

I socialized with my tourmates as the ship cruised the Beagle Channel. There was a lounge in which several people would hang out at any given time. As I'd done in the past, given all the down time, I asked provocative questions to get a conversation going. In this instance, I asked why they were taking this trip. The answers were somewhat surprising and included: special occasion; want to reach all the continents/this was the seventh continent reached; special birthday; graduation gift (including to self); and "to see a place that few have ever been to and few will ever go." Some also wanted to see the most pristine place on Earth before it gets marred or destroyed by global warming/ice caps melting, war, oil spills, military attacks, nuclear destruction, or something else. A couple of people said they wanted to "ride the high seas," and one guy wanted to "get thrashed about the ship and get soaking wet." Hey, whatever floats your boat.

People have since asked me if you can fly to Antarctica. There are no commercial flights that land there; however, there were and may still be flights that fly over it. Would you count that as having been to Antarctica? Or would it count as having been there if you see it by cruise ship but not land on the continent? I wouldn't, but plenty of people would since they were "in the waters surrounding it." To me that's like seeing the shower water running but not bathing, but to each his or her own. Note that Antarctica is not considered a country; it has no permanent human population, no government (although several countries lay claim to it), and it is mainly used for science.

I can't emphasize this enough: no matter where we were all from, what culture, socioeconomic class, race, religion or what have you, there seemed to be a communal sense of pride in taking this trip, that we were privileged to be going to Antarctica and having an experience few ever have. Short of going to the moon this was the most exciting trip you could take from Earth, and it was electric to feel this. I got goose bumps one time just thinking about it. I wasn't scared or nervous at all; I trusted the captain and crew, and all else.

I had a strong feeling this was the right thing to do – and as it turned out, it definitely was!

We all attended a mandatory evacuation drill "just in case" – a good thing since we were headed toward the roughest seas in the world including the Drake Passage and Cape Horn. Several people got sick from these passages, including a member of our posse of 8 who turned green and was in his room a few days recovering. The ship did rock fiercely back and forth with waves crashing over the bough at times; I thought at one point we're sure to capsize, but we didn't. Dishes crashed in the galley, and I was thrown hard left and hard right, crashing into the walls. I liked this in a crazy sort of way; it seemed like we should have to weather a few storms and cope with the roughest seas en route to Antarctica as a rite of passage, so to speak. I then realized what "thrash man" was so exhilarated about.

One night, as my new roommate from Montreal (a guy in his mid-30s named Jacques) and I lay in our respective beds, the waves were so huge and fierce that we literally slid up and down on our mattress as the ship went up and over each one. While uncomfortable, I still thought this was cool. I was tossed but didn't toss my cookies, yet. I realized how all alone and isolated we were should anything bad happen. Yet, this didn't faze me. The reaction among others ranged from glee to terror. I felt excited, rejuvenated, forward-looking, and thankful I could experience the experience, because no matter how this was going to turn out it would be the mother of them all. Ironically, while several passengers experienced ill effects from all the movement, I would later be on a Caribbean cruise with a guy in his 50s who told me he could handle all that – but what got to him was when the water was smooth as silk, and especially when he lost sight of land. Unfortunately you never know how you'll react on a cruise until you're on it, so you might want to start by taking a short one if you haven't been on one before. I always carry a box of Pepto Bismol® tablets, which does the trick for me.

We continued sailing for four days before reaching land. The views were magnificent including glaciers, whales, albatross, and skua birds which are indigenous to the area (brown and grey with a short tail and a weird quacking or ha-ha sound). Several people got very excited about seeing these species, and everyone got out their cameras. The whales and glaciers were awesome; the birds didn't do it for me. There were lectures at night about the fauna, geology, topography, and much more including histories about explorers Sir Francis Drake and Shackleton. Whereas prior to this trip I wouldn't have been interested, I now found myself very interested and asking a lot of questions. As my curiosity grew, so did my knowledge and interest to learn more. After the trip I found myself studying up on these explorers and others, and watching documentaries about them on TV. I would have never done this before. That's another thing I found about travel – whenever I'd see a TV program or poster, e.g., with a landscape I'd been to, I had a connection to it. As mentioned, I worked in a travel agency for seven summers (about two full years combined) and wasn't interested in the giant travel posters adorning the windows and walls of the office; now, whenever I passed by one, I would stop and stare, and sometimes literally feel a blast from the past if I'd been there before. And if I hadn't...I wanted to go.

The last lecture, the night before we landed on the peninsula, we were again briefed on safety. We once more heard that Antarctica is the coldest, windiest, and driest place on Earth. But there was a lot more to be concerned about. Issues included potential to fall into the crevasses which may be hidden beneath the snow and ice, which could immobilize or kill you if they're deep enough; wiping off your boots/stepping into a special purifying solution with them on before entering the ship because penguin poop (called guano) is a pollutant; and not trying to swim in the water (dumb as that sounds) because a woman from a very recent tour tried this and was severely wounded by a leopard seal. Other precautions included wearing sunglasses so as not to go snow-blind; wearing a lot of high-SPF suntan lotion to prevent potential extreme sunburn (yes, I said sunburn, including on your lips – the snow reflects the sun); drinking a lot of water so you don't dehydrate; and realizing that you can easily sweat after physical exertion and then have it freeze after you stop (selected breathable clothing was recommended).

What I didn't realize was that we wouldn't be docking on the peninsulas, but rather taking zodiacs to shore - rubberized, motorized rafts that hold about 8 people at a time. And you get knee-deep in water going from the raft to the shore. My boots did not come up to my knees. This made for an uncomfortable short walk to the frozen tundra, but I did it. It's a good thing I was dressed for the occasion in all other aspects. This included (all worn at the same time): thermal underwear, thermal undershirt, T-shirt, sweatshirt, fleece vest, parka jacket, jeans, waterproof pants, two pairs of socks (one wool), special high-traction fur-lined boots, ski mask (covering the ears), and warm leather gloves. I also brought hiking boots, extra gloves, and a ski cap with me as back-up. Thus, I also wore a backpack with everything I thought I'd need, including lots of bottled water and suntan lotion, as I hiked around. Others brought scarves (good idea, I didn't). The temperature range when I was there was a balmy high of about 40 degrees and low of -40 degrees (also could be considered balmy as the low there). So it was important to dress in layers. Most people had brightly colored jackets which was recommended to make it easier to spot you in case you needed to be rescued. I didn't have one and didn't plan to buy one just for this purpose, but if the boat or zodiac capsized I'd be sure to float near someone who did!

So why risk all this? The vaccinations, very long trip, weather extremes, dangerous travel conditions, and all those potential hazards up to and including death? Well, as they say, no pain-no gain and no risk-no reward. Was it worth it? Absolutely! I can't begin to describe what I saw, but I'll try. My overall impression was of this being <u>otherworldly</u>, much more so than Iceland, which to that point was the clear champ in this category. It looked like you were on another planet or frozen moon. I had lived in Buffalo, New York through a few winters, and this made Buffalo look like the desert. Ironically, Antarctica is technically considered a desert because there is so little moisture in the air! Why? Because it freezes before it reaches the ground. For this reason there are no lakes or rivers, but you do get a great view of the ocean. Prisitne white mountains everywhere. Snow and ice everywhere. Penguins, seals, skuas, and other creatures roaming around freely. Feeling like it was this way millions of years ago. Incredible views all around. Just standing there, taking it all in, thinking maybe this is what it feels like to be walking on the moon, or being victorious after the final play of the Super Bowl. I remember the look on everyone's face as we stepped onto the continent for the first time. Amazement, awe, and a total wow! It surpassed everyone's highest expectations, and we gushed about it after returning to the boat (again having to wade through the water). It made "spettacolare!" seem "just OK" by comparison, and that's saying a lot.

Then there were the glaciers, wow! I had been to Alaska and took a boat tour of the fjords in Seward, which were incredible. I never thought I'd see glaciers any better than that. But here they were, the iciest blue color you'd ever seen. I learned that the ice-blue color forms when snow falls on the glacier and is compressed into it. This is the most striking color I've ever seen, and there were different hues. The ice glistened in the sun, sparkled, embellishing all around it. And these glaciers and ice sheets were mammoth in size, gigantic, stories and stories high. But the best part was when they cracked, or calved, with a loud explosion that reminded me of the M-80s we blew off on July 4th in Brooklyn, and huge chunks fell into the ocean. I could have watched that all day long. I saw some of that in Seward, Alaska but this was even better – louder explosions – KABOOM! – bigger chunks falling, more glacier ice floating around. Some tourmates and I went up a snowy hill and slid down it. The view from atop was great. I had my ski pants on but still got a bit of a burn. Good thing I didn't go on my belly like a penguin; better my butt hurt a bit than my belly (debatable which offered more protection after the big steak dinner in Argentina). If you recall being a kid playing in the snow, losing all track of time and space, multiply by 10 and that's what this was like. A thrill, a spill, and a big chill all in one!

We had learned all about the penguins, and tried to find the four different types: Adelie (white ring around its eye), Chinstrap (black stripe around its chin, looking like a tie for a hat), Gentoo (white patch on its black head, orange feet), and Macaroni (strands of orange hair looking like a Mohawk haircut, red beak, orange eyebrows – funny-looking creature). There is also the Emperor penguin which can stand up to 4 feet tall and weigh up to 90 pounds! I saw the first four types but not the Emperor, which is the rarest to see (would any of the others dare tell him he has no clothes?).

It was fascinating to see the penguin colonies, thousands of these funny-looking creatures everywhere, waddling around like Grandpa Munster, sliding on their bellies, and swimming in the

Antarctic Ocean. Several were running, quacking like a duck, and molting (shedding feathers). They were not afraid of humans at all, and seemed just as curious about us as we were about them. The "rule" we were told was that we couldn't get within 15 feet of a penguin, unless they walked up to us. Staff members watched us regarding this and for our safety. Several penguins did walk up close to us, and one of the tour leaders pointed and motioned to me to look down. There at my feet was the cutest penguin! I held out my hand but the tour guide quickly told me to withdraw it because penguins do bite! Many of us got extremely close for photo ops, and that was harshest on my hands and fingers because I had to take off my thick gloves and ready myself to snap the photos. When the right time arrived, I clicked off the photos as quickly as possible, and then put the gloves back on rapidly. My hands and fingers froze, went numb at times, and were often red, cracked, and bled around the knuckles. It looked like I had just gone a few rounds with the Mike Tyson of Emperor penguins. It's a good thing I brought hand lotion as advised before the trip. There was guano all over the place so you had to watch where you stepped (it smelled like motor oil and stayed with you if you got exposed). My camera batteries froze (still didn't have a digital camera) but I'd wisely brought lots of extras and kept changing them out. I also brought a back-up camera that took the same batteries, and a charger. Thankfully, there was one spectacular weather day during which we didn't need to wear gloves or even a hat!

We were also warned not to step on any moss or other vegetation – it could take 100 years to grow back. I went on a hike with a bunch of the others. The hiking was treacherous – lots of rocks (could easily twist an ankle), ice (could easily fall and break something), and other hazards including the potentially deadly crevasses. We looked out for each other as best we could. I followed behind because I hadn't been on a lot of hikes. My foot fell into a small, hidden crevasse in the ice which hurt my knee. I'd later put on an ice pack, ironically, which helped. I was fine – fortunately.

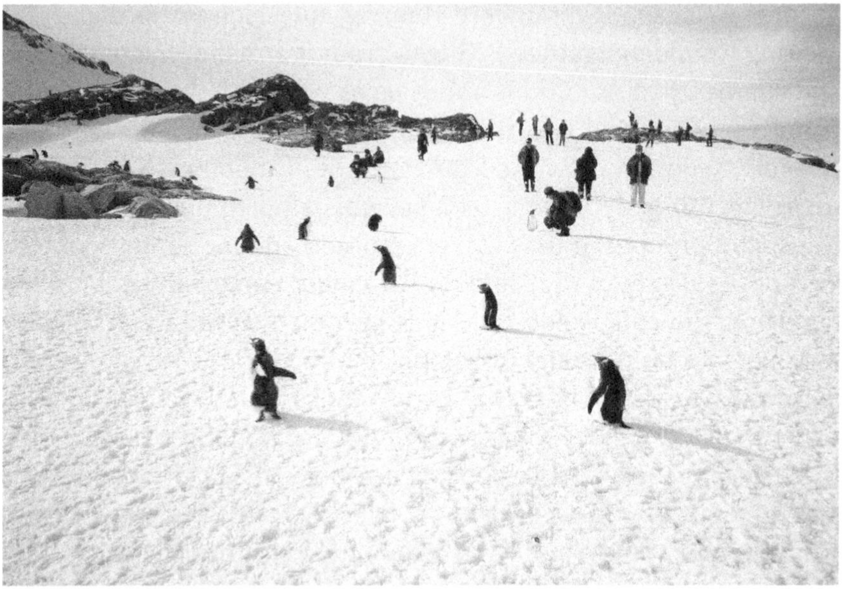

Penguins were everywhere, free as a bird, so to speak. They were as curious about us as we were about them - after all, this is their environment we were visiting.

My favorite part of the trip was rafting around the glaciers in the zodiacs. This was incredible! The raft held about 8 of us plus a tour guide. We all were in life preservers, and good thing too based on subsequent events. To enter the zodiac you had to wade through the water and hold the guide's arm, "forearm to forearm," for stability (hand to hand was too slippery). We would need to get into and out of the zodiac many times during this trip, so doing it properly was paramount. We motored around the ice floes and saw magnificent views. An ice-blue glacier upfront is really something to behold. There were collective sounds of awe, pictures, and looks at each other like this is so amazing! The visibility was decent, a bit cloudy, and definitely frigid. My teeth were chattering and one of the other Americans, a gal maybe age 30 sitting opposite me, looked totally frozen. I'd estimate the temperature to be at least -30 degrees with the wind-chill factor (I knew what this felt like from a brutal winter in Michigan).

But what made this all worth it was the majestic, spectacular view that is Antarctica. Thankfully, we had terrific weather during most of the trip, including three consecutive sunny & clear days for the landings, which we were told is extremely rare – another "spettacolare" moment! A tour guide, Jim, told us that the weather had been "miserable for the past three weeks, and you don't realize how fortunate you are to have come during this time." The ship's captain would later state and restate that in the 20 years he's been running ships to Antarctica this was the best week of weather he and his crew had ever seen. He said this emphatically and really meant it. Others from the crew would say the same thing independently of each other throughout the trip. In my mind I pictured getting 777 on a slot machine; it sounded that rare and fortunate. If there was a slot machine anywhere nearby I would have played it based on this good fortune – it was all going right.

Ironically, in the zodiac the view was a reverse-Jungfrau situation in that the panorama was from the bottom up, not top down, which added to the fascination. From bottom to top you saw the pure white mountains reflecting in the glass-like blue water, ice floes, seals, penguins, birds, then the mountains themselves towering over the landscape, and an azure sky with puffy white clouds. Everywhere you turned was like a post card setting. Remembering what I'd done in Alaska, I shot photos from the views all around including behind us. I did not bring a video camera as so many others did because I just wanted to focus (literally) on the photos, and then put the camera down, take it all in, and make a mental image that I could retrieve later. I subsequently put the photos into a magnificent album, and created a panoramic effect from the photos taken in these many directions.

There were two unusual moments during this excursion, both a not-so-subtle reminder of the dangers of being in Antarctica: we saw a forlorn-looking seal sitting on a chunk of ice with its tail bitten off, probably by a whale, and bleeding. We felt sad for the seal but couldn't do anything. The tour guide said it's going to die. Also, as we motored back to the ship we were followed by a leopard seal that bit the zodiac and punctured it! Had we been further away from the ship who knows what might have happened? Fortunately, we made it back OK. One of my zodiac-mates captured a photo of this and later shared it. Scary? Sort of. What you should expect? Maybe. Exciting? Yes. Take nothing for granted while here? Definitely! Undaunted, I would take the zodiac ride twice more before the trip was over. I did not see any seals in the vicinity during these rides. Obviously a big difference from zoo to native habitat, as I also could have learned the hard way in Australia had I approached that kangaroo.

Rafting around the glaciers and mountains of Antarctica was unforgettable, with the most magnificent scenery I have ever seen! Bundle up - the temperature could reach at least minus 40 degrees.

We returned to the ship. After wiping off my boots, and stepping into the guano-and-other-germ-eliminating solution, I returned to my cabin. That shower felt great! I was frozen yet had also sweated. The group had dinner, and afterwards I continued reading the book I had brought along, "The Power of Your Subconscious Mind," which I was re-reading for the 8th time since college. This book and "Looking Out For #1" are my favorite and most-read books; I highly recommend each one, which has helped form who I am today (I re-read the latter on a Club Med trip soon after this one). Each night there was an activity to keep us entertained. One night there was an auction for sea-faring and Antarctica-related items. I didn't have any room in my luggage for anything a decent size, and really didn't see anything all too appealing (my photos were my best souvenirs). After the auction the captain was making the rounds and we spoke for a bit. I told him

I collect things from my world travels, especially little things such as fridge magnets and baseball-style caps. He told me where I could get a fridge magnet at a later stop we'd be making (poor quality – fell apart quickly) and then said he had something for me. He returned with a beautiful cap that said Antarctica across the front, and gave it to me! I was stunned and so thankful! This cap is rare and I take such good care of it to this day; I only wear it in good weather, and protect it as if it were a rock not to be removed from Antarctica.

At the end of the voyage, the captain reiterated that in talking with the crew they felt this was the best-ever weather they had in the 20 years the ship has been making this sailing, and how fortunate we were. He said that just in the past couple of weeks there was a blizzard and hurricane that prevented any landings – yet we were able to make all of them. All this was just another cosmic confirmation to me that I had made the right choice in going, and was in the right place at the right time.

So it was a bit late and a few of us were hanging out, just chatting, getting to know each other. As with just about any group, be it co-workers, classmates, tourmates you're going to get your different personalities from A – Z, and in world travel you get, well, a microcosm of world personalities, and also an interesting array of thoughts and ideas. I enjoyed these late-night chats because people really opened up. There were no media aboard ship (TV, radio, Internet) so this was a welcomed discussion forum for an eclectic group of people who, whatever their reason and situation, decided to take this expedition. Much of the conversation had to do with travel, but world politics made its appearance as well.

Two such interesting people were my respective roommates, Jacques from Montreal, and Sebastian from Holland. Jacques told us that he's traveled extensively throughout Europe and Asia. He had a boring occupation, but seemed to get off on travel to exotic places. I like when he said that he's taken well over a year off to just travel while he's young, and has offset this cost by putting his stuff in storage during this time so he does not pay rent. Excellent idea, and I admired his desire to live his dream. I suppose he had the five essentials I mentioned to do all this (not the least of which is stamina). He was about 15 years younger than me and preferred to hang out seemingly exclusively with the 20-something crowd, so we didn't spend much time together except a few comparison-notes chats in our cabin. He was a good roommate – quiet, considerate, and sharing of his world-travel experiences.

At this same session, Sebastian opened up as well, but in a much different way. He was a smart guy and had very strong opinions about what was happening in the world. He wasn't crazy about Americans and was definitely against President George W. Bush's policies. He ranted about American Imperialism, and how we are bullies to the rest of the world. Yet, he loved his home country, Holland, which he never called that – instead calling it the Netherlands which is a much larger region that includes Holland. He was historically-minded and seemed to trumpet his country whenever he could, and bash some others, especially England and the U.S. We just listened and let him speak his mind, inflammatory as some of it was. I was not going to let something like this bother me. At times, Sebastian was annoying when an American on our tour would do something wrong and he'd tell others, "the American did this" or "the American did that." I didn't like that and told Sebastian the next day as the two of us had breakfast. Marcus had heard of what happened the night before and came over to us. He's a bigger guy than Sebastian and gave him a good piece of his mind about trashing America and Americans. I told Marcus I'd already talked to Sebastian about it, but Marcus wanted to make it totally clear, and did sternly before walking away. In general, Marcus seemed the laid-back type so his anger was a bit surprising to me. Sebastian didn't make an issue of it, and I said I'd appreciate it too if he didn't criticize us, refer to us like we're all the same, and basically keep his negative opinions to himself – especially since we're all here to enjoy the spectacular vacation. Sebastian said he was was OK with this, but you could tell not really.

That's when a very interesting turn-of-events occurred. I could tell that Sebastian was bothered by what just happened. He was quiet and in thinking mode with a bitter look on his face. I tried to change the topic back to our trip, but he said something to the effect of, "The Netherlands was very powerful back in the 1600s and 1700s" and went on to detail its glory days. I asked about its relationship with America, citing that in New York City, where I'm from, there is Stuyvesant Town, the Holland Tunnel, and a major street named Amsterdam Avenue. When I asked if New York City was originally called New Amsterdam (which I knew to be the case) he said, "Yes!" I asked about my home borough, Brooklyn, and asked if that means anything in Dutch. He said it does, "Breukelen" means "broken land." I told him this could be because Brooklyn is actually part of Long Island, which is separated from New York City. Sebastian's face then lit up and he started telling me how the Dutch helped America during the revolutionary war against their hated rivals, too, the British; how the Dutch were the ones who funded and armed America against them. He seemed gleeful at this point realizing this U.S.-Netherlands connection. "See, our two countries are friends," I said. "And here we are, together, representing them."

Sebastian nodded, and to my surprise opened up and told me more about a woman he loved many years ago who broke up with him, married another guy, realized she still loved him, but won't break up with her husband with whom she has two kids. Sebastian seemed wounded just telling this story, which happened 20 years ago. I empathized with him, told him about Doreen, but that life goes on. We acknowledged each other's pain, but Sebastian was still feeling the sting whereas I was long over it. Poor guy, I really did feel for him.

That day we cruised the Drake Passage, one of the most rough and dangerous stretches of ocean in the world, where anything can happen. Better bring a strong stomach with you. Here we encountered incredible-sized waves that rocked our boat relentlessly, creating crashing sounds that rivaled the KABOOMS of the glaciers cracking off from a distance. The ship sailed at funny angles as we went up and over these waves. This was at once scary and exhilarating, in that order. I didn't expect this at all. The captain reassured us several times. Sleeping was again difficult between the noise of the waves, the howling winds, the rocking of the boat, and the steep upward and downward angles of the boat. Walking around the ship was difficult as well, throwing us back and forth from wall to wall. To me, this was part of the overall experience, and if you can't handle the waves get out of the ocean, to paraphrase an old expression. Lots of people got sick during this stretch including me. It was the first time

I "lost it" in about 30 years (there went a prized streak), since I had vertigo as a teenager. Barf bags lined the railings. One staff member made a funny comment: "You can tell who the drunks are aboard the ship – they're the ones walking in a straight line."

At meal times I sat with a variety of different people so that I could meet everyone. Most were very polite, but gave me an earful about how they hate U.S. foreign policy, they think President Bush is "an idiot," how Gore really won the Presidential election, how Americans don't know anything about the rest of the world, how we force our culture on others, shouldn't have gone to war in Iraq, and are big bullies in general. I wanted to say, "Aside from that, Mrs. Lincoln, how was the play?" I wasn't about to enter into a debate on this; I wasn't interested in politics, would probably have been verbally attacked if I did try to defend our actions, and most importantly, I did not want anything to hinder this once-in-a-lifetime trip. As a reminder, most of these people were from Europe, and from as far away as Australia. I would encounter similar sentiment in future travels as well, with some relief in countries where people liked us. There were other political points made, too, not involving the U.S. (worldwide ecology, poverty, save the whales, etc.), that others thankfully decided to chime in about to divert the discussion.

I went to a movie and lecture at night. This time it was about the explorers Shackleton and Amundsen (Norwegian) who raced to be the first to the South Pole, and the hardships they endured – Amundsen won by a month. Many of Shackleton's men froze to death 11 miles from a food depot that would have saved them. I found this story highly interesting. The Italian scientist who had permission from her government to collect soil samples also gave a lecture. I didn't find this interesting, but others did. We all applauded. On occasion, a whale, seal, or albatross bird would be spotted on the port or starboard side of the ship. Many came running with their fancy digital cameras. I'd take a look and maybe some photos if the visual was spectacular, but wouldn't just take photos of a bird flying around or just the whale's tail unless it was totally upright.

The next day we landed on another Antarctica peninsula, and this was one of my favorites – Cuverville Island. This was the most incredible place I'd ever seen to this point in my 20 years of travel!

It encompassed my previous description and more – worthy of repeating: snow-covered, pristine white mountains; gorgeous ice-blue glaciers; seals, penguins, and humpback whales; beautiful azure blue sky; loud, attention-demanding explosions, visually yielding huge chunks of ice breaking off from the immense glaciers, creating mini-tidal waves (big trouble if they create big tidal waves!); and then, as you looked back, there was our little red ship looking like a toy boat (seriously!) in the engulfing blue ocean. This was paradise to me as a photographer, and I clicked-off nearly 200 photos in 2 hours. Not all of my tourmates made this landing; several were still seasick. I ran to a group of others to share my glee, and they shared theirs as well. It was more like delirious euphoria!!! I spent time roaming around with a couple of the younger gals in their 20s, from Vancouver and Sweden, which were two favorite places of mine as well. I had won two Journalism awards in college and had an outstanding vocabulary but really couldn't find the words to describe this, at least not in English. So my mind immediately searched its foreign rolodex. "Gute fahrt" or some other variation didn't "cut it" (sorry for that bad pun), nor did even "Spettacolare! Spettacolare!" from the first Jungfrau mountain sighting by the Italian Eurail passengers in Switzerland. I asked the gals I was with if they had any words to befit what we were seeing. They didn't either. We just kept looking around, turning, pointing, gaping, making sounds like "oh!" and "ooh" and "wow!" followed by lots of picture-taking.

The sunny day made a huge difference, I'd imagine; that was the whitest snow I'd ever seen. More "quacking" from the penguins (mainly Gentoos), roars from seals, splashing by whales, and cawing by the birds amidst all this. We saw thousands of penguins in their colonies, standing totally upright at attention, waddling around, flapping, molting, and more. We only had a few hours there before going to our next peninsula landing, Neko Bay. I could have spent all day in either place. Neko Bay was just as gorgeous, maybe more so than Cuverville Island. OK, this was my new favorite place in the world, beating the old one which was a few hours ago! I remember the mirror-like water with ice chunks, atop which there were some seals, but especially the smaller ice dotting the ocean giving it a shimmering luster in the sun. Several of us hiked up a snow-covered hill that overlooked a glacier and the bay. “Spettacolare! Spettacolare!” – and multiply by infinity. Chunks of ice were again calving off the glaciers, dropping into the bay, and floating downstream. To the thousands of penguins, seals, and other wildlife in the vicinity this was probably just another day in Arctic paradise. But to us, it was definitely a “wow!” I especially liked seeing the mountain reflections in the ice-streaked waters. The water right next to the glacier chunks was a color I’d not seen before, an iridescent greenish-blue. The closest I’d seen to it was in Alaska, but this color looked even more striking and brilliant. Maybe it should be called “spettacolare! blue.” Perhaps some artists out there can develop it into a color for mainstream usage. There were other gorgeous blue-family colors, too.

Another awesome view occurred on a zodiac ride immediately after the hike down the hill. We went in shifts since only about 8 people could fit into each zodiac. Several zodiacs were out at once, and I took photos of my fellow zodiac-mates both inside my own and also of others motoring nearby. We saw a few humpbacks and out came the cameras. An interesting photo in itself was of the others poised to take photos of a whale, with their long lenses held rock-steady, pointed at the water, just waiting. We saw several. I knew whales were big, but this was the closest I’d got to one and it was gigantic. Several were “logging,” lying flat face-down looking for food. Their habits were explained to us. We were just amazed; this was all surreal! And the weather was such a help. It actually got up to 40 degrees at one point, so like the penguins, we started shedding – our layers of clothes, that is. For reference, the warmest temperature ever recorded in Antarctica was 55 degrees Fahrenheit, and the coldest – which is the coldest ever recorded on the planet – was -128 degrees Fahrenheit (without the wind-chill factor). To be in 40 degrees along that continuum, with dazzling sunshine, was nothing short of incredible.

Wow, isn't this grand! That's our ship in the background, looking like a toy boat in the vast Antarctic Ocean. Don't forget the sunglasses, suntan lotion, and water bottle - you can get very sunburned and very dry on this frozen continent.

During the ride back, everyone on the zodiac said how this trip is so worth the money. This later came up as we compared notes with the others on our expedition. The consensus: no-brainer - this was the best vacation any of us had ever taken, and there were still a few more days to go. That night on the ship we had an outdoor barbecue, if you can believe it. The weather was holding up nicely, and this being summer in the Antarctic, there was lots of daylight. We even had a beautiful sunset on top of all else. More photos, smiles, raves, and drinks! The ship was adorned with flags from around the world. Standing under the one from Israel was an Israeli gal in her mid-20s, Naomi. We had a brief and pleasant conversation about the amazing journey so far. She asked if I've been to Israel. I said no, but that I'd like to go someday. She highly recommended it and provided some places to visit. She hadn't been to the United States yet, and I returned the favor.

That night, a bunch of us sat around discussing life in general and travel in particular. We were from the U.S., Canada, England, Scotland, Australia, and New Zealand. There were some interesting stories; it seemed like everyone had loosened up during this trip and recognized we are all comrades in travel. One guy, Dave, an American in his 30s, told that he has a seven-month-old son at home but felt such a yearning to go on this trip that he pleaded with his wife to do so. Finally, she relented and he's glad he went – although he misses his wife and son a lot. As it turns out, Dave told about his roommate from "the Netherlands" – and yes, it was Sebastian! Without saying anything about knowing him, I asked how that's going. After a bit of hesitation, Dave said, "Fine, we're getting to know each other." Sebastian toned down selected opinions the rest of the trip and everything with the "issue" we discussed was fine.

Three Australian guys who I sat with at dinner a couple of nights earlier told of a funny story about Americans in their tiny hometown called Alice Springs - population 60,000 or so, and a couple of hundred miles from the famous giant sandstone formation, Ayers Rock. One of the men, Jack, told how the U.S. had a "secret" military base there with 1,000 G.I.s; however, this "secret" base was visible when you fly over it going in and out of Alice Springs' airport. The local Australian residents knew about it, but when you asked any American what they did in Alice Springs they'd reply, "janitor" – probably told to say this by their commanding officer if asked. So one of the Australian guys said to us on the ship, "Imagine that, in a tiny Australian town of 60,000 people, there are 1,000 U.S. janitors!" We laughed. As it turned out, one of these Australian guys said he used to work in the United States, and when I asked where, he said, "For NORAD in Colorado Springs," and in case I wasn't familiar with it he described that NORAD monitors and controls airspace in North America. "Were you ever in Colorado Springs?" he asked. I said, "Small world – I used to live and work there for four years - we're neighbors yet again halfway around the world!" When I asked what he did for NORAD he replied, "Janitor." We had another good laugh. I truly enjoyed these delightful late-night conversations; not only did they pass the time well, but I learned a lot and felt a real connection with people from around the world.

We had more travels during this trip, and they did not disappoint. We went to Petermann Island through the Lemaire (pronounced Leh-mere) Channel, where there were abundant Gentoo and Adelie penguin rookeries. It was this cool circular bay, not very long, from which you could view very interesting-looking glaciers including an ice arch. The mountains were dark brown and ice-capped, reminding me of those in Alaska. The weather was overcast which made for a more foreboding landscape than what we had seen in the bright sunshine. Lots of slippery rocks, so you had to be careful when hiking around. I nearly slipped and fell a couple of times.

Next we cruised to a different landscape. Deception Island was in the South Shetland Islands, and was volcanic. Volcanoes blew twice there in the late 1960s and did considerable damage. The British had a base there in 1944 but had to evacuate it in 1967 when a volcano caused massive destruction. We took a two-hour strenuous hike up to and around the rim, which was very interesting, but what was more so was when a group of us got into our bathing suits and soaked in the natural thermal waters of a crater-like hole by the lagoon. This reminded me of the Blue Lagoon in Iceland but on a much smaller scale. It was freezing when we got out (even if the temperature was still a balmy 26 degrees Fahrenheit). Yet another cool experience, soaking in the waters of Antarctica! A funny thing happened just after this, when one of the younger guys on the tour decided to test the waters, literally, and run into the ocean. Dumb move given what could have been lurking out there, but this was a moot point. After about three steps in he immediately turned around and ran back to the shore. Yes, the water was that cold! Duh. Several of us had our cameras out to capture the inevitable shocked look on his face upon run-back. He didn't disappoint.

We also sailed to Hannah Point which had more Macaroni penguins. There were more birds flying around looking for penguin eggs and other food. Finally, there was Aitcho Island, another volcanic isle on which we took a hike to the end of it to get a good view. There we saw the surrounding islands, and more seals. These were generally elephant seals, the largest ones we saw. They seemed pretty mellow and didn't bother the penguins moving past them to the water. Once again, everything was just breathtaking. I really didn't want it to end, and tried hard to make a mental picture of what I was seeing so I could retrieve it without relying on photos. Much as I tried, the images in my mind faded over time – so it's a good thing I got all those photos! It might be worth the price of hypnosis to mentally revisit there.

Our tour leader obtained permission for us to visit two military bases: Argentina and Ukraine. We were provided with a tour of each upon arrival by selected military personnel aboard. We saw how the guys lived, were given some history, and asked questions. Many said they get bored and lonely but amuse each other. There were many posters and calendars of scantily-clad gals on the walls. There was a small gift shop there with very limited selection of items where I bought the Antarctica fridge magnet, made of wood. This wasn't good quality and cracked soon after purchase. I glued it back together and still have it on my fridge. I wished a better-quality one was offered.

On the return trip through the Drake Passage, we passed through a place called Kodak Alley because of the spectacular scenery (glaciers, mountains). This was amazing. At night, a crew member surprised us all with a video retrospective of our trip featuring over 100 photos he clandestinely took of us passengers. We were all represented in at least one photo and cheered as each one of us was shown. I was pictured holding my backpack up against a mountainous backdrop while standing on the pristine white snow. I got a loud roar, louder than most, which really surprised me. I took this in a good way; several people there really liked me. Aside from the passengers, one was a very cute Filipino maid on the ship. Every time I looked her way she seemed to blush and then smile at me in that special way. I thought about initiating something, but we had been warned not to do anything illegal or get into any trouble, because Antarctica is part of a multi-country treaty that makes it very difficult if you have a problem. I simply did not want anything to tarnish such a great vacation.

At the end of our trip passengers who had digital cameras were allowed to upload their photos onto a selected website using the ship's private computer, and from these a CD was made for each of us. These photos were sensational, and basically replicated the ones I had taken and then some! While I valued photos back then, the older I get the more I cherish these not only for their initial capture of my vacations, but for the connections they now recreate upon further review. Years earlier I had taken an adult education course in which the instructor told the class to "just keep shooting" because the cost of photos is relatively inexpensive and the memories are priceless. He was right, and I always kept that in mind.

I went to the lounge and initiated more discussions. One such question I asked is where each person would recommend others travel to for a visit. Sebastian and a guy from Canada recommended a safari in Africa, in Kenya or Tanzania, and provided some companies they'd go with. Others recommended South America, using our current tour operator. More recommendations included Slovenia (from a guy whose heritage was this), Patagonia in Southern Chile, Nepal, Greenland, Wales, Alaska cruise through the inland passage, Mongolia, and the Canadian northwest territories including Baffin Island in the Canadian territory of Nunavut. I would end up going to most of these in the coming years.

We also marveled at the weather again. This seemed to be a big topic many were buzzing about. Obviously, it was a major concern when going on a trip like this; it's beyond your control and can be an all-or-nothing deal-maker or deal-breaker for the entire trip. A couple of people said, as they did before, that they're still hoping for some more rough weather to relive that real Antarctic travel experience. Others politely told them to shut up. I joked that if we didn't get a snowstorm I would mix-in some of my Buffalo, New York photos with the Antarctica photos for my photo album. As it turned out, Mother Nature would have the last laugh, "relatively" speaking, because we continued to have wonderful weather. Temporarily, at least.

Well, it had been quite a day and I ended up sleeping 15 hours that night as we headed back through the Drake Passage toward Ushuaia for the next two days. I had a bit of a cold and had taken some medication that knocked me out. I recovered very quickly; if a minor cold, small knee injury, and one-time seasickness were all that happened to me throughout a trip like this, I was happy. Others didn't have it so good and had hurt themselves in various ways; a few were in casts or splints. The next day we just chilled out on the ship, chatting and reading, attending more lectures, and watching for whales along the sides of the ship. The next-to-last night we all got together and recounted our wonderful trip. The captain yet again gushed about the terrific weather for it and how fortunate we were; indeed, it probably made a huge difference. He did, however, say that there's some nasty weather just ahead, and we hit right into it the next day.

We ran into a near-hurricane and the ship again was a-rockin'. A gal from Michigan, and also a tour guide aboard ship, got their wish to "ride the high seas," and were as excited as little kids opening Christmas presents, running over to the port windows and checking out the action. One final movie that night told more about Sir Francis Drake, and how his ship got blown off course during a hurricane. How appropriate to see that movie at that time; the sound and rocking effects of our ship sure made it seem like you were right there aboard his ship! As we exited the theater room, we saw the barf bags out again and lining the railings. This didn't look good, literally and figuratively.

After the hurricane, our little ship hit into a blizzard, which made for more theatrics. Some were nervous, some were scared, some thought this exciting, some thought this could be the end. High drama on the high seas! (Incredibly, a few short years later I would face even more drama than this aboard another ship.) Someone yelled, "I knew our trip was too good to be true!" given how great it was in the world's most unforgiving place. At this point that old movie slogan came back in my head, "In space, no-one can hear you scream." This was it, do or..." Thankfully, the captain and crew navigated out of this and we were all fine and safe. That was close. Sleeping that night was no easy feat. My roommate Jacques and I again slid up and down in our respective beds as the waves swelled to tremendous heights (maybe 15 – 30 feet was one estimate). We went up one end of the wave and down the other, time after time. That got lots of people sick again, but I was able to "weather the storm" with a combination of my little pink pill Pepto Bismol and also Bonine® for motion sickness which, thankfully, also made me very sleepy. I was also very sore from the landings, hikes, carrying heavy gear, and contorting into awkward positions.

"Was it worth it?" I asked myself again the next morning, as we prepared to disembark. "No doubt about it!" was my answer to myself, and later to many others asking this same question. In fact, as we approached the shore, a couple of older members on the expedition walked over and commended me for taking such a trip and accomplishing so many world travels at a relatively young age. They wished they had or could, but told me how sick and tired (literally) and sore they got, in some cases preventing them from going on many of the landings. They encouraged me to keep traveling and do it while I'm young and healthy. They appreciated my provocative questions, conversation, information, and jokes. I left them with one last one. A few of them had been to Alaska as well, near the North Pole as had I. I told them now we can tell people that we're "part Polish – we've been to or near the North and South Pole." One final laugh, a handshake, some handshakes and hugs with the others, and it was the end to a magical mosaic! Many people exchanged names and contact information, but I didn't, except with Marcus, who asked me for my email address. I just knew that I wouldn't be seeing these people again – that's how it goes with these tours, and I just didn't want to be disappointed. We said our goodbyes and wished each other well. As it turned out, Marcus didn't contact me. However, this would not be the last time we would be in contact...

My final thoughts about this Antarctica experience were **"WOW!"** and New Year's Resolution accomplished! I was so happy I got to take this trip, and was deeply appreciative for all the events that unfolded to allow it at just the right time. To this day, it stands alone as the greatest trip I ever took! This expedition was another reason I decided to write this book, so I can share this experience, and my other travels, with readers. But there was still more to follow, both on this trip, and in many future and wonderful sojourns.

At last, we made it back to Ushuaia! Real land! Hot weather, and time to defrost! From 90 degrees to -40 degrees back to 90 degrees. What a sensational trip to Antarctica. Everyone raved about it. Although several people ended their tour with Gap Adventures upon this landing, mine continued (as prepaid) back in Ushuaia and in Buenos Aires for a few days afterwards. Several of us continued the tour, and Sebastian and I were once again reunited as roommates. I emailed my brother to tell him and our parents that I returned safe and sound to South America. My mom worries a lot. Only by reading this book will she find out what really happened in Antarctica!

Back at the hotel, I relaxed and had dinner with Sebastian. We spoke mainly about our respective travels and shared experiences. He asked me if I like waterfalls. I told him yes, and that I lived near Niagara Falls, which is the most visited attraction in the United States. He enthusiastically told me of two other waterfalls he said are even more spectacular, that I'd never heard of: Iguassu Falls in South America, and Victoria Falls in Africa. He said he's been to all three and rated them in that order from least to best: Niagara, Iguassu, and Victoria. He explained to me why – that Iguassu was much larger than Niagara Falls, and Victoria is very high and steep, and in the middle of a jungle. I shrugged and said I'd take his word for it since I figured I'd never see the other two. I was impressed that he knew all this, confirming that he was at a higher strata of travel experience than I was. I admired his knowledge in this area and respected his recommendations; he was like a traveler role model to me, maybe what John from the Bermuda cruise was like at his age. Afterwards we returned to the room, where I got a good night's sleep.

The next morning, our last in Ushuaia before the flight back to Buenos Aires that evening, I chatted with our local South American tour guide, Benjamin, who called me over to sit with him at breakfast. He was a very nice guy who smiled a lot. He delighted in helping people, and loved being a tour guide. I told him how terrific the trip was to Antarctica – which by that time he had heard from many others. He was glad about that. He said that because I'd be leaving a day earlier than the tour officially ended (due to flight arrangements), I would be missing the prepaid free dinner and tango dance show. I said that's OK, and "no refund required." He smiled and said he arranged for me to see the performance that night! I asked how that can be when we didn't arrive into Buenos Aires until midnight. He said there was a show that was performed from 1:00 a.m. – 3:00 a.m. "The reservation has been made," he said, "so go." He was such a nice guy that I didn't want to disappoint him, and I really appreciated him doing that for me. So I smiled happily, said OK, and added "Gracias." Benjamin replied, "De nada."

During the discussion I told him that this trip enabled me to get to two new continents, and that I only needed to get to Africa to achieve a travel goal. I also told him I aimed to get to 50 countries eventually, and that I'd been to more than half that already. He asked if I'd been to any other South American countries. I said no, but I'd like to go. Benjamin then told me matter-of-factly that there is a ferry you can take from Buenos Aires to Uruguay, and if you take the "fast ferry" for just a little more money it will get you there in an hour. I was quite surprised, and said I'd check into it. I did so later that day and learned that there's only one ferry that would get me there and back in time for my return flight to San Francisco, but it left at 8:00 a.m. This seemed dubious because the tango show ended at 3:00 a.m., I wouldn't get back to my hotel until 4:00 a.m., I'd then have to get up at 6:00 a.m. and get to the ferry dock by 7:00 a.m. for the 8:00 a.m. sailing to Uruguay. That's nuts – and I was so tired already from the grueling expedition (and sore, too). I realized I couldn't do both events, so I figured I'd go to the dinner/tango show, leave after an hour, and sleep in the next morning before my afternoon flight. However, this was not what would happen...

We had 8-1/2 hours to roam around Ushuaia. My tourmate posse of 8 originally now swelled to 16 and co-opted me into joining them for this walk-around. The conversation wasn't to my liking, so I politely excused myself and went off on my own, walking down the main street (Saint Martin), sightseeing and taking photos. I was happy my camera still worked and hadn't frozen. A funny thing happened when I stopped into a photocopy place to make an additional copy of my main passport page, in case anything happened to my original passport (always keep an additional copy or two apart from your passport – and give a copy to someone from home, too). The cost was 10 cents in Argentine currency (pesos). I didn't have any local change with me so I showed the female clerk a U.S. quarter which she took from my hand and examined. The gal of about 20 smiled and, not speaking English, said "uno momento," motioning for me to wait. She returned after presumably doing the calculation, and not only gave me my photocopy, but three Argentine quarters back as change for my one U.S. quarter based on the exchange rate. Despite not speaking each other's language, we both laughed. I gave her the change back, clasped her hand, and said "keep it." She understood the intention, said "gracias" and smiled. After having high drama on the high seas, it was nice to share a pleasant little moment in a pleasant little town.

I continued my stroll. The city looked a lot like one in Alaska, or in a Colorado ski village, with rustic stores and a towering mountain in the background. I stopped into a place with a sign reading "Backpackers Welcome" and sat in a comfortable chair – in which I ended up falling asleep for an hour, which rarely happens. I didn't realize how tired I was. I ate an empanada for lunch, a popular dish there, which was very good. Then came some wild weather: sun, fog, rain, snow and more sun – in that order. I had a feeling that the tour group after mine going to Antarctica was in for a rough time with the weather. By now, the weather my group had is probably folklore. As mentioned early in this book I had spectacular weather in general throughout my travels, telling me that these trips were meant to be. It's good to go with the flow, but not with the tidal wave! In the coming years sea travel to Antarctica would be increasingly limited: the glaciers were melting at a rapid pace, making it dangerous to pass through the area. In fact, a couple of years later the little red ship we were on struck an ice glacier off the coast of Antarctica, was lying on its side before sinking, and thus made international news! More than 150 passengers were evacuated and fortunately rescued by a Norwegian cruise ship that was in the vicinity. That could have been us. And, as mentioned, there are hungry seals and whales there looking for a meal. The passengers ended up being OK, and got a misadventure to go along with the planned adventure (no extra charge, I imagine).

Speaking of which, it was time to seal the deal and wave goodbye to Ushuaia. My tour group boarded the plane for a four-hour flight back to Buenos Aires. Some people were leaving the next day, others were spending additional time there, while others spent extra time in Ushuaia as several others had done on the front end of this trip. On our flight I sat next to the older couple from Wales who I'd met at the airport in Buenos Aires and whose luggage was lost. It literally "missed the boat," and they told me was not found as yet. I felt really badly for them. They asked about mine and I said it barely made it. We wished each other well with the rest of the trip...and return flights, including luggage. They were nice people, and I admired how calmly they handled the situation.

We arrived at the hotel near midnight. Benjamin called ahead to the restaurant/tango place, Bar Sur, to ensure my reservation for 1:00 a.m. Was I really going to do this, being so tired? Well, I did. Sebastian wanted to chat with me – we were becoming closer – but I told him of this plan and that I may not even return to our hotel room because of a potential early excursion to Uruguay. He was surprised that a ferry ran between the two countries; as with me, he didn't know his South America geography. I said I'd be back to chat with him afterwards, and before my return flight home later that evening.

The hotel concierge called me a taxi which took me to Bar Sur. I liked the place; it looked classy, like an old supper club. The few patrons there were leaving, and by the time I was served my dinner (lomo steak again, wow!) I was the only one left. The manager, in his 50s, came over to me and I thought for sure he would ask me something like, "Is it OK if we cancel the 1:00 (a.m.) show?" Instead he told that the dancers will be out in a few minutes. His English was not that good and I wasn't sure what he had said. My Spanish, however, was worse than his English. I tried to tell him it's OK if he or the dancers want to cancel the show since it's only me here: "No tango solamente" I said, recalling my high school Spanish from 30 years ago, trying to communicate that they don't have to do the tango for only me. He replied, "Si, dos," which didn't make sense to me based on what I thought I'd said. A few minutes later, as I was about to leave, the show began. I later found out that I had said, "Don't tango with me alone," to which he replied, "Yes, two." I guess he meant "it takes two to tango"! No wonder I got a 'C' in Spanish class, and ironic that he said the word "Si" back a lot in response. These things (and worse) can happen when you're tired in a foreign country at 1:00 a.m., are by yourself and don't speak the language. But if I survived Antarctica, surely I could survive this. My mind even amused me with a joke to keep me awake, recalling a comedian on TV saying that Americans should walk around saying "B" because Canadians say "Eh" and Mexicans say "Si."

Anyway, the big meal made me even more tired, but the dancers were now on the floor with the lights out and a spotlight on them. Oh definitely a "siesta" atmosphere for me with the lights out after a big meal at this hour, but I had to watch it. The main dancers were excellent, and the female dancer had one of the best figures (along with a pretty face) I've ever seen to this day. She reminded me of a praying mantis, the way her legs stretched out and toes pointed outward (weird analogy, but that's what I thought at the time, in a complimentary way). There were lively tunes (the horns kept me awake), romantic ballads, and some slapstick comedian in various costumes rambling in Spanish as the dancers changed for the next tango, which added a surreal element to it all. At one point the comedian was pointing to me because I think audience participation was part of his act. He would then laugh, make some clown-like gestures, and motion to me to come sit on a chair in front of him. I shook my head no and waved him off – thank goodness that's universal. He got the idea.

The tango show continued, and I showed the camera to the manager who nodded that it's OK to take photos (universal gestures were working now). The dancers at times played to the camera, holding the pose, which I appreciated (especially the gal's leg over the guy's knee). It went through my mind that maybe they think I'm somebody really important, because the show is going on only for me. Little did they know that if my Spanish was any better they could all be home sleeping by now.

I moved around to get different angles, and closer to them from where I'd been sitting. They seemed to like this, and the manager said something in Spanish in a tone that indicated approval. The comedian also seemed to like this, and I got a photo of him, too. I was getting a second wind, and getting "into" the tango dance as the music heightened. I sat through the entire two-hour show and felt strong, even at 3:00 a.m. After the show ended, the dancers went backstage and I figured the show is over and I could leave. The manager took me to the dance floor and took a photo of me on it. He then said something loudly and the female dancer appeared, still in her sexy black dance outfit. She came right up to me, and – I'll never forget this – in broken English said, "Do you want to tango with me?" She was even more beautiful and sexy than I had seen from afar. I mumbled, "I don't know how." She said, "I will teach you," and placed my arms on her body where they were supposed to be. The music played, and she glided us through the dance. I stepped on her feet a few times but she said, "Don't worry." I didn't, mainly because I was mesmerized. She wore fishnet stockings, low-cut top, slit skirt, and spiked heels, all in black. It seemed like a dream, and good thing there were photos to prove it wasn't (I'd hate to wake up and find myself clutching Sebastian, who also had a ponytail). The manager took photos of us, and the male dancer came out in his costume, too (no, I wasn't going to dance with him). He laughed as did the few staff remaining plus the comedian, as the gal and I tangoed around the dance floor. She had to keep on her toes, literally, because I stepped on them a few times. But she kept on her game face. Everyone was having a good time.

Now here's the kicker (almost literally): at the end of the dance, after I'd almost kneed the gal by accident, she held out my arm, turned her head, positioned me just so, kicked out my left leg, bending it a little, and with her hand around my shoulder put her leg on my knee and held it there! The manager ran and said, "I get camera" and took a few photos of this. I was thinking "Spettacolare! Spettacolare!" or whatever the Spanish equivalent is. I was so energized that I stayed another half hour taking more pictures, when the guy and gal started dancing again. When it was time to leave, I shook everyone's hand, and the gal gave me a big hug. All of us were happy and smiling, laughing and enjoying. And I'm thinking, "This is the way life should be. How great was that?!"

As they were all conversing amongst themselves in Spanish, I was walking out the door. As an afterthought, I turned to them and said, "Adios!" That one word I knew meant "goodbye" - and may have saved my life. I walked out into the street at that early-morning hour and was hailing a taxi that happened to be right there. I had my hotel's card in my pocket so it was set up to be an easy ride back. I was about to step into the taxi when the manager literally ran after me in the street and said in very broken English, "I call you taxi" and escorted me back into the club. I'm thinking what the heck is going on? Another guy who worked there, who was in his 20s and I hadn't seen before (maybe the cook?), spoke English well and said that the taxi drivers there can be dangerous - they pick up passengers, drive them to remote areas, rob them, and maybe even worse, especially during the late hours. He said there is a specific taxicab company they deal with for their customers. He called it for me, and the taxi arrived in about 15 minutes. We all said goodbye again, and I thanked everybody. Another lesson learned: the situation when traveling could change as fast as the Ushuaia weather - you have to be careful! I would have several other transportation "situations" later on that will be described, one of which dominated international news.

I was back at the hotel room at 4:30 a.m. and got a couple of hours' sleep. Sebastian, an early riser, was up at 6:00 a.m., the time I needed to be up. I told him about the tango place and he was amused. We agreed to have dinner together at 7:30 p.m. and catch up after my return from Uruguay, before I headed to the airport for my overnight flight back to the U.S. I had the hotel front desk clerk call me a taxi for the short ride to the ferry dock on this Saturday, and also had him arrange a taxi pick up in the evening at 9:00 p.m. to take me to the airport, which I later confirmed. The taxi driver to the ferry arrived on time. Upon arrival at the ferry station, I asked him to wait there while I made sure there was indeed a ferry at 8:00 a.m. as I was told. There wasn't; on weekends the 8:00 a.m. ferry runs at 10:00 a.m. I had the taxi driver take me back to the hotel so I could get some additional sleep (desperately needed), and arranged for him to pick me up in two hours. "Dos horas," I said. I just hoped, based on my Spanglish, he didn't return with two prostitutes (well, if he did, then have fun, Sebastian). He knew what I meant and said "Si." I napped for two hours. I was still tired but had enough juice to make it through this long day. I figured I could sleep on the ferry, and later on the long plane ride home. I'm like that on vacations – leave it all out on the field because this is what I live for and who knows if/when I'll ever be back.

The taxi arrived on time two hours later, and I gave the driver a nice tip at the ferry dock. I took the "fast ferry" from the Buquebus ferry company but didn't sleep on it, instead opting to take photos on this clear day. The ferry arrived in Colonia, Uruguay a little more than an hour later. This is the oldest town in Uruguay and I was surprised to learn is Portuguese, not Spanish. It was taken over by Spain, but later returned to Portugal a couple of times. I walked around for seven hours, checking out the rocky beach area for starters. The beach reminded me of the lakefront beaches in Buffalo, New York and the bluish-gray water had very low but sweepingly wide waves rolling in. The city seemed rather sparse, not much going on. I took a short walk to the historic section. Lots of cobblestone streets going back to the 17th century. Several stone houses, too, and a lighthouse that is a main attraction there but didn't impress me (I'd seen better in New England). I wasn't really sure what to do there and asked some locals, a group of younger people in their 20s. They spoke English fairly well and basically said this is it; the old historical section is the tourist area. A cool-looking guy named Leonardo suggested a restaurant at which I could have good food – especially the ravioli. I balked at that saying I'd had that in Buenos Aires and wasn't impressed. He insisted this place is good, and he and friends go often. He pointed the way and I checked it out. It looked nice inside and I tried the ravioli again for $3 U.S. (huge plate). This time it was good. If the first one in Buenos Aires was "wide right" (sorry, Bills fans), this one was through the middle of the uprights.

I was in a rare position of having lots of time to stroll around without having to be back to the motor coach, ship, or meet anyone at a specific time. There were lots of people riding around on mopeds (only $8/hour) but I didn't want to risk injury before heading back. I'd already injured my knee (which was recovering) and saw that the moped drivers were aggressive, as in Firenze. I thought it better to just keep walking, although it was 90 degrees. I walked around the shops and plazas, took my usual large amount of photos, chatted with the locals getting by on my high school Spanish, and just mingled. It was nice to just sit and relax a while with a local beverage ("yerba mate" which tasted like green tea). I have certain questions I routinely ask of the locals, in addition to what there is to do. One is how the city or country got its name, and what it means. Most people don't know, even in the U.S. For example, most people I asked in the U.S. didn't know that "Colorado" translates in Spanish to color red, named after its red-colored river or rocks. Or that Nevada means snow-covered (for its mountains). Or that New York, New Jersey and New Hampshire were named for their counterparts in England, York, Jersey, and Hampshire. I just find it an interesting factoid that might give a clue as to the sightseeing there. So I asked and found out that Uruguay means "river of the colorful birds." I saw the river, but not the birds – I wasn't there too long, however.

Since I was in a foreign country not related to my tour – and thus out of its jurisdiction – I had to be very careful. This included even little things we take for granted such as drinking the water. I knew all about Montezuma's revenge, so I was super-careful when in selected foreign and underdeveloped countries, but wasn't sure about Uruguay. So I ate and drank only pre-packaged items, and dined in the better restaurants. It's a good rule to follow – if you're not sure, don't chance it. Often times there were street vendors around who seemed OK. They could very well have been, but if there was any doubt I wouldn't make the attempt in general (risk/reward).

While Colonia wasn't anything to write home about, it was somewhat interesting and further whet my appetite for travel to South America. I would later return to Uruguay's capital in Montevideo where there was more to see and do, but for now this was a nice side-trip addition to what was already a phenomenal vacation. It was like this entire trip was meant to be, and thank goodness for that. You can't put a price on realizing your dreams.

After I took the ferry back to the hotel in Buenos Aires, I had dinner with Sebastian there. It seemed fitting to finish off this trip with the first person I met on my tour upon arrival. To my surprise, Sebastian was sad about my leaving. He enjoyed my company and we toasted each other, and to a better world. Despite what he had said about the U.S. in the beginning, he did come around – at least part way – in saying that "most Americans are OK, I just disagree with the politics," and that "you need to separate the people from the politics." This was an important revelation for him, and realization for me. Sebastian said that I helped him like the American people more; he was surprised how much I knew about other countries, and was impressed that I was taking time off to see the world and learn more about it. We did not stay in contact, however, and just wished each other well before parting. I have to admit it was nice meeting him. I didn't know it then but his insights and recommendations would become important considerations for me in the future that changed my trajectory – and would literally have a far-reaching effect in more ways than one. Sebastian was also a good roommate, and his being hurt by the woman he loved is universal. I hope he finds true love and true happiness.

Well, I packed my bags and it was time to head to the airport. The taxi driver that the hotel front-desk clerk called for me arrived 15 minutes early, which turned out to be very important. I got into the taxi and was sad that this magnificent vacation was ending. But there would be one more curve in the road ahead: the taxi driver took me to the wrong airport! He realized his mistake when retrieving my luggage from the trunk, and was seemingly good enough to tell me about this before I walked into the terminal. He was berating himself for this mistake, which cost me time in making my overnight flight. Now the scramble was on to make it in time.

He drove like a New York City cabbie (a good thing in this case), barely making it to the correct airport in time. However, once there he wanted me to pay the metered rate – which included going to the wrong airport! I already knew from the front-desk clerk the approximate price of going to the (right) airport so that I could plan having enough local currency left over to pay the taxi driver. I politely pointed this out to the driver, but he wanted me to pay the additional amount anyway (his English was suddenly better). I wondered if this is why he showed up early, and if he planned this, knowing I'd be squeezed for time. I remembered what the Bar Sur manager told me, but this cab was called by my hotel clerk and I assumed would be legitimate. What to do?

I paid him the price for going to this (the correct) airport. We argued, and he soon found out the meaning of "Brooklynization." He was, however, holding my luggage hostage in the trunk, and time was on his side (but I didn't let him know that part.) The winning point came when I said that I'd let the hotel know what happened if he doesn't take this money (plus decent tip) right now. It was risky threatening this, which might have jeopardized his future business, but my New York City instincts kicked in and the gambit paid off. He accepted it grudgingly. I didn't want the trip to end this way, but I would have felt lousy if I were ripped-off. I would end up returning to Buenos Aires two years later, and encounter more, shall I say, "unusual circumstances" which will be later described.

I got some well-needed sleep on the plane and arrived back in the U.S. without any problems. I processed over 1,000 photos on a picture-maker machine (zooming/cropping as needed), and printed out the ones from the collective CD as well. They came out great! Another reason I take so many photos is to later relive the trips upon viewing them after processing – with yet another vicarious trip back when putting them into photo albums and showing them to others. I combine post cards when possible (none were available in Antarctica) to enhance the photos, often starting with a panoramic photo or post card of the area and then focusing in on the details (including some food shots, like the lomo steak). I'm not all that creative with the photos, but do assemble them in ways that can portray a landscape, e.g. to give the viewer a sense of the panorama I saw. I do not show my albums to many people, but a high percentage of those who see them exclaim "Wow!" a lot.

Here's a favorite anecdote regarding this. Back in California, as I was putting the Antarctica photos into a massive album later at a big table in a coffee shop, a couple of college gals looked over several times, seemingly intrigued, when one finally asked me what I'm doing. "Putting my photos of Antarctica into an album. They came out great! Would you like to see them?" I cheerfully offered. The two gals looked at each other and shook their heads. "No, thanks, came the answer." When I asked why not, one gal said, "Because we don't want to see pictures of your Aunt." They thought the photos were of an Aunt of mine named Arctica! I just laughed and said, "OK." That gives me a chuckle to this day, and was the gift (of laughter) that kept on giving because I thought about it again when doing the same with my photos from a later trip to Monaco, featuring my "Uncles," Monte and Carlo. And they probably wouldn't have wanted to see photos of my "Nice" in France, either.

# Chapter 10

## Jetting Off To The Far East, Southern Europe, And North Africa

I was living in Northern California, near the Bay Area, and eager to explore the area in the warmer weather. I went to nearby San Francisco a lot, being a big-city guy, and enjoyed it. The views were awesome near the Golden Gate Bridge and overlooking the city. Chinatown, downtown, cable cars, sporting events, and more. Another paradise for a photographer. There was also Napa Valley, which I toured on my own, taking the train through wine country and lots of small, scenic little towns along the highway. This was outstanding and a whole different vibe than New York City.

I had to be realistic about my future travels in that I did not have unlimited funds. I had accumulated lots of free air travel miles through frequent flyer programs but had to use them within an allotted time or lose them (many airlines' mileage programs had expiration dates back then). These miles would cost me significant money if they expired and I had to buy them. I thought about my situation and decided that the best way for me to live out my dream is to teach full-time, yet have the summers off, if possible. I searched around and there was a rare opportunity further north, in a small town that is part of the State University system, where I could teach as a "Lecturer" without a Ph.D. I would be accepted based on my master's degree in business, 20 years' marketing experience, and accomplishments. The pay was little more than half what I was making, but I was single with no dependents or debts, had saved a lot, and the salary per year would easily support my lifestyle including significant travel. And the best part was I would not have to teach during the summers (optional), thus having more than four months off during the year including winter break. Because I was a full-time employee, the job came with full benefits, including medical, dental, and a pension plan. After interviewing with my eventual boss (Department Chair), I was offered and accepted the job, which would begin in August. My role was to teach four classes per semester of Marketing Strategy, the core course for this department, required for all business majors (and an elective for others). It was now early June and I had nearly three months to roam before starting. Thus, I lined up several trips, one each month including, in order: Hawaii/Japan; Spain/Portugal/Morocco; and last but not least, Club Med – Turks & Caicos Islands, the place of first and last "resort" when I have a major change in my life.

As long as I was on the West Coast I figured now would be a good time to go to Japan, much closer than from the East Coast. As it turned out – and here's a good lesson learned – the airline didn't mention this but I asked if I'm entitled to a free stopover on the way. The answer was yes, and I selected Hawaii. My other trips thus far did not allow this (except maybe to Australia but I hadn't thought to ask), but from this point forward I always would ask this question and would often use the allowable stopover if it included somewhere I wanted to go. In this case, Hawaii was a no-brainer – at least to defrost from Antarctica, if nothing else. I spent time in Honolulu, Kauai, and Molokai for a week, having another excellent time there. In my first go-'round of visiting all the states, Hawaii was my 50$^{th}$ state visited. Within a year I would go to Alaska and thus visit each of the 50 states at least twice – and get to every state capital in the process when reaching Juneau. Within just a few years afterwards I would end up visiting all 50 states at least 4 times each in total.

I was very fortunate on my flight out of San Francisco to Hawaii to be sitting next to a 20-year-old Japanese student attending Berkeley in the U.S. named Kazuko, originally from Tokyo and returning for a visit. Kazuko was at a make-or-break point with her boyfriend, who was the jealous type, and still lived in Tokyo. We discussed her situation for a while, and I gave her my opinion, as she sought. Then she was very helpful in explaining the Japanese culture to me, including that "Japanese people like Americans," which turned out to be true from my experience there. She taught me some basic Japanese words, and asked me to tell her about South America because she planned to go there someday. I told her all about the tango place in Argentina and what happened there. She laughed. We then napped simultaneously. When we awakened, we were approaching Honolulu and I needed to deplane. I told Kazuko that I wished I could meet her and her boyfriend in Tokyo, but that knowing how I mangle translations I'd probably say to him, "My name is Steve. I slept with your girlfriend on the plane." She laughed and said that she wouldn't be there by the time I arrived a week later. We said a fond farewell, and wished each other a good trip. The look on Kazuko's face was priceless because this was a major turning point for her with her boyfriend. I said to her the only Japanese word I know, "Sayonara."

A week later, continuing from my Hawaii trip, I arrived in Tokyo circa 7:00 p.m. after a 10-hour flight from Honolulu. I exchanged currency and took a taxi to my hotel, which was elegant but very expensive at $200/night for 5 nights. My taxi was ride was expensive too, and I kept wondering if there was a less expensive/low-cost way to get to my hotels in the future. The New Prince was a business hotel and had a lot of amenities, with a good restaurant and bakery in the lobby. This bakery was very good for me. The prices in Tokyo were through the roof, I'd say more than double that of New York City. But the bakery had these breads into which cheese, vegetables, and other ingredients were baked for only $3 U.S. each and they were delicious. A standard breakfast there cost about $20 U.S. so for a fraction of that I had a quick, filling morning breakfast and/or lunch. The "bell girls" looked like retro airline flight attendants in mini-skirts and white stewardess-style caps, and helped with my luggage. I would soon encounter many other familiarities in Tokyo.

My hotel room had a nice view of the city and, I have to say, the most sophisticated toilet I've ever encountered. It was like a rocket ship with lots of gadgets; I thought there would be an instruction manual for how to flush, but I figured it out (I just didn't want to be sucked-down ass-first). I would encounter more of these engineering feats later in the trip. All the TV stations were in Japanese, except for the British version of CNN which I watched at night before going to bed. A bummer was when I'd find an American program (e.g., sitcom) but it was dubbed over in Japanese. I walked around the hotel area, taking a hotel card at the front desk right away in case I got lost. I was told by the concierge that Tokyo is very safe, especially in that vicinity, and it seemed to be. I was tired, went back to my room, and to bed. On the way back to my room I noticed that the elevator did not have the floors 4 or 9. I was later told these are bad-luck numbers in Japan and that no hotel has them. I later learned that four is pronounced "shi" in Japanese which sounds like "death," and that nine ("ku") sounds like the word for agony or torture. I thought, "Good thing I didn't wear a San Francisco 49ers football jersey - people would run from me like I was Godzilla!"

The next morning I got an early start, unusual for me. Wanting to do as much as possible, I did not have a big sit-down breakfast but instead had a cheese-bread or whatever it's called, which was very good. As I was leaving I saw a parade of businessmen enter the hotel in line formation, all dressed in dark suits, apparently heading to a business meeting. They looked so homogeneous you would think it was only a few guys and a bunch of mirrors. This gave me an insight into the business culture (if not the mainstream one) of conformity. I seriously wondered if everyone had "got the memo" to wear the dark suit, white shirt and dark tie to the meeting. Each person was dressed this way, and there were at least 50 of them.

Out in the street, the first thing I noticed was the stifling humidity, which Kazuko had told me about. I thought she was kidding based on her strong description of it. She wasn't kidding. I was quickly saturated, but that didn't stop me. I asked directions from a gal named Yumi (was she named after the humidity? I wondered). I knew from experience that the younger people tended to speak English more than the older ones, so I stuck to this plan. Good thing, too, because a lot of older people didn't speak English. The younger people in particular had lots of electronics. I'd never seen so many people have so many devices. As in Hong Kong, lots of cell phones, and a lot of iPods as well. So my first impression was:

humid, conformity, and electronics. Let's see what else I could detect beyond 50 feet from the hotel. I soon found out: there were several American restaurants right next to my hotel: T.G.I. Friday's®, Outback Steakhouse®, McDonald's and Wendy's®, too, with both the English and Japanese lettering. I felt right at home, sort of. As I walked around the city I noticed something else "American": at 5'8", I was taller than about 75% of all the males and 95% of all the females. This made me feel about 6'2" in U.S. terms. Maybe with the exchange rate I was.

Since I was on my own in a new city, I planned a city tour in the afternoon. I made sure there was an English-speaking guide. Not only did she speak it well, but she was formerly a reporter for a Tokyo news station. Our group of about 30 was informed that Japan has 127 million people in a country the size of the U.S. state of Montana, and that Tokyo is the most crowded capital in the world at 13 million people. More than 32 million people live within 50 miles of Tokyo. The average salary for a man in Tokyo is $52,000/year. However, their jobs are so stressful, and it is so shameful to lose a job, that for 7 years in a row over 30,000 people have committed suicide because of this. Interestingly, real estate is at such a premium that the average 3BR condo in Japan costs $450K-$650K, and a round of golf costs $160. Entire families often live together in these condos to consolidate expenses. We drove along and were shown the Gingko trees that lined the streets, followed by the Banyan trees when we arrived at the park (these have twisted branches, and I saw these in Hawaii, too). I was starting to realize that there are several places in the world with things that look alike. Also, like the British, the Japanese drove on the opposite side of the road compared with Americans, so you had to be doubly-careful when crossing the street.

We also went up into the Tokyo Tower to get a panoramic view of the city. We were given the history. It was built in 1958 and measures over 1,000 feet tall. The tower is modeled after the Eiffel Tower in Paris, and was painted white and an international-colored orange to be in compliance with air safety regulations. I left the tour group after that to take photos; it was getting crowded by the windows. There were many impressive views. You could see from up there how congested the city really is. Wall-to-wall buildings, and people. There's even a bridge that looks like the Verrazano-Narrows Bridge in Brooklyn. I realized that Tokyo is looking very similar to New York City. I'd see even more of this similarity later. There was a museum, restaurants, and shops in the lobby. I bought my post cards, as usual, one of each, and fridge magnet.

I met a young couple on the tour from Finland. They were shocked that I, an American, knew so much about Finland and had been there. They really warmed up to me upon hearing this, and were also impressed that I had taken the ferry to Tallinn, Estonia from Helsinki to spend a day there. Our tour then went to a pearl factory to learn about how these are made. A funny thing happened there. The tour leader told us all to select a number out of a box to potentially win a pearl in a drawing. I picked out the number 4 but put it back, remembering this is a bad-luck number there. I picked out another one, and wouldn't you know – 4 was the winner. I was surprised that number 4 was even in the mix. Further, because I was the next-to-last one to draw a number, the person after me selecting the winning number from the box probably picked up the one on the top – the one I had just put back. I didn't know what the pearl was worth, and didn't want to know after this event.

We continued our tour to the downtown area. This place definitely reminded me of New York City with lots of well-dressed people hustling and bustling around, very crowded, and lots of little shops (remember, space is at a premium and very expensive). Following this we went to a Buddhist shrine; our tour guide told us that the vast majority of people in Japan who claim a religion are Buddhist, followed by Shinto, and Christian – which is growing. However, many people did not adhere to a single religion or were non-religious. I bought some small gifts to take home, including for a friend's then-teenage daughter who was "into" Japan (she's Caucasian). I stepped outside while the rest of the group shopped, and a couple of interesting things happened. A few school girls asked me if I'm American. When I said yes, they asked to take a picture with me. I said OK, and as the photo was snapped they made the peace sign with their fingers. Soon after this I noticed several teenage gals passed by wearing Mickey Mouse T-shirts, which was perhaps worn more prevalently than in the U.S. I stopped and chatted with them for a few minutes. There was a clear positive affiliation with America, at least among the younger crowd (the older crowd, who remembers the wars, not so much). Also, and this was very weird, as I walked down the street several Japanese women would keep their head down as we passed in opposite directions, but then as we were parallel they would look up abruptly and stare right into my eyes, then keep walking! I never did get a reason for this – but I'll say that there were times I walked around Tokyo for hours and did not see one other Caucasian. Maybe I was among the few Caucasians they ever saw. The tour ended and we were returned to our respective hotels. I found the tour a good introduction to the city.

I was feeling really good, and wanted to do something special that evening. The concierge told me of a tempura dinner- kabuki theater performance combination, explaining that kabuki was a Japanese play. I got dressed in an evening outfit and took a train to the bus that would take me to the meeting point (the concierge assured me this is totally safe and much more inexpensive than a taxi). Another funny incident happened as I was in the train station, and asked the Japanese lady behind the counter for directions: I didn't speak Japanese and she didn't speak any English. We played what I'll call "international charades" including her coming out from the booth and spreading out a subway map for us to review my route. This took 10 minutes but she was very patient and cooperative – as were all the Japanese people I met. I finally understood what she meant based on her creating, for lack of a better word, a trip-ticket using marker on the map. There was one other thing she communicated, and it was important I know this: I needed to take the #1 train uptown, but when returning I needed to take the #2 train back to this same station. In New York City, for example, each train retains its same number or letter whether it goes uptown or downtown; you just have to stand at the appropriate side of the platform. The Japanese system was more intuitive when I thought about it.

I got to the restaurant and met the rest of my group, upon asking for the tour leader whose name was given to me. To my surprise, there were several Americans on this tour, especially several gals near my age who were from Boston. As it turned out, one of them recognized me from being on her tour that morning! She told me that after this trip she is continuing on with her friends to other Asian countries. There were also three gals from Houston, Texas in their 20s who said that Houston has similarly high humidity to Tokyo. They still didn't like it, however. There was also a very pretty, upscale-looking and well-dressed Caucasian recent college graduate named Liz there from Ohio, who attended with a well-dressed Japanese man in his 50s. This seemed odd at first because she kept calling him by his first name, so it wasn't her dad. It turned out that he was her chaperone. Her dad was a respected professor in Ohio, and this gentleman (I'll call Hiroshi) was his colleague from Tokyo who agreed to escort her around Japan as her dad's graduation gift. He also would be escorting her all around Asia. Nice dad, nice gift! Liz and Hiroshi, upon hearing that I like translations of foreign languages, told me that ironically "Ohio" translates in Japanese to "Good morning." Also, "thank you" in Japanese is arigato ("ah-ree-gah-toe"). I would use both of these expressions throughout the remainder of my trip, and they were appreciated. I wondered if "toilet" in Japanese translated to "rocket science."

The tempura dinner arrived and was the best I've ever had – not that I eat a lot of Japanese food. The apple-flavored dinner rolls and Kirin® beer were also excellent. We all walked around after dinner since there was time before the play. The locals were very accommodating in taking photos of me and with others in my group. They were expert photographers in general, and even voluntarily climbed atop low-lying surfaces to get a better angle. I was impressed! They seemed pleased I was using a Japanese-made camera, and I was surprised they looked to notice. We walked around some more. Tokyo seemed like other big cities I'd been in, especially New York and London. Downtown looked a lot like both combined, as if the Japanese had copied the best of both. There was even an area that looked like Times Square, including a giant neon sign for what else, Fuji® film, just like in New York City! Our tour guide told us that the Japanese are famous for copying things, which is why the Tokyo Tower, which I went up during the morning tour, looks very much like the Eiffel Tower in Paris. So, interesting concept: copy the best of all worlds and put them in one place. This probably makes a lot of tourists feel right at home.

Next was the kabuki performance, which was the equivalent to Broadway. We were told that this theater is very famous in Japan. This type of play is a dance-drama. I thought the play was interesting but weird. Several actors/actresses were in white-face make-up with wild hair and in kimonos. They contorted their bodies into unusual positions, and many of the actresses shrieked. Sometimes there were musicians on stage with the actors. There were several acts, and many of the sets had brightly-colored neonics. The last scene was by far the best with the most startling, brightly-colored set design I've ever seen; one actor in a kimono even got into a hunch on all fours, contorting his body in a most unusual way. I listened to the play through a transistor radio I was given with earpiece upon entry; the play was translated into English (and other languages, too).

I was bored at one point and asked the tour guide if I could go out to walk around and stretch my legs. He wasn't wild about the idea, but escorted me out and walked a bit with me. Just as we exited – what luck! – we saw one of the actresses in full kimono without the white-face make-up. She was beautiful! I asked if I can take a photo with her. She bowed and indicated yes. I gave my camera to the tour guide and asked if he would do the honors. He seemed very nervous, like this was a famous actress, and he took two photos of us which ended up coming out really well. I thanked the actress and we bowed to each other again, which lasted longer than just a few seconds. The tour guide waited for her to leave and excitedly told me how fortunate I am that this happened given the rarity. "That was just an amazing coincidence!" he beamed. I smiled and said, "Beginner's luck." I should have told him how I put the winning number back into the box during the pearl drawing. He then strolled toward the theater and I said I'd be in soon. Later, I'd hear him excitedly tell others what happened.

I walked around the theater alone and asked permission of the employees to take photos of various posters and other kabuki-specific memorabilia. Once again, they were very gracious and accommodating. I also bought several post cards of the theater, which were expensive, knowing that I'd mix them in with the rare kabuki actress photos at a later time, to give the album I planned to assemble that special appeal. I spare no expense when it comes to photos, post cards, and albums since these will be my legacy someday. I returned to the theater, and later on the actress that the tour guide and I saw appeared on stage. He looked over to me and smiled. I usually give a thumbs-up but didn't know if that's offensive in the Japanese culture, so I played it safe and just smiled and nodded. The play ended, and I returned to the hotel at 11:00 p.m. What a first day – two full tours after a long flight and a major time change! I'd end up sleeping for 12 hours, however, and was refreshed the next morning to continue this most unexpectedly pleasant and interesting trip!

The next day I spontaneously decided to go to the zoo in Ueno, a Tokyo suburb requiring two subway transfers, after it being recommended by one of my tourmates the previous night. I left the hotel after having a delicious apple-melon flavored roll for breakfast. I walked to the Shinagawa train station. This was my first time taking the train during the morning and it was packed, more so than even New York City trains. There is no shortage of people willing to push you forcefully from behind to jam you into the train car, including little old ladies who turn into blocking backs on the goal line! Not only did I see this happening frequently, but I also was on the receiving end of a couple. "Moving the pile" is what they call it in football, and it probably had a similar translation there as well. I remembered Kazuko telling me on the plane that once she was in a subway car so crowded that a man put his newspaper right on top of her head and turned the pages to read it! I was a head banger as a kid and now had a flat spot on top of my head – so maybe there was a way to monetize this over there to some taller train travelers, including a place to put the coffee cup (only kidding).

I arrived at the zoo area by train and walked 10 minutes to get to the zoo itself, stopping off for photo ops along the way of some interesting sculptures. The weather was cloudy but about 70 degrees and pleasant. I'd been to many interesting zoos around the world, and this one fit right in with them. It featured a giant panda, gorillas, spider monkeys, elephants, lions, llamas, and lots of colorful, exotic birds including eagles, ostriches, flamingos, parrots, and a white owl. I was also intrigued by the penguins, which harkened me back to Antarctica, and a giant anteater. I saw a few cute Japanese kids playing by the animal statues, and their mom was taking photos. She asked me to take one of her with the kids, and I obliged. She then asked if it's OK if I'm in the photo with her kids! I said "Sure" and she took a few photos with her camera, from different angles. She then asked if I want to have my photo taken with my camera with her kids. I said OK, and she took several. They came out excellent, especially the ones at the panda statue. When I travel I try to get photos with others, especially locals, because they provide variety to my eventual albums, accenting it by showing scenes of everyday people in everyday life there. I'm glad this situation came about with the photos: a win-win. It did, however, heighten my awareness of how different I was in Japan.

I had an excellent time walking around the zoo, but it was cut short when the skies darkened and the rains came down heavily. I was thinking about going to see the Yomiuri Tokyo Giants baseball game that night at the Tokyo Dome but thought it might be rained out. When I told this to the concierge back at the hotel he looked at me funny and said, "The games are never rained out. They play in a dome." He was right, of course, and I felt dumb. Maybe he thought I'd loaded up on the sake. I still decided not to go with the pouring rain. Instead, I had a nice sushi dinner (not my thing but another "when in Rome...") and worked on my journal in the room. I also sat in the lobby and chatted with other out-of-towners.

Next I walked to the currency-exchange store near my hotel, and waited in a long line. When I got to the clerk, she didn't speak any English. A Japanese guy seven or eight people behind me did, stepped off the line, and bailed me out. He was very helpful and advised me to go to a different place nearby where they speak more English. I did so and thanked him. He gave me his card; he was an Associate Professor at the University of Tokyo. I didn't keep in contact with him, but should have; I ended up teaching university soon after this trip. The people in Tokyo were very kind to me, and this helped make the trip more pleasant. I had also helped many international people navigate around the U.S., so maybe this was good karma.

The next day was sunny and warm, a beautiful day, and I returned to the zoo to finish up my stroll and take more photos. Afterwards, I changed into my New York Yankees baseball T-shirt and cap, then took the train out to the Tokyo Dome. I didn't realize the popularity of the Tokyo baseball team (Giants), and was very fortunate to get one of the last remaining standing-room-only tickets for 1,000 yen, or about $10. The team was technically called the Yomiuri Giants then, and I figured this was a section of Japan like Brooklyn was to New York. Having some time before the game, I walked around the stadium and took lots of photos, especially with a cute gal I met in a floppy hat named Sakura, which, she told me, translates to "cherry blossom." There were many giant-sized, glass-encased laminated posters, not only of the Japanese baseball stars in Japan, but those in America as well including (and especially) Ichiro Suzuki (Seattle Mariners), Hideki Matsui (New York Yankees, formerly of the Yomiuri Giants), Hideki Nomo (Los Angeles Dodgers), and a relief pitcher named Shigatosi Hasegawa (Anaheim Angels and Seattle Mariners) who pitched for nine years. There were lots of souvenir stands outside of the stadium, and the stadium itself is adjacent to an amusement park featuring a large ferris wheel and roller coaster. Together, this area is called the Entertainment Complex, and also includes a bowling alley (there was a seven-foot high bowling pin near the stadium). I thought that including a stadium, along with an amusement park, as part of an overall Entertainment Complex was very interesting. This was similar in concept to Tokyo including replicas of Times Square and the Eiffel Tower within the city itself. In my marketing career I also borrowed features from other products and incorporated them with the standard products my employer's company manufactured. I was starting to really like Tokyo: so different, yet so similar.

I took photos on the stairwells around the stadium named after famous Japanese players, the most conspicuous being for Sadaharu Oh, the Babe Ruth of Japanese baseball, who hit 868 home runs in his career (154 more than "The Babe"). Oh also played his entire 22-year career with the Giants, and managed them for a few years afterwards. He is a giant celebrity (pun intended) in Japan. Numerous fans, especially kids, were swirling around the stadium wearing jerseys of their favorite players, just like in the U.S. From the outside it looked very similar to American baseball stadiums, with a few tweaks as noted. But inside was a different story.

A massive line for the remaining tickets had formed and lots of people were turned away. I was "that close" to not getting a ticket; one more photo at the zoo and I probably wouldn't have got one. I thought about scalping my ticket but first of all I really wanted to see the game, and also who knows what would have happened if caught doing this in a foreign country? It was bad enough I was chased by Hungarian police in the train station a year earlier for not realizing another fare had to be paid to switch trains. Also, I had gone to the Super Bowl and am so glad I did not sell my ticket to that once-in-a-lifetime-experience; I could have got maybe 10 times its face value.

This was an interleague game, and the Hakone Hawks had a better record coming into it. I was in what we know as the Standing Room Only area, way out in center field. The section I was in was packed like a Tokyo subway train, but we all got along fine and were respectful of what little space we each had. The interior of the stadium reminded me of the Toronto Sky Dome where the Blue Jays play, which I went to the previous year, and also the Minnesota Twins' Metrodome indoor stadium, both with their artificial turf and big white dome. That's where the difference ended. There were a lot of signs in Japanese all over the stadium, both professional advertisements and artistically-drawn from the fans to motivate the team. Here's another striking combination: American baseball combined with college football! There was a college football atmosphere throughout the game, including at least 20 different chants that the fans sing, very loudly, as they practically stand on top of each other. Many have orange plastic bats that they rhythmically bang together in unison while chanting, and they scream during every pitch leading to an eruption if the Giants get a hit, score a run, or make a good play in the field. I've been to a Super Bowl, and World Series game at Yankee Stadium, but I never heard anything human this loud (being indoors probably had something to do with this, along with it being done by so many people in unison). People waved huge flags, there was a live bugler right near me in the Standing Room Only section, and cheerleaders entertained the crowd between innings with dances, flips, splits, and pyramids. The fans did "the wave" with military precision, perfectly, like I've never seen before. These fans knew exactly what to do and when to do it in synchronicity, all throughout the game, in words and actions. This generated a tremendous amount of noise and excitement.

I was crowded-in but stood during the entire game with no problem. Everyone was gracious to me. I met a couple of cute gals in uniforms with whom I took photos, and even a police officer in the Standing Room Only section who, despite strictly enforcing fans remaining in this section, escorted me to a better vantage point at a lower level of the stadium so I could take photos from a closer range. Interestingly, an American guy from Atlanta saw me looking around for someone to take a photo of me with the field in the background, and came down several rows to do so (these came out very well); the Japanese fans were so absorbed in the game I dared not disturb any one of them. I volunteered and did the same for him with his camera. I realized that I've now been to three "Giants" games in sports: New York football; San Francisco baseball; and Tokyo Japanese baseball, all at their home stadiums, a nice trifecta!

Back in my section, an English-speaking Japanese gal and guy who had been to an American baseball game explained some of the major differences to me. In Japan, the ball is smaller, the field is smaller, the game can end in a tie after 12 innings, the game cannot go beyond around 10:30 p.m. so fans can catch the last train home, and there are cheering sections for each team. Also, when I asked why the Giants, who play in Tokyo, are called the Yomiuri Giants, the guy (named Tsuyoshi) said that the teams are named after the company that owns them, and that Yomiuri is a company that publishes newspapers, maybe like the New York Times in the U.S. I didn't know any of this, but was glad I found people who could tell me.

The game itself was good, but the visiting Hakone Hawks won, 5-2. When the game ended, the helpful police officer who escorted me to the better photo vantage point sought me out and shook my hand with a nice smile. That was really awesome. He seemed like he wanted to escort me out of the stadium, but I waved him off and said it's OK. Afterwards, I wondered if he was being so nice because I'm an obvious tourist, American, Yankees fan, or he thought I might be harmed by unruly fans because I wasn't wearing a Giants shirt or cap. I'll never know but encountered no issues. I even lingered outside the stadium to take night photos of it all lit up. Because I got out relatively quickly, I could have just taken a few photos and boarded a relatively uncrowded train back to my hotel. Instead, I wanted photos with the fans coming out, and took several. Many other people took similar photos, and I got some photos with these fans dressed in team garb. Once again, people were very friendly and helpful. I also took some photos of the amusement park rides outside the stadium lit up at night. There was a total carnival atmosphere to this whole experience, and that was a good thing.

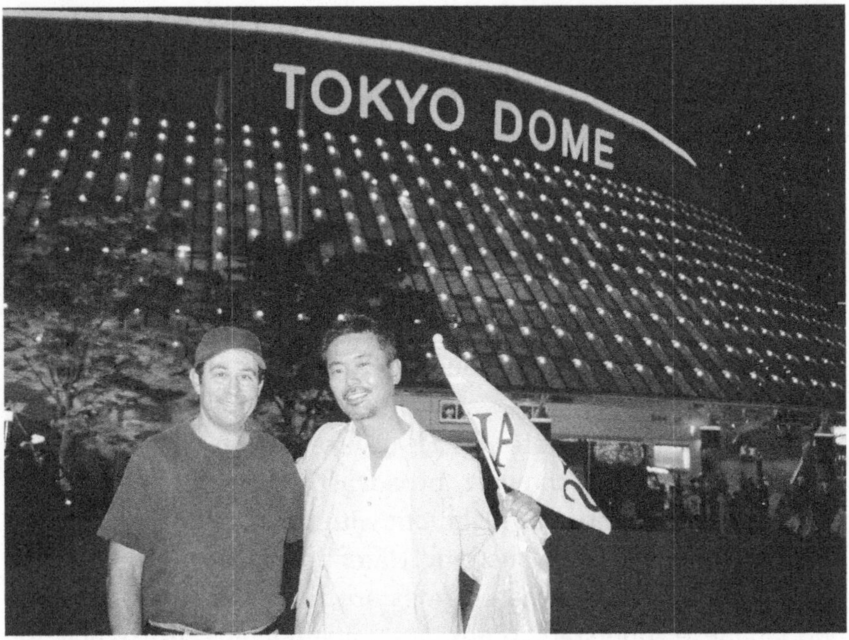

In Japan, this photo was taken after the local baseball team played. This guy was one of those fervent Tokyo Giants fans waving his flag in unison with the others, chanting rhythmically, and singing the various songs that are as much a part of the game there as the game itself. Note that the publisher of this book removed the Yankees logo on my shirt and cap for legal reasons.

Now it was time for another popular "ride" in Tokyo: the train crusher, as I called it. This was the most grueling train ride I ever endured, and that says a lot after riding the New York City subways daily for over 20 years. It was so crowded that when I tried to move one way I was totally spun in the opposite direction and pushed by others making their way past me. Remember: I was the "big guy" at 5'8"; it was the little old ladies who had the force of the Fearsome Foursome (LA Rams Defensive Line back in the day). This spin-around happened to me one other time, in Times Square in New York City on New Year's Eve, after the ball dropped, as I was trying to make my way across the street. So, here I was again, one decade and half a world away. I wasn't hurt at all, and it was kind of fun in a way. But now I can understand how people get trampled at concerts, e.g.; you have to be on your toes, figuratively speaking.

Japanese subway cars not only had traditional poster ads on the walls but also a TV screen that showed 10-second ads for individual products. Fortunately, it also showed the names of the upcoming train stations. I exited at Shinegawa station, had a yakitori chicken-and-vegetable stick (popular there and delicious), and went to a nearby Starbucks to relax and reflect on my excellent day today over a $5 (U.S.) cup of Joe. I was having a really good time on my own in a foreign country in which most people didn't speak English, and taking the public transportation around, too. My confidence as a traveler was rising, and I had come a long way both literally and figuratively. In retrospect, this trip would be a platform for future solo travels to other foreign countries as well.

The next day, Sunday, was a big travel day. In the morning I flipped on the TV and there was a live New York Yankees-Minnesota Twins baseball game showing, broadcast in Japanese! The game was being played Saturday night, but with the time difference I was watching it live on Sunday morning. I later heard that several Yankees games and Seattle Mariners games are broadcast there because two Japanese superstars, Hideki Matsui and Ichiro Suzuki, play for these teams, respectively, and still have a large following in Japan. I watched a few innings and then had to be on my way. This reminded me of watching the Super Bowl in Cologne, Germany a decade earlier that had been broadcast in German.

I took one final group tour, this one a long ways away. It required a 2-hour motor coach ride, 1-hour "bullet" train traveling 240 m.p.h. (like Eurail on steroids), a ferry, and a tram up a mountain just to get there. This was in the Hakone mountain region, home of the team that played the Giants the previous night. It seemed that Japanese baseball was ubiquitous. Our tour guide was very informative, providing little factoids along the way such as that the word "karaoke" literally means "empty" (kara) "orchestra" (oke). This popular activity originated in Japan, and is still very popular today (I later went to a karaoke bar but didn't sing). She also told us that the word "Fuji" means "never die," hence the name of the mountain (and the film). Speaking of which, we arrived at our first destination, Mt. Fuji, but unfortunately cloudy weather obscured the peak of Japan's tallest mountain. However, 15 minutes before we left, so did the clouds, and we got to see the peak – which I later heard is not so common due to visibility conditions. Naturally, I took lots of photos in those few minutes. Mt. Fuji is 12,300 feet high or about 2,000 feet less than the tallest peak in the U.S., Pikes Peak. But what made it stand out was the shape of the mountain, a symmetrical cone at the top and snow-capped. Mt. Fuji is surrounded by a Western-U.S.-style village including lots of clothing and souvenir stores. Although I was using Kodak film at the time, in deference to Japan and Mt. Fuji, I bought a few rolls of Fuji film there and used them to photograph Mt. Fuji.

Next we all had an included lunch at a fancy hotel near an amusement park. I strayed from the group, as I often did, and took several photos of the immense roller coaster which we were told is the third largest in the world. It looked like at least two "Cyclones" from Coney Island (in my home town of Brooklyn, N.Y.) combined; with the way Japanese people copied things, I wouldn't be surprised if this was just what was done (not a bad idea). There was also a Toyota go-cart track nearby. I wished there was time to take a ride. We then went to a beautiful Buddhist temple that included a white dome with a gold Buddha in the middle of an arch. There were stone lions leading to the temple on a tree-lined path. The lions had different city or country names listed on them, such as Shanghai or Thailand. Most were white; some were brown or bronze. Whatever the color, the detail was exquisite. I waited my turn to have my photo taken with the Buddha. Then we took a ferry on Lake Ashi, and took an aerial tram up a volcano called Mt. Komagatake for a great view. This sort of reminded me of taking the Sandia Peak Tram in Albuquerque, New Mexico between the mountains. It also reminded me of the aerial trams I'd taken in Gatlinburg, Tennessee; Jackson Hole, Wyoming; and also in Switzerland as well, among the mountains. Once atop the volcano we had an excellent view. Finally, to complete our long, interesting travel experience, we took the Shinkansen "bullet" train back to Tokyo. I asked a Japanese guy standing next to me on the platform to take my photo as the train was approaching because it had an unusual shape, pointed in front, like something that would move at the speed of light. He did so, and then sat next to me on the train. As it turned out, he was a salesman for Olympus – the company that makes my camera! We had an excellent conversation all the way back to Tokyo; I then knew more about cameras, films, and picture-taking than ever before. He was originally from Malaysia and told me about his country, too. What a nice man.

After exiting the train, I had dinner at T.G.I. Friday's to compare it to that of the U.S. (it was the same), went to Starbucks for coffee, had some sake at a local bar, and then back to my hotel room. I was very contented with the trip, and packed that night for my upcoming flight home. Overall, I had a wonderful time – Hawaii and Japan were both outstanding!

So, it was back to California and all that abundant sunshine which I missed. The weather was warm and it would have been a good place to remain until my teaching job began. But, I was on a roll, and wanted to continue traveling. Further, I was improving as a "travel athlete" and building up my stamina with these long-distance trips, probably a silver medalist by now. I wanted to keep that momentum going; I only traveled in coach class and had even learned how to position myself in the small plane seats with little leg room to sleep comfortably. Even after a 20-hour flight, I was feeling fine with no aches at all. It was mind over body, or was it mind over matter, or was it what does it matter, I'm going overseas?! In any event, it somehow worked.

At this point I had traveled to six continents, and had a goal to reach all seven. The one that was missing was Africa. The next month

I found a motor coach tour, through Cosmos again, that went to Spain, Portugal, and Morocco. That would do it – and get me to two new European countries as well. I had the time, and the price was very good again. So, off I went – "alone again, naturally," looking forward to meeting new people, exploring new places, and gathering new learning. Once again, Cosmos came through in a big way.

This would be a 16-day tour, my longest-ever to that point, and the trip to Europe would be more difficult because I was now living on the West Coast, much further away than when I was in New York. I took a flight from San Francisco with a change of planes in New York (I did not stay over), and then headed to Madrid, Spain for a full day on my own before meeting up with the tour group. Upon arrival, I asked at the guest services desk (where they speak English) how much is a taxi to my hotel, and was told 35 euros which was approximately $45 U.S. I then asked the key question: is there a safe bus or train I can take for less that is quick? The answer was "Si"; there was a train (it's called the "metro" there) that took me right near my hotel for 1 euro, or $1.35 U.S. So that's what I did, luggage and all. Quick, easy, and saved me dinner money. After checking into the Praga Hotel, I took the metro again and walked around the city to get a feel for it. There were plazas at seemingly every turn, and most tourist sites were within a short distance of each other. I quickly learned my way around the train system which was easy, strolled down the streets, admired the architecture, and had tapas, a local favorite. There were a ton of choices for these hot or cold, bite-sized little appetizers in Plaza Mayor (pronounced "My-orr"). I had a couple with cheese (cold) and calamari (hot). I liked them so much that I would get these on occasion back in the States upon return, whereas I hadn't ever before. I also had churros (donuts).

The city was colorful and vibrant, and for the most part people were friendly. Because I have dark hair and eyes and could pass for Spanish, some people talked to me in that language initially, assuming I was a native. Upon learning I'm not, they spoke English if they could, and I tried to compensate for anything lacking in the conversation with my Spanglish. This generally worked out. I also had people in Italy assume I'm Italian and speak to me in that language, and later on this very trip it happened in Morocco, too. Perhaps I have some of this mixed into me – but not as far as I know. One storekeeper was arrogant with me, however, and I was later told by another patron who knows him that he doesn't like "gringos" (foreigners). I was walking around the store, which sold meats, and didn't see anything I wanted to purchase. As I walked out he asked why I didn't buy anything. I told him that I just arrived in the morning, already had lunch, and was just looking around the stores to see what there may be of interest for future purchase. He was upset with me for not buying anything. "Don't worry," I said, "I won't be back. And maybe neither will the 40 people on the tour with me." With that, I walked out briskly. I don't base my impressions of anywhere on just one person or even a few; this guy was the exception not the rule in Madrid. However, I would encounter a similar attitude later during the trip.

I met my tour group for dinner, including the guide, Maria, and the bus driver, Renaldo. They were excellent throughout the tour. We received introductions and, of course, the itinerary, rules & regulations, and more. There were 27 others on the tour. Almost all of them were in their 50s, 60s, and 70s, married, and from Australia, Great Britain, or Canada (the usual). There were a few East Indians now living in the U.S. but who retained their Indian roots, and also married couples from Tasmania and Sri Lanka. Although I had been to Australia, I wasn't sure where Tasmania was. My tourmates from there told me it's an island south of the continent, and that they're from the capital, Hobart. Throughout the trip they gave me more history about Tasmania as I'd asked, and I told them about the U.S. if they asked specific questions (there weren't many). There was only one person younger than me, Maureen, who was a college student from Canada going to school in Spain and traveling on this tour with her aunt from Montreal. I spoke with Maureen the most during the trip (mutually beneficial), but made it a point to talk with every person on the tour. When I travel I get into my happy zone, and I was perceived (so I was later told) as very lively, humorous, well-traveled and outgoing. However, I was also seen as aloof because I often strayed from the group during sightseeing after viewing the parts I liked, and then moving on. But, I made it back to the motor coach on time – most of the time. Details about that later.

There were two important factors that greatly contributed to making this an excellent trip, and either one not being the case could have very much trimmed this success: everyone on the tour was pleasant, helpful, and supportive; and the weather was fantastic (65-75 degrees and sunny every single day) after three consecutive weeks of heavy rains . Regarding the former, at the end of the tour our guide remarked that we were among the best-behaved, and most cohesive tour groups she ever had. Regarding the latter, the magnificent weather made a huge difference in visibility, colorfulness, and vividness in general for the trip three times over: while there; in my photos; and in my mind's eye when I recall it. Also, since I was the only single guy, I again received a private room for the lower "share" price. As mentioned, I've had good roommates and not-so-good, but in general having a private room is preferable – especially if I meet a nice señorita! (Unfortunately for me this trip, the closest I came to that was meeting a senior citizen on this tour named Rita.)

The best way to present this trip is in chronological order, so you can "ride along with me" and see how the trip builds. The first day we toured Madrid and received Maria's narrative, often prefaced for some reason with the expression, "Wella, you know..." (just these three words put me back on that motor coach when I think about them; this was part of that tour's signature for me). We learned that Spain is the largest producer of olive oil in the world, and many olive trees were pointed out. While not as exciting as a banyan tree like I saw in Hawaii and Japan, these olive trees were interesting in their own way; some leaves looked frizzy, and some trees seemed to have what I'll call a wide wingspan horizontally. We then passed by the Jewish section and learned there are still many Jews in Spain; the Jews from this region are called Sephardic. We stopped off and viewed several cathedrals, nice architectural structures, and large fountains. There are over 200 churches in Madrid so we could only see a small sampling, and stop into even fewer. They were impressive, and what always gets me is the ancientness of the building. It makes me realize how young the United States is, or modern, if you want to look at it from that perspective. I'm not a history buff by any means, but seeing these historic structures evinced a majesty about them that you can't get from a TV documentary, movie, video, or book;

seeing these live is like black-and white to color by comparison. At least in my book. Literally.

We had a rest stop every couple of hours during this tour, often at a place that sold food and of course had toilets. Sometimes we just stopped for a snack, and other times this would be where we would have lunch, at a predesignated restaurant approved by the tour operator. Often times they were in scenic places where you could take photos and I did that a lot. Also, throughout the main tour there were optional tours you could take with a local guide – some were included in the overall tour price, and some had an additional fee. I often opted out of them unless they were really something different; many of these included shopping at the end and that really wasn't my thing except for a quick in-and-out. In my opinion, the main tours were planned out very well. These so-called "comfort" tours were geared to older people, so I understood that they would be very safe and slowly-paced; often times on this tour, Maureen and I would venture off during these stops for a long walk, and take photos of and with each other. When we decided not to go on the optional tours, which could last up to two hours, we would just hang out and chat, dine, sightsee, etc. So if you take a tour like this, you might want to bring a book or recreational activity to do during the long down times.

We returned to the hotel in Madrid, where I took the subway again, this time downtown for dinner and to mingle with the locals. I returned to Plaza Mayor, which seemed to be where a lot of the action was taking place. This plaza was larger than I thought earlier in the day when I was hustling to see as much as possible, and reminded me of the parliamentary square area I had seen in Brussels, Belgium – lots of restaurants, shops, outdoor cafés, portrait artists, and tourist groups from several different countries. I had an excellent dinner (paella, with seafood) and walked around on this beautiful evening. I noticed that, as in Japan, I seemed taller than about 75% of all the guys there although I'm only 5'8." I chatted with a few male locals, and also met beautiful women (of which there were many) who asked my name, where I'm from, why I'm there, etc. (the usual). I told them about the tour, and how it includes that we're going to other parts of Spain along with Portugal and Morocco. Three of them said half-kiddingly that they want to go with me. I said I would let them if I could, but this cannot be done.

I returned to the hotel room and got a good night's sleep. In typical fashion, we had to put our luggage outside the room by 7:45 a.m., eat a breakfast included in our tour price, and then be on the motor coach by 8:30 a.m. (with head count before we left). We continued touring Madrid, departing by early afternoon. We went to Plaza de España at which there was a huge statue of Miguel de Cervantes, novelist and playwright who wrote the book Don Quixote. This stone statue overlooked bronze sculptures of Don Quixote and Sancho Panza on horses. The novel Don Quixote is thought of as one of the greatest fictional works ever, and there sure was a lot of homage paid to it there. Tonnage, too; Sancho was looking a bit portly, and it was explained that "Panza" means "belly" in Spanish. There were two skyscrapers, the Royal Palace nearby, and a lot within walking distance. The metro train was there, too.

Later that afternoon I took an optional tour to Toledo (pronounced "Toe-lay-dough"), which had a few different aspects of interest to me. All except seven of my tourmates took this excursion – in part, I believe, because the alternative was to roam around a relatively desolate area. Note that these optional tours and their highlights are distributed to tour members prior to the trip, and you can sign up ahead of time or on the tour. Toledo was the former capital of Spain and is a fortress city with impressive architecture. We went to a beautiful cathedral that houses the actual crown of Queen Isabella, who ruled circa 1500. Although she's the one who sent Columbus on his voyage to discover the new world, she was also the one who expelled the Jews and other non-Christians during the Spanish Inquisition.

We also went to the El Greco Museum, ironically in the Jewish quarter of Toledo, and viewed the artist's impressive work. Another cathedral, Toledo Cathedral, was from the 13$^{th}$ century and is the third-largest Gothic cathedral in the world. It was gorgeous both inside and out. Although I had seen a good amount of cathedrals to this point, I have to say that this was one of the more impressive to this day. We would later go to another cathedral in Granada, Spain that is the third-largest cathedral of any kind in the world, after the Vatican and Taj Mahal. I was even more impressed with this one; several former kings were buried there, too. This cathedral was built in Spanish Renaissance style in the early 1500s. I cannot adequately convey the sense of majesty and history from seeing this up-close, and walking around both the interior and exterior, but would encourage you to see this for yourself if you're ever there. Although I had no interest in cathedrals before I began traveling, I was now moderately interested in them, having seen many, and being awe-struck by them. Not only were the ones I was viewing that day built in the Renaissance era, this was part of a Renaissance for me as well in becoming the traveler, and hence person, I am today. That said, I was "cathedraled-out" by the end of this optional tour, magnificent as they were, much as I was with the museums in England and Italy when with Mike. I had hit my threshold but was glad I saw and experienced what I did. The rest of the optional tours I took during this trip would all be outstanding, which certainly enhanced the entire vacation. Interesting how within a month I went to Japan and learned that "Ohio" is Japanese for "good morning," and then went to Spain where I visited Toledo, which is a city name in Ohio (U.S.). What goes around comes around, you might say.

We then hit the road and headed to a city called Avila, which we would go to the next morning. We got into our hotel and had dinner. It was fairly quiet when I decided to spice things up. An older Welsh couple was sitting next to me, and we had chatted earlier. They had a good sense of humor and the guy had laugh lines around his eyes. I figured, well, maybe he likes to laugh. So I asked why we can't show "naughty bits" on TV in America as they do in Great Britain. He really got into this, as did others, with the upshot being that America is conservative, puritanical, uptight, or some other derivation that was mentioned, but in a nice way. It seemed strange hearing that from mainly British people, who we Americans sometimes think of in the same stuffy way. They liked that I was a fan of the British comedies Monty Python's Flying Circus and The Benny Hill Show, both shown on TV when I lived in New York during my teens (the former on PBS). I went through some of the routines with them. The guy did like to laugh, his wife a little less so. But it made for interesting discussion which we kept primarily amongst us so as not to disturb others' conversations, or those who wanted to dine quietly. All I had to say was "I'm a lumberjack and I'm OK" and the guy was practically shooting his beverage out his nostrils.

The next morning we got out early and toured new cities. First there was Avila, a "walled city" featuring a very old fortress and a very high number of churches (Gothic and Roman) relative to its number of inhabitants. This city looked really ancient, and we were told goes back to pre-Roman times in 5$^{th}$ Century B.C. It is almost 4,000 feet above sea level, and it was there that we had our worst weather – cool and foggy, but then it lifted and became sunny. There was an interesting history told to us, how it was conquered by Romans, then Arabs, among others. This was the first time I'd been in Europe and heard about Arabs, but we would hear even more about them as we moved further south and toward North Africa on this tour.

Next we rolled into Salamanca, a quaint college town. I roamed around on my own for two hours, again eschewing companionship so I could maximize the number of places I wanted to see and things I wanted to do. I met an intelligent coed from Cyprus who told me a lot about her home country. I had no plans to visit Cyprus and wasn't sure where it is. It's a good thing I paid attention because I did end up there a few years later and remembered one of her recommended restaurants to visit. Soon afterwards, I heard two gals talking with American accents. I figured they were fellow tourists. They were waiting for me to be done talking with the student from Cyprus because they heard my American accent and wanted to talk with me. They were pretty blonde exchange students there from Pasadena, California. We chatted for 30 minutes. They were very informative about Salamanca, life in Spain as an American, what there was to do, and how they're faring there. Overall they liked it but missed the U.S. They were going home after that semester, and missed their friends and family. They liked Spain in general, spoke the language but not fluently, and were glad they did the exchange program. They hadn't been to New York but would like to visit someday. So I exchanged contact information with these exchange students (how ironic), but we never did connect although I was then living in California. No matter; I would soon see thousands of students like them when I began my teaching career, and get to know many of them.

Our tour group then took the long ride toward Portugal. The lull of the rolling wheels plus the pre-recorded mellow acoustic guitar music played by the tour guide as we drove there put me and many others to sleep. I was having pleasant dreams, however, while living my dream as well. We had another fine group dinner, one in which the passengers started bonding. The seat rotation on the motor coach helped; not only did everyone have a chance to get a window seat, but to mingle with others near them if they so choose. I returned to my room and watched the BBC, the only English-language channel. No Monty Python, Benny Hill, naughty bits or lumberjacks in drag. Only news. Boring.

The next day we rolled into Coimbra, the former capital of Portugal, a beautiful city with houses atop hills overlooking the city, reminding me a lot of Catalina Island in California. This was my 30$^{th}$ country visited and I was very proud of this achievement. We took a city tour, during which time I walked around and had a custard tart (local delicacy) in this cool-looking bakery with Art-Deco design. I also saw some interesting antiques from yesteryear, and many reminders of Portugal's past (paintings, posters, books, statues, war memorials, and more). We went to the University of Coimbra. You have to climb at least 100 steps to get up there. Many of my tourmates couldn't do this and turned back; Maureen and I were among the few who did. This reminded me of climbing the seemingly endless stairs at the Vatican.

Once on the campus, I chatted with more of the locals. Unlike several of the Spaniards I'd met who had an edge to them, the Portuguese were very humble. Although quiet and seemingly aloof in the beginning, I found them to be very open and friendly if you initiate conversation with them. I really liked all of them. At the university there was a graduation ceremony taking place, including 10 pretty gals in these elegant black robes, having their picture taken by a professional photographer. Afterwards, I chatted with them as a group, telling them I'm from America on tour and we just got into town. I couldn't resist asking if I could take a photo with them for my album, "but only if it's OK. If you don't want to I understand." All of them happily obliged, and I got one with me in the middle. I thanked them and they wished me a nice trip. That was sweet of them, and it's those little things that make me appreciate people no matter who they are or where they're from.

Our tour group then went to Fatima ("Fah-tee-mah") – you guessed it, another cathedral. The town thrives on religious tourism and can attract up to a million people on selected holy days commemorating sightings of Virgin Mary apparitions in 1917. Once more there were lots of steps to climb, but these were considerably easier. The building was white and made for a good photo op against the bright blue sky. We had lunch in the area, and then drove to Bathala where we visited a beautiful old monastery with masterful Gothic architecture. I liked the impressive arch, and took several photos with that in the background. Inside was just as impressive with its stained-glass windows and cloisters. These Abbey Cloisters are a World Heritage monument, and built in the late 1380s! They looked sort of Arabic featuring more arches. Afterwards, our group did a wine-tasting at a local vineyard. These wines were terrific and the vineyards reminded me of those in Napa Valley, near where I was then living in Northern California. There seemed to be a strong California-Portugal connection – one more was awaiting in Lisbon, and it was a big one (literally)! The weather was great and everyone seemed pleased with the tour thus far (a buzz was developing).

We then drove into Lisbon, which is called Lisboa there. We were provided with the history as usual for each city visited. Lisbon is one of the oldest cities in the world, hundreds of years older than London, Paris, and Rome. At one point it was captured by the Moors, who I remembered learning about in school but hadn't heard that name in decades. I wasn't sure where they're from so I asked. They were Berber people from North Africa and often Black, but not always. I recalled reading "Othello" in my "Shakespeare" course in college, and that's where I had last heard the term since Othello was a Moor. I was finding the history of the places we visited more and more interesting, giving relevance to things I had learned about (but didn't care much about back then), and was at least asking questions about it out of curiosity. My friend Mark in New York is a history buff and his influence also had an effect; he would often later expound upon my trips with his historical insights which embellished the overall experience. Mark later told me that my descriptions of the places I'd been also helped embellish his historical readings and references. My tour group stayed at the very nice Roma Hotel, where I again watched the BBC on TV, but also checked out the local stations in Portuguese. Back in college I dated a Polish gal who had lived in Brazil before coming over to the U.S. The main language in Brazil is Portuguese, which she pronounced as "Por-tu-gay-sah." I thought she was mispronouncing it, but that's how the locals say it in Portugal. I then referred to the language that way, and the locals seemed to appreciate it. I later researched the language and learned that over 230 million people speak it worldwide, more than I thought (there are a combined 200 million people living in Brazil and Portugal, the vast majority of these in Brazil).

The next day was one of my favorites of the trip and in all my travels. I did not take the optional city tour but instead took the metro train around town and into the center of Lisbon. I happened upon a tower overlooking the city and went to the top for a panoramic view. Atop the tower was a very attractive blonde in her 20s taking photos of the city, who asked me in broken English to take one of her with her camera. Ironically, this is the line I often use to meet women. As I was taking a photo of this gal, named Libena, several gals from Ireland were there at a nearby table having lunch and asked us if we wanted them to take our photo together, assuming we're a couple. I laughed and said to the one who stood up to take it, "Sure, this is our first date, a blind date, and we flew here from different countries to meet at this very spot." Libena was charmed by this, laughed, and played along. We hugged each other and pretended to be lovers, cheek-to-cheek with a few pecks on the cheek thrown in. After the photo, the Irish gal told her friends about our "date," and they invited us over to their table to have beers with them. Libena shrugged, as did I, and we joined them. So there we were, me and seven pretty girls atop a tower in Lisbon having drinks together – and two minutes earlier I didn't know any of them! We had a grand old time for a half-hour, after which I said, "Well, this has been so much fun, thank you all, but I really need to spend time with my new girlfriend since this is such a special occasion." Then I looked adoringly at my "date" and said, "Please come with me, dear, and let's chat overlooking the city on this beautiful day." Libena then waved goodbye to the Irish gals, who wished us well, and I sat with her for the next two hours. In a sense I felt like Francois, my former "room-mate" from Club Med. Every now and then he'd pull a stunt like that, and on rare occasion it actually worked (to his surprise).

Libena was so amused by what just happened she just gushed about it. Then, almost as an aside, she said, "What's your name and where are you from?" It's a good thing the Irish gals were out of earshot. After all that we did not know each other's names or where each other was from! I said, "My name is Steve and I'm from New York City but now live in California." This impressed her; one of Libena's dreams was to get to America and go to both places. She seemed very interested, leaned in and touched my arm a lot, and we looked like...well, lovers. She introduced herself as Libena and told me she's from Bratislava, Slovakia. When I told her "I was there last year" she almost fell off her seat. I started naming things I remembered about Bratislava, including the statue of the guy with the manhole cover. She then told me that they soon changed the design because motorists were driving over it and careening into the nearby storefronts. This meeting with Libena (meaning "love" in her local language) was just wonderful – as in full of wonder. We just kept talking, laughing, smiling. This seemed too good to be true. Imagine if things worked out between us and people would ask, "How did you two meet?" What a story that would be!

Well, it was too good to be true. In fact, in light of what just happened, the rest of the story is coincidentally amusing. I asked Libena what she's doing in Portugal. She said that she worked last summer in a restaurant in Italy, where she met this Italian guy who now goes to college in Coimbra, and she's meeting him in another hour for dinner. I was like, "huh?" and "duh." She had to be going soon but wanted to keep in contact. We exchanged email addresses and have kept in contact to this day. However, we never did see each other again. This was a weird, funny, and delightful experience all in one. I took it lightly and just chuckled when it was all over – oh well, to what could have been!

But wait. The best was yet to come a couple of hours later. Libena had told me of a bridge in Lisboa, the Vasco da Gama, by the sea. I took the metro train down that way to see it. The train system in Lisbon is tricky and included two transfers (no police chase this time), but I figured it out and got to my destination. The bridge was magnificent, and was the longest suspension bridge in Europe. However, not too far away was another bridge which, if you had blindfolded me, drove me to it, and took off the blindfold when we were there, I would have confidently told you was the Golden Gate Bridge in San Francisco (same shape and color). But it wasn't; it was a bridge called the 25 de Abril Bridge (named after a 1974 revolution). It even connected from Lisbon to a city called Almada (sounds like Alameda), and was built by the same company – American Bridge Company – that built the Bay Bridge that connects San Francisco to Oakland. Another connection to California - how strange all this was!

As I was taking photos of the 25 de Abril Bridge, I wanted to be in one with it in the background to show people in California. But for a long while there was nobody around to take it. I waited and saw a guy about my age walk by, dressed nicely, and asked him if he speaks English. He said yes, and despite being Portuguese, spoke English fluently. I think he was an executive of some sort from the dapper way he was dressed. I asked him to take my photo by the bridge and he was very accommodating. He asked me where I'm from, and when I said "America" he wanted to talk with me.

We had a wonderful discussion, for one hour! He told me about Portugal, and I educated him about America. Now here's the thing: similar to Sebastian, this guy who I'll call Filipe, did not like America – its policies and people, who he said are ignorant about the rest of the world. I told him I can understand his point of view, and I've heard this from others. However, I took the high road and explained to him how I've been traveling to explore the world, value other people I meet wherever they are from, and here's the upshot: when he asked me what was the one thing I learned from all my travels, I looked him right in the eye and said, "That we're all the same. We all live, love, laugh, cry, bleed, hurt, and everything else we humans experience as emotions, and the more I thought we were all so different, the more

I realize that we're all that much more the same." I then told him of my tourmates and how well we all get along, and how "we should all just appreciate what each other has got and how lucky and blessed we are to be living in the world we do, at this great time in history." I added a comment Sebastian made, with which I fully agreed, stating: "You have to separate the people from the politics." Then I added, "People are just wonderful, even and especially in some poor countries I've been to. The human spirit is an amazing work of art! Love life and it will love you!" Filipe was hanging on every word. His eyes became bigger and I must have struck a responsive chord that resonated with him. He suddenly got tears in his eyes and – I will never forget this – put his hands on my shoulders, looked me right in the eyes, and said, "Thank you. Thank you for opening my eyes and making me aware." Then he looked away briefly before looking back. "Thank you for helping me to understand. Thank you for being here today. Thank you." He then gave me one final direct look, and started walking away. After walking several steps, however, he turned back to me, returned, and asked if I could meet him with his girlfriend the next day in this same spot at this same time so I could tell her what I just said to him. I said I would if I could but the tour was leaving in the morning. I again said how nice it was to meet him; he knew from my look, tone, and genuine sincerity that I meant it. Filipe thanked me again, and walked away for good this time. I think I know what he told his girlfriend that evening.

I may have changed this man's mind about America and its people, and realized that like it or not, I had become an unofficial goodwill ambassador for the U.S., as Americans often do when they interact with others not from our country (assuming they make a good impression). I would continue to do this when encountering people hostile to Americans in general – and there were no shortage of opportunities coming up. Sometimes I would help make a difference, and sometimes not. I did that day which made me feel really good; it's a feeling that dollars, escudos, or euros can't buy. As with Libena, I never saw Filipe again – we were two ships passing in the night (near a bridge!), but we had all benefited – laughing and/or crying – from the day's events. These experiences are what can make travel so wonderful. The ones you won't find highlighted in any tour book, and are not for sale.

I then took the train back to the hotel. I went back a different way and noticed some fantastic art in the train stations – even better than in New York City subway stations, which can be pretty impressive. Some were very colorful, some used a combination of art and blank white tiles, and there were several creative and colorful sculptures, too. Everything just clicked that day, went really well, all on my own. At the group dinner several tourmates said they "missed" me and wanted to know what I did. I gave them a recap, but not about Filipe, which I considered a private, and somehow sacred, matter. They liked my story with Libena. As it turned out, the optional tour costing $50 went to the same places I did – but what I had experienced was more of a "de-tour" in life that would have been hard to top.

So it was no surprise that to top off this special day I had a wonderful conversation with a fellow tourmate from Dublin, Ireland, an elderly lady traveling on her own in her 70s. We hadn't spoken before but were sitting next to each other at the group dinner. She told me she's a "dreamer" – and recently made her dream come true when traveling from Ireland to San Francisco to Hawaii to Fiji to Australia to India. I could see that just talking about her dream trip rejuvenated her; she positively sparkled like an emerald, and had been so quiet all trip thus far! This lady, I'll call her Glenda, totally lauded my decision to leave the business world and teach so I could travel around the world and make my dreams come true, too. "Do it while you can, while you're young and healthy," she said with a beaming smile. She reminded me of my grandmother who had passed away several years earlier, and with whom I was very close. There was an instant and wonderful bond between us, two souls who had found each other through a mutual dream. It was rewarding for me to see someone that age fulfilling her life's goal in her waning years. I'm sure she deserved it, having come through life's grinder still so excited about life and all it has to offer. God bless her!

The next morning we left Portugal – now one of my favorite countries – and headed into the southern part of Spain called Andalusia. The mountainous countryside featured olive, fig, and cork trees; spinach plants; gypsies in open wagons; sheep, horses, and storks in their nests; windmills, and castles! Quite a colorful variety, just what I like. We stopped into a small town that included small caged partridges in the backyard of the restaurant at which we had lunch (I hoped these weren't on the menu). After lunch, we reached our destination city of Seville, called Sevilla locally. Did any city have a name we Americans called it? I wondered.

I really liked this city which had new/trendy and old traditional sections, winding streets, and little plaza squares instead of the giant ones in Madrid. I'm not much into fashion but I even liked the stylish hat that so many men wore, I think it was a fedora of some kind. I settled into the hotel room, rested a bit, and did a rare optional tour at night going to the dinner and Flamenco dance for which the city is popular. The beautiful Spanish women looked great in their colorful Flamenco costumes, stomping their high heels and clicking their castanets synchronously with their steps, sometimes even holding a rose in their teeth. There was a certain machisma to this – proud, bold, daring, and sexy. The show was well worth it. I took two rolls of photos (about 50 pictures) during the performance, stayed out at night after the show, and enjoyed a fun and vibrant nightlife. I went to one of the bars, and the locals sure can drink! The people were friendly, more so than in Madrid, and more laid-back, too. I returned to my room and had a real scare. I had put my carry-bag, with all the canisters of film, directly below the room's heater, and after the few hours there the canisters were hot, even inside the little black plastic cases inside of a cloth bag. I worried that my film might be ruined, which would be a real tragedy. Damn, that song "The heat is on" (Glenn Frey) kept going through my mind. The next day I became even more concerned about this. I opted out of the city tour and took a roll of the film to a local camera shop, where I had it developed. The photos were fine – thank goodness! – and the owner reassured me the rest would be, too. Very fortunately, they were, but lesson learned about storing film.

Although I missed the "included" city tour, the one I ended up taking on my own was probably better the way things turned out. I strolled around this charming city and went to a cathedral (don't ask me why but I was starting to like them) and a nearby park. Then came the highlight of my day. I found a bullfighting ring called Plaza de Toros. There were five sexy Flamenco dancers having their photo taken by a professional photographer outside the ring. I had taken several photos of this because it was so colorful, and cool – not something you see every day. There were many other spectators watching but none taking as many photos as me. The female business manager in a suit came up to me at the end of the pro photographer's shoot and asked what I was doing. I told her that I'm a tourist from the United States, and I hoped she didn't mind if I took a bunch of photos from the distance because the ladies and costumes are so beautiful, and I'd never seen a bullfighting ring before. Her expression changed from semi-scowl to smile. I made a couple of well-timed quips, and she laughed. I figured I had nothing to lose, so as the Flamenco dancers were getting ready to leave I asked if it would at all be possible to get a photo with them to show my friends back in New York and California. She at first seemed like she was going to say no, but then gave it a quick thought and said, "Wait here." After talking with a few people, she said "OK, one photo" and took it herself of me and the ladies. As usual, I said, "Please get the heads and the feet in, and I'm happy" with a smile. She did so, and the photo came out great! I was very happy about this.

I lingered around and ended up talking to the guy who guarded the bullfighting ring. I told him the same "tourist" information about myself, and asked him if I could take a photo, from behind the wooden fence, of the bullfighting ring itself. He let me do this, and was such a nice guy that he said I could step onto the dirt portion inside the ring for a photo he would take of me there. I sort of trusted him, but didn't know if this was a good thing to do. I did it, going all the way to the center of the ring. He spoke English fairly well and said, "I'll take a photo of you now." I yelled, "OK, take one – but if the bull chases me around take all the photos you can!" He laughed. Fortunately there was no bull. He then told me there is a bullfight museum right next door. I was intrigued and went. I found it interesting. I didn't stay for the bullfight (nor would I), but enjoyed myself in this area.

I had some bland pizza for lunch, and then took a long walk to the river area (or "ree-ver," as our tour guide later pronounced it). There I met two sets of college students from the U.S. who were exchange students in Seville; two from Minnesota, and two from

Texas (the two groups of gals did not know each other). We had enjoyable conversations. One of the Texas gals, Luz, told me to go to the Feria – a Spanish festival celebrating the Spring harvest that lasts a whole week and gets up to a million people. She told me how to get there, and I walked another two miles (very pleasant day and views). The festival was tremendous – guys and gals dressed in fine clothes, Flamenco dancers, music, food stands, festivities, and they even dressed the horses drawing the carriages in colorful floral arrangements! It looked like New Orleans' Mardi Gras and Rio de Janeiro's Carnival combined in Spain. I took lots more photos, and just laid it all out there energetically, knowing we had another long motor coach ride the next day, and I could sleep then if needed. I had a grand old time there, mingling, trying new foods, laughing, drinking – lots of unexpected fun! Despite having done a lot of walking already, I walked back to the hotel, making it over five miles of walking for the day. I didn't mind all the walking because you can easily get cooped-up from all the motor coach riding; I needed to get my circulation going and would walk whenever feasible. And this helped me lose a couple of pounds I had gained during the trip. I went to bed tired, but very happy, after another excellent day!

The next day was very special for me, because it was the day I reached my seventh continent, Africa! Our tour group took a ferry from Southern Spain to Morocco, passing the Gibraltar Straits and Rock of Gibraltar on the way. We were provided with the history and folklore, including that, pre-Columbus, beyond this point was considered the edge of the Earth, and going beyond it meant you'd fall off. I thought the Rock was just, well, a rock, but it's an island city that has a lot to see including great views, shopping, a botanical garden, and monkeys running around. We arrived in Tangiers, Morocco and exchanged our local currency for Moroccan currency called dirham ($1 U.S. = 8.46 dirham). It's important to remember the exchange rate so that you pay the proper prices and receive back the proper change. We didn't tour Tangiers immediately, but would later loop back to it.

Our tour group was soon met by three local guides in robes named Khalid, Mohammed, and Abdullah – just their names and appearance helped me feel like I was in a different world. They provided city tours throughout our trip to Morocco. Other names they said on the tours were Berbers, Phoenicians, and people from Carthage – names that would make my eyes glaze over in history classes but now were relevant, so I was suddenly at least a little bit interested. I was starting to get a thrilling sense of anticipation about this part of the trip; it was much different than Spain and Portugal, and different than anything I'd ever seen before. I could see already that this was going to be a whole new experience, from the women's kaftan robes to the men's fez hats. Once again we lucked-out with the weather. Morocco was very hot the previous week – up to 110 degrees – but there was a "cold snap" at a "brisk" 85-90 degrees when we arrived, corresponding to almost exactly the number of days we would be there. Amazing timing with the weather once again!

We went through Customs, and then drove more than three hours through the Moroccan countryside to Fez, with some beautiful views of the coastline. Some spell the city Fez and some spell it Fes. I saw it spelled both ways there. To me it's "tomato-tomahto" since it's pronounced basically the same. On the road we saw donkeys pulling wagons, men in skullcaps, women in veils, dromedary camels (one hump), people yelling in French and Arabic, and many Berbers – mountain people of the Barbary Coast – also in colorful outfits. This looked like a land that time forgot, but I would get an even better glimpse of it the next day. Our first tour guide, Mohammed, was my kind of guy. He was friendly, smiley, funny, and called himself "Momo," which means baby, because he's the youngest of 12 in his family. He also liked to provide the history of names and informed us that Morocco – called Maroc over there – translates to "where the sun sets." Momo said that the northern part of Morocco is primarily Spanish while the southern part is primarily French, and that the languages spoken throughout the country are in order: Arabic, French, and Berber. Also there is a Jewish Quarter – where the Jews were given sanctuary after being expelled from Spain during the Spanish Inquisition circa 1500. I hadn't thought of Morocco as being Jewish-friendly, but then I knew.

I chatted with Khalid to get a sense of Moroccans as people. He told me that "Moroccans are friendly, peaceful, and love everyone."

We stopped off and did a little shopping. Maria, our tour leader (who was still aboard with the three guides), told us not to drink the water in Morocco and to buy bottled instead, and also to buy toilet paper and carry it with us because many rest rooms do not have this included. Further, she explained, there is a fee you have to pay to use public rest rooms, so keep some coins and smaller bills with you. The things we take for granted! We arrived at the <u>beautiful</u> Menzeh Hotel in Fez. The lobby décor was outstanding, and really made you feel like you were in an Arabic and African land, somewhere far, far away, somewhere new and different. I was impressed. I got to my room and was very tired from the long trip. The bedspread had this Arabic pattern that seemed just right. If I were to dream of a hotel in Morocco that gave me a sense of adventure, it would look like this. I wanted to go for local cuisine somewhere close, and asked the hotel personnel for recommendations. I wanted a place in which English was spoken and was, above all, clean and safe. I was referred to a local establishment at which I had the kofta, which were spicy meatballs. As I had learned in Thailand (and later, other places), our definition of spicy and the local definition of spicy can be entirely different. So I had a lot of water with the kofta, but it was only mildly spicy and very good. I went to bed early – big travel day, big meal, still a hot day near 90 degrees, and more upcoming travels.

The next day would be one I'd never forget. We went on an included-tour to the Medina. This is a large, outdoor flea market, for lack of a better term, with each individual narrow store called a souk (rhymes with "kook"). Because almost the entire tour group was elderly, I knew that if I stayed with them the pace would be slow. I like to zip around to see as much as possible in the limited time available. I asked Maureen if she wanted to join me, but she was obligated to go with her elderly aunt. I was on my own again, which Maria warned me against doing there, but seeing I was determined she said to be "very careful." I said I would be, and went about my business, camera in an opaque shopping bag so it – and my being a tourist – wasn't obvious. As I began walking around a young Arabic guy in his early 20s, dressed in jeans and a T-shirt, approached me and started speaking Arabic. I immediately said "English" and he understood. He then spoke to me in pretty good English. He wanted to sell me a carpet, and referred me to his store. I politely declined. He asked if I'm Moroccan. I said, "No, why?" He said I could pass for one; something about how my eyes were shaped. I was unaware if there was any Moroccan in my background (I don't think so, but you never know). He was pleasant and we told each other to have a nice day.

I arrived at the entrance to the Medina, and immediately started thinking of the rap song "Funky Cold Medina" by Tone-Loc. There was funk, all right. And total mayhem, too. Lots of people rushing around, yelling, hustling, bustling, and jostling. There were guys in colorful outfits carrying carpets, guys trying to sell you everything under the sun, and people begging for change – including lots of kids who walk up to you with their hand out saying, "Give me 10 dirham." They were very persistent and aggressive. I saw them shame one old lady into giving them money by saying several English-language curse words in a row. Many of these beggars, kids and adults, appeared very dirty, and also cough/sneeze without covering up. I did my best to avoid them, using my New York City speed-walking skills as needed. There were men pushing wheelbarrows, others calling out to you, and just seeming chaos. I didn't see a lot of police around, either. There was the smell of spices, seeds, smoke, and fragrances permeating the air.

Prices had to be negotiated. This reminded me slightly of Orchard Street in Lower Manhattan, where there are prices listed (for tourists) but locals know to negotiate instead. There were only men running the souks; I didn't see any female workers out of the hundreds of stores I passed. I noticed that the men and women were standing and conversing separately throughout the Medina. There were narrow winding streets, and skinny sidewalks that made for a potential disaster. That's because when someone yelled "bellek!" this meant that a mule pulling a wagonload of people and/or merchandise was barreling down the road and, as Maria had warned us, "They don't stop and they don't carry insurance." I saw a few near-misses, and translated "bellek!" to mean "Move your ass, or mine will cause you to be kissing yours goodbye!"

I conversed with an Arabic gal in her 20s dressed in a black body suit from head to toe called a burqa. You could only see her eyes. My first thought was that she must be very hot in there (possible pun intended). She spoke English well, and told me basic things about Morocco. I asked this gal if I could take a photo of her and with her. She said OK. I didn't think people in burqas allowed themselves to be photographed, but I guess I was wrong. After the photos this gal ran up to me and asked me to pay her the equivalent of $5 U.S. for the photos she allowed me to take. I said we didn't discuss a price, and that I didn't think I had to pay anything. Several of her friends came running over (all female) and argued with me. We settled on $2 and that was the end. I was wondering if there was a "sheikh-down" syndicate there, as I called it, maybe including the kids who curse in English until you pay up. I should have learned a lesson from this experience, but didn't – similar situations would be repeated, as will be described.

I walked away briskly and forgot about this incident. Then a young Arabic guy in his 20s grabbed my arm from behind and hustled me toward some others in a slightly out-of-the-way area. This happened very quickly, and for a split second I thought I was being kidnapped. Just as I was about to struggle, I was pushed to the ground in a seated position, and in a flash I had three large snakes around my shoulders, with a guy dressed as a snake-charmer playing his flute seated opposite me! The guy who grabbed and pushed me down then ran and got a cobra which he held in front of me; both were staring at me, this guy and his cobra, which was a few inches from my face! I couldn't fathom this immediately, but then a crowd gathered around, mostly of Arabs in garb, who watched and cheered. If I'd heard the word "bellek!" I'd know I was in really big trouble. The snakes were moving on my shoulders and were fairly heavy. What was happening here? This was a bizarre bazaar!

Well, what was happening was another "sheikh-down." The cobra was trying to get at my bag, in which I had my camera. The young Arab guy who grabbed me spoke English well, saw there was a camera in my bag, and asked me if I want to have photos taken. I thought very quickly and said "Yes" for a couple of reasons: if something really bad happened, like the snake(s) bit me, I'd want there to be photos in my camera to alert whoever finds it as to what happened (I had quickly recalled a story I'd seen on TV of a guy who was missing, but they found his camera, exposed the film, and found the last picture was a close-up photo of a bear – you can figure out the rest); and also, if I made it through this unharmed, I sure would want these photos! We negotiated briefly – I would say he had the upper-hand, literally – and we settled on 10 euros (about $13 U.S.). He took my camera out of its case, and the photos were taken as the snake-charmer – and the snakes – did their thing. I'm thinking, "Well, I've skydived and walked on Antarctica, so I can get through this if I stay calm and relaxed." I saw it was a show, that this is what they do, so it's not like I was going to be harmed unless something went awry, although it certainly could have (which is why I did not participate in the elephant show in Thailand).

After the initial photos with the three snakes, the young Arab guy takes them off and replaces them with a big, heavy cobra. "Hold still" he said to me. "Don't worry, I will!" I said. My mind then warped into playing a variation of The Hollies lyric, "He ain't heavy, he's my cobra." The crowd around me was getting bigger. I just kept looking at the snake-charmer and wondering if that was a flute or a clarinet he was playing. Anyway, the cobra was around me, I did not make any moves, and just hoped it wouldn't bite me. I was surprised there wasn't a snake-oil salesman there. To keep calm, my mind went on autopilot again and made mental jokes – including the thoughts, "I wonder if I have "Cobra" medical coverage at my new employer when I return?" and "I wonder if this includes wrap-around coverage?" I made a mental note to check these out. The snake-charmer music kept playing; people were oohing and aahing, taking photos, and just looking at me. Some were pointing, and told their young kids to look. I just smiled. It all was surreal. At the end, the Arab guy removed the cobra, people clapped, and I got up and took a bow (or was that, boa?). I was given my camera – after I paid the 10 euros, shook hands with the Arab guy, waved to the snake-charmer, and left. Well, that was...interesting!

I met with the tour group back at the bus on time, but strangely, did not tell of this experience. I think Maria would have freaked out, and others might have been frightened about potential kidnapping. Several tourmates made small-talk with me, asking how I liked the Medina and if I did any shopping. I merely said, "I found it...charming," and quickly asked what they did. As a side note to all this, in addition to buying post cards, I bought a red T-shirt that read Hard Rock Café, Maroc on it. I had asked the merchant if this would shrink a lot in the wash or if I'd have any problems with it. He said, "No problems." I later found out not only is there no Hard Rock Café in Morocco, but the red color came off easily in the wash – and I led the league in red-dyed clothing for a while (which I had to toss out). There were human snakes there, too, so you had to be doubly careful. However, everyone else I met was just fine.

Back at the hotel I freshened up (didn't think "essence of cobra" would attract any women), and decided to get a late lunch/early dinner at a nearby restaurant. The hostess was extremely attractive, a blonde Berber gal in her 20s named Izlane. I thought she was a knockout from the second I saw her, and we instantly liked each other. She was so sweet, too! Izlane spoke Arabic, French, and very good English. She had never left Morocco, and told me it's tough to get a visa. She was interested about life in the United States. Since I was the only customer that late afternoon, Izlane sat with me for almost my entire meal, and we chatted. She had a particular beauty like I had never seen before, like an Arabian Marilyn Monroe, that was very alluring. She asked to see me that night so we could continue our discussion. I said that I would stop by after 10:00 p.m. when she was done working. Izlane had changed into a great-looking red shirt and looked fantastic! I mean, wow! However, perhaps having second thoughts, she said she didn't want to go out, but we can talk outside the restaurant. I was disappointed but said OK, and so we did.

Izlane told me more about Morocco, and I answered her questions about life in America. Music, fashion, the types of places you can go, and the things you can do. After a half-hour she had to go home. We hugged goodbye, and we just kept staring at each other. I tried one last time to convince her to come out with me, saying that early the next morning we're off to Marrakesh. I was smitten, but she was forbidden, it seemed. At the end we exchanged contact information, but didn't get in touch with each other. However, we found each other years later on social media, and have remained in contact to this day (she's now married). She still looks great, and is very pleasant. Speaking of sweet, I sampled some local candies and fruits at a nearby store; at least there I got a "date" (ha). I then returned to my hotel room, and went to bed very tired after a most interesting, and overall excellent, day!

The next morning we embarked on a huge travel day to Marrakesh, Morocco – nearly 300 miles. We stopped at a place called Ifrane for a morning snack, where I took photos at a large stone lion. I had pistachio ice cream, a popular flavor in Morocco, which I grew to like and would have often at comfort stops. As we continued in the motor coach, our local guide, Mohammed, saw someone he knew herding a bunch of camels and coming our way. He told the driver to stop, and said hello to his friend. After a brief chat, he motioned for us to get off the bus. We did – and we were offered a chance to ride atop the camel for free! I was one of the few who took this offer. The camel herder had the camel sit down, and I was to mount it between its two humps. At first I thought a two-humped camel was called bi-cameral but I was confusing this with the U.S. legislature (too much desert sun)! The camel herder became distracted, and I ended up sitting in the wrong spot, behind the second hump. The camel rose up and off I went. One of my tourmates, seeing what happened, told me to hang on tight. I did but it was hard hanging on. There is no gear you wear, no stirrups, or anything. The camel herder was yelling in Arabic at the camel, who didn't respond, and "Momo" looked like Tony Romo (Dallas Cowboys quarterback,) trying to direct the camel into the open field. Maria grabbed my camera as I'd asked her to and took photos. I saw later, after they were developed, that because I was sitting so far back on the camel it looks like I'm "humping" it in the photos! And the camel is smiling (the bastard)! Well, they got me down after the ride and my tourmates were chuckling (as was I – after I was safe, that is!). I gave a nice tip and we were on our way. This was the highlight of the day; the rest was pure travel with some rest stops, lunch, and chatting with more tourmates. At the group dinner, over coffee, one of my smarmy tourmates asked if I wanted sugar. When I said yes, he replied, "One hump or two?" There's a wise-guy for you. We arrived in Marrakesh at 11:00 p.m. I went straight to the hotel room, and to bed.

The next day our tour group went to the Marrakesh Souk, similar to the Medina in Fez. This one seemed less intense, and this time with no snakes. I still had to avoid those merchants calling out to me, and even trying to catch up with me. Afterwards, we strolled around the city and I enjoyed the Arabic architecture. They really put the "arch" in "architecture," with some looking like elaborate giant keyholes in a mosaic of finely decorated orange stone. I was getting a real appreciation for this style. There were some fine gardens, too, and a mix of old town and modernization. There were a lot of Berbers there, along with numerous French, German, and Brits. There is some dispute as to whether the word Berber derives from the word Barbarian, which would not be complimentary. Izlane had said that Berbers prefer to be called Amazigh (free men). We passed by several colorful markets. The sunset that night was awesome, turning the buildings colors – red, orange, pink. At the hotel, several tourmates were in the lobby and raved about the optional tour, which included seeing a beautiful valley from atop the mountains and having tea in a genuine Berber home. In retrospect, maybe I should have done this tour – especially after having met Izlane who is Berber. I heard that the Berber people were very nice, but also very poor. Another tourmate chimed in that, according to what he's heard, many Moroccan houses could take years to complete because building them is done in stages. Thus, there are many unfinished houses on the streets.

I signed up for the optional dinner show to see the performance "1001 Arabian Nights" at a local club. There's a funny story about the dinner. At the restaurant, we were served an appetizer in a fancy dish, and after tasting it I tried to figure out what it was. Quail? Duck? Pheasant? As we were eating it, our waiter walked by and a tourmate asked him. "It's pigeon," the waiter matter-of-factly replied. Half of us then spit it out, including me. It didn't taste badly, it's just that it was, well, pigeon. An Indian guy in our group asked the waiter to take his portion away from the table; he didn't even want to see it. I asked the waiter to do the same. I looked at my Indian tourmate and said, "I guess we're birds of a feather." He didn't appreciate the humor, and was very upset that he ate pigeon. I think he was ready to "fly the coop" and not stay for the dinner or show. The main meal was good (couscous), and I liked the mint tea afterwards as well.

The show began and there was a lot of dancing. Much of it was belly dancing, popular in the region and done well. But there were acts from "mountain tribes" that featured drum beating, yelping with tongue rolled in a peculiar way, snake charmers, and the best of all, acrobats who were terrific. It was a good show overall. I was glad I went. Hard to believe that in a little over 24 hours I rode a camel, had snakes around my shoulders, and ate pigeon!

We continued on the next day to Casablanca. It doesn't look like what you see in the famous movie, which was filmed in Hollywood, but there is a Rick's Café in town that includes many facets of the movie, from a player piano to the interior design. The seafood was good there. Aside from this there was not much else of interest to me, except maybe viewing a huge mosque which we didn't visit. We went to a large cathedral outside of the city, and continued along the countryside where there were lots of white houses on hills overlooking the city ("casa blanca" means white house in Spanish).

Our next and final destination in Morocco was Rabat ("Rah-baht"), the capital, where the King of Morocco lives. We went to the Royal Palace where we saw the changing of the guard, and then this immense fortress that dates back many centuries. There was more splendid architecture around the city, and interesting floral arrangements. We continued our drive along the Barbary Coast and arrived at our fancy hotel, the Mercure, at night. I had a quick dinner and got to bed early for a 5:30 a.m. wake-up call.

The next morning we took the ferry back to the port at which we arrived, where our motor coach driver was waiting for us. The coach was thoroughly checked because some Moroccans stow away under these to get into Spain. It was cleared. We took a final tour of Tangiers and then rode back to Spain, arriving four hours later in beautiful Costa del Sol. There were lots of long, narrow, sandy beaches there that reminded me of Southern California. Lots of fine restaurants, too. One of my tourmates was an elderly man who was very late in getting back to the bus, and the tour leader became worried. She went out to find him but no signs! We almost left without him after 15 minutes but he finally showed. This almost happened to me earlier in the tour, at the maze-like souks, and I was a few minutes late after sprinting at top speed. One big piece of advice: make sure you are back to the motor coach or bus on time – the tour bus may leave without you, and it is your responsibility to make it to the next destination if you miss it. A trick I learned later on, when I had a digital camera, was to take a photo of the spot where the bus left us off – this way, if lost (and it does happen), I can show some locals (or the police) the photo, and they can tell me the location. I had to do this once in a remote area. The alternative would have been worse. If you are late back to the bus, holding up others, at least expect a "Bronx cheer" when you return from the rest of the passengers who had to wait, if not a reprimand from the tour leader.

After this we headed to Granada, Spain, that name supposedly meaning "Great castle," but we also heard it could have been named after its pomegranates. Just when I thought the trip was winding down and I'd seen its best, along came the Alhambra Palace and Fortress. This place was <u>magnificent</u>, especially the architecture. We learned about the history of the Moors in Spain, followed by when the Christians conquered in 1492 (Queen Isabella again). The Christians destroyed just about everything but left the Alhambra intact because of its beauty and grandeur. I'm glad they did because it's a spectacle to behold! The Islamic architecture and the Muslim art are beautiful. I returned from this trip with an appreciation for them, having none before (because I had no exposure). To this day, the Alhambra is up there with the Taj Mahal regarding the most beautiful buildings I've seen.

After another overnight, we returned to Madrid, our starting point, and said our farewells. I told Maria and Renaldo what a wonderful time I had, thanked them heartily, and tipped them mightily. I also said a nice goodbye to Maureen and the others. They were a great group, and to this day one of my favorites on any tour. I stayed an extra day because I had used frequent flyer miles I'd accumulated to defray the expense of this trip, thus having to wait the extra day to use the free airfare. It was well-worth it to me. And it didn't even cost me another night's hotel fee. That's' because I had a very early flight out the next morning, and decided to stay out all night; despite all the trip activity, I was energized and wanted to maximize my stay. So I arranged with the hotel porter to have my bags stored for a small fee, and off I went.

That afternoon, I took the bus from my hotel and, inspired by the Alhambra experience, went to the famous El Prado Museum. I enjoyed that, too (if Mike could see me now!) and also strolled around Plaza Mayor and Plaza del Sol on a picture-perfect day, literally! I had a fine dinner (gazpacho – cold tomato soup, and gambas – prawns, which were both excellent) and then returned to the hotel area by train. I met some more locals and we chatted about life in our respective countries, keeping it on a light note. I arranged with the hotel to have a taxi (via a company they recommended) pick me up at 3:30 a.m. for my 6:45 a.m. flight back to San Francisco. I then stayed out all night locally before leaving. The taxi connection and flight all went smoothly, and I returned home safely.

That was some trip, truly outstanding! I saw and learned a lot – a common theme that would increase with each successive trip. In retrospect, this was another steppingstone vacation that would vault me higher on my way to becoming the traveler I would eventually be. I was as comfortable being away from home as I was in my own city. I processed my photos which came out great (over 1,000 pictures), and...slept well that night with pleasant dreams to last.

Even with these recent travels, I still had some time before the Fall semester began as I switched to my new teaching career. I reviewed the textbooks from which I'd be teaching, prepared my lectures, familiarized myself with the university campus, and was ready to go a few weeks ahead of time. So, I had one more place I really wanted to visit, a place that had become a perennial transition point for me; a place where I could count on having an excellent, relaxing time and return fully recharged. And that place was, once again, Club Med – Turks and Caicos Islands in the Caribbean, despite having to travel there from the West Coast this time. I would again choose to travel there by myself, enjoy the most beautiful beach I'd ever seen, the amazing chocolate bread (dark and white!), and hopefully meet great new people. Well, what was old was new again – and even what was new would be new again, too.

I arrived there and, despite some recent rains at the Club the week before, once again had excellent weather all week. This was becoming the norm, and amazingly would continue even to the present day! So there I was, back at my home away from home, and still my overall favorite spot. The Club seemed to be getting more modernized each year – wired, commercialized, and even corporate somehow. I didn't like this evolution, but it was progress I suppose. The customers needed to stay connected to their home or office, and Club Med needed to accommodate this. The world was changing, and even the average age of the Club visitors was increasing (now maybe to 30-35 at Turkoise) to where I was becoming the old guy. There were very few singles clubs left as well, and another reason I went then was that the Turkoise village was still mainly (but not exclusively) for singles, and still had a large contingent coming from New York City. I missed those wild & crazy New Yorkers, so here was a chance to reconnect. I met several from my home town, Brooklyn, and people from all over the world once again.

I had my usual excellent time there. I chose the roommate option one more (and last) time, and came up a winner with a guy originally from Philadelphia who was a physical trainer, a nice guy a few years younger than me who was in great shape and did not follow me around saying, "There is my room-mate!" Evan and I got along from the get-go; we went around together but gave each other our space. We would become friends, and later he would also move out West to a nearby state. We got together only one time after he moved, but remain in contact to this day via social media, mainly. We'd meet girls and help each other, including with photography, a mutual hobby. He had a digital camera then but I still did not. We debated which is better. I still preferred film, and back then the digital photos were not as advanced as they are today (precipitating my switch a few years later). The shows were magnificent and full of energy, and there were the usual "Hands Up," "Crazy Signs," and other songs and dances (a few new ones were added). A few members of the staff, who were rotated every so often, remembered me. I remembered them, too. It's nice when the sun isn't the only warm thing at Turkoise!

The most unusual event happened as I was strolling down a winding pathway along the beach at night heading back to the room. There was one other person on that path, a tall guy who appeared heading toward me. We would pass like two ships in the night, as I did with so many others to whom I'd smile and say hi. But this would be different in 3...2...1 as we came parallel to each other in passing, and glanced over to see who the other person was. Would you believe...it was Marcus! Yes, Marcus from the Antarctica cruise a few months earlier! We just stared at each other, not believing our eyes. First randomly sitting next to each other on the flight from San Francisco to Buenos Aires, then being on the same cruise to Antarctica as two of only a few Americans, and now here we were on an island in the Caribbean! We greeted each other in amazement, and I said we should play the lottery together (I wasn't kidding, but we didn't). Marcus was there with his mom, as a gift to her on a major birthday. This was unbelievable. I saw my roommate, Evan, and called him over. We told him the story. He was amazed, too. What were the odds? You see, it really is a small world. This was Marcus's first time there; by this time I was a veteran of the Club and gave him pointers - including "Don't step in the guano," which made him laugh.

I would see Marcus later, and we each enjoyed the rest of our stay; we kept in contact sparingly after this trip. I ended up visiting Marcus a few years later at his California home, with my then-girlfriend, Lana. At his beautiful home, Marcus showed us, on his big-screen TV, a montage pictorial he had put together from his Antarctica photos. That was impressive. Lana really liked it, too. So how about that, perhaps Club Med and Antarctica have something in common: both are "the antidote to civilization" in their own special way.

I began my teaching job at the university a short time later. I adjusted well to my new surroundings, career, faculty, and students. My officemate, Bev, was also new to teaching full-time, and a nice lady who helped me a lot with the computer work. I helped her in whatever ways I could as well. We remain in contact to this day, despite neither of us still teaching. Everyone else was very helpful to me, too. I was simultaneously a student in learning all you can about teaching, and teacher while performing my role. Upon hearing my work experience, several students referred to me as "The Ring Pop Professor." Ironically, I was marketing Ring Pops, Push Pops, and other popular candies to them 10-15 years earlier, when they were in my "target market" of kids ages 6-12! Now, here I was teaching them. There was little formal training; it was almost all on-the-job. I had an interesting perspective about my new situation – it was like being on tour again with new people of different backgrounds and personalities. The Department Chair was excellent at leading us as a group, and developing me personally as an instructor, patiently answering my many questions as I got started. This helped my overall experience be a very good one. Perhaps best of all, as mentioned, I had positioned myself to have a solid job with full benefits, and more than four months off to travel and explore! Soon after starting my job there, and realizing it was going well, I looked into booking a vacation over the upcoming December-January winter break. I wanted someplace warm. I thought I'd found the right place at the right time, but then...

# Chapter 11

## Central America: Adventures and Misadventures

After teaching my first semester in California, I had more than a month off for winter break in December-January. I was focused on traveling the world, gaining a new adventure, and living life to the maximum, having broken the corporate shackles. Gap Adventures had a vacation that tied-in nicely with the time off I had, a three-week trip through Central America: Guatemala, Honduras, Nicaragua and Costa Rica. Was I ready for another extreme adventure? I thought, "I had an excellent time going to Antarctica with Gap last year, so why not?" Two thoughts emerged after the trip was over: just surviving this trip was half the battle; and five words that came to mind were: harrowing, exhilarating, exhausting, dark, and grungy.

This tour was limited to only 12 people; in fact, there might be only 12 people in the world crazy enough to take this trip. Once the trip was booked, I had to get vaccinations for hepatitis A and hepatitis B, was given a prescription for Cipro® in case I got extreme diarrhea, and a supply of malaria pills – which I'd be required to take before, during, and up to a month after the trip. Typhoid and tetanus shots were also necessary but I'd had these vaccinations last year before the Antarctica trip. I was informed that the side effects from the malaria pills may include hallucinations, coma, or death in rare cases. Certainly this was at least a pause for concern, but I decided to go ahead with it. Fortunately, I tolerated all of these medical precautions well. The specifications for luggage allowed were rigid, in that it could not have wheels, was limited to two pieces, and should be soft & flexible. I later learned that's because it would be tied to the roof of vans (of wild & crazy drivers), and these rules helped the drivers manage it better. A flashlight was also recommended to take along and I would later find out why; however, a torch would have been more appropriate. I also knew that several of these countries were politically unstable, Americans had been recently kidnapped and/or killed there, and there was a high crime rate – especially in Nicaragua which had a particularly high unemployment rate. The U.S. State Department issued numerous warnings to Americans traveling there which sounded dire. Robbery victims were urged not to resist in any way; one person who had recently resisted was killed instantly. Despite my entire family and all friends telling me not to go, I decided to go anyway. A motivator for this decision was a perennial one for me regarding many major decisions – if I didn't do this, I'd wonder what it would have been like had I done it. This was a factor in my decision to go to Antarctica, and also to leave the corporate world to teach at a university full-time as well. Both of those turned out very well.

I had a long trip just to get there: two-hour shuttle van to Sacramento Airport, seven-hour flight via Houston to Guatemala City, Guatemala, and a two-hour van ride to Antigua, Guatemala to meet the tour group at a specified hotel. I had a bite to eat at the airport where I figured the food was safe. It was, but I'd learn on this trip not to assume anything was safe, including the water (again I drank only bottled). The hotel was "OK" and I was surprised I had my own room after booking a share at the lower rate. Maybe I was again the beneficiary of being the "odd man out" having not yet met the others on the tour. I thought maybe the other guys were much younger than me so they were paired-up together, or maybe I'm the only guy, wouldn't that be something! I was very tired but it was New Year's Eve and our tour leader, Brian (from Colorado), an athletic guy in his mid-20s, invited the group out to a bar where we would all get to know each other. So without even napping I went with the group, a range of worldwide people from 20s – 40s. I was one of the oldest people on the tour. That didn't bother me, but what did was that the bar we ended up at was smoky and loud, not my scene on either count. I asked Brian if there were any New Year's Eve festivities nearby we could go to. "Not really," he replied. I told him I need to walk around to stretch my legs after so many hours of sitting. I added that this bar isn't my scene, and that if I don't return there I'll go back to the hotel and be prepared to leave early the next morning to start our trip. Brian said OK and those familiar words, to "be careful."

It's a good thing I went out on my own. It was 11:00 p.m. and I walked to the center of town, alone and a bit wary, arriving at a major plaza. It was relatively empty then but only a few minutes later many people were gathering. A short time later the crowd got much larger, around a thousand, crammed into a small area. You could sense that something big was about to happen. As it turned out, there was a huge New Year's Eve celebration in the offing. The police came by, mounted on horses, and separated the huge crowd using these horses and their nightsticks. This separation happened right in front of me, literally, with the back of a nightstick poking my belly, as the crowd standing straight ahead was ushered to the other side of the plaza and made into a circle. The area was cordoned off and, as fate would have it, I was in the first row! I turned around and there were hundreds of people standing right behind me. A few minutes later, from seemingly out of nowhere, came a variety of entertainers including acrobats, costumed performers on stilts, and fire jugglers – right in front of me! There was music, fireworks, people shouting – a real spectacle! I was getting really into this; it was like Feria and Mardi Gras combined. The festivities were so loud that I figured it attracted the entire town, including my tourmates, and that we'd talk about it the next morning.

Meanwhile, I was fortunate again in having brought my camera; by then I'd learned to bring it everywhere on trips because you never know. It would have been a major bummer had I not carried it with me that evening. I got some incredible shots, including from directly behind one of the fire jugglers passing lit clubs back and forth to another fire juggler, and later on, with the costumed people on stilts. Everyone was going wild, many wearing party hats reading Feliz Año Nuevo, and many who were drunk. But they were fun, smiling, laughing, having a grand old time. This was another moment when the merriment transcended everything: age, race, nationality, religion. Partying is the universal language! Near midnight the crowd was going wild, and I was "woo-hoo"ing it with them, really getting into the frenzy on a natural high. At midnight several guys shook my hand and many gals hugged me. Taking my cue from the party hats I shouted, "Feliz Año Nuevo!" to which many said the same and much more that I didn't comprehend, but instead just smiled and gave the gals a second hug (why not?) if I thought it was something good. I ended up taking approximately 75 photos that night, and had a great time to start this trip. I arrived back at the hotel and got a delightful night's sleep, which I really needed, that included very pleasant dreams about the New Year's Eve celebration. Little did I realize then that this evening would be the highlight of the entire trip for me. Nor did I realize that my tourmates did not attend the spectacular celebration until informed the next day.

The next morning I met the rest of the group. They included people from the U.S. (two others), Canada (one), New Zealand (one), Asia (one), and Europe (mostly U.K.). They had a wide variety of occupations including actor, chef, lawyer, and cartoon animator. I found out a few things based on early discussions with them and Brian: the trip started two weeks earlier in Cancun, Mexico; most of the group members already knew each other, and were paired-up with the rooming; and I, as the lone single to that point, would be paired-up with Billy, a new arrival that day and guy my age also from the U.S. (New England), starting that evening. I was not a good fit with this group: they were nice people but liked to party at night in the bar, and also most were smokers which I don't like being around (nothing against the smoker, just the smoke). One person was also heavily into politics and sparked a few debates. I also didn't want any part of that. I tried hanging out with them a couple of nights but it just wasn't my scene. I politely excused myself and didn't join them again. Thus, I was seen as aloof, but in an independent way, so I was told. I found lots to do on my own, however, and these were some of the best parts of the tour based on my preferences.

The trip was grueling, dangerous, and scary in many ways. I did not expect this. It wasn't until I arrived that I was told there would be 73 hours of travel – by motor coach, vans, and a couple of ferries. With delays, this ended up being closer to 85 hours. Often we were up between 3:30 a.m. – 4:30 a.m. to leave by 5:00 a.m. – 6:00 a.m. One day we traveled 18 hours. The local drivers we took did lots of things they show not to do in the driver training videos: drive way too fast, tailgate, pass other vehicles in narrow areas (going way too fast), not signal, stop short, etc. It seemed that the biggest vehicle on the road wins, including horse-pulled and donkey-pulled carriages. Many buses were psychedelic colors, a throwback to the 1960s. I thought this was cool, however, and took several photos as they passed by. Most of the roads were unpaved; several were uneven; and I don't recall seeing any speed limits, traffic lights, or even stop signs throughout the trip. In the local vans, which held 15 people, there was a lot of bumpity-bumpity-bump for many hours, with rest stops every four hours or more.

Our luggage would be tied to the roof of these vans, and we had to schlep our own luggage between vehicle changes. Often we took "chicken buses" – yellow school buses packed with locals. I met some nice people on these buses, but they were crowded and with no air conditioning amid hazy, hot and humid weather conditions (there was no air conditioning in any vehicles or hotel rooms during the entire trip). I sweated my butt off both indoors and outdoors. Perhaps worst of all was that one bus we were on emitted truly nauseating fumes to the point where myself and another guy on my tour were about to puke. I was watching him, and if he did, I would have, too. I was able to get through this awful smell by a score of 51-49%, it was that close.

On our first full day we took a city tour of Antigua, Guatemala. The city name translates to "Ancient Guatemala" and there were lots of old colonial style churches there dating back to the 16th century. I felt as if I were back in that time based on the old-style buildings, serenity, and cobblestone streets. The small city (population of about 35,000) was surrounded by volcanoes. I was struck by the colorful buildings (not literally, but with some crumbling structures this could have been the case), including a beautiful yellow church called San Francisco. There were columns with licorice-looking twists on the outside, and beautiful paintings and sculptures inside. The center of the city featured a giant fountain in an area called Central Park. I was surprised that there were a lot of older Americans who lived there; one such guy told me Americans and Europeans retire there for the climate and low cost of living. I was told the city has excellent chocolates. Having a sweet tooth, I had to try these. They were very good, but not as creamy as the milk chocolates in Europe.

Our group then went to Copan, Honduras. The city was a bit rundown and primitive, but we spent most of the time at the Mayan Indian ruins. These were as good as or better than the ones I saw in Tulum, Mexico 20 years earlier and, according to my tourmates, as good as or better than the world-famous Indian ruins in Chichen Itza, Mexico. I took some nice photos, had them taken of me by tourmates, and returned the favor. We then had a very long van ride to Roatan Bay Islands, still in Honduras. We came upon an impassable road due to remnants from Hurricane Katrina that passed this way several months earlier the prior year, plus some new flooding. Brian, who spoke fluent Spanish, discussed this with the driver. There was nothing that could be done by vehicle, so we all decided on-the-fly (literally) to chip-in and take a charter flight. We saw lots of fallen and twisted trees in the region, and I had seen the same in the panhandle of Florida a few months earlier. As a side note, I was in New Orleans two weeks before Hurricane Katrina hit there as one of my last travel flings before teaching began. Timing can be everything.

We were briefed on Roatan Island and told that it was a real dive, literally – it's known for its scuba. The clear and colorful blue waters would remind me a bit of the beach at Turks and Caicos, but the beach wasn't as nice as that. The weather there was expected to be very hot and humid. We were advised to spray ourselves with insect repellent (containing at least 30% DEET, which mine had). I did this, but in retrospect wondered if the fragrance of my repellent attracted, rather than repelled, the bugs. Upon arrival to the outlying areas there were numerous insects, especially sand fleas, which bit a lot of us up pretty good leaving large pink "pimple-like" marks, especially around the ankles. I had at least 30 bites on my legs and ankles, while Sabrina, a Swedish college student with her blonde hair, blue eyes, and milky-white skin, had at least 100 bites (no exaggeration). These itched but weren't painful. Two guys on my tour from the U.K. had spent time in the Amazon just prior to joining our tour and one had what looked like a mosquito-bite necklace around his ankles. He seemed proud of it, showed it off, and was declared the unofficial winner for both symmetry and overall number of bites after displaying most of his bare skin.

I was surprised these tourmates were not concerned about malaria. I sure was, especially after being bitten by a mosquito. There was signage all over the countries we visited about malaria and dengue fever, too, regarding how to protect yourself. I checked with the CDC and my physician before this trip, and was taking prescribed malaria pills during it. Malaria is rough stuff and you wouldn't wish it on your worst enemy. I heard from my tourmates and the locals what I'd previously been warned about from my physician: these pills can cause hallucinations or even death, and that the adverse reactions from the pills could be worse than the malaria itself. I had no problems with the supposedly "horrible" taste of the pills (which I swallowed whole) or any hallucinations. I know people who did, though, and some, even on my tour, did not take malaria pills despite the high incidence of the virus in some of the countries we visited. Subsequently, I learned more about it and was relieved based on the very small odds of contracting the virus if bitten, since it needs to be from a particular species, and that mosquito, itself, needs to be infected.

Here's WebMD's explanation: "Malaria is spread when an infected Anopheles mosquito bites a person. This is the only type of mosquito that can spread malaria. The mosquito becomes infected by biting an infected person and drawing blood that contains the parasite. When that mosquito bites another person, that person becomes infected. In the United States, people who develop malaria almost always got infected while traveling in parts of the world where malaria is common." I did not see any research stating that the mosquito also needs to be pregnant, as I was told in Central America. I also didn't get malaria, thankfully! The good news is that it is now curable if caught early enough.

We then approached the city. Roatan was all dirt roads, with one main road in and out of the city. Some parts were so rural that to go to the toilet you had to dig a ditch and cover it when done. The main road was lined with gift shops, restaurants, diving gear stores, and bars. This is where several people from my tour started drinking heavily. A few stayed two extra days in Roatan and paid extra for a flight to meet the rest of the group in Nicaragua. There were a lot of armed police in the area, which created two questions: why are there so many armed police – is it because they have a high crime rate? And is it safer because they are there? The answers, I learned, were yes and yes. Youth gangs contributed to much of the crime – high unemployment, drugs, and not much to do there could have been factors individually or in combination. After a basic city tour, we found ourselves with little to do. Most went to the bar, where I heard two of the gals "put on a show" by sexily dancing with each other and attracting guys like "moths to a flame," as one tourmate later put it. I went out on my own, and used my New York City street smarts when walking around. I met a few interesting people, mostly beach and diving folks, who raved about the calmness and clarity of the waters there.

The most interesting person I met was about 12 hours later, a white-haired, flamboyant American guy in his 60s from Alabama named Ken I met on a jitney boat I was taking to the beach the next morning. He paid the locals to bring him conch fish because he said 1 in every 10,000 has a pearl in it. He then sells these pearls via the Internet to customers in the U.S. He showed me some of these pearls, explaining that the ones that have better roundness and pinker color are more precious. They were beautiful. He said his "hobby" helps him spend winters scuba diving in Roatan and the rest of the time back in the U.S., plus other travels. He also said there is an annual conch festival in Providenciales, Turks & Caicos Islands, in November. That's where I go on my Club Med vacations, yet I never heard of this. Well, I just learned a few new things. He also told me he has a 21-year-old beautiful girlfriend in Roatan. I raised an eyebrow in disbelief, and then he reopened his hand containing the pearls. "Oh," I said. As it so happened, on this same jitney was a gal from my tour named Beth who accosted me as the jitney docked. She was also going to the beach to do some snorkeling and overheard my discussion with Ken. I told her that I didn't believe he has a young, sexy girlfriend. Beth said she did – because she saw him with her the night before at the Twisted Toucan Bar being "very frisky and amorous." Beth said she is gorgeous. I wouldn't be surprised if her name was "Pearl."

Beth and I went to the beach together. I walked around and took photos while she snorkeled. This was good bonding for us because we hadn't got along so well on the tour thus far, especially since I didn't accompany most of the group to the bars at night. The beach was gorgeous, circular with white sand that sparkled along the edge of the Caribbean Sea. It was very picturesque with boaters, kayakers, and snorkelers on a magnificent sunny, 78-degree day. While roaming around, I met a lawyer with a great figure in a sexy bikini named Reyna. I took photos with her and asked her to join Beth and I. She politely declined, saying that she's been at the beach a while and is roasting in the sun. But she provided a good overview of the island and its people, saying it's a fun, laid-back place to relax. It sounded like a Central American Club Med to me, and that was a good thing.

I swam in the warm water, and had a one-hour conversation with an older couple from Boston while in there. We just marveled at the beauty of the island. I spoke to Beth a lot after she returned from swimming, and we sunbathed. She headed back to the hotel before me via the jitney boat while I stayed on and got some great sunset photos. Back at the hotel, I met the tour group and we headed to dinner. Once seated, we all shared our day's events. Many went diving, some went swimming, and a few went hiking. Beth, a fellow New Yorker, and I got into an animated what we'd call a discussion, and others would call a debate, which entertained and amused the others (lots of facial expressions, hand gestures, and "oh, I don't think so's!"). Unfortunately, one of our tourmates, Pam from The U.K., was chewing when she thought something Beth said was funny, and began choking on her food. She kept on coughing and got out of her seat. Something was definitely wrong. My roommate Billy knew the Heimlich maneuver and performed it on her, forcing the food out, and saved the day. He was our hero for a while. Beth looked at me and said, "Oops." That ended our discussion/debate/group entertainment. As frightening as that was, there were other dangers lurking out there about which you had to be very careful.

On a ferry ride, I met a guy from Switzerland in his 20s wearing a backpack named Mathias. We had an excellent conversation. He was traveling by himself and told me of meeting nice people, seeing the countryside, and overall having an enjoyable time. However, he'd been robbed by a youth gang at knifepoint in broad daylight on a crowded street in Managua, Nicaragua. They were yelling at him in Spanish but he couldn't understand what they were saying, or wanted him to do. They cut off both straps of his backpack and took off with it. He didn't fight back because he was "paralyzed by fear." He considered himself fortunate that they didn't kill him. Thankfully, our group had no such incidents.

The next day we marched onward, literally. There was a lot of trudging on this tour – sometimes in the mud – with heavy backpacks. Brian took a photo of me that he later emailed showing me trudging up a steep hill with backpack after we exited a ferry sometime around 8:00 a.m. I looked so weary, and was! You could see the bottled water bulging from my backpack. It was very important to keep hydrated, so I carried extra water (especially since I liked to veer off on my own and hike for miles). It was important on this trip, as cautioned, to drink only "agua purificado." This included using it for brushing your teeth and washing your face. You also had to beware of ice cubes in your beverages, and salads that may have been washed in local water. I avoided these altogether, not wanting to chance anything. Showering was another story – I tried not to let the water get in my mouth, and as far as I know no-one on our tour became ill from the water. By the end of the trip I had lost seven pounds – mostly water – due to sweating a lot. This byproduct of the arduous "vacation" wasn't a bad thing, since I needed to lose a few pounds anyway.

At night, it was so dark outside you sometimes needed a flashlight to see a few feet in front of you. It's a good thing I brought one, which was recommended in the pre-trip notification received by the tour operator. A torch would have been more appropriate; seriously, it was that pitch-black. I also brought a roll of toilet paper, as recommended, because not every rest stop had it, or even a toilet, as previously mentioned! And to complete the trifecta of things we may take for granted such as lighting and rest stops with toilets/

paper, I'll also mention paved roads because we traveled so far for so long on dirt roads that my butt was getting sore. Good thing I'd brought the good toilet paper, with the two-ply and extra softness. There were some dangerous creatures we encountered such as a tarantula and, as our local tour guide in the jungle told us, "a snake that emits cyanide, so be very careful where you walk." There was a snake very close to us at the time, which may have reminded him to tell us about this. Wonderful.

Aside from all this, I had an issue rooming with Billy. He was the darling of our group having rescued Pam from choking with his Heimlich maneuver, but for me was a nightmare. He was a heavy smoker and, perhaps consequently, a heavy snorer, which drove me nuts. To make a long story short I asked Brian, our tour leader, if he could do something about this. Two other guys on the tour who were roommates offered to rotate with me (that was nice of them). However, after a short while they wanted to return to their original roommate status, leaving me with Billy again. I tried as best I could to cope with this, including wearing earplugs and a Walkman® to bed, but they didn't help the overpowering snoring. Billy and I ended up arguing, although we each realized it wasn't the other guy's fault. I really thought the rest of the group would come down hard on me, but people blew it off as "just one of those things." I later apologized to Billy, who accepted.

I lost sleep the rest of the trip, but not just to Billy's snoring. One night everyone else (including Billy) in the group was out extremely late and several got very drunk, coming back rowdy to the hotel at 2:30 a.m. Some were nasty, angry, profane, and doing other things. Sonya couldn't control her laughing at Gordon, because he was rolling on the ground making a weird hee-hawing wheeze like a donkey. Although I was pissed that they were going on with all this for three hours until the wee hours of the morning, practically outside my door, I didn't want to chide them in their current state, and also based on what already had happened with Billy. The "donkey" comment at least made me laugh, because he did indeed sound just like one. Then again, in that rural town it could easily have been a real donkey. That particular night, just as I got back to sleep, a rooster awakened me. Damn. It was loud. "Please cockadoodle-don't!" I thought. But it was too late. Billy returned and was snoring, I couldn't fall back to sleep, and we had to be up in an hour anyway.

There were other room-related situations and snafus, too. One time I held the shower curtain rod as I was stepping into the tub, and the whole shower curtain and rod came crashing down. There were frogs, geckoes, and assorted insects in the room at any given time. One gecko climbed rapidly across the ceiling as I chased it, trying to get it out of the room. It climbed up and down the walls with ease. I was later told that the geckoes are good; they eat the mosquitoes which may contain malaria. I still didn't want them in the room.

Regarding eating, I had another adventure, or misadventure, depending on the situation. The food was very good in general. I especially liked the fruit – very juicy and flavorful – but you had to be careful it wasn't washed in local water. I usually stuck with the safe dishes such as chicken and rice, nothing too exotic. One time, when dining on my own, I was served my fish dish, and just before the waiter put it down in front of me all the lights in the restaurant went out – another power outage, which we encountered several times during the trip. Although I couldn't see two inches in front of me, I was hungry, started cutting the fish with my fork, and eating it. When the lights came on a few minutes later I saw the fish on my dish – its head was still on and one yellow eye was looking up at me. Yeeeoooow! Somehow I felt like Shaggy in Scooby-Doo, and just wanted to make a run for it (to where, I don't know, especially since it was pouring rain outside). I couldn't eat any more of that fish.

The next day we had a very long motor coach ride into Nicaragua. At least this motor coach had a bathroom on it, unlike the others – what a pleasure (little things meant a lot on this trip)! Then we transferred to a yellow chicken bus. I sat next to a local gal and we had a long chat. She was very interested about life in the United States and dreamed of going there someday. She told me of a Nicaraguan U.S. baseball pitcher named Vicente Padilla, who was recently traded from the Philadelphia Phillies to the Texas Rangers, and is a big hero in Nicaragua. She thought he was the only native-born Nicaraguan to be playing in the U.S. major leagues. We arrived into Nicaragua and transferred to a van waiting for us. We made a rest stop at a place so primitive that after you went to the toilet you had to dump a bucket of water into the tank for the next person so they can flush. "Like Robinson Crusoe, it's primitive as can be" (theme song from "Gilligan's Island"). Brian gave our group the option of spending an extra day in Granada, a colonial town featuring volcanoes, in lieu of the day we were to spend in Managua. I had the feeling he had been alerted to the crime spree in Managua and was going to steer us in that direction anyway. I was the first to agree to this without mentioning my encounter with Mathias – but had the others voted for Managua, I would have mentioned it.

So, we spent three days in Granada starting with a volcano hike in the nearby town of Masaya. A few tourmates hiked all the way up the 14,000-foot high Concepcion Volcano. While very proud of this accomplishment, they were also very sore upon return. At the base of this mountain I met a woman from Western Colorado who was waiting for her husband to come back from his hike up the volcano. We chatted for over two hours; having recently lived in the state, I had been to her home town and we both loved Durango and Silverton (a historic railroad connects both cities). This woman told me her whole life's story, including some shocking details I'll let be private. This was yet another example of a total stranger telling me his or her life's story – including her statement to me that, "I'm telling you things I've never told anyone else." Sometimes it just works that way. I've done something similar, but not to any great extent. I've learned that you may end up seeing these people again, even years later and halfway around the world.

I hiked quite a bit, also getting high into the atmosphere. I almost had a mishap when a big gust of wind came and nearly blew me off the mountain as I got too close to the edge to take photos! I learned my lesson then and did not get that close to the edge again. Back on the bus, my tourmates and I exchanged hiking stories, ending with wishing each other "happy trails" before we parted and settling into our hotel rooms. I liked the city of Granada, which is warm year-'round, and again met some very nice locals. I continued to be very impressed by how friendly, cheerful, and helpful they were despite being dirt poor, and literally living in shacks along dirt roads. I gave some local kids a few coins and they treated these as if they had won the lottery. However, they followed me around after that looking for more, with their friends joining in. They complied when I firmly said "that's all, no more." Although they were somewhat aggressive, a few months later I would run into extremely aggressive kids who seemed to be professional beggars in Eastern Europe.

I stayed in the center of town a lot, on my own by choice, just letting life happen. There was a yellow church with a red dome; horse-drawn carriages; street vendors; and a mercado (market) several blocks long that made for good photo ops. There were also old women walking around with a fruit basket tied to their head and guys carrying sacks of flour over their shoulder. Because of the very favorable exchange rate, I had a big lunch for $4 U.S. and a very large dinner for $8 U.S. I also sampled some local sweets, including an incredibly good, flavorful, home-made coconut patty. I noticed that in other countries I visited the food seemed to taste richer there. I'm not sure if theirs is just made differently, contains ingredients we don't have, or maybe even contains ingredients we're not allowed to put into ours – but in several cases the foods I've had in many countries were definitely tastier than comparable ones I've had in the U.S. In fact, to this day, that was the most "coconutiest" flavor I ever tasted, and I love coconut.

The next day, our group was led back to the center of town, and we went to the "Old Mercado" built in 1891. This was a giant flea market which had cheap prices for clothes, fruits, fish, fragrances, spices, and more. Lots of colorful buildings, a park nearby with fountains, young people hanging out on the steps of various old buildings, and a slow pace in general – not the hustle and bustle I've seen in other outdoor shopping areas. And no-one yelling "bellek!" as an alert to potentially getting run over by a donkey-drawn carriage as in Morocco. Just a laid-back area with people moseying along, which was refreshing.

After leaving Granada, our group took a ferry the next day to Ometepe (pronounced "Ahm-eh-teppie") Island, which is dominated geographically by two giant volcanoes and features a lush jungle. I went into the jungle and saw white-faced monkeys and some exotic birds. We stayed in a mid-tier resort area right on Lake Nicaragua, which is the largest lake in Central America and second largest in Latin America after Lake Titicaca (located between Bolivia and Peru).

At 99 miles long, it's about half the length of Lake Erie in the U.S. The resort area was very rustic, with bamboo huts and hammocks overlooking the Lake, reminiscent of the hammocks at Club Med in the Turks & Caicos Islands. Many, if not most, if not all of us were tired at this point, and took turns in the hammock which was a pleasure to be in. I rested a lot in this picturesque location, taking photos and chatting with my tourmates.

We were then off to Costa Rica, the last country on the tour, and by far the most Westernized. During a three-hour layover at the bus depot, Sabrina built an impressive house of cards. I got a photo of this, and the look on her face was great as if to say, "Ta-da!" (or Swedish equivalent). Our group first went to La Fortuna, a little town featuring yet another volcano, this one called Arenal. While impressive, I'd seen enough of the volcanoes for a while and had recently flown over one spewing lava in Hawaii. So, I mainly rested in this town, catching up on much-needed sleep. There was also a TV in the hotel room and I watched the NFL playoff games in Spanish. I enjoyed this, especially how excitable the announcers got when there was a touchdown (perhaps consistent with the "Goooooooaaaaaaal" calls made for fútbol/soccer by announcer Andres Cantor).

Our group next took a ferry to Monteverde, where we hiked in the jungle with a professional guide in the morning, then visited a hummingbird sanctuary. A couple of tourmates brought high-powered binoculars and got excited when seeing a two-toed sloth. They let me see it through the lens. It didn't do anything for me, but to them this was like a "Goooooooaaaaaaal!" so I acted excited. There were some gorgeous, colorful birds in the rain forest (lots of mud, too) making all sorts of noises I hadn't heard before. Back in the "concrete jungle" of New York City you might hear "Yo, Ralph!" followed by "Hey, Louie!" as two guys yelled out the window to each other at all hours of the night, but they were nothing like these amazing creatures in the real jungle which were a delight to behold.

Several tourmates went zip-lining across the rain forest, which they invited me to do. But my back was aching from the hikes/heavy backpacks, plus some bad mattresses, so I didn't want to chance anything bad happening at that time, since things were screwy on the trip in general. An older corporate executive officemate, who looked out for me, once gave me advice in this regard when stating, "Just take it easy when things are out of whack - you want to live to fight another battle." Perhaps if I return I'll give zip-lining a run. I did, however, walk the canopy bridges over the jungle for a bird's-eye view. This was cool, tied-in with how I like to get an overview of the landscape (literally), and made for more excellent photo ops. This move to a higher elevation is a trademark move of mine; even in New York City nightclubs during college I'd go up to the highest point so I could look down at the crowd, select the gals I wanted to meet, then "swoop down" (as my friend Harvey reminds me to this day) to meet the desired women. This often worked, so maybe I had an eagle-eye. Or maybe I was an eagle in a previous life, explaining why I felt so comfortable doing this and in places indigenous to eagles on my vacations.

Which leads me into another high-elevation situation. While driving back to the hotel in a van, which was exclusively for our group, we came across several people bungee jumping from a bridge. Brian convinced the driver to stop, thinking there would be tourmates wanting to do this. But no-one did; either we were too tired or felt it was too risky (it looked like a make-shift operation). So, we were all just standing there, when finally Brian decided to do it. He was hooting and hollering on his way down; I think he'd done this before, maybe many times based on his calmness. He was OK after the jump, and then another tourmate, Sonya, decided to do it and was also OK. We had time for one more before the van returned. Poor Sabrina was goaded into being the next candidate, and she looked petrified as the rope was being tied around her ankles. Although she was encouraged by the others and putting on her game face, I could see that she really didn't want to do this. I walked up to her and said, "Sabrina, if you really don't want to do this, then don't. It's OK." I was jeered by several tourmates, but Sabrina told the guys tying the ropes to stop, and they did. She seemed very relieved, and later thanked me in private. Having done a skydive a few years earlier, I may have attempted the bungee jump, but with my back aching I thought the wiser of it and didn't.

Finally, we traveled to San Jose, Costa Rica by motor coach, and of course my mind immediately played the Dionne Warwick song, "Do you know the way to San Jose?" which was a light, airy tune befitting of the mellowness we had just experienced in the jungle. By this time I was very tired, and only went into town briefly, visiting the impressive-looking National Theater. San Jose is the capital and largest city in Costa Rica. I went to an overlook and saw how crowded it was, especially compared with the smaller cities and towns we had just visited. By comparison, it seemed like a cacophony compared to its airy, melodic namesake in song.

The tour ended for me the next morning, and I said goodbye to my tourmates. This was no Antarctica trip, but there still was a tourmate connectedness we had having gone through this grueling marathon (at least to me). Sabrina said an especially hearty thanks to me, probably because of my rescue of her during the bungee jump. We kept in contact briefly by email afterwards, since I was planning another trip to Sweden in the future. When I told her this she quipped, "I'll warn all the women before you arrive." I wondered if that included from the higher elevations. Well, I did go there again and had a great time, but by that time Sabrina and I were no longer in contact. I liked her and hope she's happy with whatever she's doing now. I said a fond farewell to Brian, too, and even to Beth with whom I bickered from time to time – but who I think respected my opinions, even if she disagreed with them. And I even made peace with roommate Billy. We understood what had happened, and it was "just one of those things." This was not one of my favorite trips, but I learned a lot and am glad it happened. Based on the dangers posed by this trip, for subsequent vacations I started using my credit cards a lot for purchases in foreign countries, and told my family that if anything bad should happen to me to check my statements as a literal paper trail regarding where I may have been when the music (and credit card charges) stopped.

As a side note here, people often ask me about health and safety issues, such as: should I travel by myself? What if something happens and I need medical attention? I can only say let the traveler beware. You can buy trip insurance ahead of time, which can include trip cancellation if something happens before you even leave, or if you need to go home sooner, or if you do need medical attention abroad. Early in my travel career I took the insurance; later I did not. I'm also asked about traveling solo, especially by females. I've met several solo female travelers, from 18-85. It depends on your level of desired comfort. I've met hippies, missionaries, college grads taking time off to explore before entering the work force, business travelers, adventurers, backpackers, hikers, bikers/trekkers, those who live off the land (country to country), thrill seekers, writers, photographers, those trying to "find themselves," those trying to find others (e.g., soul mate), those wanting to find God, those wanting to commune with nature, and more. I say if you have the passion then go for it. Be careful, be respectful of others and their culture, but most of all, be you and become the future you that you aspire to be as a result of these travels.

Upon return home to California, I slept very well and prepared to teach my next semester. Little did the students know that their teacher had just learned a few more lessons – about himself, the world, and life. Early in the semester I told the students how we never stop learning. We never do, and thank goodness for that!

# Chapter 12

## Eastern European Mosaic

After teaching that semester I had three months off for summer! Thus, I planned a whirlwind vacation to Eastern Europe to last half of this duration, 8 countries in 42 days total, including the Balkans and their capitals utilizing two connecting Cosmos tours via an overnight train. This would be grueling but I was up for the challenge and filled with enthusiasm. I took a plane out of San Francisco and visited with my family and friends in New York. Following this, I took an overnight flight from JFK Airport to Budapest, Hungary, arriving early morning there and ready for what I hoped to be another exciting adventure. It was too early to check into the hotel, so I left my bags with the concierge and had the day to myself before meeting the tour group later that evening. I was to have a roommate on this trip and thus paid a lower price; that said, if I couldn't be assigned a compatible roommate I'd have my own room for the lower price. You would think after what just happened in Central America I'd be opting for a single room, but I had a good feeling about this trip. I'd soon find out what was behind hotel door number three.

Remembering what happened a couple of years earlier in Budapest, I took the subway downtown but made doubly sure that I had the right tickets with the right stamps at the right price and was going in the right direction. I make mistakes like everyone else, and was well-aware that you can have a beta of 10 in this regard when you're away from home, alone, and in a foreign country in which you don't speak the language. But, I like to learn from my mistakes, seek opportunities, and become even better. So, second verse same as the first – and this time there were no problems. I even alerted the tour group later that evening about what had happened to me on the subway there two years ago. No-one else planned to take the subway, but the tour guide made a note of my taking it in case anything happened.

I walked around one of the main plazas – to which I would return three weeks later after the tour group looped back to it – and around the Parliamentary area. I also again walked across the bridge separating the cities of Buda and Pest along the Danube (not blue, but greenish in color). I walked around the Opera House, which is a magnificent structure inside and out. The weather was unseasonably cool for this time of year; thus it turned out that my last-minute decision to pack a lightweight jacket was a good one, not only for there but other countries as well with cooler-than-normal temps. I bought a lot of post cards, knowing I'd assemble a photo album of this trip at some point, to mix-in with the hundreds of photos I'd invariably take.

Back at the hotel, I went up to my room. Upon opening the door I saw a pair of legs hanging off the edge of one of the beds – man's legs, older man's legs, then as I continued opening the door it revealed more of him until we were staring at each other's faces. We both gaped, recognizing each other. Upon seeing the legs I sure hoped it wasn't Billy again...and it wasn't, thankfully. But it was Fred, a nice white-haired, white-bearded guy from Missouri who had been on my Central European tour with Cosmos two years earlier! I didn't speak with him that much back then, but we did have a drink at an English pub in London at the end of that tour. Now, here we were again. As it turned out, Fred was an excellent roommate – nice, quiet guy, mechanically-oriented, who even fixed my camera at one point in the trip. We chatted, caught up, unpacked, and headed down to the group dinner. There we met our tour leader, Alina, who is from Transylvania, attractive in her mid-20s, and sounded like a female Bela Lugosi – who, ironically, was Hungarian. We would visit Transylvania later in the tour. The rest of the tour group members were mainly older retirees, as expected, and there were 45 of us in total. One exception was a Korean gal named Nancy from Southern California, who was in her late 30s and traveling by herself. She would be a big help to me throughout the trip, and I would help her as well. The vast majority of the tour group consisted of Brits, Australians, and New Zealanders (Kiwis), and there were only 5 Americans (including a married couple in their 70s). At night came the big question: would Fred be a snorer like Billy? Thankfully, no! This helped make the night, and the tour, a most pleasant one in that regard.

The next day we began our tour through Hungary and met our motor coach driver, Rocky. I had brought a book to read this time, called "A Short History of Nearly Everything" by Bill Bryson, so I found it an interesting coincidence when our guide began with an unusual fact: the paprika spice from Hungary, made from red peppers, is among the finest in the world. I just learned something new...that wasn't in the book. We didn't spend too much time in Budapest, but did see a number of interesting and unusual castles on the outskirts of the city. We also saw homes decorated in gypsy style (very colorful) - the mention of that word triggered my mind to play "Gypsies, Tramps and Thieves" by Cher, and indeed we did see some gypsies roaming around in their garb. The audio-visual combination again gave the trip more authenticity, not that it needed this. It's like a reverse daydream – a song may cause you to think of what's being sung about, but at times like this the visual I was beholding, and perhaps the words being said by the tour guide, triggered the song to play in my mind.

We went to an artist town called Szentendre that had European charm – cobblestone streets, horse-drawn carriages, museums, galleries, artists, and outdoor cafés, in addition to several churches. It was on the banks of the Danube river adding to the charm and the accessibility. People were friendly, but that's the business there since it hosts many tourists. Szentendre had a very large Serbian population in its past, centuries ago, and still does today, but not nearly as large. That country would be our next stop.

We arrived at our next destination: Belgrade, Serbia in the Balkans. We learned all about Serbia, one of six republics of the former Yugoslavia – its involvement in two World Wars, relatively recent ethnic cleansing of Albanians, and more. There is still a significant

Albanian community there but more than half the population is Serbian, plus some small populations from Montenegro, Hungary, and other places in the region. Belgrade did not get a lot of tourism, but this was changing, slowly. Our tour guide was very concerned and overprotective of us here, warning us not to go downtown because of the crime. As such, although this was not a luxury tour, we stayed at a beautiful hotel, the Intercontinental on the outskirts of town, probably for safety since it was very well-protected. The hotel itself was enormous, with art galleries in the lobby. Fred accompanied me around, unusual for him to suggest this but he may not have wanted to be alone. Sure thing, and we walked around the gi-normous lobby checking out the shops. As usual, I looked for post cards, fridge magnets, and little knick-knacks to bring home because I had very limited room left in my luggage after packing. Also as usual, I struck up a conversation with a local Serbian gal named Milinka who I'd estimate to be about age 22. She worked in one of the art galleries and was very friendly when we walked in. I was smiley and chatty, too, while the reserved Fred just looked on and let me take the lead. He had previously complimented me on how I meet the locals and get a real feel for the places we're in by chatting with them, saying he wished he could do that. Another "as usual" was that I had my camera with me, and good thing I did. I asked Milinka if I could take a photo of her and with her, "so that I could tell people I know back home how pretty and friendly the Serbian women are." Milinka was flattered and Fred took the photo of us together, after I had taken one of just Milinka. Well, that was as good as it would get.

The next thing Milinka asked was, "So where are you guys from, Australia?" I was surprised that she could not detect our obvious (to us, anyway) American accents. I said, "No, we're from the U.S." "Really?" Milinka said, surprised. After we nodded she immediately turned off to us, literally, twisting her body at a 90-degree angle and barely looking at us. Her smile was quickly replaced with a scowl. While her body turned 90 degrees, her personality did a 180 and she snapped, "Half of all Serbians hate Americans for bombing Kosovo for no reason!" She followed by steaming, "Tito ruined our country by allowing Albanians into Serbia because they have 10 kids to our 2 kids." I looked at Fred and he looked at me. I looked at Milinka and she looked at me. Then Fred. Then me again. I said, "I really don't want to get into a political discussion about that. We're tourists here and want to have a good time." Fred backed me up, and he's so polite (to my occasional aggressiveness). I'm glad he did.

Milinka did not apologize, but instead said, "Have a nice trip" and started to walk away, as did Fred. My next move was audacious, even for me. I said, "Milinka, wait a second." She turned back around. Fred stared at me. "Would it be OK if I took a photo with you being angry, because you are part of our Serbian experience and I already have the happy Milinka photo which you wouldn't want me to show to other Americans, right? Because that was before you knew we were Americans, and now that you know, that's not how you feel." Fred's look was like, "huh?" Even I couldn't believe what I was saying. I don't think even my "Portugal" speech would have worked here. We were fortunate she didn't throw a vase at us or something. But Milinka, still steaming, said, "Yes, you may do that because you can show it to your American friends and tell them not to come here." So I handed my camera to Fred, and Milinka stood next to me with a scowl. Fred took the photo. I now had the pre and the post in pictures. I looked at Milinka and said, "Thanks for being so honest and allowing us to take your photo. Have a good day." "Bye," Milinka said abruptly. Needless to say, we didn't buy any artwork. But she herself was a piece of work. Yikes! And I could then see why many Americans say they're from Canada and/or place Canadian stickers on their backpacks, luggage, etc. so as not to be confronted. I would have an experience involving this option a few years later, which will be described. If you're going to do something like this, be sure you know what that alternate-"citizenship" country's (e.g., Canada's) relations are with the country you're in – who knows, it could be worse.

So, Fred and I walked away. When we were out of Milinka's earshot (and hopefully throwing distance) he looked at me and said, "Well, that was...an experience." "You still want to hang around with me, roomie?" I said. He said, "Yes" after a slight hesitation – but we didn't really do this much since we each liked to explore on our own. He added that this experience had "interesting dialogue" and was "revealing." Sooooo, I decided not to go downtown if what we just experienced was any indication of what to expect. Fred easily convinced me to go to dinner with the group in the hotel, and he cajoled me into telling the story we just encountered. There wasn't much reaction (remember, most tourmates were not Americans). The tour guide, Alina, immediately took a head count at dinner – we all were there and she seemed relieved. There was only a short time between our arrival/getting settled in the room and group dinner, so people didn't have much time to go out, anyway.

The dinner was elegant and included Greek musicians. I'm not sure what it's called in Serbian (too many little markings above the letters) but I had minced meat and also plum brandy, which were two local popular items. There were also various kabobs on skewers, and noodles with poppy floating around. Appetizers and dessert, too. Mostly meat dishes, and very few vegetables. The food wasn't bad but no-one raved about it. The music was the best part, and there were people dancing. It was "all Greek to me"; after only a short time there I'd had that pointed discussion with Milinka, and we were listening to a Greek band in a Serbian restaurant. I'd heard that Belgrade has a great nightlife and wanted to check it out, but we had a mandatory meeting (including more safety tips for the next day's excursions) and it was raining. And based on what already transpired, passing on that seemed like a good idea. Fred and I didn't talk about Milinka again. I got a good night's sleep, and so ended an educational evening.

The next morning we drove over an hour and toured Novi Sad, a city of about 400,000 people including its metro area, which featured an old cathedral, lots of little shops, and a long, dark tunnel leading to the Danube River. (How long is that river, anyway? It seemed to be everywhere.) The town square was rather small, but easy to get around with lots of hotels there, along with large bronze statues of statesmen and war heroes, and those lamps like you see in the Dracula movies (there would be plenty more of those later on in Romania). There were a lot of orange brick buildings around – maybe that was the "in" color 400 years ago. It rained, and I probably shouldn't have exposed my camera to so much moisture; this is where my desire to take an abundance of photos worked against me, because my camera stopped functioning! However, Fred took a look at it, fiddled with it, opened and closed it, and ultimately figured out how to repair it. I had a back-up camera but it wasn't as good, so thanks, Fred!!! We continued by visiting a fortress area, a museum, and a synagogue. The rain was a real damper, so to speak; I'd been so spoiled with great weather for so long, and now I saw what a difference it made. So there was a lot of "sad" here – the city name, the weather, and my camera stopping functioning (until Fred fixed it).

After this, we drove around the rest of the day and settled into a hotel, not nearly as nice as the Intercontinental we'd been in, but still good. We had a whole new experience waiting the next day. Before falling asleep that night, I thought how I enjoyed the anticipation of visiting a new city, and likened it to the anticipation you have when getting a gift-wrapped present – as we roll into a new town, it's like the first sight of it is the wrapping, and then you create your own gift by what you make of the experience. Even Belgrade and Novi Sad were fine; not every gift is what you hoped for, yet these make the ones you do like seem that much better.

Following breakfast the next morning in the hotel lobby, which included primarily meats (bacon, sausages, wieners), we were off and running again into Bulgaria. We started in the capital, Sofia, which has over a million people. I knew a bit about Sofia because the previous semester I had an exchange student in my class from there. In fact, when I told him when I'd be there, he said he would be there during this time because he would be attending a wedding. We kept in contact while I was in Bulgaria but we just missed seeing each other by about two hours (he got delayed). I saw him the following semester and shared my photos with him; he was impressed that we did so much in his home country. I was fortunate to make it back safely, because the drivers in Sofia made the taxi drivers in New York City look like slowpokes.

We took a tour of Sofia, and what stood out to me was this huge structure with five or more domes on it in radiator green or gold colors. It was neo-Byzantine and built in honor of Russian soldiers. Having been to all 50 state capitals by this time, it reminded me of a combination of some of those domes, but all on one building. These domes had rows of arch-shaped windows beneath them that made the whole structure look gorgeous! I wasn't much for churches or cathedrals, as previously mentioned, but I was really starting to get into the cool architecture. As beautiful as this cathedral was, there was even a more amazing one soon to follow.

About an hour's ride from Sofia, in the mountains, we went to an old Turkish monastery called Rila. I liked the Turkish architecture ever since my trip to the Alhambra Museum in Spain the year before. This building was very impressive as well, including beautiful paintings on its exterior. I loved the rows of striped symmetrical archways and their stark colors. There were a few very impressive architectural buildings in the complex. I had stopped going on the local church tours in general because it was getting to be like "You've seen one, you've seen them all" – but to the credit of the tour operator, the churches and monasteries we were visiting were truly magnificent. Rila is a UNESCO World Heritage Site, and having seen a few of these by then (including the Alhambra Palace), I began realizing that buildings with this stamp on it are worth the trip to see if you are in the vicinity. I even found the history of it interesting, and I don't normally care for such things. Rila was founded in the $10^{th}$ century and rebuilt in the 1800s after a fire. It's the oldest monastery in the Slav world. It has a spiritual and artistic past that I won't go into, but it does chronicle the tortuous and torturous history of Bulgaria itself.

We had a little extra free time so I decided to look for a new camera. Mine was acting up again, and my being without a camera on tour was like a person in the desert being without water. I ended up walking around with Fred and buying an East German (now German) camera with the brand name Praktica (another point-and-shoot) for about $100, made by Pentacon company in Dresden. I had never heard of it but Fred had and said it's a very good make. I went for it and used it for the rest of the trip. It turned out that the quality was excellent; I used it for the next 2 years and 10,000 photos. It seemed fitting that a traveler like me would use a camera purchased in a foreign country.

Our last stop in Bulgaria was Veliko Tarnovo – a former capital of Bulgaria and site of two uprisings about a hundred years apart against the Ottomans (circa 1600s). As such, there was an old stone fortress called Tsarevets in the hills. Fellow American Nancy asked me if I want to join her on a hike up to it during some free time. I agreed, and up we went, including a lot of stone steps and curves. There were great views of the city and the Yantra River – which leads into the Danube (of course). My former Bulgarian student had told me that the fortress lights up at night – which it did in multi-colors – and that the bells chime. I like when the historical meets the modern, and this was a spectacle to behold (viewed from both the city square and the large window in the lobby of our hotel). I could easily imagine a laser-light show there done to medieval-sounding rock music, like E.L.O.'s "Fire On High" for example (I can't get enough of those laser-light shows). My marketing mind never stopped working, as even some of my students had commented. As it turned out, our motor coach conked out on this hot, humid day, and we waited around for over two hours for a replacement. When it arrived, we headed into our final country on this tour, Romania – where my paternal grandfather was from (the town bordered Russia, but no time to visit). Upon arrival, our bus was sprayed with bird-flu disinfectant. As if that wasn't bad enough, we later learned that some of the meat we ate for breakfast our first morning there was horse meat, which gave some a post-breakfast queasiness (the "pigeon" effect, if you will, as mentioned in Morocco).

In a rural town, just before we headed into the main city, there was a wedding going on. Our motor coach slowed down to observe it. A lady who was part of the event invited us in for a drink. We were warmly welcomed, took a rest stop there, and crashed the wedding. I took photos of – and with – the bride and groom. That was a nice unexpected event. I wasn't about to start collecting wedding photos from other countries, but would later also get photos with the bride and groom from other countries in Europe, Asia, and Africa (all outdoors). Some brides and grooms even asked me to be in their photos taken by the professional photographer, so today they're probably looking at the wedding photos and asking, "Who is that guy? I thought he was from your side of the family."

In Romania, we started in Bucharest – a cosmopolitan city with some huge buildings. I walked around the university and also the Parliament building, which is enormous, the largest such building I'd ever seen by far! We were told this is the world's largest civilian building, and I even had to stand way back to get it all into a photo. The city name locally is Bucharesti, but close enough (unlike Florence Italy being called Firenze, and more like Lisbon being called Lisboa). Interestingly, we were told in Hungary that there was a movement to rename Budapest PestBuda because of its similar-sounding name to Bucharest, but this never happened. I was surprised to learn that Romania has 22 million people, much larger than I'd thought. I would soon learn there were other aspects of Romania that were large, if not super-sized, as well. The people there were extremely nice and welcoming of us. I'm sure the tour operator scouts out these places to ensure we are comfortable – which is why I go off on my own to see the real deal for myself. Even the surly Serbian gal was an education I would not have obtained had I just stayed within the boundaries, which I took as a net positive.

After the hike together in Bulgaria, Nancy and I became a little closer. She surprised me when offering her glib services in helping me meet pretty Romanian women with whom to take photos. For example, in one of the shopping areas, she would catch my attention in the jewelry shop she was in and have me come over. When I did, she would introduce me to the pretty employee and suggest that we take a photo together after some chit-chat. I don't think Nancy was being flip; I think she liked how I operated, having observed me doing my thing, and wanted to help. Nancy also did this in the pizza shop soon afterwards where several of us went to lunch. As it turned out, one of the servers was a model – and was featured on the cover of the menu! Obviously, another photo op – let's call this one part of the "special ops" unit: photo of the young lady, the young lady with me, the menu, the young lady with the menu, and me with the young lady and the menu. I try to get numerous photos for several reasons: some don't come out well (due to lighting, etc.); some have heads, limbs, etc. cut off depending on the photographer; I can select the best ones given more choices; and I need several photos to make a spread in my albums, which have two facing pages of six photos each (slip-in pockets). For years people had tried to get me to buy a digital camera, but I resisted, preferring film for the quality. But as the quality of digital cameras got better, I relented and did later buy one – especially so I could see the photographs immediately.

The most unusual event regarding Romanian women came that night at the hotel in Brasov. There was a young female singer named Dhalma, who was entertaining at a trade convention in the lobby. As she was singing the Frank Sinatra song, "New York, New York" (with a Romanian accent) to end the show, I happened to be coming down the steps behind her wearing a New York Yankees T-shirt and baseball cap. Some people in the audience who realized this coincidence started laughing, and she seemed flustered. I waited for her to finish the song, and then approached to introduce myself. I explained what happened and said they were not laughing at her. This made her feel better because she could not figure out what happened. We chatted for about a half-hour outside, in a park, and educated each other about our respective countries. She had to go back inside, but we would keep in contact by email for a while afterwards. Dhalma wanted me to sing a "New York, New York" duet with her at the end of the next show, but I wanted to have a night out on the town. We hugged goodbye. Well, no king of the hill that night, but there were no little-town blues, either.

I met more locals that night at a nearby bar and they were very friendly, relaxed, and interested in our tour (where it went, where it was going, how I liked Eastern Europe). The conversations were lively, curious, and refreshing. However, and this cannot be overstated, there were lots of stray dogs everywhere that curtailed my evening. This situation was out of control and a serious issue in the country. One bite could ruin the trip, so I did the "Stray Cat Strut" back to the hotel after midnight, and to bed. I definitely felt like I was in a Bela Lugosi movie at times, between the accents of the locals, the dark streets, the "Goth" look (including the street lamps), and even some little kids with long hair curls down to their cheeks. This was the real "Goth" before it was fashionable. Sort of cool, sort of scary. Soon enough, we would be visiting Transylvania – and Dracula's Castle.

After a bad night's sleep (nightmare about vampires, including Barnabas from a favorite childhood TV show, "Dark Shadows"), we toured Brasov before leaving it. It was a steamy, hot day and I didn't feel like doing much, plus I was tired having not slept well. We went to Peles Castle and Palace which I was reluctant to visit because I was "palaced and cathedraled-out" again, but Nancy – who was playing an increasingly important role – convinced me to go in with the group (saying I could sleep on the bus later en route to our next stop). I reluctantly agreed, and was soon glad she convinced me. Wow!!! Outside looked beautiful, but I've seen palace exteriors like that before. But inside...this was the most ornate "anything" I've ever seen! Red carpets, gold, art, sculptures, the immenseness and immaculateness...even the chandeliers were among the most impressive I've seen anywhere; combined, it created a synergistic surreal experience. I was awed, and put it up there with the most impressive buildings I've seen to this day. I thanked Nancy, who walked around with me, and also made another excellent suggestion in having us go to the botanical gardens.

We walked around a little more, and I noticed that a lot of guys in Romania, well, looked like me, and vice-versa. I could definitely see that I had family roots there; many people even approached me and started speaking Romanian thinking I'm a local. I became aware that while I'm an "American," my ancestors came from elsewhere, and this intrigued me because I never had a reason to give it much thought. I never did do an ancestry tree, but I probably will in the future as a result of this. I also thought about the drummer in the Vienna symphony orchestra; maybe he was Romanian, because we looked so much alike.

Finally, we went to the famed Dracula's Castle in Transylvania, called Bran Castle, in the Carpathian Mountains. Naturally, as soon as we arrived my mind started playing the Rocky Horror Picture Show tune, "Sweet Transvestite From Transylvania." We were given the history prior to arrival. A warrior named Vlad The Impaler, who fought over 500 years ago, is thought to be Dracula. His father was Vlad II and belonged to a group called Order of the Dragon ("Dracul" in local language) that was to protect Christianity in Europe. Vlad the Impaler fought off the Turks by impaling them and showing these bodies to prospective attackers outside the city as a way of warding them off. I guess between Dracul and the stakes through the bodies (and the blood), the legend of Dracula was born. In 1920, the castle was a royal retreat for the Queen, after which the Communists took control of it, after which it was returned and became the site it is today. Interestingly, many historians don't think this is the same castle from the Bram Stoker novel "Dracula" in 1897 because he didn't know of it then, but it became "the" place nonetheless.

There was definitely a well-done "atmosphere" about the castle. It looked spooky from the outside, up alone on a steep hill, surrounded by forest, with lots of orange (there's that color again) spires, and a bell-tower you could easily envision bats flying around. There were also some excellent views from above, at which I took lots of photos of the grounds below. There were lots of old-style horse-drawn carriages, too, amid the hills and forest, adding to the ambiance. We learned that "Transylvania" translates to "across the forest." There were lots of gift shops outside hawking everything Dracula. A little too commercialized for my taste, and this detracted from the spooky experience. The weather was a bit cloudy; some good soaking rain – or even mist – and thunder would have better befit the Dracula Castle experience.

It was not nearly as spooky inside but there were secret passageways and medieval-looking furniture making it plausible. Interestingly, the Romanian accent of the internal tour guide enhanced the spooky experience, at least to people like me from the U.S., which he may not have realized. The creative marketer in me wanted to see more of a spooky experience. I really think that if there were a surprise visit from "Dracula" appearing out of a creaking coffin, baring his fangs, and maybe running after selected people from the crowd, with fake bats being released, that would be sensational (and a real photo op). Some fog and sound effects would be good, too. This would be similar to the special effects used at Universal Studios®, e.g., with a visit from Jaws coming from the depths and baring his sharp pearly whites to a "boat"-load of tourists; or when "Frankenstein," appearing as a lifeless dummy, was a real-life guy and scared my friend Chris half to death by growling and grabbing him around the throat as he passed by. Those were many years ago, so maybe the rules have changed today with liability issues and all that (e.g., literally scaring people to death).

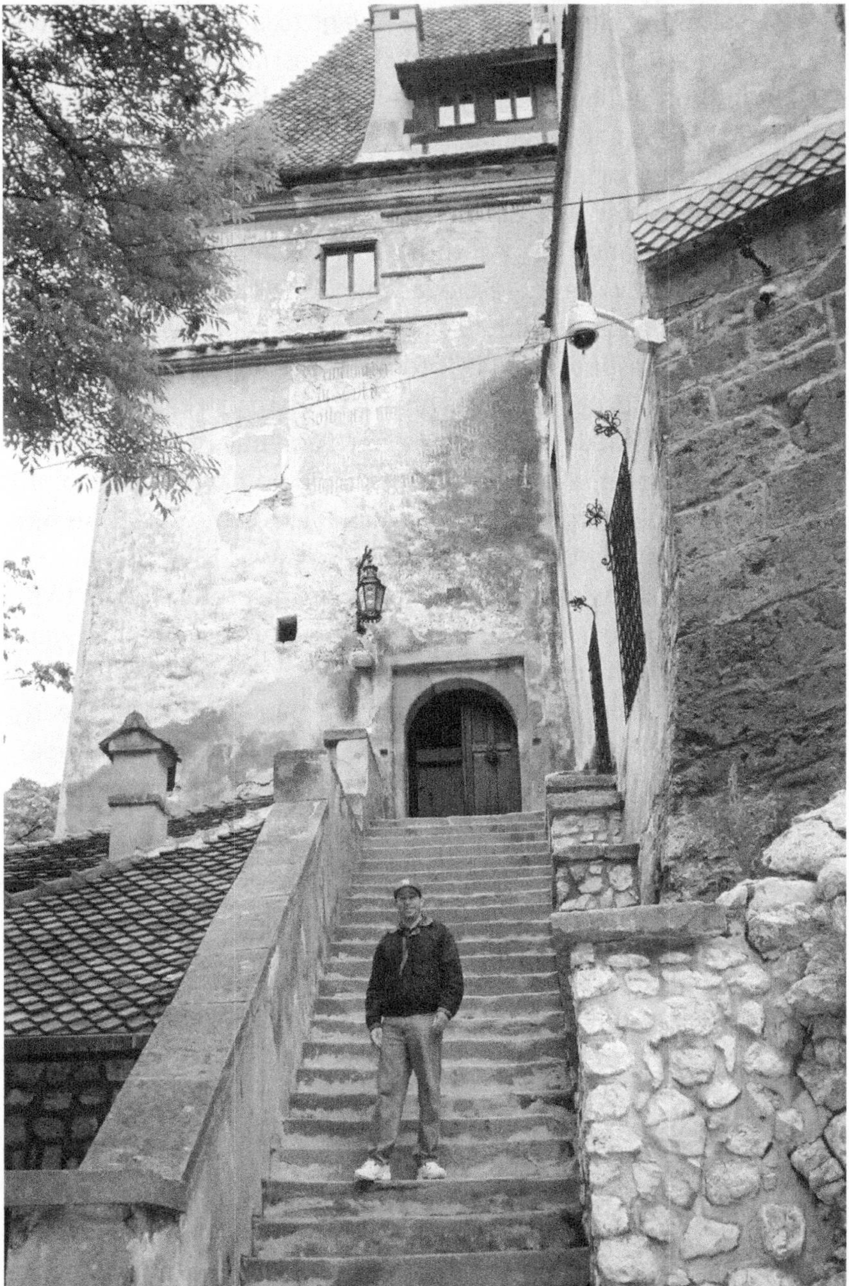

Bran Castle in Transylvania, Romania is also called "Dracula's Castle." More majestic than spooky, it features a secret passageway inside, and a balcony overlooking the forest in the Carpathian Mountains. There are lots of merchants outside the castle hawking everything "Dracula."

During some free time afterwards, I went to a coffee shop across the street. I said to the clerk, in my best Lugosi impression, "I vant to suck some coffee," but she just looked at me blankly, so I ordered in traditional English after feeling stupid. As I sat down, a guy there in his 20s, overhearing my bad impression, told me he's American too, and invited me to sit with him and his girlfriend who's from Romania (Brasov). James and the beautiful Viviana were living together in New Jersey, and were there on vacation. They liked it in Romania, but James had an issue with having to pay 50 cents every time you needed to use a public toilet. I told him about what I called the "burial ground" toilets in Central America where you had to refill the water tank in a muddy area, or dig a ditch and bury it, and suddenly he wasn't so upset. We took photos; it would have been cool if I got one with fake fangs (readily available across the street) to bite his girlfriend's neck, but I didn't ask. Where was Nancy when you needed her? – she was on a roll with getting me pretty women to be in my photos. I said a nice goodbye to James and Viviana, then went to meet up with the tour group.

Our tour group parted after hearing more about the dearly departed at the hands of Vlad and the fangs of Dracula. We headed all the way back to Hungary to end our tour, passing by more ornate gypsy homes adorned with silver tinsel-looking decorations. Some of my tourmates caught a cold, including my roommate, Fred – who unfortunately gave it to me. This would bother me for the rest of my vacation. However, I had an excellent tour and said my goodbyes before dashing off. We were delayed getting back to Budapest, and I barely made my connecting overnight train to Ljubljana, Slovenia to begin my next tour. Interestingly, I was struggling with my luggage which I had to hoist above my head to get onto the train car. Just then, a huge, extremely muscular guy I'll call Lerch, an employee who was already in the train car said, "I vill help you" and took the luggage from me. Had he not been there I'm not sure that I would have made the train. He later voluntarily brought me a pillow and some blankets for the long trip. That was very nice of him. In fact, nearly everyone I met in Eastern Europe was very nice to me in part, I believe, because I was respectful of them and their culture; smiled and was friendly; and attempted to speak their language, if only a few basic words.

In my train car were three young American students from Berkeley. They were cool guys I took photos with. They talked a lot about weed and drinking. I didn't tell them I was a university instructor within driving distance of their campus – partly because I didn't want them to feel uncomfortable with me, and partly because at that time I was Steve the traveler (I do not take the job on the road with me, unless the trip is for business). They were having a blast traveling through Eastern Europe, being rambunctious, and living la vida loca – and I commended them for that. I had to work my way through college, and never got to do this, I told them, so I'm making up for lost time now. They thought that was cool as well.

I met another young guy in his 20s on this train, from Korea, who told me of the perils of taking overnight trains, especially in this region, having done it before. I thanked him – but sure enough the next morning he was all upset that someone had come into his cabin and stole his camera! He had thought he locked his door but maybe hadn't. I felt badly for him; he was such a nice guy. Fortunately, he had a back-up camera, but it wasn't nearly as good. I told him about my Praktica, but he was into digital.

Another scary moment happened when an announcement was made soon before our arrival, in a language I wasn't familiar with. I was in a back car of the train and ignored it. "Lerch" again saved the day – he informed me at the last minute that I need to move to the front of the train because at the next station it sheds into a smaller one with the last several cars left overnight in the stockyard. Wow, thank goodness he told me!. Between "Dracula" and "Lerch" it was a "creepy and spooky, mysterious and kooky" experience that day – but I was learning a lot and experiencing life, and that's what mattered most!

I arrived in Ljubljana, Slovenia (pronounced as Lube-lee-ana, Slow-vane-ee-ah) at 5:00 a.m. to begin my next tour. I had signed up for the roommate option again, but this time did not have one. Good thing, too – my cold was worsening. I napped for only an hour because there was a 6:30 a.m. wake-up call for a group breakfast. I had missed the orientation meeting the previous night, but would be briefed along the way by the tour leader. It's a good thing I had notified the tour operator, again Cosmos, before the trip that I would miss the orientation because of the travel necessary for me to get from the first tour to the second one; had I not done this and was delayed, the tour may have well left without me. There were only 19 people on this tour, which went to Slovenia, Bosnia, and Croatia. My tourmates were once again older (retirees) and mainly from the U.K., Australia and, New Zealand.

We first went to a spectacular cave called Postojna. I had been to other excellent caves such as Waitomo Cave in New Zealand and several in the U.S., but this one was best. We took an electric train through the cave and it was immense, the largest I've seen. The cave is an estimated 2 million years old and about 17 miles long! After the train ride, we took a hike inside the cave with our guide, and saw immense limestone pillars, stalactites, and stalagmites. These seemed larger and longer than the ones I'd seen before, and were well-illuminated for tourists. The cave was "cool" in a couple of ways: the temperature was about 50 degrees - which was invigorating given my lack of sleep; and also the formations were otherworldly, ancient, and even had water passages with unusual-looking salamander-like fish swimming around. I had marveled at American buildings that were 200 years old, European buildings that were 2,000 years old, and now here were calcium formations 2 million years old! They sure did look prehistoric, and it was amazing to see this. My photos from the cave came out dark, which I suspected would happen, so I was glad I bought post cards from the gift shop at the end of the tour. I took some photos outside the cave entrance in the sunlight, which came out fine.

We then toured Ljubljana. My overall impression was that the city reminded me of a cross between Eastern Europe, Western Europe, and the Mediterranean, a hybrid of sorts. It wasn't quite any one of these but had elements of all three: there were the charming, colorful, European buildings and outdoor cafés along cobblestone streets. There were those orange-brick buildings again, with yellow and pink-colored buildings scattered throughout. There was another impressive castle, lots of pointy spires like in Romania, and large statues dedicated to politicians, war heroes, and others. Plenty of dragons and gargoyles, too, giving it that medieval feel. There were also artsy drawings, sculptures and other creative endeavors around the city. At several elevated points I got excellent panoramic photos of the city – lots of white buildings with red roofs amidst the trees. There was a river with several bridges over it, and many cafés alongside them. There I stopped in for a snack and met some local college students. They spoke English well and wanted to talk with me a lot, especially about the U.S. and my impressions of Ljubljana. I told them I just arrived with my tour group, but the cave was spectacular. One guy was part Italian so I said "Spettacolare!" and he smiled. These students (two guys and a gal) were into the arts and asked me about the museums in New York City. I gave them a briefing, recommending they see them some day. They aspired to go to the U.S., especially New York, and were more excited about doing so.

Our next stop was in Bosnia & Herzegovina which, like Serbia, was a war-ravaged country. Our motor coach had to follow a "mine sweeper" heading into the country that looked for unexploded bombs! This was not in the trip plans but if it had to be done, then it had to be done. After keeping a safe distance behind the automated device, the motor coach driver was given the all-clear to proceed. There was destruction all around, with some signs of a slow rebuilding. Here we saw numerous airfire bullet marks on the buildings still standing. It was the first time I had been to a place that showed so many signs of being in a war zone. We first rolled into Mostar, a Turkish shopping mecca, where I had a slice of pizza that looked like quiche and tasted like neither. Always the collector, I like to get pizza when possible in different world cities, and observe the different tastes. This one had none, and as Roseann Roseannadanna from "Saturday Night Live" used to say, "You don't know what it is." But that's what I get for eating pizza in a Turkish city in Bosnia.

Next we went to the capital, Sarajevo, in a valley with mountains around. This didn't start off well, but would get better. I immediately had a dispute with a local merchant over currency exchange. He had given me back too much change but I didn't realize it. He followed me around, spoke no English, and I thought he was harassing me, so I "Brooklynized" him (anger is universal). Our tour guide intervened and spoke to each of us. She explained that he gave me about a

U.S. dollar's worth of extra change, and verified this with the item I'd bought and the Bosnian currency I had taken as the change. I gave him the overage, he smiled and said something that probably translated to "thanks," and shook the tour guide's hand. I had the tour guide apologize to him for me. Everyone smiled and everyone was happy. Whatever.

Just after that, however, a very cute blonde came up to me and asked if I'm American. She may have heard me speaking (yelling) my second fluent language, Brooklynese, which engendered her approach. It turned out that she was a college student in Arizona, of Bosnian descent, and was there visiting her roots. Sanja was sightseeing with her mom, to whom she introduced me. We all had a pleasant conversation, and I would later keep in contact with Sanja via social media. Sanja looked similar to many female California students I was teaching, blonde and shapely, but I did not tell her (or most people) that I'm a college instructor for the reasons previously mentioned. Plus, in this day and age of social media, my explorations and exploits could be out there in no time. Interestingly, even on campus where I was teaching, I dressed down on my days off, causing students in my classes that semester, and even some faculty colleagues who passed me by on the street or campus, not to recognize me (I look 5-10 years younger in T-shirt/jeans/baseball cap). I also don't define myself by my occupation, and don't want others to define me that way, either. When I'm on vacation, I'm Steve the traveler; I'd already been identified as an American by various others, and that was enough of a stereotype to deal with. I'm even using a pen name for this book.

In Sarajevo, we stopped at the site where the Archduke of Austria, Franz Ferdinand, and his wife, Sophie, were assassinated by Serbians in June 1914, starting World War I. We saw the route of the motorcade procession and were provided with details of the assassination; the U.S. equivalent was the JFK assassination almost exactly 50 years later. It was eerie seeing and hearing about this, given the worldwide implications of this one action. There are different types of Bosnians in Sarajevo: Serbs, Croats, and Muslims called Bosniaks. I found the people there profoundly patriotic, and eager to rebuild the city. They were friendly in general and tried to sell me lots of things. I balked, but did take one person's advice and bought a pastry called burek which was minced beef in a filo-pastry ball, which was pretty good. I just walked around, bought my post cards, took lots of photos (especially of the war-ravaged places, which was something different I hadn't seen much of), and then returned to the motor coach. I found the visit worthwhile for the historical perspective.

From there we headed into Croatia, another part of the former Yugoslavia, and our motor coach again had to slowly follow a robotic minesweeper which searched for unexploded mines ahead of us that were still believed to be there from the recent Bosnian wars (lovely). To take my mind off becoming a potential fireball in Bosnia, I struck up a conversation with a tourmate who was a reformed rabbi and graduate of Harvard, Oxford, and Columbia for his undergraduate, graduate, and Ph.D. degrees, respectively. He started the Reform Jewish Movement in Israel 35 years ago, and was an incredible guy to talk to - very smart and articulate. An older married couple on my tour from Chicago gave me some cold medication they brought along that made me feel better. That was real Midwestern hospitality. I spoke with a few more tourmates; because there were so few of us, we were spread out quite a bit and it was no problem getting a window seat for the view and photo ops. But the down side was if you wanted to talk to others, you had to work at it since there might not be anyone sitting next to or even near you.

We arrived in Croatia, a very beautiful country on the Adriatic Sea, which itself had gorgeous turquoise waters. We headed down the Dalmatian Coast where I saw several Dalmatian dogs, white with black spots, where they originate. We went to Plitvice Park, which had picturesque waterfalls, and water color that was reminiscent of the "radiator green" hue I had seen in Lake Louise, Canada. Then we viewed an ancient city called Zadar, followed by the capital, Dubrovnik. There I hiked an impressive-looking fortress overlooking the hills with those orange rooftops again, lots of them! Were orange bricks on sale back in the day or what? If these manufacturers' ancestors somehow made their way to Egypt, the Pyramids might be orange! They looked neat and orderly, however, making for a striking panorama as viewed from above, especially against the blue sea. The city afforded many other panoramic and excellent views, including the waterways and even streets/plazas, especially in the Placa area with lots of cafés and bustling crowds. There I had a really strong espresso. I was still feeling the effects of my cold, but did not let it stop me from doing anything I would ordinarily do. We didn't spend a whole lot of time in Dubrovnik, but I would return a few years later and have more time then – including a neat experience with some trendy young Canadians.

Our next and final stop on the tour was Zagreb. We did the usual city tour, and then had time off on our own. Most people went shopping for the two hours, or to see more churches/cathedrals as we had done earlier. I walked around on my own, and totally lucked out by asking a local young guy what there is to do of interest there aside from the usual. He informed me that in a half hour there would be an international dance competition in a nearby outdoor square he pointed in the direction of, with costumed dancers from several different European countries. Well, I didn't expect that answer – but I was glad he told me. I returned to the motor coach just before the driver was about to drive off and got out more film from my carry-on bag. I arrived at the plaza early, just as the crowd was gathering, and took a front-row seat on the floor (there were bleachers for the viewing but I wanted to be as close as possible). Sure enough, at noon there came the buses, and out poured the dancers – in country-specific costume! They represented Croatia, Macedonia, Poland, Bulgaria and other countries. There were individual couples who danced and were judged, then many couples from that country dancing around. In sum, they were great – whirling, twirling, smiling, styling, and a few even did stop-motion right in front of me so I could capture the photo, after which I gave them a smile and thumbs-up. From the upward angle I had, a large sign reading Zagreb Bank in the local language above the dancing was visible, which gave the photos an added European flair. At the end of the performance I took photos with some of the dancers, who were very accommodating. There was a younger gal in her 20s who was rubbing my backside before a photo was snapped (was that a Za-grab?). The whole competition took about an hour, and it was wonderful – with nice weather yet again!

Back on the coach several tourmates said they didn't see me around and wondered if I'd gone back to the hotel to rest up with my cold. I then told them what I'd done, and they were in awe. The down side of telling my tourmates these things is that it can make the tour leader look ignorant of these events, but I made a point to say I learned about this from a local guy I happened to speak with, and that the event may not have even been published. That's why I do my thing locally; the churches, etc. are nice, but by asking around I sometimes find these hidden gems.

The driver then took us all the way to Ljubljana for a final city tour, and where our trip ended. I had another wonderful tour overall – and must say how impressed I was that these tour operators provided such a diversity of activities and beautiful places to go. I knew as a college instructor that my lectures needed to be a "one-size-fits-all" because there are slow, medium, and fast learners all in one class, so as an instructor you just have to pick a level somewhere in the middle and go with it. Land tours can have this diversification and more. Yet, they have something for everyone on these tours, and the free time gives the free-stylers like me an opportunity to fill the voids with activities specific to my tastes. Soon enough, I would be taking trips exclusively on my own, without any oversight, and that in itself would be a different kind of adventure.

Part of this independence began after this tour ended in Ljubljana, because I had four days left before my return home (using free frequent flyer miles to pay the airfare has its limitations), and so I had planned that after this trip I would trek around on my own to who-knows-where, being purely independent. I took a train back to Budapest where I stayed overnight. I toured the city on my own the next day, and came across a shooting in the street! No, not that type – a TV commercial. After the shoot, I spoke to the beautiful actress who was the star. She didn't speak English too well, and the director didn't seem to want me talking with her. The actress said it's OK to take a photo of and with her, and ironically asked the director to do it, which he did. Other onlookers then wanted the same but he barked at them and packed up. I never did find out what product the commercial was for (perhaps it was hair spray given the wind machine blowing into the models' faces as they walked).

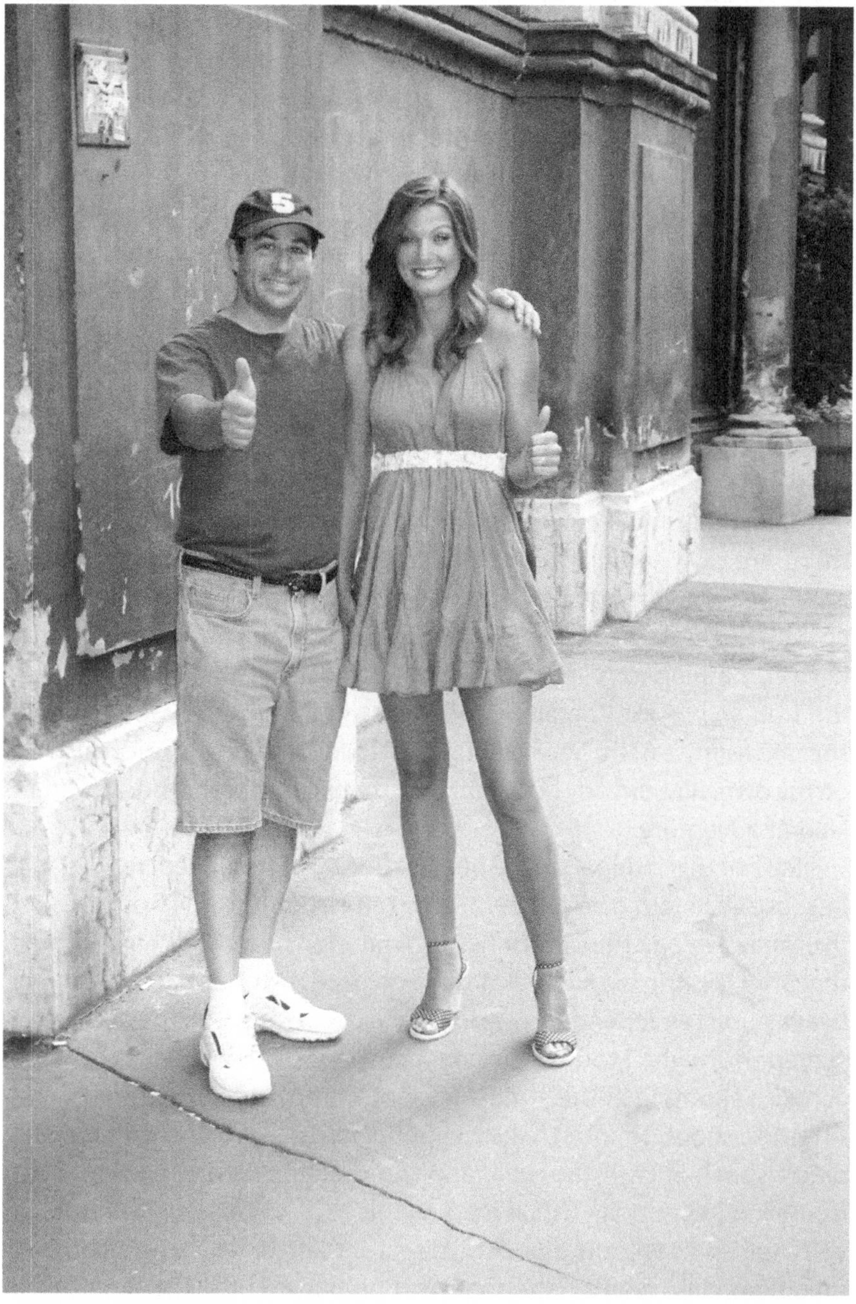

This actress-model was in an outdoors TV commercial in Budapest. I "waited it out" to chat with her afterwards. Naturally, I had to have a photo with her, in case she becomes the next Zsa Zsa Gabor.

I had planned to stay in Budapest the remainder of the time, and catch my flight home from there as previously ticketed. However, on the advice of a fellow traveler I chatted with in a café, he convinced me to take a 12-hour overnight train to Krakow, Poland which he said is a beautiful city – and would represent another country for me in my march toward 50 countries traveled to by age 50. It was well worth it. I left my luggage at the hotel in Budapest and took just a small overnight bag for the one or two nights I'd spend in Krakow (with no hotel reservations, just winging it). I sat with two lovely gals in my train car who were traveling together, one from Croatia and the other from Hungary. Both were in their 20s and spoke excellent English, as the younger folks in these countries often did. We had wonderful conversations about life, love, travel, and more. We all agreed that people are basically the same all over the world (my new "theme song" if you will, or even if you won't), war is stupid (their strenuous sentiment), and you have to separate the people from the politics (the flip side of my theme song recording, thanks to Sebastian). They had a lot of provocative ideas, were positive and invigorating, and gave me great hope for the future.

I arrived at Krakow at 8:00 a.m., found an inexpensive hotel recommended to me by an employee at the railway station, and checked in a half-hour later, planning to rest for at least three hours. Upon check-in I asked the hotel clerk if there is anything special going on that day. She told me of a tour that leaves in a half-hour going to the former Nazi concentration camps of Auschwitz and Birkenau. The clerk said I could pay her now for the ticket and get it right away, so that's what I did. I won't go into the grizzly details of what I saw, but I will say that it was shockingly moving and I became emotionally overwhelmed. Part of the reason for this was that so much was so well-preserved – hair samples, luggage with name tags, photos (and I mean more graphic than I'd ever seen), and just seeing the gates, the railroad tracks, the barracks...a great sadness just enveloped me and others there, who were openly weeping. I expected a basic, suitable-for-the-family museum and tour, not that! But I'm glad I got to see it, and more importantly, feel it. This made Schindler's List look sanitized by comparison, and that was a powerful movie.

I returned to the hotel and stayed overnight. The next morning there was another interesting tour I booked, to see the underground salt mines (something new and different). I didn't know what to expect and was surprised by what it was. This huge salt mine was founded over 700 years ago and mined table salt. But it took a long time for the miners to get in and out, so they carved religious icons in rock salt so they could worship (Catholicism) right there in the mine. These sculptures are impeccable and incredible. They include altars, religious icons, saints, even a church with chandeliers! It had a cave feel to it – chilly, waterways, but I guess you could say it was sub-lime, in a matter of speaking. This was another intriguing find, something I never knew existed.

I walked around Krakow and was impressed by what I saw there as well. It was a classy-looking place with horse-drawn carriages in the main plaza, lots of well-kept cafés, sparkling clean windows, and just lots of upscale elegance. There was also a Royal Castle called Wawel (pronounced "Wah-vel"), other historic buildings, monuments, street entertainers, and many museums. I had to have a Polish sausage, and it was delicious (flavorful, meaty). There were the usual cobblestone streets, archways, and surprise – not as many orange buildings, which gave way to lots of yellows and green-iron domes. The weather was good for walking around, and I did a lot of this as well as mingling with the locals. I met the Vice Counsel to the U.S. Embassy, a nice guy in his 30s, who helped me when I was looking at my street map, perplexed and lost. He gave me directions, and we chatted for a while (he's from Chicago). He offered me a personally-escorted city tour if I ever return, and seemed pleased that I chose to come all the way out to Krakow from Ljubljana.

I spent one more overnight in Krakow, checking out the night life, which was pretty good. The women were beautiful, so my college ex-girlfriend from Poland was the rule, not the exception! I was surprised at how small the dinner portions were in Europe in general, compared to those in the U.S. I believe this was a major factor as to why I rarely saw an obese person in most of Europe, especially in Eastern Europe. While many of these women were gorgeous physically, I did not see them being gorge-ous from a food standpoint, that is, did not gorge themselves. One told me she eats a lot of "sa-lahd" (the way she pronounced salad, with emphasis on the second syllable). I spoke to two female friends in their late 20s sitting together about this. One said the price is a factor; they don't want to spend so much money. The other said, while taking out a cigarette, that she and many other women there smoke to stay thin. "If I smoke, this replaces food for me, and it's cheaper than eating." I hadn't thought of that. I asked if this has anything to do with wanting to look sophisticated, or like the people in the movies. They looked at each other, then me, and said, "No." Later in the conversation, one asked me how I can afford to travel so much, "if you don't mind me asking." I replied, "I use my tobacco money." They asked, "What do you mean?" I said, "I don't smoke, or drink a lot for that matter, or do drugs, and instead save this money for travel. Add it up," I said, "and you will see over many years how much you can save." They made a quizzical face as if to say, hmmm. "If you stop smoking and save enough, come visit me in the States and I will show you around." I gave them my contact information, but never heard from them. My bet is they're still smoking.

After a good night's sleep, and feeling better from the cold, I spent the next 30 hours getting back home to Northern California, including a 13-hour train ride from Krakow to Budapest, 9-hour flight from Budapest to New York City, 6-hour flight from New York to Sacramento, and then drove to where I live and work 2 hours away. I was exhausted, but happy after this 42-day trip! What a wonderful time (again!). I spent the next 3 weeks editing, sorting, and labeling my 2,800 photos (an expense that needs to be considered when planning a trip – it can add up). The entire trip, all expenses included (photos, too), cost me less than I planned. I would gladly do it again, even at a higher cost, because in the end, seeing/learning/feeling/doing is priceless.

I was exhilarated at this point – new career, new city, new people, all this traveling, all this new learning – it was like a Renaissance at a time in life when most people plateau or even start declining. This natural high translated to my work – many students would comment on the evaluation form that I have a lot of enthusiasm for the subject matter, and in general. I'm glad this was evident, because several got excited about marketing, and a few even changed majors to study it, as noted in a subsequent reference letter from my boss. I taught that next semester well, and by this time was very comfortable in my new career. Soon, I was even given a second course to teach at night, Sales Force Management, that not only had a full classroom, but was also simulcasted via 2-way television to another campus 70 miles away, with 20 additional students in that class. I really felt great in my personal and professional life, and this gave me the confidence to take even more and bolder trips.

# Chapter 13

## Easy As A-B-C: Argentina-Brazil-Chile

I was in full-swing with my travels and in life. The next year I would visit an incredible 40 countries and 12 states! So much for getting to 50 countries by age 50, I was shooting for 75 now! During the winter break from teaching, I had more than five weeks off during intercession, starting mid-December, and I went travel-crazy. I sought the warm weather and vacationed for 37 days including Caribbean cruising; a visit to visit my family in Florida; and then a trip to Argentina, Brazil, and Chile for one week each, going solo again with Gap Adventures. I was told this trip was not as extreme as the Central America trip a year ago, but that it's not an easy one, either. Fine, bring it on, I wanted a rematch.

At the U.S. airport I was pulled aside by Security and "randomly" checked. This wasn't uncommon for people after 9/11, but I noticed it was happening to me more frequently – I believe precipitated by the various country stamps in my passport. Later, at my hotel, I saw that my checked luggage was also searched, but that as usual the contents were folded up more neatly than I had packed them (never anything missing). This was an inconvenience of traveling during these times in the world; it didn't bother me, but it was something to allow more time for when planning a trip (I had cut the timing too close a few occasions).

The other passengers and I jetted from Miami to Santiago, Chile on December 30th, and I took some terrific photos from the plane window as we flew over the Andes Mountains. At the airport, I asked the customer service desk personnel to find me a safe taxi, and they called one for me. Having heard the horror stories, I learned to ask (at hotels, airports) for reliable and safe taxicab companies – whose reputation with those establishments relied on safe, comfortable, and fair treatment of their customers, and whose drivers spoke English, if possible. Note that I often sneaked a photo of the taxi from behind (including plate number) in case anything bad happened to me; if my camera was found, there would be some evidence as to what may have happened. My driver was an extremely nice guy who even took me on a free city tour as we meandered our way through the city to the hotel. We went to a park overlooking the city, and the Royal Palace. Both times he let me out to take photos, and he took a few of me as well. I thanked him, he appreciated my big tip, and I checked into my room. The taxi drivers often provide tours (less expensive than the advertised tours), and the driver gave me his card in case I wanted to see more. I took the card but it wouldn't be necessary to call him.

I met the rest of my group at the hotel, another 14 people who were all very nice and representing the U.K., Australia, New Zealand, Ireland, Hong Kong, and a couple from the U.S. I lucked-out again by paying a lower trip cost to share with a roommate, but not having one assigned this time, so I had the room to myself for the same low price. The temperature was 85 degrees when I arrived mid-afternoon. I would, unbelievably, once again get lucky with the weather, just missing two heat waves in Argentina and Brazil in which the temperature was 110-120 degrees right before we got there for a "cool-down" to mid-80s each time.

I was rarin' to go, and met the group for the orientation and dinner. We had a 24-year-old French female tour guide named Veronique who spoke fluent English, French, Spanish, and Portuguese. She warned us not to go downtown to the New Year's Eve celebration the next evening because of the potential crime situation. Everybody agreed. Except me, but I didn't say anything. Veronique said she booked a dinner show for us all that night, so we would have a good time celebrating the New Year. Introductions were made. During mine I ended it by telling people not to be offended if I don't stick with the group during free time; that I tend to go off and do my own thing, but if others would like to join me darting around and photographing everything, meeting the locals, etc. I would welcome that. Some did throughout the trip; most didn't, which was fine with me. Others preferred to be on their own as well. Tours like this, which are one step away from being independent tours, attract people like that.

The next day we took a city tour of Santiago, getting an early start. I enjoyed the terrific views of the nearby Andes Mountains overlooking this busy, active city. There were the usual plazas with statues honoring war heroes, Plaza de Armas in the city's historic district, a sculpture park (I like these a lot), and free time to roam, photograph, and do whatever. So I spoke with several locals and got a flavor for the city – literally, after being recommended some food, including empanada de queso (cheese wrap) and espresso. I was told the night life is great and that downtown used to be very dangerous, but is "not so much" now. The young people I spoke with were driven to be successful and make a lot of money. They dressed well, spoke English well, and wanted to know where the tour was going. They were impressed with the itinerary, and we wished each other well. I walked around with some other tourmates briefly, and then caught up with them later after they decided to go shopping. I like to make the most of my time out; spending more than a few minutes shopping just isn't my thing on vacation, although, as mentioned, I will pick up post cards, T-shirts, caps, fridge magnets, and other knick-knacks that are small and fit into my crammed luggage. On this tour, I met some people who didn't bring more than a couple of T-shirts, preferring to buy them in cities we visited. Not a bad idea. Some even disposed of the T-shirts when we left that city, wanting to travel lightly. I thought about this again a few days later, when lugging around my 40-pound backpack to the more remote areas we'd visit, but kept to the status quo.

We went to the main part of the city in Santiago, and after another tour were provided with more free time – for me, that meant time for my first misadventure (what's a trip without at least one of these, which was becoming par for the course?). A young guy who was dressed well was handing out leaflets on the street (I didn't notice what for). I wanted to try the pizza in Santiago, and asked him where is a good place to go. He told me to follow him to a nearby place that had smoked windows, and said what I'm looking for is in there. I walked in, and as soon as I entered, a pretty, sexy hostess, wearing lingerie and fishnet stockings, sat me down and called over a half-naked girl who immediately sat on my lap, fondled my balding head and hair, and said in broken English, "What would you like?" Oh boy, here we go again! "Two slices of pizza and a Coke®," I said sheepishly." "What? she said, working her way down from my hair. "Pizza," is there any pizza here?" Believe it or not, I still thought I could get some pizza there. "We have pizza ass," yes, right here. You like me?" It dawned on me that maybe the guy with the leaflets thought I had said "pizza ass." Now, I was looking for the pizza and she was looking for the sausage, LOL. I couldn't help but smile when this thought crossed my mind – which she took as a sign of interest. Things got a little more serious after that.

I was brought over a "free alcoholic drink," which I refused in a polite way upon arrival, by another half-naked girl (making one wholly-naked girl between the two of them!). This new gal tried to cajole me into drinking it, and sat on the other half of my lap. When I said I need to be going, that I'm on a tour and the coach is waiting, one gal got up and said, "Choose one of us. Or both. Bring your coach here and you can each have one of us." There was a language barrier, although no clothing one it appeared, as this temptress was popping out all over.

I said, "Thank you for this offer, you are both beautiful ladies, but I thought this was a restaurant where I could get pizza. The guy handing out the papers outside said so." "He works for us," one gal said. "Now, are you going to choose us?" I replied, "No, sorry," and started to get up, pushing away the other gal on my lap who was resisting my movement. The more talkative of the two gals said that I have to pay "30 dollars" for the drink (I didn't touch) and the time the two girls spent with me (who I didn't touch). I said, "Listen, I got to go" and then the taller one, about my height, blocked my path. "You pay now!" she demanded. OK, time to switch into Brooklyn gear. "No!" I said, raising my voice. "I am leaving now and we are done." She immediately called over the bouncer, who held a big searchlight over his head and shined it down on me. He told me to pay. I refused. He said to go to the back room with a girl and the price would be the same as for just the drink. I said no thanks. He insisted I pay. I still refused, and wasn't backing down. At this point, at just the right second, I pushed my way past all of them and out into the street. The door opened behind me. Images of the Hungarian police chasing me down ran through my mind. But nothing happened. I just glared back at the guy. And so ended my "cheesy" pizza experience. I did go elsewhere and got my pizza. And yes, I made sure it was a pizza place before ordering anything. And yes, I made the motor coach on time. And yes, I thought of the John Fogerty song lyric, "Put me in coach, I'm ready to play" when the half-naked gal thought the "coach" was an actual person. I did not tell anyone about this misadventure except for a few select friends back home.

We went to a winery and this was magnificent. I'm not big on wines, but the scenery and the wine itself was awesome (free samples were provided)! I had recently taken the wine tour in Napa Valley, California, but this was even better. The history of the winery, and how the wine was produced, was explained to us. I learned a lot about this, which was good because wine was important to the region in which I lived; in fact, some people had names for the aficionados in the industry, such as wine nerds and cork dorks.

We arrived back at the hotel. While with the rest of the group in the lobby, I made a night-altering decision in telling the tour guide I will go downtown for New Year's Eve instead of joining the group for the dinner and show (which cost extra). This decision was largely driven by the great New Year's Eve I'd had a year ago in Guatemala, and, well, I was much older than my tourmates, not a drinker, and really wanted to experience the local celebration, camera at the ready. Veronique said "OK, but you must be very careful, and you must take a taxi that you have the hotel call for you. This is very important. Coming back you might not be able to get a taxi." I told her not to worry, I'll figure it out, and that I'd meet her and the group the next morning at the designated time. I then went to nap, but overslept! The wine plus the action-packed "pizza experience" had taken their toll. I shot out of bed, saw it was already nearly 10:00 p.m., and went to the hotel lobby. I asked the clerk if it's possible to get a taxi. He said no, this was not possible. I was determined to get downtown, and asked if there's any other way to get there. He told me that I could walk to downtown but it's about three miles and is dangerous ("peligroso"). I thanked him, and tried to flag down a taxi. No such luck. At least the weather had cooled off.

I ended up walking the three miles, but not without some detours. A policeman saw me walking by myself, dressed fairly well, and asked where I'm going. I told him, and he warned me not to walk there. Further, he said if I did, not to take the route I was going, but to walk down a few major streets to which he directed me. I wrote these down, thanked him, and continued walking very briskly, asking for direction confirmations at these points. However, at one point the streets were empty and it got a little dicey, but I just kept on the move. Finally, I arrived and there was a huge reveling crowd getting ready for the stroke of midnight. Bands, balloons, shouting, smiling, laughing – I was getting back into my happy zone from this contagion. I joined in, got some excellent photos, and I must say that the people were just as nice as could be. They let myself and other photographers in front of them briefly to snap photos of the performers, offered to take photos of me (of course I returned the favor as usual), and many hugged and kissed me, and shook my hand at midnight amid the stunning fireworks display. There was that Carnival atmosphere again, but no stilt-walkers or fire-jugglers that I saw, anyway. This was worth the effort, fulfilling, and I was very happy I went.

I stayed out until 2:00 a.m. and then...how to get back. Still no taxis available, so I started walking...and walking...and walking. A policeman again stopped and questioned me. I told him where I was going and showed him the hotel card, hoping he would drive me there. He redirected me toward the larger streets and avenues ("avenidas") and told me to be "very careful." There were still a lot of people out, and I pulled a bit of a slick trick: I walked behind a group of younger, well-dressed people, close enough where I could be perceived as being part of their group, yet far enough back so as not to arouse their suspicion (a judgment call, using my instincts again). This worked well with a couple of groups I encountered, and I arrived back at the hotel safely. The clerk who told me about the taxi situation, Raul, was still on duty, and we looked at each other. "You made it," he said with a smile. "Si," I said. I confirmed my wake-up call with him for three hours afterwards, went to my room, and went to bed. A most interesting day, and evening. Sometimes the equation can be me + adventure tour = misadventure, but generally even these are worthwhile learning experiences and are the exception, not the rule. I continue to be cautious, but undaunted, because my goal is to maximize my happiness in life without interfering with anyone else's goal to do the same. And be safe and healthy while doing it.

The next morning at breakfast I was told the dinner and show were "expensive and boring," and asked what I had done. I told them, and they were impressed I went downtown by myself. No-one (including the tour leader, Veronique) asked me how I got there and back (assumed I took a taxi), and I didn't bring it up that I walked. We left for the airport to head to our next destination four hours south: Bariloche (Bar-il-oh-chay), Argentina, in the Patagonia region, surrounded by lakes and nearby glaciers – where the weather would be refreshingly cooler (since we were far south of the Equator). Our hotel was in the snow-capped mountains, and I again lucked-out with a room that had an incredible view of them accented by a gorgeous lake (I'd heard that most people's rooms did not have a view). This was picture post card material, and I took numerous photos of my rustic cabin-room and panorama of the views. I was thinking that either Gap was making it up to me from last year's experience to Central America, or I was just very fortunate. Either way, this was awesome, and Gap was in my great graces!

The employees in the hotel, two guys and a gal in their mid-20s, took a liking to me and made me fantastic-tasting hamburgers at midnight (lomo burgers?). We had lots of laughs and fun, they were great. And the gal, Mariella, was absolutely gorgeous, and to this day is one of the most beautiful women I've ever seen. And speaking of heavenly, I walked into town a couple of times and found heavenly chocolates, among the best I'd ever had. So in my first day there I had experienced among the best views, burgers, chocolates and beautiful women I ever had. I was really liking this place! I went to the Patagonia Museum (not that interesting), but later on came across a guy with a beautiful St. Bernard rescue dog and got some great photos of and with "Bernie." For some reason animals like me a lot, and despite this guy warning me about his dog's reaction to strangers, the dog cozied right up to me and even looked right into the camera when I asked him to. There was also a show put on by the locals including mimes, magicians, comedians, and dancers against the beautiful mountainous backdrop. It just didn't get any better than this; I was having a blast, and everything there seemed to go right. I bought a Bariloche cap and wear it proudly to this day. It acted as a bat-signal years later to another guy who noticed it, had been there, and we had a great conversation about it. So Bariloche even had an excellent residual effect, and was just one of those magical places for me.

We continued into Southern Chile, moving to Punto Arenas, at the southernmost tip of the country, which featured awesome glaciers that reminded me of Antarctica. Then it was on to Puerto Montt, which featured a mountain that looked a lot like Mt. Fuji which I had seen less than a year earlier. This near duplication seemed a bit odd to me, but I suppose there were lots of them in the world I wasn't aware of. Punto Arenas also had gorgeous water at its peninsula, with a nearby penguin colony. If Antarctica is out of your reach or price range, then Southern Chile might be for you. The people there were also very friendly and welcoming – you sensed not just because you were a tourist, but because they genuinely liked people. After my total experience there, I found the name Chile a misnomer, based on the warmness of the people, anyway.

My tour group next arrived in Buenos Aires. The first thing I noticed was that the women looked incredible – even better than last time, if that was possible. We had a free day, and I told the tour leader I'd be walking downtown alone. She again told me to be very careful. On my stroll I met a woman from California named Doris who was headed toward the spot at which Evita Peron addressed the Argentinians from the now-famous balcony. We walked through a dangerous neighborhood to this location, and took photos of each other when arriving at the main site. I then continued to the La Boca area which I had visited during a previous trip, remembered well, and wanted to explore again. Once more there were those colorful buildings, and professional tango dancers in the street who dance with you for a couple of dollars' tip (one U.S. dollar equals three Argentinian pesos). I hung around this area, and ended up dancing with a tango dancer later on. I got the full leg-on-knee treatment again, and of course, more photos. I met other people, including a couple of gals with whom I stuck my head in cardboard cutouts of male and female tango dancers. There were lots of shops there, a historic Caminito cultural area which inspired the tango dance, and a seaport, too, with tall wooden ships. On my walk back, I happened to pass by the tango place I had such a good time at during my previous visit to the city, Bar Sur, and wanted to see if my favorite dancer still worked there. Alas, it was 3:00 p.m. and the establishment wasn't open yet. I never did get back there during this trip.

Finally, as I walked back to the hotel, I came across two beautiful local gals in their 20s who chatted with me over coffee. They wanted to know what I liked best about their country. I mentioned the steak, colorful buildings, tango, scenery, weather, outdoor cafés, and last, but not least, the beautiful women, which made them smile. Then my honesty got me into trouble. One asked, "So, with all your travels do you think the women of Argentina are the most beautiful in the world?" I said, "Second best." "Who is first?" this gal asked angrily. "Sweden," I said. "I like the striking Viking look." Wrong answer, to them, anyway. "You think they look better than us, than all this?" she said, cajoling her friend to strike a sexy pose with her. "Well, OK, for brunettes it's Argentina and for blondes it's Sweden." The vocal one replied, "Well, next time you're in Sweden you tell those girls that the women of Argentina are better-looking, OK?" I just smiled – not because I agreed, but because I imagined this being even better than my camera-trick to meet women. I was clever and said, "I'll tell you what. Let me take a few photos of you, and I will compare these to the photos I have of the Swedish women, and then I can decide."

The gals said OK firmly, walked me out into the street, then posed sexily individually, together, and with me to the astonishment of a few onlookers and people I asked to take photos of the three of us. Not only did I wonderfully enjoy this, but I immediately thought of "strike the pose, there's nothing to it" from Madonna's song "Vogue." In my mind I rhymed "Caminito" with "taquito" and "Buenos Aires" with sexy "mujeres" (women). I was just having fun – no worries, no stress, just being happy, and that's all I really wanted. If it didn't come to me, I was going to find it or make it happen. I later thought how I should have said after this, "You know, I'm also making a list of which countries in the world have the best women to sleep with ..."

At night, the tour group went to a steakhouse, as I had done last time on tour there, and I told everyone that the lomo steak is just fantastic in Buenos Aires. Most people ordered it (many probably would have anyway). The steak was again tender, juicy, and seasoned just right. I don't normally rave about food, but this was totally steak-tacular! All for $10 U.S. including all the trimmings. Several tourmates and I took photos of our steak at various stages of consumption, including the juiciness, and said this was the best steak we'd ever had. This time, the expression "stick a fork in it" was a positive – because you could cut the steak with just your fork! Upon asking about the steak preparation later on, I learned that the cattle there are fed only natural foods, with no steroids. I guess this makes a difference. But they don't hit as many home runs, LOL.

Next we all flew to Iguassu (E-gwa-su) Falls – the waterfalls Sebastian told me is more picturesque than Niagara Falls, and is among the top three in the world. This waterfalls separates Argentina from Brazil, is also near Paraguay, and it didn't disappoint! It's about 3 times the size of Niagara Falls, has over 200 separate cascades, is in a forest, and gets 1 million visitors a year. Funny that I hadn't heard of it until last year. The name "Iguassu" means "big water." Legend has it that a god planned to marry a beautiful woman named Naipí, who fled with her mortal lover Tarobá in a canoe. In a rage the god sliced the river, creating the waterfalls, and condemning the lovers to an eternal fall. There are walkways from both the Argentina and Brazil sides where you could see this cavernous cascade up-close. Many of us took a boat under the waterfalls, much as you can do at Niagara Falls (on Maid of the Mist), but were cautioned not to bring our cameras, which would probably get soaked. I made a last-second decision to bring my camera and was glad I did (nobody else from my group did). I got some spectacular photos, and fortunately protected my camera well from the soaking mist. I had learned my lesson about bringing a back-up camera, and had a comparable one in my luggage - the Praktica if needed, helping in my decision.

Although it rained while we were there, I took many photos during a brief patch of sunshine, and these would come out extremely well. We all got a real soaking under the Falls, but no complaints here. I'd feel as if I missed something if I didn't get a good soaking. Later in the trip a few tourmates were mildly upset with the tour leader for strongly cautioning them not to do three things I ended up doing that were major highlights of the trip for me: going downtown on New Years' Eve; walking to the Caminito area from the hotel, supposedly "dangerous"; and taking my camera on the boat to photograph Iguassu Falls. As mentioned earlier, you have to make your own judgments on these trips. At this point I was an experienced traveler, a relatively younger single guy from a big city, in excellent health, and took calculated risks. The tour leader was just doing her job, and I didn't blame her for erring on the side of caution in her role. I told this to my tourmates, but this did little to mollify some of them. We did, however, take a group photo there.

Here's my tour group at Iguassu Falls, on the Argentina side.

Our group then went in a jeep to go zip-lining in the jungle as an optional tour. I passed on this because I wanted to see if I could get into another country, nearby Paraguay, during the same duration. Veronique told me it's too risky with the timing, that I may need to pay for a visa at the border (cash only), and that if I do not get back in time it would be very expensive for me to meet the group at the next city destination's hotel. This time I listened to her and didn't go. A year later, however, I would get there – and the proximity of Paraguay to Iguassu Falls would be a topic of conversation I would have with a high-ranking person there.

We spent the next day in Brazil, seeing Iguassu from the Brazil side, which was even nicer than seeing it from the Argentine side because you can see the whole panorama. Some tourmates liked the Argentine side better, but most preferred the view from Brazil. They were both amazing, and you can't go wrong with either one, in my view (pun intended). I later learned that Iguassu Falls is a UNESCO World Heritage Site. As mentioned, these designated sites are awesome, and in the future I paid attention to which ones had this certification.

Interestingly, the main language in Brazil is Portuguese; Spanish is the main language in all the other South American countries, although other languages are also spoken. We stopped off at a small town called Paraty, 125 miles south of Rio de Janeiro, in which we spent two days. This was a charming place. Quaint shops, white stone homes with colorful doors, cobblestone streets, a boating area, bay, beach, street mimes, and beautiful busty women rivaling those of Argentina. I could have done with spending one day there instead of two, but this gave me time to sleep-in one morning and go at a relaxed pace. The women enjoyed the shopping or spa, and I watched a couple of NFL playoff games broadcast in Spanish. Maybe this was good luck because my favorite team, the Chicago Bears, beat the New Orleans Saints to advance to the Super Bowl. Back in the U.S. years later I would meet a gal from Paraty, Brazil who was shocked I'd been there and knew so much about it (including watching guys in the stores paint wooden boats that they sold right afterwards).

Our final stop on this magnificent tour was Rio de Janeiro, a must-see if you're in Brazil. It rained a lot during the past month, which was highly unusual, but when we arrived the weather was generally fine.

We took a tram up famous Sugarloaf Mountain, and also went up Corcovado to see the world's largest Jesus statue atop that mountain (not the same one as Sugarloaf, as some people think). I got some great photos of the Jesus statue, especially from an Italian guy who was lying on his back taking photos of his girlfriend so he could fit in the entire statue behind her. Before he got up I asked if he could do the same for me, which he did. I then did the same for him and his girlfriend, getting them both in with the statue. I also got superb photos of Sugarloaf Mountain, the city below, and the beautiful beaches of Copacabana and Ipanema (those two old songs came to mind, Barry Manilow's "Copacabana – the hottest spot north of Havana" and "The Girl From Ipanema"). We then stayed at a hotel near Copacabana Beach, went sightseeing in Rio, and our tour ended there. What a great trip! I was again very impressed with the variety of places we went, pace, activity options, and safety concerns (not that I always observed them). We all thanked our tour guide and driver verbally and monetarily, and then said so long to each other with appropriate contact information exchanges. I told Veronique that I will be staying three extra days in Rio, and asked for advice. "Don't go out at night," she said - "there's a lot of crime here." But she knew me by now and added, "But you go out and enjoy, whatever you do." We wished each other a good trip back. Another French person I really liked!

During my extended stay, I primarily went to the beaches, watched the beauties, met a few, and took photos. The cloudy/drizzly weather returned along with a lot of humidity. I didn't really mind. I got to know Rio, and was surprised that a city this size (10 million people) was so laid back and not hustle-bustle. I sampled the local foods, and believe it or not found great hamburgers at a place called, of all things, Bob's! Other local foods included pizza (of course) made with cream cheese, gumbo made with chicken instead of shrimp, and little shacks along the beach that had coconuts, fruit shakes, hot dogs, and more. I grazed quite a bit with little meals here and there. You still had to be careful about where you ate, making sure it's clean, and beware of tap water (again I drank only purified water). Because Rio is so diverse, there are many ethnic restaurants with good food, too. The prices were again amazingly low, so there was a lot of value to be had.

The locals in Rio were fun and friendly, and are referred to as Cariocas. They love their fútbol (soccer) there, and even told me that I should not wear the colors of the rival teams! I didn't have a pen and paper to make a list, but they weren't kidding. There's a mixture of Indians, Europeans, and Africans there, too, and even some groups from the Middle East. It was a melting pot like New York City, but with a Southern California theme with the beach, sun, mountains, water activities, and laid-back atmosphere. An interesting cross-section if you like big cities.

I walked around a lot during the day, and don't ask me how but I ended up walking on the roof of the posh Copacabana Hotel, from which I was taking photos (the police passing by made me come down). I basically took it easy and slept a lot. As it turned out, because I was so tired I didn't go out much at night, just to some places within walking distance, including seeing a Samba dance which was excellent. This turned out to be a good thing because on my flight home I had a seatmate, a guy my age, who told me he was robbed at knifepoint in Rio at night, and that the two gals who came into the police station after him were carjacked.

So, it was back to California, all happy and tan, glad I went on this trip and again appreciative I returned safe and sound for another round of teaching for the Spring semester – during which time I would meet Lana, who I casually dated for the rest of my time there. Lana was from the local area and worked in the medical field while later becoming a part-time lingerie model. She took me around to new places, all the way up near the Oregon border, where I would stump people by asking if oregano comes from there. More teaching, more learning, a new person in my life, and more happiness. This was all going very well, and I continued my upward trajectory with a nice balance of work hard and play hard, even as I soon approached age 50. I also continued planning ahead for more trips by doing the "credit card shuffle" – taking advantage of deals that provided airline miles as incentives for signing up. Many banks were giving enough to obtain a free trip after a minimal purchase, with no strings attached. Now having the free time during non-teaching months, this turned out to be an outstanding opportunity that enabled me to enjoy more travels than would have been possible.

# Chapter 14

## European Odyssey – Eastern, Western, And Central

That summer I had three months off again. My desire to travel was insatiable, and I couldn't wait to do more. I booked three consecutive tours that even my travel agent suggested I not do based on the grueling schedule, adding that she can't imagine anyone having the stamina to do it all. Further, these were via three different tour operators, none of which I had traveled with before (combined, they had the schedules and destinations I needed). However, I figured I endured two consecutive tours last year, and wanted to maximize my airfare dollars as long as I was flying all the way from California to Europe again. By now you know me: I went for it anyway, and had an exhausting but wonderful time. Ironically, it was the travel agency that couldn't handle it properly, as will later be explained (surprising because the agent did a good job before). The tours encompassed countries in the United Kingdom, Baltics, and Balkans followed by Russia, Greece, and Turkey. These would be with "comfort tour" operators and include time on my own in Turkey at the end. There would be multiple cities visited in each country. The weather would range from 40 degrees in the U.K. to 110 degrees in Greece, so I also had a lot of clothing to bring in my luggage. This vacation, too, had its share of adventures and misadventures, but in the end I was very happy I ventured out.

I arrived via overnight flight to London's Heathrow Airport, and planned to take a train from there to the area near my hotel. I was toting a carry-on bag with the tour operator's logo that was sent to me in advance, spotted at the airport by one of the reps, and told that I'm entitled to a free transfer to the hotel. I said I hadn't paid for this option but was told I'm entitled. So, I went with the group arriving at the airport near the same time I did (the tour operator is informed of passengers' flight itineraries). As it turned out, I was right and hadn't paid for this option, but the tour operator let it slide. I walked around London on my own seeing the usual sights including Big Ben, Parliament area, Tower Bridge, and excellent aquarium before returning to the hotel for the group dinner/orientation. We had a distinguished British tour guide, a gentleman circa age 55 named Simon, who was well-dressed in a suit and tie befitting the upscale nature of the tour operator and the older, upscale tour passengers. His dapper appearance and British accent added a touch of elegance to our U.K. panorama that would take us to England, Scotland, Northern Ireland, Ireland, and Wales, in that order. This was the only upscale tour I had taken thus far, and I paid the extra cost because it got me to all those places in the U.K.; had it not, I probably would have returned to see the other places missed, and spent another airfare. So, there was value in paying the premium price for this tour, if that made sense. The motor coach driver, Peter, was also British, and carried everyone's luggage onto the coach. It beat doing it myself (or having a guy like Lerch bail me out last-minute), or walking around with a heavy backpack, although more of that would be coming in future trips.

There were 45 of us – again, with the usual demographics of mostly older, retired people, couples, mainly from Australia, New Zealand, Canada (only a few from the U.K.), and only 4 Americans (the "10%" effect, again). My one takeaway from the entire trip was green hilly sprawl, mountains, oceans, beautiful landscapes, occasional gray skies that made for an appropriate backdrop against the greenery, hard-charging waves crashing against the rocky shores, and medieval castles. We started in London and traveled north to the large county of Yorkshire, which had a population of five million and was larger than some other countries I'd be visiting on this trip. On a rainy day in Leeds, there was an old-style locomotive train billowing gray smoke, and the motorman let me take photos with him. In York, I once again realized that my hometown of New York City was named after this place, for the 17th century's Duke of York. Prior to that, it had been named New Amsterdam by the Dutch in the early 1600s. Similar to New York City, York itself was very compact and easy to walk. Most major sights were walkable within 20 or 30 minutes – or sooner, if you're a fast New York City walker like me. I made the most of our time there, darting around and enjoying the historic sites as well as the cafés, at which I had Yorkshire pudding and "a spot of tea." Lots of history there, medieval churches, streets of red brick, and Bavarian homes with whimsical architecture, exposed brown beams, and hanging potted plants.

Our next country visited was Scotland, including both Glasgow and Edinburgh. As we crossed the border into a small town called Gretna Green we came upon a Scottish wedding, and a band with guys dressed in kilts playing bagpipes. I was very intrigued by this and took lots of photos after our group was granted permission. Many guys walking down the streets did so in kilts, reminding me of when I was in Bermuda 16 years earlier and seeing guys on mopeds in suit jackets and ties wearing Bermuda shorts. There were many kilt stores – lots of plaid designs, as you might imagine. I particularly enjoyed a Scottish dance we attended in a restaurant, and had a good tableside seat for taking excellent photos. After this I happened to walk outside, and had a mental orgasm seeing a lone bagpiper dressed in kilt and caubeen (Irish beret) walking around a green, hilly area playing a tune. This was the image I had in my mind when hearing the mid-1980s song "Shout" by the British band Tears For Fears, at the end of it when there is what sounds like a bagpipe instrumental to me (probably a guitar or a keyboard, however). I took photos of and with the bagpiper, and this provides another retro blast-from-the-past when I look at them today. It's not often a fantasy and reality come together, but in this case it was spot-on.

On the motor coach, a Scottish gal in her 30s, Maggie, on tour with her husband, sat in the seat next to me and wanted to speak about travel and my keen interest in taking photos. She recently started traveling and wholeheartedly agreed with my desire to capture as much as possible in pictures, adding a line that I often thought about in later world travels: "Once the travel bug bites, you're smitten." Maggie said she "suffers" from this (with a big smile) and could tell I was "infected" as well. I said, "Yeah, I have been into many small churches called mosque-itos, and got mal-area there." She laughed.

We talked about our photos of vacations. She wanted to know how I know which photos are from where after I get them back, with so many that I take. I shared with her my strategy: each day on every vacation I'd write down what I wore, so that when my photos come back from processing I'd know where they were from! I've heard many fellow travelers lament that they received hundreds or thousands of photos back from their trips, and didn't know which city or country they were in! That's why, when possible, the first photo I'd take in a new city included the city name (on a store front, e.g., or "Welcome To" city or country sign if available). I'd then know that the photos taken after that point and before the next city sign were from that area. I'd also double-check this against my clothes list to be sure. As crazy as this sounds, I continued, I also foresee that I will create a photo album later on, and therefore try not wear any article of the same clothing from another city in that same country (except shoes). So, for example, red shirt, blue jeans, white sneakers in Glasgow, and blue shirt, beige slacks, brown casual shoes in Edinburgh. I even go so far as to not wear the same exact combination of clothing in any city on the tour, although a partial combination is OK, since this may be unavoidable. Or, I told her, alternatively you can decide on the "T-shirt-from-every-city-visited option," which would obviate my methodology. Maggie thanked me for the advice, took her regular seat, and I could hear her excitedly tell her husband what I'd just said. I did not see her wearing local T-shirts, so perhaps she took my initial advice.

We headed into Glasgow, and the first thing I noticed was that there was an auditorium that was armadillo-shaped, similar to the famous Opera House in Sydney, Australia. It was the only other time I saw this design, which is striking and different. I liked that there were large banners with the word "Glasgow" hanging all around the city, because this enlivened the photos, provided the city name I sought to begin my photos from that area, and enhanced the feeling of being in a faraway and different place. We took a city tour, and I darted here and there taking photos, as usual. However, in speaking to the people in Glasgow I couldn't make out what they were saying! Not only the accent, which was supposedly in English, but some of the words being used. This was worse than the cockney accents I had heard in England, and more incomprehensible than anything "Scottie" ever said on "Star Trek." We rode around a lot, too, with the tour guide narrating the sites. I would have liked to stop off and take a photo of the Sherlock Holmes statue near Scotland Yard, but the coach kept going. These tours are well-timed so any request to stop and get off is up to the judgment of the tour leader. With many elderly people on the tour getting on and off the motor coach, some with canes, e.g., this could take a while in itself. I tried to take photos from out the windows but often was unable to do so this time when sitting in an aisle seat. I supplemented my photos with post cards, including one of the Sherlock Holmes statue.

We then headed to Edinburgh, pronounced Edinboro, birthplace of Sean Connery. This city was green and hilly, sort of like Buda in Hungary. The accent there was a bit easier to understand, and the people there didn't much like those from Glasgow (rivalry). The Edinburgh Castle, located on Castle Rock, was the main attraction, and sat atop an extinct volcano over 400 feet above sea level. It was said that human habitation there goes back to the 9$^{th}$ century, B.C. Other than that there wasn't too much that interested me. The people there seemed aloof, maybe they were shy, or maybe I just didn't meet the right people. I sampled the malt beer there, which was pretty good, but I would have better beer in Ireland a short time later.

On the ride toward Northern Ireland, our tour guide, Simon, asked if there were any questions thus far. I had a couple – and they sparked a very lively discussion among the generally reticent passengers. I asked how many countries we were visiting on this trip (so I could count them toward my goal of 75). I did not expect the shocking dialogue. Simon (from England) said that the U.K. and Ireland are two countries, and that's it. Others, including Maggie from Scotland, were in disbelief because Scotland, for example, had its own currency (Scottish pound), parliament, and other independent considerations. I had asked this question when in Scotland of some locals, if Scotland was a country, and all said yes. Well, to make a long conversation short, some felt we were going to five countries and counted them as such (others were also country-counters), and some agreed with the two.

When I returned home, I checked into this and found that England, Scotland, Northern Ireland, and Wales are technically four autonomous regions but all part of the United Kingdom, which is a country. Ireland is a separate country, so two seemingly was the answer there. However, when we got to Northern Ireland and Wales, the people there said they live in an independent country. Also, International Travel News provides its "United Kingdom Travel Award" for visiting "all four countries in the U.K.: England, Northern Ireland, Scotland and Wales." So, you decide. I also met people who counted Antarctica as a country. As one guy on my trip there said, "After all this, you bet I'm counting it!" I found it interesting that technically Antarctica is not a country, but that Vatican City is. For the record, my Aunt, Arctica, was counted as a person but not a country☺.

Another point raised was what happens if you go to a country, such as the former Yugoslavia, that now broke up into six different countries – do you count it as one or six? There was some lively debate about this as well, but more people felt that it's one if you went there when it was just Yugoslavia, and more based on each country that developed from it as long as it was an official country when you visited there. I agreed with that, and would soon be visiting these new countries. As for the converse being true, say if Yugoslavia reunited, then most people said they would still count the countries they went to when they existed, in which case you could have technically been to more countries than there were listed in the world.

After that intriguing dialogue, we still had a lot more time before getting to Northern Ireland, and I raised another question: how many countries does a person need to get to in order to be considered a "world traveler?" This one created even more controversy. It seemed everyone had an opinion – a different one. Our tour leader wisely opted out of this discussion until the very end, when I cajoled him into his point of view. The range among the passengers was from 20 - 80. Some felt that 20 was enough to get a flavor of the world, while even those who agreed stated it depends on which countries, i.e., are they geographically dispersed? Others said they should include at least four continents, while still others said the cultures need to be vastly different in at least several of them. From those who thought the higher number was appropriate, the argument was that you couldn't get a real flavor of the world in so few as 20, that you needed to visit at least five different continents (some even said six), and at least a couple of cities in each country as we were doing on this tour. Then the conversation devolved to what constitutes being "to" a country, which was "familiar territory" to me from the same question I brought up during the Calais, France motor coach ride three years earlier. Oh boy, here we go again. The range was from a few hours, especially for smaller ones the size of towns with not much to do, to days or even a week. One guy said if you set foot in it this should count, another said being in the airport should count, and one person shocked us all by saying that flying over the country should count because "you're breathing the air" of it while doing so. Everyone disagreed with that. There weren't any tempers being shown here, but several people were passionate about their opinions. Mine was 50 countries, minimum 4 continents, with enough time spent in each to get a flavor of the place, depending on your own pace.

OK, it was time for "Simon says," as I called it. Everyone looked at him, but he was ready for the challenge. His opinion was "a minimum of 40 countries, but not most being comfort countries." He made the point that you could cruise to a lot of places and not exert too much strain, even stay on the ship in port and say you were there, but that really shouldn't count. In essence, he was saying that you needed to go out and get a feel for the country, at least doing some activities that provided this. Bottom line: it's open to interpretation, and whatever floats your boat (or cruise ship, as the case may be). I did not consider myself a world traveler until my 50th country visited, which was when I reached Dominica, by which time I had already been to all 7 continents. Call me a hard grader (some of my students did), but by then I felt comfortable with this self- designation; several people felt I earned this well before that time.

So, next we traveled into Northern Ireland, Belfast in particular, and this represented a whole new landscape. The first thing I noticed was the ubiquitous big, bold, and colorful graffiti on the walls of a very political and scary nature, showing masked terrorists, guns and bombs, with anti-U.S. messages (war in Iraq), and the word "Revolution" written a lot. I had a really excellent conversation with a male college student at the university who told me of Northern Ireland's history and fight for freedom. There was still tension between the Catholics and Protestants, but not as intense as before. This guy I'll call Ben had a good sense of humor, and was very forthcoming about the pros and cons of living there, which included the oncoming change yet the slow pace at which it is coming. I came away with a feeling that Belfast was rebuilding and going to be OK, it just needed some time. I had stated my usual point of view about how we're all in this thing together, so let's make this world a great place to be, and a great life. That's why I liked teaching at the university; I fed off the energy, promise of a better tomorrow, and new ideas by the students (I did not tell Ben I was an instructor). Ben and I shook hands heartily; we appreciated the exchange of information about our respective countries, and our shared philosophies of life. I walked around a bit, but we didn't spend too much time there. I was impressed with the great architecture (Victorian), mountains surrounding the city, and people, who I found very friendly and helpful in general.

Next we rolled into Dublin, Ireland. The first thing I noticed was lots of pubs. I spent time in O'Neill's (black storefront with shrubbery above it, gold lettering, and on a street corner). I just had to have a pint of Guinness which is made in Ireland, and it was phenomenal! I'm not really a beer drinker, but thoroughly enjoyed it as I looked out the huge Victorian windows to the street and had a hearty chat with the bartender, Connor. I told him I'm interested in the derivation of names, and asked him if Ireland or Dublin meant anything in particular. I thought Ire-land had to do with anger, war, and revolution (on my mind since I'd just come from Northern Ireland with the graffiti), but he said it has to do with a historic queen who wanted the country named after her. Dublin means "black pool" but he didn't know why (was there oil there, I wondered?). Then he said his name, Connor, means "hound lover" which I thought was interesting because I love basset hounds. I didn't see any there, but did in England – longer and heavier than the one I grew up with back home which was of the French variety (smaller, and cuter). While on the topic, Connor told me about the history of Molly Malone, and a famous song set in Dublin about her. She was a hooker and there was a busty statue of her in a conspicuous location on the street, which I later visited. She looked like the Dolly Parton of her day; my Guinness mug wasn't the only thing overflowing based on the sexy statue. I met a couple of college gals from Boston at the statue who also wanted pictures of and with it. We had one taken of the three of us there as well. They loved Ireland, and were visiting their roots (ironically, they had colorful, dyed green hair).

Speaking of colorful, I was very impressed by the famous Doors of Dublin – colorful doors of the symmetrical Georgian townhouses that were said to be of different bright colors because the women of Ireland were tired of their husbands coming home drunk, going into the wrong home, and sleeping with the wrong woman! There is another story that the doors exist because, after the death of Queen Elizabeth, England ordered Ireland (still under British rule) to paint their house doors black to mourn the Queen, but the Irish rebelled and painted them assorted bright colors. However you look at it (literally), there is a colorful history behind them! There was a famous montage poster made of the Doors of Dublin by a New York City ad agency guy who was visiting there, and it was later used for the Irish Tourist Board. These houses created a cool mosaic as you walked down the street, which commanded your attention. Beautifully done!

I walked around some more, visited different pubs and restaurants (prices were steep), and spoke to more people. I really liked the Irish, who I found to be lively and fun in general. This befit many Irish people I knew back in New York City and Buffalo, too, including an ex-boss, ex-girlfriend Doreen, and current friends. They tended to be young, outspoken, bold, witty, and fun – my kind of people. Lots of laughs, and for some reason they liked to debate me. They loved their sports teams. They also loved their music; several were surprised that I saw U-2 in New York City's Greenwich Village just before they hit it big in the U.S. (I still have the 45 rpm record for "I Will Follow" which was their encore song that night). Ironically, my date that evening had the very Irish last name of Kennedy, and said she was a member of that famous U.S. political family. I also later liked The Cranberries a lot, including the haunting voice of its female lead singer, and wondered if the lyrics from the song "In Your Head" which include "with their guns and their bombs" inspired any of the graffiti I had seen in Northern Ireland, or vice-versa.

We also toured the Waterford Crystal Factory, and learned all about crystal. There's a self-guided tour you can take of different areas including molding, glass-blowing, cutting, sculpting, and engraving. There were some amazingly beautiful crystal pieces there with precision craftsmanship and perfect-looking. I liked the transformation of the heated glass into crystal; it was like nothing I'd ever seen, and mesmerizing when the fire became glass. Whenever I saw crystal afterwards I thought back to this, realizing the artisanship it took to get it from what it was to what it was going to be. In an "aha" moment, this made an impression on me: I realized that, metaphorically speaking, I, too, was transforming, having a "burning desire" to travel the world, and was "molding" myself into a new, higher-quality person. I believe in transforming yourself from time to time, because there is so much opportunity to become a new and better version of yourself – you just need to figure out what works best, before the "engraving" on your tombstone. Travel was certainly the ticket for me.

That evening, our group went to an Irish step-dancing performance, and it was great! I'd been a big fan of Riverdance, which I saw on Broadway twice, and truly enjoyed this performance as well. Afterwards, there was a cheesy comedian who basically told bad jokes about a dummy named Murphy. Boo-hiss. Bring back the dancers!

On the last day of this tour we reached Wales, featuring a number of castles. I was very impressed with Cardiff Castle, which I accessed by walking along a finely manicured green lawn on which I ended up meeting a guy from Canarsie, the section of Brooklyn where I was raised! I had asked if he would take a photo of me with the castle in the background and, recognizing my accent, he asked me what part of Brooklyn I'm from (us Brooklynites recognize it just like that). He was a fireman, and we chatted about the old neighborhood for a while. Another "small world" story. But not really – many people do not realize that Brooklyn by itself has well over two million people – and if it were a city it would be among the largest in the U.S.! There is a sign to this effect in the intro to the old "Welcome Back, Kotter" TV show of the late 1970s. That he was from my specific neighborhood was unusual, however, because it is not nearly the most populous in Brooklyn. Then again, maybe not, because Howard Schultz, Founder and Chairman of Starbucks, is also from Canarsie.

Cardiff Castle was medieval and had an impressive, well-decorated clock tower including colorful figurines of people dressed to task back in the day. The time theme was emulated in the interior as well with painted signs of sun movements and zodiacs. There was a lot of marble (including statues); colorful and impressive glass art; and smoking rooms fit for a king. This medieval symbol that still stands today seems as if it could have inspired the Excalibur® Hotel in Vegas, Dungeons and Dragons , the Goth movement, and Disney® with its large and fantastic opulence. I was able to envision what it might have been like to live there during those times, and enjoyed the retro experience, if only briefly and in fantasy.

Other "historical" notes from Wales included actor Richard Burton and singer Tom Jones hailing from there (I thought of several of his songs while there – "it's not unusual" for me to do that). Naturally, I had the Welsh rarebit there and it was delicious. We also saw Cardiff Bay and Millennium Stadium; rugby was a big sport there, and people were passionate about it! The weather wasn't bad that day (it can be inclement there a lot), so I got some pretty good photos. In a way, I wished it was overcast because the castle would look more striking against a gray backdrop, but no complaints on any sunny, warm day in the U.K. There were plenty of people on blankets on the green lawns just hanging out, reading, eating, talking – reminding me a bit of Central Park in New York, but with a giant 800 year-old stone castle behind them. There were also red hop-on, hop-off sightseeing buses riding around, but there wasn't time to take any of these. I would take these around a lot on later trips in other countries.

We then headed back to London via Salisbury, Bath, Stonehenge, and Stratford-Upon-Avon, all of which I had been to many years earlier when vacationing with Mike. I enjoyed these places yet again, took numerous photos, and bought more post cards as usual. The tour leader did me a huge favor – we were running late due to traffic, and instead of dropping me off at the hotel, he had the bus driver drop me off at Heathrow Airport so I could catch my next flight to Kiev, Ukraine. I had anticipated that I might not have time for the hotel first, based on the tight timing, and had brought my entire packed luggage with me. It was especially good that this happened because I hadn't realized that the connecting flight (within Europe) had a lower weight limit than my overseas flight to London. So, to avoid paying a huge surcharge for the overage, I needed extra time to ditch 10 pounds of clothing to make the weight limit (which didn't thrill me, but tossing an old back-up pair of heavy shoes was about half of it). The airline was very strict about this despite my explanation of the situation. This was frustrating but I learned in the future to check weight and other baggage restrictions on each flight I'd be taking within the itinerary, not just the ones to and from the U.S. Most snafus on this trip would happen at transfer points, and I would soon have another one upon landing at the airport in Kiev, Ukraine (formerly of the Soviet Union).

I was not supposed to go to the Ukraine, but my travel agent messed up and booked me on a second tour, which began in Helsinki, Finland before the first one ended! So, to make up for this mistake, the travel agency flew me to the Ukraine with one night's hotel at its own expense, and then I paid for the flight from there to St. Petersburg, Russia (second stop on the new tour), just as I would have had to pay from London to Helsinki (worked out to a lower price for me). Well, at least this got me to a new country for a day on my own that I might not have gone to were it not for this happening.

It was after midnight when the plane landed in Kiev, Ukraine. The airport was almost empty, and two guys approached me in black leather jackets. One was very large with his black hair combed back, looking like a Russian version of Bowser from Sha-Na-Na. The other was my size with blond hair and balding. I did my best to avoid them, but soon the big one (nearly the size of Lerch) said to me in broken English, "You speak English? You need taxi?" I said, "No, thank you" and walked away figuring I would ask at the front counter for a reliable taxi to my hotel. But there was nobody at the front counter; in fact, the airport was deserted except for a security guard and a couple of other passengers who soon left. I obtained my luggage, went outside the airport, and it was even more deserted. So back inside, the two cabbies were still there and approached me. "You still need taxi?" the big one asked. The smaller guy just smiled, showing his gold teeth. He continued, "No other taxis tonight." I said, "Wait here" and asked the security guard if he thought I'd be safe using those taxi drivers. In a classic statement, he looked over at them, looked back at me, and said, "For me, yes. For you, I'm not so sure." Well, that was...reassuring. My choice became sleep at the airport until morning with a lot of luggage (not an option), or chance going with one of those jokers. I returned and asked if they are both together, or separate. The big one said, "I am one and he is one," which I assumed meant that they were separate. I then said, "I will go with you," pointing to the smaller guy, with my sole rationale being that if anything should happen (e.g., attempted robbery or worse) I would have a "fighting chance."

I gave him the address of the hotel, and he piled my luggage into the trunk. At night, I couldn't catch a photo of his license plate without the flash going off and alerting him, so I memorized it. He said to sit next to him, not in the back seat. I sat in the back seat and said I am more comfortable there. I then wrote down the plate number, and stuck it in my pocket with the date and time on it. He asked me where I'm from. I replied, "New York, Brooklyn" (where there are a lot of Russians in some sections). He asked if I am Italian. I look it and said, "Why do you want to know?" "Mafia?" he asked. "Maybe," I replied, wondering if he meant Italian or Russian. He asked why I'm in Ukraine. "I'm here on a mission," I replied (well, I was: to have a nice vacation). I think this scared him, because he was quiet after that. We got to the hotel, where he helped me with my bags. I gave him a good tip (had exchanged dollars for rubles in the London Airport). He smiled, showing me those pearly golds, and nodded. I said, "da," which is one of only two Russian words I know, It means yes, which didn't apply, but it was nearly 2:00 a.m. and what the heck, I tried. The driver gave me his card, "For ride back to airport." I then thought, "I don't know about this," and the only other Russian word I knew came to mind, "nyet" (meaning no), which at that time made me think of the BTO song, "You Ain't Seen Nothin' Nyet" (I wished I could turn off that musical association part of my brain at times, but I guess my brain knows when I need a laugh).

The hotel concierge ran out to greet me, and helped with my luggage. When booking my hotel in that city, I had specifically sought one that had 24-hour service, for an occasion such as this, and often sought out hotels with this 'round-the-clock flexibility during my solo travels since delays often happen. I got to my room and fell asleep immediately. The next day I walked around the area; my hotel was centrally located so I could see several tourist sites. The first thing I noticed was how this place reminded me of Brighton Beach, Brooklyn, which is heavily Russian and nicknamed "Little Odessa." I had to have the chicken soup, latkes, and chicken Kiev! I had the first two for lunch and they were excellent, but at another restaurant for dinner when I asked why there is no chicken Kiev on the menu, I was given a strange look. They don't call it that there; to them, it's just chicken. Although the menu was in Russian only, a nice lady there who spoke a little English knew what I wanted and prepared it for me (boneless rolled, breaded, deep-fried chicken breast stuffed with garlic butter and herbs). It was outstanding! I praised her and the chicken (more smiles, with only one gold tooth).

The weather was rainy and chilly, which put a damper on my photo ops, literally. And it was Sunday, so many places were closed. However, I saw the main sites including the gold-domed buildings and the Opera Theater. These were OK, but nothing special. So I just moseyed about, snacked here and there on local foods (I checked with the hotel staff as to where and where not to go), and met more people, mainly younger ones who spoke English fairly well. But not too many people were in the vicinity, and after the taxi ride the previous night I didn't want to take much public transportation. I also had a lot of vacation ahead of me, so I made an early day of it and evening, too. I would have liked to spend another day there and maybe go to some museums, but I had to fly to St. Petersburg the next day to meet my tour. As it would turn out, almost exactly one year later I would have a co-worker in the office next to me of Ukrainian descent (name and all), and also attend a Ukrainian Festival.

The next morning I left for the airport, and had the hotel call me a "safe" taxi. It would have been funny if the previous cabbie showed, but I got a new guy who was very nice. He even let me stop off for a photo op in a shopping plaza that had the sign "Welcome to Ukraine" in English. He let me stop off for a few more photo ops as well. However, I spent so much time doing this I was late to the airport. Then I almost got screwed big-time. There was a much longer line than I had anticipated at the security section, and it was moving at a snail's pace. I was not going to make my flight at this rate. So I asked a guy way up the line if I could go in front of him (New York City moxie) after explaining my reason and moving toward the spot in front of him. He nodded, and I did (he may not have even understood English). Just then, the security guard (not the one when I first arrived into Kiev) came over and asked in broken English what I'm doing. I told him, and he said to go back where I was. Frantic, I told him I would miss my flight. The others in line said nothing. I continued with my pleas, in a very nice way, and finally the guard said, "I will let you move ahead only if <u>everyone</u> in front of you says it's OK. They have flights too. If one person says no, then you stay where you are." He then made this announcement to the waiting passengers in three languages, and seemed to enjoy this superiority.

I went to each person, starting with the one ahead of me. He said "tak." I looked at the security guard, who nodded to me ("tak" means "yes" in Ukrainian). The next person, a blonde-haired lady, looked me over and said "da." The security guard said, "She's Russian and says OK" – which made me realize right then that this was like playing Russian roulette. In my heightened state, my mind also immediately jumped to the Police song, "De Do Do Do, De Da Da Da" which was my way of hoping "da" would keep coming up (otherwise I was in deep doo-doo). The next few people said yes and, thankfully, one guy who spoke English as a second language said to the guard,

"Can you just ask everyone if it's OK?" The guard did this, and asked everyone in line up to the guy I initially asked to step in front of if it's OK. I just stood there with my hand luggage and said, "I'm really sorry, but would you please be so kind to let me in front of you this one time? It is just me with a small bag." Well, I lucked-out! I turned to the guard after only about 10 seconds after no-one said anything and asked, "May I please go ahead?" He just looked at me – and it could have gone either way. He just waved me ahead with a stone face, and I said "Thank you." I thought about trying to say it in Ukrainian or Russian but I had no idea how to say it and didn't want to mess-up by potentially insulting him. So, I made my flight but barely. Maybe I had a saint after all – great weather in general on my trips, the guard letting me go ahead, and now I was heading to St. Petersburg. Strange things would happen there, too, starting immediately upon arrival.

I arrived in St. Petersburg, Russia and had an unusual incident at the border patrol: I was detained for a few minutes because the border agents saw that I looked Russian and were surprised I was not, based on my U.S. passport and spoken English. So they had to get a supervisor who, after asking me many questions, finally believed I am an American tourist (and not a double-agent?) and let me in. I then started thinking of the Beatles song "Back In The USSR" although this was my first time in Russia (Ukraine was formerly part of it, however).

There was more confusion to follow. Upon arriving at the hotel, I learned that the tour leader was not informed that I wouldn't be meeting the group in Helsinki the first night of the tour (i.e., the previous night). He had been frantically looking for me all over, and nobody knew me or where I was. I explained to him what happened, and he reconfirmed with the tour operator at headquarters that I was not supposed to arrive in Helsinki, but there in St. Petersburg. Communications breakdown, but I was there now. This gentleman, Yuri, was a nice older, well-dressed gentleman of the Simon ilk, but who was Russian. He briefed me on the orientation he had given, the do's and don'ts, which were like the other tours. I then said I was glad my flight got in early because I was hoping to make the city tour on the itinerary for that afternoon. He said there'd been a scheduling change; that day would be a free day on our own, and the city tour would be the following day. I wasn't wild about this, because had I known about it, I could have perhaps stayed in Kiev the extra day when more attractions would have been open there. So, I met the tour group and went around on my own. I needed the day to decompress anyway; I'd now been traveling for a while, schlepping heavy luggage, and was out all the time primarily sightseeing. We were about to embark on a tour of several European capitals – and based on the extremely high prices in some of them, you sure needed a lot of capital!

One such city was St. Petersburg, the capital of Russia, with prices on average at least double that of New York City. During the day, I went to the city center on my own. St. Petersburg is a beautiful city, one of the nicest I'd seen to that point, on the Neva River. It has five million people and nicknamed "The Venice of the North." Stockholm had that same nickname when I was there so is one a pretender? Are they sister cities? Well, in my estimation both are beautiful cities and deserve this title (I later learned that other Northern European cities with canals have this same nickname). There were amazing palaces and museums that we would later visit. As with Romania, when the Russians did something, they did it big – statues (especially of Peter the Great), fountains, buildings, and they were immaculate. Palace Square was an amazing place, including Winter Palace and the Hermitage Museum which had gorgeous architecture. I learned that Peter the Great is credited with dragging Russia out of its medieval times and making it into a leader of its time, and that he was nearly seven feet tall. His statue has him up on a horse, and you had to feel for the horse carrying a massive guy that size. His cabin is also on display there, a colorful wooden house that he had painted to look as if it were made of bricks. The river area had lots of restaurants and shops, and that's where I bought some post cards and small souvenirs, since I had all this free time. I met the group for dinner back at the hotel. Nice people, older, "the usual suspects" from the usual places.

The next day our group went to the same area I had gone to on my own, and that's where I had another experience that even Yuri would say is something he had never seen before. We went to the Hermitage Museum. The interior was as beautiful as the exterior;

to this day it is one of the finest museums I have ever seen. It was immense, immaculate, and impeccable. I took a lot of photos there, and I needed to change a roll of film. I moved into a darker room from where my tour group was, and as I was changing the roll a pretty gal circa age 25 bumped into me as she stepped back to admire a painting and apologized. Her name was Kira, and it turned out she was an English teacher from there. We chatted briefly, and she really wanted to talk with me more "since you speak English so well," which would benefit her. Our group had a one-hour lunch scheduled in just a few minutes, after which we would be boarding the motor coach en route to Novgorod. I told Yuri I'd like to speak to a young lady I'd just met, would skip the lunch, and meet the group at the coach at the proper time. He looked over at Kira, raised his eyebrow (she dressed sexily) and said OK. "Be careful, she looks dangerous" he mockingly admonished me with a smile.

Kira and I talked by the sea, took photos, and had several things in common including teaching (I made an exception in telling her I teach since she was in the same profession). Kira didn't want me to leave, but I had to. She wanted to come with me to Novgorod on the motor coach. I said that I'm on a paid tour and she cannot go, even if she paid for that part of the trip. She didn't take no for an answer and, as my tourmates were boarding, talked to the Russian driver, Nikolai, whom she totally charmed in Russian to the point where I think he would have let her on. But Yuri stopped this, being firm but polite to Kira. Meanwhile, my other tourmates – a talkative group of about 35 people – were wondering what's going on, and this created a buzz. Kira then said to me, "Where are you going to be tonight in Novgorad?" I showed her the itinerary and hotel name, which she knew. She said in front of everyone that she would meet me there that night. I didn't believe it because the city was several hours away, we were about to leave, and how would she even get there (she told me that she doesn't drive)? Kira hugged me goodbye in front of everyone, and said she would see me later, again with my whole tour group hearing this. I then boarded the coach and took some razzing about this, but it was good-natured. The strong consensus, including from me, was that Kira was not going to be there. I had just met these people, so it was a funny way to get to know them. First I was thought to be a spy, then a missing person, and now a playboy?

We arrived at the hotel and had a group dinner in the lobby. There was an American guy on the tour in his 60s named Gary who looked like former Los Angeles Dodgers' baseball team manager Tommy Lasorda, and it turned out he was from Southern California. He was a bit odd and claimed to have been to 100 countries, but he counted Puerto Rico and several Caribbean islands that are not official countries. Gary also said he's been to nearly every major league baseball stadium, which I admired. My friend Mark in New York has the same goal (I've been to 12 but do not aspire to go to all of them). I was tempted to ask Gary what he feels constitutes being "to" a stadium, such as being seated in it versus walking around it versus breathing the air surrounding it as you drive by it with the window opened, but didn't want to be a wise-guy (I saved that for other occasions).

As the group was ending its dinner, a hotel clerk entered into our private dining area and asked if "there is a Steve here from California." Well, that would be me, and when I identified myself, he motioned for someone to come in, and it was Kira!!! She was dressed in the same exact clothing, and there was a loud gasp by many – including me. "Kira, you're here?!" I managed to say. "Yes, I came for you" which made me think of the Star Trek episode in which a beautiful alien woman says, "I am for you, Kirk" but if she touches him he'll die (I couldn't think of an appropriate song lyric). I asked Kira if she had anything to eat and she said yes, but that she doesn't eat much anyway and declined my offer for some food. She had taken a train, and just wanted to be alone with me, so we...went up to my room. More buzz, major buzz! from my tourmates as we headed up the stairs – a few followed us several feet to see what would happen. Anyway, Kira ended up staying overnight, and the next morning several astonished tourmates saw me saying goodbye to her as we were checking out of the hotel. Kira had an aunt in town she'd be staying with. We kept in contact briefly after I returned.

On our motor coach ride en route to our next destination in Novgorad, there was a very lively discussion about what I had done. Yuri immediately said, "Ladies and gentlemen, I will need your attention to tell you about our next stops. But before that I will say that what just happened with Steve is something I have never seen in my 17 years as a tour leader." I felt a little embarrassed, a little proud, and a little happy that it happened and made for a nice memory. With that, Yuri went on with his lecture about our next destinations. Soon after he stopped speaking, a few people from the tour, mostly older guys, sat and chatted with me. Some liked what had happened and encouraged me. They all had the same advice – which would be repeated to me many times: keep doing what I'm doing, while I'm young and healthy, because there are no guarantees that your travel plans will ever be realized, and if they are you may not be in the best condition to enjoy them. I totally agreed with them, and added that with the world changing as it is there could be additional safety, environmental, economic, and political factors that result in not being able to go places you want to even if you're able. It was this foresight that would lead to another major travel decision later on, and allow me to get to some places I would not have gone afterwards for these reasons, as will be described.

Outside of Novgorad, we stopped off at an area that had a beautiful white, sandy beach with lots of volleyball players. Gary came up to me and, along the lines of the "Star Trek" theme again, I asked him if we hit a geography warp or black hole and were now in Southern Cal. He said this looked just like it, with tan, hard-bodied guys and bikini-clad gorgeous gals included. I later thought of telling the Russian women they are #2 to the Swedish gals to pull the same stunt as in Argentina, but didn't go there with it. On the continued long bus ride to Moscow a quiet Malaysian tourmate about my age, Rahim, also traveling by himself, came up from the back and sat in the seat next to me. He asked, "How did you do that?" "Do what?" I inquired, just to make sure we're on the same page. He said, "You know, the girl." I told him how Kira and I met, and that I was the right person in the right place at the right time, who spoke English well. He was amazed by this, and said that he could never do such a thing – although he would like to. I saw that he had a fancy digital camera with big lens and told him of my "camera" routine, by which I ask a pretty gal to take my photo, and the conversation would start from there. He was too shy to even do that. So, we talked about photography and he was very helpful. Later in the trip, he followed my lead in rushing to the large back window of the motor coach to take photos when we didn't have a window seat. I would speak and hang out with him occasionally throughout the trip, but he couldn't keep up with me, and I was too independent, anyway.

We arrived at the beautiful Hotel Sovietsky in Moscow. There, incredibly, a gorgeous blonde clerk liked that I was from the U.S. ("ah, you are American!") upon seeing my passport, and we hung out a while after I checked in. We also would keep in contact after I left, but only a few emails were exchanged. She noted that, "you look a bit Russian," and asked if there is any such ancestry in my background. I told her my paternal grandmother was from Russia (the one who married my grandfather from Romania), and, later on, I did see a number of people who looked like me, my brother, my dad, my uncle, and a specific pretty female cousin from that side of the family. I also saw our family name in giant block letters on a department store as we were driving into the city but I wasn't quick enough to catch the photo of it (and never did get it). The funny thing was when I saw many of these people who looked like me and my family members, I thought they spoke English, and when they saw me, they probably thought I was Russian. Indeed, several locals did approach me and speak in Russian, and were surprised I did not. It just goes to show again how a decision made by an ancestor generations ago can affect your entire life, and that of your future generations.

The next day we went to the Kremlin on tour, and I met yet another pretty blonde, Sasha, a college student wearing trendy U.S.-style jeans with holes at the knees, who spoke English very well. I wanted to meet her and used the "camera stunt" ("would you mind taking a photo of me?") to do so. We talked for over an hour, and what a sweet gal (much like Izlane from Morocco). We found that we have a lot in common, despite our age difference, in terms of philosophy of the world. It was so refreshing speaking to her! Once again, I did not mention that I am a university teacher which could have put a barrier between us. In fact, I just said "I work in business" if anyone asked, and did not get specific. One older woman from the U.K. on my tour happened to see me speaking with Sasha, and said loudly to other tourmates she was with, "Look at him – he finds a new girl in every city." Funny thing is this is not the case back in America, where I am just an ordinary guy who does not stand out from the crowd. An important revelation for me at that point was that sometimes when traveling around like I did, I was the only game in town as far as American men in a specific classification go (e.g., much younger than most tourmates). So, with little or no competition, it was pretty easy and many times some beautiful women were pursuing me. Yes, they may have thought I have money (which I denied if suggested), but I think it's more that, just as you represent your country politically and become an unwitting ambassador, so too do you represent the social trends of your country to the younger people in particular – including fashion, music, and even McDonald's! So, at least with Sasha that day, I was the Krem de la Krem (pun intended) of American pop culture, and she was the trendy type who would be amenable to this. There were terrific cathedrals in the Kremlin area and, of course, Red Square, which was totally magnificent! I took a lot of photos all around – Sasha was a good photographer, too – and they came out well. History was everywhere, and what a historical place to be. There was also Lenin in his mausoleum, his embalmed body right there looking up at you (eyes shut). That was creepy.

Based on the history of Russia with its spies, our tour guide told us a funny true story about two American tourists visiting Russia who were in their hotel room and saw a metal nodule extending upward from the floor. Convinced they were being spied upon, they unscrewed the nodule - whereupon they heard a loud crash. It turned out that was the piece that held the chandelier in place for the room below! As it would further turn out, I would later have hotel room experiences involving a crashing chandelier and being spied upon in two other parts of the world, as will be described. Also, when I emailed Lana to check-in and see how she's doing, she later told me that my email arrived in Russian. Strange things were happening there, indeed.

Moscow was very expensive, more so than even Reykjavik or Tokyo, but many of our meals and entertainment were included there. Moscow has been known at times to be the most expensive city in the world. I'm not a big drinker but had to have the vodka, which was excellent. I didn't try the Russian dressing, nor even knew if they had it there, but I tried the pelmeni, which was like a meat dumpling, and a bit spicy. It tasted very good and I had it again another time. I also had a few things I couldn't describe – not that they were so terrific, I just didn't know what they were in the restaurant. At least there wasn't a fish-eye or turtle head staring up at me.

I found a few other things there, too. If you made an effort to talk to people there they were very interesting, warm, and even funny. But they were not forthcoming (except Kira, because of an unusual circumstance, and maybe some service personnel). The train station there was magnificent, among the best I'd been on – very efficient with only a few minutes' wait between trains, elegantly decorated (chandeliers and marble at the station stops), and fantastic art and sculptures, some with political messages. Moscow, with over 10 million people, is actually more populated than New York City, and more people use the train system there by a wide margin. Moscow was my kind of place – big city, interesting, historical, beautiful women, nice people, and good food. I felt comfortable there, and would soon enjoy some first-rate entertainment as well.

That night, I attended a great performance: the Red Star Red Army Chorus and Dance Ensemble with performers dressed in Soviet military uniforms, including singing, a high-energy dance (lots of twirling and squat-kicks), and an orchestra. I was awe-struck how good this performance was, and had never seen anything like it. The acoustics were great, and everything went off like clockwork. It was historical, military, colorful, and Broadway all rolled into one. To this day, the performance is one of the best I have ever seen, and I have been to several Broadway plays and comparable others. That this play was in Moscow at the time added to the ambiance. I subsequently learned that the group tours in selected U.S. cities, so if you get the chance, you might want to go see it.

Based on this outstanding performance, I decided to take another optional tour offered the next night, to the Moscow Circus. This, too, was awesome (and I've been to several circuses), especially the acrobats. Here was another time I ignored the rules, and it paid off. An announcement was made in several languages prior to the show that photography was allowed, but only without a flash, since a bright light could startle the performers as well as the animals during the performance. It was added that photography without the flash would not come out, so basically don't even bother. I sat toward the top row, far from the action, but had a feeling that the photos could or would come out – even without a flash – because there seemed to be ample light from the circus stage. I also figured that I could get these photos put on a CD and digitally enhance them with brightening, perhaps. Also, I had been to several Club Med performances at night (theater shows, trapeze acts) in which my photos without a flash came out decently, and then fine after enhancement. So, I took numerous photos without a flash, and from what I could see was the only one doing so (many people had put away their cameras after the announcement). As it turned out, the photos came out great! Not just from the circus, but from the Red Army Chorus show, where a similar announcement had been made, and I did the same thing. Lesson learned: don't always accept what is being said. And my camera was only a good point-and-shoot, nothing fancy.

The next day we left Russia, but I'd had a wonderful time there in only a few days. The weather was even excellent, warmer than usual with very little rain, which made it comfortable and conducive to great photo ops. There was so much history there! Although history wasn't my thing, I couldn't help but notice and appreciate the grandeur in which it was displayed. I developed an interest in it afterwards. When I saw old war movies on TV I no longer turned the channel so quickly. Being in Russia created a touch point, and made even the black-and-white historical reels seem like colorful, vivid memories to me, with a little recollection and imagination.

Next was a brief stop in Minsk, Belarus – which I didn't even know how to pronounce properly until this tour (Bella-ruce). There really wasn't anything much there, and it seemed like a throwback to the Old Soviet days with block-style, boring homes that had laundry hanging off the clothes lines. These were the least attractive buildings that I'd seen. I saw lots of huge Soviet statues in the squares, and a handful of pastel-colored buildings in an effort to look somewhat modern, but even these lacked any sort of style. However, at night I went out and there were many teens hanging out along the Svislach river. Some dressed very elegantly and liked going to the disco. There seemed to be a 1940s culture by day, and a 1970s culture by night, including the fashions (I hadn't seen in over 30 years). Many people had blonde hair and piercing blue eyes, looking Scandinavian.

There were about two million people living in Minsk so it was fairly sizeable, but also fairly homogeneous (Russian is the main language spoken, but there is a Belarusian language, too). In the end, this was good to experience regarding how it was years ago, because much of Belarus is still in a time warp. Not even Russia is this way any longer. The song I thought of there was "Let's Do The Time Warp Again" from "The Rocky Horror Picture Show." I wondered, having done the dance at the Waverly Theater in Greenwich Village where it debuted in New York, if this would catch on if I taught it there. I decided not to chance it, which may have been my best move there – dancing or otherwise.

We then traveled into Finland (Helsinki) and the Baltics, including Estonia (Tallinn), Lithuania (Vilnius,) and Latvia (Riga). I discussed Helsinki and Tallinn earlier, so I'll focus here on Lithuania and Latvia – which were surprisingly good, mainly because of the people. Vilnius wasn't much to look at beyond a large cathedral in a square, and Old Town with baroque architecture. If I hadn't seen similar types of places before I would have been more impressed – and that can be a drawback of traveling so much because you compare a lot instead of taking each place in for what it's worth. There were more orange houses among tree-lined streets, and bicyclists all over the place. The people were young, the women were very pretty (blondes in general), and most of the population was Lithuanian. There were a lot of artists there, Bohemian types, and hippies. Some struck me as weird, and even bizarre with super-crazy spikey hair, and garish clothing looking like an Italian hotel room décor you can wear. There were several sets of people I spoke with, guys and gals, mostly in their 20s, who approached and wanted to chat with me upon hearing my spoken English. I obliged, but by the end of the conversation I finally wised-up and realized that I was their English lesson for the day. They wanted me to keep talking and were hanging on every word. They laughed at all my jokes. I could have made the worst jokes and they would have laughed. I later found out there was a statue in town of

Frank Zappa that I didn't see, and that Zappa had nothing to do with Lithuania but represented the new culture, or old counterculture, however you want to look at it, and was revered.

Outside the city, we went to the Hill of Crosses which I found unique – thousands and thousands of crosses of every kind were piled high there as a tribute to Christianity, and Lithuanians' national identity. Some were tiny so as to fit in the palm of your hand, and some were several feet tall. Some were wood, some were metal. Some were very colorful, and there were religious figurines there as well, several elegantly carved. This is a pilgrimage site, and even the Pope had been there in the 1990s. It made a good photo op from afar, up close, and from the top. I had never seen anything of this magnitude before or since. I'd venture to say this is, or should be, in the Guinness Book of World Records.

Riga had a different feel to it, more subdued, and had a few bridges from which I obtained more picturesque sunset photos. There were several more cathedrals, including the Dome Cathedral which is the largest in the Baltics, and an Art Nouveau building in white, that was very impressive (renovated and over 100 years old). The people there were also very pleasant, but in a different way. They were extremely clean and courteous. Unlike Vilnius, which had mostly Lithuanians, Riga had a lot of Russians in addition to the Latvians. There was a medieval feel to the city, but a slow modernization as well, like it was trying to find itself but headed in a direction it wanted to go. Speaking of which, the best architecture I saw in the Baltics was a building called The House of Blackheads, which is an 800-year-old Gothic building (orange brick again) that was rebuilt. It stood out as a marvel among the rest, and had some cool-looking blue trim with statues around it as well. This was a background in many photos I took at the Town Hall Square, and was lit up at night. And yes, the photos came out well, without a flash.

The Baltics concluded our excellent adventure! It was then off to the airport in Helsinki, and then to Athens, Greece for my third consecutive tour. I was holding up well physically, and really psyched for this next part as well, which would include several new countries, cultures, and more surprises. I had emailed my travel agent about the mishaps and made sure that she had someone picking me up at the airport when I arrived; this was included in the package. I was assured this would happen, but good news/bad news: the driver did show up and held a placard with my name outside of the baggage claim area, but once all my luggage was loaded into the trunk, his car wouldn't start! He radioed in, and I had to wait at curbside for another half hour in 100 degree weather for the back-up. The driver apologized, but it was getting to be like a good omen in a way – a bad start portended an excellent trip. While waiting, I took a photo of a funny billboard. In big letters it read: Nescafé: A Taste Of Greece. I know what they were trying to say but it translated funny when you said it. This reminded me of a badly translated ad shown years ago in National Lampoon magazine for a vacuum cleaner that read: Nothing Sucks Like An Electrolux.

At the hotel, I met with the tour leader, a Slovenian native in his mid-30s named Bojan, or Bo for short. He was a portly and trendy-looking guy, casually dressed in button-down shirt and slacks, who seemed very happy to see a passenger under 60 years old on this tour. He was impressed that I was an American who not only had heard of Slovenia, but had been there, can pronounce it correctly, and could spell its capital correctly. During our tour he would often come up to me during breaks, and we had a few intriguing conversations about growing up in the U.S. versus Eastern Europe. He liked hearing me talk, and I wondered if I was his English lesson, too, although I didn't think so. My tourmates were again the same type as before, older, from the U.K., Australia, and New Zealand, with a couple of Asian Americans (married) in our group of under 30 people. I was surprised that I hadn't seen more people I had toured with before, given all the trips I was taking and the homogeneous nature of the passengers. Perhaps not many were serial tourists like me.

The first full day featured a significant morning, noon, and night component. We began with a city tour in Athens early in the morning. Several people on the tour, including myself, were disappointed with the city – dirty, crowded, very hot, merchants who tried to rip you off, high crime in nearby areas, and many there did not seem to like Americans. I bought a lot of post cards at one small store and, despite spending a good sum for these, the clerk wanted to charge me a dime for the bag to put it in. I refused and started putting back the post cards – at which point the clerk said OK, no charge for the bag. I should not have made my purchase there on principle but let it slide. I don't like being ripped-off in any way at any price, and would later tell my college students this story as a "how not to" treat the customers. Athens had a fast-pace, New York City feel to it, complete with lots of concrete, tall buildings, and fast drivers (so be careful!). Most people in Athens, including middle-aged people, spoke English fairly well, and almost everyone belonged to the Greek Orthodox Church. I would even luck-out later and happen to see one of the priests, who let me take a photo of and with him. Our tour leader Bo was a very good photographer, and he even scouted out photo ops for me and the others.

In the afternoon we walked around the various tourist sites. Our hotel was situated near the Acropolis and Parthenon. We toured these, and if you wanted to see some ancient buildings, you had come to the right place: these were amazing! We also climbed a lot of stairs and saw an ancient Olympic Stadium. Almost all others on the tour could not make this long climb, especially in the heat, and turned back. If only they had invented elevators back then! There was a single guy from New Jersey on the tour in his 70s who wanted to buddy-up with me. He was interesting, but all he did was complain which wasn't my scene, so I politely excused myself most times and split on my own (I chatted with him at group dinners). One even older guy, however, was fascinating and even fought in the Battle of the Bulge in 1945 during World War II, educating me about this.

There were a lot of immigrants living in Athens, including from the former Soviet Union and Balkans. I was later told by some locals that Athens doesn't really represent Greece, that I should cruise the islands to get a better sense of the country. I would end up visiting one island, Rhodes, a couple of years later and noted the dramatic difference (sort of like a Southern California resort area to midtown Manhattan on a busy afternoon). After the tour I found some inexpensive Internet cafés, from which I emailed friends and family back home, and also Lana in California.

We had dinner our first night at a nearby restaurant, with a Greek folklore show. The first act was an older lady sitting on a stool, singing, smoking and drinking intermittently, as the band played stringed instrumentals in Greek costumes. We all looked at each other like, "OK, what was that?" A Greek tragedy, perhaps – we weren't sure whether to laugh or cry, or even applaud. Our dinner included lots of souvlakis and kebobs, including turkey leg meat that's carved into slices off a rotating cylinder and put inside a gyro with French fries, lettuce and tomato in there, too. I'm not big on Greek food but have had my fair share. I have to say, great gyros there – the best I ever had! There were also interesting and tasty "donuts" (their word for tourists) that were locally called loukoumades. These were actually bite-sized dough balls, similar to zeppolis in New York City, and beignets I'd had in New Orleans, except that these had a honey-coating instead of being shaken in a bag with white confection powder.

The next day we arrived at Kalabaka, part of Thessaly, which included a small town called Meteora that looked prehistoric with giant granite rocks extending upward as if reaching for the sky. Atop these were monasteries and a convent that we visited. This was a land that time forgot; we saw a few monks, too, hand-painting religious icons. Nobody was in any rush. If you ever wanted to just escape the world and chill this would be a good place to do it (in sharp contrast to the hustle-and-bustle of Athens). We also went to Delphi, which I figured would be good based on it being a UNESCO World Heritage Site, and it didn't disappoint. This city played a major role in Greek mythology, including the oracle (the most important in Greek mythology) and where Apollo slayed the dragon. It also included an ancient theater that was rather amazing, situated in the mountains. I climbed well above its plateau and took some excellent panoramic photos looking down upon it to reveal its contrast amidst the surroundings. This is where the Olympics were thought to have begun circa 776 B.C. An impressive place overall.

We then headed north to Macedonia, Albania, and Montenegro, all former republics of Yugoslavia. As with Estonia, I didn't even know that Macedonia was still a country. Over there they pronounce it Mackedonia, with a hard "c." Our motor coach was stuck in a long line of traffic at the border there for quite a while, so we were let out for a smoking break or to stretch our legs. Although Bo said not to take any photos at the border crossing (since photos at all border crossings were prohibited), I saw an impressive-looking statue of Alexander the Great on his warrior horse there and really wanted to photograph it. I asked the guard walking around there if I could do this. He was reluctant but said OK, with his supervision, and making sure I pointed the camera only at the statue. I thanked him; he wouldn't let anyone else do this (a few asked subsequently). As it turned out, a few years later a giant bronze statue of this measuring 8 stories high and 48 tons was erected in the center of the capital city, Skopje ("Scope-yee"). I was surprised this wasn't done sooner; even the smaller one at the border was a very good attraction.

We toured around Skopje, where the locals were interested in my visit from the U.S. and the tour group in general. Very few tours went there, and many of the residents there never met an American. I noticed this as a trend; the fewer tours that visited there, the more curious the locals were to meet the tourists. Their keen interest made me feel as if I'm from another planet, but it was flattering, too. Some of the architecture (but not much) was fanciful, such as for a church that had a cave-like, dome-shaped entrance and highly detailed woodcarvings. There was also a fortress, stone bridge, and a monastery that were intriguing, but I liked the city square best with some small shops and friendly faces. I had a few casual conversations while looking out over the mountains. It was pleasant for a couple of hours. Nothing really stood out about the city – except its colorful red and yellow sunburst-designed country flag. I bought a fridge magnet of it that stands out on my refrigerator to this day. So while Skopje was a plain old hot dog, the Macedonian flag was very spicy mustard that commanded your attention against the ordinary background. An interesting combination I'd later "relish" when looking at the photos.

We also went to a small city called Ohrid, southwest of Skopje, which has only about 40,000 people living there, or less than 10% of the 500,000+ living in Skopje. Although Macedonia is mostly land-locked, Ohrid has a beautiful coastline along the ocean with those immaculate-looking orange-roofed houses, and a castle atop the hill. This place was quite a find, another little gem. I learned that Ohrid and Lake Ohrid were accepted as UNESCO World Heritage Natural and Cultural Sites. I figured there was a reason we went to such a little place. Sometimes good things come in small packages.

Next up: Albania. Despite being there only a short time, I again found myself in unusual situations. In Tirana, the capital, there was a strange mix of old Soviet-style architecture and newfangled modern buildings, as if a caterpillar trying to transition into a butterfly. There was also an impressive fountain and statues. The city struck me as an evolving place with young students all around, eager for change. U.S. President George W. Bush spoke there a week earlier, and the signage was still up welcoming him at a triangular structure called The Pyramid. I took a photo of it, after which a female college student approached me, asking if I'm American. After my experience with the Serbian gal I asked, "Why do you want to know?" She said that she and Albanians in general love Americans (based on what happened in Kosovo, and NATO getting involved). I then spoke with her freely, and took a photo of and with this gal, Alda, in front of the Pyramid positioned so that the Albanian flags were over her shoulder and the American flags still there from President Bush's speech were over mine. There were quite a lot of Albanian flags throughout the city. We then chatted quite a bit more, and I was very impressed that she not only knew the extensive history of Albania, but of the U.S. as well. She gave me a big hug at the end when we parted. Quite a contrast to the Serbian gal, but here again was an example of you representing your country politically whether you like it or not. I was also learning that no matter which country we visited, the people there were very prideful and patriotic. A lot had been sacrificed for their freedom, and why shouldn't they be? Ironically, soon after this trip I would end up visiting Albany, New York. I don't think there is any relation between the city and the country, except for the similar name.

Soon afterwards, I inadvertently took a photo of a military building, whereupon a military officer dressed in uniform yelled at me while getting out his rifle! He came closer; I put my hands up, camera still in hand (all those years of doing the famous Club Med dance paid off right then, LOL). I was so relieved when I somehow talked my way out of this. I told him I'm a tourist from the U.S. (that might have done it), and did not realize that was a military building.

I was calm about it, and he saw I meant no harm. This is another hazard when traveling to a country in which you don't speak or read the language. Had he delayed me any further, I would have missed the motor coach, which was heading to another country shortly.

When I returned to the motor coach I was the last one on, barely making it back on time. When Bo asked, "Where were you?" I replied "Getting hugged and almost shot at." One female passenger from the back said in jest, "It figures with him." After I told what happened, the same lady said, "So which one hugged you, and which one wanted to shoot you?" Very funny, I suppose. I said, "Don't worry, I'll be a good boy...until we reach our next city." My tourmates were nice, really, and Bo seemed to enjoy my escapades.

We briefly went into Montenegro, a small country the size of Connecticut that had become independent a year ago. There were lots of mountains, and a beach at the small coastline by the Adriatic Sea. Some of the beaches reminded me of the beaches by Lake Erie in Buffalo (barren, with brown sand) while others reminded me of the Northern California beaches Lana had taken me to, with giant boulders in the water and surrounded by mountains. There was an Old Town that had that centuries-old feel to it, nothing I hadn't seen before so it didn't stand out.

Our tour group made a brief stop in Kotor, which had a similar feel to it. The Old Town there was very well-preserved and another UNESCO World Heritage Site. There was an impressive ancient city wall that blended well with the stone houses from views atop the city, which were spectacular. This also looked Mediterranean with the red-bricked houses dotting the hills above the coastline. Bo and I chatted over coffee as we overlooked the city. Strangely, there was a fully-functioning wooden car that caught a lot of attention. I had never seen one, so it piqued my interest too and was good for a couple of photos. There was a lot of history there, and a lot of giant rocks as well several stories high (similar to Meteora). There were a lot of references to former Yugoslavian dictator Tito there, including statues and the Tito Restaurant, decorated with his photos. Several locals from the former Yugoslav countries I visited remarked to me that they wanted a reunification to be more of a power in the region. One especially politically-oriented university student commented,

"We wanted independence and got it, but now we cannot compete with the world powers because each of us is too small. If we reunited, and it was done the right way, we could be up there with them. Isn't that what the United States did? It has all those independent states together, and is now the superpower." My only reply was, "It can work under the right circumstances." I didn't want to discuss politics on my vacation, and rarely did, but it was interesting to hear what others thought, as I'd heard from many world residents.

I had now been to all the former Yugoslav Republics after they declared their independence (including Croatia, which I had been to the previous year and would be heading to next), another travel accomplishment accompanied by lots of experiences and learning. And with my musical mind I thought about the song "The Good, The Bad, and The Ugly" while in Montenegro, a late 1960s instrumental hit by American composer Hugo Montenegro based on an Italian spaghetti Western movie starring Clint Eastwood. This song title was befitting given my overall experience in the former Yugoslav Republics, because all three applied at some point.

Our motor coach rolled into Croatia, where I had been last Spring as well, and to the capital, Dubrovnik. This was a picturesque city along the Adriatic Sea. The Dalmatian Coast it was part of reminded me of the beautiful Amalfi Coast in Italy. We took a city tour and went to the Old Town. Lots of shops and an old baroque cathedral. Former National Basketball Association star Tony Kukoc is from Croatia (among the first NBA stars from Europe). Unlike Ichiro in Japan, however, his name is not emblazoned all over the place. I purchased more post cards, took photos, "the usual" – and no photos of anything that resembled a military building! This would be the last stop on our tour, and my last in the three consecutive tours I had taken. Despite wanting to just take it easy and relax, another interesting event was soon to take place.

After checking into the nearby hotel, I got lucky when bringing out my camera to take photos of the beautiful landscape. On a pier, I saw a young Western Canadian couple in their early 20s having lunch, Katie and Scott. I asked them to take a photo of me, and we ended up spending five hours together on another beautiful weather day. They were from Kamloops and backpacking their way around the world after recently graduating college. They would find a city they want to go to, get there inexpensively, travel light, get jobs as bartenders and/or servers, and then decide to go elsewhere when mutually ready. I was fascinated by this, and they were equally intrigued by what I was doing. Here again, travel can be transcendental – that is, transcend age, citizenship, and all else. We had a great time getting to know each other, and they happily offered food and drink as part of this newfound acquaintanceship. They were intelligent, reflective people who made this rational life choice to be happy, at least for the time being, and I respected that. You could say we were vaga-"bonding" in the best way, traveling the world and sharing our experiences, philosophies, and ideals during the several hours we had together.

Having recognized that there is no dish called "Chicken Kiev" in Kiev, Ukraine (later confirmed by a Ukrainian friend in the U.S.), I kiddingly asked if there is "American Dry" ginger ale there since we have "Canada Dry"® ginger ale in the U.S. They laughed and said no. I "impressed" them with my knowledge that Canada has a Prime Minister, not a King or a Queen, as I'd learned in Montreal many years earlier. "Very good," I was told. "Not every American knows that." We then got into a more serious discussion when they suggested a theoretical education in which students have an option to go to at least 20 countries after high school or college graduation, to get a worldly experience before entering the work force, especially in these days of globalization. They were preaching to the choir with that one, and I readily agreed. It was a refreshing meeting of the minds. We also refreshed ourselves in the Adriatic Sea with a swim. As such, a few tourmates saw me with them, and I was again part of the dinner conversation buzz ("Who'd we see you with this time?"). Generally, most of my tourmates had gone shopping or sightseeing. I liked my afternoon better. It seemed there was an intrigue about what I did, how I did it, and who I was with (which didn't thrill me, but I was diplomatic about it). This was a reason why not too long after these vacations I would often travel solo.

On our last day of the tour, I talked Bo into taking a group photo of us in a picturesque setting along the coastline. Several of us gave him our cameras, and he took the same photo over and over. I'm glad we did this, and I hope the others are, too, so I could remember all the people I shared some prime time with, not just those I met on my own. When I had this photo developed back home I thought of one last song: "The Way We Were" by fellow Brooklynite Barbra Streisand. Indeed, they were "misty water-colored memories" (Adriatic Sea in background), and if I "had the chance to do it all again"...you bet I would!

The tour ended, we said our goodbyes, and I'd had yet another excellent vacation. All three tour operators did a wonderful job. I was using my frequent flyer miles for this trip, and the only day I could get back for free was five days later from Athens. I did not want to stay in Greece another five days, and so I had booked my flight from Dubrovnik to Istanbul, Turkey, where I would be on my own in a Muslim country on the Black Sea, and then return to Athens from there. This would also give me 65 countries overall toward reaching my lifetime goal of 75. Here, too, I would have weird experiences – one of which resulted from the T-shirt I was wearing!

As with many other places I'd been, Turkey is not called that there, but Turkiye (Tur-kee-ya), and was not named after the bird we know as a turkey, but presumably after the country's first leader, Mustafa Ataturk. But this is in dispute and it's not really clear how Turkey got its name. However, I did fly into Ataturk Airport, so go figure. I soon realized that many there did not like it when you referred to their country as Turkey, so I called it Turkiye when I said the name. Turkey is so big that it is bordered by 8 countries (I thought this might be the record but France is bordered by a comparable amount and Brazil is bordered by 10). I learned a bit about Istanbul, too – it's the third largest city in Europe after London and Moscow, was formerly called Constantinople (I even remember an elementary school song about that), and part of it is in Europe, while the other part is in Asia (separated by the Bosporus Sea).

This city had a whole new vibe that was very different – and with my track record, who knew what to expect? Just the look and feel of it was intriguing, with all the Ottoman architecture, Muslims dressed in their garb, the incredible number and size of the mosques (with giant minaret spires) bellowing Islamic prayers throughout the streets, and Turkish flags all around, with the red and white crescent moon and star. As with Athens, Istanbul was very crowded and polluted. There was a lot of trash in the streets including a huge amount of cigarette butts. There were no garbage cans in the streets (that I saw), but then periodically came an army of people on pedal-powered vehicles that bagged it and hauled it away. Interesting concept, but I prefer the trash cans. There was small store after small store on the streets, the size of tiny convenience stores, and many narrow restaurants with open storefronts featuring turkeys spinning on a vertical rotisserie from which pieces were carved off to make a sandwich or platter (and it was delicious!). There were very few people there who looked like me, dressed like me, and spoke like me. I totally stood out – and this led to my next adventure.

The next day, my first full one, I decided to wear my green and white Michigan State (alma mater) T-shirt. I had recently been to the university visiting a friend, and figured maybe this would be like a bat-signal to another American. It was! As I was walking down the street I heard a voice from just ahead of me saying, "Michigan State? I'm from Michigan. I used to live near Detroit!" As I looked down it was a little old lady in her 60s, a nun in her habit named Maria, sitting there on a stool by the cathedral. We said a startled hello to each other, and chatted for a half hour in the blazing heat. She was originally from New England and heard her "calling" to come to Istanbul, where she has since lived for over 8 years. She stood up, was only about five-feet tall, and offered to show me around on the extensive tram system there which went around the city to the mosques and the Bosporus Sea area. I accepted, so off we went. I figured she's a nun, so what could be bad? Then again, with my track record of misadventures, anything was possible. Fortunately, we had a wonderful time. I thought it interesting when she told me that Muslims lump all non-Muslims together, so it didn't matter whether you were a Christian, Jew, Catholic, or other – you were seen as an outsider.

Maria and I had a grand old time chatting, joking and laughing. We garnered lots of stares but didn't care. She was genuinely excited to be with an American, and insisted that we have lunch in her friend Mohammed's Turkish restaurant – he once lived in New York, she said. I agreed, and once we were at the restaurant he ended up joining us for lunch after Maria told him that she just met me and I'm from New York. Mohammed was the consummate host (as Turkish people are known to be), providing a great lunch with delicious tea at the end as well. I had the kofte (Turkish meatballs) because I wanted something familiar to start with; a meal, no matter how good, that doesn't agree with you can ruin your trip. As Mohammed and I chatted, we learned something we had in common: he had lived and worked in Brooklyn, New York for four years, and was the former manager of a popular diner in Sheepshead Bay, Brooklyn (near Canarsie) that I used to go to with my friends! He wasn't there during the years I lived there, but he knew all the main streets in Brooklyn and details of the diner so he wasn't putting me on. At the end of the meal he gave me a fez to wear, and we took photos together. This was all bizarre but yet another welcomed adventure.

I would see Maria again, but not for a while. She had to be somewhere after lunch, and I needed to exchange more currency. The next day I took the trams around by myself as she showed me, and did my own mosque tour. These were astonishingly interesting, especially the Blue Mosque, which was the granddaddy of them all. Inside was just as awesome, as nice as the major churches and cathedrals I'd seen in other parts of Europe. And the mosque exteriors lit up at night, creating another breathtaking view. I was into Turkish architecture ever since visiting the Alhambra Palace a couple of years before in Spain. I was fascinated by the history and the majesty once again. I met some locals who told me that Cappadocia (in Turkey) is an extraordinary place to go with its unique rock formations, caves, underground cities, and potential to even take a hot air balloon over the area. It sounded great but was far away, and I wanted to explore Istanbul. I kept it in mind, however.

Another day I went to the Grand Bazaar, which is one of the oldest and largest covered markets in the world. I received the red-carpet treatment, literally: it seemed like everyone there wanted to sell me a carpet (red and other colors), which was of extraordinary quality and design. In retrospect, I wished I had bought one, but the shipping cost would have been enormous and I wasn't about to carry it home. In another "When in Rome moment," I looked for the confection Turkish Taffy there, and didn't find it. That would have been another blast from my childhood past and an appropriate place to consume it. Istanbul, like many mega-cities, was bustling with people, traffic, street vendors, street hawkers, and fast-food places. I was surprised by how many rotisserie turkey places there were. I had several such meals during my visit there, and they were delicious – juicy and flavorful. A few guys there looked like "The Soup Nazi" from Seinfeld, and I wondered if Germany had exported its citizens to Turkey, as Turkey had to Germany after World War II. Had Mohammed said, "No tea for you!" after dinner I would have fallen from my seat laughing my fez off.

I went out at night locally only. I'd been warned about pickpockets and even kidnappings, so this being my last city visited on a long tour, I wanted to play it safe. My hotel was in a central location, and the staff was excellent with advice. I thought about going to my first hookah bar, but decided not to chance inhaling anything I didn't know. Most people in Istanbul were very nice to me, but a couple of people weren't. I suppose this was to be expected given the sheer number of people I met. Overall, I found them friendly, very hospitable, helpful with directions, and even with spare change for the pay toilet when I ran out. The gals were beautiful. I wanted to see a belly dance there but there were none going on near my hotel. I was offered more than just the belly of a gal by numerous guys there ("C'mon, I show you nice girls who show you good time"), but I wasn't going for that. During a subsequent trip to another country, I would have my chance to be up-close with a belly dancer.

On my next to last day in Turkey, I saw Maria again randomly, near her usual location at the cathedral, and we went down to the Bosporus Sea by tram. We had a Coke there and hung out together, talking and taking photos, getting more incredulous stares and not caring. There were some cool statues, and a playground nearby as well. After our time together that day we said an appreciative farewell and bon voyage to each other. What a nice lady, and what a bizarre (and bazaar) experience all this was! I took a boat ride on the Bosporus and got some great views of the coastline. This helped cool me off on another scorching day. I then took the trams one last time in a "hop-on, hop-off" manor (like the buses in several major cities), stopping off at one mosque, hopping onto another tram, stopping off at the next mosque, and so on. I couldn't get enough of them after a while; they seemed to grow on you. I liked Turkey even in **hind**sight - it was **h**istorical, **i**nteresting, **n**ew, and **d**ifferent. I felt myself growing educationally, and even spiritually. Once again, the college teacher had become a student, of life.

So it was back to Athens one last night before a marathon 28-hour trip back to Northern California, leaving Athens at 7: 00 a.m. and returning to NorCal at 10:00 p.m. the same day after the time difference (flying backwards in time). What a long, strange journey that was, but a truly wonderful time with still over one month to go before returning to teaching. I spent time with Lana. We went all over the vicinity, including attending a fiddle contest in a nearby small town. There weren't many of those back in New York. I was enjoying doing anything new and different, and was brimming with confidence after successfully taking all the international trips. I went to several more states in the U.S., but had a hunger for going overseas yet again. I still had the time, the frequent flyer miles, and a new goal: to visit every country in Europe, needing only a handful more. I still had a long way to go, however, literally and figuratively.

Coincidentally, in early August I received a letter from a major airline that my 53,000 frequent flyer miles were going to expire in one month if I didn't use them, or take a qualifying trip to keep them valid. I did not plan on taking any further trips. I then called and asked a helpful male rep if it's still possible to get to Europe with this amount of miles, and at this late date since I had to return within three weeks to start teaching. He was great about helping piece together a trip that made sense for me; getting to anywhere in Europe at this late date using free miles was an accomplishment, and he even obtained one free stopover for me in New York City each way as part of the deal! But the real deal-maker was when he asked if I had a world map to follow along with prospective trips. Are you kidding? Does Superman have a cape? As mentioned, looking at a world map is my kryptonite, because back then once I did this there was a 100% chance that I would be booking a trip right away. For that reason, I did not look at my world map often, especially when the discretionary cash was low. The timing of this trip was also excellent because it gave me enough time to process my 128 rolls of film from the previous trip (another 3,000 photos), take care of other details, and return just before the Fall semester began.

Where was I going? Sacramento to Los Angeles (nine-hour layover) to Newark, New Jersey on a free stopover (spent three nights in New York and New Jersey to see my family & friends) to Nice, France (French Riviera) to Monte Carlo, Monaco (via railway) to Basel, Switzerland (one-hour flight) to Vaduz and Schaan, Liechtenstein (via buses) to Luxembourg City, Luxembourg (via railway) to Amsterdam, Holland (via Eurail) then all the way back to Northern California and start teaching three days later. After booking the trip I thought, "Am I really going to do this?" But I decided to go ahead, as the image of a poster I had above my bed at Michigan State came to mind, with a man diving off a cliff into the beautiful blue ocean with the headline, "You only live once, but if you live right once is enough." I had become a road warrior, plane warrior, and other kind of travel warrior by this time, and wanted to leverage that as much as I could while I was robust, healthy, and had built up such endurance as a travel athlete. This trip would also help accomplish two goals: getting into three new countries (Monaco, Liechtenstein, and Luxembourg) in my march toward attaining 75 countries visited in total, and getting me close to visiting every country in Europe. Sold! Plus, it was blazing hot in Northern California in August. I'd be going solo, but I was no stranger to doing this, and could do another "when in Roam" (pun intended) independent tour on my own, which many times was even preferable.

A funny thing happened on my way to France. I had a nine-hour layover in Los Angeles with nothing to do. I'm OK with layovers of three hours or less. An airport employee told me there is a free shuttle from one of the nearby hotels to the beach. I didn't see anywhere to store my luggage at the airport, so I took it with me to the beach, changed into my swimsuit, and spent a nice day there sunbathing and watching the surfers and volleyball players. I then took a flight to New Jersey where I spent time with family and friends, and also at the beach at the Jersey Shore (Long Branch) with my friend Chris – without my luggage beside me this time. I also spent time in Manhattan, Brooklyn, and Queens seeing my friends and former coworkers as well. New York City welcomed me like an old friend, and I feel the same way about it; there's nowhere else like it, but I also had a lot of other places I wanted to see and things I wanted to do.

As such, after three days there I took an overnight flight via Frankfurt, Germany into Nice (pronounced "Niece"), France (pronounced "Fronce" by the locals over there). I had only been to Calais, France very briefly and really did not see the country. I'd heard all about the French being rude – but here's an important point: not only didn't I find this in France at all, but I've had many pleasant experiences with the French throughout my life and like the way they live their lives in a work-hard, relax-easy way. Someone once remarked to me that it's because I'm from New York City that I don't notice the rudeness (which in itself is a rude remark). Well, New Yorkers are not only as nice as people I've met anywhere else, but many are genuinely warmer and friendlier than the average person. A lesson I learned in New York and France is that it all depends on the person, not the location or nationality. That said, I had not been to Paris yet, where even the other French people told me it's a different situation. My experience with the French, including this trip, and my Club Med experiences (which included many French customers there), would soon become a factor in a major decision I was going to make back home.

Upon arrival at the hotel that early afternoon, I napped for a couple of hours and then walked around the city which was, well, "nice," but under construction near my hotel. An important travel note is to know what time the hotel allows you to check-in. I ensure before booking the hotel that I can check-in upon or soon after arrival, but I've heard stories where tourists assumed they could check-in early in the morning and sometimes they couldn't until as late as 3:00 p.m. If there is no luggage room (e.g., in a small hotel), you may have to be with your luggage several hours while waiting. The weather was terrific, mid-70s and sunny. This was a pretty city on the French Riviera. I liked the architecture, especially of the Opera House and selected museums (Art Deco), the Old Town with its cafés, fountains and statues, and of course the crescent-shaped coastline, which was especially impressive seen from high above. I didn't speak French except for a few words – but, importantly, made the attempt with basic words, and this seemed to make a big difference (versus assuming they speak English). Just as I'd had waffles in Belgium, I had French Toast there which was excellent as was most of the food. I'd heard it was originally called French Toast because it was made from stale bread that was too hard to be eaten, so it was dipped in eggs and toasted to avoid throwing it out. Ironically, later that evening, I'd meet some others at a restaurant and they toasted me with their wine as a new visitor. That was a French toast of a different sort.

The next day I asked the front desk clerk the best way to get to Monte Carlo, Monaco which I'd heard was near. I was told the ride is 11 minutes by train. Simple as can be, and I was there as quickly as going from one train station to the next on the New York City subway. But this time it was from one country to another! Monte Carlo was opulently gorgeous, with fancy cars and spectacular views all over the place. There were lots of Princess Grace (Kelly) images as well; she was beloved there, killed in a car accident in 1982, and her husband Prince Rainier had passed away in 2005. It cost 10 euros ($13.50 U.S.) to go into the casino but man, what beauty! I'm not into bling or jewelry, but there sure were some opulent rings, necklaces, watches, you name it there. Good thing I brought my sunglasses, but who knew I'd need them indoors!

I walked around the immaculately landscaped grounds outside. More glamour, elegance, sophistication, and charm. There were beautiful gardens/floral arrangements, fountains, cathedrals, and a few more Europeans I met, including a blonde gal from Finland who was surprised I had been to Helsinki, citing that she heard "Americans don't travel." She asked what percentage of Americans own a passport, saying she heard it was about 10%. I said I didn't know for sure but said that maybe it's closer to 20% based on the small sampling of people I know who either do or don't have a passport. "Either way," I said, "it's probably very low compared to people in Europe because we have such a big country, and many people don't have the desire to travel overseas, the money, and/or the time, energy, or health." She thought this was odd and made a face. "Besides," I said, "many people like coming to the U.S., so I guess we have a lot to offer." She wanted to know why I travel so much. I said I like getting away and learning new things, meeting new people, and that a hundred years ago there were probably a lot of people like me who wanted to do this but the transportation wasn't available except maybe by long ship. Just for kicks, I complimented her beautiful, piercing blue eyes to see if she would say something like, "I do not need compliments, I know who I am" (maybe that was the standard blow-off line in Finland). She said thanks. No return compliment, which I figured would be the case, but it would have been funny if she had given one and then I used the "I do not need compliments" line back to see the reaction. Actually, I wouldn't have done it, but it was a fleeting thought. We parted with a smile, and I was on my way.

On the return trip from Monte Carlo to Nice I stopped off and went to a beach in a town between the two cities, Beaulieu-sur-Mer, which means "beautiful place by the sea," and stayed until sundown. I took some fabulous sunset photos, and met more tourists and a few locals. Everyone was friendly and cheerful. The weather was just delicious, and I realized on the short train ride back that within a few days I had been to a beach in Southern California, the Jersey Shore, and French Riviera. I wondered if this would create an odd-looking tan, or if the sun is the sun no matter where you are (weird thought, and maybe a question for the next motor coach ride). Anyway, the best thing was I didn't get sunburned.

The next morning I had to be up very early for a one-hour flight to Basel, Switzerland. I asked if there was a bus or railway going to the airport, and was told yes, a bus, and where to catch it (I had taken a cab from the airport to the hotel because I was very tired). As it turned out, because it was Sunday, the schedule was greatly reduced and I had to wait an extremely long time for the bus. After having dragged my luggage a ways (whoever invented rolling luggage was a genius!), I ended up flagging down a taxi driver who got me to the airport. Ironically, the bus arrived just after I stepped into the taxi (which was expensive), and passed us going to the airport.

The flight to Basel was smooth and easy. Upon arrival I was delighted by the tram system of electric trains that radiated out from the airport to all parts of the city. I asked a local if there's one that goes to or near my hotel. A nice lady who knew the trams well pointed the one out to me (tram #8 – there's that number again, a good omen), which saved me an expensive cab fare (Switzerland is very expensive!). My hotel was the Basilisk, just a lovely place in the historic district. It was clean (as things are in Switzerland), comfortable, and had an excellent breakfast selection. The room was tiny, and so compact that the sink was in a closet (which I had not seen before or since)!

I walked all around this charming city on the Rhine River – what a pleasant surprise this was! It reminded me of Amsterdam with its easily walkable bridge, canals, bicycles everywhere, old-world charm, architecture, fountains, and statues. I hung out a lot by the river and met more interesting people - students, senior citizens from the U.K. and U.S., locals of all ages, and others. It's amazing how if you just stay in one area and are receptive to meeting new people, the variety you can meet. The key is to be willing to leave your comfort zone, and be able to face rejections, too. I hadn't been to Switzerland since many years ago with Mike, but I enjoyed it just the same. There was a dollhouse museum and zoo I heard mixed reviews about; neither idea thrilled me, and I was having a good time just walking the city, so that's what I continued doing until leaving the next day. If I visit there again I would consider checking out these other two options (especially because I now have a "collection" of unusual museums to which I have been).

Next it was off to Liechtenstein, a country between Austria and Switzerland with a population of just 35,000 people. I thought it was bigger – because the long name on the world map takes up so much space! I truly had no idea what to expect there, and hadn't read up much on it. I was a big proponent of just letting things happen as they may, just wingin' it, and going with the flow. Well, if I'd thought Basel was a nice surprise, I was about to be even more surprised by Liechtenstein, a country that was like a small Alpine Village. There were no airports and few train stations in Liechtenstein, so I relied on the bus system to get to the capital, Vaduz, then another city, Schaan. After my visit there, I came away with the impression that this country is the second-best kept secret in Europe, after Iceland.

Vaduz, the capital, was this nice little city tucked into the mountains, and a combination of Switzerland and Germany. It was very walkable, had a castle, a neat little Parliament building area, a National Museum, and a Postage Stamp Museum. But its real strength was the people – how sweet and pleasant they were, with lots of smiles, happiness, and good cheer everywhere. People went out of their way to help me with directions, things to do, places to see, and were just so incredibly nice! I had a great conversation with a shopkeeper there named Andrew, who told me the history of the country, was very knowledgeable about the U.S., inquisitive as well in an intellectual way, and just the nicest guy.

Schaan, with a population of roughly 5,000 like Vaduz, had its own charm. There was a carnival there at the time and lots of merriment. You couldn't help but get caught up in the fun; it seemed like everyone was out there on another beautiful weather day (just a hint of chill in the air foreshadowing the Fall). It seemed like a pleasant little town, the equivalent of a European Mayberry. I'm not much of a small-town person but I just enjoyed it; the whole setting and atmosphere seemed just right. Perhaps it was lightning in a bottle, or maybe this was the way things were, but I just remembered leaving there with a broad smile, feeling wonderful, and thinking what a pleasant surprise Liechtenstein was. Another "who knew?" among the many I was finding.

I returned to Basel for an overnight, had a good time out on the town going to nightclubs, and the next day took the train into Luxembourg. On my Central Europe tour a few years earlier we were supposed to stop off there, but because the tour was running late the leader opted not so stop in the country, instead giving us the tour highlights as we passed through (including lots of banks, and the banking history). I did not count that as a country visited then, but here I was going into the capital, Luxembourg City, to spend a couple of days there. I took a bullet train, and I recall the conductor wearing a rich-looking purple uniform with fez-like cap without the tassel. There was also a sexy female conductress who took a photo with me in front of the train during a station stop, and she had an equally cool-looking uniform. And that was the best part of Luxembourg to me.

For some reason, I pictured Luxembourg as being upscale, elegant, and even aristocratic based on the international banking system that was prevalent there. Even the name had a "deluxe" quality about it. However, I found Luxembourg City unexciting, visually dull compared to others I'd been to, with many downtrodden, poor, and rude people. I'd heard that people from the country were generally well-to-do, with a very high per-capita standard of living, so this was surprising (perhaps they were elsewhere at the time or out in the 'burbs). There were some higher-elevation views of a finely manicured garden area, and bridges surrounded by trees, but the city seemed old and grungy with a few spotty elegant buildings. I realized that it's an ancient city, but somehow this didn't have that same charm as others in this genre. There were a few statues, cathedrals, and shopping/restaurant areas that were just OK, but nothing to write home (or in this book) about. Strangely, I had a Chinese dinner, and the waiter, who was from Luxembourg, had the so-called French attitude that I didn't encounter in France. Go figure. We bickered a bit about something he was clearly wrong about; I think he was just a foul person in general. I met several people there who loved Europe and Luxembourg in particular. I thought that was fine; you should be proud of your country. I learned that over 95% of the country is Roman Catholic, and that there are three official languages: French, German, and the local language, Luxembourgish, which was relatively new.

When it came time to leave, I took a long rail trip back to Amsterdam, Holland and sat across from two lovely French gals in their early 20s who were aspiring models and dressed Parisian style, with colorful flowing dresses and floppy hats. I needed to stay overnight in Amsterdam and hadn't made any hotel reservations. These gals were very helpful in suggesting places I stay there, and told me of a magnificent garden area at the Amsterdam Airport which blew me away when I searched it out (gorgeous tulips among others). They were just so friendly and fun, with lots of laughs and smiles (and of course, photos – maybe they'd be famous some day). This made the trip go by quickly. And their hotel recommendation was excellent (relatively inexpensive at 79 euros or $105 U.S.). I got a good night's sleep prior to my long return trip.

The next day I had a 22-hour trip back to Sacramento, California which would have been longer except that I asked at the ticket counter if there was anything I could do to avoid a 7-hour layover in Philadelphia and a 9-hour layover in Phoenix. As it turned out, there was: for $25 I was able to change my flights to go from Philadelphia to Chicago, then directly to Sacramento with minimal layovers. This was another example of "ask and you shall receive"; numerous times I had done this and, just by asking, received much better connections. From the "funny story regarding this" file I'll tell you that there was once a flight cancellation and everyone was in a panic to rebook, causing an incredibly long line at the one ticket counter. I simply got on the phone, called the airline, and within minutes was rebooked on a flight leaving soon after my original one was scheduled to leave. These days, of course, you can easily re-book online.

So, back in Sacramento, I got in my car parked at the airport and drove home for two hours, arriving there at 4:00 a.m. I'd had another excellent trip. You would think that these long trips cause exhaustion, and they sometimes do temporarily – but overall they are energizing, exhilarating, and make me feel alive! Plus, I feel a tremendous sense of learning – which I sometimes incorporated into my marketing and sales lectures for the university students as appropriate, from my first-hand experiences. I processed another 1,000 photos, and was happy with how they came out. The photo processors again came out and said, "So where did *we* go this time?" They meant this literally because of the vicarious trip they took with me when processing the photos. Many people have suggested I process my own photos, but I prefer to leave that to the experts and use the extra time for other endeavors, including more travels.

# Chapter 15

## Caribbean Cruising And "Port Collecting"

*Caribbean Cruising And "Port Collecting"*

Rather than interject each Caribbean Island visited throughout this book when traveling there, I've decided to make a chapter of it since most of these visits occurred during a relatively short time-span, I could discuss cruises in general (a major mode of my transportation), and these trips led to more extensive cruises elsewhere later on. So, what is the Caribbean? The answer is complicated, but I found a website that provides a relatively brief explanation:

*Caribbean History*

The Caribbean is a collection of islands and seas located to the north of South America and to the east of Mexico. Although this may not be apparent on a globe or world map, there are over 7,000 islands, reefs and other land masses that comprise this fascinating part of the world. These islands formerly went by the name of the West Indies and the story goes that Christopher Columbus had discovered the Indies whilst landing his ship in the Caribbean during 1492. Caribbean history has an intriguing story to match such magnificent islands.

*What Makes Up the Caribbean?*

The Caribbean itself is divided into two different areas. One is called the Antilles, which is again split into the Greater and Lesser Antilles.

The other half is known as the Bahamas which are actually found in the Atlantic Ocean.

In terms of their official arrangement, the Caribbean islands are considered to be a part of North America and 27 islands and locations are recognized as constituting the Caribbean islands. Most of these are overseas departments although some are dependencies, retaining a slight level of freedom.

*Early Caribbean Inhabitants*

If you were wondering why the Caribbean has such a name then allow me to shed some light: the Caribbean gets its name from an ethnic group known as the Carib who inhabit the Antilles.

The Caribbean is home to around 40 million people, although this has been largely dependent upon European influences. This 40 million comprises people from all over the globe and the islands are very enriched indeed. There are Indian, Chinese, British and French links; as well as hints of many other cultures across the globe that have helped to shape the demographics of the Caribbean.

In terms of language, this influx of immigrants has left the islands with a vast array of languages. The main ones are English, Spanish, French and Dutch, although a few Creole languages can be found here as well.

*European Colonization*

Every one of the islands that make up the Caribbean was at one stage a colony of a European empire. Some of them retain this status although the majority have now achieved independence. Typically this came about after the collapse of the slave trade. French Guinea is one such example of a Caribbean island that is still an overseas territory belonging to a European nation.

Due to this level of colonization amongst European countries, many of the islands have remained incredibly separate and their history in this area has meant their participation in international affairs is really quite limited.

The Caribbean history of these islands is so diverse that they are often completely different in a modern sense. Apart from their climate, very little remains constant from island to island. They all have different cultural aspects to demonstrate and very different cuisines.

Here is a more extensive breakdown:

**Island groups**

**Lucayan Archipelago**

- Bahamas
- Turks and Caicos Islands (United Kingdom)

**Greater Antilles**

- Cuba
- Hispaniola
  - Haiti
  - Dominican Republic
- Jamaica
- Cayman Islands (United Kingdom)
- Puerto Rico (U.S. Commonwealth)

**Lesser Antilles**

- **Leeward Islands**
  - U.S. Virgin Islands (United States)
    - Saint Croix
    - Saint Thomas
    - Saint John
    - Water Island
  - British Virgin Islands (United Kingdom)
    - Tortola
    - Virgin Gorda
    - Anegada
    - Jost Van Dyke
  - Anguilla (United Kingdom)
  - Antigua and Barbuda
    - Antigua
    - Barbuda
    - Redonda

    - Saint Martin
    - Saint Martin (French Antilles, France)
    - Sint Maarten (Kingdom of the Netherlands)
    - Saba (BES islands, Netherlands)
    - Sint Eustatius (BES islands, Netherlands)
    - Saint Barthélemy (French Antilles, France)
    - Saint Kitts and Nevis
        - Saint Kitts
        - Nevis
    - Montserrat (United Kingdom)
    - Guadeloupe (French Antilles, France) including
        - les Saintes
        - Marie-Galante
        - la Désirade
- **Windward Islands**
    - Dominica
    - Martinique (French Antilles, France)
    - Saint Lucia
    - Saint Vincent and the Grenadines
        - Saint Vincent
        - The Grenadines
    - Grenada
        - Grenada
        - Carriacou and Petite Martinique
- Barbados
- Trinidad and Tobago
    - Tobago
    - Trinidad
- **Leeward Antilles**
    - Aruba (Kingdom of the Netherlands)
    - Curaçao (Kingdom of the Netherlands)
    - Bonaire (BES islands, Netherlands)

So, with all that in mind, here are my selected experiences. By cruising, I would also reach my 50th country, Dominica, and only one year later I would reach my 75th country, Trinidad & Tobago. Caribbean cruising fit right in with my teaching schedule during winter intercessions and enabled me to get to several more countries in a more affordable manner than flying there. Note, however, that many Caribbean islands I went to are not official countries, and I did not count them as such, including Bermuda, St. Maarten, U.S. and British Virgin Islands, Puerto Rico, Grand Cayman Islands, Martinique, Curacao, Bonaire, and even Turks & Caicos which I had been to numerous times by this point for Club Med vacations. There were several official countries, as listed by the U.S. State Department, I visited in the Caribbean which were, in order: St. Lucia, the Bahamas, Dominican Republic, Barbados, Dominica, Antigua & Barbuda, Haiti, Jamaica, Grenada, Trinidad & Tobago, and St. Kitts & Nevis (which will be discussed in a separate section). Cuba is also counted as a Caribbean island country but is not open to tourism by Americans. Several people consider Belize a Caribbean country, but it is more a part of Central America.

I ended up going to many of these non-countries and countries multiple times because the cruise lines often visited the same areas (Eastern, Western, and Southern Caribbean), and to get to the new I also had to visit the ones I'd been to previously (not that I minded). However, I tried to avoid duplication as best I could when reviewing the itineraries. I would have liked to especially get to Aruba and Guadeloupe (non-countries) but never did make it there. I also would have liked to get to Saint Vincent and the Grenadines, the only other Caribbean country I haven't been to, but didn't get there (as yet) either.

My general takeaway from these Caribbean islands was their sheer beauty, beaches, great weather, lush greenery, smiling happy people, and history of pirates which is often played up as a tourist attraction. My first trip to the Caribbean was to St. Maarten (French and Dutch sides), and from there I was sold. The people were friendly, cheerful, smiling, and accommodating; the scenery, food, and activities (especially on the French side) were terrific; and I had a very enjoyable time coming back well-rested and tanned, after having been stressed at my job.

In my career I worked on a "gap analysis" – determining what gaps exist between your current status and where you want to be, and how best to fill them. I created my own gap analysis of a different sort by measuring the success of vacations in part by looking at how I was feeling before them and how I felt afterwards. I found that vacations elevated me to a new level I aspired to be at, and were the best way to get me to where I wanted to go, both literally and figuratively, to maximize my happiness (even relative to the resources needed to take these vacations). To quote the popular ad slogan of MasterCard®, the value of this happiness was, and is, "priceless." Ironically, I used a MasterCard to pay for many of my travel purchases, obtained credit card airline miles for them, and used the points for additional travels. The year after this vacation, I had a similar before-and-after effect in Cancun, Mexico, and the year after that a similar result after my first Club Med vacation to Turks & Caicos Islands, as mentioned. I was a work-hard, play-hard guy all my life, but was learning the extreme value of vacationing hard (or soft, as the case may be) as well. The Caribbean was a big part of that, and the results were the rocket fuel I needed to endure my upcoming often busy schedule and extreme workloads. Work-balance was extremely important to me, and I was realizing the great "treasures" to be had on Caribbean vacations.

In Trinidad & Tobago, I attended a Calypso dance. The performance was terrific, and I mentioned to the dancers afterwards that this country was my 75$^{th}$ visited. They had some paper and markers, and I made a sign to this effect, and they posed for a photo with me holding it as an excellent memento. I had just (finally) purchased a digital camera and showed the ladies how the photo came out. They were happy with it, and fascinated with the photo appearing instantly on the digital camera screen. Additionally, the women in this country were gorgeous; I'd say among the top 10 in the world that I'd seen. In New York City, I had worked for 8 years with a gal whose family roots were from this country, and she was very pretty, nice, and smiling all the time. Now I saw where she got it from.

In similar fashion, I also liked Barbados a lot. The island was colorful (especially the buildings and clothing), Bob Marley reggae music reigned supreme, and there were fun, friendly people who I met and walked around with a lot. I didn't particularly care for reggae music when first visiting the island, but as a result of the good time I had there started listening to it occasionally. My mind became like a digital-camera screen, retrieving the images of Barbados upon hearing this music. This was another connector to bridge the gap between life as usual and a vibrant feeling of happiness. There was also lots of rum, great snorkeling, and a beautiful night sky in Bridgetown. I ended up traveling there again on a different ship, and enjoyed it immensely both times (the second experience was a confirmation of the first).

Antigua had a beautiful beach, and I ended up going there three times overall. Once I ended up meeting a group of 20-somethings there (guys and gals), and it turned out they worked on the ship I was on – it was their day off and they invited me to hang out with them, which was very nice. I enjoyed playing Frisbee® and just chatting with them about what life was like working on a ship. Many of them became attached to selected passengers and were saddened to see them go.

I went to Jamaica and had a whole different experience. When shopping there, I asked an older female merchant if I could take a photo in her store of the colorful caps and clothing. She said only if I buy something. I said I'm not sure if I will and put away my camera. She then said it's OK, and so I took a few photos and she took a couple of me in the store. I bought many post cards there which were all I was interested in, and she seemed contented with that. A few weeks later, after switching to another cruise ship, we stopped in Jamaica again at the same port. I went into the same store by coincidence. The same lady recognized me, forgot I made a purchase there, and chastised me for not doing so. I was shocked she even remembered me since our encounter lasted about 10 minutes several weeks earlier. I reminded her that I did buy the post cards, which she forgot about, but she still criticized me. Her store was empty, and was empty the day I bought the post cards, too. That's what bad customer service can do. Not to mention I was on a cruise ship, and people talk to each other. I didn't say anything to anyone else about this place – but if she were polite and welcoming I would have – in a good way.

But there was an even a worse situation in Jamaica. Wandering around by myself again, a local middle-aged guy who seemed pleasant approached me with a big, friendly smile. After ascertaining that I'm a tourist from the cruise ship, he mentioned a few places I should visit while walking around. I thanked him and headed on my way. He soon caught up with me and said, "I have an idea, Tommy will show you around" and started walking with me. I figured he meant a friend of his or perhaps a local guide he knew in the area. We walked together and he appropriately steered us in the right direction for excellent photo ops. We chatted, and his answers were brief but friendly. He offered to take my photos at various sites but didn't want to be in any photos himself. Fine. We continued for a while and stopped off for some lime juice, which was the best-tasting lime anything I've ever had (I'd later go back there for more; anything coconut there was also outstanding). I treated him to some beverages for his kindness in taking me around, and having me meet Tommy shortly.

So we're walking for a while longer and I asked, "Where's Tommy who's going to take me on the tour?" He replied, "I am Tommy." Startled, I said, "What? You mean your name is also Tommy?" He said, "No, I am the only Tommy, and Tommy is taking you on this tour." It turned out he was a nut who referred to himself in the third person. He soon said, "Tommy will now take you to the main shopping area" and I said that I've seen enough and would be on my way. "Tommy doesn't like that," he said. He just glared at me. I'm thinking "Well, Steve doesn't like this, either" after he said, "Tommy wants to be paid for being your tour guide." To make a long story short, after some "negotiations" I gave him a few bucks to get rid of him, and he left. I shouldn't have gone anywhere with this guy but he seemed pleasant enough, and I was so charmed by the environment that I was too lax. Always be on your guard, because there are tourist predators out there looking to make a quick buck. Fortunately, I did not go into any remote area with him, and the word "police" scared him a bit.

On the plus side, Jamaica had beautiful beaches, and there was a lot of Bob Marley and Jimmy Cliff music played there (both Jamaican-born), as elsewhere in the Caribbean, too. The people were very friendly and smiled a lot, making me feel comfortable. I just had to be sure not to feel too comfortable, based on the lulled-in experience with Tommy. I also liked those colorful rasta hats. "Yeah, mon," good stuff, colorful and emblematic of the Caribbean.

Puerto Rico was interesting and fun. My ship went to Mayaguez, and this was the first time any cruise ship entered this new port. There was a big party for our arrival that included Puerto Rican flags emblazoned all over city hall, music and dance performances, and the mayor making a welcome speech. New York City had a large Puerto Rican population, and this remotely reminded me of the annual parade there, making me feel comfortable. The beaches were as pretty as the women. I would later cruise to San Juan on a different ship, and enjoy myself there as well. I almost met-up with a former business associate who had moved there, but we missed each other by a few hours.

As mentioned, I love Turks & Caicos, but had only been to the Club Med village in Providenciales. However, a cruise I was on went to Grand Turk, and the beach there was just as spectacular. There were several good restaurants in the area, the pirate history was played-up, and of course there was lots of shopping. Anything with "Turk" in it was becoming a good experience, be it Turks & Caicos or Turkey.

Many people don't realize that the Dominican Republic and Haiti are two countries sharing one island (called Hispaniola), with Haiti occupying the Western third. Yet the former is Spanish and the latter is French based on their respective histories. So, it's not like Brooklyn, Queens and Long Island in New York City which also share one piece of land but are fairly similar. This is a good example of how the Caribbean is a chain of islands but, despite having a similar geography, can be vastly different – even on the same island. I won't go into the histories of this, but just give my overall impressions based on selected experiences there.

In the Dominican Republic, what jumped out at me was there was a major emphasis on baseball, including that in the United States. I saw lots of kids wearing Sammy Sosa jerseys, but there are so many current and former American stars that also came from there it made you wonder if there was something magical in the water. I'm talking about many dozens of players, and some of the best to ever play the game, including Albert Pujols, Manny Ramirez, Pedro

Martinez, Robinson Cano, Jose Reyes, and the three Alou brothers (Felipe, Jesus, and Matty) who played in the 1970s. Baseball was a way of life there, and many aspired to be like their big-league heroes. Kids ate, drank, and dreamed baseball, based on what they told me. They also had a tremendous knowledge of the game (statistics, etc.), and enthusiasm when just talking about it. I found this refreshing and so full of...hope. I also enjoyed watching them play baseball; you never knew who might be the next star. Interestingly, I would be an ultimate approver of kids who were casted in TV commercials for candy brands I worked on, and two of them became fairly famous, including one as a star on Broadway years later, and the other as a star on a hit kid's TV show. I wondered if any of these Dominican kids would someday be the next major league superstar, and truly hoped they were able to realize their dreams.

Haiti, on the other hand (or land, if you prefer), is one of the poorest countries in the Western hemisphere, and it showed. There was political violence and other bad things in its history. Add in a devastating earthquake and you just have to feel so sorry for the people there. But you know what? As with the teens and kids I met in the Dominican Republic, there was a sense of hopefulness there as well. I saw a lot of happy, smiling people there, kids playing games and enjoying themselves, and many happy adults, too, as I had seen on the other side of the island. One local lady said to me, "Always happy, just always be happy whatever you do." You know, sometimes it is just that simple. I remember a colleague at work later asking me two provocative questions. The first was: "Would you rather be rich and miserable, or poor and happy?" After having seen these people, I'd say poor and happy, actually, because to me happiness is the end-game (some people wince at that answer, but to each his or her own). The second question was: "If you had $10 million and lost $9 million, would you be happy?" My answer was yes; see the above for the reason (others wince at this one, too). Ironically, I wasn't happy when I ended up losing a pair of glasses in Haiti on the beach; despite an extensive search assisted by the police officer there, they were gone. Fortunately, I brought a back-up pair.

As a quick tour of a few other places in the Caribbean, the Bahamas had gorgeous water but was a dangerous place. The cruise line docked at one of the "cays" off the mainland, where we were heavily guarded. Bonaire was a cute little place, picturesque with blue-green waters and easily walkable. Grenada had an old fortress, beautiful waterfalls, and some stunning views from above.

A funny thing happened when a British lady at dinner one night complained about the tour she went on that day to see flamingos. She was totally hilarious as she loudly told us and anyone else within earshot what happened. "They took us on a tour to see the flamingos, showing us a brochure with lots of flamingos on the cover to get us to join. So we go there, the driver goes by the area real fast, and there are no bloody flamingos! When I asked where are the bloody flamingos, he told us that it's mating season and there are none here! And so we didn't see any bloody flamingos!" (her voice rising). People were laughing at her delivery more than anything else. I still laugh when thinking back to the way she described this event. She would probably have liked the Monty Python's Flying Circus routine regarding there being "a penguin on the tele" (exploding penguin skit); she even sounded a bit like one of the people in that skit (shrill voice).

The other places I'd been in the Caribbean were also a joy. It's no overstatement to mention that I've been to the Caribbean a whole lot, both at Club Med and on numerous cruises, because it's gorgeous. If you're looking to just kick back and relax, pamper yourself or be pampered, ride for comfort or ride the waves, then go find your sweet spot and enjoy some of the finest beauty and nicest people the world has to offer. "Sweet dreams are made of these" as the Eurhythmics sang, and, take it from me - I travel the world and the seven seas – "everybody's looking for something" (primarily happiness). Many people – locals and vacationers – found it there.

I also became very familiar with ship travel since this was the most affordable way to see many places at once – with the ship being your hotel, meal provider, and entertainment provider as well. As with land tour operators, cruise lines are stratified into low-, medium-, and high-end as well. I took most major cruise lines at each level and found some better than others relative to their price, but it's a matter of preference. The one I most preferred was Holland America Lines, which had impeccable service, excellent food, and the size/style ships I liked. The crowd tended to be older, but I'm very adaptable, and am not big on little kids running around anyway. Royal Caribbean Lines and Carnival offered good value, with these two improving their food along the way when others were cutting back (especially on portion size). I did not like Princess, but things may have changed since my one cruise with the company a few years ago.

Often I would book these trips on my own, but in the beginning I used a travel agent, who I told my aim was to see as many countries and islands as possible for the best value during the specified time periods. When checking around, she came across a term she said befit me: a "port collector." There were others out there looking to cruise with the same aim I had to the Caribbean – and indeed, around the world. So, in subsequent visits to the travel agency I was known during that time as "Mr. Port Collector." The name would become more appropriate with each subsequent happy adventure and future booking. I never thought of myself as a "portly" guy, but if the name fit, then so be it. I've been asked if I believe travel agents are worth the extra cost. I believe that depends on your level of convenience desired. I would say yes if you are comfortable turning over your request and having one-stop shopping (the agency may even have access to special deals not made public), and no if you're a do-it-yourselfer who doesn't mind comparison shopping and exploring additional options the agent may not have time to do. To this day I mainly book my own trips, but sometimes turn the booking over to a travel agent who then gets a discount from the travel provider and passes part of that savings along to me (e.g., when I book Club Med vacations). I've found online travel sites hit-and-miss, and often came up with better deals on my own.

As for the ships, they are getting Larger and LARGER and LARGER. Some can have full-size malls in them, and on one ship I saw a Mardi Gras parade down "Main Street" – made to look just like a big city street, with actual room balconies from which you could watch it. Basically, large cruise ships these days are like floating hotels. There are spas and gyms. Olympic-sized swimming pools and saunas. Theaters and lavish dining rooms. Libraries and discos. Medical facilities and fitness centers. High-caliber entertainment, seminars, and lectures. And maybe a casino. Lots more, too. Especially on a world cruise, but more about that later. The staff is there to ensure you have a good time, and I found they do an excellent job overall.

When booking your room cabin, know what's above and below you, and where you are on the ship. There are noisy areas and quiet areas. Cabins with balconies, portholes only, and no windows. Suites, and rooms that are basically big closets. I had some great rooms for the price, and some not so great that I needed to change. Reasons included excessive ship noise at night (e.g., from the engine room); being in a room directly below the swimming pool where the staff dragged the deck chairs (across my ceiling) very early in the morning; and things not working right, especially the TV. In general, however, the rooms were good, I was comfortable, and all my change requests were accommodated. If you're a steady customer, or book at the right time, you can receive upgrades. I also receive my luggage quicker than most – not because I'm special or pay more for this, but because I prefer to take it onboard myself rather than checking it. This way, although it can be a hassle, I can unpack quickly and iron what I need instead of waiting several hours for luggage delivery. The ship isn't going anywhere at that point, so might as well get all unpacked and ready.

Since I've done so much cruising I've been asked a lot about seasickness, which inhibits a lot of people from going. There's no one answer; it depends on the individual. I did not get seasick on a ship (except a mild case on the small one to Antarctica), and happen to like the gentle rocking because it puts me to sleep at night. But this malady can happen to anyone at any time so do be prepared. I've met people who don't like the rocking or the roughness of the seas; some don't like when the water is still; and I even met a guy who gets seasick if he no longer can see land (and, similarly, a guy who wouldn't take a plane because it was merely "a tube in the sky"). In general, I haven't heard about an abundance of people getting seasick on any major cruise I've taken, but I never knew all the passengers. And during a rough trip, even those with iron stomachs can be afflicted. There are medications you can take before, during, and afterwards should it happen (including the travel "patch"). Sometimes it can be mind over (land) matter, so don't psyche yourself out before going.

If you haven't cruised before you might want to try a short one to "test the waters," so to speak. But remember that the waters and weather change, so one experience may not be like the next. The size of the ship and the deck you are on can also make a difference. On a separate note, there is always a mandatory lifeboat drill soon after you board, but this is standard operating procedure with nothing to worry about. You may see a message from the captain on your TV and receive periodic broadcasts from him as well with information and updates.

I enjoy speaking with and learning from the photographers at the studio onboard, who work for the cruise line. They've helped me improve my picture-taking and they also sell photos of various passengers they photograph, including upon entering the ship, when sailing, and sometimes on tours. I have 24 8x10's of selected photos from around the world, and they make a nice mini-album – a high-quality leather one I obtained for free by purchasing a selected amount of photos during a promotion. I've taken some of my best sunset photos from ships; remember to go to the back of the ship as well when taking photos from it, where most people don't think to look, but where you can obtain some awesome photos as well. Because I take so many photos, several passengers have mistaken me for the ship's photographer! Similarly, when dining alone in selected restaurants, especially when I'm well-dressed, I recall being treated extra well, beyond the extraordinary, with lots of questions about everything being OK. I realized later I may have been perceived as a food critic, and thus received better food and service. Such can be the case when you travel solo, which has its advantages. I've also had the same happen when not cruising; it took me a long time to figure out this may be happening.

I've often been asked about dining alone. I do not give a second thought to it and am very comfortable doing this. Often times, a pleasant atmosphere with soft music helps me get into a good "thinking zone" to resolve any issues I'm having. I've met many people who are self-conscious about dining alone, so here are some things I do that I'd recommend you consider. I do not gaze at other people, or care about who may be noticing me alone, or what they may think. Chances are the others in the restaurant couldn't care less, so don't let this intimidate you. If you're in a foreign country, even better – chances are you won't be seeing these people ever again, and if you do, would they even remember? Or care? And does it matter?

There are challenges to being a solo traveler, including on cruises. Generally there is a steep upcharge for singles, and I do not know of any cruise lines that arrange for roommates, as Club Med had. I heard it's too unpredictable, and if you get a bad roommate on a ship this could be difficult. The seating at meals can also be tricky. I've been seated with a family of seven from Asia who spoke only their native language, so as to fill-out a table; with a couple on their honeymoon, when my seat was put to the side of the table as they fawned all over each other; and my (least) favorite, at a romantic table for two with a pretty señorita near my age – who dressed extremely well, seemed to know a lot of high-level people (she may have been a well-known person) – and who didn't speak a word of English! I didn't speak her language, either, so we just stared and smiled at each other a lot. We did dance; however, the whole situation was strange. In each case I had my seating changed, but I usually ended up with much older people including a "singles club" of older women one time, at which I was fresh meat.

So, I finally wised-up and requested open seating, which meant I could go to either of the two seatings for dinner and sit wherever there was an open seat, if available. I preferred this flexibility, would scout out my preferred seating ahead of time (i.e., which table and with whom), and tell the dining staff where I wanted to sit. This was fine most of the time, but there were times where the people at those tables were into their own cliques and preferred to keep it that way. Often, the older people were at the first seating so they could go to the theater show afterwards and then to sleep. I often sparked excellent conversations at these meals to the point where I was quite often invited to sit at that table every night (I would often return but not all the time). It was also a great way to meet a lot of different people on the cruise. A couple of times I was invited to sit at the captain's table, too, and at other times, usually late-nights for snacks, I would sit with the crew members in the dining room or lounge and chat it up with them. It seemed that everyone had a story about why they're there, passengers and crew alike (explore the world; wants adventure; not sure what next move is so do this in the meantime; "port collecting" like me; and crew that basically needs the money or likes being in the hospitality business). Some people did the math and figured they could eat their way to profitability, going to both seatings and gorging. On later world cruises, reasons included people who were dying and wanted to see the world before they leave it; the sheer elegance of the trip; and even a lady who calculated that the world cruise is less expensive than staying in a nursing home (albeit the medical treatment wouldn't be as good). I found it all very interesting.

And now for something completely different. Well, almost. Romance onboard ship. I'll just state a few words about it. Yes, it can be like "The Love Boat." It can blossom under the sunlight, the moonlight, at mid-day or midnight. You can tell when it happens, and what a beautiful setting for it to be this way. A dream-come-true, in a post card setting, amidst a galaxy full of stars in idyllic weather. It's beautiful and makes it a voyage to remember. It can also be like that but without the "love" part (you fill-in the substitution). The wolves come out at night, too. And so do the cougars. The hunter can be the hunted. There are also crew-organized "singles mingles" events at times to accelerate this, where you learn which passengers are available and looking. The crew is not supposed to have "guest relations" with the passengers. I say supposed to because it can and does happen. Breakups from these happen, too. Sometimes loudly. Sometimes with things being thrown. By people with good aim. The ship hits the fan, so to speak. I have heard from crew members that relationships amongst the crew members are encouraged. Tight living quarters. Long work days. Long journeys that can last months. What's one to do? I've met several crew couples who met this way, and others who came to work on the ship as a couple. I've also seen some, shall I say, very odd pairings that, if they were menu items, might be called the boss-admin. assistant assortment; rich lady-boy toy appe-teaser; and much older gentleman-not-his-(grand)daughter grill-mates. I make no presumptions here; I'm just stating what some others would say is the obvious. Whatever happens on land can happen at sea, too. But does what happens there stay there? You could end up cruising for a bruising, so be smart, beware and be careful. I've seen and heard plenty, and had a couple of my own "Love Boat" experiences that were enchanting, and not.

There are port excursions the ship provides that you can book ahead of time or when onboard. I've taken several of these, and they're very good. I've also gone on my own and split taxis with other passengers to have more flexibility and save a few bucks (to apply to other excursions). As always, if you go by yourself or with others from the ship you must be very careful. The ship lines assume no liability if you do this and, as you may have heard about on the news in these situations, "stuff happens." Also, you must be back at the ship before it sails, or more precisely, before the doors close before it sails. This is your responsibility; unlike the land tours I mentioned, where they might wait a short time or even come looking for you if you're not back in time, the ship has thousands of passengers and will need to sail as scheduled. You would then have to meet the ship at the next port at your own expense (which may be very costly). That's why it's a good idea to have the ship's itinerary with you, and also the corporate headquarters' contact information. I almost "missed the boat" twice – once when my airline flight was very late and I literally sprinted with all my luggage yelling, "Don't leave!"; and another time when there was incredible traffic when returning from the tour I booked on my own and there, but for the grace of my running speed to the port entrance, did I barely make it. I have heard of people missing the boat and being stranded. Also, funny as this may sound, there may be many ships in port at a given time, and you could get confused as to which is yours. It happened to me a couple of times as I was rushing, and I was redirected to my ship. Now I take a photo of my ship in port, not just for a subsequent photo album, but as a reference on my digital camera if I get lost amidst the many ships that could be there at one time.

One final note about cruises, a lighter note, if you will. In the lounge late at night when the crew chats with passengers over a few drinks, I ask about funny questions from passengers. One older gentleman asked a crew member if the moon they're looking at now in the Caribbean is the same one that he sees in Florida. And a lady asked on a cruise passing over the Equator if she could be notified when the ship gets there, because she wants to take a picture of it. That reminded me of a time a customer came into the travel office at which I worked in Brooklyn, and asked the quickest way to get to Chicago (nearly 800 miles away). Another customer in the waiting area jokingly told him to go out the door, make a left, and just keep walking – and then he darted away before anyone could stop him! That guy might still be walking today, many years later, and wondering if that's the same moon he saw in Brooklyn.

So, in January, when I was off from teaching for winter break, I took two cruises for three weeks total to the Caribbean. The first cruise was to Panama and Belize. Our stop in Panama City yielded a view of the famous Panama Canal, one of the Seven Wonders of the Industrial World, connecting the Atlantic Ocean to the Pacific Ocean via the Caribbean Sea and using lock gates. This, in turn, obviated the need for ships to sail all the way around the southern tip of South America at Cape Horn – and, having done that aboard ship en route to Antarctica, I can tell you that it's no fun. It was amazing to see ships passing through there, which can take 8-10 hours to navigate. I had also been to Hoover Dam in Nevada and admired that engineering feat as well, but this was even more impressive, saving 8,000 nautical miles via the connection and seeing how the canal equalizes the sea levels of the two different oceans that meet there.

But there was more to Panama City than this. There was an Old Town area including lots of churches, museums, and outdoor markets selling Panama Canal-related merchandise, including jewelry and wide-brimmed Panama hats (ever since my trip to Seville, Spain I became somewhat interested in unusual hats of all kinds). The people were friendly and had big, welcoming smiles – not just the merchants, but nearly everyone. There were also many U.S. major league baseball players from Panama, including Hall of Fame second-baseman Rod Carew and current New York Yankees' superstar relief pitcher Mariano Rivera (a future Hall of Famer), two of my favorite players. Both have broad smiles as well, and are masters at their respective crafts.

I found Panama to be quite diverse, with those colorful buildings like I had seen in Central America, the locks area, and a modern section with glistening skyscrapers that looked like a mini-Manhattan off the water. There was a distinctive Latin feel, with salsa music blaring from various locations, but no dancing in the streets as in Buenos Aires. You had to be careful where you walked given the high crime rate, but I felt safe in the tourist area; the police were abundant and rode their bikes around. There were lots of buses and taxis if you wanted to get around the city, but I preferred to hang around the tourist areas this time and just gaze at the modern marvel that was well worth seeing.

Next was Belize, located between Mexico and Guatemala. Here were a variety of people and cultures including ancient Mayan Indian ruins (similar to what I had seen in Cancun), Creoles, East Indians, Asians, Arabs, and Europeans. Most people there speak English (the official language) since it was under British rule for over 100 years, and was formerly known as the British Honduras before becoming independent in 1981. The country has a beautiful coastline and an exotic Caribbean flavor to it, unlike any other place I'd been. This was based on its unique blend of people, cultures, and even animals such as baboons and monkeys (which howled like basset hounds). We went on tour to Belize City which, unfortunately, like Haiti and so many other places, was dirt poor (literally a lot of dirt roads). Lots of huts, outhouses, and destitution. There were also a lot of "jerks" there – not the people, but the chicken, which was delicious, along with the spicy rice (reminded me of New Orleans cuisine). I also had the shrimp and catfish, both dishes I also enjoy and consider special treats when prepared right, which these were. A young lady there taught me how to do a Calypso dance. This instruction came in handy, because a year later a Calypso dancer in Barbados looked for volunteers to join her on stage, saw me smiling at her, grabbed me, and had me dance with her in front of the audience. I did well, based on the lessons I was given that day in Belize. Because of the country's beautiful coastline, Indian ruins, and diversity, I thought a good slogan for it would be "Seeing Is Belizing." I told this to a few shopkeepers but they just smiled and shrugged. I still think it could work to attract tourists, and is "ownable" given the country's distinct name.

Once again I walked around and met the locals, including a good chat with a police officer, middle-aged people, senior citizens, and students who provided the country's history. They seemed contented in general – and I found that a lot of people who hadn't seen any better, didn't know any better, and so were happy. This was a revelation to me, and got me thinking about the meaning of happiness, that is, if you can outsmart yourself, literally, by knowing too much and thus not being happy because you know better. Although there was high poverty and crime, they got by OK. There was a vibrant pulse to the city, reminding me of New York City in some ways (maybe it was the blaring Latin music), but with a leisurely overtone. I found myself smiling and laughing a lot – and that was most important. I found the wood-carved crafts around the city impressive, but a little large for my luggage with all the travels yet to come and little knick-knacks I was bound to pick up. In retrospect, I wish I had bought one. The rum punch was delicious, but as for the seaweed shake being sold...I'll pass.

The latter cruise was to the Southern Caribbean. In addition to reaching Trinidad & Tobago, we also went to Isla de Margarita, also known as Margarita Island, off the northeastern coast of Venezuela. Venezuela was dangerous at the time for tourists, so I did not go onto the mainland. However, the beach was excellent – crystal clear water with a turquoise-green color I hadn't seen before, that you could walk far into while standing up. There were white-sand beaches with swaying palm trees against a backdrop of mountains, reminding me of Southern California. There were lots of green rolling hills around, too. Over 100 miles of coastline included more than 50 beaches, many just little coves that you felt could be your own private beach if you were wealthy. What separated this stretch of beach from those in Florida was that they were not in hurricane alley, and there was very little rain year-'round. Just a lush, tropical paradise that didn't get too crowded, either.

The island was not overbuilt so it had that primitive feel to it, yet mixed with the new when viewing the exquisite women in string bikinis (and less). Not only were many gorgeous and tanned, I found them fun and friendly. I told a few locals on my cruise ship that I'd be going to other South American countries soon afterwards. I was told to be very careful, but to have a good time (in that order). I met a few people who were there for snorkeling and scuba, and raved about it. Also, they encouraged me to take a taxi around the island, which cost next to nothing because gas there was extremely inexpensive due to the vast oil supply. I would have liked to, but wanted to just enjoy the fine beach and weather with the limited time we had from the ship. This limited time, while a fair amount, is what encouraged me to take independent trips later on, so that I could have more time to do what I liked and not be so time-constrained. I'd be starting my "independent trip" (so-called by the travel company) to South America on my own in just a few more days, once the ship returned to Barbados. But right then and there, I was relaxing on the beach, sipping a drink, admiring the views, taking lots of photos, and thinking this is Paradise.  But no-one gets away that easily. There would be a price to pay for all this, for I learned that not everything when vacationing was "priceless." And that payment was now coming due.

# Chapter 16

## South America: Not As Easy As A-B-C

The ship returned to Barbados, and so ended another fine cruise vacation. Then the rough stuff started – three weeks on my own in South America, and not so much the tourist places as when I traveled to Argentina-Brazil-Chile a year earlier. No, some of these countries would be much more challenging. I thought I'd prepared well, but you never know – especially with an independent traveler on a less-structured trip to some less-traveled places with several unforeseen circumstances. This trip got off to a bad start when my flight to Fort Lauderdale was cancelled, and I was rerouted to Miami. Then this same airline lost my luggage during the transfer, but found and delivered it only two hours before I left for South America. I was stressed-out by this – the airline had undone some of the cruise relaxation benefit, but I just took a deep breath, gathered myself, and began this new "independent" trip with an open mind. I'd be traveling to, in order: Quito, Ecuador; La Paz, Bolivia; Asuncion, Paraguay; Lima, Peru; Cuzco, Peru; Machu Picchu, Peru; and Bogota, Colombia which would get me to five new countries and the vast majority of the South American countries in total by the time this trip was done.

The main issue with it, shockingly, came from the travel agency miscommunications and mess-ups on both ends – the one I had communicated with, and the ones they had communicated with in South America. I won't mention the reputable agency I dealt with, but will say it even had a specialty department that booked trips like this one, in which I was flying point-to-point to various cities and would be met by a local tour guide who would provide a tour in each location. I liked this option – on paper, anyway – because it provided the flexibility I was seeking, yet provided someone who knew the city, spoke the local language, could advise me of specific do's and don'ts (not that I always comply), and who also would meet me at the airport or hotel. Since several of these places I'd be visiting were fairly dangerous, it was important to have my ducks in a row and not become a sitting, or dead, duck. I thought the details had been buttoned-up, but apparently a zipper was needed. In the end, however, I would do it all and be pleased with the outcome. But it should have been easier and more relaxing.

I arrived into Quito ("Kee-toe"), Ecuador and stayed in a classy hotel, Rio Amazones, near the city center. I strolled around narrow streets and observed the colonial buildings and city landscape, accented by the Andes Mountains. There was also an active volcano nearby that as recently as two years earlier had spewed ashes on the city, closing the international airport. The people and city had a warm charm: lots of smiles, helpfulness, friendliness, and old buildings well-maintained with several impressive churches (one of which had dual bell towers). It was strange that I even went into these churches after being force-fed so many on European tours, but they had grown on me. I also wanted to note if there was a difference compared with those from Europe (not really, but I'm no expert). I later learned that Quito and Krakow, Poland were the first two World Cultural Heritage sites declared by UNESCO, in 1978 – which may explain why I was charmed by both. There were also large plazas, including one named San Francisco, which was a popular name of several places I had been including in Europe (and, of course, California, near where I was living at the time). The full name of Quito, in fact, is San Francisco de Quito.

The people in Quito – as with elsewhere in South America – were crazy about their fútbol (soccer), and I passed by the stadium when it was empty (no games while I was there). Red, yellow, and blue are the team colors, and coincidentally (or subconsciously), I wore these colors around town a lot which may have earned me some "brownie" points with the locals. I would later make a point of wearing the country's team colors – and avoid wearing major competitors' team colors – in other cities on this trip which had fútbol teams. I found that wearing local sports team colors does help in some cases, including in U.S. cities (totally unofficial study but you may want to try it if abroad, or even domestically). I would have liked to go to a fútbol game, rowdy as the crowds are said to be (I had survived an Oakland Raiders football game sitting in "the black hole" with the fanatics).

My tour guide showed up as scheduled and provided a nice day tour that took me to the Equator. At this site was another tour guide who demonstrated some feats involving gravity. I volunteered for one. The tour guide asked me to clench my thumb and forefinger together, and hold it tightly. She tried to break them apart but couldn't. Then she asked me to take three steps to the left, having me stand on the Equator, and was able to pull them apart easily, despite my attempt to keep them together. This was repeated with several other tourists. This same tour guide also balanced an egg on the head of a nail. Both feats were interesting and impressive, garnering a lot of looks of surprise. Also, Quito has a high elevation (over 9,000 feet), so the altitude might take some getting used to. I was used to this high altitude when living in Colorado, and unlike others who were new to the area, I did not have any issues with it there nor in Quito.

I had a little issue with people speaking English in Quito (not many did), but I spoke a little Spanish, so the "Spanglish" combination was enough to get me by. In general, as mentioned, throughout my travels the younger people spoke English fairly well having learned it in school; therefore, I would often seek them out when needing assistance. The food was very good – especially the fish and the fruits, which were both flavorful. I met a few locals, took lots of photos ("the usual"), and was having a good time there. I heard that the nightlife was good but was geared for the much younger people. I was advised to stay within a specific perimeter at night. There were lots of police around, which either indicated the area would be very safe, or potentially very dangerous requiring their presence. I had just started this vacation and didn't want to find out, so I remained within the area, which still had some bars and other nightlife.

Overall, I enjoyed Quito and would consider going back – especially as a gateway to the Galapagos Islands. In retrospect, I should have gone there from Quito being so relatively close. I later heard from people who had been to Galapagos how awesome it is. So, it's on my list, but I had many other places to see and things to do as well.

My next flight was to La Paz, Bolivia. This city is inside of a canyon and, like Quito, has a population comparable to that of Philadelphia or Phoenix. It had lots of hills with orange-roofed houses on them, reminding me somewhat of the Dalmatian Coast in Croatia. My first impression, upon arrival into the city, was that it's like a giant flea market in a ghetto; there was extreme poverty everywhere (67% live below the poverty line) – and I was jostled quite a bit for handouts from poor people sitting on the pavement with a blanket as their bed. It was sad. I gave a little here and there, especially to the kids and elderly. A U.S. dollar went a long way in that country. People sold anything and everything seemingly everywhere, especially while sitting on the pavement, just to survive. Ironically, like Ecuador, the country also had an abundant oil supply. I kept thinking that there must be some way to leverage that into a better way of life for the people.

During a tour, we were told that the country was named after the independence fighter, Simon Bolivar, but lost a lot of land in wars, especially to Peru, Argentina, and Brazil. Bolivia also reminded me of other countries I'd been to in some ways: there was a lot of political graffiti on the walls as in Northern Ireland; the city was at a very high altitude like Quito, 12,000 feet up, and is the highest-altitude city capital in the world; and, as in Serbia, it seemed from my experience that 50% liked Americans and 50% didn't. These "American-unfriendly" places have very small sample sizes because once I ascertain that some people there don't like Americans, I don't say where I'm from. Once again, I also encountered locals who couldn't tell from my accent whether I'm from America or England, or even Australia. I wondered if people in South America could tell what country in that continent a person was from based on the specific accent. Later, some said they could do this, but they also observe the style of dress and selected words spoken.

The city was very dangerous! I was warned several times not to go certain places, especially at night. There were riot police outside of my hotel daily (I stayed in one of the better hotels, thankfully), and I got into an argument with a young drunk guy circa age 20 who was peeing on a wall in public, in broad daylight, with little kids walking around. Speaking of pissed, that's what happened to me and several others at Customs after landing at the airport when selected people, foreigners such as myself, were pulled off the line and forced to pay $100 in cash for a visa to enter Bolivia, although there was no such official requirement at the time (at least, that I was aware of). A female visitor, who also had to pay this fee, got very angry with the border agent and she screamed "Estupido!" at him a lot. I was surprised she wasn't hauled off to jail, perhaps with me too as an accomplice, because I wasn't thrilled either (albeit I was calmer). But I knew better than to exacerbate the situation; maybe this was a very new requirement. And what was I going to do, not pay it and go home?

That might have been a good option based on what was about to happen. My tour guide showed up by bus and thought that I was driving us to the sights I wanted to see! Holy miscommunication, Batman, how did that happen? He ended up leaving, and I ended up not paying, all amicable as a misunderstanding. I went downtown for a stroll around and came across a parade. I waved at some young guys and gals holding signage who waved back and came out of the parade to talk with me. I wondered, if as with the nun in Turkey, if I was wearing something that piqued their interest. It wasn't that, they just wanted to chat with someone who they thought (correctly) was an American. In some ways, they reminded me of the very nice young people I'd met in Southern Chile the year before. Also, they spoke English fairly well and perhaps wanted to practice with me as had the young adults in Lithuania and Latvia. As for me, I was glad to be talking to non-beggars there who spoke English. We chatted for a while, and they were very pleasant. They invited me to join in the parade. I figured this would be a good photo op, and I asked if they could take my photo with the parade in the background. They said sure, and told me to hold up the sign they had made, which was all in Spanish. I figured this gave it a more authentic Bolivian look, not like I'm at the St. Patrick's Day parade, e.g., with signs printed in English.

I wasn't paying attention to the parade, just focusing on them and the conversation we continued having. I should have been more aware, at least surveying the situation. We all started marching, with me holding the sign. Soon afterwards, the riot police came, swinging their clubs and throwing stuff into the crowd (tear gas, I think), and I just ran with the rest of them. The crowd dispersed in several directions, and chaos ensued including several protesters turning on the police. Lots of shouting, running, clashing, and water-spraying ensued in the smoky haze. It turned out this wasn't a "parade," but a military protest against the Socialist party which was in power, and the riot police came in to break it up. I just wanted to get out of there. Not even I dared to turn around and take photos because, as I learned at the Customs point and elsewhere, guess who might be first to be singled out? In what was not a Kodak moment (more like a Kodiak moment with those giant cops bearing down), I made haste down a side street, not knowing where I was and perhaps putting myself in more danger. But I relied on my instincts again, and just walked very briskly until I found a shopkeeper who spoke English and directed me back to my hotel (fortunately, once again, I had taken the card from the front desk with me). Well, it "reigned" on my "parade," but I did "rally" from that low point and "march" ahead. I should have known better, the signs were all there. I just couldn't read them – literally or figuratively.

So, was there anything good about this place? Yes, of course. Many people were kind to me, helping me out with directions, "safe" places to eat, and activities to do in "safe" areas. I also liked the colorful shawls and "bowler" hats that the ladies wore. These hats were ill-fitting (too small) and seemed more like men's hats, the type worn in England maybe 150 years ago at an equestrian event. Yet there were lots of women there, called cholitas, who wore them as a fashion statement. I wondered how they kept them on their head, which seemed like a feat because a good breeze could knock them off. It was cool up there in the high altitude (50s and 60s), but

I found this refreshing. Normally, it rained a lot there in January, but once again I had good weather throughout my trip. I also took to the altitude fairly well. I saw many foreigners struggling to breathe, and I was very mildly affected but not enough to stop me from doing anything. I later learned, however, that just a few days after I left Quito, Ecuador there was a volcanic eruption that forced the evacuation of 1,000 people. Compared to that, I suppose La Paz was pretty darned good.

I thought about buying an Alpaca sweater but didn't want to remember Bolivia. Better yet, I did an "I'll-packa" my luggage and got the heck out of there. I had ambivalent feelings about Bolivia – glad I got to see and experience it, but glad I was leaving safe and healthy. It was important for me to obtain many diverse life experiences, which inevitably would include some mishaps. I considered these bumps in the road, so to speak, and learning experiences that prepared me for later travels. However, I was not done "learning." My next flight was to another capital, Asuncion, Paraguay, and another adventure-misadventure scenario.

I wasn't thrilled with this place, either, a land-locked country where things went awry just after landing at the airport. From the "get-go," I didn't "get" and I didn't "go." That's because the taxi driver to my hotel arranged by the travel agent never showed, leaving me in a precarious situation I worked my way out of with the help of airport security who called me a "safe" taxi. Soon after my arrival at the hotel, the chandelier in my hotel room crashed to the floor, shattering and nearly injuring me (I hoped the people in the room above me weren't unscrewing it thinking it was a spy piece!). There was high poverty and crime there, aggressive child beggars, and lots of dank, dark places with massive cracks in the sidewalks. Political corruption and drug smuggling were two other issues facing the country. There was also a certain feeling that you were in a time warp, circa late 1950s or early 1960s. I saw several weird-colored (including pastel) Volkswagens and buses there. I'd heard there were some interesting places to see (e.g., small waterfalls), but either didn't find them or my tour guide didn't know of them, which was hard to believe. I took a city tour with my guide and there were few places of interest we went to except a palace, a cathedral, and the waterway area - Paraguay means smaller body of water leading into a larger one. That larger one could well end up at Iguassu Falls, which was not too far away but most people think of Argentina and Brazil when they want to visit there.

This brings me to an interesting conversation I had with a senior hotel management employee, a nice guy in his 50s who was very interested in my perceptions of Paraguay as an American, and how it could be promoted as a destination place for Iguassu Falls. I told him what I thought should be done (especially advertising and promotion), in particular noting how much less expensive it is to stay in Paraguay for budget travelers. I also mentioned the city needed to be spruced-up. This gentleman said he agreed, had some sway with certain higher officials in the country, and would let them know my thoughts. I admired that he wanted to make a difference there; he seemed enthusiastic and genuine about wanting this change. He talked a lot about the upcoming election, which had a solid challenger to the long-ruling Colorado (red) party, stating at that point each party had declared victory. Thus, he feared potential riots. Thus, I decided not to go out at night, opting instead to rest up and prepare for my big trip to Peru, and finally, Colombia. Besides, in just a short time I'd already had a few lowlights there, and during this trip in general. As Jackie Gleason might say in "The Honeymooners," it was "a regular riot." The expression from the show "bang-zoom" also applied, regarding the crashing chandelier and zooming in by the riot police.

My first stop in Peru was Lima, and I was not impressed there, either. The city was "just OK" and featured a park overlooking a bay, more cathedrals, the tomb of conqueror Francisco Pizarro, and more colorful buildings that were dull by comparison to the ones I saw in the Caribbean. There was a clock tower, statues, and plazas. If I hadn't seen it all before I would have been more impressed, but by this time I had seen more and better, so I just finished the city tour and rested up for the main attraction, Machu Picchu.

The flight between the two cities lasted an hour. Cuzco was the ancient capital of the Inca civilization; today, it is an aesthetically clean, beautiful masterpiece. Cuzco featured fine colonial architectural buildings combined with vestiges of the Inca civilization, against the backdrop of the Andes. It was easy to get around, and I even sat and relaxed a while just staring at the majesty of the place. It's still one of my favorite cities, sort of like a South American Prague.

Several musicians showed up, and I just loved their Peruvian Indian music. I bought a cassette tape and still play it to this day (my old Camry still has a cassette deck). A couple of years later, I would see guys like these playing in the Times Square train station in New York City, where I bought another cassette tape entitled "Music From The Andes Mountains," and chatted with them about my Andes experience. I'm also a fan of Native American Indian music and have cassettes of it bought in New Mexico that I also enjoy very much. Music is a connecting point to many things I want to remember, so if I had the chance to relive the wonderful memories there via the music I was all for it. I suppose many tourists think of Cuzco as merely a gateway to Machu Picchu, but there is a lot to Cuzco which shouldn't be overlooked in its own right. It's historical, colorful, beautiful, and musical all in one little charming place.

The main part of the city is called Plaza de Armas, and there are streets above that give a good overview of this area as well. There were a lot of Peruvian Indians walking around with their colorful garments, and again I saw those bowler hats I like. The people there loved their fútbol, too, and there were several crafts stores around selling local handiwork. The finely-laid cobblestone streets of the city were but a peek at what I was about to observe at the world-famous Machu Picchu ruins.

I almost didn't get there. The next day, the only day I had to go there, my wake-up call didn't arrive, and I had to rush like mad to make the train to get to Machu Picchu! Although Cuzco is only about 50 miles from Machu Picchu, getting there is difficult through the mountains. I took a train for three hours to a small town called Aguas Calientes near Machu Picchu, followed by a 20-minute bus ride up to the gate leading to the ruins. I met my tour guide at the bus depot; he was holding a placard with my name. We rode up together to the 8,000-foot plateau overlooking the ancient civilization's structures. He was a nice guy who provided the Incan history, and was also a good photographer as the photos would later bear out. The structures we were beholding were built circa 1450, and the war hero Francisco Pizarro conquered the Incas about 100 years later. It was said, however, that an epidemic of smallpox brought there by Europeans was what really wiped out the Incas. The site now known as Machu Picchu was discovered by an American explorer in 1911, and what a find it was!

The weather was iffy that day; it was mostly cloudy and rained up there a bit, making our hike slippery and muddy. But the sun did come out briefly and that's when I took many of the photos. However, the foreboding cloudiness also made for good photos. Two songs came to mind up there: "Macchu Man" (pun intended) by the Village People, and "Here Comes The Sun" by The Beatles. The views of the panorama were stunning; you *felt* the history. I had been to several Native American Indian places in the U.S., but this felt totally different based on the history; with only a little imagination, you could visualize what it could have been like back then. We climbed a lot of steep steps, walking around to different vistas of the ruins. The more I saw of it, the more in awe I was. The most amazing part was that the walls were built with no mortar or cement - or anything binding them. Again the Andes, and the clouds, made for a dramatic backdrop framing the stone structures, and were accented by the plethora of greenery. There were a lot of llamas (and maybe alpacas) up there as well, and backpackers, too, who looked like they were prepared for a couple of days there or more.

Based on all my travels thus far, it was hard to get a "rush" because I had seen so much, but this place provided that. There was the Temple of the Sun, Group Of Three Doors, Fountains area, and others that made you wonder how they did that. What I also noticed that impressed me, particularly as a casual photographer, was how the stone doorways framed the mountains when you looked directly through them. I noticed that up-close the stones were larger than I'd imagined when seeing them at the bird's-eye view. At this point in my travel career I wanted to see the best of the best, and this was in that genre. It was awesome just being there! I later learned that both Cuzco and Machu Picchu are UNESCO World Heritage sites. Of course they were; if they weren't, I'd be worried about the organization's judgment and selection process.

Machu Picchu was also voted one of the Seven New Wonders of the World by the New7Wonders Foundation, along with such other famous sites as the Taj Mahal, Coliseum, Christ the Redeemer statue in Rio, and Petra in Jordan. By this time I would have been to, or would soon get to, all of these. By the time of this writing I had not been to the Great Wall of China or Chichen Itza in Mexico – the other two making the list - but these are places to shoot for in the future.

I thanked the guide, and took the bus down the mountain and train back to Cuzco all in the same long day. It was well worth it, however. I had one more overnight at the hotel, and wouldn't have stayed there if I hadn't already pre-booked it as a non-refundable due to the non-wake-up call that nearly cost me seeing this magnificent site. I let them know about my displeasure in a diplomatic way, also alerting the travel agency. I realize that these things happen, but I had made extra sure that this call would arrive as scheduled (I didn't and still don't bring an alarm clock with me, but maybe should). As it turned out, there was a miscommunication between the night staff and the day staff. Fortunately, my internal clock always seemed to come to the rescue, and it did that time for sure. I didn't let this bother me much, but I learned another lesson about ensuring your wake-up call: don't assume anything.

Finally, to end this trip, I flew to Bogota, Colombia and checked into my "four-star" hotel which I booked based on a high recommendation for its safety, proximity to attractions, and it being my last stop on this tour where I figured I'd be pretty tired by then. Also, since I'd heard it was dangerous to walk around at night, I wanted a place I could just spend some time in that had a pool and bar in the lobby. I met my tour guide(s) there. This is where I had a "double-header": two guides showing up when only one was booked! I had no idea how this happened. The two guys argued over whose client I was and, after everyone called his respective travel agency, we collectively agreed that they'd both show me around and split the fee. This worked out better because each guy knew different sections of the city well – one guy the North district (upscale), and the other the South district (poor). However, they both warned me about the same thing: do not go out alone at night and walk around, which is what I asked them if I could do. Nearly everyone I asked about this urged me to "be careful," which I appreciated; heeding this was another matter.

We traveled high above the city where they gave me an overview, literally, and then to several plazas within the city, including Plaza de Bolivar with its twin bell towers (Bolivar's name was all over South America). There were many vending carts, with colorful umbrellas, selling food and drinks. I liked the arroz con coco a lot, which was steamed rice with coconut milk and sugar; I'm big on anything with coconut or lime. I also had the popular local dishes, including chicken with rice (arroz con pollo). I was urged to try the bananas, and did – they were so good that not only did I have these throughout my trip, but I started regularly eating bananas from that point on (my dad had been trying to get me to eat these for years). Beyond this, I found the people to be very friendly, friendlier than I thought they would be based on some of my ordeals to this point. One even taught me to salsa in the plaza. I wanted to put it to the test at a nightclub, but remembered what I was told about going out by myself at night.

However, I did walk around alone at night, but used my New York City instincts. I wanted fresh air, nice weather, and exercise but was very careful. I'd already had my South American and European (Spain and Russia) taxi misadventures, and didn't want to chance anything taking one there. I ended up being fine. That I could pass for looking Colombian in the dark maybe helped, plus walking briskly as if I knew where I was going. I had no problems – but it bears repeating that I do not recommend doing such potentially dangerous things. There were a lot of military police around as well, which made me feel a bit more comfortable. Later, I learned that several women had been attacked and further, that blonde women were especially vulnerable (I'd heard about this latter point in other parts of the world, too – mainly where blondes were not prevalent, and therefore perhaps more desirable).

The next day, my last, I stayed around the hotel but also walked around a lot to nearby plazas, cafés, and shops. I had some fruits which were delicious. I didn't even know what some of them were, but a few locals urged me to try them since they're popular there. One called a mangosteen supposedly has a great health benefit, and tasted OK. Once again – and this bears repeating – the food and beverages there tasted much more flavorful than the comparable products in the U.S. Of course, in another "when in Rome" scenario, although I am not a major coffee drinker I had to have a couple of cups – which were the best cups of coffee I ever had. As a result, I bought a large bag of coffee candy (one of my favorites) that lasted me a long time after I returned home. The candy was perhaps the most flavorful of any candy I've ever had, which is saying a lot because that's the business I was in for many years. I also bought a bag of coffee beans for my dad who drinks coffee often, and he shared it with his co-workers who thought it tasted great.

That night, I stayed in, packed up, and readied myself for a big travel day all the way back to California. It took 20 hours for me to return to California; I had taken 14 planes (including connections) in the last 14 days. On the flight back, I realized I had now been to about 80 countries - the total of John from the Bermuda cruise. And I was more than 30 years younger than he was by the time he had done this. Traveling was more than a hobby for me, it was a passion. A passion that would grow into later what I would refer to as a pillar of my life – no longer a hobby or interest like bowling, the Yankees, or photography – but a <u>foundation</u> that was shaping my life, like education and career. I figured as a college professor with summers and other time off, I could just keep traveling to places I wanted to go (provided I had the resources), but soon learned that in other parts of the world I wanted to visit the best time to go would be in February to May, when the weather was best and the crowds were light. I was unable to travel during this timing due to my teaching schedule, but kept this thought in mind.

I still had one free week remaining before teaching began for the new semester. I had some expiring frequent-flyer airline miles that had to be used quickly - use them or lose them. I kept careful tabs on these because the miles were worth real money if you used them. Northern California was in its rainy season, so I thought why not skip down to the Caribbean again and get a nice tan before I begin another semester? I thought about returning to Club Med, but since I was eager to see new places, especially visit new countries, I took a quick trip to St. Kitts & Nevis, another country in the Caribbean that a fellow traveler had recommended. This beautiful island had lush greenery that accented the emerald-colored water, and also had finely manicured lawns and gardens. Just a delightful place. I didn't do much there except go to the beach and lounge around in the hotel. I was in recuperation mode, and this was the right trip at the right time. As it turned out, my timing for this was excellent not only with the weather, but also because I would not have the upcoming summer off as anticipated.

Back at home, I prepared for another semester of teaching that Spring – which unknown to me at the time would be my last there. It went well, and the university wanted me back. However, there was a tricky part to this in that recruiters from the corporate world, with whom I had kept in contact, told me that having been out of corporate for three years is the maximum before interest in me would significantly diminish, even with my accomplishments. Plus, there was a recession looming, and companies were already tightening up the hiring. At this same time, universities were looking to reduce expenses based on budget cuts from the state, and were laying off teachers. I was safe, but was not provided with a longer-term contract beyond one year (renewable at both parties' discretion).

In a very tough choice, I ended up taking a corporate job in private industry landed via a national recruiter – would you believe, back in Buffalo, New York? This was pure coincidence. The company that hired me was a major multi-national dairy processor based in France; that I liked the French in general was a significant factor in my decision. Well, the job was good in the beginning, and I even made a new business friend at my level named Akym, who was from New Jersey. He was of Ukrainian descent (and surprised I'd been there), and I enjoyed his sense of humor. As business team leaders of large brands, we were sent to France to present the company's marketing plans for the products our respective teams worked on, and both did an excellent job. There were two things I realized the French there seemed to appreciate more so than back in the States: that I taught at the university level, and especially that I traveled to 80 countries by then, including nearly every country in Europe. In that regard, I was the beneficiary of a good twist of travel fate. To make a serial phone call story short, the company would save a lot of money on airfare if I was willing to spend the weekend in Malta (a country I hadn't been to), instead of returning on the previous weekday as scheduled. So that's what I did to create a win-win (others on the business trip needed to return before the weekend).

Although I stayed in St. Julian's, which had a pretty harbor area and good nightclubs, I spent much of my time in the country's nearby capital, Valletta. I took a city tour and met a tall, pretty blonde Russian tourmate in a red dress on the motor coach who I went around with during the stop-offs, although she spoke no English. But that didn't matter for either of us; we had a fun time anyway with no words spoken, roaming around hand-in-hand. There was a lot of history there including a big cathedral and palace, along with a beautiful harbor that we observed from Dingli Cliffs on the west coast of the island. We didn't see any Maltese falcons there, but we did visit a glassware factory and a National War Museum. The next day I met an Italian model who, after the magazine photo shoot, I took photos of and with. She was very pleasant and told me about the fashion world of modeling in Italy – and all the work that's involved preparing for the shoots. Once again, the weather was excellent, and the people were warm and friendly, too. I had gone to college with a gal who was Maltese, and would meet a Maltese lady soon after this trip back in the U.S. Both were flamboyant people, and I like people with a lot of life to them as the people there in Malta had. Even if they spoke only Maltese...or Russian.

The trip to France and the attendant side-trip to Malta were the highlights of my experience at this company. After that, I was less enchanted, missed the freedom I'd had to travel when teaching, and eventually left before the year was over with no regrets. I could have returned to teaching, but I had a new calling, one that by now was as familiar as an old friend.

As I did in business with preparing marketing plans, and as I did in teaching with preparing the syllabus and lectures, so too did I make a personal plan for myself at the end of each year. And when I sat down and thought about what would really make me happy, I realized that my true love at that time was travel. I was still single with no commitments, I had the discretionary income, desire, health, stamina, and now the time I needed. <u>I had visited nearly 80 countries</u>

and decided to go for 100! I was very good at realizing goals, and went about determining the best way to make this happen. It would take a while, but I came up with the ideal solution: the most viable and economical way to accomplish this was via international cruising. I wanted to travel sooner rather than later since the U.S. had just entered an economic recession that was diluting the value of the U.S. dollar. I had the resources, so off I went again into the wild blue yonder – not the sky, but the sea.

# Chapter 17

## Asia Fantasia: 9 Asian Countries in 24 Days – From China To Singapore And Beyond

This vacation almost didn't happen, but I'm very glad it did. I was making plans for my 50th birthday in February, on Valentine's Day, and wanted to be with a female. I never thought the "she" in this case would be a ship! Lana was to visit me from California, but had to cancel due to job demands. Being with my family in Florida was another option, but then I thought, "Why not do something different, as I had for my 40th birthday when going to Australia and New Zealand?" And why not keep with the theme of my **FINE** travel strategy that had worked so well – **F**un, **I**nteresting, **N**ew and **E**xciting?

During my research, I was surprised to find that a mainstream cruise line that usually did not travel exotic routes had a ship traveling through Asia, starting on February 14th. Further, two major airlines I was affiliated with had just merged and I could combine frequent flyer mileage to get me there and back for free, flying into Shanghai two days before the cruise, and returning home from the Philippines after it ended. And the best part was that the cruise line, which had been booked solid for this trip for months, had just one cabin left in my desired price class due to a cancellation, and the price was excellent! It seemed like this trip was meant to be. However, in the intervening hour between the time I learned this information and checked if I could use my frequent flyer mileage to these departure cities, the cabin was booked by someone else and then the cruise line was sold out! Damn! But wait: being a veteran traveler and marketer, I knew that cruise lines provide blocks of rooms to travel agencies, both brick-and-mortar and online for these ships, and that just because the cruise line itself had no availability this did not mean that there weren't any cabins left. So, I called around and struck pay dirt with an online site big in its field. This company, too, was sold out, but I was so persistent with callbacks after midnight that I was able to snap-up a cabin that had been cancelled, at an even lower price than the one I could have had from the cruise line! It was Super Bowl time when this fortunate event happened, and I realized metaphorically that I had received a "Hail Mary." It wasn't the Queen Mary, but in this case just "touching down" where I needed to go would be the victory I wanted.

I was on my way a week later! The ship would sail to, in order: China (Shanghai, Xiamen, Hong Kong, and Sanya); Thailand (Pattaya City); Viet Nam (Danang, Nha Tran, Tau Vang); Cambodia (Sihanoukville); and finally, Singapore (Singapore is also the city name). From this last port I would then spend a week on my own flying to Malaysia (Kuala Lumpur); traveling to Indonesia (Batam) by ferry; and then flying to the Philippines (Manila). And, amazingly, I would receive a free stopover in South Korea (Seoul) on my return to the U.S. because, again as a veteran traveler, I knew to ask about this given the distance of the trip. The very helpful reservationist (who was rooting for me) was totally accommodating. This trip would get me to seven new countries, plus two that I'd been to before (the first two). Unlike the South America trip, I would not have a tour guide meeting me in each city after the cruise, and would just be wingin' it on my own the whole time. As long as I stayed away from "parades" and things that went crash-in-the-night, I figured to be OK.

My home was well-secured and looked after, so I left with peace of mind. I would remain in Buffalo during this time because the rent was very affordable for a nice place, and why pay more when I wouldn't be around for long stretches? I flew to Shanghai on February 12$^{th}$, arriving the next morning and spending the day exploring the city (again). It was the same as I remembered it. The crowded city looked like a big version of Chinatown (naturally), with huge vertical banners outside the storefronts, mostly in red or yellow with Chinese lettering. I had "Chinese food" for lunch, consuming a chicken dish with rice. The taste was similar to that I've had in the U.S. with three notable differences: it was more flavorful, saltier, and the chicken pieces were smaller. In talking to locals who spoke English there, I learned that food is prepared differently in various parts of China, so that the same dish could taste a particular way in Shanghai and another way in Peking. Some chefs used more spices, sauces, salt, or even vinegar to enhance the flavor. Also, it is impolite to discuss inflammatory topics in a group at the table, such as politics. "The meal is meant to be an enjoyable experience, and save the politics and debates for later," I was advised.

I was surprisingly refreshed, having slept well on the plane, had no jet lag, and did not need to nap after the 20+ hours of flying. I was still a travel athlete, even at 50, from the previous conditioning having done this so often. After a good night's sleep I took a taxi to the ship, only three miles away. The check-in was very organized, even with few people speaking English, and I got to my cabin quickly. Unfortunately, there was a problem with the air conditioning and heating system there, but I was moved to another comparable room when another passenger disembarked at the next port. After the safety drill, I went to have lunch and meet other passengers.

As suspected, the vast majority of passengers were retirees. Fortunately for me, there was a very nice upscale "younger" South African married couple on the ship named Andrew and Nadine, who were in their 40s, professional, fun, and lively. We sat together at the dinners; I enjoyed their company immensely (he's a psychologist and she's an artist). Despite being from different continents so far away, it seemed as if we had grown up in the same neighborhood. We thought the same way, and had the sense of humor. This definitely was a boost throughout the long cruise, and I learned a lot about their home country in the process. They highly recommended I go visit there, and as it turned out I would be sooner than we all thought. At dinner, the staff surprised me with a delicious birthday cake and balloons for my 50th birthday (perhaps Andrew or Nadine tipped them off, or they knew from previous bookings based on my birthday). That was very sweet, and there were sweeter parts yet to come.

China in total was a mixed bag on this trip. Xiamen (Shah-men) was rather dull. Its main industries are fishing and shipbuilding, among others. The weather was unseasonably cool (temperatures in the 40s) and damp. We only stayed a day, and I was underwhelmed. But better things were coming. In Hong Kong, we visited Kowloon Island where I had stayed on business. I even got to re-visit the posh Peninsula Hotel in which I stayed. It still had the same elegance. We took an organized tour to a floating restaurant that was on its own island, a colorful kids' park with giant Chinese doll figurines, and a tram up to Victoria Peak overlooking the city and harbor, which I had done my first visit there – the spectacular view was worth repeating. Hong Kong had been returned to China by the British after a 99-year-old treaty had ended, but still seemed the same to me as 14 years earlier. At night, Hong Kong's tall buildings lit up the sky with a light show, with beams shooting out all over like a laser-rock performance (no music, though). I watched this from the port side of the ship. It was as if Hong Kong was saying goodbye to us, sending us back to the sea with a colorful display of its final hospitality.

Next came the best part of China for me, in a place I'd never heard of before now, Sanya. Instead of taking the ship's shore excursion, I took a free shuttle van into town and walked around on my own. The weather was beautiful, sunny and about 75 degrees. Many others from my ship were in this shuttle van. While they went shopping for two hours, I walked in totally the opposite direction, a long way, before which I noted the exact location and time of the van pick-up for returning us to the ship. I came upon a beautiful white-sand beach, at which I saw many cute Chinese gals in their 20s in bikinis taking photos of each other. I didn't know there was a beach anywhere around, so I did not have my bathing suit. I walked onto the beach anyway, and asked if the gals speak English. They didn't, but seemed intrigued by me and were very friendly.

Using hand gestures, I asked if they would take a photo of me using my camera which I gave to them. They agreed and took a few. Then one of the gals handed me her camera, ran down to the shoreline, and wanted me to take photos of her and her friend, obvious by their posing, which I did. The two gals then said something to each other and laughed. They ran back to me and one grabbed my hand, bringing me to the chairs in which they were sitting under a bamboo umbrella. Her friend ran up laughing, and then pushed me down on the seat, sat on my lap, and put her arm around me as if I was her boyfriend for a photo op. Her friend took photos, and they were cracking up. Then they reversed positions, and the other gal sat on my lap. I didn't mind, and after they were done I got out my camera and asked for similar photos, which they obliged. We had lots of fun despite not speaking each other's language; even many other people on the beach (mostly Chinese) were amused and gawking. I might have been the only Caucasian on the beach, which was crowded, and probably the only one not in a bathing suit, which added to the odd scenario. These gals were so much fun that they reminded me of Akko from Japan who was on my tour in Scandinavia. And if I'd had my bathing suit and suntan lotion, you know that I would have asked for the multi-handed backrub like I got at the Great Barrier Reef in Australia.

The shuttle van would be arriving soon, and I would have to go. I wished they could have come back to the ship with me, heck, and stayed with me during the trip. It was a laugh-a-thon despite the age and language differences. At one point all three of us couldn't stop laughing, though we didn't know why – laughter is not only universal, but contagious! They hugged me goodbye and we did a group hug, too. As I turned back one last time, they were still looking at me and waved goodbye. I had a really fun time there, and I think they did, too. More happiness was created in the world, suddenly, unexpectedly, humorously, at no-one else's expense. This sounds good to me.

At dinner that night, Andrew and Nadine asked me how my day was, and I told them. I didn't think they believed me but I had my digital camera and showed them the photos. Then they believed me. The funny thing was the other guys at our table for 8 (3 couples, me, and an older woman) wanted to see them, too, with the wives sitting right next to the married guys. Andrew passed my digital camera to them. Later, in private, both these other guys came over to me and said to keep doing what I'm doing, living my life this way, and enjoying every minute of it before I get too old. These comments triggered lyrics in my mind from my favorite Billy Squier song: "Learn how to give/Learn how to take/Learn how to live/Before it's too late." These lyrics still resonate with me big-time today, and often drive me to live life to the max now while I can.

We next docked in Laem Chabang ("Lame Sha – bang" – I liked the name), Thailand. Many passengers took the long road trip to Bangkok, but I had been there and wanted to go elsewhere. This turned out to be another good choice. I took an organized tour to Pattaya City, and had another excellent time there. As with Sanya, this was another city I knew nothing about until I got there. The main attraction was a cultural show that featured colorful, ornate, gold outfits, slow-movement dancing that seemed Polynesian/Hawaiian (lots of hand movements), and also an elaborate stage set looking like something out of "The King Of Siam" (which Thailand was called prior to 1939). There was also a kick-boxing match that I enjoyed even more than the cultural show, and then there was the elephant show, which I enjoyed most. These decorated elephants played soccer, rode tricycles, threw darts with their trunks that popped balloons, and even painted very well with watercolor brushes! The grand finale was that they would give backrubs with their feet to selected audience members. Perhaps because I was taking a lot of photos, the ringmaster selected me from the crowd of about 500 people to be the "rub-ee" under the elephant's foot. I was cajoled by the crowd, but decided not to. One slip from that elephant and it would have been all over. I opted for safety, this time, but took a lot of photos that came back surprisingly well given how far away I was (my camera had a high zooming capacity that came in handy when editing the photos to look closer-up).

After the event ended, the ringmaster came up to me, and we chatted. He liked Americans and told me to wait until the crowd left, if I could, for a "special surprise." I told him I had a shuttle bus to catch, but that it would take a while for the others to board so I had about 15 minutes, seeing that the bus hadn't arrived yet. When the place was empty he let me into the ring, where the elephants were, and got one to lay down in front of me as the camel had in Morocco. He then told me to straddle it and give him my camera, which I did. I trusted him, and by association the elephant, too, which then raised up! I held its leash; there was no other support, such as a saddle or even helmet for me. The elephant walked around a bit, and I was sliding around on its back, holding on with a firm grasp; I was happy I had done my set of 40 push-ups (as I had every morning since I was 15) because it wasn't easy holding on. The ringmaster took a few photos that ended up coming out well. That was a new experience, for sure; in fact, it was **FINE** all rolled up into one: **F**un, **I**nteresting, **N**ew **E**xciting. Maybe **TUSK**, too: **T**ricky, **U**nusual, **S**cary, **K**razy!

That's a real elephant in Pattaya City, Thailand that just finished a performance playing soccer, throwing darts at water balloons with its trunk, and giving backrubs with its foot to selected volunteers from the audience during the show. I rode it around for a while, and felt like I was in the circus.

At dinner, Andrew and Nadine again asked what I had done that day (they had gone shopping). I didn't say a word, just showed them the photos of me on the elephant. I then explained what happened. They and my other dinnermates got a real kick out of this. I told them that's what I would have got had the elephant mistaken me for a soccer ball. Our group of 8 got along very well, with more from the U.K. and also Australia chiming in. I was becoming ringleader, sparking the discussions, before yielding to others when they became emboldened to do the same (even Andrew was reluctant to address all in the beginning). I learned more about Andrew and Nadine – they had met on a dating website about a year earlier, and it worked! Nadine had pretty much given up on it based on the guys she was dating, but then along came Andrew and it was magic. They did make a very nice, good-looking, and fun couple. I thought there could even (as in *even*tually) be hope for a free spirit like me.

I spent a little time at Pattaya Beach the next day, where it was about 100 degrees in the shade. During lunch I nearly burned my mouth off when eating the hot and spicy Thai food! I never before and never to this day tasted anything that hot! I almost wanted to put suntan lotion in my mouth to soothe it. That stuff should come with a warning label. Funny thing was I had asked for the "mild" version. Afterwards, I photographed an old church, orchid garden, and went to a gem factory with a pictorial flowchart and video of how the gems are mined, polished, and cut. I would later meet an elegant lady aboard another ship who was a gemologist, who would be impressed with my knowledge of gems, and wonder how I knew so much about them. Prior to seeing this video I knew zero about the process. So, going to this place in which I had virtually no interest turned out to be a sparkling idea. And so was going on this cruise as a last-minute decision; in the end, my travels would go so well that I needed no other confirmation that I did the right thing in sailing right out of the corporate world and back into the rest of the world. "Sea world" then took on a whole different meaning to me.

Next we were off to Viet Nam's three ports. There were many Viet Nam War veterans on this cruise who had come onboard specifically to return to the scene they remembered all too well. Some of the conversations were really intense, including among vets who had just met on this cruise. Whether they were there to exorcise their demons, or relive the memories, or whatever, there was a lot of emotion behind it. Several went into the former Saigon, now called Ho Chi Minh City or HCMC, and returned with their stories. I did the same also from Vung Tau (an hour away), but of course it wouldn't have the same significance to me since I was a little kid when the war started and a mid-teen when it ended.

This country had a whole new vibe compared to China and Thailand: poverty (again). Lots of people were walking around without shoes, and in tattered clothing. I gave some money to selected people who really appreciated it. But once more, the people were what made it a warm and friendly place, and delightful, actually. I took organized tours in each port to get a lay of the land before venturing out on my own; this was an opportunity to see places to which I might want to return. Later, I did just that. One tour guide tried to be a comedian; his jokes weren't funny but I gave him credit for trying. He said, "You may have heard that we eat dog here. We do – hot dog."

The first thing I noticed in general were the crazy drivers, including numerous people on motorbikes and bicycles, followed by the disorganization/chaos. In Ho Chi Minh City there was a lot of hustle and bustle, reminiscent of other larger cities, but also lots of little boutiques, street peddlers, street beggars, and piles of various industrial materials left unattended in residential areas where you wouldn't expect to see these. We were warned about pickpockets as well, so I was constantly on the alert. The city was divided into many districts, and we were in the downtown area in District 1 once called Saigon. There were many statues, gardens, temples, pagodas, and old ladies in conical hats with chin straps selling books, local crafts, silks, and other items. I strolled around being extra careful, ending up in various shops, and not taking any chances roaming away from the main tourist venues as I had in the other cities. I was also careful about the food, given my near-death mouth experience in Thailand, and of course even crossing the street required full attention. I saw several war memorials but didn't make the trip to see the now-famous Cu Chi tunnels that Ho Chi Minh war guerillas used to attack

Saigon. In retrospect, I should have spent more time seeing the war memorabilia.

We came across an outdoor wedding and, as I had done in Romania, couldn't resist taking a photo with the bride and groom who were all too willing to do this. They were each short, maybe five-feet in height, so I looked very tall compared to them. Their friends also took photos of the three of us; they thought it was funny (I was dressed in street clothes). We said goodbye, and I wished them well. I'm not sure they even spoke English, but we knew what each other meant. Another "who was that guy?" moment. Note: I just take the photos and do not crash the wedding.

Since I'd had fun on the beach in Thailand, I went to one in Viet Nam as well and had another really good time. First I met a Swedish gal named Erika who was touring the area. We hung out together for a while; she was also into photography and we took numerous pictures of the landscape and of each other. Note that I take so many photos that I need lots of them with others so I can balance out those with only me and only landscape for my albums. Even if I took only 5% of my photos of or with others, that can still be up to 150 photos per long vacation I need to shoot. Erika and I had a good time, and she had to get going back to her ship, but I would soon sweep a gal off her feet – literally. I met a tiny little gal named An, about age 20, who was maybe five-feet tall and had the cutest smile. She came over to me as I was taking photos with some other Asian gals I'd met and spoke very little English. She wanted to be in a photo with me by the shore, and she walked me toward there. I don't know what came over me but just before the photo was taken I reached over and picked her up – right out of her sandals! An had such a look of surprise on her face as I cradled her, and you can see her sandals at the bottom of the photo which held her feet just seconds earlier. We all laughed.

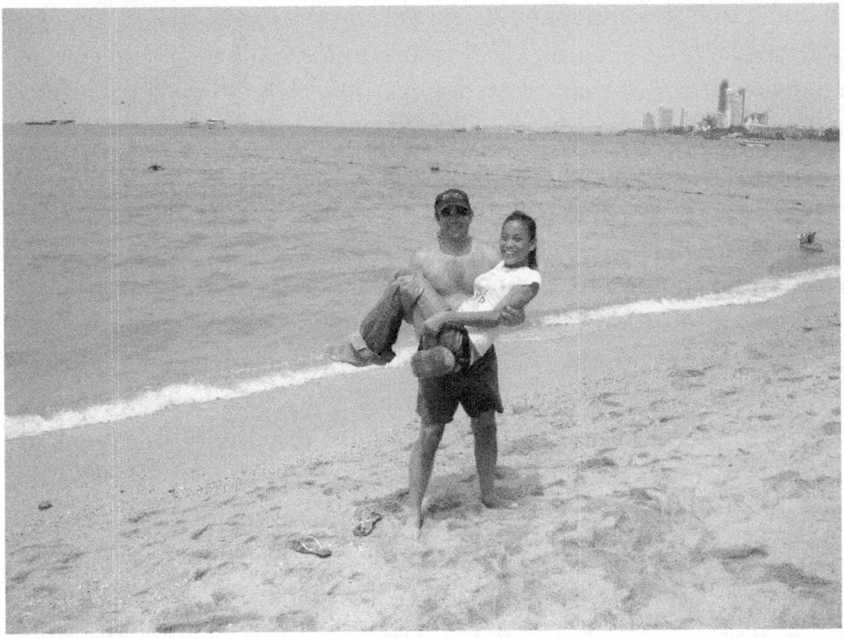

Here in Viet Nam, I made a spontaneous decision to lift this gal up just as the photo was being taken. As it turned out, she came right out of her sandals! Talk about "picking up a girl on the beach!"

Soon after this, I was walking around and met another cute little gal named Linh in her 30s, who was selling sunglasses with her mom at her side. She had a lovely smile, and wore an orange shirt with a floppy white hat while holding a wooden tray with the sunglasses. We got into a very good conversation, and she told me about the city. She was very interested in America. After our chat, she looked up at me and said, "Can you take me back with you to America?" Her mother, who spoke a little English, cracked up. I laughed, too. I said, "You're tiny so I think I could fit you in my luggage, if that's OK." Linh just smiled, and I said, "I wish I could, but I can't, sorry." Then Linh stunned her mom and me by saying, "Will you marry me?" She was serious! I told her no in a polite way, but thanked her so much for asking. I didn't want her to feel badly for asking, and she was OK with my reply.  I bought a cheap pair of sunglasses from her, gave her a hug goodbye, and went on my way. How sweet was that? And why didn't I marry her? I thought. Maybe I should have. Sunglasses for life! In many poor countries I've been to, and some not so poor, locals perceived all Americans as being rich. I later learned from a gal in China that she and many Asian women she knew looked for a guy with the "five c's": "credit card, cash, condominium, car, and career." I had only three at that point. Not a great catch, oh well. Ironically, I would soon travel the "seven seas."

I then walked around and bought a T-shirt. At 5'8, 155 pounds, my size there was XXXL (compared to a Medium in the U.S.). I was again like a giant in an Asian country. I later heard of a guy who was 6'5 with blond hair and blue eyes who went to Bhutan – and was followed around like a deity. I bought a cap as well, to "cap-off" another good day. At dinner aboard ship that night, Andrew and Nadine just looked at me and said, "OK, let's have it, show us the pictures" without even asking what I did. Andrew intriguingly scrolled through them and wanted the stories. I told him and the rest of my dinnermates. They just shook their heads incredulously. "Will the whole trip be like this for you?" Lewis from London asked. "I hope so," I replied with a big smile. "I sure do hope so." That night I slept 15 hours; I must have needed it. Maybe it was due to the video replay in my mind, also known as pleasant dreams.

The cruise sailed on, and we ended up in Sihanoukville, Cambodia, so named after one of the country's independence-fighters from that region and translating to "Jaws of the lion." Sihanoukville was the place of the last official battle of the United States army in the Viet Nam War, although the incident took place outside Viet Nam. We were provided with the history of the country and it is ugly, including dictator Pol Pot during the Khmer Rouge regime killing his own countrymen, especially those who had the capacity to oppose him, including teachers and other intellectuals. Cambodia recovered from that, but the situation was still very bad there; it is still one of the poorest countries in the world, with a per capita income of only $2,000 U.S. a year. Take what I said about Viet Nam's poverty and crazy drivers and double it, from my standpoint. Near our port was a large shantytown with garbage everywhere. In other poor countries, I saw people on bikes come by and put the trash in bags to be hauled away. Here it just stayed. Many people walked around with white surgical masks over their mouths - and they didn't work in the medical profession. There were loose chickens running around, kid beggars seemingly everywhere, and most people walking around barefoot. Your heart really went out to them.

There were lots of motorbike drivers who had no helmets, drove wherever they felt like (including sidewalks), had no mirrors, and seemed to be very early teens who shouldn't be driving anything motorized. Part of this was due to there being no public transportation system there, except for independently operated vans called tuk-tuks that jammed people in the back and shut the door. However, you would see people in the back without the door shut, which appeared very dangerous. There did not appear to be a lot of police enforcement, and you had to watch where you went, even if you had the right of way. Essentially, this was "bellek!" with a motor.

There were, however, a couple of positives about the place, which I suppose was why we were there. Among them were several Buddhist temples, and huge golden Buddha statues that were quite ornate. There were other golden statues, too, and several large stone lions. Another major attraction was the white sand beaches. These were very good, reminding me a lot of the Caribbean beaches. I then had a strange Canadian – Cambodian connection that would span more than one year. On the beach, I met a couple of Canadian college students from Vancouver. I had been to Vancouver a few times, and to this day it's one of my favorite cities. I told them about my photo albums and asked if they knew where I could get Cambodia post cards; I hadn't seen any around. They didn't know, we finished our nice chat, and I was heading back to my beach blanket.

Just then a boy about age 12 ran toward me (I was hoping he wouldn't offer me a ride on his dirt bike). He asked if I'm from the cruise ship. I said yes. He then said he could get me whatever I needed. I asked if he could get me some post cards. He said he'd try, but didn't return. I forgot about the interaction. However, this kid must have said something to someone because a few hours later a cabbie (or I should say a guy who has a car who charges people whatever price he feels like for a ride) came by our dock as the ship was boarding and yelled out, "Post cards, who wanted post cards." I came over to the rope separating us, discussed it, and we worked out a price. I told him to hurry because we're leaving in a little over an hour. He did, and I met him back there in 60 minutes as planned.

But he wanted five times the amount! Despite this being a relatively small sum ($25 vs. $5), I wasn't about to be "taken for a ride" by anybody, and refused. I tried to negotiate, but he said that he was also charging me for the gas to get the cards from the other side of town, which wasn't in our conversation. I was willing to pay him double, but he gave me a hard time. If he was nice about it I still may have done it at the very high price, but I refused because of his attitude. He also gave me some chatter about all Americans being rich (probably meaning the ones who can afford to visit there). I informed him that's just not true, and walked away. I ended up not getting the post cards, which I regretted because I needed them for my photo album. Here's where a Canadian came to the rescue. A year later, through some travel connections at Gap Adventures, I ended up being referred to a Canadian woman I never met who was going to Cambodia as part of her vacation. Via email, we arranged that she would get me the post cards, mail them to me upon return to Canada, and I would pay her when she returned, which is just what happened. I offered to pay for the postage as well, and despite her refusal I paid it anyway. But if she had charged me the airfare to get them...

These ornate gold statues were in sharp contrast to the poverty of Cambodia. But the real riches were in its people, who had endured a lot but were determined to be happy.

A few passengers took the 13-hour tour to Phnom Penh (optional excursion costing extra), but I couldn't see riding 9 hours with those crazy drivers for spending only 4 hours in the capital. At dinner, I spoke to a married couple who went. It didn't sound so "phnom"-enal – they said there was extreme poverty and chaos, but that its shining moments were the opulent pagodas, palace, riverfront area, and museum. Reasons for going included the history, the movie "The Killing Fields," and what else was there to do near the port? (good point). Well, I was "OK" with my stay there in Cambodia. Not every trip was going to be wonderful, and it's good I saw the palpable poverty because it brought out my human empathy side in a big way. I understood more by seeing, helping me reconnect with my feelings, and thought deeply about it while in that environment. Viewing stories about poverty in the movies or on TV, or reading about them, is one thing; but when it's right there in front of you, literally staring you in the face and assaulting your other senses, you realize what it really is. This was like a smelling salt of reality for me, and I have also often thought about it since.

Next we sailed to Singapore, the last port for this cruise. Unlike the two places we just were, Viet Nam and Cambodia, this country was aesthetically beautiful, and so clean you could eat a meal off the pavement. However, it was weirdly obsessive about this. On the declarations statement they wanted to know if you're bringing in weapons, excessive cash, and among other things, chewing gum! They do not want litter, and consider gum a potential "menace" (my sarcasm) in this regard. Had I said "I have 'Bazooka' on me" I might have been arrested for both weapons and gum charges.

Our tour guide told us more. There is a steep tax for importing a car (e.g. $40,000 total cost for a Corolla), and a tax for dog owners, too, because of the pollution/litter that can be created, respectively. Weapons of any kind (possibly including toys) can get you into big trouble, and the same but to a lesser extent with porn (even risqué lingerie), and pirated movies and music. If a cop pulls you over for speeding there is no arguing – you get a ticket in the mail and are expected to pay it (no pleas are accepted). Our tour group saw this in action while on the motor coach. If you're caught with drugs, there is an automatic death penalty. There are some religious materials restrictions, too. It was then that I realized why the news-making 19-year-old U.S. teenager who spray-painted cars there received four months in jail and was caned with four strokes, causing bruising and bleeding. So be forewarned, if going to Singapore in particular, check about restrictions ahead of time – they're serious! Note, too, that in a couple of countries visited I had to undergo an infectious diseases medical exam on-site at immigration (everyone entering did). So beware that this may be required to enter the country, irrespective of yellow card vaccinations, e.g., and that you could be denied if not deemed healthy on-the-spot (including viruses). I had a funny thought if I happened to sneeze when being inspected; that if questioned whether I have a cold I would deny it and say that I was asking for the whereabouts of Dr. Ah Choo.

There was an extensive public transportation system in Singapore, including monorails and trams, to keep the place less polluted and ineffably clean. The taxi drivers even dressed in suits! I took a half-day tour – if for no other reason than especially in Singapore I wanted the "protection" of a tour guide who might save me from myself given the situations I sometimes got myself into. We learned that Singapore is a "city-country," meaning this is the only city in the country, and is one and the same. Singapore is the size of Chicago, so it's not big for a country, but it is for a city – you can see how strange it all gets. We rolled through Singapore's Chinatown and Little India areas. However, each has a significant population in the other's community, prompting our tour guide, a lovely Singapore lady, to say, "They didn't get the memo" in her slow-speaking, clearly-enunciated, deliberate manner with a broad smile. I wanted to say, "If they got the memo I hope they didn't litter with it afterwards" but maybe wisecracks on an official tour would be considered mutiny and I'd be caned (or based on my confectionery marketing experience, candy-caned). We toured a neatly manicured botanical gardens with mini-waterfalls where there were some interesting huge plants – one of which looked like a giant feather in an Indian's head-dress. I noticed a robotic efficiency about the country, everything very orderly, on schedule, finely manicured, and meticulous; this reminded me of Switzerland, but there it was even more pronounced.

I had brought poster board and a black magic marker with me, to create a sign with the date reading, "I am now in Singapore – my 85th country visited." I held this up in three separate locations for a future photo album insertion, including in front of the Buddha Tooth Relic Temple, an icon of the city. One female passerby who was British said, "Congratulations!" and I would later take a photo holding the sign with a local Singapore gal at my side. I traveled to more than 100 countries but stopped creating the signage after the 100th. I had thought for sure that my 50th or 75th would be my last country visited; had I known I would get to the 100th I probably would not have made up these other signs. But once I had them, I thought I'd keep going every milestone until I reached the magic number (to make an interesting photo album page out of them someday).

After the tour, I walked around on my own and had Singapore noodles, which like the Thai food, were super-spicy and practically burned-off the inside of my other cheek (the one inside my mouth, not the one they cane). I spoke to a few locals who were friendly, especially the younger people, who struck me as very proper and British-like. The cruise then ended, and I said goodbye to my cruisemates, especially Andrew and Nadine who I'd keep in contact with via social media. Excellent cruise and trip overall – once again, I saw and learned a lot!

I took a taxi to my hotel, at which I was staying only one night, where I learned that there was a ferry to Batam (pronounced Bah-tom), Indonesia that took only 90 minutes to get there! I didn't have a visa, but was informed that I could get one there upon arrival. Intuitively, I quickly decided to go there, and had to hurry to make the last sailing of the day. Without thinking much about it, I packed my essentials and raced to the dock, barely making the last ferry outbound. I was virtually the only Caucasian on the crowded ferry, and received further stares when taking a general photo of the interior, and having someone take a photo of me on the ferry in the seating area. I definitely stood out, but this wasn't new to me.

Upon arrival, I had to stand in a separate line to acquire a visa. It cost only $10 and was very colorful – inexpensive and a nice souvenir! I went inside the ferry terminal, a relief because it was blazing hot outside. I thought the clock there was broken because it showed the time being an hour earlier than what I'd thought. As it turned out, that clock was correct – there was a one-hour time difference earlier, so I had an extra hour to spend there. To be sure, I asked the ferry personnel about this, and they confirmed that the time for my return ferry is based on Indonesian time. The security guard approached me. He told me to be "very careful," and added that the area "is not safe." He didn't mean just pickpocketing, he meant physical attacks. I changed dollars into rupees and went out, but not far from the terminal. I didn't realize that Indonesia was such a populated country – the 4th largest in the world with 238 million people! Jakarta is the largest city there with nearly 10 million people (more than New York City), and Batam has nearly 1 million, so it wasn't small. There are 17,000 islands to Indonesia, but only about 6,000 are inhabited.

During my wanderings outside, it was time to switch on the New York City instincts – walk briskly, be alert, nothing in back pockets, nothing flashy showing, look like I know where I'm going/what I'm doing, and also note if any police officers are nearby and their whereabouts. I'd been in that situation before, so I was not nervous. There really wasn't much in Batam, some nice buildings and a harbor area in this highly populated Muslim city with a tourist industry. As such, there were police officers around – but again, I had been warned. Many women at the harbor area dressed, shall I say, provocatively, looking for some action. I strolled around without incident, taking photos and admiring the views. I had learned to "stop and smell the coffee" more as a photographer – not just shoot and run, but stand there and take in the environment, be aware how it affected my five senses, and this often made a difference. I did not sample the food outside of the port terminal because I had no more cheeks left to burn, and needed my tongue for future conversations.

I returned to the terminal and spoke to several locals there who were welcoming and curious about the U.S. I had an especially good conversation with a pretty gal dressed in Muslim attire who told me lots about the Indonesian culture. She said it is a montage of various cultures that includes Buddhists, Hindus, and Islams, plus many others having roots in the Middle East and Far East. She told me about the food, in particular rice dishes, tofu, and satay which I'd heard of but I didn't know what it was (skewers of meat or fish dipped in peanut sauce). I asked why the food is so hot. To them it's not. Lots of red chili peppers was the answer. I'm not a peppers eater, so maybe that's why I burned like a disco inferno, thinking fire would flare from my nostrils. I had a bite to eat inside the terminal where there were restaurants, and had a good meal for only two U.S. dollars in equivalent rupees. Nothing spicy, and I asked a few times to make sure given the potential language and taste-bud barriers. I bought extra white rice and bottled water just in case, but was fine.

As it turned out, a year later back in Buffalo, New York I met an Indonesian gal named Tika who I dated for a while before she moved to the Midwest. Tika invited me to a family Indonesian dinner with some relatives and I accepted. They were very nice, the food was very good, and I bought a mini-fire extinguisher to put in my pocket just in case (just kidding). Tika had a very interesting story, although I'm not sure how typical it was. She was married to a prominent guy in Indonesia for several years, when he suddenly decided that he wanted four wives and that they should all live together. She got divorced, which shamed and humiliated the family, and she therefore left the country to live with relatives in Buffalo before they moved to the Midwest, taking Tika with them. That's the last I saw or heard from Tika after a few dates. I would have settled for three wives in total, but there went that idea. Soon after my brief relationship with Tika, I attended an Indonesian cultural dance performance aboard a cruise ship that was outstanding. So, I was exposed to and liking Indonesian people, food, and events in just a short period of time, after hardly knowing anything about the culture. After that, nothing further relating to Indonesia crossed my path.

I returned on the ferry and lost an hour in time, so it was late and dark back in Singapore. I walked around the hotel area and talked to several young adults who were hanging out. They liked Indonesia, but each of them had not lived anywhere else although they wanted to someday. I didn't tell them this, but I noted throughout my international and domestic travels that if people hadn't lived or traveled much outside their local vicinity they tended to like their city/neighborhood better. Conversely, if they had been exposed to other (better) places they didn't like their own area as much and even moved around a lot to other cities, realizing that there may be better ones out there. Although I had lived out of New York City by then for more than a decade, I still appreciated it – but was glad I was exposed to the other cities I had lived in as well to offer balance and perspective. Even living in Queens, as I had for 8 years, was a whole different vibe than living in Brooklyn, despite both being part of the same city. I'd like to get back to Indonesia someday and check out the major cities and tourist destinations such as in Bali and Jakarta. But I'd had a small sample, a buffet plate so to speak – and perhaps best of all, I didn't get burned by the experience, literally.

The next day I left for Kuala Lumpur, Malaysia by plane. I had no idea what to expect as I ventured out on my own, also in a heavily Muslim city, just looking forward to letting life happen and making the most of it. The weather was extremely hot and humid, like a sauna. I found a hop-on, hop-off bus in the center of town that took me around to a number of attractions for a reasonable price, a double-decker that had ample seating on the inside and also atop the bus in the open air. The concept, if you're unfamiliar with these, is that you are dropped off at various designated points of interest of your choosing, and then you hop back on another bus that comes maybe every half hour to an hour and do the same repeatedly to other tourist spots at which it stops. Unlike being with a tour group, you are not time-constrained at any one particular area. I would later use these buses in other cities, including in the U.S., and am a proponent of them.

It was so humid in Kuala Lumpur! I walked over five miles that day and lost seven pounds, important since I gained weight from the cruise. I even have a photo in my gray Brooklyn T-shirt showing nearly the entire garment soaked with perspiration. The city was very polluted, and there were more crazy drivers which seemed par for the course during this trip. In fact, our tour guide in Singapore had said that if you go to Malaysia you will find that compared to Singapore "it is like Felix Unger and Oscar Madison." She was right. I had an excellent time, however, and was particularly impressed with the helpfulness of the people – be they well-to-do or dirt poor.

The one exception, at least initially, was an outdoor Muslim crafts vendor who was surly to many people. When I approached to look at the merchandise on his table, he snarled at me, "Where are you from? United States?" I saw that he was going to be hostile if I said yes, and wanted to see if the "Canada" response would be better. So I said, "What if I said Canada?" without actually saying I was from there. I then realized that perhaps this was worse, because I didn't know the history between Canada and Malaysia – what if they had a war and people in Malaysia were still bitter over it? As noted in my travels, people today were still upset about wars their country lost hundreds of years ago. Maybe I should have said I'm from a neutral country like Switzerland, but it was too late now.

Fortunately, this guy's facial expression and demeanor changed 180 degrees immediately upon my mentioning the word "Canada." He smiled and said, "Ah, Canada." It was as if his happiness switch had been flipped on. He was then very friendly, and told me to take my time looking around. Perhaps something good happened to him in Canada or he liked Canadians, or there was something positive between the two countries, but whatever it was I had inadvertently said the magic word. Had I said American this may well have triggered an inauspicious outcome. I later learned (upon research for this book) that Canada was one of the first countries to recognize Malaysia's independence, and established diplomatic relations that are strong to this day. Ah, what a relief!

I went to Chinatown, and then the "Little India" region including the vast mosque area. There I met three Norwegian gals who got dressed in the Muslim regalia so they could enter the mosque. They wanted to be dressed appropriately so as to be respectful to the culture, which was admirable, covering their skin as needed. At the outdoor prayer area there were lots of people praying barefoot and seemingly sleeping on the floor. Then I met two tall, blonde Swedish gals who were a lot of fun. They probably would have let me hang out with them had I asked, but I wanted to maximize my time in the city, getting around to different locales by the bus, whereas they were sauntering around that one area. They were very liberal and welcomed me to take a lot of photos of them making funny facial expressions. No problem.

It was a good thing I stayed on my own because I saw some excellent sights, such as the famous Petronas Towers, 88-story twin metal skyscrapers that are among the tallest buildings in the world, with an upscale mall inside including stores such as Hermes, Versace, and Cartier. There was also a pewter factory, and a park with impressive gardens nearby. As with the Christ the Redeemer statue in Rio, I saw a guy lying on his back taking photos of friends in an effort to get them in frame with the towers to the top in the background. When done, I asked him to do the same for me. He did, and I later returned the favor to him and others looking for a photographer to do the same. The view from the top was spectacular, and what was even more spectacular was feeling the air conditioning inside the mall!

After visiting an orchid garden, I had a delightful conversation with a pretty Black gal from South Africa named Jaha (a Swahili name, she told me) who, like the aristocratic gal in Tokyo, was being escorted around by a dignified-looking man. Jaha was by herself, and the man was escorting only her in a sleek black limo. Jaha told me her perspective about South Africa, and I told her mine about America. We had similar world views. Her escort/chauffeur took photos of us together, and upon handing me back the camera out of Jaha's earshot said to me, "She likes you, and that's a good thing, a very good thing." "Who is she?" I asked. He just smiled as Jaha approached, and didn't tell me. I had to be going and never asked Jaha about her situation. Maybe royalty. Maybe a lottery winner. Maybe a famous actress, singer, dancer, or other performer - she was beautiful. I wasn't too interested, figuring I'm not going to South Africa anytime soon. Jaha gave me her email address. I took it graciously and caught a glimpse of the escort/chauffeur, who I think would have high-five'd me had not Jaha been right there. I never did contact Jaha. Little did I know that I would end up in South Africa in a little over a month – and have a very interesting encounter with a different Swahili gal there.

I'd had a really good day in Kuala Lumpur and returned to my hotel. I wanted to reward myself somehow for losing the seven pounds and asked the concierge about dining at a good restaurant. He recommended one, and the waiter there suggested the noodles with prawns. Oh no, I'd learned my lesson about the food there I called "scorch." However, the waiter said he hears a lot about that from non-indigenous people and could make it mild for me "so as to please your palate." And he was right. It was delicious and very flavorful (had some soy-based ingredient). The iced tea I ordered was also exceptional, including orange slices in the tea. This was the best iced tea I'd ever had, and I drink a lot of iced tea. Not only was the American music played in many international places better than that in the U.S., but so too did the food and beverages taste much more flavorful in many restaurants, as mentioned, with this one being no exception. I never became ill from anything I ate overseas, and in cases like this was very happy with the taste. And for a much lower price, too. So, Malaysia was a pleasant surprise, but nothing like what was in store.

The next flight took me to Manila, Philippines, where at Rizal Park, near my hotel, there was a big sign exclaiming, WOW Philippines as the country's slogan. I had a "Thrilla in Manila" (no relation to the famous 1975 boxing match between Muhammad Ali and Joe Frazier referring to this), and this part of my vacation was one of the best. As with Viet Nam and Albania, the U.S. had worked its magic in the Philippines (World War II), and the people there still appreciated it. As I was learning, people all over the world were beholden to their history, even for centuries, and many responded accordingly to others indigenous to those areas. I thought this strange; however, I decided to go with the flow there since Americans had a halo effect and were treated well. So, what are the Philippines? Basically a chain of 7,000 islands – not as large as Indonesia's 17,000 islands, but still fairly sizeable. There was a large urban sprawl that included everything from modern skyscrapers to shantytowns; more poverty there as well, and pollution. The city was very crowded, and driving was slow and difficult at times from what I observed. But the strength of the city was its people – they were so very friendly and helpful. I was predisposed toward liking Filipinos based on past experiences; I had worked with several in my corporate jobs, and had dealt with many in the hospitality industry, especially on cruise ships.

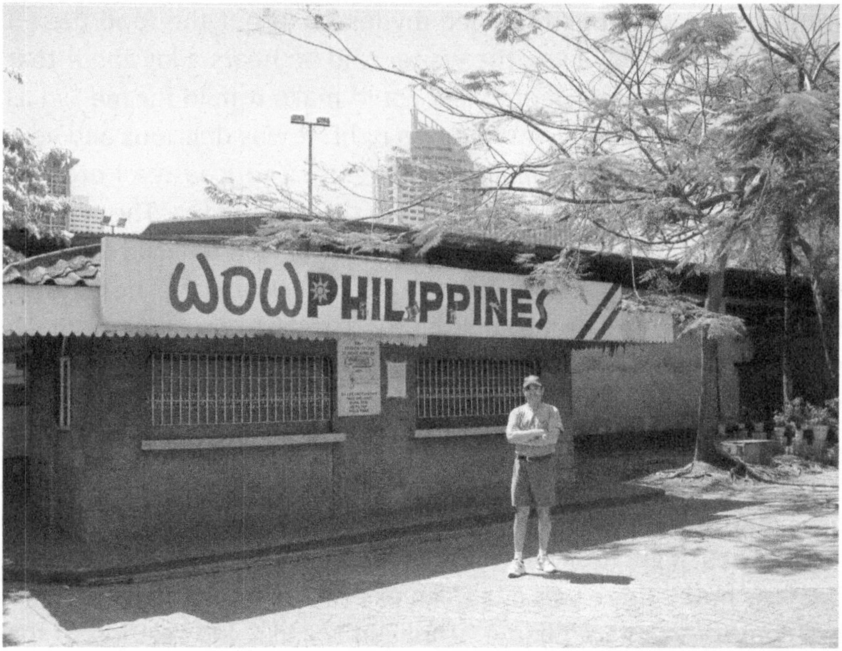


The sign says it all - great people, great adventures, and even great hamburgers from a local chain that's most popular!

I took a personalized, customized city tour. The driver was late arriving, apologized profusely, and gave me the tour for half-price. There was an old church, a fortress, the city market, a waterfront, nothing special. But one thing you couldn't help but notice was the tuk-tuks ("tuke-tukes"), also called jeepneys. They were all over the place, run by private operators, and are described as follows by Mandy Bartok of Asia Insider: "This cheap form of transportation came into existence following the Second World War, when the victorious American forces sold off large quantities of surplus automotive equipment – used in the retaking of the island – to local Filipinos. With a transportation system decimated by the ravages of war, forward-thinking city residents began running the jeeps as shared taxis, often spicing up their appearance with bright-colored paint and metal roofs to protect passengers from the elements. Before long, the revamped military transports were a ubiquitous sight on the streets of Manila." I observed smaller ones as well, the size of golf carts. I found them efficient and the drivers safe.

My fun started when the sun went down at a gorgeous, colorful sunset over Manila Bay. I met several people there who were warm and friendly, chatty and smiley, and they told me of a shortcut to walking back to my hotel after I had taken a tuk-tuk (three-wheeler) to get there. With the weather now cooler and remembering how the long walk in Malaysia was great exercise, I walked all the way back using that same route. I stopped off for a quick bite to eat at a hamburger place the locals highly recommended called Jollibee, which is a chain I'd never heard of but which I would subsequently see in other countries. These burgers were among the best I've ever had – juicy, flavorful, and totally delicious! In fact, I returned there the next day to reconfirm this, and it was that good! I asked the locals about McDonald's and other fast-food places popular in America found nearby. There, at least, it was Jollibee all the way by a wide margin; however, I noticed throughout Europe and Asia that the American fast-food establishments were often more popular to the comparable local ones if they existed.

I continued my walk, and came across an older woman selling some crafts across the street from the hotel at which I was lodging. I looked over and saw a gorgeous sight – not the crafts, but the beautiful gal in her 30s standing next to the cart in a black leather jacket. I passed by a few times to take additional looks, and to see if she was with anyone. The answer was yes – the older woman selling the crafts, and no-one else.

Walking over, I began a conversation with the older woman. She liked me, and introduced me to her niece, the very attractive Lisette. She was shy at first, but I cracked some good jokes and got her laughing. I believe that my long, aerobic walk put me in just the right spirit to be at my best, and learned the value of these moving forward (pun intended). Lisette and I had a few things in common and her aunt, perhaps knowing something I didn't, suggested we go across the street and sit in Rizal Park to chat. Well, let's just say that her aunt was right; Lisette and I had a wonderful time filled with laughter, romance, and happiness. She was such a sweet gal. We passed by my hotel, and the doormen there were very impressed that I had just arrived and met such a beautiful gal. Later, they treated me like royalty with big smiles after seeing us exit together holding hands. I had a blast from the past when one of them asked how I did that, reminiscent of the Malaysian guy asking me this on the bus ride in Russia. I told him to "take a long walk," which came out wrong, so I changed it to, "Continue smiling and being happy, and it'll all work out." He smiled and nodded. I felt like a "Jolly Bee," having created such a "buzz" among them. They knew that I had my "Thrilla In Manila."

The next day, Lisette and I spent more time together, including at Rizal Park (Rizal was a national hero) with its many flags, statues, and war memorials. I really liked Lisette. She had young kids from a previous marriage; between working with her aunt and tending to the kids as a single mom, she had little time for much else. That may be why her aunt saw this as a good opportunity for Lisette, whose shyness may have reduced her desire to go out at night (there was also some crime there). The time passed quickly, and I had to be leaving soon. Lisette and I would keep in contact, but after a while the sun would set on our relationship, colorful as it was. But overall, WOW Philippines – I had a wonderful time there, and another **FINE** time as well.

The next morning I left for Seoul, South Korea, which was the free stopover I obtained by asking about it when booking this vacation, and which represented another new country during my Asia trip. And yes, I did think of the song "Soul Man" by the Blues Brothers. In fact, the locals there had a lot of soul – friendly, fun, and even frisky. After checking into my hotel I inquired about city tours and was told there was one in a few hours. I signed up and went. I distinctly remember an ornate Buddhist temple with three giant golden Buddhas inside – much larger than even the mega-sized ones I had seen in Cambodia. There was a pageantry parade outside the temple, and I got some fun photos with the performers afterwards. We also went to a cultural village and a statue park. There were even more people in South Korea on mobile phones than in the Philippines - Samsung, of course. To give you an idea of the magnitude of Samsung, according to Wikipedia, "Samsung produces around a fifth of South Korea's total exports and its revenues are larger than many countries' GDP." Because I had taken so many photos during this trip, I was down to my last few remaining bytes of storage for my digital camera and looking for additional memory cards. I found some great bargains there despite Seoul being an expensive city in general. The electronics there were of good value, and I purchased a 4gb memory card for my digital camera for lower cost than a comparable buy in the U.S. As it would turn out, these extra photos I was thus able to take would be precious.

Seoul was a crowded city, with a population over 10 million. I met some very pleasant Korean gals in their 20s there who educated me about the country. They were being educated at a local university, and I had worked in education, so we all learned something during the exchange. They liked Americans because of the food, music, and culture rather than the history or politics with the U.S. (older people there identified more with the latter issues). We shared a few laughs, and they recommended a restaurant I should try nearby before we split. So I went in during a busy lunch time and was seated by myself at a table for two. Without my even being asked, a few minutes later the server brought over a guy to sit with me, a businessman in a suit and tie in his 40s, who introduced himself as Mr. Kwon. As it turned out, he was CEO of a sporting goods company there, and we talked a bit about business at his discretion, but not too much.

In Seoul, South Korea I visited the Jogyesa Buddhist Temple, featuring three huge golden Buddhas inside. The exterior was quite colorful and ornate. I continued meeting locals, such as this nice young lady, from whom I could learn about the country and its culture.

He spoke English very well and helped me order my meal; I told him I'm not equipped to handle super-spicy, which "can do a number on me" (he didn't understand my vernacular, and I then remembered not to use colloquial expressions when overseas). I went for a more basic stir-fried chicken dish Korean style which was still a bit spicy. There were a number of side dishes as well including cabbage, and something called kimchi fried rice. I was tempted to try the eel but didn't go there; instead, I had the dried codfish soup. All the food was excellent, and at the end we said thank you and goodbye to each other. He was a good lunchmate, very knowledgeable, professional, pleasant, and polite.

I went sightseeing on my own. The city had numerous shopping areas, everything from street vendors to major malls, but every area I traversed was very clean and the people were very helpful and extremely polite, making my walk a happy venture. I felt very safe there, no problem. There was lots of leather there for sale – in almost any type of garment. I took the advice of some others I met to have Ginseng tea, which was very good. I would have liked to take the subway, but the weather was good and I just felt like walking (I needed a new pair of sneakers upon return home, and maybe feet, too). I returned to the hotel and went out a bit at night, heading to a club and dancing with some hot Korean gals who were dressed in sexy silks. There was a great light show, and later I had a rice wine which was delicious. This knocked me out, and I had a good rest during my final night of this long, happy trip before my return flight the next morning.

The day of departure there was one more surprise in store for me, maybe a cosmic reward for having spread some education and laughter in the world. I was wearing an old maroon and gold sweatshirt a Topps Regional Sales Manager had bought for me when I visited to assist on sales calls in Minneapolis. It was from the University of Minnesota. I usually wear this sweatshirt on long flights because it's so comfortable. How did this come into play? Soon after arriving at the Seoul Airport I looked over to my left and saw a large group of female college students wearing the same style university sweatshirt I had on – they had just arrived, and were walking around carrying their hand luggage. We all stared at each other; I went over and started the conversation with them. They told me they were the University of Minnesota's female dance team that was in an international competition. How amazing was this! And what a good thing it was that I had just bought an additional memory card for my camera the day before so I could get additional photos. I asked a security guard there if you can take photos in the airport and he said it's OK. I had to have a photo of them, in yet another "it's-a-small-world" story, and the gals happily complied.

Lots of people looked as I took photos of the dance team in a group pose. I then asked a passerby if he wouldn't mind taking a few photos of me with the gals, which he did with my camera and, upon their request, with their cameras as well. This was reminiscent of what happened in front of Skansen in Stockholm; ironically, there were many blonde, Swedish-looking women in the dance troupe since Minnesota has a large Scandinavian population. We all laughed at this coincidence; what were the odds of this happening? This was a fun finish to an interesting, diverse, and excellent trip as I marched toward getting to 100 countries. I was feeling wonderful, like an excited kid all over again, marveling at the world I had never known. WOW – as in World Of Wonder, and what a great place it is!

I returned to New York and processed thousands more photos. A funny thing happened when the lab technician, a guy about 60 or so who worked in the back, heard it was me at the counter coming to pick up the pictures. He told me how much he and others enjoyed my photos – "we feel like we are on a vicarious trip with you." They know more about me and my travel escapades than anyone else, and occasionally, upon picking up my photos, I'll get a wry smile from the technician who processed them. One slyly said to me, "You don't look like an international playboy." I replied, "Let's keep that our little secret." "When's the book coming out?" I was once asked. "I'm not writing one," I replied. "You need to write it" was the answer. "And include your photos!" "When I get to 100 countries," I replied. "Oh well, I guess I won't be seeing that book in my lifetime" one of the older technicians said, not knowing I had already been to 89. "Stay tuned," I responded. "You never know what will develop."

# Chapter 18

## The Middle East And Africa On A World Cruise

The weather was still frigid, snowy, and icy in Buffalo, New York in March. I stood out even in my own city, walking around with a tan – yet shoveling my car in and out of parking spots. "Shoveling" off to Buffalo wasn't my favorite pastime, so I was open to new opportunities. Then I discovered my kryptonite – a brochure I had received in the mail months earlier about a world cruise. I didn't know why I still kept it, because at the time I was working full-time with no end in sight. But situations change, and just thumbing through it piqued my imagination. Reading became imagining. Imagining became calling – "just for information and pricing." Calling became thinking about it. Thinking about it excited me. Talking about it motivated me. Paying for it meant I was not turning back. Packing meant I was going. I had a quest to be in 100 countries in my life – and this long trip would yield just that.

WOW didn't apply to just the Philippines, but also to the "segment" of the world cruise that took me from the Middle East to Africa, 32 days in total, including 23 days on the ship portion followed by 9 days on my own; 11 countries that would get me to 100 total lifetime. In order, they were: Bahrain, Jordan, Dubai in the United Arab Emirates, Oman, Seychelles Islands, Kenya, Mozambique, South Africa, Zimbabwe, Botswana, and Zambia. This segment trip from Dubai to Cape Town was part of a larger 114-day grand voyage leaving out of Fort Lauderdale, Florida and I was very fortunate to be able to get on it at all because this excursion often sells out a year in advance. I ended up getting the last single cabin (after persevering), after the price was reduced three times due to the severe global recession. When I subtracted out my expected expenses in New York from the total cost, it was do-able, and these countries were places I wanted to get to. Cruising, albeit on this highly upscale voyage, was the most economical way to reach them all. Additionally, I utilized my former employer, the AAA, to receive a further discount, and a free dinner aboard the highest-end restaurant on the ship, too! I was also very fortunate in being able to use a large frequent flyer mileage amount to obtain free airfares for the outbound and return portions that worked with this itinerary. I asked about the free stopovers again, and the very helpful airline supervisor assisted me in securing two to Arab countries, one to Bahrain and one to Jordan, which were not ports of call on the cruise – no long layovers, either! The situation just seemed like I was meant to go on this trip, so despite being tired from the previous one, off I went on another adventure to "Sheikh It Up," as The Cars tune goes.

I had a good flight to Bahrain, including sitting next to a lovely gal going to visit family there. We joked, laughed, and were mutually excited about our respective vacations. On the contrary, during the connecting flight a lady my age told me her life's story that included spousal abuse, a nasty divorce, and her kids no longer talking to her after siding with her ex-husband – all after an "ideal marriage." She left her job, now had nothing remaining of her former life, and was depressed. Our conversation was cathartic for her, and I truly sympathized. I had heard similar stories from other travelers, and this was the reason they were traveling in some cases, to get away from it all, decompress, and recompose. They say that time heals all wounds, but travel may get the assist. For me this flight was quite a contrast from the start, and a harbinger of things to come.

The plane arrived in Manama, Bahrain which the locals pronounced "Ba-ha-rain." I had barely heard of this place until I received the free stopover, and had little idea what it was like except that it was an Arab country. And there sure were lots of Arabs, mostly in a red-and-white head dress I later learned is called a keffiyah. My taxi driver also had this on. I'd not been to an Arab country before, so this was a whole new experience which intrigued me. The hotel I booked online two days earlier, and was now standing in, also had that Arabian ambiance to it based on its décor; if I'm in Arabia then I want to feel like I'm there. There were jungle-themed couches and throw-pillows in the lobby, and photos of various sheikhs on the wall in the Reception area. There was also a belly dancer in one of the rooms in the lobby entertaining some businessmen. I peeked in the cracked-open door when passing by, whereupon a big Arabian guy in head dress closed it on me (private show, perhaps?). My room was plush with a great view of the city; I was very happy with the accommodations at a very reasonable price after securing yet another last-minute deal.

I was there for two days, and spent most of my sightseeing time walking around. There wasn't much there except a waterfront with a few nice buildings called the twin towers of the financial harbor area. I also ventured into a mosque where I had another interesting experience. I had gone on a free tour and taken approximately 30 photos, the most of anyone in my group. Afterwards, the older Arabian gentleman who gave the tour, dressed in full garb, stopped me as I headed out and showed me a special photo I can take. He asked if my camera has a timer. I said yes. He positioned me in a particular location and told me to place the camera on the floor, facing upward, with the timer on. I did so. As I was standing there he joined me, and the flash went off. I saw what he meant when I looked at the photo: our heads were centered in the dome right above us, making for an excellent picture! I noticed, however, that based on the upward angle my arms were cut off, so we took another one. I did my signature move, "thumbs-up," which prevented the arms-cut-off look in the photo. A few years ago I got the idea to do "thumbs-up" photos when taking pictures with some college students from Europe who imitated this American gesture for the photo (maybe they had seen it in the media). I joined in, and from then on thought it would be cool to get photos with others from around the world doing this same pose for a photo album I would eventually assemble. Here was a good opportunity with an Arab guy dressed in appropriate attire, and so we took a couple. He had to go quickly for the next tour, so I thanked him and went outside the mosque.

Because Bahrain was my 90th country visited, I had made a poster board sign indicating this with the date in black marker. I really wanted to take a photo holding this sign with the Arab tour guide, but he wasn't available. Fortunately, there was a young woman standing outside dressed all in black, including veil, so all you could see were her dark brown eyes. She spoke English, and I asked if I could take a photo with her. I was surprised that she agreed, and I got someone to take it of us. The photo came out well (head-to-toe). I couldn't have asked for better; it was pure Arabian. Despite the guy who closed the door to my viewing the belly dancer (who may not have been from Bahrain), I found every other person there more than kind to me. I did mention to selected people that I am American just to see what the reaction would be. To my surprise, not only was it positive, but there was a U.S. naval base on the other side of town!

The next day I took a cab to the naval base in a town called Juffair, about five miles from Manama, where I walked around the area. There were all kinds of American restaurants there, including McDonald's and Pizza Hut®, T.G.I.Friday's, and American-style shops selling clothing, electronics, and more. For those few blocks around the base you wouldn't know you were thousands of miles away from the U.S.; it was as if the Americans had their own part of town geared to them. I asked an officer if I could take a photo of the base. He said no (politely) – it's policy. I talked to one of the Navy men sitting outside at the Starbucks, and he was from the same little town in California at which I had just taught! He graduated from high school there only a few years ago. Small world once again! We had a good long chat, and he told me that the locals there like Americans. Perhaps it was his being from California that sparked a Beach Boys tune I couldn't get out of my head the rest of the day: "Bah-bah-bah, bah-bah-Bahrain!" Of course my mind would think of this at this time, it was a natural (it later went into "Help Me Rwanda" but I never made it there, and "Serban USA" – yep, made it there). Interestingly, the U.S. Navy SEALS would later play a major role in an upcoming event in which I'd be involved.

Next it was on to Amman, Jordan on my own as well for two days. Soon upon arrival I was told by a cabbie that there are two types of Jordanians: "native born who are OK with Americans, and Palestinian-Jordanians who dislike or hate Americans due to supporting Israel." This cabbie was the former, and was quite informative. He urged me to go see Petra as long as I'm in the area. I'd heard of it, but wasn't quite sure what it was or where it was. He told me it's a long bus ride away but worth seeing. I thanked him and looked into it later. After chatting with some locals at the hotel I just had a feeling this was going to be a boring couple of days, but that was OK because I was resting up for the world cruise. Safety was my main concern, but I did want to get a sense of the country.

Meanwhile, I walked around Amman alone - which the hotel personnel warned me not to do for safety reasons - meeting the people and seeing the sights. The city was in a hilly area, and the temperature was cool for that time of year, in the 60s. I took a bus near my hotel and went to King Hussein Mosque, taking several photos after ascertaining it is OK to do so. I walked around all over the vicinity which featured historic buildings but little else of interest to me. Amman is near the desert but I didn't want to venture there since my upcoming world cruise would include that, preferring to just amble around the city and ramble with the locals. Most important was to be safe and not eat anything that didn't look right, taste right, or seem right because one mess-up there could ruin my trip.

Ironically, it was when I was seeking safety that I had my best time there. I approached a Military Policeman (with rifle over his shoulder) asking for directions. I had difficulty understanding him, and kept asking. Soon we were approached by a portly, distinguished-looking man in a suit who asked the M.P. in Arabic what it is I wanted. Upon ascertaining it was for directions, he asked me in English who I am and what I was doing there. This man, who I'll call Ahmed, seemed a bit hostile at first. He seemed important because the M.P. deferred to him. I thought I was going to have another "Malaysia" experience and was prepared to trot out the "Canada" routine – except that Ahmed seemed the type who would ask for ID. If I thought eating the wrong food might get me in trouble, imagine the potential difficulty in impersonating a Canadian (besides, I only knew the first two words to the country's national anthem, "O Canada," and those were it). I asked Ahmed who he is, and he told me, "A retired Jordanian Army Colonel who served with King Abdullah." Stunned, I could only utter, "Oh, okay." I didn't know what else to say.

I told Ahmed I am an American tourist who was looking for directions to a particular mosque. Once I said "American" his demeanor changed. He was relaxed and asked me what I'm doing in Amman; his English was excellent. I told him just sightseeing before my world cruise starts in a couple of days. I had said a couple of magic words that piqued his interest: not "just sightseeing" but "world cruise." He was interested in world travel and astonished that I had already traveled to 90 countries (he asked how many I've been to). In retrospect, maybe I shouldn't have said that because with a camera in my hand he might have thought I was a spy, as did the guy in the London pub seeing me taking so many photos. But Ahmed was cool with this, and in a way I felt comfortable with him because he physically and personally reminded me of my former boss and department chair at the university – a guy several years older than me with a good personality and sense of humor. Perhaps Ahmed picked up on this, because he warmed up to me, too. We talked for a half-hour, including him giving me a detailed history of Jordanian wars, and recent wars in the region. I was hoping he didn't get into any Jordan-Israel conversation with me, or anything potentially inflammatory. He didn't, and we even shared many pleasantries and several laughs. He said, "I see you take photos. Is this your hobby?" I said yes, and emphasized it's just a hobby, adding, "I put the photos into albums back home, so I can remember the good times and share them with others."

Ahmed then asked me if I wanted to take a photo with him. I said, "Definitely!" and I did. I then had the moxie to ask if I could take one of the M.P., who looked to be in disbelief as to what was happening. Ahmed asked him (or perhaps told him) in the local language, and so I did that, plus got a photo with him taken by Ahmed. I thanked them both for their graciousness. Then the three ladies Ahmed was waiting for arrived, two daughters and a daughter-in-law, to whom he introduced me. They all spoke English well and we chatted for a few minutes. Ahmed seemed impressed by my travels and mentioned this to them. I asked if I could take a photo of them, but they were shy and politely declined. Ahmed then asked me if I want to come back to his home and dine there! I really wanted to say yes and do it, but I just couldn't chance it, so I politely declined. Ahmed seemed disappointed; he really wanted to continue our chat. We parted warmly, and I felt like I was very fortunate things turned out this way. I smiled to myself thinking a strange thought that popped into my head: that I took Ahmed up on his offer, had dinner at his place, and over tea he told me that he's originally from Brooklyn (as was Mohammed from Istanbul). What a nice man he was!

The temperature was getting cooler, which was refreshing during my walk all the way back to my hotel, about three miles. I walked about seven miles in total that day, which seemed to be my limit. After sweating profusely, I took one of the best showers ever with very soft water. Down in the lobby, I asked the hotel clerk if I could get into nearby Syria (which would have been a new country visited for me). He said no for two reasons: first, I'd need a visa ahead of time, and second, it would be extremely dangerous for me there. This time, I took the advice. I asked about Petra. He gave me a brochure and said he could call me a taxi to take me to the bus station. I said it would have to be the next morning because I'm leaving after that. He found that there is a very early bus leaving at 6:30 a.m., and I instinctively said OK. He booked the taxi for me and arranged a wake-up call for 4:00 a.m. I had a quick dinner based on the hotel clerk's recommendation (sharwma – pitas with sliced chicken with hummus and salad – "hold the pickle") which was tasty. The next morning I was off to another experience, Petra.

I was up bright and early. It was pitch black outside. The taxi driver arrived on time and said he'd wait with me at the bus depot until the station opened so I could buy my tickets. It's a good thing he did because after a half hour the place was still deserted. I became concerned. The driver radioed-in, and learned that he had taken me to the wrong station! He profusely apologized and brought me to the right one a few miles away; unlike the taxi driver in Spain, he did not try to charge me for the extra mileage. I barely made the 6:30 a.m. bus to Petra, with about two minutes left. At least I was on – and just hoped this was the right bus! It was. The ride took three hours, and was uneventful, but ultimately took us to this famous location between the Red Sea and Dead Sea. I wasn't sure what to expect; I just knew that Petra had been around since prehistoric times, and inhabited by the Romans and others. I later learned it was another UNESCO World Heritage Site.

Upon arrival, my first impression was that it looked like Garden of the Gods Park in Colorado Springs, Colorado. There were orange rocks and unusual rock formations. But here there were many horse-drawn carriages and Arabs on white horses riding around. I even met a Black Arab guy who was a pleasure to speak with and showed me around. The main attractions were buildings built into the rocks: temples, tombs, religious artifacts, and remnants of a city long since gone after existing from early A.D. to medieval times. It was a beautiful day to walk around, sunny and 70 degrees, and I had seven hours to do so before the bus returned to Amman. The place was magnificent, and again had what I term "the majesty of the history." Once more, as in Europe and other places I'd now been, the historical feeling I had from being in a place like this was far superior compared with the historical places I'd been in the U.S. which were teenagers (or younger, even down to infants) by comparison. For this reason alone, places like Petra are worth seeing, and imagining what it might have been like back then.

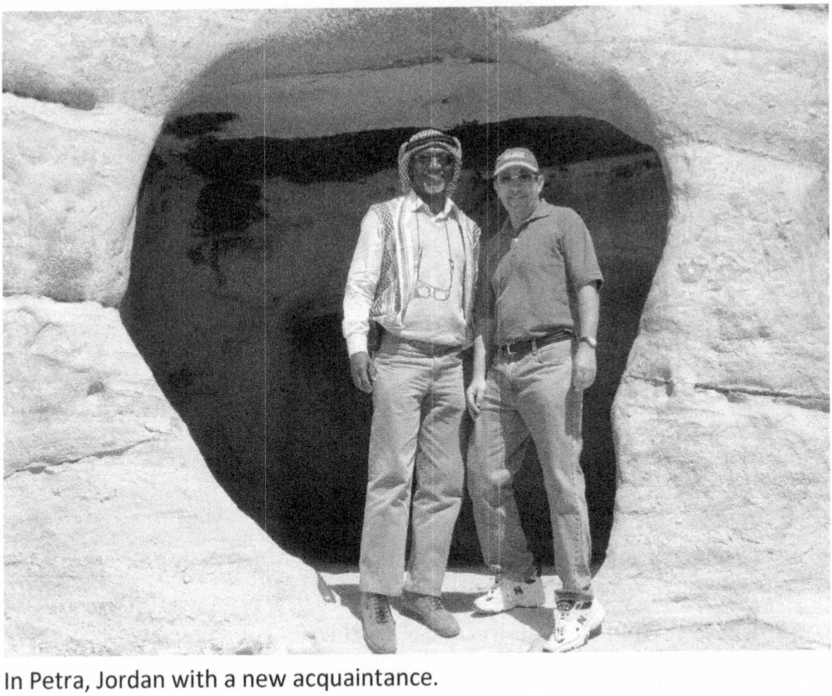

In Petra, Jordan with a new acquaintance.

There was a surprise human element here, a surprise highlight of the trip, which occurred when two little kids (decently dressed but looking for money), boys age 12 or so, offered to take me up a steep hill to see a prehistoric bank and other buildings that most others didn't get to see because of the daunting climb and no roads going there. I declined several times, but they were persistent and convinced me to follow them – which I did very carefully and always keeping the main road in sight. But, they were right – there were some very cool buildings up there including a bank, churches, and others with lots of ancient columns. The kids ended up taking very good photos of me, too, and I rewarded them with a nice tip we had agreed to ahead of time. Beyond that, however, they were a lot of fun and excited that I was excited by the new find. They would say, "Over here, see this building!" and "Look, more over here!" and run to the site. They reminded me of the two boys in "Slum Dog Millionaire," although not Indian.

Even after I gave them the money they willingly helped me down the hill (tougher than getting up there and easy to slip/fall/tumble), taking my hand, leading the way, guiding me from in front and behind, making sure I was safe and unharmed. They were impressed I was from America, and their feeling for me was genuine. I really liked those kids, and felt a real sadness when I turned back after leaving and they were still looking at me sort of sadly. I waved goodbye and they did the same, with simultaneous smiles, looking at each other, then at me. One kid gave me my "thumbs-up" sign I had done in a photo. This event reminded me of being a kid again – climbing, exploring with others, delighting in what was found, and being happy for no other reason than finding happiness. It was great sharing kindness with kids a quarter of my age from another part of the world who were poor but happy. I even had asked them if they're happy and they said yes. I believed them. It's a spirit you don't see much of anymore. As I left I thought, "Hmmm, rich and unhappy or poor and happy. Definitely poor and happy." Of course, rich and happy is better, but I'm not so sure that's in abundance – even after speaking with several wealthy people in my life. I would soon be among lots of rich people in Dubai, and then on my world cruise.

The bus arrived on schedule, and I made it back to Amman for a final dinner there. Not wanting to take any chances with unfamiliar food dishes, I went to a restaurant and had another pita with charred beef that was carved off a rotating spit and served with veggies, which was pretty good. There were also chickpeas but I'm not a fan of them. The restaurant wasn't crowded, but the service was slow. I was in no rush, and was tired from all the walking. Back in my hotel, I packed and prepared for the trip to Dubai and my first world cruise, wondering what was different about it than a regular cruise. I was very happy with my trip to Jordan – having no idea what to expect when arriving, yet meeting a distinguished former Army General, seeing a world-famous site, and meeting two delightful kids who were happily going about their business, hustling tourist tips, and hustling around enthusiastically as kids their age do.

The next morning I took a two-hour flight to Dubai in the United Arab Emirates, again having no idea what to expect. Upon arrival at the airport my mind played a variation of the Beatles song, "You Say Hello, And I Say Dubai." I wondered if my mind ever took a minute off. I also wondered what an Emirate is and learned it's a territory ruled by Muslim dynasties. There are seven of them in the UAE, the largest of which in population is Abu Dhabi followed by Dubai (combined they make up 69% of the Emirates' total population). So, I headed for the ship by taxi, and the cabbie voluntarily showed me some of the sights around the city (for free) since I had lots of time before needing to board. We went along the main drag, where I saw these gleaming ultra-modern buildings that looked futuristic, including twisted, curved, and a few shaped like rocket ships. One looked like a huge, vertical flat-screen TV, and as it turned out the tallest building in the world called the Burj Khalifa was planned to be completed the next year - which would be nearly twice as tall as the Petronas Towers I had seen in Malaysia! This was opulence at its architectural finest, and very impressive! Dubai is a rich country with its oil and gas exports, so maybe they figured why not be creative and make a statement? There were many Porsches, Ferraris, and Maseratis there, too, plus others luxury cars driven by Arabs with their head dresses flowing guided by the wind. Later, when walking around on my own, I went to the Grand Mosque; several souks, where merchants were peddling spices, perfumes, gold, and more; and saw many "chic sheikhs" on fancy mobile phones.

On the other side of the Dubai Creek were the historic buildings, many going back over a thousand years. According to Wikipedia, the first human settlement in Dubai was 3,000 years ago and inhabited by nomadic cattle herders. There were wind towers there and a distinctively "ancient" feel to it. I liked the modern side better, and this was the largest gap between old and new in any city I had ever seen (to this day as well). If I'd had the time I would have liked to go into the desert and see a Bedouin dance a couple of locals told me about. But I had to board the ship which was the top priority, and I left plenty of time to do so not knowing how many passengers were boarding there. As I boarded the ship, I turned a final time to see the opulence of Dubai, whereupon my mind played a variation of the one-hit wonder song by Steam, "Nah-nah-nah-nah, hey-hey-hey, Dubai."

The first thing I noticed aboard ship was that there were a lot of very old people, 70s and 80s and maybe more, with no younger ones in sight. I asked if I'm on the right ship, and was told yes. An old adage holds that "the sea is Mother to us all," but here Father Time joined in as well: I soon learned that the average age of the world cruise passengers was over 75. This wasn't a bad thing (I got along well with older people), but I was hoping to find some people closer to my age as I had found on all my other cruises. I later learned that many people on this cruise were wealthy, and were onboard for the duration of 114 days. I would be onboard for 23 days, from Dubai to Cape Town, South Africa which doesn't sound like a lot compared to 114 days, but I remembered thinking that 10 days was my absolute limit after some cruises. I even created an acronym for what happens on day 10: I go BOOM – Bored Out Of my Mind. Aside from the crew members, I later learned that there were only three others younger than me – all attractive gals in their mid-20s traveling with an older relative (they were from Holland, the U.K. and Spain). Fortunately, all passengers I met aboard the cruise were very nice, and many of the older women on there were maternal toward me, especially those I sat with at dinner. The high-quality service and food onboard was among the features that warranted the higher pricing compared to other cruises; this was the best of the best for this class of world travel. I would later say, "I only live like I'm rich when I'm poor" (not working, but thus have the time). Yogi Berra would have been proud. He also might have liked that I have lived by one of his famous expressions, "When you come to a fork in the road, take it" (I even thought of naming this book that title).

When booking the cruise I was asked about my seating preference. I had asked for a dinner table for 8 of younger people, if possible. I was seated with those mostly in their 60s and early 70s – not quite what I had in mind, and when I inquired about this aboard ship I was told "this is the youngest table." As it turned out, four people from this table had met on a previous world cruise and made plans to take this voyage and sit together. These included a former nurse I'll call Lillian (rumored to have lived with a wealthy doctor); an attractive older woman in her late 70s I'll call Vivian, who I'd guess was a very hot number in her day; an older guy near her age I'll call Jack who was also widowed and supposedly was an item with Vivian; and a Japanese lady in her late 50s I'll call Miki who had a black belt in judo, exceled in many areas, and was a dynamic person. All were American or Canadian.

There was another newcomer I'll call Victor, a bachelor in his late 60s from the U.S., who wanted to pal around with me. He had the hots for one of the women who was a guest speaker on the ship (an attractive Australian in her 60s) and, having not dated for a long time, asked my advice a lot. I didn't really know what to tell him, and just gave him general advice – including letting her know how he feels and maybe asking her to dance later on after dinner. Victor kept warning me about the "cougars" on the ship, older women on the prowl for younger men, and that I was "the most eligible bachelor on the ship so be very careful." He had heard conversations about this and felt it his duty to give me a head's-up, maybe in exchange for the dating advice. Meanwhile, I was more interested in the younger women but they were too young for me and, in some cases, fiercely guarded by their older relative. So, the hunter was the hunted, interesting. As it turned out, one of the older ladies I met had a romantic interest in me and would attempt to hold my hand, which I politely rebuffed.

Maybe her mind played Beatles tunes, too, such as "I Wanna Hold Your Hand." However, mine countered with "Help!"

I was a big hit at the meals with my international travel stories, and I learned a lot as well. Many of my dinnermates – and overall passengers on the ship I met – had been to many countries, but not nearly as many as I had been. That's because even the veteran cruisers can only get to so many countries by ship (those having coastal ports); and I had gone to many interior countries that many of these older passengers didn't want to or couldn't venture to. Thus, by having already been to 90 countries I was constantly asked about several they hadn't been to – even followed around after dinner to continue the discussion. It was only then that I realized the accomplishment I had made in this area, how far as a traveler I had come, literally and figuratively. I'd thought these much older, veteran travelers had easily been to 100 or more countries, but no-one I met knew of anyone that had. That revelation would also be my first impetus for my writing this book, to "tell the story," as so many had requested.

They were all very nice people, but I would spend my time hanging out with the crew and the younger gals in the after-hours bar near the top deck. However, the older people on the ship and I bonded in one way: they were very well-traveled and we shared many very interesting stories I wasn't able to hear or share anywhere else (my friends and family generally didn't travel much, and certainly not a lot overseas). The stories were fascinating and motivating for me to do more; everyone said I'm doing the right thing in traveling while I'm young, and many of these people had significant health problems. One older guy now realized the fallacy of working 40 or 50 years in a row and only then getting to travel, after you're old and maybe unable to do certain physical activities, or even stay awake as needed. He added that most people need the money, and so have to work consecutively, but questioned the whole system. One lady noted a reason for her taking the world cruise was the fine medical staff aboard ship, while another lady was dying and wanted to see what she could of the world before she left it. There was a lot of "medical" talk, and I often would either politely listen or get away as fast as I could if I could since I wasn't interested (this was Club

"Med" of a different variety, you might say, although they had the "bread," even if not chocolate).

I also noted that many aboard the ship proudly displayed various articles of clothing (mainly shirts) from other parts of the world with various country names emblazoned on them, which was very cool. I had some clothing like that, too, especially my caps, which initiated a few conversations, but I was not ostentatious about where I'd been as were many others. A lot of the crew were from the Philippines, and while I said nothing about my "Thrilla In Manila," I mentioned I was there, leading to several nice conversations about the country. In fact, one crew member was a finalist in the Miss Philippines contest a few years earlier (and was very beautiful)!

The first port of call was Muscat, Oman. I took a city tour, where we went to the Grand Mosque (of course), palace (of course), shopping area (of course), and I took a lot of photos (of course). There was an old historic town, and a more modern section. Overall, this was a pleasant place with some notable highlights. I climbed to the high point on the tour and took in the panorama of the city with the mountainous backdrop against the Arabian Sea, which was an outstanding sight. The Sultan Qaboos Grand Mosque is the third largest mosque in the world, but wasn't as opulent or architecturally appealing as others I'd seen (still, it was impressive). There was the Mutrah Souk (indoors), which featured just about anything and everything with emphasis on local crafts (e.g., wood carvings and jewelry). There was food, too, especially fish, but I settled for some local tea outside by the waterfront, which is where I spent most of my free time before the torrential rain (after which the sun came back out). I really liked the head-dress of the men, which included two versions: the smaller one with flat top and Arabic-embroidered design called a kumma, and my favorite, what looked to me like a combination turban and pirate's bandana of various designs and colors, called a mussar. I could see this catching on as a fashion trend, even in the U.S. and everywhere else. Most men wore long white robes as well. The pace in the souk was slow, but there were periods of chaos with locals yelling to each other (no different than some other souks I'd visited). Thankfully, no-one yelled "bellek!" there.

We were to travel to the countries of Comoros and Madagascar, but didn't due to rioting there at the time (labor disputes). I wanted to add those countries to my list, but we would end up substituting an extra day in Kenya (which worked out even better for me) and Richards Bay, South Africa to replace these. The cruise ship I was on in January did not stop in Guadeloupe as scheduled, also due to rioting, so I missed out on some other new places, but these things happen. Obviously, the cruise lines put passengers' safety first. However, they could not foresee what would happen next – which would make international news!

Our next stop was the Seychelles Islands, a chain of 115 islands off the East Coast of Africa. There had been significant activity in the area by Somali pirates, but when we arrived the situation had intensified. An American cargo ship had been seized and the captain held hostage for ransom. We were watching the news on the main deck as we were in the vicinity. President Obama was addressing the situation on national television. Notifications went out that our ship was taking on additional security personnel, getting out the hoses to ward off a potential attack, and preparing for evasive maneuvers if needed. There seemed to be two sentiments on our ship about this: holy crap!! (predominantly), and isn't this cool?! (me and a few others). We were told that we'll be safe, but you never did know in a situation like this. We couldn't see any pirate ships from our vessel (what a great photo op if so), but they were out there firing mortars, and dangerous. People weren't freaking out but there was a great deal of concern. I waited a long time for the ship's Internet terminals to become available, and then emailed my family, with my brother as point man, notifying that we're OK. I've been accused of being overly optimistic but wasn't really concerned. Fortunately, U.S. Navy SEALS arrived and three of them shot the captors, killing three pirates with three bullets fired simultaneously. The captain of the seized cargo ship was freed, and the event was over. And I thought this world cruise might be dull. Not! I wondered if the Navy SEAL I'd met in Bahrain was involved, but never found out.

After that thrill, it was back to sailing as usual. We docked in the Seychelles, in the Indian Ocean, ending up on Mahe Island, the largest in the chain and surrounded on three sides by mountains. I walked around the city called Victoria. This was a quaint little place with pastel-colored buildings and a notable silver clock tower with the clock face on all four sides. People sold crafts primarily on the corners but also mid-street, and the pace was slow-lazy. I went to the botanical gardens which featured lush greenery, flowers, plants, trees, and 100-year-old tortoises, which were friendly and moved at the pace of this relaxed island in general. I had a local guy take photos of me with them but, unlike other tourists, I did not sit on their shells (nor would I), which seemed cruel. When someone did sit on a shell it made a small popping sound as if sitting on and slightly indenting a piece of hard luggage. An embarrassing mishap occurred when I saw a cute Filipino gal dressed sexily, and I tried to pick her up (hey, it worked in the Philippines). She stunned me when, after my introduction as "Steve," she said, "Yes, I know. Don't you remember me? It's Angelique from the ship – I work in Dining." "Oh, yeah," how are you?" I said sheepishly. "I didn't recognize you without your uniform." "Today's my day off," she said. I felt like crawling away as the tortoise in front of us was doing (probably laughing its shell off), but instead I asked her if she would be in some photos with me, with the tortoises all around. She agreed, and was very pleasant about it. "Well, see you later," I said. "Bye," Angelique said with her nice smile. I was embarrassed, but oh well.

I ambled around and noticed how small these gardens were. But they were peaceful, and a good way to spend half a day. Just getting off the ship after days at sea and walking around was important; that's another reason I took few land excursions (except for something special in most cases), because you go from sitting on a ship to sitting on a motor coach or bus. I need to be out and active, to burn off some extra weight gained by the gourmet food served, and to circulate both literally and figuratively.

The real attraction of the Seychelles, however, was the beauty of the surrounding azure water. I went to a high point and observed the island against the backdrop of the ocean, a splendid view. I could see the beaches, but there was not time to go on one. Something came over me as I was just staring at this gorgeous sight - a feeling of "wow!" Not just about the sight itself, but how fortunate I was to be there beholding it. This is what I had studied and worked so hard for, to be here, now, beholding this, loving and appreciating every minute. I was quite aware of the rarity of being able to do this; many people on the ship, aware of their advanced age, wanted one last (or even first) glimpse of the world at its finest before they leave it. For me, this was an awesome sampler cruise, buffet-style if you will, and I would return to certain places we visited. This was one of them. And I would later see the most incredible beaches that I've ever seen to this day.

I returned to the ship, and there were still a bevy of vendors selling merchandise there. It took me a while, but I finally found someone who sold post cards. I bought a few that captured the incredible color of the water. Back onboard ship, I had my dinnermates saying "She sells seashells in the Seychelles" between the appetizer and main course. Most people said they went shopping, and some went to the botanical gardens. Overall impressions of the latter were that it was "just OK." I just hoped we weren't having turtle soup that night. We didn't, but we would soon find out about another creature of the sea, one moving quite a bit faster, that would shock us.

We quickly learned there was more pirate activity as we headed to Mombasa, Kenya. We had several lifeboat drills, and maintained the additional security force and other protective measures. I again found this thrilling. Fortunately, we made it there without incident, and I had a great time in Kenya in which we would spend an extra day that was substituted for not going to Comoros. The first day I went on a safari, organized by the tour department of the cruise line onboard ship, to Shimba Hills. There were 8 people to a van (a good-luck number), each with comfortable seating and a short set of stairs in the center leading to an opening in the roof from which you can view and photograph the wildlife. I dumbly thought you could get out of the van and take photos – what was I thinking? There were several vans following each other in a procession, each full of passengers poised to shoot photos. We traveled for an hour on a long stretch of red dirt road but didn't see too much wildlife at first. Then several passengers theorized and complained about our collective vans having a caravan effect, making so much noise that they scared away the animals! So the drivers slowed down, giving more space between vans, and then we saw a lot more – which was awesome, including lions, elephants, giraffes, impalas, water buffaloes, baboons, and colorful birds. Plus, there were excellent waterfalls later on in a tropical rainforest.

Back on ship, during the dinner we discussed our respective experiences on the safari for those who went. There were raves about seeing the wildlife in their native habitat. In separate but related news, three "cougars" aboard ship cornered me at the bar after dinner. These women were very attractive, from the Deep South, and in their 60s I'd say. One was extremely wealthy and told of her vast opulent possessions. They had their eyes on me and edged closer, surrounding me on both sides in the booth so I couldn't get out. As in Buenos Aires, when surrounded in a much different situation, I bolted out after pushing my way through. This time, it was tougher to escape but did with what I'll call diplomatic pleasant persistence. I was called after with an American accent but much different than mine: "Y'all come back soon, ya hear." Right after that, I watched the passengers dancing to the orchestra music on the main deck. Lillian had been trying to get me to dance with her the entire trip, and this time she cajoled me just right so I gave in. She noted that I danced very well. She told this to the other ladies at our dinner table the next night, who then wanted equal time. Maybe I should have danced with them, too, but I didn't want to be locked-in to anything; I enjoyed my freedom and spontaneity, and besides, there were paid male dancers aboard ship for just that purpose, to dance with the older women. A gruesome story regarding this soon followed.

The next morning a terrible tragedy occurred. The ship hit some rough seas, and a man not too far behind me fell down a flight of steps and was laying there motionless. I was close by and ran over, as did others, who immediately called for the medics. The man, in his late 50s I'd estimate, was taken away and at first rumored to be dead, after which it was said he was seriously injured. As it turned out, this man was one of the dance instructors Lillian and I had been right next to the night before! I had seen elderly or handicapped people holding onto the rails for dear life when the ship swayed, but nothing like this, especially from a relatively young, robust person. This incident was a real shame, and I hoped he ended up OK. He was in the wrong place at the wrong time. I later heard that several people on the ship pass away during these cruises and are taken by air ambulance (Medevac, e.g.) off the ship stealthily, so as not to alarm other passengers.

Another time we hit rough seas, and the water was heavily spilling out of the on-deck swimming pool, first to one side, then the other as the ship rocked mightily. You have to be careful at all times and not take anything for granted. Hang onto the railings, and if the ship is a-rockin' do come a-knockin' for the staff to assist you if needed. On a different ship, I had a bad fall – slipping on the freshly mopped floor outside the dining room (caught on surveillance tape) after dinner ended, with no signage posted as to the wet floor. I went to the medical department and was found to be OK. It could have been a lot worse for me, or someone else to whom it may have happened. So, one important takeaway from cruising or any other type of travel, is not to let your safety guard down because you feel protected being on a cruise, escorted tour, etc. Anything can happen anytime, anywhere – and when you're in unfamiliar surroundings, your risk could be even higher.

We arrived in Mombasa, Kenya, my 95$^{th}$ country visited, a coastal city along the Indian Ocean, and second largest in Kenya after Nairobi. I toted my little placard sign to hold up in selected locations for later inclusion into my photo album. The most prominent place was at the entrance to the city, which featured giant elephant tusk replicas at least 20 feet high that crossed each other slightly beneath their pointed tips. I had a local guy take several photos, and he was amazed by my camera; he was thrilled to see that you could view the photos immediately, as if it were magic. I still remember his big smile and look of amazement. The culture was Swahili, a mixture of Arabic, Indian, and African cultures. Swahili was a main language as well, but many people I met spoke English fluently, especially the younger folks once again.

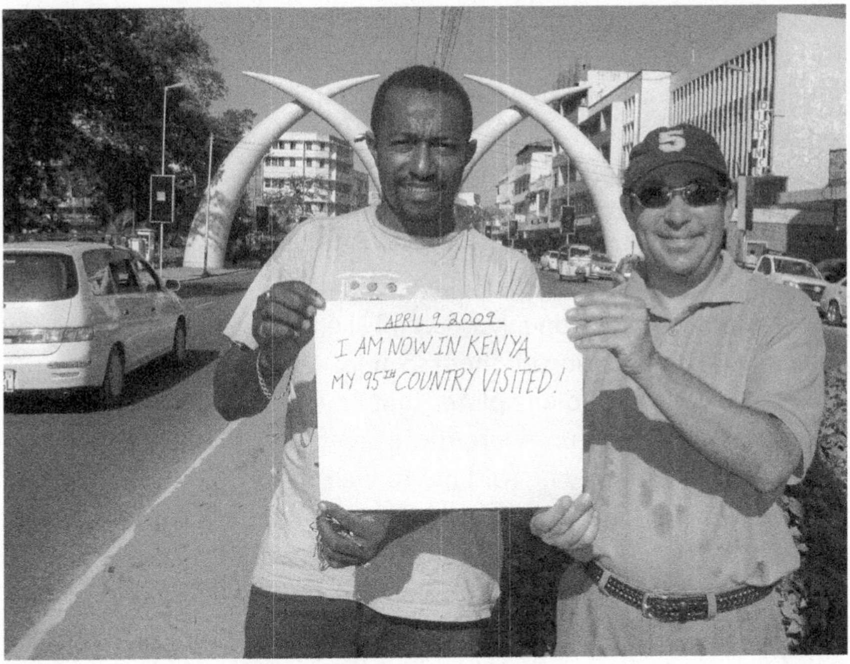


The count was on to reach 100 countries. Here in Mombasa, Kenya a local gave me a hand with the sign, literally (make that, two hands). I would later see more giant tusks - on an elephant roaming freely and glaring at me in my 99th country visited.

I took a city tour via the ship's excursion office, mainly through the Old Town area. The highlights were a colorful church, lots of crafts stores, and an artist's village where we observed bare-chested men carving wooden souvenirs, including those representing elephant tusks. These were expertly done and the whittlers were intensely focused on their craftsmanship. Later, while touring the city, we observed several doorways carved with Arabic characters that were also well-crafted. There was also an old fortress, Fort Jesus, which had impressive canons. It was fairly hot and very humid so I didn't walk around too much, just went with the group slowly along (Kenya lies near the Equator). Besides, we had an extra day there due to missing out on Comoros, so no rush. The real charm for me, however, was the locals in colorful clothing, going about their business, slowly milling around. As in South America, they were very adept at balancing baskets of food on their heads – some had ties to fasten them, and others it appeared were able to balance them with no ties. I heard the beaches were excellent but just wanted to explore the culture; I had been on many gorgeous beaches and hoped to meet some locals. So, I continued just walking, photographing, and exploring.

The next day, I explored Mombasa entirely on my own. A funny thing happened outside of our cruise ship where many vendors set-up shop (the "shop" being a piece of pavement). One aggressive vendor wanted to sell me a decorative plate with a safari theme painted on, and it was very well-done. However, I like buying souvenirs that say the name of the location on them so at least I know where they came from. I asked if he had any plates that have the word Kenya written on them. He did not, nor were there any from other vendors there. As I was walking away he told me to wait there, and with the plate in hand went to talk to a guy sitting nearby and drawing. It turned out he was the artist who drew the plate artwork. The vendor asked if he could write Kenya on it. The artist looked over to me, back at the vendor, and took the plate. He then artistically added Kenya in a good size along the top, and I bought the plate. I mentioned to the vendor that having the country name on his products might help him sell more (I'm always the marketer). Other vendors overheard and asked me about this. Soon, there were about 12 of them listening to my marketing tips – I felt like I was back teaching in California. Several then went to this one artist and others hanging around, and had Kenya put on some of the merchandise. I don't know if they sold any more by doing this, but they were happy I was trying to help them. Later aboard the ship, I asked my dinnermates about this and most agreed this would entice them to buy it. "Entice" was a good word to use based on what would happen the next day.

During a "free" day there (no planned activities), the free shuttle from the ship brought me downtown where I roamed around aimlessly looking for excitement and adventure, although these possibilities seemed as remote as the city itself. There were lots of people just sauntering around languidly, mostly locals, and a few tourists, some of whom dressed as if they were going on safari, although that was mainly up north in Nairobi. There were also a lot of clothes lines outside the homes, women carrying babies, and in a strange way, "the sounds of silence." I had some local roasted meat and coconut-flavored rice for lunch, which was OK but not as good as I expected given my passion for coconut, and a banana which was flavorful and delicious (tour leaders in the past informed that any fruit having skin or can be peeled is OK to eat).

More walking around, bored. Nothing going on, until I came across a Kenyan dance performance in an open shaded area including several sexy women in headdress and loin cloths shaking just the lower half of the bodies, followed by just the upper half. They were rhythmic, coordinated, agile, and talented. The fast-beating drums added to the sensuality. And they were beautiful – great shapes, sexy bodies, and big smiles. I watched for a while and really got into it. I took several photos, but couldn't get any with them at the end of the performance since they scurried away (probably from guys like me wanting photos). This fed into my next adventure.

Soon afterwards, toward mid-afternoon, I spotted a very attractive local woman who looked to be circa age 30, whose beauty stood out from the rest, just walking around slowly like me. We were drawn to each other. She was at least as pretty as any of the dancers, and dressed in tight-fitting jeans. I asked her to take my photo (using that old trick) just to break the ice. She was very receptive and let me take photos of her, too. She liked that I was American – President Obama, whose father is from Kenya, is hugely popular there. Her name was Tuliza and she was very interested in talking more with me. Tuliza suggested we go to a bar/restaurant across the street. And so we did. She just finished lunch and only wanted a Fanta® soda to start, and I had one, too. We entered into an excellent conversation. I asked her to speak Swahili to me and she did, which I found interesting. Tuliza told me how hard life can be in Mombasa (including high unemployment), but that the people are friendly and easygoing. We were engrossed by each other, and the Paul McCartney song "Ebony and Ivory" began playing through my mind.

Tuliza then brought me to a local bar where we sat in the back room and had a drink. I normally don't drink much alcohol, so this went to my head. Tuliza was very interested in the ship I was on, and wanted to see what it was like onboard; she had never been on a ship. There were only a few hours left before the ship was to set sail. Tuliza sweet-talked the shuttle driver in Swahili into taking her back to the ship with me – to the astonishment of other passengers on the ship who were also heading back on the van, exceeding what Kira from Russia was able to accomplish. There were few seats left, so she sat on my lap on the way there. At the security gate, Tuliza couldn't be let in even though she was with me. The security officer said I could talk to Guest Relations and see what could be done, but Tuliza had to wait outside. I did just that, but was told that I needed to give at least 72 hours' notice to obtain a guest pass for security reasons. I understood the explanation but was very disappointed. I wished we had another day there. Tuliza and I kept in contact by email, but she ended up getting married to a European guy and living there. In her final email to me she stated that I was her first choice (had I pursued her) but she knew that I didn't feel the same way. Because I was into other things and valued my freedom, I didn't want to be tied down with anyone at the time, which I explained to her. "Lord I was born a ramblin' man" as the Allman Brothers sang, and I just kept on ramblin' geographically, while others rambled about this event conversationally.

At dinner that night our table was buzzing with what happened, and several people came over to me wanting every last morsel of information. Victor (Mr. Malaprop) said, "I told you, Steve's the horniest guy on the ship," which garnered a few amorous stares in my direction from much older women. I really didn't want to discuss any of it, and downplayed the whole thing telling them nothing happened. Victor hounded me later on, and in a helpful piece of advice I told him of my camera routine as to how Tuliza and I met. "The rest of what happened," I said to him with a smile, "is confidential." "I'll bring out my camera more," Victor said. "May the film be with you" I retorted, parodying the famous line from "Star Wars." I hoped he "clicked" with someone soon because he was seriously looking.

The next stop was Mozambique, which was an economic mess after a civil war, famine, and strife. According to Wikipedia, "It is estimated that 80% of the city's population live in slums without running water or electricity, but the city has little money to invest in infrastructure." And it showed, immediately. We docked in Maputo, where I recall seeing many barefoot women wearing head scarfs down by the river washing their clothing and carrying the basket loads on their heads with a baby in their arms (quite a balancing act). Some of the clothing (sarongs and wraps) were quite colorful. The city featured beautiful white sand beaches which we observed from high above the bay, but again I preferred to walk around and mingle, which had just worked so well in Kenya. In retrospect, I should have gone to the beach. The country was extremely poor, and I got a distrustful vibe from the locals maybe because I was a foreigner, White, American, or something else. This place was definitely not as friendly as the other places we'd been to; maybe they hadn't ramped up to tourism yet. Or traffic lights (many crazy drivers ignored them). I liked the huge wall murals, which looked like a cross between those I had seen in the Caribbean (colorful) and those in Northern Ireland (political), for their artistic value.

There were many kids in the street just hustling, begging, dancing, some looking forlorn and some smiling, laughing. The country seemed like it hadn't changed in hundreds of years, and was backwards. There were probably better parts, but I didn't see them (this was really a bad situation if these *were* the better parts). This extreme poverty made me take notice of the way the world really is in so many places, and made me appreciate what I have even more. I felt sorry for the people there. I did not talk to many nor did I have any meaningful conversations. It wasn't a wasted day by any means, but not one of my better ones. Even seeing the bad can be a good education. A few months later I would meet a college student in Buffalo wearing a T-shirt with the word Mozambique on the back. This gal had worked as a volunteer there, and told me it *was* as bad as I had seen, maybe worse, including high crime. She did not renew her contract there because of the potential danger.

That night, in a total disconnect to what was in Mozambique, we had a "formal night" on the ship with men dressed in tuxedos and suits, and women in lavish dresses. There were fancy decorations, balloons, ship photographers taking formal-pose photos, exquisite food, and gourmet appetizers after hours. I felt guilty partaking in this after what I just saw, but did. I also got a photo with a professional singer aboard ship from Australia, who was talented and pretty. This was the most lavish party I had seen, trumping the one at a

CEO's home of a former employer who brought jungle animals with a trainer into his mansion. There, his wife's shoe closet was so large that during a house tour I asked if that was the master bedroom (before seeing all the shoes along the floor). Oops! In this way, the world cruise was far superior to the regular cruise ships' gala events, although some of those were extraordinary as well.

The ship stopped at three ports in South Africa: Richards Bay, Durban, and the final stop on my portion of the world cruise, Cape Town. Richards Bay was boring, except for a picturesque harbor area (largest in South Africa). Based on the missed day in Madagascar, we would be spending a second day there, which I found equally as dull – I went to the beach but there were hardly any people on it, so I went to a nearby mall instead. There was a highlight, however, and it had a related event that was equally as excellent. This was Zulu country and, as such, the Entertainment Director arranged for Zulu dancers in full costume to give a show outside the ship the next morning before we sailed. I had wanted to see African dancing, and even suggested a theater show for such to the Entertainment Director en route to Africa, so I was very happy to see this. There were a few hitches, however. The passengers were unaware this was happening, and many were departing for excursions at this time, heading to the tour buses by the hundreds. They wanted to see the dancers but had to leave. Meanwhile, the dancers wanted a passenger to dance with them, and scanned those who were watching from the entrance of the ship and those encircling them a bit closer.

The leader of the troupe must have seen lots of old people, some with canes and in wheelchairs. Then he spotted me way in the back (with my camera, naturally). So he ran into the crowd and pulled me out by the hand. It was early, and I really didn't want to do this, but before I knew it I was among them with a female dancer giving me a quick visual lesson on how to move my body. There was also a lot of "stomping" as part of the dance. I followed along, and soon the ship's photographer was taking photos (to sell to me later, of course). I gave my camera to another passenger who took excellent photos – especially of me bowing my head forward and lifting my knees in unison with them. I did this fairly well, and got some kudos afterwards. At the end of their performance I stuck around and took photos with all of them, which came out very well.

That night there were other Zulus performing at the theater show aboard ship – different Zulus, who told their story through interpretative song and a softer style of dance. I sat in the second row shooting close-up photos (no flash allowed). This group was also excellent, and I hung around a half-hour after the show ended hoping to get photos with them to round out the planned Zulu-dance section of an upcoming photo album. I figured they had to come out sometime, and there was only one way out. Besides, nothing else much was going on that night, and I had done something similar in Barbados and Trinidad that resulted in terrific photos. Sure enough, they exited. I praised their performance, and asked if I could take photos of and with them. They were hesitant at first but then I showed them the photos I had with the daytime Zulus (maybe they knew them – or some were them). They smiled, looked at each other, and said OK. I asked a passerby passenger to take them with my signature comment – "please get our feet in" (because I can edit the photos later to be more close-up if desirable, but cannot include feet that aren't there to begin with). He did a good job, and I "bought" him a drink later (the trip was all-inclusive). My dinnermates had by this time started requesting to see my photos. I showed these to them, among selected others, and they liked but "envied" them. I asked Victor if he's been "using his camera" as we discussed, with a wink. He said, in my pun-intended style, "Yes, but nothing has developed yet." I just hoped he wasn't "flashing" the women.

We then sailed to Durban, South Africa which featured buildings along the beach having a distinctive African theme. This included, for lack of a better term, "spear art" - giant decorative spears accenting the bamboo huts dotting the coastline. I took a city tour on my own via local taxi driver. We went into the city but this wasn't nearly as nice – we were warned about high crime, especially at night, and to be careful during the day, too. Some parts of Durban reminded me of the area near Penn Station in Manhattan – very crowded, dirty in some areas, and a lot of small stores (many of these were run by Hindus). I went to the Indian part there – lots of turbans in Durban – and it didn't seem like I was anywhere near Africa. A fellow passenger saw me walking around and came up to me in a frenzy – he had just been robbed, but was physically OK. He took the free shuttle back to the ship and dealt with it there. This man ended up making a police report, and seemed to be fine afterwards. I repeat: you can never let your guard down, even on vacation. I was never robbed, but met several people who were – even big, tall, very physically fit guys in their 20s and 30s.

Durban seemed like the place to go to the beach, and so I did and had a good time. The water was beautiful, and there were several snack shops there. The area featured a large mall nearby, which I walked around and bought many post cards from one shop. I got a good tan that day, but on the shuttle back to the ship I lost my sunglasses! This was no ordinary pair – this pair had been around the world with me and had great sentimental value. I asked Guest Relations if they could assist me, and it was good news/bad news – yes, the tour operator found them after they fell down the space to the side of my seat (I shouldn't have put them in my shorts with the wide pockets), but because the tour operator was closed already and our ship was leaving the next morning before they opened, I could not get them. I was very upset about this, and offered to pay for a taxi there and back so I could retrieve them. Although Guest Relations tried, the situation was no-go. This was one of those little things that would have meant a lot. I later had them mailed back to me in the U.S., and received them a month later (the cruise line graciously paid the postage). I had a back-up pair that looked similar with me, so not a huge deal, but I would have liked to have these back (I still have these sunglasses to this day, and they have been to over 75 countries with me).

At dinner that night a few passengers said they weren't thrilled with Durban, and had thought about going to a nearby country called Swaziland; they were aiming at specific travel goals including number of countries visited (many were trying to get to 50). I had looked into this as well but was told although the mileage is not that far, there could be trouble at the borders (long waits, e.g.) and the ride is through rough terrain so there were no guarantees of making it back to the ship on time. I learned that if an excursion booked via the cruise line is late getting back, the ship will still be there when the group returns; however, if you go on your own and don't make it back in time, it's on you to get to the next port at your own expense (a good idea since nearly all your possessions are on the ship!). The trip, as I had configured it, would get me to my 99$^{th}$ country, but I still wanted to get to one more if possible to make the 100$^{th}$ on this trip. It wasn't going to be Swaziland, but a surprise was in store that would get me to one I hadn't even thought about.

Our next port – the last on this amazing world cruise for me – was Cape Town, South Africa which I'd heard was beautiful. I never found out. There was a tremendous wind storm heading there that kept us from docking for 8 hours (a rare time when this number was not good for me) until 9:00 p.m. So, we had lost the day of sightseeing there, which was my only day to do so since I had to be up the following morning at 4:00 a.m. for a 6:00 a.m. flight to Victoria Falls, Zimbabwe, which started the solo portion of my trip. I almost made a big error in assuming there would be a taxi available to meet me at the ship at that early hour to take me to the airport – Guest Relations wasn't so sure, and this not being the case would have imperiled the rest of my pre-paid trip (it's always in the details). Fortunately, Guest Relations arranged this taxi pick-up for me, and there was no problem. So, I missed Cape Town which I really wanted to see – but I would return there, as fate would have it.

Overall, this world cruise was outstanding! It was a once-in-a-lifetime experience not many get to do - especially at such a relatively young age. I saw and learned a lot – and the cruise was an experience in itself. I had a positive feeling about it, after all was said and done – it sure beat staying in Buffalo, or working at an unsatisfying job, for that matter. I didn't go BOOM (Bored Out Of my Mind) as thought after day 10, although I was getting there by the end of the trip. However, I did go BUST in a good way: Beautiful Upscale Ship Transport. I said my goodbyes and received a lot of kudos from the passengers and crew who enjoyed having me – a factor that would play into my future plans.

Meanwhile, the next morning I boarded my early-morning flight as I began my trip to the interior southern portion of Africa. My first stop was to Zimbabwe and Victoria Falls – the very place Sebastian had told me about four years earlier on the Antarctica cruise, which he claimed is the best waterfalls in the world. He had been right about Iguassu Falls, and so would this trip be worth it? I'd bet you 100 trillion dollars but it's not worth very much in Zimbabwe money – you see, their economy collapsed, and their bills in this denomination were now on sale there for $1 U.S.

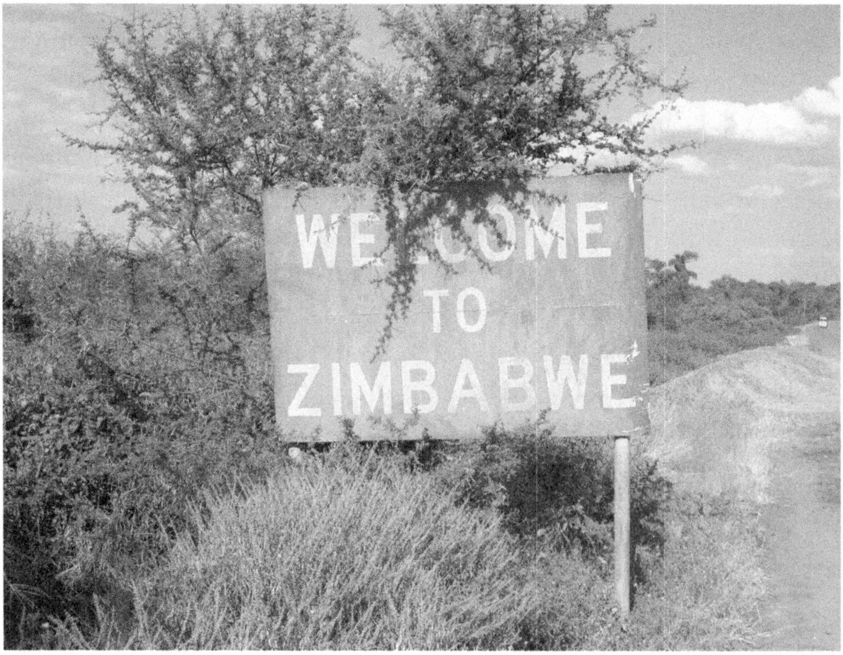


It was hard to believe I was in Zimbabwe.

# Chapter 19

## The Interior Of Africa, India, And Return To The Middle East

The flight went well and I arrived circa noon at the classy resort I had pre-booked (expensive at $250/night but I needed the best for safety). Although Zimbabwe is a poor country, it's expensive getting there, and the price of good-quality hotels is expensive as well. That said, there were baboons and wart hogs roaming around freely outside – and it was said that the baboons could be dangerous (scratch and bite, and hard to control). I was amazed at how fast they could climb, even straight up. They were ravaging some house across the road as I entered the hotel. I had my own developing situation upon check-in: the clerk could not find my reservation and told me that they were sold out for the two nights I was supposed to be there! That's' not what I wanted to hear after a long early-morning flight and nowhere to go after my taxi had left. The people in Zimbabwe spoke English, so language was not a barrier. Finally, after the manager and two others got involved – and I showed my receipt – the issue was resolved after they called my travel agency. I almost thought a shakedown was coming, but it all turned out well. The hotel was posh and had a jungle theme. Literally, it was a jungle out there, as I was soon to learn.

The manager asked what my plans were, and if I needed a personal guide. I said to sightsee and yes, respectively. He told me that the guide is also a taxi driver and wanted to know if there's any place special I wanted to go aside from the obvious Victoria Falls. I asked what else is around, and even asked if Swaziland was anywhere close. He laughed and said no, "but Botswana and Zambia are." I had him repeat that, especially the part about Botswana (I had already planned on going to nearby Zambia). He told me that it's a two-hour cab ride away, but his driver/tour guide could come immediately and give me a good price for U.S. dollars. I had planned to take a nap, but that information exhilarated me; going to Botswana, a country I hadn't planned on visiting, would be the additional country I needed to get me to the magic number of 100 lifetime.

The driver showed up in 20 minutes. His name was Sundai and he brought a male friend, Khumo, who was a taxi driver in Botswana (Sundai was not allowed to drive a taxi there), so they would switch off driving in the respective countries. That was fine with me. Both guys were extremely nice, especially Sundai who was approximately age 30, a happy-go-lucky guy, and who really cared about my safety. Such was the case when we came across a mother elephant walking in front of its calf, the calf's trunk around the mother's tail, crossing not too far ahead of us. I sprang out from the back seat to take a quick photo. Sundai yelled "No! – get back in the taxi!" because he knew what might happen: big momma stopped, stared at us, and I really thought was about to charge – huge tusks and all. After a few seconds – which seemed like eternity – both elephants kept walking. I then clicked the photo from the vehicle. Sundai and Khumo just looked at each other, and then told me not to take photos like that unless I ask them first – elephants have been known to charge. I apologized, and tried to defuse the situation with humor, telling them I know how to stop an elephant from charging – take away his credit card. We were safely out of harm's way then, and they laughed. After that, everything was fine, and we got along extremely well.

Elephant crossing in Botswana. I was admonished by the tour guide for attempting to take a photo outside of the vehicle - and glared at by a large elephant as another reminder not to. Despite being a teacher, I learned my lesson.

We finally got to Botswana. There was really not much there – very sparse, very desert, and very deserted. In fact, Botswana is one of the least populated countries in the world with only just over two million people in a big geography. It's also very flat. The main industries are livestock and especially mining, where it is known for its high-quality of diamonds. The drivers took me to the Safari Resort where I mingled with the locals for a few hours while the they went off on their own for some of the duration (thank goodness they returned!). I had lunch there, including some kind of seasoned beef with rice (didn't taste that great). I learned that the big sports there are football (soccer), cricket, tennis, track and field (lots of top runners from there), and even handball which I played as a kid in Brooklyn.

The locals spoke English well, and seemed contented with their slow-paced life. I actually enjoyed this laid-back mentality because I was such a go-go person; for the first time, I realized that working so hard is nuts. Yes, it gets you material things but there's a lot to be said for the work-life balance. I knew so many people who were stressed-out/burned-out, and wondered how it ever got to such a sad state (keeping up with the Joneses? Wanting to impress others? I wasn't like that and didn't want to be like that). I remember that it hit me there, to really enjoy life as I was doing. Yes, being single and having discretionary income helped, but I can truly say that these people I met in Botswana, and other poor people I met elsewhere, seemed as happy if not happier than most people I knew. And when you consider that money is just a means to an end, that end being happiness, maybe they are better off and the rock group Boston was right when singing, "I understand about indecision, and I don't care if I get behind/People living in competition, all I want is to have my peace of mind." And yes, that song lyric ran through my mind a lot there – and afterwards. An epiphany in Botswana. Who knew?

We returned to the hotel, and I'd had such a good time that I arranged for Sundai to pick me up the next morning and take me around Zimbabwe and Zambia. That's what he did – including to the major site, Victoria Falls, which straddles both countries. He let me roam around there, picking me up many hours later. As with the U.S. and Canada separating Niagara Falls, you can walk from one country's side to the other (and get a visa as needed at the border). Upon viewing them, and in a close call, I do believe these are the best waterfalls in the world. As Wikipedia describes, "while it is neither the highest nor the widest waterfalls in the world, it is claimed to be the largest. This claim is based on a width of 1,708 meters (5,604 ft.) and height of 108 meters (354 ft.), forming the largest sheet of falling water in the world. The falls' maximum flow rate compares well with that of other major waterfalls."

The water tumbled into a gorge, and, well, the whole panorama created a "gorgeous" sight. However, that's not the half of it. The roar of this natural wonder was unbelievable, like an approaching subway train, and there was massive spray creating a soaking mist. It's a good thing I brought an umbrella and several plastic bags for my camera! I got soaked despite wearing a raincoat provided there, but obtained several excellent photos of both the waterfalls and me getting soaked next to them by a brave lady from Scotland who co-soaked with me while taking them (I did the same for her). And while mentioning Scottish, according to Wikipedia again, "David Livingstone, the Scottish missionary and explorer, is believed to have been the first European to view the Victoria Falls — which he did from what is now known as 'Livingstone Island' in Zambia, the only land accessible in the middle of the falls. David Livingstone gave the falls the name 'Victoria Falls' in honor of his Queen, but the indigenous name of 'Mosi-oa-Tunya' — literally meaning the 'Smoke that Thunders' — is also well known." It's no surprise that Victoria Falls is a UNESCO World Heritage Site – and well-deserved. You really have to be there to behold this spectacular cascade; photos don't do it justice. If I'd had more time I would have considered taking a helicopter up and viewing it from above. I crammed in a lot on this last day, but in retrospect should have stayed one more day.

Victoria Falls in Zimbabwe, Africa. Sebastian was right - this is the best of them all.

What's a nice boy from Brooklyn doing in a place like this? Getting soaked by Victoria Falls in Zimbabwe, Africa - and loving it!

I had my signage with me, that I'm now in Zambia, my 100th country visited, and the date. I had a photo taken of me holding the sign in several locations – but could not do it close to the Falls because of the soaking issue. So I did this first, before going to the Falls, by the bridge crossing over from Zimbabwe to Zambia, in front of the sign that said Welcome To The Victoria Falls/Zambia. It was cool having Zambia as my 100th country visited because it's an exotic location that most people don't get to see, even veteran travelers, because it's in the interior of Africa and not available by cruise ship. I tried my best to preserve my hand-made sign, but it ended up getting soaked. There were bungee jumpers at the bridge connecting the two countries, but I wasn't about to chance doing it. I saw a woman coming from Zambia over the bridge toward Zimbabwe who was not only beautiful, but was wearing a colorful African-art dress. She looked like she could be Miss Zambia. I asked to take a photo of her and she graciously said OK. The photo came out well, and I showed it to her. She was dazzled by the instant appearance of the picture on my digital-camera screen. I offered to mail her a photo, but she politely declined. We chatted and then parted with a smile and gratitude. It was just a nice moment on a nice day with a nice lady and doesn't sound like much, but it's the little pleasantries in life that can add up to a lot.

I met with Sundai as planned, after being soaked by the Victoria Falls mist and perspiration. He was glad I enjoyed it after my rave review! Then we drove along the Zambezi River and took photos there, having another good time laughing it up. I really missed him when we parted; he gave me a big hug to show he felt the same. The feeling was genuine from both of us. What a great guy! This had turned out to be quite an adventure, and I can still visualize and "audiolize" the Falls. I mailed Sundai photos as he requested, and made copies for Khumo as well, along with a long note expressing my appreciation not only for the transportation and communication, but for the education and camaraderie as well.

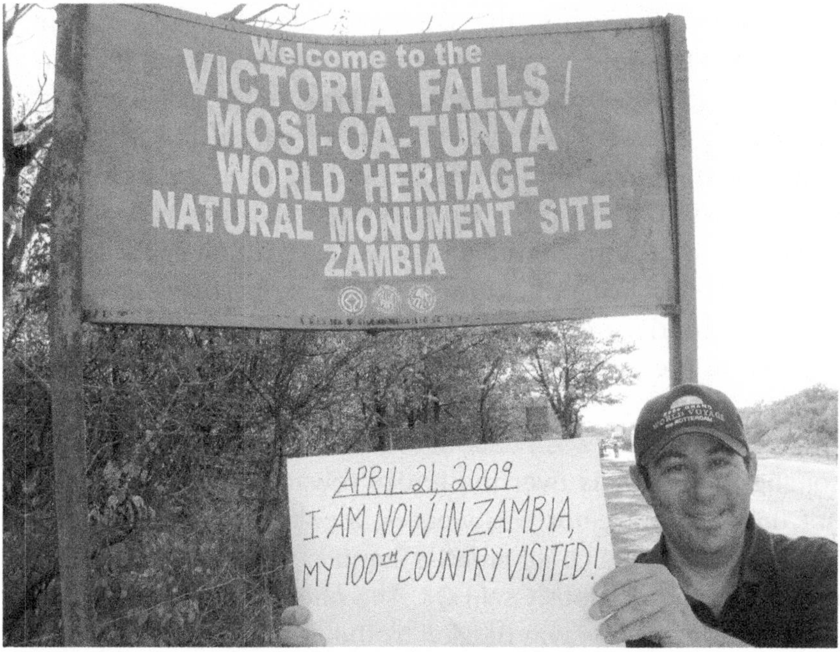


I finally made it! I've been to more countries since, but this one was special, having accomplished the goal.

My last act was to buy a 100,000,000,000,000 (100 trillion) dollar bill in Zimbabwe, which was part of the actual currency there before the economy crashed. These were now hot souvenirs. I had mine framed at home: the bill cost me $1 U.S. and the frame cost me $5. But my experience there was worth more than the value of any currency. Some things, like this trip, and travels in general, were and are priceless.

The vacation ended and I was so happy I had gone! I would have one more hurdle to clear before being home-free, however: one of the airlines I connected with as part of my itinerary wanted to bump me from the full flight in favor of a paying customer (I was again using my frequent flyer miles). I had noticed this as a trend: a few airlines viewed those using free airline miles as having a lower status than a paying customer, when you should have at least the same status since these miles were garnered via being a frequent flyer and thus paying a lot to have earned them. The better airlines realize that and treat you as such. This was a key point I made to the connecting airline personnel to retain my seat – but this airline was an international *partner* of my main airline in the U.S., through which I obtained the miles, which may explain its reluctance to keep me on the flight (which, where I'm from, is called the "tough noogies" rule; I'm entitled and I'm going). It all worked out in the end, and I did let the base U.S. airline know about this situation (I received an apology, and the issue was checked into). I was extra vigilant about this in future trips - getting stranded is no fun. This did not happen again with any airline.

Upon safe arrival home, I realized what a tremendous life experience this all had been! I had taken nearly 3,000 more photos to capture it all, and the photos came out great. I had an incredible excitement about life, and was just turned-on to travel in general. Although I had reached my travel goal, I still wanted more. What about seeing the Pyramids? Taj Mahal? Israel? And maybe getting to every country in Europe now that I was so close? These were all pleasant yet exciting thoughts on my long plane rides home. And that's another thing: when you have such beautiful memories, these make for great dreams. Just think how much time you spend dreaming and you realize yet another multiplier effect of your travels! Are "sweet dreams made of these?" You bet!

You would think that getting to 100 countries is cause for celebration, but I didn't do anything special afterwards except have a fine dinner with a lovely date, and no-one did anything special for me. Nor did I expect or want anything; the travel experiences and happy memories were their own rewards. But I did receive a good life lesson which was even more valuable that I will share with you. I only told close family and friends about this accomplishment, and learned there are those "friends" who rejoiced with me and were genuinely happy, and those who were genuinely envious, with a few even saying so. My overall relationship didn't change with these people, but I was told a few things that were revealing and shed a new light on where they, ironically, were coming from. Here's what happened, and here's how I learned to best handle this potentially delicate situation. When the friend or other close person asked how my trip was, I downplayed my travels, just providing the basics, and letting the other person ask questions to the degree he or she wanted to. I did not boast, and if I sensed that someone was not interested in hearing about them beyond a certain point, I moved on, or went along when he or she changed the topic. Later, I developed a better tactic in that upon return from my trip, I'd start off by asking about how the other person is doing, because when I led off, the other person often was more reticent in replying, sometimes even saying, "Well, I can't compete with what you've done, but...", and then tell me about his or her routine events. One friend even told me that hearing about my travels made her realize how boring her life is. So, bear in mind that even if others do not come out and say it, they may feel compelled to compete with you, or feel badly if they cannot. I found that being humble was the best way to go about it, but I have met many travelers who will shout their accomplishments from the top of the highest peak (however, paraphrasing one person who did this, all he ever heard back was his echo). Therefore, in my opinion, it's best to continue things as they were, and know within yourself how fortunate you were to have experienced all this in the myriad of ways travel can expand your horizons and you as a person.

The corporate job market continued to be very tough at this point. I still had ample resources to wait it out, including investments that continued to do well, and was looking for the right career opportunity. I also began consulting in Marketing, which paid well and gave me the needed flexibility to take advantage of travel opportunities. So, I decided to return for a few days' vacation to my favorite place in the world, Club Med – Turks & Caicos Islands in the Caribbean, which I had not been to in four years. It was the same wonderful place I had enjoyed and missed – including the beach, beautiful women, "Hands Up" and "Crazy Signs" signature songs, gourmet meals, and that delicious chocolate bread! But there were a few changes: no more roommate options, and the place had become more commercialized, like a resort, with all-inclusive packages including alcohol. There were more couples as well, and the average age was closer to 40 than 20 as it was years ago. The former "antidote to civilization" was becoming more like civilization itself. As a marketer I understood the reasons for doing this: vacationers were looking for all-inclusive luxury and willing to pay for it, especially those days when they were working so hard to keep their jobs. Being pampered was perhaps a need more than a want. Yet, due to the recession and competition, the land package prices were very reasonable, and I was again able to take advantage of last-minute deal pricing and use of frequent flyer miles – a benefit of being flexible due to not working full-time. I wasn't a "frequent flyer millionaire," as one person had asked me about, but I had built up quite a lot of miles that were not worth anything unless they were redeemed.

To paraphrase the Malaysian guy who thought I was Canadian, "Ah, Club Med!" With a beach like that and still a party atmosphere at its core, this Club Med village already had a "hands-up" on the competition. In fact, this beach on the island of Providenciales would later win tripadvisor's® Travelers' Choice Award for two years in a row, 2011 and 2012. But then, those of us who had been going for so long already knew that (there went the best-kept secret). The staff continued to make for a fun atmosphere, yet you could go off somewhere and relax without anyone hassling you to join in.

I had another excellent time, featuring the usual fun in the sun. I met people from Southern California and asked why they made the long trek all the way to the Caribbean when there are so many beautiful beaches there. The answer was the same: the gorgeous beach, with its warm blue-green clear waters, and a lecture on how this differs from the Pacific Ocean which isn't as warm or clear. Many of these people were snorkelers or scuba divers, and to them this made all the difference. Club Med also offered scuba diving certification courses at this village. The shows at night by the staff were outstanding, better than I had remembered (especially the dancing in "Cleopatra"). There was also an excellent "foam party" whereby the main area outside the swimming pool was cordoned off, and soapsuds were sprayed in for frolicking in one's bathing suit, bikini, or dental floss masquerading as a bathing suit. I noticed that the food quality wasn't quite the same but was still excellent. I re-read a favorite book, "Looking Out For #1" by Robert J. Ringer, which I read in college, recommended back then by Harvey, and I also re-read it every few years since then as a refresher. The book, contrary to its name, is not about stomping on other people to get ahead, but how to maximize yourself in several different areas, personally and professionally. I still subscribe to the author's philosophy of life which has served me very well, and I convinced others at the village to check it out when they returned home. Ironically, I would later read "Pulling Your Own Strings" by Dr. Wayne Dyer – and see him running along the coastline of Fort Lauderdale Beach as I was reading his book there!

I returned to Buffalo all tanned and ready for the warmer weather there. I did some volunteer work, including teaching at a local inner-city high school (ironically, about how to get a job), with more explorations of the Western New York vicinity. There was a lot to do there, and I was out every single day leveraging my freedom. I entertained several visitors, including Harvey, Mark, and Lana from California, who I took to the annual Buffalo Wing Festival where she spotted the gorgeous official St. Pauli Girl® spokesmodel dressed as on the beer label at the company's booth. Naturally, I had a photo op with her – including with her photo on the poster behind us in the booth. I spoke with her and, surprisingly, she wasn't from St. Paul or even Minnesota, but from Slovakia. She was very surprised I'd been there, and that I'd also been to neighboring countries and around all of Europe. We chatted for a while about it, and just as we got into the best part of the discussion, she was dragged away by the booth people to be in photos with others who were waiting. This included with one little boy who said excitedly, "Daddy, look!" Daddy was looking, all right, and mommy wasn't too thrilled.

I continued my domestic travels and achieved the milestone of getting to every state a minimum of four times (Alabama being the last one). As the weather turned colder, I looked for a desirable full-time job opportunity. When none appeared I looked for an international travel opportunity. Plenty of those appeared. I still had enough frequent flyer miles to take several trips. I managed these well, knowing how much I needed to purchase with each airline credit card to achieve selected mileage for free trips. It was well worth the effort. One such opportunity using these miles (and saving me thousands of dollars) was a trip back to the Middle East, with a side-trip to India, to kick it off in early Fall (when the weather was cooler there). The airline's frequent flyer desk was once again very helpful and patient in assisting with the itinerary. I was off and running to 10 countries (most new for me) and 4 continents in 24 days – half by land, and half by sea. Building up to being a travel athlete greatly helped during this trip; the travel itself would be arduous in that I'd spend 40 hours on planes, 20 hours in buses/trains/motor coaches/taxis, and 11 days at sea. There would also be several climate changes, and a lot of luggage schlepping. However, the sun shined for 24 days in a row, I made it through in fine shape, I had another excellent time, and became a mental travel athlete as well through all this new learning. Previous travels were a big benefit here because I had developed an innate sense of where to go, what to do, what to eat – and what not to, so that I could keep safe and healthy. I once again went by myself, by choice. Few I knew had the resources to take a trip like this, including the endurance.

The first stop on this trip was New Delhi, India, a real challenge before I even got there with 17 hours of flying plus 7 hours of layovers. Add in a big time difference and climate change, and it resulted in being very tired and just wanting to rest up (I left on a Tuesday at 7:00 p.m. and arrived on Thursday morning at 7:00 a.m. including 12 hours' time difference forward). But, based on the airline's limited flexibility to even get me there on short notice, I only had two days to stay there, so every minute counted. I changed currency, obtaining rupees, and took a taxi to my hotel. I had planned to relax and sightsee New Delhi that Thursday and go to the Taj Mahal in Agra (several hours away) on Friday as my must-see site that would hopefully make it all worthwhile. I checked into my upscale hotel (only $25/night for a "superior deluxe" room with the excellent exchange rate for U.S. dollars), and inquired about trips to the Taj Mahal for Friday. I was informed that the Taj Mahal is closed on Fridays for prayer – so I would have to go that day or not at all! Yikes! I inquired as to the best way to get there, and was told my only viable option was to take a taxi for nearly five hours each way. The good news: the cost was only $40 U.S. each way, the taxi driver would wait for me, and one could be available in 20 minutes. The bad news: unpaved roads, no rest stops, and, for lack of a better term, "bellek!" with oxen all over the place. My biggest concern: could I go without peeing for nearly five hours? The answer was yes, barely, because I recalled that eating salty foods or snacks helps inhibit this, and it worked (I had brought potato chips with me)! I wasn't sure if the price I was paying was good or not, but it sounded great; under the circumstances, I was thankful to get it.

The taxi was called, and I would nap in the back seat for an hour on the way there. I should have napped more because India was filthy with animals such as camels, mules, and silver ox roaming the streets with no-one cleaning up after them. There was garbage all over the place. Poor people were pacing around, yelling a lot. And because India was so crowded, the small cars on the road drove very close together. I had to brace for impact at least five times, and really thought we were going to crash. There were several construction delays as well. But the driver did a good job evading the animals and avoiding the vehicles. I was glad he would be waiting for me during the four hours I was there because I trusted his driving skills.

Upon arrival, I was told that vehicles are not allowed to drive to the entrance to the Taj Mahal, about a half-mile away, so I'd have to take either a mule or a camel-drawn carriage for $2 U.S. I chose the mule, perhaps because of my previous experience doing the "Humpty Dance" on the camel I rode in Morocco. My taxi driver rode another mule alongside me. As we arrived, a young Indian guy in his mid- 20s I'll call Neville approached us. My taxi driver knew him, and they conversed briefly in the local language which I later learned was Hindi. The driver said he would meet me back where he parked the taxi at a little after closing time, roughly 7:30 p.m. I besieged him to wait for me no matter what (in case I got caught in human traffic while exiting). Neville then spoke English to me, stating that he is my tour guide. I knew nothing about this, and asked about a fee. He said, "Don't worry, you're taken care of" and showed me what looked like an official ID with his photo on it. So I assumed this was included somehow (bad assumption). Neville was very good. He was very Westernized and even "cool" by American standards, including his fashionable style of dress. Neville was able to cut through the long line and get me a ticket quickly, and then guided me along.

This photo was taken directly after a very long flight and taxi ride, but visiting the Taj Mahal on this beautiful October day made it all worthwhile. Wow! This defines "the majesty of the history" I mention in the book.

My very first and strongest impression was that the Taj Mahal was gorgeous (white marble, with pond in front and minarets on the sides), and this was the most incredible building I had ever seen. The sunlight bounced off the white marble creating different colors on it toward sunset – purple, orange, pink and more. By this time I had seen plenty in my life, but I was awed looking at this jewel and just kept staring (there were other structures nearly as grand that I saw during our ride there). There was a reflecting pool, garden, trees, and two mosques on the grounds. This all seemed just perfect, and unlike anything I had ever seen. Neville was eager to show me around and please me as his customer. He was fun, sort of an Indian version of Sundai from Zimbabwe; we had a good time with lots of laughs. I was exhausted, however – perhaps literally from the toxic traffic exhaust fumes – but was energized by being there among one of the Seven Wonders of the World (and a UNESCO World Heritage Site). I learned some of the history as well. The Taj Mahal is actually a tomb ordered built by the Emperor to memorialize his favorite wife, who died in

1629 A.D. I went inside and was very surprised to see how small it was in there! I expected it to be like a museum, but it's actually a mausoleum, and takes only about 15 minutes to get a good glimpse before you leave. You have to remove your shoes or cover your feet to enter, but there are socks provided there to do that. You also have to cover your legs, and I was very fortunate to have not changed into shorts (despite the very hot weather) because I was concerned about insect bites. Women had to cover their shoulders. The tomb is beautiful, with marble and gemstones. It took 22 years to build the Taj Mahal. Now that's what I call love!

There wasn't a whole lot to see there aside from the magnificence of the Taj Mahal and I wondered what to do for the remaining three hours. Naturally, I took a gazillion photos. Neville turned out to be an excellent photographer. He was very impressed when I received permission from a beautiful Indian gal in flowing white dress to take photos with her – including romantically holding hands. She was "waiting for someone," and I didn't want to be there if the Indian equivalent of Bruno showed up. I also had Neville take a photo of me amidst the crowd, surrounded by numerous Indians including some in traditional garb. And I took a few of and with Neville because I wanted to remember him, had lots of time before meeting the taxi driver, and wanted photos of others to diversify the myriad of landscape photos I would later put into my albums.

Aggressive beggars swarmed the tourists, but by then I was used to them. They sold cheap souvenirs and I bought a few small ones, including a fridge magnet of the Taj. It was nearing the bewitching hour when I had to return to my taxi – I sure hoped the driver was still there. If I'd had more time I would have checked out Fort Agra, but seeing the Taj Mahal was great and it couldn't have worked out better with the transportation, weather, tour guide, and of course the majestic "wonder" I was beholding. This seemed too good to be true, and sure enough at the end there was a little snafu. My tour guide Neville wanted me to pay him $200 for his services! I reminded him that I asked him about a fee and said I wasn't going to pay one if he charged it. His idea of my being "taken care of" and my interpretation widely differed. I had planned to give him a nice tip, and told him I'll give him $20. He demanded more, which really ticked me off, "Agra-vating" me, so to speak. He was slightly tarnishing my nice time, trying to screw my happiness, and largely diminishing my high opinion of him – all of which I told him. Money was the name of his game, and I didn't like his attitude. For some reason I used a few American idiomatic expressions involving animals that he didn't understand, but seemed intimidated by, such as "You're beating a dead horse," "You're taking the bull too much by the horns" (calm down), and "Don't kill the golden goose." He was stunned that I withstood his best attempts, and ended up taking the $20 (which I later learned was more than plenty – think how far that goes when I was paying only $80 for a 10-hour round-trip taxi ride with the driver waiting 4 hours for me!). Neville was further stunned when I put my arm around him and said, "C'mon, I'll also pay for the camel ride back." He accepted, and even smiled. We ended up parting cordially, and doing a big-city handshake by locking thumbs. He would have rivaled Sundai for best tour guide ever, but blew it. Perhaps the lesson he learned about trying to intimidate a tourist paid off literally for him later on, when hopefully he was diplomatic and thus received bigger tips.

My taxi driver waited for me all this time - and I was so glad to see him! I had taken a photo of him with his taxi before we parted so I would recognize him – or, if he wasn't there, hopefully find someone who knew him and would call. I took one last look at the magnificent Taj Mahal, nearly enveloped in darkness by this time, and couldn't help think of the song that popped into my head, "Goodbye Rupee Tuesday" – even though it was Thursday. I was very glad I went – and had a "Sun day" for viewing it and taking photos.

I was feeling a bit queasy from all the action, and not eating properly, so I did not want to chance eating traditional Indian cuisine that night, plus it was nearly midnight upon return to New Delhi. Ironically, there was a McDonald's near my hotel that was still open, so I went there. I ordered a traditional hamburger (which tasted the same as in the States) but they offered local variations including curry (in New York City there is a fast-food takeout place called Curry In A Hurry® but I did not see it in India). It would have been cool to have a deli sandwich in New Delhi, but there were no restaurants there serving such meats. The main beer in India was Kingfisher®. I had seen signage for this around New Delhi and decided to try one. I'm no beer expert but it tasted bland and a bit sweet. Not bad, though. Kingfisher called itself "The King of Good Times," which may sound familiar to when Budweiser®called itself "The King of Beers." The Kingfisher TV ad I saw had this complicated theme: guy drinks Kingfisher, guy gets girl. Some things are universal.

I had difficulty navigating through several people there when exiting the restaurant. One homeless lady clutched my shirt, nearly ripping it, looking for a handout. Then very aggressive merchants I'll call urban turbans approached me to hawk their wares, speaking English well, and beginning their sentences with, "My friend, where you from?" One really dirty, smelly guy put his hands on me and I just lost it, screaming at him never to do that again. New Delhi was so filthy I didn't know what was on them, and I sure didn't want to find out. There were feces all over the place, which brought lots of flies and mosquitos. There was garbage strewn everywhere with no trash cans in sight. The smell was intense. My "superior deluxe" hotel room wasn't so wonderful, either, with sagging mattress and lots of street noise (no air conditioning, so the windows needed to be open). I should have upgraded to the super-duper superior deluxe room for $30 (in total, not extra) which may have eliminated that foul odor of something I couldn't quite identify (but got the clerk to bring up the industrial aerosol spray they kept on hand to eliminate it). However, I did like the Indian music videos on TV – including lots of non-verbal romantic interludes on the beach. TV soap operas were big there as well. This was the home of Bollywood, after all. Many of the women were gorgeous.

The next day was my last one there. I took an inexpensive taxi tour around the city in 95-degree heat. The taxi driver's native language was Urdu, but he spoke English very well. I spent time at India Gate, a war memorial similar in design to arches I had seen in France, Italy, and even Washington Square Park in Manhattan. I also visited the financial and commerce center called Connaught Place, with an area called Central Park nearby, the name of which also harkened me back to New York City. There was also a gigantic, colorful statue of an Indian figurine towering over a highway above us, called Hanuman Statue. There were other towering statues of Indians as we drove around, too. Perhaps as in Romania and Russia, when they did something big in New Delhi, they did it really big! The Grand Bazaar was another example. There were so many items for sale, especially handicrafts, books, miniature statues, spices, and incense. The whole city felt like a chaotic hustle, from the bazaars to the malls, to the streets where there were so many small vehicles driving so closely together (including tuk-tuks also called auto rickshaws there), to the pavement where there were so many poor people that the poverty was almost palpable.

As I toured some more, there were several impressive mosques, smaller bazaars, and Buddha statues. I finally did have an indigenous Indian dish, although I do not like Indian food in general. Since I'm a big fan of the Ramones (who are from New York City, and who I saw play before they were famous not far from Rockaway Beach), I had the Chicken Vindaloo, which is mentioned in my favorite song by the group. It tasted pretty good but didn't convert me over. Ironically, after returning from India, I noticed a restaurant called India Gate back home in Buffalo, New York and had the Chicken Vindaloo – it tasted about the same (hot). Both times I had gone alone, which is ironic because the Ramones song mentioning the dish has the lyric, "Hangin' out all by myself/I don't wanna be with anybody else..."

Once again, I got out and met the people. I was predisposed to liking Indian people based on several I had met already in the United States, including a college girlfriend and former boss at the university. Speaking of which, it was a real pleasure chatting with the university students in India, who were very smart and optimistic about the future. Many had a good sense of humor and asked a lot of good questions about the U.S., focused on politics and economics (I'm no expert on either). Several were congenial, and they spoke English very well – I'm always impressed by people who speak more than one language. Most were Westernized, wearing American-style clothing, and very knowledgeable about the U.S. and Europe. I'm almost embarrassed to admit this, but many international people I've met from around the world know more about the U.S. than I do, and I believe the average American citizen does, regarding our history, politics, and geography (several foreigners stunned me with their knowledge of the juxtaposition of our states). This may not be surprising given our influence in the world, but watch any "Jaywalking" segment of "The Tonight Show with Jay Leno" and you get some idea, albeit perhaps exaggerated for TV viewership, about our lack of knowledge. The tour ended, and I stayed out late checking out a local club that I didn't particularly care for (crowded, smoky, didn't like the music).

Although I spent only a couple of full days in New Delhi, it felt like a lot more. I was out a lot and didn't get much sleep, maximizing my time there. I'd seen enough – the day at the Taj Mahal made the whole trip worthwhile. The rest was a jumble, but with a few pleasantries that made for good memories. I still had a lot of travels to go. A benefit of my upcoming long flight was finally getting some good sleep on it. I'm one of those people who sleeps better on a plane or a cruise ship than in his own bed. Maybe I should get a white-noise machine with the sound of these engine noises for home use.

I felt refreshed when arriving in Athens after a seven-hour flight covering nearly 3,000 miles. From there I went straight to my hotel, which cost "only" $75/night instead of the usual $109. I took a short taxi ride to the dock to board my 11-day cruise (4th of the year: Caribbean, Asia, Africa, and now Mediterranean), but things went poorly there: lack of signage, few people to direct you to the appropriate location, and very long lines. While frustrated, I knew from past experience that a bad start often leads to a good trip – and such was the case once again. I finally got to my cabin aboard the ship and, like the sun breaking through the clouds, it was quiet just as I had requested and everything was in good working order. Our first stop was Cyprus, an island country that is part Greek and part Turkish, with a history of many occupiers including Egyptians, Persians, Venetians, Byzantines, Greeks, Turks, British, and even Alexander the Great from Macedonia based on its strategic position. We visited the second largest city on the island, Limassol.

I'd heard from other passengers who had been there that Cyprus has good shopping, but little else of interest if just walking around. Having seen some of the best of the best in shopping and sightseeing, and after doing my own research, I opted for going to the beach for the day. There I met another passenger who I hung out with for several hours, Dana, who was celebrating her 30th birthday by herself on the cruise. She was a nice lady who was a nurse's aide back home and liked cruising. Dana and I compared notes about cruise lines, discussing the pros and cons, giving each other a few pointers. We agreed that cruising is an efficient way to get to many places inexpensively, but that you lose a lot of flexibility and time being on the water so long. We had both met many people who never left the ship in port; they just liked the experience of being on a ship and cruising. And if you had bad weather the day you were in a selected location, such as happened with me in Cape Town, South Africa, there was no waiting it out until the next day.

Yet, if you liked cruising, it was an extravagant experience – and affordable, unlike earlier times when only the wealthy could go. Often, a cruise was a major event, perhaps a once-in-a-lifetime experience, that was now an affordable luxury and a major life highlight. We agreed that you can recognize the people on their first cruise by their wide-eyed enthusiasm, and that's a good thing.

Our next stop was Israel. Back in my hometown of New York City, it was often mentioned that there are more Jews in New York City than in Israel, but it wasn't even close: according to Wikipedia, there were 5.6 million Jews living in Israel that year and, according to the New York Times, there were slightly less than 1 million Jews living in New York City a few years earlier (although this figure was estimated at 1.4 million including the suburbs). Tel Aviv is the most populous Jewish city in the world with 2.5 million inhabitants. I thought this was going to be an interesting experience no matter how you added it up. We docked at the port of Ashdod in Haifa. The city looked rather dull with blah-looking square buildings in tan or off-white color. The streets were crowded and smoke-filled, with lots of military police around. They made me feel safe but then again, as with past trips, I figured so many were around for a reason; I was aware of potential imminent danger given the country's volatile history. Some of the women were stunningly beautiful, and I took a photo with one dressed in an army uniform who could probably kick my ass (and I don't mean the one I rode in India). Years earlier, back in New York City, I dated one such beautiful Israeli army gal, and not only was she very skilled in mortal combat as trained by the army, but she could assemble and disassemble car and airplane engines. I found that an intriguing combination that I never came across again, although there were probably plenty of gals there in Israel for whom this was common.

The people were mixed regarding how they acted toward me. Some were as friendly as could be, helping with directions, suggesting places to visit, and glad I had come to visit. Others were not so much, pushing past me (and others), rushed/stressed, screaming on their mobile phones. I saw a funny T-shirt that read "Don't Worry, Be Jewish." The best attraction was not related to the Jewish culture but the Baha'i religion, where this was the world headquarters. Their temple was way up on Carmel Mountain overlooking the city and was gorgeous, including an impressive flower garden. I had heard about the Baha'i religion from a prominent university administrator who was my seatmate on a flight from New York City to Virginia after I graduated college. He was a nice guy and explained the religion to me. He asked me to call him, but I never did. I had no idea I'd ever be at the site of the organization's world headquarters, and that it was so stunning. I also walked around nearby Haifa University and met many smart, inquisitive college students. Unlike the students I'd met in Germany and India, e.g., these students were more like the ones in Northern Ireland, very interested in politics, national security, and the U.S. I avoided these discussions as best I could, again not wanting to get into a debate about these sensitive subjects during my vacation.

The next day I took a tour of Tel Aviv instead of going to Jerusalem, as many did. I didn't want to battle the crowds as I had done in India. That evening, I heard from the people who went to Jerusalem that they were hustled in and out so quickly that they didn't have much time to see anything. Plus, there was an extreme military presence that made many uncomfortable. I repeatedly heard the same comments: too crowded, too many police, and didn't get all the photos they wanted. However, I know others who went and loved it. Tel Aviv was also very crowded, with lots of cafés and Mediterranean beaches. There were many young soldiers, some of whom looked barely old enough to shave, with rifles over their shoulders. This time I didn't meet any retired colonels as in Jordan, but I did "rub elbows," literally, with a few people who bumped into me in passing (some were even faster walkers than me).

I wanted to have some authentic Jewish food so I had matzo ball soup, bagels, latkes, and kugel. All were delicious and like the ones I had in New York City, especially on the Lower East Side. I even found some Bazooka Bubble Gum there with comics in Hebrew. After watching some artists and street performers, I went back to the ship. I was hoping Hebrew National hot dogs would be on the menu but no-go. Or any brew, such as an Israeli beer (there's one called He'brew®, calling itself The Chosen Beer), but no-go to that as well. I don't regret my no-go to Jerusalem, but if I'm in the vicinity again I would probably go just to be part of the experience – but not on a tour if I can help it so that I could spend adequate time there.

Egypt, our next stop, was a whole different story. I enjoyed it a lot and was very active, including fending off super-aggressive merchants. Here's a good tip: whenever you hear someone calling you starting with, "My friend," run! I took an all-day excursion to Cairo and Giza to see the Pyramids, which were amazing! The weather was sunny, warm, and clear making for great photos with my new 12-megapixel digital camera (which I still have to this day). There were several Arabs walking around with camels, offering to give rides for "only one dollar." Our tour guide warned us, "Don't take one – they charge you a dollar to go up on the camel and 20 dollars to get down." I already had my camel experience in Morocco, and I saw some here spitting which didn't look too auspicious, anyway. I got a nice photo of me holding the rope of a camel as if I were walking it around, and one standing next to a young Egyptian merchant with the Pyramids in the background. As with the Taj Mahal, an hour or two is all you need there, and these also were tombs (built for the ancient pharaohs). They were amazing to look at. Even with as much as I had already seen in the world I was still in awe by viewing these (when you're "hooked" on travel you need a bigger and bigger "fix," and this was one of them!). I took lots of photos and had an enjoyable time there. Our tour guide tried to be a comedian. He said "We have KFC here, too: Kentucky Fried Camel." Maybe he should join with the tour guide in Viet Nam who mentioned they have "hot dog" there and form a comedy team. I was later asked if I "walked like an Egyptian" while there. I not only did that, but a bit more as follows.

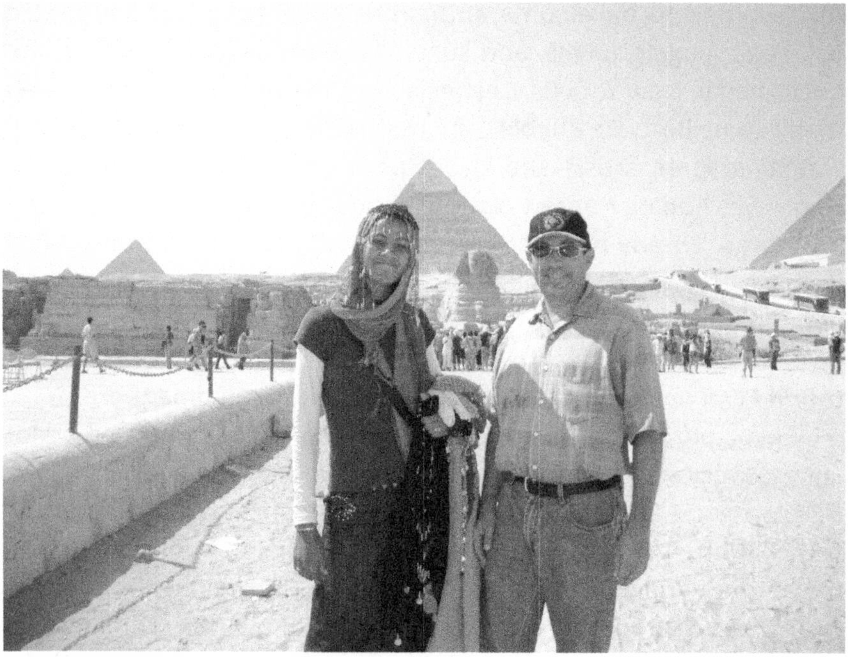

The Egyptian Pyramids are amazing! There are over 100 of them in the country, but the ones here in Giza are most visited. The famous sphinx is also right there, helping create a delightful desert panorama.

As part of this tour we also took a cruise along the Nile River, which not only afforded excellent views but a delicious lunch, too. There was a belly dance performance, and in a lucky break reminiscent of what happened at the Kabuki Theater in Tokyo, I came across the belly dancer walking around a remote area between performances and got a couple of photos with her. During her next performance she looked at me alluringly while swiveling her hips, and danced right around my seat. Then she motioned for me to join her, and I did on stage. My tourmates were hooting and hollering, and one guy took a few photos of me up there with my camera. I tried to belly dance as she wanted me to, but let's just say that if she were Queen of the Nile, I was King of DeNial when asked how I did (my circular hula-hoop motion wasn't the ticket). Naturally, this made the dinner discussion aboard ship that night and got a few "belly laughs."

The next day we went to Port Said (pronounced "Sy-eed") which, like New Delhi, was filthy. I walked around the city and later went to the beach, which also was filled with litter. There were more aggressive merchants there who I out-talked and out-walked to get away from them, including the statement, "I am NOT your friend, so please move on." Sometimes on a hot day I can get a hot temper when provoked. This time I walked like a New Yorker- away, quickly. Back aboard the ship, I met up with a guy a few years older than me from South Florida. He had a pretty Latina girlfriend with him – although I use that term loosely because she walked away to be on her cell phone a lot, and was in the bar area quite a bit. But that gave Ira and me a chance to become acquainted, and we were very similar (he's originally from New York City). We exchanged contact information but never did get together. Once again, I found that if you talk to certain people long enough you'll find a few things in common. Another good example was at dinner that evening when I spoke with a married couple from California near my age. As it turned out, the guy was from my home town in Brooklyn, and the gal had attended the same university at which I taught in California! At night, I watched Al Jazeera TV, and this was "radically" different than in the U.S. There were more extreme war scenes shown (including dead bodies), and had anti-Western protest themes. I could not tell what was being said because it was in Arabic, but realized through the photos that the news in the U.S. was highly sanitized by comparison (or theirs was ultra-graphic).

Our final cruise stop was Turkey. Ah yes, Turkey, back again, this time to the port city of Kusadasi ("Koo-sa-dah-see") before heading to Istanbul, our final cruise destination. I walked around both cities extensively, and met more locals and shipmates. One gal I met was a weather reporter in Germany, although she was born an American. Another was a sexy Russian shipmate circa age 60 who was a cross between Marilyn Monroe and Zsa Zsa Gabor! She was very pretty, extremely active aboard ship (and an especially good dancer), and flirted with just about every guy. She also dressed extravagantly, from head to toe, and even wore a ship captain's cap one night earning her the nickname "The Captainess" from jealous women. But she was more like "Captain Of The Heart" to the men, who lined up to dance with her and take photos (er, yeah, I was one of 'em). She hung around with a Russian female friend who didn't say much. In fact, I never heard her say anything (in any language).

In Istanbul, I looked for but didn't find Sister Maria. Perhaps had I wore my Michigan State T-shirt again she would have spotted me – and we could have talked about the basketball team having another fine season! I even went to her friend Mohammed's Turkish restaurant to look for her, but he wasn't there, either. I felt very comfortable in Istanbul, and knew where I was going on the trams. I went back to the mosques, the Bosporus Sea, and even had more of the rotisserie turkey from the same place I'd had it before. I even remembered that old tune I learned in elementary school, "Now it's Istanbul, not Constantinople..." And there was plenty more history there as I wandered into a cultural center and art museum. I just loved Arabic and Turkish architecture and art – two excellent new interests as a byproduct of my travels. And in another "bazaar" thought, that's where I went back to. I had forgotten how immense this indoor flea market is, and noticed it is much larger than even the Grand Bazaar in New Delhi. I later learned that it has over 3,000 shops attracting between 250,000 - 400,000 visitors daily! This time I was used to the hustle and bustle and aggressive merchants, taking it all in stride, literally, walking for coolness (to get out of the sun), exercise (fast-walking), and observing anything new I missed the first time. I had another nice time in Turkey. Or should I say Turkiye, which triggered the song "Tequila" by The Champs in my mind (maybe that's why I don't drink or need to – my mind creates its own intoxicants that keep me smiling).

The cruise ended, and I enjoyed it very much. I had another whirlwind one-week vacation remaining. First I went to Tunis, the capital of Tunisia, and yet another new country visited in North Africa. In a word, yeeech! The taxi driver tried to rip me off (and actually did overcharge me after I messed-up on the exchange rate), I was constantly given wrong directions, there were lots of Muslims who did not like Westerners, and it was 95 degrees with high humidity on top of all that. In retrospect, I should have gone to the beach there (a major attraction) instead of walking the city. The main highlight was the market area, where I spoke with several merchants and enjoyed flavorful fruit. As later events would show, Tunisia was nearing a crisis back then. A little more than a year later a merchant would set himself on fire, engendering rioting over economic and political conditions that would spread to several other countries in the region, topple governments, and eventually help reshape the Middle East. I felt uncomfortable in Tunisia in general, like people didn't want me there, and I didn't belong. I was there only for a couple of days and thought, "Oh well, you can't win 'em all." However, I knew a "G.O." at Club Med from Tunisia who was wonderful – pretty, shapely, bubbly, and even performed a great belly dance at a show one night. So go "figure."

Next I was off to to Barcelona, Spain where I spent three days and had a wonderful time amidst great weather (sunny, low-70s). The downtown area was bustling along the wide avenues, especially La Rambla, with mimes, musicians, artists, and people dressed to entertain, making for excellent photo ops and fun times. There were lots of cafés and street vendors there; it seemed like a daily mini-version of Feria. I visited a couple of old cathedrals that reminded me of others I'd seen around Europe, but there were also very impressive modern buildings. This was no Dubai architecturally but had its moments. For dinner, I ate paella, the national dish, at a place recommended by the hotel staff. I started eating paella more often when I returned to the States, so this was another food that left an impression on me. My stomach was also learning a new language – that of international cuisine, which I was exploring more and more based on my travels (including back home, too, where I would sometimes seek out these dishes).

Many people there lived in apartments because space was at a premium, and they were crazy about their fútbol (soccer). I watched a soccer match on TV at a local bar; the fans were riveted to every move. Since the sport is low-scoring they cheered wildly at every goal. Much of Europe is like this, so if you want to fit in there wear a fútbol jersey – of the local team, of course! And don't call it soccer. I'd like to see a live game someday, which would be a new experience. Also, recognize that many people there are Catalonians (or Catalans). I still wasn't sure what the main difference was after it was explained to me, so I went to my old pal Wikipedia and learned that people of this origin from various parts of Spain, France, and other places form a "historical nationality" in Spain but do not necessarily align themselves with the country. Sort of like (Oakland) "Raiders nation" in

American football, with that team's fans all over the country devoted to the black-and-silver. I also learned that Andorra – a land-locked country between Spain and France I planned to visit – has Catalan as its official language. Which leads me to Andorra, literally.

I took an 8-hour round-trip bus ride to this tiny country – there are no railways, ports, or airports. I especially liked the Pyrenees mountain vistas along the way, which made for excellent photo ops out the bus window (prompting others to get out their cameras and take similar photos). By this time I was good at making "over-the-shoulder-catches," meaning that if the bus made a sharp turn before I could take the desired photo, I would quickly take the photo over my back shoulder as needed, guesstimating where the desired object would be. Often I'd capture the desired scene or object somewhere in the picture, albeit not centered, and edit the photo later to frame it properly.

I'd heard that Andorra was known for its tax-free shopping, and attracted a lot of people from Spain and France. So, combined with there not being much else of interest for me there, I did something most people do on tours that I generally didn't – shopped! I bought a few shirts, and of course post cards. The country was tiny but the shopping was pervasive including very high-end merchandise. The city was modern and clean with an adequate amount of police patrolling. I was careful about potential pickpockets, given that this was known to be a shopping mecca, and encountered no problems. Once again I took the precautions previously mentioned. I walked briskly, although I wasn't sure where I was headed in some cases.

The weather was cool that day with a bit of rain, which was a plus given the heat I'd been in most of my vacation. When it cleared, I took a good walk and several photos of the mountains from a high point. I learned that Andorra's capital is the highest in Europe at over 3,000 feet above sea level. Because of its small size, Andorra had a hint of Liechtenstein to it, but without the fun/party atmosphere. It seemed like a transient place where people came and went. Indeed, the country only had a population under 85,000. However, perhaps based on life being so easygoing and fairly prosperous there, these factors contributed to its people having the fourth highest life expectancy in the world at 82 years at birth – or maybe their shopping included defibrillators.

The ride back was fairly uneventful except for more mountain photos out the window and a guy who was on my bus who said, "ooh, that's right" and followed my lead doing the same (including to the back of the bus/empty seats there for shooting out of the back window). I chatted with several passengers but nothing too exciting was discussed. Many people showed what they bought, and mentioned the deals they got on it. Many just slept. I napped as well. It was a dull ride after the mountain part. So, if you're into shopping, Andorra may be the place for you. And if not, it's still a good place to stroll around and meet an interesting cross-section of people, mainly from Spain, France and Portugal. "Daytripper, yeah" as the Beatles crooned.

Back in Barcelona, I attended another Flamenco dance at night as I had in Seville. The women were beautiful and brimming with an alluring confidence as they stared into the audience. I was getting into the different dances of the world, and this one also was terrific. Whirling, twirling, and unfurling (of the revealing red dress) along with the heel stomping and clicking castanets ruled the night. Inspired, I went looking for the ladies and met some nice señoritas in a dance club until early morning. One last fling, and thus ended my time in Barcelona and Andorra in a most pleasant way.

My final destination was also a repeat performance, back to Italy again. I arrived at Rome's airport and quickly learned there was a train I could take to my hotel area instead of an expensive taxi. The trip in was smooth and hassle-free. So, when in Rome (literally) what do you do? Go back to the Coliseum, where I had been with Mike? Yep, and this time the weather was better, encouraging me to take an official tour to see parts I may have missed. This was a good idea because there were several passageways with wonderful ancient art. And the history was pretty amazing as described by the tour guide. I stayed back to take photos - which the tour guide said not to do – and ended up getting detached from the group, which the tour guide said could happen. I was paged at the Coliseum – I didn't know they could do that – but couldn't find the location of the page, so I never did catch up with the group. However, this turned into a positive because it gave me a lot more time there (and what I missed on the rest of the tour was not too exciting, I later heard). So I went all over the Coliseum, inside and out, shooting lots of photos including at sunset, which gave it a whole new look. There were also a lot of statues outside the Coliseum that made for excellent photo ops. I later photographed selected nearby buildings with interesting architecture that created a panoramic mosaic of the area in a subsequent photo album.

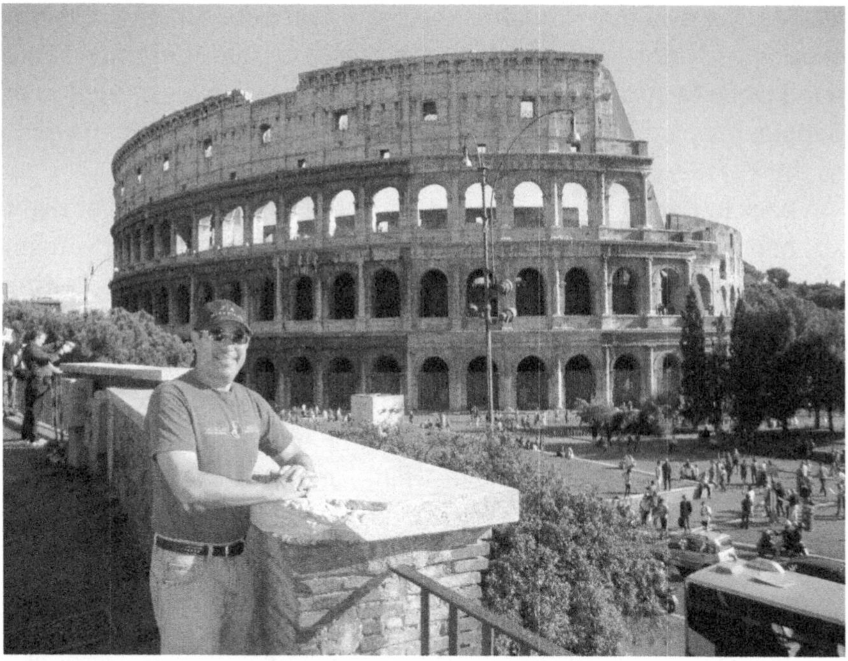

The Coliseum in Rome, looking as magnificent on the outside as it does on the inside. This awesome structure is roughly 2,000 years old, and is a reason why you might want to travel overseas to experience such history. Photos do not do it justice.

Finding my way back to the hotel by bus was fairly easy. This time, the driver stayed with the bus and passengers the entire trip, unlike one time during my first visit to Rome nearly two decades earlier. Strangely, the hotel I stayed in had an owner who loved the Kennedy family in the U.S., and the lobby was adorned with numerous photos of them! My room was small but had interesting tile art in the shower area. It was also in a good location, walkable to several main attractions. I had traditional Italian food for dinner, chicken with pasta, with gelato for dessert; all were delicious. The people were generally friendly, but you had to watch out for pickpockets and speeding drivers. I walked around at night; the city was not wild and crazy like I'd thought, but pretty mellow. The cooler air felt wonderful. However, stray cats were everywhere, so there were not only cat calls to the pretty women there but to actual cats as well (the former by adults, the latter by little kids).

I left Rome after a couple of nights, and needed to fly back to Athens for my return flight to use my free frequent flyer miles for the trip. So, one last night in Athens did the trick, at the same hotel I stayed in earlier. The employees there remembered me and welcomed me back. I emailed family and friends to let them know I was OK, and left the next morning for the long flight back to New York. Overall, this was another excellent trip including the "three gems": Taj Mahal, Pyramids, and Coliseum, plus the cruise and other travels. I was in my glory, but getting a job was another story. Not to worry, I had another plan if that didn't pan out. And guess what that was...

# Chapter 20

## World Cruise Part Two (And Then Some)

When I received the call from the cruise line about going on another world travel experience at a great discount, I was excited yet hesitant. The prior year's cruise had its highs but also its lows – much like the ocean waves the ship sailed upon. Generally, the world cruise brought me to places I had never been, but the law of diminishing returns was in effect since I had already achieved getting to 100 countries and more. Still, a big discount was enticing and it was winter in Buffalo again, making the choice that much easier. Taking the cruise also gave me another opportunity to celebrate my upcoming birthday in yet another memorable location.

Excited at the prospect for more exotic travel, and able to secure appropriate flights using my free frequent flyer airline miles once again, I made a spontaneous decision to "go for it." I would be sailing two segments this time: Buenos Aires to Cape Town, South Africa; and Cape Town to Mumbai, India. The travel arrangements were not that simple, however, and would become even more complicated. I couldn't return using my free airline miles from Mumbai so I arranged with the cruise line to disembark at the previous port in the African country of the Seychelles Islands (requiring special permission for me to do so), from which I would fly to Tanzania (another new country), and back home from there several days later. There was a further complication that threw a wrench into the works: due to continuing pirate activity in the area, the ship's captain decided at the last minute not to go to the Seychelles Islands - from which I already had non-refundable plane reservations! So, I had to scramble, and was helped out by the ship's staff in making travel arrangements to fly to the Seychelles from the previous port of Mauritius, and then head off to Tanzania from the Seychelles as scheduled. The flight was not cheap, and neither was the hotel – but I had to do what the circumstances required.

To begin the trip, I arrived a couple of days early into Buenos Aires to spend extra time in a city I liked, and especially because during the winter in Buffalo flights could easily be canceled due to inclement weather. This could cause me to possibly "miss the boat" if planning to arrive the day of the cruise (which disembarked late afternoon), or even the prior day depending on the severity of the weather in Buffalo. I stayed in an inexpensive but good hotel, and walked around the city. I made sure to have the "Bife de Lomo" steak again to reconfirm its greatness! This steak just melted in my mouth and was flavored just right; it was just as good as the time I declared it the best steak I'd ever had – winner, and still champ. I revisited the upscale Recoleta area and also the tango place I'd gone to, Bar Sur, but it was closed for the day, and I never did return.

I was glad to be aboard the ship, and happiness/relief often triggers my humor hormones. Upon being welcomed by the hostess, who gave me a run-down of the amenities on this world cruise, I said, "I assume the cruise line arranged for the girl in my room." She was stunned, and thought I was serious. Looking at her checklist, then at me, then the checklist again – then at me again, she told me to wait there and ran to check with her boss before I could stop her. The boss arrived and asked me about my "unusual special request," but with a smile that said, "What can I do to help?" I didn't think it would get to that point, and quickly retorted that I was just checking if there is daily maid service. He answered "Yes!" with a friendly smile, and everyone was relieved. Note to self: they take you seriously here even if they are fluent in English. I carried my own luggage to my ship cabin and got settled. Everything was pretty much the same as last year – upscale older people from all over the world, especially the U.K., other parts of Europe, Canada, and Australia, with several

Americans and Asians (about 10% for each). There would be a few "characters" on the ship to liven things up, which wasn't bad at all.

After the mandatory lifeboat drill – important because there were still pirates in the area – I went to the dining room and awaited not only the dinner, but who my dinnermates would be. I had no idea if last year's dinnermates were onboard (they weren't). So, I was all decked out, since at the time of my reservation back in New York I had requested a table for 8 (largest they had) and to be seated with young people. I was assured that my emphasized request would be communicated to the appropriate dining room staff; I had even mentioned this on the previous year's post-cruise survey.

I had a pleasant greeting by the dining staff, some of whom remembered me from last year, and was led to my table. It was a table for two – and sitting there was a very old American man, well-dressed in a suit and tie, who greeted me with a handshake and said that his name is Don. I thought this was a joke – retribution in a fun way for the one I had made when boarding, perhaps? It was a couple of months before April Fool's Day, so that couldn't be it. I pulled the dining room staff member off to the side and, with no disrespect to Don, told him I am supposed to be seated at a large table with young people. He told me to look around – there were no young people, and the average age of the passengers on this cruise was 78 (older than my parents). Don later told me he's age 90! I couldn't leave him sitting there by himself, so I figured I'd join Don for the one night only and then get my table changed. As previously mentioned in my discussion about cruising in general, I had a few snafus like this (on different cruise lines), including being seated with a honeymooning couple ("Just the three of us, we can make it if we try?"), a large Asian family of seven speaking only their native language and me ("I think I'm turning Japanese, I really think so"), and a single wealthy Latino lady who spoke no English (was she "Living La Vida Loca"?). So what happened here? Upon inquiring after the fact, I learned that either: 1) my request didn't get properly communicated; 2) the dining manager was going to do what was easiest for him - in fairness, several tables were already decided based on some passengers' requests to sit with people they knew or closer to their age; or 3) in figuring out the Rubik's Cube® regarding seating, the manager may have just decided, "OK, here are two American guys who don't really fit anywhere, so I'll seat them together." Nationality could have been a factor that trumped age.

In any event, Don was a former Ivy League graduate, military commander, and long-time lawyer from New England before retiring to the South of France. He was also a widower from not too long ago, a very intelligent and interesting guy, and a nice person. I sat with him through the dinner and listened to his war stories, literally. This was good for a night and we ended on a pleasant note. The next evening I was still without a table while the staff was "figuring it out," and I gave it one more night with Don, which went fine. There really weren't any other young people (even in their 50s) who I saw, so I decided to dine by myself at the buffet several nights and chat with the staff, primarily. However, before doing so, I noticed that there was a table behind Don and I at which a person was a no-show for the previous two nights. The people seated there were much older than me, very nice, and invited Don to sit with them. The gentleman that he was, he asked me if it's OK, realizing he'd be leaving me alone. I said OK (wink-wink to the ladies), and everyone was happy. I later sat with Don again on and off, when he parted from the ladies and wanted some more one-on-one chat with me. He called me "one of the most interesting people" he's ever met, in particular because I had been to 107 countries to his 90, and I had taught at a university after a successful business career. I felt the same about him. We became fond of each other and I looked out for him when I could. It must have been difficult for him to be on this trip by himself after being married for over 60 years. He told me that he's on for the full 110+ days after leaving out of Los Angeles, California a month earlier.

As it so happened, I was connected to another elderly passenger on the ship! My friend Mark's elderly cousin, Grayson (in her 70s and with a cane), was also on the cruise. I knew about this ahead of time from Mark, met up with her, and we had some pleasant chats over tea. She was also widowed, and in retrospect maybe I should have introduced her to Don (I had a little cupid in me – responsible for 3 friends getting married 25 years ago who are still married to this day). Maybe I needed to aim an arrow at myself – although I "quiver" at the thought.

The previous year there was an American guy near my age on the world cruise with a beautiful, younger Filipino wife. He was wealthy, having invented several products, and his first line to me was, "So, how did you make your money?" The assumption was that everyone on this world cruise was wealthy – and that was probably right for the vast majority of people. I wasn't, but easily blended in with them despite the money and age gaps. However, I really resonated more with the middle and even lower classes in general. The President of my former employer had said that I "helicoptered well" (a term I had never heard), meaning I got along well with those above me and those below me in the corporate hierarchy. That's because I'm this way in general, and my work persona was a subset of my overall personality. Interestingly, Don physically resembled that President, and looked like he could have been his dad! Which made me wonder: Do rich, successful people look alike? A lot of passengers on the ship seemed cut from the same mold – aristocratic-looking and sounding.

At the lounge that night I saw a female passenger I hadn't seen since the cruise last year. She was a few years older than me, had a lot to drink, and got frisky with me from the get-go (I frisked back). She had been onboard since the beginning of the cruise and, well, I know how she must've felt. She had a female friend who was very big and boisterous – make that, outrageous – who really knew how to party hard and drink the guys under the table. She was flamboyant, fun, and definitely livened up the place. Many from the crew (mainly Filipino and Indonesian) got a huge kick out of her. I spent more time up at that bar than I ordinarily would because there was nowhere else to go after 10:00 p.m. that was nearly as interesting. Things happened there for me on occasion, but what happened there stayed there (remember, this is not a kiss-and-tell book).

There was one final character to describe: an old guy age 91 I'll call Walter, who described himself as "a dirty old dog" to the middle-aged women, and he laughed hard at his own jokes. Once he laughed so hard that his false teeth almost went flying out in front of several "Mrs. Howell's" and me! This instantly brought back a memory as a kid, seeing the wind-up chattering teeth toy my friends and I used as a gag, spinning and chattering around. This guy was a riot, and I was very impressed by his spryness. He was by himself and, if I had to guess, may have been Don's dinnermate before I came aboard (they're polar opposites, like Felix and Oscar, or Singapore and Malaysia). I asked Walter what his secret was to life, and he emphatically replied, "Never take yourself too seriously." I always remembered that, and always will because he's totally right. My friend Harvey's dad, who is also very successful, was fond of saying, "Never believe your own bull." So maybe successful people not only look alike, but think alike, too. I had a grandfather (mom's side) similar to Walter who lived to age 92, and was very healthy despite smoking cigars. He was a jovial guy who worked until his mid-80s – and he loved his job, his family, and life in general. If we could only bottle and sell this stuff we could have a huge economic boom. World cruises for everybody!

I was reseated at dinner the third night at a table for 8 with "younger" people, primarily in their 60s. They were all very nice, and included a husband and wife from Pennsylvania, and two American gals named Caroline who met when one, a realtor, happened to show the other, a highly-tenured airline employee, her future home. Both ladies were single, attractive for their age, and one lived in the South of France! I introduced her to Don, another American who also lived in the region, and they hit it off immediately. In fact, Don became a guest at our table when someone didn't show, which was often. The ship was like a small town, and eventually most people knew of – and about – each other. This was like a face-to-face Facebook® without the book part, and often times the tables were a-twittering with the latest saucy ship news. Each table seemed to have "whine" on it, too, but that was a different story (health and other complaints).

One reason I decided to write this book is that my dinnermates and others aboard the ship found my travel stories anywhere from interesting to fascinating, with several following me around to hear more. I did not volunteer any of this, but when asked directly the extent of my travels, as they had shared, I told them, and they were in awe (many had been to 30-70 countries). Don may have also spread the word based on our one-on-ones, in which he also asked me the extent of my travels. I enjoyed being among these fellow travelers despite our vast age difference because, as deserves repeating, I could not relate to anyone I knew back home about my alternate travel life (most hadn't even been to 10 countries, and many had never left the U.S. given their family priorities or lack of resources). I was also glad to meet some retired teachers aboard ship to share our professional experiences for the same reason, and we had our own private meetings in the lounge after a while. Even with all these passengers I met initially, the best was yet to come – but they were hiding and few knew who they were. There's more about that situation later.

Our first port was Montevideo, Uruguay, the capital, which had a lot more going for it than Colonia, to which I had been five years earlier. I stayed around the city center and walked to the oceanfront. There were beautiful beaches in the area as well, but near the port were old colonial buildings and Mercado del Puerto (market) with quite a good selection of fruits, veggies, meats, and other foods, plus books, handicrafts and other souvenirs. I found the people to be mellow for once in an indoor market; there wasn't only an "air of aromas" but an "air of sophistication," too, at least compared to similar market areas I had seen. There was also an outdoor market in the vicinity that featured a lot of fish but was mainly a "meat market" in more ways than one. There were several antiques and clothes, but with a flea-market atmosphere as opposed to the upscale indoor market.

Independence Plaza was a popular tourist spot and featured a huge statue of a war hero on a horse. The nearby buildings were Spanish, Italian, and Art Deco, all making for good photo ops on this "caliente" day of 85 degrees and sunny. The taxis around town were safe, but a little high-priced. Last, but certainly not least, Uruguay was a fútbol (soccer) mecca, and even hosted and won the first World Cup in 1930. Several locals had on their jerseys and shorts. I like when fans ardently support their teams. In New York City, whether you're Yankees-Mets, Jets-Giant, Knicks-Nets or Rangers-Islanders-Devils, you can count on strong loyalty and fervent fandom forever. I'm glad I went to Montevideo. The city changed my impression of

Uruguay for the better, having only seen Colonia, and I now had a better sense of how the city pulsated with a good blend of old, new, picturesque, and Mediterranean charm.

Back on ship we prepared for 8 consecutive days of sailing across the Atlantic, a stretch in more ways than one. I scoped out the ship for activities to do, and ended up spending time in the gym, library, lounges, and reading the book I'd brought. The staff had to keep us busy and entertained without the help of the ports. This was a daunting task, but they figured out a way and did it well. So there we were, a tiny little ship sailing this great big ocean en route to Namibia on the West Coast of Africa (most ships do not sail to the West Coast, which has several underdeveloped or dangerous countries, but does include the tiny republic of Togo☺). During this time there were two outstanding parties onboard ship at night: Valentine's Day (my birthday), and Mardi Gras. The decorations for each were exquisite and there was music, dancing, food and more. The ship photographer captured great pictures, as usual, during events and everyday life aboard the cruise, displaying them for sale. I'm not big on fashion, but most passengers got all decked out (pun intended) for these events – including men in tuxedos and women in gowns. Many passengers dressed in costume for the latter party, and their costumes were very ornate. Mardi Gras featured a masquerade, lots of colorful tinsel, New Orleans-style music and food, and lots of drinking! One wasted Australian gal near my age was licking my face in the lounge later that night. I said, "Who's your crawdaddy?" and she thought that was the funniest thing she ever heard, rolled on the floor, then virtually passed out.

As for me, I took a licking and kept on ticking, dancing with young and old alike, and having a good time. A strong benefit of the world cruise was that the staff members will dance or dine with you if you're alone (and want them to) to enhance your cruise vacation experience - and everything is done with TLC (albeit Tequila, Liqueurs, and Cognacs in the bars). I took many photos, and also discussed photography with the staff at the studio, receiving a few good pointers. My photos came out well, and I was very impressed with how these parties were done – you could tell a lot of work went into them. I expressed my delight to the ship's Cruise Director and entertainment staff. I took photos with selected crew, staff, and a performer on the ship. This included a guy who was seven feet tall, a gal who was seven feet tall in heels, a photo standing between the two of them, and an Australian singer who performed in the theater. All these photos were keepers.

We approached Namibia, and soon after docking there was an "African Safari"-themed party and dinner aboard ship, which was one of the best parties I've ever seen! This included an actual safari jeep hoisted onto the ship, African foods (meats, fish, and vegetables such as plantains and yams), and sitting areas decorated with zebra stripes, tiger stripes, and other jungle themes. There were singers and dancers who entertained then and later on stage in the theater. During the latter event I "waited them out," as I had done in other places, and took photos with them in their street clothes. Their dancing was absolutely awesome and really got me going when we arrived in Namibia. I was really starting to like the African culture – so colorful, soulful, rhythmic, genuine, and upbeat! And the people were so nice, friendly, fun, happy, and smiling – for me, it really did boil down to those simplicities of being what life was about at its essence. "Happy" was a way of life in Africa, regardless of economic status, and I truly admired that!

Meanwhile, not to be outdone, the Indonesian staff performed its own magnificent show in the theater one night, and that, too, was one of the better performances I saw. Whereas just a few years ago I had almost no interest in other cultures, now, through osmosis if nothing else given my travels and exposures, I was very interested. Even when I returned back home I would flip the channels and see things that I once had no interest in and watch them with great interest (e.g., African life, strife, and wildlife, among many others). Travel was transformational, transcendental, and transcontinental, too!

So there we were in Namibia, and I wondered what this place was all about. In a word: desert. In another word: poverty. Yet, in an ironic third word: diamonds. We docked in two ports, Walvis Bay and Luderitz, respectively. Walvis Bay, which is German for Whale Bay, really didn't have much to it except for the bay, which I found to be ordinary except for the pelicans. The best part was seeing where the "sand meets the sea," that is, the desert meeting the Atlantic Ocean. I was amazed that after all that traveling I was still in the Atlantic (New York to South America to Africa) – which gave a perspective as to how large this ocean really is! The Namib Desert was a good size, too, stretching for 1,200 miles along the Atlantic coast and into neighboring countries as well – plus it is thought to be the world's oldest desert. On tour, we took a four-wheeler over the immense dunes where, surprisingly, there was some unusual-looking vegetation. The weather was beautiful, sunny and in the 70s. Overall, this was a good time, and I did my usual routine in wandering off to take photos. I also learned more about diamonds after seeing some high-quality gems in a local store and asking questions. De Beers had a strong foothold in Namibia, but the Russians were coming in trying to get a grasp of this huge business, according to one jeweler there. The Namibian government also partnered with mining companies there regarding diamonds, he said (with a twinkle in his smile, and his watchband).

At the next port, Luderitz, I took a taxi ride around the city with a trendy cabbie named Johalis, who reminded me a lot of Sundai in Zimbabwe. We had a bunch of laughs, and I loved his happy-go-lucky attitude. He even took me to some extra places most people don't see, including a place called Kolmanskop, a ghost town from the 1950s. About 100 years ago diamonds were discovered there and it became a mining town, only to become this ghost town after the diamond business went downhill, literally, when people abandoned town and the sand took over the houses, sinking them. So, the town was "deserted" in more ways than one, and there are claims that it's still haunted. Who would think you'd find something "chilling" in the desert? Meanwhile, Johalis thought my digital camera was possessed or something of the like – he was totally fascinated with how the photo image appeared on the screen immediately afterwards, as if by magic. He wanted me to teach him how to take photos – and the ghost town was a great place because it was deserted when we arrived and there was no-one around to take my photo (although occasional tours go through there). He did a really good job; this made his day (and mine), and he kept shaking my hand by locking our thumbs together. It didn't take much to make him happy, and I later thought about this when I was bothered by something trivial at work or in general that really didn't matter in the long run. He had it right.

Back aboard ship we next headed to Cape Town, South Africa which I had missed last year due to a wind storm. It looked like a repeat this year as severe winds delayed us in getting there. I thought it would be "deja-vu all over again." However, we made it through, and what a wonderful place this turned out to be! I would later tell people onboard that I would even think of living there, to which many replied, "Me too." We had two full days there. The city is aesthetically beautiful and culturally diverse, but deeply divided. My first impression was that this was like San Diego, with its marina, mountains, beach, and overall grandeur. But it sure was windy! Thus, the funicular that ascended Table Mountain did not go all the way up to overlook the city; however, it went up high enough to get a magnificent view of the area, including the blue-green water. And that's the only color I was interested in, because a few locals there tried to get me into the Black-White political discussion, which I avoided.

I took an open-air, double-decker, hop-on, hop-off tour bus around town on my own and went to Mariners' Wharf as one of the stops on the Blue Line. After having an excellent seafood lunch overlooking the wharf, I met two pretty teenage blonde sisters there named Millie and Mie (pronounced "Me"). They were dressed mostly in pink, looking like junior versions of the lead character in "Legally Blonde," and handing out soaps carved in jungle animal shapes from a wicker hand basket each carried. Not only did they perform (acting) and were known locally, but here's their trademark: they talk in synchronicity. I would ask them where they're from, and they would immediately say, "Cape Town, South Africa. Isn't it beautiful here?" in perfect unison and harmony. But that wasn't the trick, either. It was that they could do this on-the-spot with long, complicated answers, such as to the question, "Where should I go to have a good time tonight, and what should I do?" They would immediately synchronously respond and not mess up, as if singing a duet they had rehearsed a hundred times.

I thought they were twins but they weren't; one was 17 and the other, 16. Upon closer look they were slightly different, but only slightly. I also thought I was on some kind of TV program and said, "OK, where's the hidden camera?" They insisted (in unison) there was none, but I still wasn't so sure. They gave the politically correct answer to the question I asked, but the real answer was that you didn't want to go out at night because of the high crime there (we were warned by a tour guide). I decided to match wits and try to stump them by asking a question they probably didn't prepare for. They answered well and in sync again. I had fun talking with them, and had to pass by several times as I strolled up and down the wharf taking photos. I have lots of photos with them, and we kept in contact for a short while after I returned home so I could follow their careers.

This was strange - these two sisters (but not twins) in Cape Town, South Africa spoke synchronously in response to questions. They were selling jungle-animal shaped carved soaps, but you were in for more than you bargained for when speaking to them. They insisted there wasn't a hidden camera for some TV program, but I wasn't so sure...

I also went to the Kirstenbosch Botanical Gardens, which was among the nicest gardens I'd been to (a distant #2 to the Butchart Gardens in Canada's Victoria, British Columbia). This not only had a magnificent landscape, but great surrounding views as well against the mountains. Peacocks and other brightly colored birds added to the scenery, and there were a few interesting animal statues there as well. I saw flowers and plants there that I hadn't ever seen before, became curious about them, and later researched them. This never would have happened even five years ago, so my thirst for information may have rivaled the plants' thirst for water. As "the most interesting man in the world" says in the Dos Equis® beer commercials on TV, "Stay thirsty my friend." And I plan to. Especially if we go to any more deserts.

The next day I continued with the Red Line, which again took me to the Table Mountain area. The tour guide explained that it is so named because the clouds sit atop the mountain as if on a table (a factoid that I used as trivia at dinner that night). I also went to Camps Bay, at which I chatted with several locals who extolled the virtues of living in Cape Town. Back in New York City, I dated a gal briefly from Cape Town who had said much the same thing. It was interesting that back then I had no idea about or interest in Africa, South Africa, Cape Town, or even caped crusaders any more. Yet that day I was standing right there, admiring, learning, yearning, and at times burning when the sun beat down on me. At Camps Bay I went onto the beach, which again reminded me of the beaches in Southern California with white sand surrounded by the palm trees, mountains, and blue skies. So, half a world away from SoCal - in Cape Town, South Africa - I could have been blindfolded and when it was removed thought I'd been taken to Laguna Beach (similar to what I saw in Russia).

I returned to the ship before nightfall, heeding the warnings of the tour guide (for a change) as I was nearing the end of my vacation and not wanting to chance anything dangerous. Back aboard ship, my dinnermates and I compared notes about Cape Town, and everyone loved it (aside from the wind). There was one more spectacular party with a pirate theme (of all things!) as we headed around the Cape of Good Hope, and then to the East Coast of Africa, where the

Somalia pirates were still making lots of international news. Once again passengers, staff, and crew dressed the part with a heavy dose of eye patches, pirate hats, and swashbuckling swords. Thankfully, we didn't encounter any real pirates out there on their skiffs with AK-47s, mortars, and rockets. I wondered what they would have thought had they come aboard our ship during the party (maybe that other pirates already captured us?).

And right after that another passenger captured my attention: Candace. She was 28 years old and traveling with her mom, Joan. The two had kept to themselves most of the trip, remaining practically hidden, and I happened to meet Candace as she was walking by the Reception Desk at a time when I was asking if any younger people had boarded the ship at recent ports, say in Cape Town? But Candace and her mom were aboard since the beginning, from Los Angeles, and were staying on until the end, back in L.A. 110 days later. Joan had met one of the instructors on the ship, an American guy I'll call Craig, and they had become friends. So Candace, who was engaged, was available for hanging out, and we became friends.

Candace turned out to be the most precocious person relative to her age I have ever met. She was born in the U.S. but raised in Saudi Arabia, where her dad worked for an oil company, before returning to the U.S. Although she looks typically American, she is fluent in Arabic, and has also traveled extensively with her mom to over 85 countries! This made for great conversation that would last 5 hours per night but seem like 20 minutes. We remained in contact after I exited the ship in Mauritius, and to this day. In fact, Candace was the inspiration for my writing this travel book, with not only persistent calls and queries, but especially a passionate letter regarding why I "must" write this book to share with others. This resonated with me because I long felt there was a reason I was unharmed given all that could have happened, had incredibly great weather, and enjoyed such wonderful experiences (plus some not-so-wonderful but worthy of sharing). It all seemed cosmic, like it was meant to be. So, when time permitted, I wrote my story.

But back to the sailing. We headed to Port Elizabeth and Durban, South Africa, in that order. Port Elizabeth had little of interest for me, except the Nelson Mandela Metropolitan University. This university was really three previous schools merged into one a few years earlier, and had a few thousand international students who could study all the way to doctoral level. One of the city's nicknames is "The Windy City," and I'd had enough of that in Cape Town. So I shopped a bit and spent more time on the ship, going to the exercise room and walking around the deck. I also browsed the ship's library materials – and, I really don't want to admit to this, studied the big globe there. If I look at a local road map, I tend to drive somewhere. If I look at a USA map, I tend to fly somewhere. If I look at a world map or globe, I tend to plan another major trip. That could be why the ship's booking department for upcoming cruises was not far away from the library or globe. They know the correct "fly-trap" location, and value of good kryptonite for world travelers.

The next port was Durban, South Africa where I had been the previous year. I spent most of my time at the beach area there back then, but did not go in the water. I went back to the same spot, and had another good day there, this time going onto the beach and swimming in the warm, luxurious water. Afterwards, I bought even more post cards despite buying a bunch last year (choco-holic, photo-holic, and post card-holic). I also bought a few small African crafts, and got into a conversation with a store owner who was also a singer. She told me of a language I never heard of that she spoke and is popular in South Africa called Afrikaans, which is similar to Dutch. I later learned that this language was also popular in some other African countries I had visited: Namibia, Botswana, and Zimbabwe. According to Wikipedia, "it is estimated that the number of people speaking Afrikaans ranges between 15-23 million" (which exceeds the population of many countries). You learn something new every day. I later learned through online research that the South African actress Charlize Theron is fluent in Afrikaans. Before leaving for Durban I made sure not to bring my favorite pair of sunglasses, which I had lost there last year and were flown to me back in the United States. I brought my back-up pair, and another pair as well on this day, just in case I had a propensity to lose sunglasses there. Fortunately, this time I had all my belongings with me when I returned to the ship.

Next was Réunion Island, off the East Coast of Africa, and a location that may have been selected because it was out of range of the pirate ships (so it was rumored by several passengers). I was curious about the name, and here is the winding history according to Wikipedia: "Réunion" was the name given to the island in 1793 by a decree of the Convention with the fall of the House of Bourbon in France, and the name commemorates the union of revolutionaries from Marseille with the National Guard in Paris, which took place on 10 August 1792. In 1801, the island was renamed "Île Bonaparte," after Napoleon Bonaparte. The island was invaded by a Royal Navy squadron led by Commodore Josias Rowley in 1810, who used the old name of "Bourbon". When it was restored to France by the Congress of Vienna in 1815, the island retained the name of "Bourbon" until the fall of the restored Bourbons during the French Revolution of 1848, when the island was once again given the name "Réunion."

I'd heard there wasn't much going on there except a tour to the volcanic mountain area. But too late – the tour was sold out and I stayed around the city center, rather bored. A few photos, a few post cards, and that was it for a half-day. Not everywhere was going to be exciting. Besides, I had been to other volcanic areas, and wasn't so sure one was much different than another, at least to the ordinary observer.

This was the last night of my voyage, and my dinnermates surprised me with a bon voyage party! This included wine and cheese, and a nice fruit selection. I learned that this was orchestrated by the two Carolines and...Don! That was very nice of them, and a few staff members came by to join in. One told me that this rarely happens; most people who leave early just receive their farewells, so I must have made a good impression. I also said a separate goodbye to Candace and Joan, and Candace almost crushed me with her hug. We kept in contact, and she encouraged me to "write the book."

The next port was the island country of Mauritius, which has an interesting history. According to mauritius.org.uk "The island was discovered by the Arabs in 975 A.D., and then occupied by the Portuguese, Dutch, Danish, French, and finally British. Slaves were imported from Madagascar and it was also a penal colony. Colonization attempts failed based on cyclones, drought, floods and plague." And after all that, "In September 1715, Guillaume Dufresne d'Arsel took possession of Mauritius in the name of King Louis XV of

France. He named it the Ile de France, placed the French flag near what is now Port Louis, drew a document witnessed by his officers declaring the island French and sailed away after three days."

Aside from all this, the country is known for being one of the few habitations of the now-extinct dodo bird which could not fly (thus was easy prey), and was described by the Dutch as "a feathered tortoise" (it stood about 3 feet high and weighed about 45 pounds from paintings and written accounts). The Dutch also named the island after the Prince of Nassau in 1598. The country became independent from the British in 1968, and today is a resort area known for its beaches, mountains, and desert. With that as a backdrop, I was intrigued by what would happen there.

I disembarked the ship in Port Louis, Mauritius and spent most of the day taking a tender (ferry) from the port to the main shopping area on the island before returning the same way. There were "the usual" items there including jewelry, bracelets, necklaces, clothing, food, and more. It began drizzling, so I returned back to the ship and planned my departure, saying goodbye to the staff and crew. I was called a taxi which took me to my "upscale" hotel. The driver, George, was a fun guy who I would later call to take me on a private tour around the island as he offered for a nominal price. He called the island "Maurice," which he said is how the French refer to it. I wished he hadn't said that because my mind immediately played "The Joker" by the Steve Miller Band with the lyric "Some people call me Maurice..." which I couldn't get out of my head for the next couple of days.

Soon thereafter, I had a weird experience befitting of the history of the island. The first thing I noticed was that there was a spy-cam (my word for it) video camera in my hotel room mounted to the wall! And the camera moved its position so the lens could follow me around! I immediately went to the front desk and questioned this, but was told all rooms had this security feature, which was common in hotels on the island. I took photos of it and was later told not to cover it up. I saw a security guard that night who was monitoring the rooms via these spy-cams. He basically said that's the way it is there. I thought of trying to unscrew it, but I remembered the story about the American couple in Russia who unscrewed what turned out to be the fixture holding the chandelier in place for the room below, causing it to crash. I also figured either this is one of the safest places on Earth or one of the most dangerous, necessitating this monitoring device.

After a good night's sleep, as the security guard might attest to, I headed out the next morning. The hotel was in a remote bushy area with no street names in the vicinity. I remembered where it was based on a tall TV tower nearby, which was my landmark (the hotel had no cards with its name and address on it). I stayed out all day and returned at nightfall circa 10:00 p.m. after walking all around the small contained area I heard was safe (I'll bet there were surveillance cameras all over). But at night I could no longer see the TV tower due to the darkness (no light on it); suddenly, everything was pitch black in this remote area. I waited around about 20 minutes, but there were no taxis or police around – the streets were empty except for one guy who looked like a "character" – mid-30s, wild bushy hair, dressed in unmatched colors. I hesitated to talk with him but did so out of necessity. English is the official language of Mauritius so there was no problem with communication. He said he knew the owner of the hotel and told me how to get to his nearby home. This made me nervous because it smelled of a set-up. This guy didn't walk with me there which I found a relief, but that didn't mean I wouldn't be followed or accosted upon arrival. Now I was wishing *I* had one of those spy-cams!

So I got to the home and rang the bell, prepared to do whatever was necessary for my safety. I had my camera in my hand and thought of making a split-second decision to take a photo and throw the camera far away into the bushes if there was anyth*i*ng I didn't like, hoping someone would find it and see the perpetrator. Crazy things can go through your mind in a situation like that. The door opened. An older Indian gentleman answered. He seemed normal, and I asked him if he's the owner of the hotel I was staying in, mentioning the name. He said yes and invited me in. He introduced himself as Raj. I saw his wife and two kids sitting there watching TV (hopefully not of the hotel guests), and walked inside. He introduced me and said he would drive me back to the hotel. And he did. I felt embarrassed and apologized. He said this happens to a lot of people, and don't be. I couldn't help ask about the spy-cam in the room. He would only say it's for the guest's safety, but I also figured it's to have a record of any damage that may be caused. I thanked Raj upon drop-off and felt better.

The next day I took the taxi tour around the island and obtained George's card from him, in case I ran into the same trouble as I had the night before. He was local to the area, said this is a good plan, and to call him if needed. He took me to the volcanic area, an excellent choice since I didn't get to do this on Réunion Island. George showed me "the crater," which had a pond at the bottom. I found this very interesting and thought that maybe all volcanic areas aren't the same. He, too, found my digital camera fascinating and played with it. Much of the island was volcanic, and George also showed me the sugar cane plantations. We ended up in a shopping area – which I told him not to take me to – so I strolled around there for a bit. I noticed that on many tours and private taxi rides, the group or individual ends up at a shopping area. I suppose this is appropriate, but I do wonder if there is any monetary encouragement from the vendors to bring people there (I've heard several people complain about being left at the shopping area for too long at times).

Finally, we ended up at the beach area (Grand Baie and Mont Choisy – pronounced "Shwahzee"), where it rained. As we were leaving the beach George happened to say to me, "Have you ever heard of Club Med?" I was stunned, and asked him why he'd asked me that. It turned out there was a Club Med village within easy walking distance, all the way out there on this island in the Indian Ocean! I walked toward it, then stopped. Not only was it raining harder, but Mauritius in general was weird and I just wanted to leave. Club Med – the one I adored in Turks & Caicos – would still be there when I was ready, and seeing the one there from afar put the idea in my mind about going to my favorite village again.

I returned to the hotel during daylight, and had a good dinner. The spy-cam was still bugging me (possibly literally), and I threw a towel on it to block its view of me as I prepared to take a shower (no door to the bathroom, although the toilet and shower were seemingly not in the spy-cam's view). But I thought something bad could happen by ignoring the warning not to do this, and removed the towel. It was like that song, "Always something there to remind me" because occasionally the camera moved around from side to side in surveillance mode. Ironically, the name of the group that performed that song was "Naked Eyes."

The next day, my last there, I was on the Internet letting my family and friends know I was fine, and that I'm on schedule with the itinerary I had provided to them before leaving. Interestingly, Candace would later inform me about the rest of the cruise after I left the ship. She said after I disembarked the Mauritius security people came aboard *twice* to recheck everyone's passport – unheard of even among veteran travelers. Maybe they were concerned about pirates, or planted a spy-cam on our ship and saw our "pirate party," which scared them. Security was a top priority, but they may have gone "overboard" with it. I had a few more hours left and took a bus to the nearby beach. It rained so I didn't get to sunbathe, but I talked to several locals. I decided not to mention anything about the spy-cam because the locals, for whatever reason, may be overly suspicious in general. I returned to the hotel and then walked to the nearby marina, having an early dinner at a nearby restaurant. The view was good, with the mountains overlooking the Indian Ocean as the sun was setting – and that was my signal to get back to the hotel, to avoid another nocturnal miscue. One last night of spy-cam and I was done. "The Spy Who Loved Me" may have been a James Bond movie, but I did not bond with this place at all.

Better times were in store, however. I traveled by plane alone to the Seychelles Islands. As mentioned, this flight was necessitated by the continuing pirate activity in the area, requiring the cruise line to change its itinerary to avoid the Seychelles. Upon learning we would not be docking there, I sourced an online travel agency via the ship's Internet to make these alternate flight reservations, since I also had booked a non-refundable flight that was leaving the Seychelles for Tanzania the following day (I did not take the insurance option covering cancellation – you win some, you lose some). Upon arrival at the airport, I had to go through massive security checks, as did the other passengers (no surprise there). I couldn't have been more scrutinized if I wore an eye patch, had Mr. Yo-ho-ho as my name on the passport, and carried a bottle of rum with me.

So there I was again in the Seychelles, on this little island in the Indian Ocean, nearly 1,000 miles from the next land mass. Yet, this remote location was part of its allure. I found a taxi driver who took me to my hotel once again on Mahe Island, where I had been last year with the world cruise. I lucked out because hotels on the island were super-expensive (hundreds of dollars for basic rooms), but I got one for free using hotel credits I had accrued from an online hotel travel agency. The deal was I could get a free room up to a $400 value for 10 qualifying stays, which I had recently completed back in the U.S. However, because most of these were at a budget hotel for under $40 each, I had spent less than the $400 in total to get this $400 room in the Seychelles last-minute (I noticed soon afterwards that this online company revised its policy to reflect the free-night maximum dollar value to be the <u>average</u> of the collective 10 stays – a big difference). So, what was a $400 room like in the Seychelles? It was moderately nice, like a mid-range hotel chain in the U.S., but not phenomenal as you would expect for that price (not even a good view). I'd estimate its U.S. value to be about $120. And it came with all the tiny ants you can imagine after heavy rains. This was another place in which the front desk could not initially find my reservation, but finally did. There were no other hotels to be had nearby, I was told (the pirates had reservations, LOL).

I would only be there for one day, so I decided to take a taxi around the island. Once again, I totally lucked out because the weather broke just at that time after heavy rains for several days. The sun came out at almost the same time my taxi arrived. The driver was a pleasant, chatty, and smiley native islander in his 30s I'll call Gaston, who took me around to the beach areas. Last year at the Seychelles I stayed in Victoria, but now I would see the rest of the island. I had no idea what I was missing, and would be amazed by the amount and beauty of awesome remote beaches at every turn. The sand was so white and the water was so clear that it seemed to shimmer and sparkle in luminescent blue-green. Add in swaying palm trees and each beach looked like a post card! I took photos like crazy and used far more than expected because I thought each beach was the most beautiful I'd ever seen – and then would come an even better one, and so on.

Although I had seen many of the world's most beautiful beaches by this time, including several in Hawaii, Australia, and Turks & Caicos, these were the winners. If I had to pick my favorite 10 of all time, at least 5 would be from here. Beau Vallon ("Bo Valone") was especially beautiful, with its azure water, and I liked the way Gaston said it with his French accent. Some beaches had a striking color of turquoise water that I hadn't even seen in Turkoise (Club Med), and some other waters were an otherworldly emerald-green color. They were so pristine, not surprising since the island was so far away from other land, was so expensive to live on, and was expensive just to get to (and more difficult now with the pirates). I had heard that Praslin Island also had gorgeous beaches, especially Anse Lazio, and if I'd had more time I would have gone there. Many divers went to the Seychelles as well for the spectacular coral.

I had brought a bathing suit with me to go onto a couple of beaches for a little while if there was time at the end of the tour (there was and I did). Gaston, like several others in Africa, was amazed with my digital camera, and I taught him how to use it. He took good photos, and I would yell to him my trademark expression: "get the feet in" (Candace often teased me about this line, saying it should be on my tombstone). Sometimes I would have him stand far away to be sure to get me full-body, with sand at the bottom frame and lots of sky at the top for an even wider view. Gaston shocked me and others on the beach with a very unusual expression he used before taking each and every photo: "OK, I'm coming!" which he shouted on the long-distance shots. I'm sure he didn't know the American colloquial meaning of this, but others on the beach did and turned to look whenever he yelled this. The funny thing (literally) was that it made me give a genuine smile each and every time right before he snapped the photo. And after that we'd be going.

I asked Gaston about the pirates. He said they are wreaking havoc not only on the high seas, but with tourism there. He hoped the episode would end soon and things would get back to normal. Upon return to the hotel, I had a fast dinner and pleasant dreams about the amazing beauty I had just seen. Although this was a rescheduled stop and expensive to fly there, it was worth every dime; you can't put a value on beauty like this! I brought back some seashells from the Seychelles, wrapping them so they wouldn't break. They, too, are beautiful and enduring reminders of the most amazing beaches I have ever seen.

My next and last stop was a flight to Tanzania. Had I not taken a safari in Kenya I would have done one there, starting from a recommended city up north called Arusha, a gateway to such popular game reserves as Selous National Park (one of the largest national parks in the world), Serengeti National Park, and Kilimanjaro National Park. In retrospect, I should have done this anyway. The plane landed in Dar es Salaam, and I went to my upscale, American-based chain hotel. There was a military policeman standing outside with a rifle over his shoulder, so here we go again: super-safe or super-dangerous necessitating his presence there? It turned out to be the latter. Not long after my arrival I walked down the street to get dinner at a recommended restaurant, and had a rock hit me in the arm thrown by a Black kid I'd say was age 15. I was angry and instinctively started running after him, but decided not to as he scampered back to his buddies. And there were a lot of them. I yelled at him, "What the hell are you doing?" Let's just say it was because I was White. The hotel manager later coached me on the do's and don'ts there, of which there were several (including protection from potential malaria).

Almost all the people I saw were Black, but there were many Arabs as well. Many people were pleasant to me there, but some were not. Maybe it was reverse discrimination, or there I guess it would be called discrimination (against Whites). I sensed the difference in pleasantness level was whether or not they were involved in, or affected by, the tourist business. As the gal in Serbia had told me, "We like your money, but we don't like you" (Americans, and others responsible for bombing Kosovo). Once again I was asked if I'm from the U.K. I told them I'm from America, proudly. I did not pull the Canada stunt, which I shouldn't have in the first place. I was taking more and more pride in being from America as I traveled, and why not? I was now realizing how much better off we are than most people. I did not flaunt or even mention this to others, but was thinking it as I again looked around at the poverty. While I empathized with those without, I was appreciative of all we have as a country within.

I was there for several days only because I couldn't use my free airline miles on another date sooner for my return flight, and the cost difference justified the extra nights' stay. I walked around the local area. The temperature was stifling, with high humidity which made the heat index 105 degrees. But I lost the additional poundage I had gained on the cruise, so that was the upside (or downside, as the case may be). I heard Zanzibar Island was a two-hour ferry ride away, and wanted to go there. But, wisely, I checked with the hotel manager first. He strongly advised against taking the ferry due to selected passengers possibly being dangerous. He said, however, I could take a 20-minute flight, which was not too expensive and included a city tour. So I did that.

I took some excellent photos from the small plane. The water was almost Seychelles-like in color. Zanzibar was largely Muslim, and the big tourist attraction was Stone Town with its maze of cobblestone streets, artists, and bistros. This was a Swahili trading center with intriguing Arabic and Indian architecture, among others - and another UNESCO World Heritage Site. However, while there were some interesting things about Stone Town, I wasn't overwhelmed by it except by the scent of spices. Generally it was very mellow, non-aggressive, and touristy. The locals were friendlier there, but more so if you were looking to buy something.

There was an unusual museum there I re-visited after the tour: The Slave Compound, which included a Slave Monument of Black men shackled together. Inside was the actual location where slaves were kept in cramped quarters before being sold to locals back in the day. There was a dungeon-like atmosphere, and it was incredible how many slaves were fit into that small space. Some of it was very graphic, including whipping posts. Maybe that's why a rock was thrown at me back on the mainland. As mentioned, people don't forget so quickly – even after hundreds of years, because the stories are passed down from the generations. After a sumptuous lunch, we were taken to a high point overlooking the city. The plane returned us back to Dar es Salaam, where I went to the beach the next day. I didn't do much more after that except roam around carefully and not be part of a "rock concert." Thankfully, I was safe during the rest of the trip and checked-out with no further problems.

It took me 18 hours to return to New York City, where I visited family and friends using a free stopover, before returning home to Buffalo. This was another wonderful trip that expanded me in many ways (my mind, not my belly thank goodness). Now I needed a vacation from my vacation. And what better place to vacation than...Club Med, Turks & Caicos in the Turkoise village once again. Anything turquoise or "turkoise" had a halo effect after seeing that magnificent-colored water in the Seychelles. I couldn't wait to see more of it in the Caribbean.

I went to the land of "Crazy Signs" once again to decompress, recompose, and reconnect with my "old friend" Club Med. I attach to selected things as well as people – Zoi, the basset hound; my old Toyota Camry that I've driven in 38 states getting me through almost every major climate condition; and Club Med, even with its evolution toward mainstream civilization. This trip was typical of the previous stays there. I ate well, slept well, and came back feeling well. A highlight was meeting a veteran pilot of a major airline who aspired to do what I've done. He was there with his wife and two teenage daughters, and we often sat together. He wanted to hear all about my travels, and have his daughters hear the same, which perhaps would inspire them, too. Kevin was more proud of me than I was of myself regarding my travels. Being a family guy, however, he couldn't do what I had, at least not yet, until retirement, and he had no desire to visit certain places I had been. But we had mutual admiration for each other.

I also walked along the beach and came to the city center, where I chatted with a Canadian gal in her 20s near the Seven Stars Resort, a magnificent-looking hotel. She was aspiring to travel a lot, and had been around Canada and the U.S. I offered the advice she requested before departing. She had never been to a Club Med before, and I recommended it – telling her that's how I first learned about it, serendipitously from people at the village (in Cancun) when I was there on vacation. She said she would check into it.

Upon returning home I felt very relaxed. I attended a few local events, and readied for my next adventure. By this time I was two countries shy of having been to every country in Europe. As I researched this I found that there is no one official list of all countries in Europe; some included Armenia, Azerbaijan, and Georgia, while others didn't. Many now include Kosovo; however, as of this writing, fewer than half the countries in the world officially recognize its independence, per Wikipedia. So I went to International Travel News and looked at its list. Based on this list, indeed I needed only two more countries to have visited every one of them in Europe: San Marino and Moldova. There was my incentive.

To answer a particular question posed to me, I believe that if you have gone to all countries on a continent at a time when the last one visited provides you with such an achievement, then you have reached this goal irrespective of new countries declaring their independence afterwards. That is, if a new country declares its independence after you had heretofore visited every country in Europe, e.g., you should not have to go visit that new country to make this same claim. That is just my opinion, but let your "continents" be your guide.

# Chapter 21

## Conquering Europe – Visiting The Remaining Countries

Being goal-oriented, and "so close yet so far" from visiting all countries in Europe, I called upon the airlines and another "old friend" to which I had become "frequently" attached, my frequent flyer airline miles. I still had enough left in one airline's account that allowed me not only to receive a free trip to Europe, but two free stopovers (one each way) based on my inquiry. The itinerary I booked was, in order: Venice, Italy (I had never been – using free stopover); San Marino, Italy (primarily by railway round-trip); Chisinau, Moldova; and Frankfurt, Germany (via second free stopover).

After an overnight flight I arrived in Venice early the next morning. I adjusted well to the time change, and didn't even need a nap. I accessed a water taxi to my hotel, then checked-in to my tiny room that was about half the size of a budget hotel room in the U.S. (the pre-booking photo looked better than the reality, but no matter). I walked around the particular part of Venice I was in, Lido. This reminded me of Rome with narrow cobblestone streets, outdoor cafés, and shops. The forecast was for some rain each of the three days I was there, but every day was sunny and beautiful, in the low 70s, with just a light rain one night. It was truly amazing how I continued to luck-out with weather during my trips. A nearby beach I visited was scenically beautiful, but littered and polluted. Renting a bicycle or moped was an option, yet I liked traveling on foot given the great weather and frequent stops for photo ops. The Italian food was excellent – similar to that in the U.S., but not as heavy or rich on the sauces. I took the water taxi around to several nearby islands, which were also beautiful. The people were lukewarm to me at first, but friendlier when, as in Rome, I told that I'm from Brooklyn, New York – which I did on purpose knowing a lot of Italians live there. Several locals in Venice told me they have relatives in Brooklyn. This friendliness was not the case with a young female travel agent in her mid-20s from whom I sought to obtain travel tickets to San Marino for a day trip. I was in for a "trip" of a different kind.

The travel agent I'll call Marcella, translating in Italian to "warlike," told me there is no way I can get to San Marino and back in one day from Venice, and wanted to book me into an overnight hotel there. I had checked this out ahead of time and knew it was possible, but difficult, involving several modes of transportation requiring tight timing. I also had a non-refundable hotel payment for the three nights in Venice, and was a road warrior, which she didn't know. I had Marcella book my trip the way I wanted it and she was unhappy about this, continuing to warn me about what I was doing. Her presentation was "warlike" but the information was factual. I did not care for her attitude, including things said under her breath in Italian with a nasty look. Perhaps in Italy what the travel agent says, goes (literally), but where I'm from the customer is always right. Marcella told me to return in a couple of hours to pick up my tickets, at which time I would make payment. I just wanted this to be done right and to get going, so I strolled around the vicinity for two hours.

I asked a few locals what there is to do of interest. Gondola ride came up a lot, but I wanted to save that for a special occasion, and it's not as much fun going alone. Also, this was expensive at over $100 U.S. for a half-hour ride or less. In case you were wondering, I did not see any Venetian blinds in Venice, and supposedly it's a myth that they were invented there. I was told about a golf course in Lido, the only one in Venice, but I didn't get to it and generally don't golf. The Venetian Film Festival was a big upcoming event there, but that was during Labor Day weekend. Other than that, not much was going on. So I took the water taxis around for some excellent coffee, pastries, and other snacks. Although people said the canals smelled badly, I did not find this to be the case. But I was told I was there "at a good time" regarding this, "before it gets really smelly in the high heat." I returned to the travel agency to pick up my tickets, and ran into a situation that really stunk!

Marcella signaled for me to come over, and had a rude attitude. She gave me my tickets and then demanded an extra $20 for the extra time she spent getting me these (water taxi, bus, and railway train). I said no, that we did not agree to this, whereupon she got her friend to come over, another female travel agent, and started speaking Italian to her, seemingly insulting me. I asked them to speak English if they had anything they wanted to say to me, and they refused. Marcella wanted her money right then (at which time she reverted to English), and I refused. She had made one critical mistake: not getting my approval and payment earlier (I wouldn't have agreed). Now I refused and was under no obligation. It wasn't so much about the money as it was about the attitude. Well, we all got into a massive argument – the voices were raised, the hands were flying (I talk with them too when angry), the insults were hurling, oh this was intense! The manager came over and tried to end it, but he was a demure guy and the gals verbally overpowered him. So we all kept arguing and eventually, continuing to be feisty, I just walked out. We were done. "Fintio!" was my last word. Not only was I in a sinking city, but I had a sinking feeling after this encounter. I can be outspoken when necessary, but don't like doing it.

While flustered about this at the time, I soon forgot about it and even thought how authentic this experience was. Then my mind played the song "Hot Blooded" by "Foreigner" (how appropriate) with appropriate lyrical substitutions: "I'm hot-blooded, check it and see/I've got a temper and not paying your fee/You should have asked me in advance/I'm not paying, not a chance." Over time, this ended up being a net positive because I went to each of the three transportation sources and bought separate tickets that were less expensive than from the travel agency, had no fee attached, and no attitude, either. On a literally brighter note, there was a beautiful sunset over the water that night, and I snapped about 35 photos of it at various stages and angles. Others did the same. Venice had among the best sunsets I've had the pleasure of viewing and photographing.

The next day I showed up very early to Central Terminal via water taxi, bought my tickets for a round-trip ride to/from San Marino, and was headed to a landlocked country of only 24 square miles with a population of only about 30,000. The landlocking is exclusively by Italy, which surrounds it on all sides. Despite its diminutive size, San Marino is only the third smallest country in Europe – after Vatican City and Monaco, respectively. I had a full 17-hour day, but made the trip successfully. This required two hours by water taxi, four hours by bus, six hours by train, and five hours in San Marino (in which there's not much to do). Once the railway train arrived in Rimini, I took a bus into San Marino. But in Rimini, which is on the Italian Riviera, you can get some excellent photos of the city from high above. Generally, once in San Marino, a walled city, walking around is the thing to do; most attractions are accessible by foot. The country reminded me a lot of Andorra – small, in the mountains, steep inclines, with lots of shopping, no taxes, and beware of pickpockets when in a shopping mecca. Naturally, I had to eat Italian food, so I had Spaghetti Bolognese since we were near Bologna, Italy (about an hour's drive) - and it was delicious! I obtained my post cards, and brought home a souvenir or two just because it was such a ballbuster to get to. I'm also proud of the colorful passport stamp I received upon arrival for this same reason.

Most people there spoke Italian, but many spoke English. The place had its charm with outdoor cafés and souvenir shops selling practically everything, including lots of BB guns for some reason. There were many statues, too – religious figures, war heroes, and others. I learned an important lesson about the return bus – be there well before it leaves because it runs only every hour. I was one of the last passengers to make it on, and had I missed this I would not have made my train back to Venice that night. But I made all the transportation back that I needed to. I especially enjoyed the water taxi back to Venice, seeing the city all lit up, as viewed from a distance through a misting rain, making it look romantic. A pretty gal named Tina on the ferry next to me noticed the same thing, and maybe felt the same way because she held my hand and smiled at me. So, one day I was in a screaming match with an Italian gal, and the next day another holds my hand on a romantic evening. Venice the Menace or Venice the Vixen? Tina told me she is leaving in the morning to see a friend up north, but we had a nice time together. My last day there I strolled around the waterfront, taking in one final colorful sunset.

Next was a flight to Moldova, another landlocked country, this one situated between Romania and Ukraine. It was also a former part of the Soviet Union until independence was declared. The country still looked Soviet style, with homogenous block buildings and archaic in many areas. Once again there were numerous clothes lines on the balconies and people carrying baskets of items. Yet, ever so slowly, it seemed to be modernizing, including an impressive glass building with the giant letters AVON on it. I'm not sure if the cosmetics had anything to do with it, but my first pleasant surprise there was that the women were beautiful. I landed in the capital, Chisinau (pronounced "Kish-now"). There was lots of green there including parks, trees, hills, and ecologically green too with trolleys to go along with the taxis, buses, and jitneys. This "Kish" was on my list (with all deference to Hall and Oates) in a special way which will be described.

So, what's a Moldova? Surprisingly and refreshingly, a U.S. wannabe! The young people there loved the U.S. fashion, music, and culture. There was even a "USA store" with red-white-blue logo and a poster of President Obama inside. The jeans sold for $300 each, and I joked with the gal running the store that had I known this I would have brought nothing but U.S. jeans in my luggage, sold them to her for $200 each, and paid for my vacation. I thought of selling her the jeans I had brought with me on the trip – "worn by a real American!" – but she wasn't buying it, literally or figuratively. This gal, named Marina, was sweet, and I'd later learn that Marina, Maria, and Ana were very popular names there after meeting several of them.

I went to a park featuring several cathedrals where weddings were taking place. The wedding parties came outside for professional photos, and I have to say it again – the ladies were beautiful! I took several photos of them being photographed (as did several other casual photographers), and of course I got into a few with my "American" citizenship. Two professional photographers wanted me to be in the official wedding photos – I wasn't sure if because I am American, or because I had nice jeans on that day. Perhaps just the bottom-half of me is in their albums, or some Moldovan's head is photoshopped onto my blue-jeaned lower extremities.

Moving to the nearby park area, I met more young Moldovans who were eager to talk with me upon finding out I'm from America. By then I had wised-up to my being their English lesson, but I was into education, and so what if this was the case? Since this was my last country visited in Europe, I again trotted out the poster board and marker, creating a sign including the date that read "I Am Now In Moldova – Thus Visiting Every Country In Europe!" I asked my new acquaintances to take my photo holding this sign, which they happily did (and, unlike in Africa, were very familiar with a digital camera). I had photos taken of me holding the sign in several locations, including the weekend bazaar, in front of Russian-looking mosques, and the posh Hotel Chisinau. Note that I do not frame such photos or display them back home; they merely go into a photo album for my personal collection, or are viewed by others if they ask to see photos from the specific locations. I have seen other travelers with huge displays of their travel accomplishments in their homes, but I like just having an ordinary-looking residence.

I almost had a communications issue when I asked a local guy where I could buy post cards. He told me the post office. I had been steered to the post office in other countries for this purpose, only to learn once there that they did not sell post cards, but I could mail them from there. So, I didn't think this gentleman understood my request. However, in this case he was right – and not only was it one of the few places to buy them, there were excellent prices, so I bought a couple of booklets (10 post cards each). Roaming around, I came across a central-city outdoor wall that people wrote random things on, so I wrote "Steve from USA was here" with the date. I returned to the site a couple of days later, and someone wrote under it "Bring USA jeans." Near this wall was an outdoor kiosk featuring an unusual local beer I just had to try. It was mixed with Vanilla Coke®. I had watched others drink it and monitored their reactions.

After a few happy souls walked away, I went for it. The combination tasted pretty darn good! I went back for more later that day, and the next day, too. Afterwards, I had a local favorite called mamaliga, some kind of polenta or porridge (neither of which I like) that had a soft consistency and tasted like mushy cereal. I wasn't wild about it, ate the whole thing, and lived to tell the tale. As mentioned, you have to be careful when trying new consumables because you don't know what's in there, and if you become ill that could mess you up physically, emotionally, and vacationally.

I returned to my hotel early that evening. When I asked the clerk the best way to walk to a snack place I had read about, he urged me not to go out at night, citing that it's dangerous, especially because the hotel is not in a well-lit or populated area. It's ironic, if not moronic, that I'm so careful about the food and beverages I consume in a foreign country, yet tend to ignore warnings about going out at night for safety reasons. I suppose that's due to choices available: there are lots of consumable choices, but at night the choice there was to stay in the hotel room watching Moldova-TV (that's what it's called) in the local language, or go out and take my chances. So, I took what was behind door #2. As soon as I walked outside I felt like part of a Dracula movie again – even more so than when I was in Transylvania. It was very dark, foggy, and there were dogs howling stronger and longer than the basset hound I'd grown up with. If someone came up behind me and said, "Boo!" I would have jumped.

I walked toward the main street, happening upon a place that was two levels up (above a hotel) from which I could hear excellent, pulsating rock music, and saw through a window lots of people dancing. I went up there hesitantly. I could only see their shadows at first glance, so I took a few steps inside. A couple of sexy gals dressed all in black came up to me and one said, "You like to dance?" with an alluring look. She was a wild-looking gal with piercings and a shock of black hair combed in early 1980s punk, and who-knows-what-else that was shocking. I danced with her, and then some of her female friends joined in. So I was dancing with five gals at a time – something Mike once dared me to do in New York, and I accomplished. But in a situation like that you never know who's watching, waiting, and wanting. Several guys came over looking like The Fonz wannabes, in black leather jackets with hair slicked back (albeit some were blonds) and dark glasses (indoors, mind you). They just looked me over. Was I dancing with one of their girls? Were they potential friends or foes? Were they going to make a scene? They talked amongst each other, and then started arguing in Moldovan with the gals. I didn't like the situation and excused myself quickly. As the cartoon character Snagglepuss would say, "Exit stage left."

My vacation ended on that note, and I returned to New York after an interesting trip. This wasn't the best trip I've had, but I was impressed by Moldova in particular. As it turned out, when I went to a local T.G.I. Friday's back home, I met two servers in their early 20s there who were from Moldova! These gals were very attractive, with one having those piercing, bright blue eyes. We ended up getting together so I could show them my photos. They couldn't believe they met a local guy who had just been there. This got them reminiscing and pining for home. But they had friends and a job here in New York, and seemed to like the U.S. Soon afterwards I assembled my Moldova photo album to show them, and they enjoyed it! So, Moldova - who knew?!

Before returning to New York, however, I had a free stopover in Frankfurt, Germany, where I spent overnight (at my expense). There was not a lot to do in Frankfurt from a tourist standpoint. I spent most of my time that morning at the nearby Main River. It was a fine, sunny day, I had a limited time there, and was told there's basically few attractions aside from some museums, an Old Town, and a cathedral. One local guy suggested going up to Cologne to the Rhine River, so I headed up there for several hours. I had been in that city on a business trip only, many years ago, and this time got to see it as a tourist. It took less than two hours to get to Cologne by high-speed train. I walked around a lot and ended up visiting the Cologne Cathedral, which was the centerpiece in Cathedral Square. This had awesome Gothic architecture, and afforded a great view of the city from the top level. There were some neat statues there and in the vicinity, from religious figures to gnomes. There were also very old, pastel-colored houses with, of course, places serving great German beer nearby.

I couldn't wait to have hot dogs there, since the best ones I ever had were in Germany during previous visits. These didn't disappoint, either. I met some locals in a restaurant there and ignited an interesting conversation. There was one thing of interest to me that was not in any tour brochure, and please pardon this culinary interlude: who invented the hamburger and frankfurter? I had always thought that hamburgers originated in Hamburg, Germany and frankfurters in Frankfurt. But upon speaking with locals there, and later conducting my own research, I learned this may not true. While the roots for both meats may have been in Germany, their descendants the way we know them today are in doubt. For example, some research claims that hamburgers go back to medieval days, to the Tartars in Asia, and some state that hamburgers as we know them today were first presented at the 1904 World's Fair in St. Louis, Missouri and mass-marketed broadly by White Castle® starting in 1921.

Some research claims that frankfurters go back to the 13th century in Germany, but it wasn't until circa 1920 that they were put on a heated bun and served the way we know them today. Hot dogs and wieners have their own theories. So I got curious about French fries, and learned that these may not have been invented in France, but in Belgium circa 1680, which then got me curious about waffles, only to discover that these may have been invented in Ancient Greece. Does tartar sauce come from the Tartans? Even Wikipedia goes light on that one (pun intended). Baked Alaska does not come from Alaska; it was Chinese, then French who called it a "Norwegian omelet." So now I'm not sure where anything comes from, but as long as it tastes good it doesn't matter to me. In discussing this with some locals, it was fun to watch them follow along, especially a few bright college students I met – even if they couldn't "ketch-up" with it all ☺.

I returned back to Frankfurt after having a nice day in Cologne, staying overnight. My return flight from Frankfurt was ironically through Boston (nicknamed "Beantown"), which I termed my "Franks and Beans" flight, and then I connected to a flight back home to Buffalo (sitting between the "wings"). The job market was still lousy, and I still had enough frequent flyer airline miles available for a few more trips. So I went back to Ol' reliable, Club Med - Turks & Caicos Islands a few more times over the next two years. I always had such a good time there, and these next visits were no exception. The Club continued to change with the times, catering to the older crowds 40+, and couples, too. But it was still one of the few Club Meds left for adult singles like me which helped bring those people together from around the globe (still a large contingent from New York City). I met a guy there named Norm, a few years older than me, who I befriended in large part because I liked the way he operated. A fellow Brooklynite, Norm was not the best-looking guy, but endeared himself to the ladies by wearing shirts with funny sayings, bringing inflatable animals, and using his excellent sense of humor. And you'd see him surrounded by a few lovelies. Those are the people I admire most: not necessarily the biggest, strongest, most handsome or beautiful, but those who make the most of what they've got. People like "Rocky Balboa." People like Norm. And people like the poor, struggling ones I met worldwide who seemed to smile much more than the average person I knew, despite having significantly less in material possessions. I learned that it's not about *those* possessions on the outside, but what's on the inside that counts most.

The retro '60s and '70s parties Club Med threw were awesome, including psychedelic signage. Several of the G.O.'s recognized me and welcomed me back. Many were from Montreal, Canada because they spoke both English (main language of the guests there) and French (main language of the ownership, French-based). If they have a need for someone speaking Brooklynese (a lot of Brooklynites go there), I could be for hire. The only kind of bread they would have to pay me is in that delicious chocolate bread – in both white and dark, still the best-tasting bread I've ever had! For me to go to the same place twice is a feat, so my continued vacationing to this same destination speaks volumes about this village (in French, English, and Brooklynese). I would have one last visit there, to make it "sweet 16" Club Med visits in total (14 of which were to "Turkoise"), and this was among my best, as described in the next chapter.

# Chapter 22

## Revisiting My Favorites

After all these travels it was hard to stay in one place for too long, but I had to settle down sometime. I continued my domestic travels at a leisurely pace, going to both familiar and new places. As after a great big, delicious meal, it was time to just digest after all this. But it was hard to quit cold Turkey (pun intended), so to ease my transition I found several international festivals to attend in the Buffalo area, and was surprised at how many there were. These included Irish (third largest St. Patrick's Day parade in U.S.), Italian, Polish (called Dyngus Day, billed as the largest Polish Festival in the U.S.), Greek, Macedonian, Lebanese, Ukrainian, Puerto Rican - and Scandinavian, which many locals didn't even know about but was terrific! I was so inspired by the costumed people singing and dancing in celebration of their local heritage that I booked another trip – to Sweden, one of my favorite places! It would be my first return after 15 years, and I would have 5 full days to see the city of Stockholm where I would exclusively stay. I also wanted to keep my "travel athlete" abilities and not go too long before taking a long-distance flight. I still endured these travels with ease, and even had a very interesting seatmate who was a Ph.D. student in Anthropology at The University of California, Berkeley. I learned more about Anthropology during that discussion than I had ever known. Ironically, we had to keep our seats locked in an upright position throughout much of the flight.

Upon arrival more than seven hours later (after connecting in New York City), the weather was drizzly. But I would benefit yet again after a prolonged rainy season there, and have gorgeous, sunny, 70-degree days for my entire stay. Even the locals told me that I "came at just the right time." Everything this trip went right, just as it had the first time, as if Sweden was welcoming me back after all these years. I went to the Information Desk at the airport and learned that I could take two connecting buses to my hotel for $35 (210 kroners) instead of an $80 taxi. This is what I did, and it went well. Sweden was more expensive than I had remembered, and I barely had enough cash in the end after thinking I had plenty to spare. As mentioned, however, I prefer using a credit card for the airline mileage points and as a tracking device to my whereabouts should anything bad happen since I traveled solo.

Feeling refreshed after a brief nap, I strolled around the local area, had an all-inclusive buffet lunch for "only" $20 U.S., and then learned how to take the bus and train from my hotel downtown to the central part of Stockholm. In fact, I had selected my hotel in part because of its proximity to public transportation to get me there. The hotel itself was less expensive as a result of being further away from the center, and it only took 30 minutes to get downtown. This was a part of Stockholm I had not seen before; it was like most major cities with excellent shopping, restaurants, and attractions. The latter part was mainly by the Baltic Sea, which afforded great views, photo ops, and lots of people to meet – the trifecta for me. In speaking with a few locals, I learned that Sweden is very gender-advanced in that women often work while men stay home with the kids. The people I met were once again fun, lively, intelligent, interesting, and helpful. I stayed downtown until sunset (circa 9:00 p.m. in early May), and photographed a beauty with bright orange sun. Another sunset in the same spot a few days later showed a bright red sun, just amazing! This made me think of the song "Red Skies At Night" by The Fixx, although that song's lyrics didn't have to do with the weather. I always wanted to see a red sunset when thinking of this song, so another mental orgasm and dream realized, as happened with the instrumental song-ending to "Shout" by Tears For Fears when seeing a lone bagpiper playing in Scotland.

Sweden had some unusual words and store names, to say the least. "Infart" (remember that word?) was the word for entrance, and there were stores named C.U.M. and Wacko, among others. Some very liberal billboards were around town as well, I believe too liberal to be shown in the U.S. (e.g., nudity). There was a very interesting old part of Stockholm called Gamla Stan, dating back to 1252 when the city was founded, where Lake Malaren meets the Baltic Sea. This well-preserved, charming medieval town was a highlight that I returned to three days in a row. There was lots of shopping and excellent sightseeing, including an immense Royal Palace. The narrow, winding, cobblestone streets reminded me of Greece and Italy, and had many outdoor cafés. The oldest square in the city is called Stortorget, and made for excellent photo ops with colorful old buildings. This had an old-meets-new feel to it, making it historic yet vibrant. There was even a train station stop right there, although I preferred to exit the train at the previous station and walk a mile to Gamla Stan along the water. I met numerous people there who extolled the virtues of Stockholm to me – both locals and tourists – but I told them all that they didn't have to sell me on it, I was already a believer. While sauntering around I came across an outdoor celebration called "Brazil Day in Stockholm," featuring a Swedish band that had an attractive blonde lead singer named Lucy who was also a fashion model. Her rock band was excellent, and after the show we conversed and took photos. She was a neat gal, and I wished her well in her singing and modeling careers. I also thought of the Swedish band ABBA while there; the group's famous song "S.O.S." could have stood for "Stunning Outdoor Scenery" to befit what I was beholding in Stockholm.

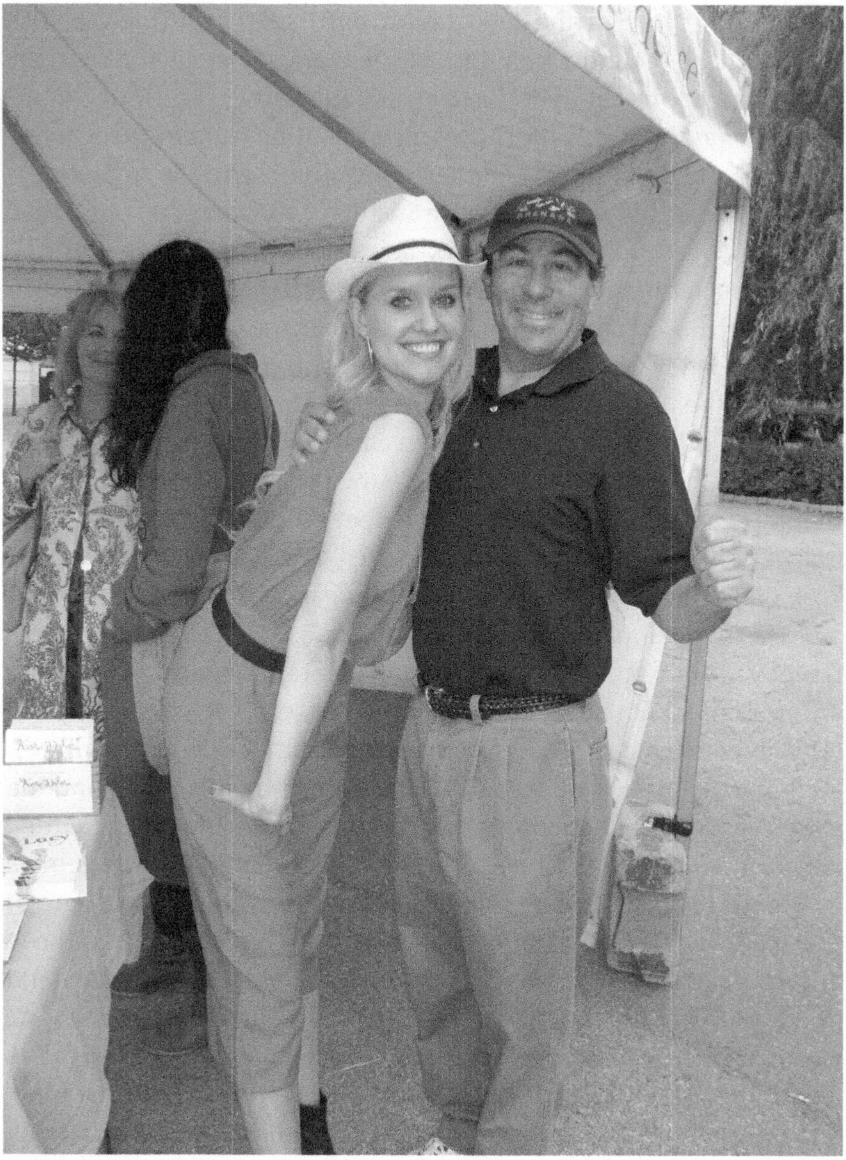

Here's Lucy - not the famous redhead we know in the U.S., but a blonde from Stockholm, Sweden after her musical performance during an outdoor concert. I revisited Sweden for the first time in 15 years, wanting to verify if it was as good as I remembered it being. It sure was!

Which brings me to the next point: did I still think that Swedish women were the most beautiful in the world, after seeing so many additional countries? The answer is... (drumroll)...Yes! But what I decided was this: while there are more beautiful women "per capita" (as a percentage) elsewhere – including and especially Argentina – the most beautiful women I saw in Sweden were more beautiful than the most beautiful women I saw anywhere else. If there were 50 women each from Argentina and Sweden and I had to pick the top 10 combined, 6 would be from Argentina and 4 would be from Sweden. But the winner would be from Sweden, and maybe the runner-up, too. So if the Argentina gals want to take that as a victory, so be it.

I met other fashion models in Stockholm as well who were beautiful. One, who I met in a park in a mini-skirt, seemed to have legs that just kept going (she was over six-feet tall), while another was an Italian fashion model visiting the country, and was interested in New York City. If I'm interested in meeting a gal overseas, or just about anywhere, I will play the following cards as needed: international traveler, American, New York City, can you take a photo of me?, and are you a model? – not necessarily in that order. That's often why and how I meet so many models, to the astonishment of my tourmates. I dated a beautiful model in New York City when in my 20s, and the main reason was I had enough courage to go up and start chatting with her (well, actually, I was "pushed" into it, literally, by a female co-worker who shoved me in her direction). I learned that some of these gorgeous women sit home alone on Saturday nights without a date – because guys assume they must have a lot of dates and don't ask! That was a major revelation that helped me date several extraordinary women overseas, and in the U.S., just by asking. I've met a few other ordinary guys who dated extraordinary women, and they all had one thing in common: no fear of rejection, and an unrelenting ability to diplomatically keep pursuing the woman they wanted until they won her over. And good for them; again, I admire this determination in "making the most of what you've got."

As a related side note, I happened to notice a beautiful blonde actress in some recent television shows and movies named Malin Akerman. I usually do not pay special attention to these beauties because there are so many in Hollywood, and I do not watch a lot of TV. But after seeing the movie "Wanderlust" I noticed something familiar about her. Upon doing some research, I learned she was born in Sweden, and her mom was a model. I wasn't so much surprised that she's Swedish as I was that I could identify this look. If you Google® her, check out those eyes – those match the type I've seen all over Scandinavia, but especially in Sweden and Iceland, as described in this book. I also learned she grew up in Canada, less than an hour from Buffalo, New York. Damn, had I only known!

One night in Stockholm I went to a McDonald's that was conveniently located outside the transport depot, as I waited for the return bus to my hotel. I was dining alone when a couple of female high school students sitting at the next table looked at me and asked if I'm American. They were interested in the United States, and knew that McDonald's was based in the U.S. We had a pleasant chat for a while, and then the marketer in me couldn't help but ask them if and why they liked McDonald's. I thought it was because it represented America or tasted good, but they strongly stated that it's because it's "cheap." I had heard this from teens in other countries as well. Although McDonald's in Stockholm cost the equivalent of $10-$12 U.S. for a basic meal (sandwich/fries/drink), by comparison a medium-sized pasta dish at a medium-priced restaurant cost $30, and a fine-dining meal could cost $70-$80 minimum. A can or small bottle of Coke cost $3 or $4 there. When I told these gals that prices in New York City are half as much as in Stockholm they were very surprised, i.e., that their meal would cost about $5 in the U.S. But the McDonald's there had a TV screen so maybe there was a theater ticket price built into the cost. They also told me that they thought McDonald's was "a plot to supersize the world and make people obese." Obviously, they were aware of the documentary about this. I did notice in Sweden and elsewhere how much slimmer people were on average compared to Americans; in some places, you rarely saw an obese person. Perhaps it's due to the U.S. having a higher standard of living, so we have more to spend. Or that in other countries less food is put on the plate. Or that prices are more expensive in many countries (especially Europe) relative to income. Or maybe lack of or fewer fast-food restaurants. I didn't let these thoughts weigh on me, so to speak, but I was still full of curiosity and wonder, even at this advanced point in my travels.

While I had the low-end, medium-end, and a couple of high-end meals there, I stocked-up on the delicious candy I found including chocolate-covered marshmallow bananas, and also aseptic fruit drinks. Once again, the flavor of foods there tasted more robust than in the U.S. in many cases. I was having a really good time, but it wasn't due to any one thing. I believed it was a combination of all the little things going well (transportation, people, activities, weather, safety, etc.); not having done a trip like this in over a year; and that it was in Stockholm, an excellent place to be in general. When I booked my trip I could not get the hotel into which I was booked for the one last night I needed it, to tie-in with my return flight home to New York (for which I used my free frequent flyer award miles). As such, I almost did my first "couch surf"- an organization I joined just prior to this trip, which is a global network of people willing to give a traveler a place to stay in their home for reciprocation of the same (not necessarily to the same traveler). I had an email dialogue with a local lady there willing to put me up for the one night in case my hotel did not have another room available for me, but the morning I was to check-out another guest cancelled and I was able to stay in my same room. The couch-surfing gal sounded a bit hesitant, anyway, and seemed busy with her young kids, so perhaps this was for the best.

I continued going downtown on my last full day there and saw yet another beautiful sunset, as if Sweden's way of saying goodbye with a smile. I heard that after I left more rains came, but while there the sun was there to greet me and chaperone me around. What a nice trip that was! Glad I returned, and happy 15-year anniversary, Sweden! I hope to return again someday. I even saved a reason to go back: get some Swedish meatballs! And yes, Swedish meatballs have their origin in Sweden.

The following year I revisited Iceland for the first time since my initial trip there 8 years earlier. Despite having some rough weather just prior to my arrival, the skies cleared and I had five days of sunny, albeit cool weather, in May. Locals there told me that this was the first such stretch of more than three consecutive days of sunny, non-precipitation weather in several months. Iceland, as had Sweden, seemed to welcome me back. I stayed the entire time in Reykjavik again, at the same lodging place, the Salvation Army Guest House (which is nicer than the name implies). The price was again reasonable at $70 U.S. per night, and the location was very centralized, which again meant I'd be walking a lot.

Since I had seen many of the major tourist attractions last visit, I ingrained myself in the local culture, mingling with the people of Reykjavik in coffee houses, restaurants, on the street, and in other venues. I mentioned that I like **FINE** things, as in **F**un, **I**nteresting, **N**ew, **E**xciting – and this time it wasn't only the city itself that provided that, but the people, too. They had a great sense of humor about themselves, their country, and the world. I was informed that two Miss World's came from Iceland, confirming that the women there were beautiful (not that I needed any confirmation of this - seeing was believing). I attended a one-man-show theater performance there called "How To Be Icelandic in 60 Minutes," which was hilarious. The skits included Icelanders' physical reaction to the swirling rains, especially when hitting them coming up from the ground, and the men's Viking mentality when it came to how they related to the women. The performance was at a relatively new venue there, the Harpa Theater, a very expensive green-glass building by the waterfront providing great views of the mountains. The theater itself was lampooned in the show because as it was being built the country's economy was crashing. As for food, the salmon there was terrific- Norwegian and Icelandic, plus the herring was among the best I ever had. I also tried whale meat, which tasted like roast beef. Despite the economy crash, Iceland was still very expensive, with prices averaging double to triple that of New York City, same as last visit. I suppose that's because the U.S. economy crashed commensurately during that time.

I attended The Volcano Show again, inside the same volcano-ographer's home theater as last time. I mentioned to Villi Knudsen, who was still there hosting his documentary, that I was there 8 years ago and really enjoyed it. He was pleased to hear that. The show was the same movie as last time, but it was worth seeing the riveting footage of actual volcano eruptions he and his father had videotaped once again. After the show, I complimented Villi again. And he said that he's now working on a similar documentary about the eruption of Eyjafjallajokull a couple of years earlier, the volcano that snarled international airline traffic (this name was also lampooned in the "60 Minutes Iceland Show," including the 47 Scrabble® points it represents). He offered me a sneak peek, but I needed to be going and figured this might be incentive to return to Iceland again someday. I took photos of and with Villi. Interestingly, his Volcano Show is not well-promoted there; a senior travel agent had to look it up and call Villi's home to ascertain that the show is still running with the dates/times. I was able to walk there from my hotel (half-hour), and I also was one of only three people in the theater at the time.

And of course, I went to the most featured attraction in Reykjavik among the many, The Blue Lagoon – twice. This outdoor natural thermal spa continued to be awesome, with temperatures ranging around 100 degrees Fahrenheit. You lose yourself in this giant blue-green basin, swimming with others from different countries, under the walking bridges, through a few canals, and overlooking the mountains. The sun and cloud variations turned the water different shades, from greenish to turquoise, which made for good photo ops both in and around the lagoon. I took some terrific photos from landings atop the restaurant, which I didn't notice the last time I was there, to get an overview of this spectacular panorama. **Wow!** Afterwards, I hung out there for a while and had a bite to eat, awaiting the tour bus that would bring me back to the hotel. I chatted with other visitors, who were also in awe. You couldn't help but smile while being there. So being a creature from the Blue Lagoon wasn't scary at all, just another day in thermal paradise and well worth the visit – and revisit(s).

And then there was my ultimate paradise, Club Med – Turkoise in the Turks and Caicos Islands, Caribbean one last time. I realized that it was my 25th year anniversary of not only my first time there, but of arguably the best vacation I ever had. I even thought of looking up the others online from back then and seeing if we could meet there, but decided not to. Solo was the way I needed to go, as I had become accustomed to, and had worked so well for me. This time was no exception. Club Med had all the usual beauty and usual suspects – the amazing beach, great food, and fun staff, several of whom remembered me (albeit from only the previous year) and welcomed me back. The crowd was even a bit older this time, with many in their 40s, 50s, and higher, but there were the 20-somethings and 30-somethings as well. I was staying there only a little less than a week, but that was enough time to soak up the sun, eat well, sleep well, and relax as I was nearing the finish line in completing my travels and this book.

During my third day there I saw an attractive gal sitting alone outdoors at breakfast, and asked if I could join her. She agreed, and we sat together overlooking the Club on a picture-perfect day (more great weather for me yet again, despite it having rained there "all last week" I was told). Felicia had arrived there the day before, this was her first time at any Club Med, and at the last-minute her female friend couldn't make the trip so she was there solo. As it turned out, Felicia was from New York City, and living in Manhattan after attending college and working there. We got along well. She added that this trip was for a special occasion, her 29th birthday, and she wanted to "spend it someplace exotic." I related to that, and told her how I had marked selected birthdays with major travels. I did not mention my age, but when Felicia matter-of-factly asked me later on I said, "I'll admit to being over 40" – which is more than the usual "39" I say and leave it at that. As mentioned, I can still pass for a much younger age, even late 30s, and do not divulge my real age because I use it as a bonus question on exams when teaching.

By coincidence, Felicia and I had dinner separately with an older, fun couple there in which the guy was a retired urologist (he called himself a "pecker-checker") and his lovely lady friend (or more) was a flight attendant. There looked to be at least a 25-year age difference between them, and they were a nice, romantic couple. Well, they became the role models for Felicia and I, who were soon walking around the Club holding hands, embracing, and more. In fact, the Club photographer gets a major assist because, thinking we were an established couple, he had us take photos in selected romantic poses including his urging us to kiss at the end – which we did. On the beach. In the water. At the pool. In the pool. At the bar. And more.

Felicia was one of the prettiest and sexiest gals at the Club so this raised a few eyebrows, but we didn't care. In fact, Felicia said that the only thing that matters to her with a guy is that he's nice to her and treats her well, and I applauded that she didn't care much about age, status, material things, and more that others do. I "bought" her several drinks (included in the package price), and we spent most of my remaining time at the Club together.

Felicia thanked me for helping make her 29th birthday special, and I thanked her for helping make my special trip...special. And what better place for romance to blossom than in paradise! Interestingly, one of Felicia's hobbies was "reading trashy novels," and she was very intrigued by my writing a book, albeit travel. She wanted me to include her in the book using her real name, but I decided to go halfsies – in the book, yes, but real name, no. And, since this is not a kiss-and-tell-book, I'll leave the romantic part to your imagination, which may have included being under the stars, under the covers, or under the influence... And so I said my au revoir to Club Med - Turkoise. It ended as it began, with a wonderful experience, assisted by a hometown New York City gal, great weather, and probably in there somewhere a great number 8, such as the number of consecutive hours spent with Felicia at any given time.

I took over 1,000 photos from each of these three revisited places, and made duplicates of most. They came out great, and I quickly placed them into albums. I look at these occasionally when I want a vicarious visit, as I do with selected other albums. That's a major benefit of having gathered all this raw material from around the world – more to choose from, including in your memory, in your heart, in your dreams, and to share. And so ended my outstanding travel odyssey.

I hope you have enjoyed this trip around the world in a few hundred pages. And maybe I will see you soon, somewhere in this amazing world.

**If you have any questions or comments about this book, you can email the author directly at stevefreeman100@hotmail.com**

# Chapter 23

## Frequently Asked General Questions...And My Responses

Since I have been asked so many questions about my world travels, here are several posed to me and my responses which may assist you. Following this are travel tips in selected categories, including money-saving advice, to enhance your trips. Remember, this is based on my personal experiences, but that said, many of these apply universally.

1. **How can you afford to travel, especially at such a young age, and while not working some of the time?**

Many people who asked me this later told me they were waiting for me to say something like my parents are wealthy, I inherited a fortune, or I won the lottery. They were stunned to learn none of the above was true, and that I was just shrewd about saving and spending. Remember, I came from humble beginnings, worked my way through school, and paid back my loans without assistance. I knew, and still realize, the value of a buck. I also educated myself well, worked very hard, and succeeded in my career. I don't have any major vices, but the money I save from not doing these is applied to travel, which I refer to as my "Big Bang Theory" – save, save, save and then spend it with a bang!

Which leads me to the next point. Some of you aren't going to like this, and no offense intended – as stated in the beginning, what works for me may not work for you, but here goes. I don't smoke, drink, use drugs, gamble, or have other major vices. It all adds up to a lot of savings that I use for travel. For example, just based on smoking a pack a day at $5/pack x 365 days/year = $1,825 x 30 years = $54,750; x 2 packs/day = $109,500 net, which means at a 30% tax rate you'd need to make over $140,000 to keep the $109,500. Add in more than two packs/day, more than 30 years, the rest listed above, or whatever else applies and it can really add up. And yes, I don't have a wife and kids, and yes, if you didn't smoke you might eat more, etc. I am not making any judgments, but am just answering the question I am most often asked based on my individual situation. Thankfully, after all this traveling I ended up safe and in excellent health. Now if I could just stop being a choco-holic, photo-holic, and post card-holic (see, I do have vices)...

**2. What's your favorite country?**

Well, my favorite place as you know by now is Club Med – Turks & Caicos Islands in the Caribbean. But that's not a country. My favorite country to visit was...<u>Iceland!</u> But, because I said "to visit," I haven't really answered the question, have I? OK, here is my answer: My favorite country in the world of the 112 I have been in is...the United States of America! You may have noticed that throughout this book I (purposely) alluded to several world sites being similar to those I saw in the U.S.: the 25 de Abril Bridge and the Golden Gate Bridge; Bondi Beach in Sydney and the landscape of Cape Town, South Africa compared to Southern California; and selected others including mountain ranges, geysers, and sculptures. We have a great country – the most-visited in the world for a reason. But that said, we do not have it all by a longshot, and there is a majesty to the history of other countries that goes back thousands of years to our 200+. This "majesty" goes beyond our purple mountains to include literal translations such as palaces and castles that are absolutely stunning. I must say this as well: go travel! Even if you have traveled extensively throughout the U.S. (as I have), there is so much more to see worldwide that will enrich you in ways you never dreamed possible. Go see it for yourself, and literally expand your horizons. I'm glad you're reading this book, and I truly hope it has been like a travel buffet for you, but the main courses are out there, and they are not only selectable, but delectable, too.

3. **What are some of the lessons you learned from your travels?**

These are sprinkled throughout the book. In general, I learned that people are basically the same all over the world!!! I expected there to be vast differences, almost as if aliens versus humans, in an "us versus them" way, e.g., Jews/Muslims/Arabs; Serbs and Albanians; Yankees and Red Sox fans. We all want the same things, inhabit the same planet, and yes breathe the same air – although that does not mean you have visited all the world's countries, as might be debated on a motor coach ride somewhere in the world. I now see us as one, with a lot of kinks to be worked out.

Then there are the connections. Not just the people connections I wrote about, but the connection to our planet, humanity, life beyond your locale. I wanted not only to see for myself what it was like, but also use all my other senses – smell, taste, hear and touch. I am a much different, and believe a much better, person as a result. There are more touch points besides these, such as viewing a scene on TV that I never would have been interested in before – now I will not only watch it, but want to learn about it, and can connect with it as well. Socially, I can connect with so many more people about so many more things. Instead of using my camera caper, I now just ask, "Where are you from?" Chances are I've been there, and can talk intelligently about it.

I wanted to do all this sooner than later in life, because it would give me more time to have these connections and recollections, and I'm glad I did. That's where the photos and albums also come into play. To this point, there was a seemingly innocuous event that happened when I was about age 20 that had a deep effect on me. My grandmother's sister passed away at around age 80 and left behind lots of beautiful black-and-white photos that were fading. No-one knew who the people in the photos were. Her husband had passed away, they had no kids, and the photos weren't labeled. An aunt from my parents' generation just happened to remark to me, "What a shame. We'll probably just toss these out." I have a close uncle, who was related to that elderly aunt, who is today also in his 80s. He now realizes the value and legacy of photos, started scanning his pictures onto CD's, and is also writing his memoirs. I think that's great. After all, when you really think about it these will not only survive you but, ironically, bring you to life to future generations. I was moved by this event happening with my aunt's photos, and starting then I understood their long-term importance. I started taking lots of photos, labeling them appropriately, and preserving them in albums. And along with other factors, that event also motivated me to write this book years later, to preserve these travel memories and pass them on. Palpable to pulpable, I suppose (unless you're reading this book online). And as my wise uncle told me, "After you're gone, all that's left of your existence are documents and photos."

### 4. What were the major pros and cons of your travels?

I was very fortunate in many ways, including being safe and healthy - both of which were in no ways givens. Either one of these going awry could have been a deal-breaker at any time, but I took precautions (see list in the next chapter) and was also intuitive enough when I didn't. I also did not get jet lag. And I was also lucky at times, which you need.

Great weather also helped tremendously! This cannot be underestimated, and resulted in more outdoor activities and terrific photo opportunities than would have been possible. And all that learning, knowledge, and wisdom transformed me into a different and better person.

As mentioned, I learned more about others based on their feelings toward my doing all these travels. Most people were very supportive and truly shared in my happiness and adventures, even if vicariously. However, on the flip side, not only did I experience much envy among some I thought were pulling for me, but other world travelers I spoke to went through the same thing and lost friends as a result. I found it beneficial to know this and even weed-out some of these people – good riddance if they can't be happy for a "friend's" achievement! But in the end, it didn't matter to me. World travelers are a special breed who are generally goal-oriented and are going to do it regardless. And what a great way to make new friends based on this common bond. What I learned to do is say very little, and let the other person drive the length of the conversation by asking questions – or not – about my travels. Some people wanted to talk for hours, and just couldn't get enough. Others said something like, "Did you have a good time?" And after I'd say "Yes" they would change the subject without any specifics being asked.

Also, ironically, despite (or maybe due to) my travels to so many countries, I had difficulty getting back across the Canadian border at Fort "Erie" (aptly named), 15 minutes from my home. I was more frequently searched (beyond "random," in my opinion, with never anything found), and decided not to go back there again – not worth the hassle, and we have so much right here in the U.S., as mentioned. My decision not to return there also had to do with the attitude of a few particular border patrol agents who thought that a "badge" is a license to "badger" innocent Americans. Other Americans also feel the same way about going there for a similar reason and aren't returning, which affects businesses in towns at the border. Some Americans think this is retribution for how Canadians are treated when they come to the U.S. through this border. I learned, however, that you need to separate the people from the politics, so I still like Canadians in general. Besides, for now I am "border-patrolled out," "cruised out," "motor coached out, "and "airlined-out" (especially with the new security regulations and cramped seating). Riding a camel or donkey might be the ticket, or a "horse with no name" if you liked my lyrical tie-ins. I feel that I traveled at just the right times, and was extremely fortunate with the way it all turned out.

5. **Your home must be full of incredible treasures you brought back, right? It's only natural to want to impress people.**

Paintings, carpets, giant statues as one of my cruisemates ordered from Asia? Not a chance. As mentioned, I jammed my luggage full of trip necessities and could only fit small souvenirs afterwards; also, I do not live in a big residence at all. I do have a vast collection of caps, post cards, and fridge magnets, but I'm not a guy who shows things off. My photo albums and memories are my treasures. Relatively few people have seen my albums, and I don't tell new people I meet how extensively I've traveled. If people ask about my hobbies I will include travel. If they ask if I've been to Europe the answer is yes. If they ask how many countries I've been to in Europe I'll tell them. And if they ask how many countries I've been to overall I'll tell them that, too. But I don't volunteer this information, boast about it, or use it to gain favor with others. There were no parties or even cards for me when I achieved going to 100 countries, and that was fine with me. I haven't even joined the Century Club for people who have been to 100 countries.

I will say, however, what makes 100 countries a true feat is that cruise ships can only go to so many; if you want to get to 100 you have to do a lot of the rough stuff. I will restate this: I was not going to write this book at all, but did so as part legacy, part wanting to share my story, and part having this survive me so that 100 years from now when a family member looks at the family tree and says, "Who was he?" I have a tangible asset that can be provided with the words, "Here, read this." I'm also self-publishing to tell my story my way, which may in the process help readers like you. Plus, this was my project during winter in Buffalo – which, ironically, was the warmest on record (there it goes again with the great weather). Almost every winter I've spent here has been warmer than usual, with many record-breaking days to the upside.

6. **What's next? Any more trips planned? Will you ever stop traveling?**

One of my favorite songs of all time is "Runnin' Down A Dream" by Tom Petty & The Heartbreakers, which inspired me to travel because that was my dream. Well, I ran down that dream and it was fantastic! I will never be done with travel, but after all those wonderful experiences I will be slowing down. As it turns out, the timing is right because I achieved all of my travel goals, am nearly out of free frequent flyer airline miles, and by coincidence, I'm just about out of space to store any more physical photos (which I much prefer to online). Sometimes you just know when it's time – but what a great ride it's been! Also, I cannot just stop – it would be like trying to stop a speeding airplane. It doesn't work like that, and I've met several world travelers who tried to completely stop but couldn't.

That's why, figuratively speaking, my landing gear is down, and the brakes are being applied gently. I still have a few more trips to take, but less frequently, and perhaps less strenuously. Travel withdrawal, as mentioned, is curable but takes time. I know people who suffer from this in a major way, and why not? Not many things can match the grandeur of world travel – if travel is your thing.

Speaking of musical inspiration, my all-time favorite song is one few people have heard of, by a group not too-well known in the U.S., "Sense of Direction" by the Climax Blues Band. The song is a metaphor about life, at least the way I interpret it. The first part is frenetically fast-paced like life itself, especially the kind I had in New York City – school, job, relationships, responsibilities, hustle-and-bustle, overwhelmed...and then slowed down substantially to the relaxing pace, using mainly an instrumental ending - travels, peacefulness, searching, finding your "way to go." This song especially resonated with me regarding "wandering over the seven" (seas), and later inspired me to take several cruises for this purpose. If I listen to that song these days (which I purposely limit), I would be inclined to travel somewhere every time.

A friend suggested I sign up for the space shuttle to go to the moon. Not likely, but maybe you will find me having something to do with Mars® - the candy company, that is. I became a candy consultant to ease myself back into the work force, and may even end up with a new career in travel afterwards. After seven summers at AAA to start my work life, spanning from high school through grad school, this would bring me back full-circle, and somehow seems appropriate for me to be in this industry. You may have noticed I didn't mention Paris. And with good reason: I never went there! I'm saving it for a special occasion, perhaps a honeymoon if I ever decide to settle down, but if not, a special birthday or other occasion will do just fine. I look forward to going there.

7. **Do you feel any differently after doing all these travels? Has it changed or transformed you?**

Transformed me, yes, in terms of lots of newfound knowledge and how I view the world. Changed me overall, not really. People are very surprised to hear me say that, but I am still the same person, down-to-earth even though I have traveled around it. My family and friends haven't noticed any difference, and I have 8 friends of at least 20 years who haven't noticed any significant changes. I'm very thankful to have had this opportunity – and that I emerged safe and healthy. I have a BBA in Advertising, an MBA in Marketing, and now a PHD in Travel, irrespective of the paper recognition. PHD, by the way, is short for **P**assion-**H**appiness-**D**reams that can come true!

**8. Any regrets or anything you'd like to do over again?**

Yes and no. Yes, I wish I took even more photos during my earlier trips. And no, aside from that, it all went beautifully. Even as a tough grader, especially with myself, I'd give it an A. You can't put a price on the immeasurable amount of knowledge and happiness I obtained through these travels. In fact, when there are company holiday gatherings and parties, it's the President or CEO who's sometimes seeking me out to talk to me about my travels – that's what they'd like to do if they had the time, and could ever stop thinking about the business (I met a few who cannot).

**9. Any advice for beginners?**

Yes, begin! Take small steps, such as to an English-speaking country, going with others, or even a short cruise to see how you like it. Look at my chronology. I started that way and gradually built up to what I eventually accomplished. If you start small and gradually build up, then each trip seems like a bigger step. Just as with walking, you need to take baby steps, then bigger steps, then before you know it you're off and "running." Also, respect the culture and do not try to impose yours on the locals! Listen and learn. Be open-minded.

**10. Anything else in general?**

Smile and be polite. These are universal. Relax, you're on vacation. Have a good time. Let go. Forget about your worries. My best times were when I was "in the zone," so happy I was there that I was probably emitting all kinds of "good vibrations." As you get older, it's so much harder to feel like a kid again. But with many successive travels I found such amazement that it was like being a kid again, and it was wonderful – as in full of wonder. It was like opening a pack of baseball cards or holiday gifts or scratching off lottery tickets – you never knew what to expect, but the hope and anticipation practically justified the price. And that's another thing, don't think of it as a one-week vacation. If you're like me, it triples: for example, one week of anticipation, one week of travels and all the joys they can bring, and one week of decompressing/feeling no pain/reliving the trip through photos. So three weeks for every one week of vacation sounds like a great deal to me. I also have met people who anticipate even a short vacation for months.

# Chapter 24

## 100 Travel Tips, Money-Savers, And Ways To Make The Most Of Your Vacation

Over the course of my travels I jotted down several helpful hints to keep in mind. I have put these in categories for this book in order to assist you. Here they are in no particular order. As a reminder, there are many more than just these so check online, with your travel provider, and use your common sense and judgment.

*Before You Go*

1. Expect to have a great time, you're going on vacation! You worked hard, saved up, deserve it, and are about to experience things that could be among the greatest memories of your life! Sure there are situations you need to be aware of in a foreign place, but your attitude will determine your altitude. And to paraphrase an expression, don't let your trip be filled with great tragedies, most of which never happen.

2. This sounds basic, but review all itineraries, confirm your flights and reservations, and bring these confirmations with you. Things change all the time. An overseas airline wanted to bump me on a full flight in lieu of a paying passenger because I was using frequent flyer airline miles through its U.S. partner airline; a travel agent booked me on a second international tour before I returned from the

first one; a few hotels lost, misplaced, or said I didn't have a reservation there – but I showed my itinerary to prove I did and got the room.

3. Give a trusted person a copy of your itinerary and passport. Things can go very wrong, and you need someone who knows where you are supposed to be in case you're not there. If you lose your passport (and copies you should bring with you), at least this can be provided as needed by someone from home.

4. Make sure you have all proper paperwork, and more, that you'll need. Passport, visas, vaccinations/yellow card, other proofs of citizenship, and bring extra passport photos which I found to come in handy for impromptu visas at the borders of countries you may not expect to be visiting (I bring at least two extra photos). I also arrange to email people back home periodically to let them know I'm doing OK, or if anything has changed.

5. Make a checklist of what needs to be done at home before you go. Paying bills, throwing out foods that spoil, arranging for someone to check on your home, stopping the mail, caring for people, plants, and pets, and other checklist items as applicable.

6. Bring extra cash/travelers checks. Many places overseas do not take credit cards (or even travelers checks), and in my early travels I needed to get to ATM machines, which wasn't always easy and can be costly. Now I bring more than I think I'll need, just in case. Also, be aware that some countries (like Russia) will only take crisp, new bills (Singapore probably needs them to be dry-cleaned). Some merchants do not take bills larger than a $20. Check this out ahead of time.

7. You might want to leave the flashy stuff behind. Or at least be very careful about showing it. I sometimes go the extreme (especially in poor countries) of walking around with my camera in a plastic shopping bag to both hide it

and blend in. If you bring the bling don't make it sing (or have it sing solo – "so low" that nobody can hear it).

8. Bring extra film, memory cards, batteries, and other necessities that you might run out of and may not be readily available overseas. On my checklist is also a camera-battery charger (and I bring two), which is customized to my brand of digital camera and may not be available where I'm going. Early in my travel career I ran out of film (before digital cameras), and from then on always brought extra (which I would almost always end up using). One guy on my tour sold an extra roll of 24 exposures he had for $10 (normally costs $2) to people who had run out – and he got it easily.

9. Learn a few words of the local language. I only learned a few, such as please, thank you, and toilet (mandatory, to avoid a game of "charades"). I found this made a big difference. Many foreigners do not like when you (a foreigner to them) try to impress your culture on theirs, especially expecting them to speak your language when you don't try to speak theirs. So making this attempt is often a big help. Also, in some rare situations, it is not clear which is the ladies room and which is the men's room (many places do have visuals, but sometimes show just the words). Knowing these words can help avoid an embarrassing situation.

10. Smile ☺. This is not to be underestimated. Americans in particular can be – and may come across as – stressed-out and demanding, which are not good things. In most places I have been the pace is slower, people are more relaxed, and they don't want to be rushed. Smiles are universal (and the longest word in the English language with a "mile" between each "s" ☺). Also, be aware that some hand gestures we use as positives can be construed as malicious negatives elsewhere, including thumbs up, the peace or victory sign, and the "OK" sign. Check these out before you use them.

*Precautions*

As stated, I was very fortunate during my travels. So many things could have gone very wrong, and at times I was within inches of something really bad happening. There are plenty of websites providing precautions which I haven't even viewed. I'm providing these here from my personal experiences to increase your chances of having a safe and pleasant trip. This is not meant to deter or scare you, just inform and remind you.

1. Don't display valuables. If your hotel has a safe, consider putting them in there – but don't forget them (happened to me once – realized it in a taxi headed to the airport). Keep your wallet in your front pocket, not your back pocket (even if buttoned). Keep your luggage and other belongings in front of you, and keep watching them. Do not leave them unattended, especially at an airport which can look suspicious and cause them to be taken away by Security. Beware of someone who tries to distract you.

2. Don't assume you're alone. Spy-cams in the hotel room, Internet browsings and emails that may be monitored, and suspicious people who wonder why you're taking so many photos. It happened to me, and can happen to you, too. Be careful what information you share with whom (never give personal information to strangers). And don't unscrew any chandeliers, even if you think they might be bugged.

3. Taxi drivers can be great or terrible, in more ways than one. Some were wonderful, happy, chatty, informational, helpful, provided what amounted to a free city tour en route to my destination, provided inexpensive official city tours compared to local tour operators – and took my photos as well. They enhanced my overall trip. Then there were the others. Bad attitude, tried to overcharge me, potentially dangerous to the point I was called back inside by the store owner to have a "safe" taxi called for me, and one who took me to the wrong airport (unintentionally,

I still believe), but who wanted to charge me for this. If you suspect anything bad might happen, take a photo of the taxi's license plate if you can (if anything bad does happen and your camera is found it could lead to the perpetrator), or at least write down or memorize the plate number. Get an approximate price ahead of time, and watch for fast meters. Most taxi drivers post the rates on the exterior of their vehicles or other conspicuous places. Beware of well-dressed people offering you a limo ride for an inexpensive price (this could be legitimate, but if it seems too good to be true...).

4. <u>Ask the hotel personnel for safe places to go,</u> places you shouldn't go (if any), recommendations for restaurants, attractions, and the like. I prefer these from the locals, but hotel staff is usually very good about this, too. I just wonder if they get paid for these recommendations, and if they're more prone to provide the standard places to go that don't reflect the true flavor of the city.

5. <u>Take the hotel's card and your ID with you</u>, including contact information, in case you get lost or even forget where you're lodging. Bring a copy of your passport page and a picture ID, especially if police "randomly" request this (remember, chances are you stand out in a foreign place).

6. <u>Use common sense</u>. If someone or a group of people are headed toward you who look ominous, simply cross the street. It's a good idea to know where the police stations are just in case, and walk toward one. This next point sounds simple but may not be so: always look both ways before crossing the street. In England and other places I've been, motorists (and non-motorized vehicles) drive from the "opposite direction," so if you're used to looking only left, you could be flattened from the right. I've been asked this many times: is it more dangerous for women? I'm not one and can't say for sure, but in general I would say yes based on things I've witnessed and stories I've

heard (including that some women even dye their hair darker). I've met some single female travelers who asked me to escort them places, or just stay with them for the train ride, etc. which told me they were concerned (some looked scared). Blondes were especially vulnerable in places there weren't many. Others had no problem, so let your conscience, and judgment, be your guide.

7. Sometimes a place is fine to go during the day, and much different at night. Some areas are better than others. Some streets are better lit. Some have mules barreling down them, so know what "bellek!" and the like means. Mosquitos in certain places can be a huge issue. During the day, no problem. At dusk and night, huge problem. Be prepared and protected as needed.

8. Watch what you eat and drink. Go to reputable places. Vending carts can be hit or miss. Do you really want to miss? Anything you peel is OK (e.g., bananas). There are other precautions, such as boiling versus washing, so check on these before you go. If you have food allergies, be extremely careful. "Mild" food has different meanings in different places. I like the "hot! hot! hot!" song to dance to in a conga line, but my mouth didn't appreciate the "mild" spicy noodles in Thailand. Be very wary of drinks with ice cubes in them. People remember not to drink the water, but ice cubes count, too, and can make you just as ill. Bottled is best, but if you can't obtain this or prefer not to, ask for no ice. Same issue with fruits, vegetables, and salads, which could be washed in local water.

9. Beware if you wear shorts or other pants with wide pockets. I lost several small items from these (some found at the sides of my bus seat later on, some never found) including sunglasses and little knick-knacks I bought and stored there. I later learned to zip everything up in my carry-on bag. Also, these are the pants that pickpockets target. Ladies, watch those handbags, hold them close

to you and not loosely so as to invite snatching. Beware of chain snatchers.

10. Use your camera and credit card as a tracking device. If anything bad should happen, the credit card company knows where you last used it and that's a good clue. Tell people from home about this plan and the company name so they can contact the company if needed. You may not want to give out your credit card number, but even if not, there's probably a division at the bank that can track you without it based on other information provided. Your camera, too, is valuable in this situation, as mentioned. I'm not a cop, and don't watch too many police shows, but I would look at the photos and deconstruct from there. "WWMD" as in "What Would McGarrett Do?" - the one from the original "Hawaii Five-O" TV series (by the way, Jack Lord, who plays McGarrett, is from Brooklyn, New York).

*Money-Saving Tips*

I am often asked about ways to save money, and I have found several. I believe that just these tips alone will more than pay for the price of this book. Many are sprinkled throughout the book. Some are standard, but others are not so obvious. Based on my experiences, here is how I saved big.

1. Obtain specific credit cards and get the free airline miles. This is the best deal going if you're a traveler, qualify for the credit cards, and can use them for travel based on your schedule. Some cards have no fee and offer enough airline miles for a free round-trip just for signing up and making any purchase, even a candy bar. Many cards have a fee, but even these may be worth it. I've had no problem using these miles; it is as advertised, and like money in the bank depending on flight availability. You can also earn miles directly via the airline travel; I've read where some people took advantage of selected airline

travel promotions, flew all over the place, and racked up huge mileage that not only was applied to future free travels, but included upgrades to elite status as a result of attaining so many miles in total. Car rentals, hotel stays, and more may be able to be converted to airline miles if those companies are partners with your frequent-flyer airlines (inquire about this). I recently joined a dining club for this purpose, and receive several airline miles for each dollar spent at selected restaurants. New ways to earn miles are popping up all the time. But the fastest way to earn a lot of miles for travel is through airline credit cards.

2. <u>Go online to check trip prices, and inquire about travel insurance</u>. Re-check prices before you go since they can change rapidly; some travel companies may refund you the difference if a lower price becomes available prior to your departure. Also, do not assume that online prices are lowest. I have obtained better prices from in-office travel agents, and directly from the airline, cruise line, and hotel. And if you hear that something is sold out, check with another vendor because often times the rooms or seats are sold in blocks elsewhere. One vendor may be sold out while others have inventory. Last-minute deals are also wonderful if you have the risk-tolerance and patience for them. I have saved many thousands of dollars in this manner, but of course had the flexibility to wait. Should you take the insurance? Again, it depends on your risk tolerance. I did at first, but then stopped. One time I took and needed it when my luggage was delayed, and bought two days' worth of items including clothing to the amount allowable. One time I didn't take it, and had to pay an airfare when my cruise ship needed to avert pirates and thus did not sail to the Seychelles Islands, which I needed to then fly to from another port in order to connect with a non-refundable flight I had already booked from there.

3. Get someone to travel with you to avoid the sometimes steep solo-traveler upcharge. If you plan to travel alone or cannot get another person to go with you, ask about being assigned a roommate. Recognize, however, that it's hit-or-miss, as described. I made a couple of friends this way, but also had some bad experiences. I figure if it is a bad match maybe this can be changed mid-stream, so it's worth a try. But you can't count on that and Club Med, for example, no longer assigns roommates. Neither do any cruise lines as far as I know.

4. Use coupons. They're all over the place, including online and printed materials. I know from my marketing experience that a very low percentage of coupons are ever redeemed, but these are among the best ways to take advantage of a deal. One minute of research and clicking or cutting could save you thousands of dollars. Now there's a great return on investment!

5. Recognize your real cost. Factor-in how much you would spend if you stayed at home. Food, transportation, entertainment, utilities, miscellaneous. Subtract this from your overall trip cost to get the "net" cost of your planned excursion. When I did the math I found that some trips weren't costing me as much as they first seemed. Factor-in intangibles, too. Quality time with your spouse? Being away from the kids for a while (for some it's a plus, for others a minus)? The life experience of cruising? I met people on cruise ships who calculated how much food they'd have to eat to break even (or even profit), and went for it. Even people on the posh world cruise told me they factored-in the medical assistance available. And one young guy on my Antarctica cruise put all his stuff in storage for a year and traveled around the world on a budget – paying for it, in large part, by the rent and utility costs he was saving. Yes, there are other associated travel costs which could include who watches the kids/pets/plants/other, photo developing

(runs roughly an additional 5% - 10% of my trip costs), and of course your ability to get away in the first place (the "big 5" I identified). So net it out – traveling may be less expensive than you think.

6. Negotiate. There are websites where you can do this, but I'm also talking about with the overseas merchants directly. In some countries this is expected, such as at the bazaars or souks. Some taxi drivers expect this, too – just do it before the ride begins. If you take the first price then that's it. Even in America I negotiated some excellent salaries, bonuses, and benefits. I could write another book: Just By Asking. My best advice in this area: Ask! The worst that can happen is they say no. If you offer value, recognize it, and "appreciate" it, literally.

7. Can you monetize your travels? I suppose so, and many people do. For me, it's the memories that are priceless. I have not framed and sold my travel photos, e.g., gone on lecture tours, or anything like that. However, I am writing this book, but more in the hopes of helping others, and as a legacy. If additional good comes from it, and ironically this book takes me to new places I never dreamed of, so be it. I do know this much: I've invested in myself through traveling, and the return on this investment has been immeasurable.

8. Take advantage of any and all discounts. Traveling during off-peak can save you a fortune over time – it all adds up. Pre-booking can also be a money-saver, as can last-minute deals. Try to find companies that will guarantee prices even if there are subsequent price increases, and provide lower prices should the price drop. Airlines and cruise ships' cost structure is heavily dependent on oil prices, and these fluctuations can affect prices either way (for a while cruise ships were including an oil surcharge to cover increases). There are discounts for seniors (e.g., via AARP), war veterans, students, teachers, club store members, groups, travel clubs, and many others. Be sure

to ask – these aren't always disclosed. Also ask about package deals including hotel and car rental, e.g. But you may be able to do better booking these individually (online or not), and not be locked into the narrow offerings that come with that particular deal. Back in the day, and maybe even today, there was a huge airline discount if you were able to stay over on a Saturday night, the savings from which often more than paid for the additional cost of doing so (lodging, transportation, food, entertainment, etc.). Also consider the exchange rate of the countries you are visiting as a money-saving (or additional cost) factor. As examples, Mexico, Poland, Argentina, Central American countries, and others provide a big relative bang for the buck, so to speak, while Scandinavian/Nordic countries, Russia, and Japan can be extremely expensive. Factor this exchange rate into your budget.

9. <u>Find rooms where you can prepare meals</u>. Several times, especially in expensive places such as Hawaii, I obtained a hotel room or efficiency with a refrigerator and stove for a few more dollars per night. In so doing, I prepared my own meals instead of eating in restaurants, which saved me hundreds of dollars a week. I still ate out often, but a basic breakfast could easily cost $10-$20/person in expensive areas compared with the glass of orange juice and bowl of cereal with skim milk I traditionally have, that costs me under $1. Also, ask if your hotel includes breakfast, free parking, and other amenities (in Alaska, the hotel at which I stayed was relatively inexpensive, but parking was $20/night). Also, strange as this may sound, I know people who stay in local hotels or motels and pretend they are elsewhere to help ease travel withdrawal, and also as an inexpensive way to recapture that "get-away" feeling. I haven't done this – yet – but may give it a try (especially living near Niagara Falls).

10. Find low-cost alternative food and beverages instead of paying a lot elsewhere. Japan was super-expensive, but I found these delicious breads with cheeses, vegetables, and other goodies baked-in for a fraction of the cost. These made a good, inexpensive lunch and could be taken on-the-go. Same with smoothies and various fruits. This saves time, money, and can be more nutritious. Just ensure you shop in reputable places, as mentioned. I've had no problems with street vendor products, but I'll usually buy packaged products such as ice cream or soft drinks from them. I haven't had any issues with non-packaged foods purchased from them, either, but have not bought too many of these. Be careful, just as you would be in your home country.

*Airline/Security/Luggage*

1. OK, let's get this out of the way first: going through airport security sucks, but there's no way around it, so just do what's requested/required within reason (that definition is up to you). Make sure to take all your personal belongings – lots of possessions get left behind, and it may take a while to get them back. I'm not wild about the X-Rays and frisking – "Hands Up" is great at Club Med, but not when being patted down. I became increasingly frustrated with this to the point of not wanting to travel anymore, and strongly believe I was profiled due to being a single traveler with dark features, and possibly because I've been to so many countries. I don't buy the "random" checks when it happens a high percentage of the time (I asked what "normal" was, and mine was at least double what I was told during some later travels).

2. Don't check bags if you can avoid the situation. Airlines are charging a steep price beyond certain sizes, weights, and quantities; it takes longer to get them upon arrival; they could be delayed/lost; and they may not make a tight connecting flight (all four have happened to me).

Learn about the regulations, and travel lighter if needed and possible. There is a lot of luggage sold in specially-designed sizes to fit in the overhead compartments.

3. I like to pack using what I call my "bag within a bag within a bag" process, including some smaller-size bags for day-trips or toting around on hikes. Also, it's best not to zip luggage to the corners because this is how zippers can break when luggage is checked (I zip to the middle from both sides). This advice was provided to me by a friendly, helpful baggage handler at the airport.

4. To maximize what you can take on the plane/fit in your luggage, roll-up your clothes, which also helps prevent wrinkling. Although this helps jam more in, watch the weight limits – not only on domestic flights but connecting international ones, too. As mentioned, I had to dump a lot of clothing to make the international flight's weight limit – which was less than on my domestic flight (ask about this ahead of time when booking).

5. Make your baggage identifiable and unique. So many look alike these days! Not only did I almost walk off with someone else's luggage bag, but someone almost walked off with mine. A "walk-off homer" is great in baseball – but not with someone else's luggage. I don't put my address on the bag tag but only a name, phone number, and email address. I wouldn't want to have strangers know I'm away and have my home address, but I'm very cautious. In this regard, I'd also rather have "Strangers In The Night" only be a Frank Sinatra song.

6. Planes are more crowded – the good old days are gone. Nowadays, due to fewer passengers, there are fewer planes. This generally means more people per flight. Exit rows provide more leg room and are beneficial for taller people in particular. I have a traveling friend who's about 6'4" and ends up like a pretzel after long trips these days. You can change seats during the flight if they're open – but

check with the flight attendant. The back row seats near the toilet can be stinky. The empty three-seater across on a long trip can be like hitting the jackpot on a slot machine. I always travel in coach – as mentioned, I've adapted comfortably to it, and it saves on money.

7. You can get some great photos out the airplane window at the designated times, and I have taken many of these that came out fantastic (mountains, waterfalls, cityscapes, cloud formations, sunsets, and one over Niagara Falls when the pilot alerted us all and flew closer to it on a picture-perfect day). Sitting by the wing can obscure your aerial views if you take photos of the landscapes. If there are two empty rows of seats opposite each other, this can allow you to toggle back and forth to maximize your exposures for the photo ops – but importantly, remember: safety first.

8. Bring snacks and good reading material for longer trips. Prices at the airport are very high, and nowadays there is a charge for snacks onboard (but I find some of these reasonably priced and good-tasting). If you require a special meal (e.g., vegetarian, kosher) make these arrangements ahead of time.

9. You can meet amazing people seated next to you. Talk with them, and be receptive if they talk to you (of course, this can backfire but give it a try). I've even obtained free medical, dental, insurance, photography, and travel advice from professionals who willingly offered (I never even asked). I've laughed and commiserated with some, and even stayed in contact with a few afterwards.

10. Ask about free stopovers. This isn't always mentioned, but be sure to ask; I've saved thousands of dollars by using these. Sometimes this benefits the airline if the flight you're booked on that night is overbooked, and the one the next morning is empty, e.g. Sure it's an extra hotel expense, but this could well be worth it. Also, if

your flight is canceled, you may be entitled to a free overnight hotel stay and meal(s) so be sure to ask. Also, not to be underestimated, sometimes if you need to travel only one-way you can get a less-expensive fare buying the round-trip ticket (with a fictitious return date) and not taking the return flight. Check this with a travel professional because restrictions may apply.

*Taxis*

Generally I've had few problems, but these can also be great or terrible. You've read my stories but I'll provide a few generalities.

1. Agree on the fare ahead of time, and if it's by the meter, make sure it's not a fast one. Some cities limit the amount you can be charged going to/from the airport to a particular destination based on distance, e.g. Remember to negotiate if this is an option (in some places it's expected). Also agree on who pays tolls – I've seen it go both ways, you or the driver. I've also found it helpful to know which route you want to take - this may avoid what I'll call an "end-around" (borrowing from American football) so that you're not paying a much higher price by taking the long way.

2. Memorize the plate number, driver's name if shown, and take a photo of the license plate if you can (e.g., while walking around the back to the passenger side) if you have any suspicions. Importantly, do not be overly suspicious when traveling abroad, but do take care. I've had enough happen over yonder because it was obvious I was not from the area. But I was savvy enough about taxis from my New York City days to not be taken for a ride, so to speak.

3. Use the taxi trip as a sightseeing opportunity. You can ask to be taken the scenic way to your destination, but check ahead of time about the pricing to avoid a potentially unpleasant surprise. If you like the driver, ask him or her

for a personal or group city tour later on if so provided. Bring your hotel card, or itinerary with its name and address on it, with you so if you get lost and need a taxi you can show this to the driver.

4. Be courteous, smile, but don't give too much information to the driver or any other strangers. I like telling the driver that if he or she does a good job I may call for my return trip – and I ask for a card. This way there is incentive for the driver to do a good job, not that this incentive may be necessary.

5. In several places I've been there are "safe" taxis, which also means there are not. Ask in advance at your hotel, the tourist bureau, chamber of commerce, or the like. The vast majority I've encountered have been fine, but if you are uncertain then do ask about this for safety and reliability.

6. Check if there is public transportation to/from the airport. Look into taking a shuttle van, bus, or train for example, which can save you money in lieu of a taxi to and from your hotel or other destination. As mentioned, I've used these and saved extensively. Plus, I often arrived to my destination faster.

7. If you have a lot of luggage, it may not fit in the standard taxi trunk. You may need a larger vehicle, and need to arrange for this in advance. I've seen tourists and their pick-up drivers at curbside with that "now what?" look on their faces upon seeing there is too much luggage to fit into the smaller-sized vehicle there. Ask questions ahead of time about the capacity relative to the amount, size, and weight of your luggage.

8. Know the exchange rate of the local currency. I once overpaid because I confused it with the country I was previously in and gave about $5 too much on a $10 fare. The good news: the seemingly lax taxi driver shot up

out of his seat and ran to help me with my luggage, and I believe would have carried it to my room if the porter didn't snatch it from him. Do not just show a wad of local bills and ask the driver to pick out what's appropriate (I've seen people do this).

9. Ask the information desk personnel at the airport what the approximate fare should be to your destination, and have the personnel secure the taxi for you if possible. Often times there are kiosks inside the airline (or other transportation) terminal with personnel who take care of this, and also can book your hotel, excursions, and more.

10. Keep your valuables with you, not in the trunk of the taxi. I put my most important items in a carry-on bag that I keep with me in the cab. This way, if there's a dispute and the driver simply drives off after you exit the vehicle with your luggage still in the trunk (I've heard of this happening – another reason to get the plate number), at least you have your necessities/valuables with you.

*Hotels/Motels/Other*

1. Check ahead of time to see if there's a free pick-up or shuttle service offered. Many people don't realize this is included in the price.

2. Make sure you're at the right hotel before the taxi driver (e.g.) leaves. Step inside and ask. Some cities have multiple locations of the same hotel chain, others have hotel names that sound alike, while others, as mentioned, may not have your reservation for whatever reason. Make sure you're at the right place at the right time; you don't want to be stranded with your luggage who-knows-where, maybe in the middle of the night in a non-secure area.

3. Equipment may not work the way you'd expect. I'm no rocket scientist, but I'm no dummy. I've had difficulty operating the bath/shower, TV (sometimes the red light means "on" and the green light means "off"), phone, lights, and even toilet where, in Japan for example, these can be very complicated (heated seats, and which button, lever, or switch flushes?).

4. Have a safeguard against missed wake-up calls. Many times the staff did not do this on time as requested, or at all. I learned the day clerk didn't tell the night clerk; this was not written down to begin with; there was a door knock or call to the wrong room; and people just forgot. Luckily, my internal body clock woke me up during these mishaps – even at 4:30 a.m. – or I would have missed my ferry, train, plane, tours, etc. Have a back-up plan, like an alarm clock or travel partner (if you have one) wake you up. Yes, this happens domestically, too, but I found it much more frequent overseas (possible communications issues, more relaxed attitudes, maybe they don't like people from your country).

5. Do yourself a favor: bring a room freshener. I have been in some real stinky rooms, even in nice hotels. And even if you have a "non-smoking room" do not assume the previous guests abided by this, including smoking cigars. This could be another "you-don't-know-what-it-is" Roseann Roseannadanna situation (including stuff on the mattress), and don't assume that the property has aerosol sprays/room fresheners.

6. Ask about a room safe or hotel safe to store your valuables. And don't forget to take them! I've not had anything stolen and most of the time did not use the safe. However, better "safe" than sorry could apply here.

7. Check the views from the room. More often than not, even in less expensive hotels/motels, I had a good to even great view, affording excellent photo ops. Also,

there may be a deck or large window on the top floor of the lodging facility from which to get the same. Ask about this or check it out. There may also be a nice lounge, swimming pool, or other amenities up there that are open to all customers.

8. Do not assume the room is a standard U.S. size, or even has air conditioning or heat. Many don't because it may not get too hot or too cold in that vicinity. But it can still get uncomfortable, so realize this ahead of time. I also like to bring a small travel pillow, and sometimes wish I could bring a travel mattress, too.

9. Some things can appear creepy. I've been in a few hotels in which the hallway lights are motion-activated to save on cost. So the hallway can appear pitch-black, but don't worry, the lights go on when the sensors detect you're there. Also, beware of anyone who appears to be following you (in which case go right to Security personnel or the front desk). Some elevators can be daunting as well (old, creaky, heavy doors that you should not assume open when a hand is detected). Sometimes I'll take the stairs, or a different elevator if available. Even in "good" or "excellent" hotels I've had in my room ants, geckos, and there was also that spy-cam...

10. Check if there's free or nominally-priced Internet in the room or the lobby. This can be a money-saver, as well as convenient. Often there are abundant Internet cafés near the hotel if not in them – these store operators understand that the hotel guests may be seeking this service, and geographically position their stores accordingly.

*Motor Coach (Land) Tours*

1. There are different levels and prices. The main difference between the high-end and low-end that I found is the quality of the hotels and perhaps better restaurants visited. I mainly use the hotels to sleep in, so I don't need a fancy one for a higher price. You'll get a higher-end clientele on the more expensive tours, but I get along just as well if not better with the budget travelers. These people often include younger tourists (e.g., college students).

2. Bring lots of reading material, music, puzzles, etc.! There are long, long rides with nothing to look at. The tour leaders often provide the history of the next country to be visited, and maybe even show a movie, but it can be dull for hours. Many people sleep during this time, but you can also use it to get to know your tourmates. As on planes and other modes of transportation, I've had many wonderful conversations with new and interesting people on the coach. These days this is a dying art, with younger people being on social media so much, but I much prefer personal interaction to share information, pleasantries, and even jokes. You can't hear people laugh on Facebook®. Most people I've met on these tours, generally traveling through Europe, have been from, in order, the U.K., Australia, New Zealand, the U.S. (only about 10%) and Japan/other Asia. I'm sure there are plenty of others who prefer to go with their local-language tour operators, assuming they operate in the desired travel destinations.

3. Beware of motion sickness, although it's rare, and about all that sitting... One passenger on my motor coach tour in her 20s had me read to her to focus her attention away from the motion discomfort. You never know until you go, so be prepared. It's never happened to me, but I've seen people get it. You might want to bring a hemorrhoid

remedy, too. I've not had this, either but some people got it from all the sitting (maybe bring a cushion) and poor-quality toilet paper (maybe bring a cushioned roll as I did, which helped).

4. Remember that the people who generally travel are older retirees, and you get the occasional college students on the standard tours (sometimes a younger relative of an older person on the tour). There's nothing wrong with this at all, but just be prepared in case you were expecting something else. There are tours specifically designed for younger people, older people, religious groups, and others so check which might be right for you. The destinations can also drive the demographics.

5. Many of these tours are fast-paced, and "Where was that again?" You might literally have a situation in which "If it's Tuesday this must be Belgium." I like this pace, but it can be daunting for some people. Also, a good idea is to write down what you wear in each place so as to know where you were after the photos are processed (I would not have remembered all of these without doing that). For this same reason, I take a photo standing next to the sign of the name of the city where possible, or with it in the background.

6. As with any group, there are norms and relationships that develop. All the same characters are there – the talkers, the quiet ones, the photographers, those who nothing bothers, those who everything bothers, the complainers, and more. The right people often find each other. I've had couples want me to hang out with them, and I've seen singles who want to be left alone. So I can't tell you that your group will definitely be this way or that, but I can say that you should be open to new people, places, and things to expand your network and universe.

7. Often times there is a local tour guide who shows you around a selected city. This additional guide supplements

your tour group leader and knows the landscape much better. Tip this guide as well if not already included in your package. There are usually guidelines provided or told to you. I find these people very friendly, helpful, and happy to be showing you around his or her city. Do not feel obligated to stick with the group to see (yet) another church, museum, etc. But if you depart the group, make sure to tell the tour guide, and know when and where to meet the motor coach – it may not be where you were dropped off!

8. <u>Yes, there is a restroom on the motor coach</u>, but usually only one. There are rest stops along the way, maybe every two hours or so, but I've been on some for four hours. As mentioned, I bring salty snacks to inhibit having to "go," but others take medications if there's an issue. Sometimes the restroom is out of order, and then, well, it's wait until the next stop.

9. <u>Reminder to get a window seat and shoot photos out of it if so inclined.</u> This includes the back window if available (front window is best, but a seat may not be available next to the driver/reserved for the tour leader). Seating is often rotated to give every person a window seat and the opportunity to meet others on the tour, which I think is terrific.

10. <u>There are things that happen beyond anyone's control</u>. Stuff happens. Roads are blocked and even washed out. The minesweeper event I described. Heavy traffic. Border crossings that take forever. Tourmates getting lost or sick, causing delays. The bus driver who angrily left the bus - and the passengers all stranded. There's not been many of these issues on my tours, but all of these happened on them – and more. Be prepared, patient, and go with the flow. I still endorse motor coach tours, and have generally had an excellent time on all I've taken.

*Cruising*

1. A great experience that can be amazing. For many this is a once-in-a-lifetime opportunity and incredible memory. There are passengers who put on the ritz with dressing up, taking the shore excursions, and enjoying the fine-dining options aboard ship. There are others whose goal is to eat their way back to the cost paid, lay out and tan (as appropriate), and generally hang around the ship which may include shopping, the casino, gym, spa, lounges, and theater shows. Whatever floats your boat.

2. There are shore excursions you can book via the ship line or on your own once in port. Be aware that if a minimum number of people don't sign up for an excursion it can be canceled. From a pricing standpoint, you're better off planning your own – often there are taxis or other tour operators in port there waiting for you, most of whom are not affiliated with the cruise line and who charge by the car or van load (so the more people, the less cost to you individually). I've done several of these and had no problems, but you never know. With a cruise line excursion the ship will wait for you if you are delayed, but on your own this may not be the case, and you're responsible for getting to the next port of call. I also like to walk around after a long ride (either motor coach or ship) to stretch/exercise so I don't always just jump into other transportation upon arrival or soon afterwards.

3. This may sound silly, but remember what ship you're on! Often times there are many in port that look alike. I've met people who went to the wrong ship, and had to scramble back to the correct one before it sailed. This almost happened to me, and it's a good thing I took a photo of the ship when it was in port so I recognized where it was.

4. Seasickness – yes, it can and does happen. But don't let that stop you. There are many remedies, and people

react differently to the same cruise. As I advised a friend who's thinking of taking his first one, start small – go for just a few days and see how you like it. But just because you fared well on one doesn't mean all will be like that, and vice-versa. I've had almost no problems after taking more than 15 cruises (except for a short time going to Antarctica), and most people I've spoken to haven't, either, except on rare occasion. I can't say how you'll react if you haven't taken one, or even if you have already, but these are my observations. Note that some parts of the ship rock less than others (in terms of deck location, and front or back of the ship), and the larger-weight ships (tonnage) are more stable. Check this out and inquire ahead of time if you think there will be any issue.

5. <u>The staff onboard is there to please you, and is generally very accommodating</u>. If you have any issues do bring them up right away, including repairs needed in your cabin, excessive noise (from the ship or even the room next to you), and dining. As mentioned, I've had some weird seatings that I had corrected, and often times have just seated myself where I felt appropriate if not accommodated properly. There's also the Lido Deck or other such comparable place where you can dine alone or with others buffet-style versus full sit-down dinner (many do this). I find the dining room the best place to meet new people, share information, and give or receive advice. One other note: do not let the staff put a sticker on your passport when you check-in! It is difficult to remove and may deface a valuable and memorable piece of property. Ask what alternatives are available.

6. <u>As with land tours, the cruises are stratified into low, medium, and high in price and quality</u>. I've gone on budget cruises to world cruises (top of the line). There is a definite huge difference, but I can go with either just the same relative to the price/quality. As mentioned, the expensive ones generally get the older crowds with

the money, and the inexpensive cruises may attract budget travelers with families. I find the budget cruises to be very good or even excellent. These days, with the overbuilding of ships and a steep recession, the prices are terrific – and you *can* eat your way to breakeven (not that I recommend this). Be careful on wet decks and wet floors inside – or you'll be cruising for a bruising, which happened to me after I slipped up.

7. Some upscale cruises have extra amenities. These may include seminars provided by professionals in the field, fine-dining options (that cost extra), spas, personal fitness trainers, and salons among others. First-class all the way, and a great life experience if you can afford it. Remember what I wrote about discounts/deals, and just asking about/negotiating these (could be unpublished deals).

8. Yes, bad things can happen on ships too, but... this is rare and can happen on the road, in the air, in your own home, and everywhere else. I've not been daunted from going anywhere. But, "just in case," make sure to attend the drills onboard (mandatory), and take all the other precautions. This is another reason to ensure that others back home know where you are. I found the pirate situation near Somalia exciting while others were almost fainting. Be aware that anything can happen anywhere at any time. If you don't have the stomach for this, then cruising may not be for you. The good news is there is a medical staff onboard with limited equipment.

9. Some theater shows and parties onboard have been among the best I've ever seen, including comparable to Broadway performances. These were not only on the fancy cruises. I saw a Mardi Gras party on both a mid-range cruise and a world cruise that, in their own way, rivaled some of what I saw in New Orleans during that city's famous festival. One world cruise had four outstanding themed parties within two months.

10. Cruising is another good way to meet new people from around the world, and with whom you can make a new acquaintance or friend. I've cruised with several people who met on a previous cruise and became friends/travel partners/more.

*Rail/Bus/Other*

1. Rail is a terrific way to get places quickly and inexpensively. I find this form of transport safe, reliable, relaxing, comfortable, and an excellent way to see the countryside. I've also met some wonderful people this way sitting next to or right opposite me. Bullet trains/high-speed rail are especially appealing if you like going fast.

2. Be careful in which section you sit on the train. As described, the train can detach at a selected station to carry less weight/move faster/make sharper turns or whatever. If you're in the wrong section, for example the back of the train, you could be left in the stockyard. Do not assume you'll be automatically awakened or moved; that's up to you. If there's an announcement that you don't understand, ask someone who can interpret it and inform you, if available. You also need to be in your assigned seat with your train ticket evident to the transit employee who checks it.

3. Know the name of your city and station in the local language. Florence, Italy is called Firenze over there. Sometimes there are station names that sound similar and are close together, so be careful.

4. For local trains, make sure you understand the rules. Tickets may need to be stamped for connections, beyond certain zones, and past selected times (which may require a new fare). The way you understand how a train system operates back home may differ from the transport in another country – such as the #1 train going both north and south in New York City, but the #1 train

going north and the #2 train going south in Tokyo. Also, "mind the gap" wherever you are as appropriate – this signage is placed all over the "tube" station and trains in London, meaning there's a space between the edge of the platform and the arriving train's doors so don't injure yourself by stepping into the gap as you board or exit the train. I now see similar signs in New York City subways, too.

5. Local buses can be unpredictable. They vary widely. I've been on lovely double-decker buses with outstanding outdoor views, to the crowded, smelly, insanely-driven "chicken" buses in Central America that may include people transporting live chickens. Generally, these are fine but do know the schedule – in particular on any local holidays they may not be running; timing for the last bus (take the next-to-last one in case the last one doesn't show); and if the route changes on weekends versus weekdays (which happened to me, and I ended up who-knows-where). In many undeveloped countries the roads aren't paved, so you're going to feel the bumpity-bumpity-bumps (reminder about that hemorrhoid medication and cushion). Check if food or beverage is allowed on the bus – sometimes yes, and sometimes no.

6. Hop-on, hop-off buses became my new friend. In case you're not familiar with the concept, these are double-decker buses that have various drop-off points throughout the city, and you could pick up subsequent ones every half hour or so thus allowing great time flexibility at any given tourist site. These were generally on schedule, had an inexpensive day-pass price (maybe $20 U.S.), and went long distances including places the trains (if any there) didn't go. They were clean, efficient, and ran throughout the day until mid-evening. In a way, that's how I did my travels – hop-on, hop-off, but by many different modes of transport, and all around the world.

7. Reminder to shoot photos from the back window of the bus where few seek to venture, and from where you can get some excellent alternative photos. You probably will inspire others to do the same, so get them while you can before the window seats get too crowded.

8. Small plane and helicopter tours can provide spectacular views. I mentioned the one in Iceland by plane, and I also took a phenomenal helicopter ride over the volcanoes in Hilo, Hawaii. These may not be for the faint of heart because you can dipsy-doodle and move at weird angles. This didn't bother me at all, but others had issues even if not afraid of being airborne. But by then I had skydived (in Colorado), so I was unfazed.

9. I also rode by mule, elephant, camel, horse, tram, monorail, bicycle, moped, tuk-tuk, funicular, speedboat, catamaran, and others. All were fine and got me from point A to point B. Just be careful on the animals because they're higher up than they appear; one fall could be the end or close to it. I have not hitchhiked, as some have asked me, nor would I chance this. I've also not driven a motor vehicle overseas.

10. And the best way to get around is by...walking. I've walked for what seems like hundreds of miles, all over the place, wherever and whenever and however, including backpacking and hiking. You can go at your own pace, meander, be spontaneous, stop and smell the roses (which I made sure to do literally and often), and just stop and appreciate nature, life, and a great sunset! If you can't walk or have difficulty doing so there are other ways to get around, but the point is to get out and do it if possible. This can also help you shed unwanted weight gained from sitting on transportation for so long. "Just do it ™." Where have I heard that before?...

*Solo Traveling And Photography*

1. Traveling solo has its rewards, but down sides too. Among the benefits are freedom, flexibility, no-one to answer to, no compromising, and going at your own pace. I have traveled solo, with friends, with girlfriends, with groups, and with family. All were fine, but I prefer solo, and have adapted to it. You could lose out on the social aspect – except if you're adept at meeting new people, which can turn this into a reward. If you're not sociable, are averse to risk, or don't like being by yourself/alone, this option may not be for you. At first traveling solo was a function of others not having the free time, discretionary income, or matching schedule to go with me. But over time I realized the benefits. Don't confuse alone with being lonely. I've met amazing people, made new friends, and had terrific times with new acquaintances. I've also been introduced to myself in many different ways going out of my comfort zone: overcoming fears, becoming more sociable (I used to be shy, which people find hard to believe), and bringing out the explorer in me. There's a song lyric I like: "Nothin' I know beats this feeling of not knowing where you're going, or what you're gonna find" (Partridge Family). That goes for people, places, and things when traveling.

   There are down sides such as if you want someone to talk to/dine with/accompany you/be with you in a medical situation; not being able to have a shared memory with others you know; and generally not being able to split costs as applicable. But I found that the benefits far outweigh the downsides – especially after you become skilled at solo travel. Many other solo travelers I've met feel the same way, but it takes an independent personality and lifestyle to accomplish this.

2. Dollars and sense. It costs less to travel solo instead of paying for others, and this savings could be applied to future travels. But, as mentioned, you don't have the social/sharing part unless you create it. You also become a puzzle piece in the seating for dining on ships, for

example, which may result (at least initially) in your not being seated where you want. The world is mostly couples, and with kids, so you have to be comfortable being single (many people I've met aren't, feel "lost," or can't handle dining alone, for example). It's an adaptable situation that can pay big dividends, and with so many singles these days there's no stigma to it at all. Many cruise ships even have a "singles mingle" so that other singles can meet and go off together, even as travel partners, if they so desire.

3. My camera – my best friend. Overall, this has been a great plus with all the photos and memories provided. I have a vertically-integrated hobby of travel-photos-photo albums, which is a major source of pride with something to show for all my efforts and experiences, that nobody can ever take away (you can lose your job, house, and even family, but photos and memories are enduring). I also find photography a challenge and continuously hone my skills – without any courses, just based on developing an eye for things. And I've been called "The Picasso of photo albums." Another great benefit, as mentioned, is that I use the line "Would you mind taking my photo?" as an ice-breaker to meet beautiful women, which has worked out very well. So that's the good news.

4. My camera – my worst enemy. As with the basset hound I grew up with, Zoi, when she was good she was wonderful, and when she was bad it was a howl-fest. Similarly, my camera isn't a Polaroid but has been polarizing. The issue is not so much my camera as what I do with it, and how I've been perceived or misperceived doing it. I've been suspected of being a spy because I took so many photos. Been reprimanded by military police for unwittingly taking photos of a military building. Angered a few boyfriends of gals who liked me by using my camera caper (no major issues). At times my photos have been checked and always proved I was nothing but a tourist. I knew that,

but to overly suspicious people - like Mr. Scotland Yard I met in a London pub and selected Security personnel I mentioned - it can look a different way. Especially if they don't like people from your country, have a quota to fill of suspects, or are overly suspicious by nature.

5. Bring extras and accessories: camera/film/memory card/batteries, chargers, and others. My camera malfunctioned a few times during trips - got wet, was dropped, was exposed to excessive heat, and other situations. I ran out of film/memory space/batteries at inopportune times, and lost my camera once. I now always bring back-ups.

6. Just because someone has a fancy camera does not mean they know how to take good photos – and vice-versa. I prefer asking someone with a high-quality camera to take my photo. But, in general, I found minimal difference in the photo-taking capability between the people with excellent cameras and those with a point-and-shoot, disposable camera, or even having little or no photographic experience. My standard line, as told to the photographer, is "get my feet in," so that I can edit the photo later, giving me a full-length or zoomed-in (cropped) option. Several guys and gals in Africa who never saw a digital camera ended up taking fine photos (they've seen post cards and tried to make it look like that, some said). Sometimes I'll watch others take photos before asking them to take some of me – you can often tell if they know what they're doing by watching. I offer to return the favor, and volunteer to take others' photos, especially when there's a group and the photographer wants to be in the picture.

7. Get a group photo with your tourmates. Sometimes the tour leader will suggest this or have a place selected for it, most times not. I have suggested this formally, and also taken the photo informally if none was planned, with most other tourmates doing the same. It's easy to overlook this and go straight to the overlook, e.g., but

when you look back on the group photo it really does help you remember the entire trip better. And you may see some of these same people again, as happened to me a couple of times.

8. Ask people to take a photo of you who you can outrun. I mention this half-kiddingly but I do this, just in case. I've seen a few grab-and-goes when the criminal was unwittingly handed the camera to take the photo. However, the younger people in many foreign countries tend to know how better to use a digital camera, so if I ask a younger person it's usually somebody who I feel I can outrun. I use my judgment, am fairly cautious, and never had a problem with this.

9. Take lots of photos! On a digital camera you can instantly see them and delete the ones you don't want. Sometimes you get that gem and are glad you took these extras. You don't even have to be a pro – the auto settings will adjust the camera for you, and since you may never return there/have that opportunity again, you might as well make the most of it photographically. Besides, as mentioned, the cost of photos is relatively small compared to the overall cost of the trip – especially if you upload them online instead of getting them printed. Sometimes I take so many photos I am mistaken for the official photographer, including on ships and at weddings I've happened onto!

10. Look at the photos from time to time, and share them with others. It's amazing that so many people I meet take the photos, store them somewhere, and don't look at them again. What a shame. They're a great way to relive your trip vicariously, bringing back all those wonderful memories, and you can preserve them in albums (online and store-bought). That's why there are reruns on TV, I suppose. They work!

As a final thought regarding cameras and photos, perhaps fellow New York City compatriot Paul Simon said it best: "Kodachrome, you give us those nice bright colors, you give us the greens of summers, makes you think all the world's a sunny day, oh yeah! I got a Nikon camera, I love to take a photograph, so Mama don't take my Kodachrome away."

On that musical note, I hope this book has edu-tained you, taken you to far-away places, allowed you to vicariously accompany me as I wandered about, and brought you to the threshold of your own curiosity about the world we live in. We're at the end of the road, my friend, and I hope that in some way I have inspired you to discover more about these places and, in the process, learn more about yourself. Whether you say Cheers, Skol, Salud, Lechaim (Israeli), Oogywawa (Zulu), or something else, I wish you a bon voyage and safe travels.

And finally, I thought I'd end with a funny anecdote from my temporary home in Buffalo, New York. After watching a documentary about the Soviet Union, I put on my Russia cap and went into a local restaurant to get dinner. The server came over to my table but, while taking my order, kept nervously staring at my cap with the letters spelling out Russia on the front. "Don't worry," I said, "I'm not Russian." The server then replied, "That's good, because our food is prepared fresh daily, and may take a little longer." We ended up having fun with this using the universal language: laughter. It was good to be home.

# Acknowledgments

I'd like to thank those who supported me in writing this book, from friends and family to fellow travelers who suggested and even insisted I write about my adventures. Candace, another world adventurer, was particularly motivating in this regard.

Thanks also to my former colleague in California, Shekhar, who encouraged me to write this book, noting my enthusiasm for travel and the stories I had to share.

Thanks to my friend Mark, in New York City, for reading my first-draft manuscript and offering his insights. Who says a Yankees fan and Mets fan cannot get along?

Thanks to Izlane, in Morocco, who provided the proper spelling for the word "bellek" cited in this book, and verifying its meaning. I will never forget that word.

Special kudos to Amber Ritchie, the nice customer representative at Trafalgar Tours who, upon hearing that the company's travel bag I was given on tour was so traveled-out as to no longer be usable, went out of her way to find me the very last one the company had left and mailed it to me gratis. This new travel bag has made it to at least 30 more countries after that, and is still going strong.

Worldwide thanks to all those I met during my travels, each of whom in his or her own way not only influenced me as a traveler, but helped shape me as a person.

Last, but not least, thanks to you, the readers, for following my book of world travel adventures to the very end. I hope you found these adventures worthy of your venturing out to buy the book and read about them.

# References

Wikipedia.com was used as the main reference for facts and statistics. Other specific reference sources were cited in the text, with additional sources listed below in alphabetical order:


About.com

Answers.com

Boliviaweb.com

Ecuadorexplore.com

Family-crescent.com

Globalpost.com

Historymyths.com

Islandflave.com

Itsvery.net

KenyaAdvisor.com

Mauritius.org.uk

New York Times.com

Siakhenn.com

SimpleToRemember.com

The Cities Book

Time.com

Visitstockholm.com

Volcanolive.com

WebMD

# About the Author

Steve Freeman possesses a master's degree in Marketing, 20 years' corporate business experience, and full-time university "professionally-qualified" teaching status. His biggest passion in life is for leisure travel. He has traveled to more than 100 countries encompassing all 7 continents. Outside of traveling, Freeman enjoys sports, photography, volunteer work, bowling, and planning his next trip.

Made in the USA
Las Vegas, NV
17 November 2022

59688244R00319